Residential Design using AutoCAD 2005

Daniel John Stine

ISBN: 1-58503-182-8

SDC
PUBLICATIONS

Schroff Development Corporation

www.schroff.com
www.schroff-europe.com

Forward

To The Student:
The intent of this book is to provide the student with a well-rounded knowledge of Computer Aided Drafting (CAD) tools and techniques for use in both school and industry.

It is strongly recommended that this book is completed in lesson order. Many (pretty much all) exercises utilize drawings created in previous lessons.

To the Instructor:
This textbook starts with a basic introduction to AutoCAD 2005 and then begins a house floor plan. Using step-by-step tutorial lessons, the residential project is followed through to create elevations, sections, details, etc. Throughout the project, new AutoCAD commands are covered at the appropriate time. Focus is placed on the most essential parts of a command rather than an exhaustive review of every sub-feature of a particular command.

The 2004 version of this book has been "test driven" by Mr. Stine's first year Architectural Technology CAD class; they have found most of the errors!

An Instructor's resource guide is available with this book. It contains:

- Answers to the questions at the end of each chapter
- Outline of tools & topics to be covered in each lessons lecture
- Suggestions for additional student work (for each lesson)

About the Author:
Dan Stine has twelve years experience in the architectural field. He currently works at LHB (a 140 person multidiscipline firm; www.LHBcorp.com) in Duluth Minnesota as an Architectural Technical Designer. Dan has worked in a total of four firms. While at these firms, Dan has participated in collaborative projects with several other firms on various projects (including Cesar Pelli, Weber Music Hall – University of Minnesota - Duluth). All of these firms have their own CAD standards and customization. This has given Dan a fairly well rounded knowledge of optimizing and implementing CAD standards and customization. Dan is a member of the Autodesk Developer Network (ADN) and teaches CAD classes at Lake Superior College, for the Architectural Technology program, including an Advanced AutoCAD for Architecture class (a class based on his book; "*Essentials for Architecture using Architectural Desktop R3.3*" published by SDC Publications. Appendix A is an excerpt from that book.) Mr. Stine also has a book titled "*Introduction to Autodesk Revit 5.0*", also published by SDC Publications, and is currently working on an updated edition for Revit, release 6.0.

You can contact Dan with comments or suggestions at **dan.stine@charter.net**
Please do not email with general CAD questions unless they relate to a problem with this textbook.

Thanks:
I could not have written this book without support from my family; Cheri, Kayla & Carter. Again, they had to bear with me while daddy had to work on "the book". I love you guys!

Thanks to the individuals that provided images contained in this book; with an extra special thanks to Ron Stanius.

Many thanks go out to Stephen Schroff and Schroff Development Corporation for making this book possible!

Table of Contents

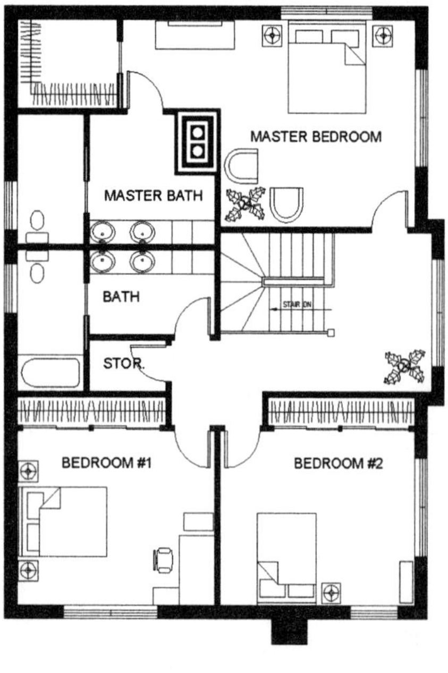

Image from Lesson 7, page 33

This is the floor plan that the reader will draw in this book; including:

- Walls
- Doors
- Windows
- Hatching walls
- plumbing fixtures
- Furniture
- Stairs
- Windows
- Doors
- Text & Dimensions

Lesson 1
Getting Started with AutoCAD 2005::

This chapter will introduce you to AutoCAD 2005. It will cover the User Interface; you will also learn how to open and exit a drawing and adjust the view of the drawing on the screen. It is recommended that the student spend an ample amount of time learning this material, as it will greatly enhance your ability to progress smoothly through subsequent chapters.

Exercise 1-1:
What is AutoCAD 2005?

What is AutoCAD 2005?

AutoCAD 2005 is the world's standard Computer Aided Design (CAD) software. AutoCAD 2005 is a product of Autodesk, which also makes Autodesk Revit, Autodesk Architectural Desktop and 3D Studio Max. The Autodesk company web site claims more than 4 million users in 160 countries. Autodesk's 3,600 employees create products available in 20 languages.

What is AutoCAD 2005 used for?

AutoCAD 2005 is used by virtually every industry that creates technical drawings and designs.

Just a small sampling of AutoCAD users include industries like:

- Construction (Architects, Manufactures and Contractors)
- Aviation
- Automotive
- Ship Design
- Facilities Management
- Art

Why use AutoCAD 2005?

Many people ask the question, why use AutoCAD 2005 versus other programs? The answer can certainly vary depending on the situation and particular needs of an individual/organization.

Generally speaking, this is why most companies use AutoCAD:

- Many designers and drafters are using AutoCAD to create highly accurate drawings that can be easily modified.
- As the "standard" CAD software among many industries, transferring drawings (i.e., sharing) is very simple.
- The large set of features and ability to handle very large, complex, drawing projects.
- Many people are trained to use AutoCAD. Whether at a previous job or in school. An employer is more likely to find an employee trained in the use of AutoCAD than any other program.

Many universities and colleges exclusively teach AutoCAD. Many companies require potential employees to know how to use AutoCAD.

What about the Architectural Programs?

Many architectural firms still use AutoCAD even though there are several software packages that are specifically designed for architecture. The general reason has to do with cost and staff knowledge of the software.

The architectural programs, like Autodesk Revit and Architectural Desktop (ADT), cost quite a bit more than AutoCAD, and for good reason. For example, ADT is built on top of AutoCAD. That means that ADT has everything AutoCAD has plus many additional features geared specifically towards architecture.

Architect's office *Image courtesy of Stanius Johnson Architects www.staniusjohnson.com*

Exercise 1-2:
Overview of the AutoCAD 2005 User Interface

AutoCAD is a powerful and sophisticated program. Because of its powerful feature set it has a measurable learning curve. However, like anything, when broken down into smaller pieces, we can easily learn to harness the power of AutoCAD. That is the goal of this book.

This section will walk through the different sections of the User Interface (UI). Like any program, understanding the user interface is the key to using the programs features.

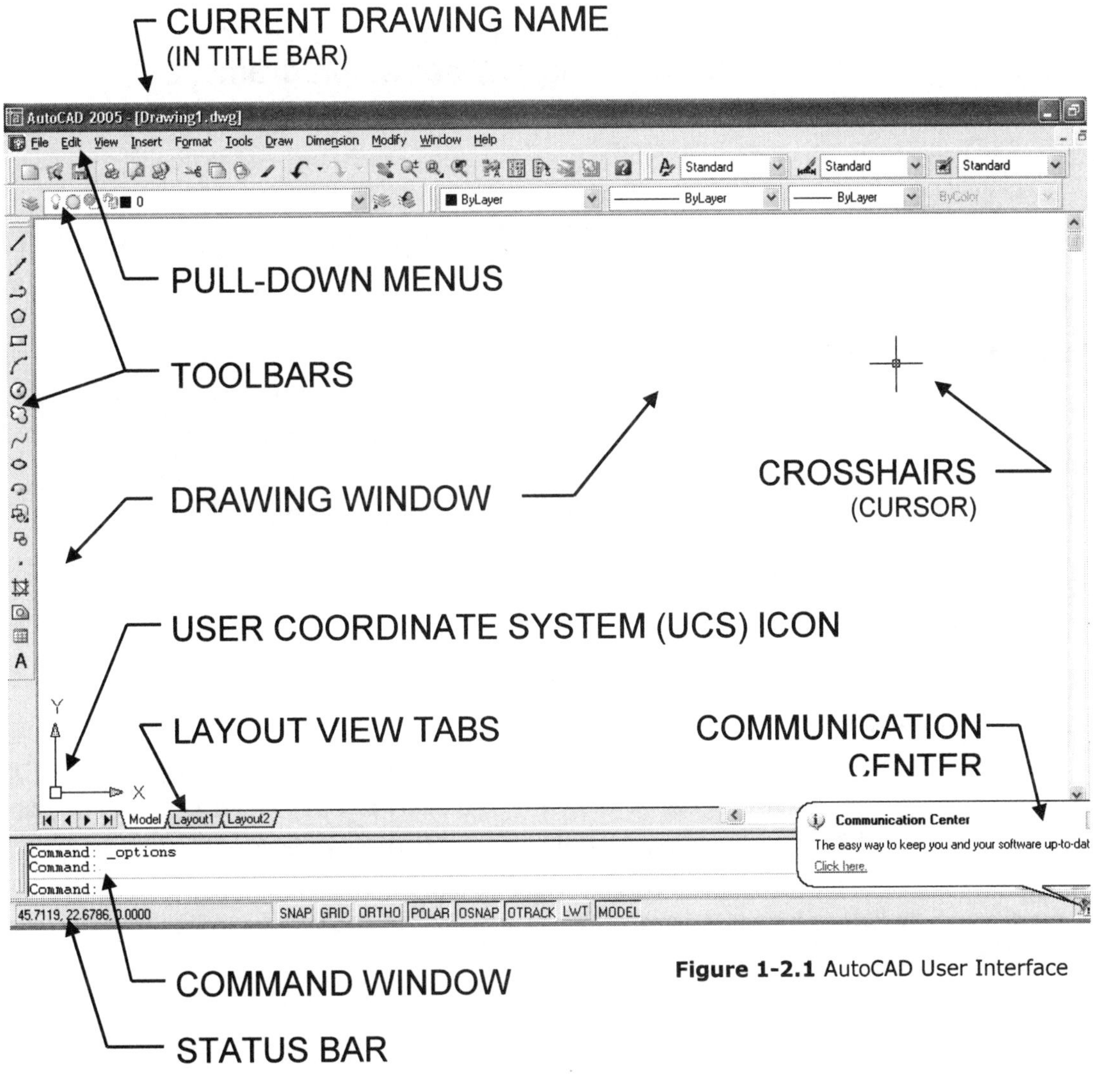

Figure 1-2.1 AutoCAD User Interface

The AutoCAD User Interface:

Menu bar:

Like all Windows programs, AutoCAD has a series of pull-down menus across the top of the screen. Click on each of the menus to explore their contents. Many of these commands are graphically represented by icons in the Toolbars.

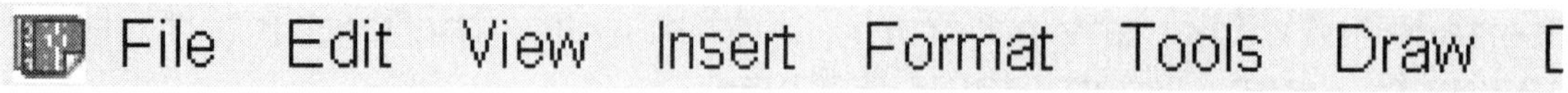

Toolbar - **Standard**:

The standard toolbar contains commands found in most Windows programs. Some examples are: Open, Save, Cut, Copy, Paste, and Print.

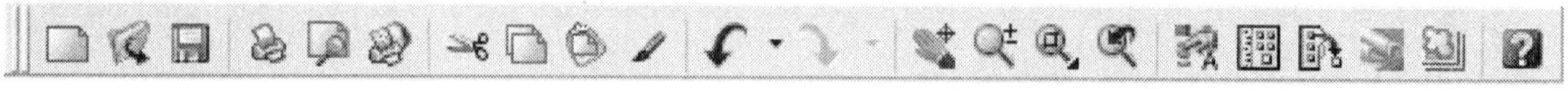

Toolbar - **Draw**:

This toolbar allows you to draw basic 2D lines and shapes as well as text, hatching, tables and blocks *(blocks are drawing entities, such as lines and text, which are grouped together).*

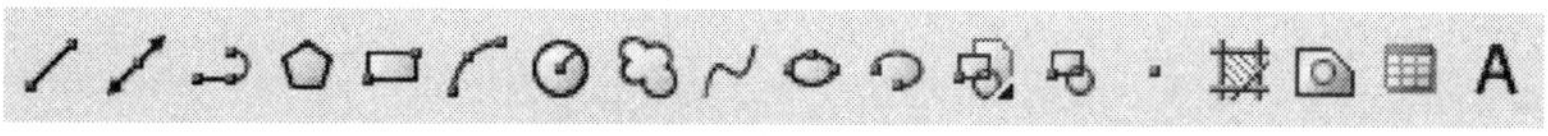

Toolbar - **Modify**:

Contains commands that modify objects in the drawings, i.e., Move, Mirror, Array, Stretch, Copy, Offset, Rotate and Erase.

Toolbar - **Layers**:

Contains tools to create and manage drawing layers. Layers allow you to manage the display and the organization of drawing entities.
TIP*: When nothing is selected, the Layer drop-down list displays the current layer; when something is selected, it displays which layer the selected entity is on (if multiple objects are selected the display is blank).*

Layout View Tabs:

When you are ready to print a drawing you create a Layout View. Each Layout View, represented by the tabs after the Model tab, contains various settings such as paper size and drawing scale. These tabs allow you to switch between these views quickly.

Command Window:

The Command Window allows you to type in commands and displays options and prompts for specific input for a command.
TIP*: New users need to pay close attention to the Command Window until they learn how a particular command works.*

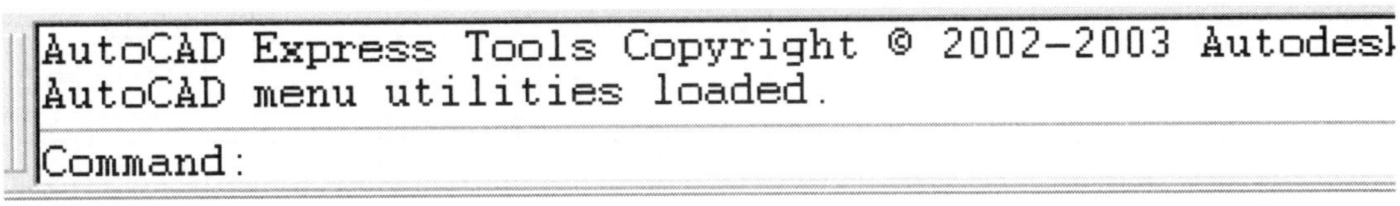

Status Bar:

This area indicates the status of various settings and the coordinates of the cursor (cross-hairs) on the screen. It also displays the length and angle of a line while it's being created. The words like SNAP and ORTHO are buttons which toggle wheatear that feature is on or not. You can right click on the buttons to adjust the settings associated with each tool.

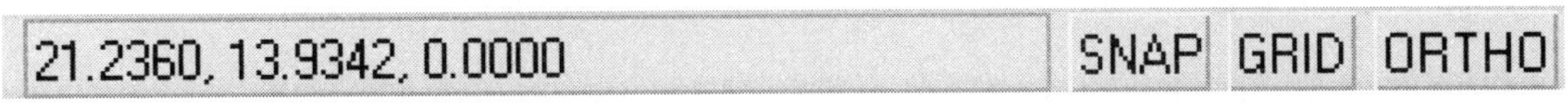

Title Bar:

The Title Bar lists the program name and then the name of the drawing that is currently active. ***TIP***: *The Window pull-down menu lists all the drawings that are open for editing and places a check mark next to the active drawing.*

UCS Icon:

This symbol helps to keep track of your drawings orientation relative to the X, Y, Z coordinate system. It also serves as a visual indicator of current display mode; 2D view, 3D view, perspective and shade mode for example.

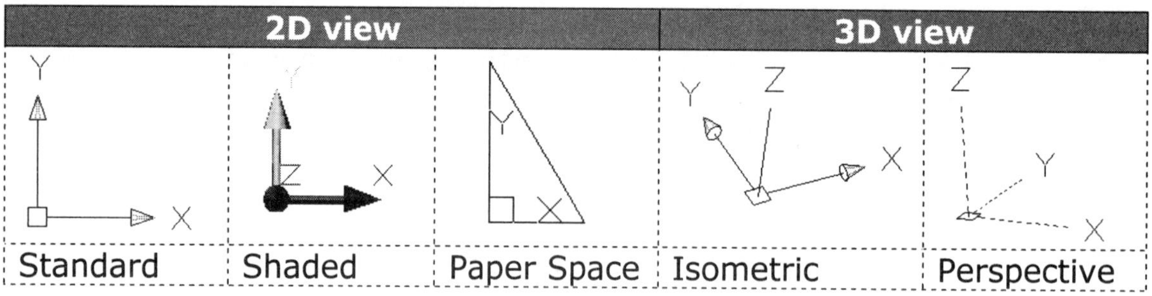

Communication Center:

The Communication Center is a live internet connection to Autodesk. This enables the makers of AutoCAD to notify you of updates and technical issues. Clicking on the "satellite" icon allows you to adjust this features settings. This feature will also notify you when external drawings need to be reloaded.

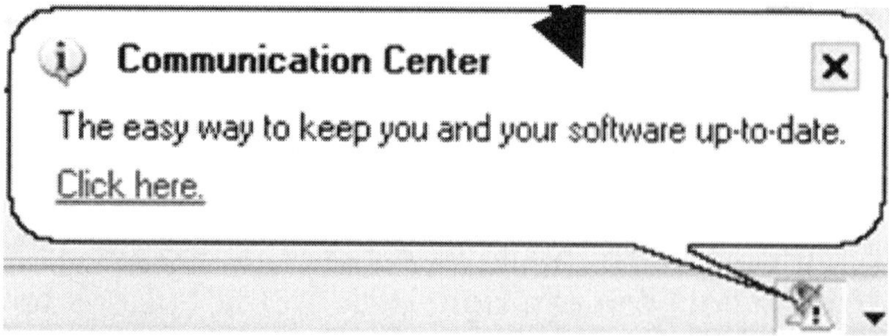

Resetting the User Interface:

If the User Interface shown in Figure 1-1 does not match your computers display, you can reset it. Figure 1-1 is the default screen layout after installation. You or someone who uses your workstation may have customized the location of the toolbars on the screen; the next steps will describe how to reset the screen configuration.

> ***NOTE:*** *This is not necessary to work through this book. It is simply offered for the individual that may have an extremely customized display and wants to reset it.*

1. **Open AutoCAD** (see the next chapter for instruction on this).
2. From the **Tools** pull-down menu select **Options.**
3. Select the **Profiles** tab (at the top of the dialog box). (see Figure 1-2.2)

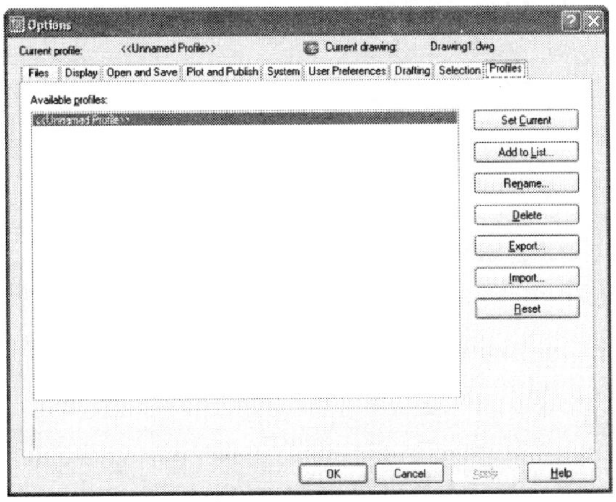

Figure 1-2.2 Options dialog, Profiles tab

4. From the list of Available Profiles, select **<<Unnamed Profile>>.**
5. Click the **Reset** button.
6. Click **OK** to close the Options dialog.

You can create new profiles for individual users on one computer. In fact, your instructor may require this.

Controlling Toolbar display:

If you need to add (i.e., turn on) a Toolbar, follow these simple steps:

7. Select **Toolbars...** from the **View** pull-down menu.
8. Check or uncheck the Toolbars you want displayed.

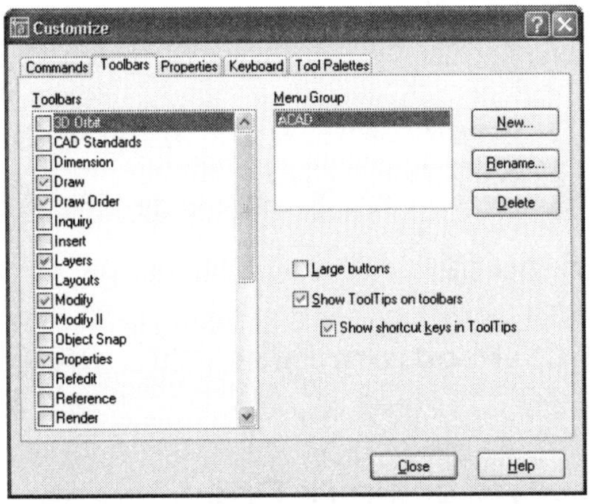

Figure 1-2.3 Customize dialog, Toolbars tab

This concludes our brief overview of the AutoCAD user interface.

Exercise 1-3:
Open, Save & Close an existing Drawing

Open **AutoCAD 2005**
Start → All Programs → Autodesk → AutoCAD 2005 → AutoCAD 2005
(Figure 1-3.1 – *Note:* Windows XP Start menu shown).

AutoCAD 2005

Or double-click the AutoCAD icon from your desktop.

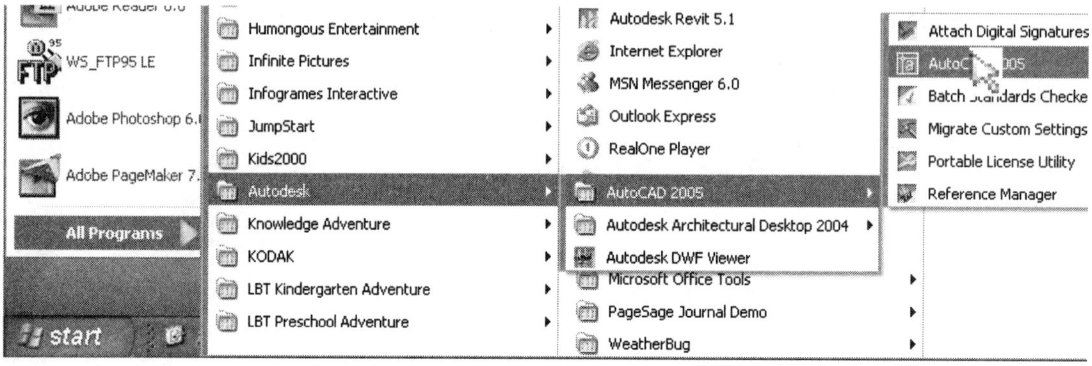

Figure 1-3.1 Start menu (windows XP shown)

This may vary slightly on your computer; see your instructor or system administrator if you need help.

Open an existing AutoCAD drawing:

By default, AutoCAD will open a new (empty) drawing. So, the first thing we will do is close this drawing.

1. Select **File → Close** from the menu bar.

Next you will open an existing AutoCAD drawing file. You will select a sample file that was installed with the AutoCAD program.

2. Select **File → Open** from the menu bar.

3. Browse to the following folder: **C:\Program Files\AutoCAD 2005\Sample.**

4. Select the file named **Wilhome.dwg** and click **Open.**

The Wilhome.dwg file is now open and the last saved view is displayed in the *Drawing Window.*

The *Window* pull-down menu on the menu bar lists the drawings currently open on your computer.

5. Click **Window** from the menu bar. (Figure 1-3.2)

Notice that the Wilhome.dwg drawing file is listed.

The current drawing (i.e., the drawing you are working in) has a check mark next to it. You can quickly toggle between opened drawings from this menu.

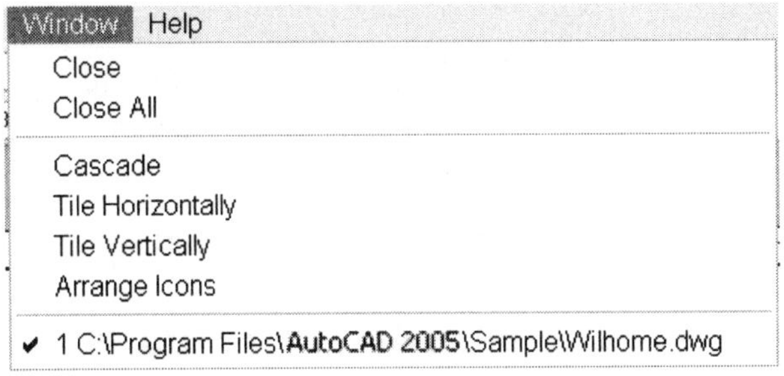

Figure 1-3.2 Window menu

Open another existing AutoCAD drawing:

AutoCAD also lets you open more than one drawing at a time.

6. Click **File → Open** from the menu bar.

7. Browse to the following folder: **C:\Program Files\AutoCAD 2005\Sample.**

8. Select the file named **Taisei Detail Plan.dwg** and click **Open.**

9. Click **Window** from the menu bar. (Figure 1-3.3)

Notice that the *Taisei Detail Plan.dwg* is now listed.

Try toggling between drawings by clicking on *Wilhome.dwg*.

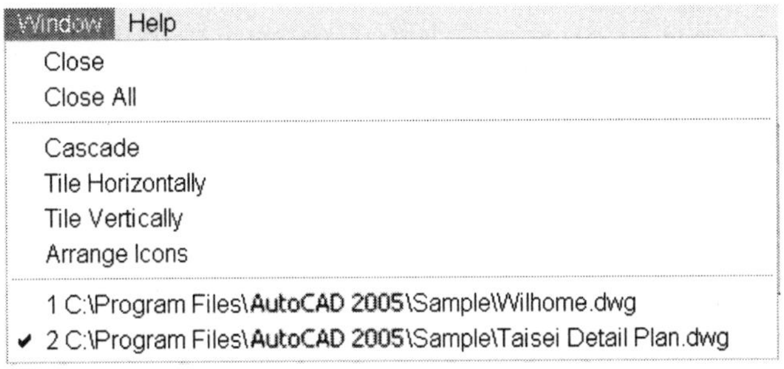

Figure 1-3.3 Window menu

Close an AutoCAD drawing:

10. Select **File → Close** from the menu bar.

This will close the current drawing. If more than one drawing is open, only the current drawing will close.

11. Repeat step 10 to close the other open drawing file.

If you have not saved your drawing, you will be prompted to do so before AutoCAD closes the drawing. **Do not save at this time.**

Saving an AutoCAD drawing:

At this time we will <u>not</u> actually save a drawing.

To save a drawing, simply select **File → Save** from the file menu. You can also click the save icon from the *Standard Toolbar*.

You should get in the habit of saving often to avoid loosing work due to a power outage or program crash.

Closing the AutoCAD program:

Finally, from the *File* pull-down menu select **Exit**. This will close any open drawings and shut AutoCAD down. Again you will be prompted to save (if needed) before AutoCAD closes any open drawings. Do not save at this time.

You can also click the red X in the upper right corner of the AutoCAD window. (*The icon is red in Windows XP only.*)

Exercise 1-4:
Creating a new Drawing

Open **AutoCAD 2005**

Creating a new drawing file:

The steps required to set up a new AutoCAD drawing file are very simple. As mentioned earlier, simply opening the AutoCAD program starts you in a new unnamed drawing file.

To manually create a new drawing (maybe you just finished working on a previous assignment and want to start the next one):

1. Select **File → New...** from the file menu
   OR select the *New* icon from the Standard Toolbar. 

   Either way, you will get the **Select Template** dialog box (Figure 1-4.1).

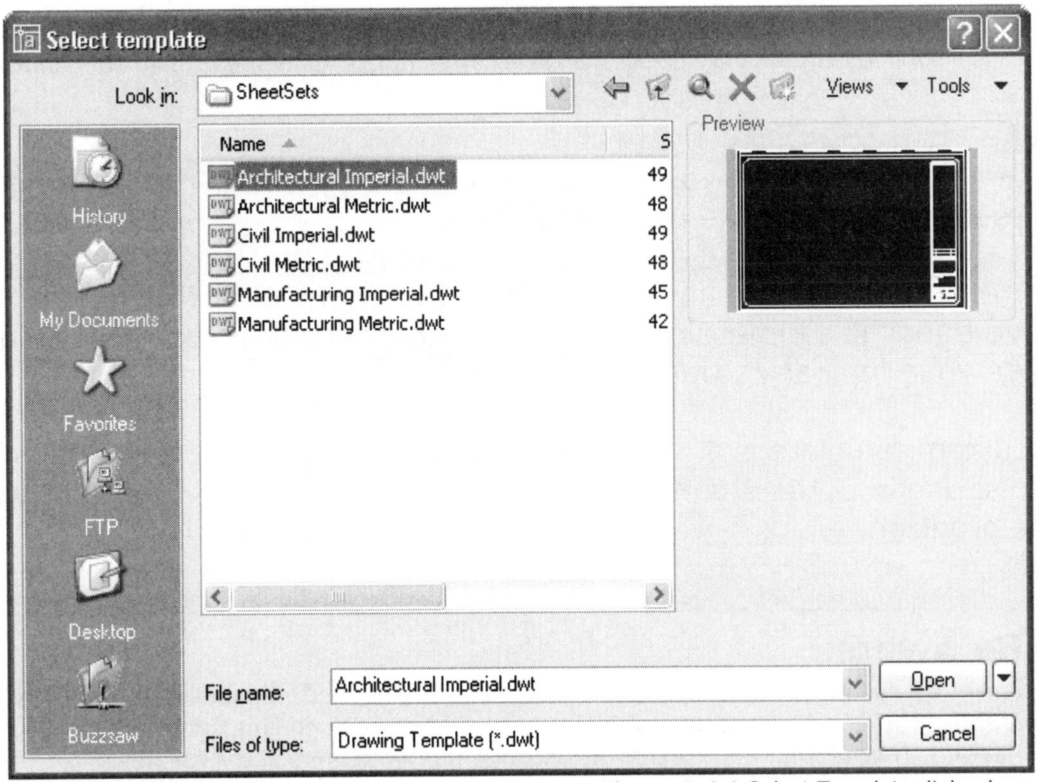

Figure 1-4.1 Select Template dialog box

The *Select Template* dialog box lets you specify the template file you want to use. The template file is explained below.

2. Double-Click on the **SheetSets** folder to view its contents.

3. Select the **Architectural Imperial.dwt** *Template file.*
   FYI: *You need to scroll to the right to see the file details*

   IMPORTANT: This is the file you will use to start all drawings created in this book. The SheetSets feature will be covered in Lesson 8.

4. You now have a new "unnamed" drawing file.

To name an unnamed drawing file you simply save. The first time an unnamed drawing file is saved you will be prompted to specify the name and location for the project file.

5. Select **File → Save** from the menu bar (you do not have to actually save your drawing at this time).

6. Specify a **name** and **location** for your new drawing file.
   Your instructor may specify a location or folder for your files in this class.

What is a template file?

A template file allows you to start your drawing with certain settings preset the way you like or need them.

For example, you can have the units set to Imperial or Metric. You can have things like dimension and text styles preloaded, etc. You can also have your company's title block preloaded.

A custom template is a must for design firms using AutoCAD and will prove useful to the student as he or she becomes more proficient with the program.

> **Be Aware:**
> It will be assumed from this point forward that the reader understands how to create, open and save drawing files. Please refer back to this section as needed. If you still need further assistance ask your instructor for help.

Exercise 1-5:
Using Zoom & Pan to view your drawings

Learning to Pan and Zoom in and out of a drawing is essential to accurate and efficient drafting and visualization. We will review these commands now so you are ready to use them with the first drawing exercise.

Open **AutoCAD 2005**

You will select a sample file that was installed with the program.

1. Select **File → Open** from the menu bar.

2. Browse to the following folder: **C:\Program Files\AutoCAD 2005\Sample.**

Select the file named **Wilhome.dwg** and click **Open** (Figure 1-5.1).

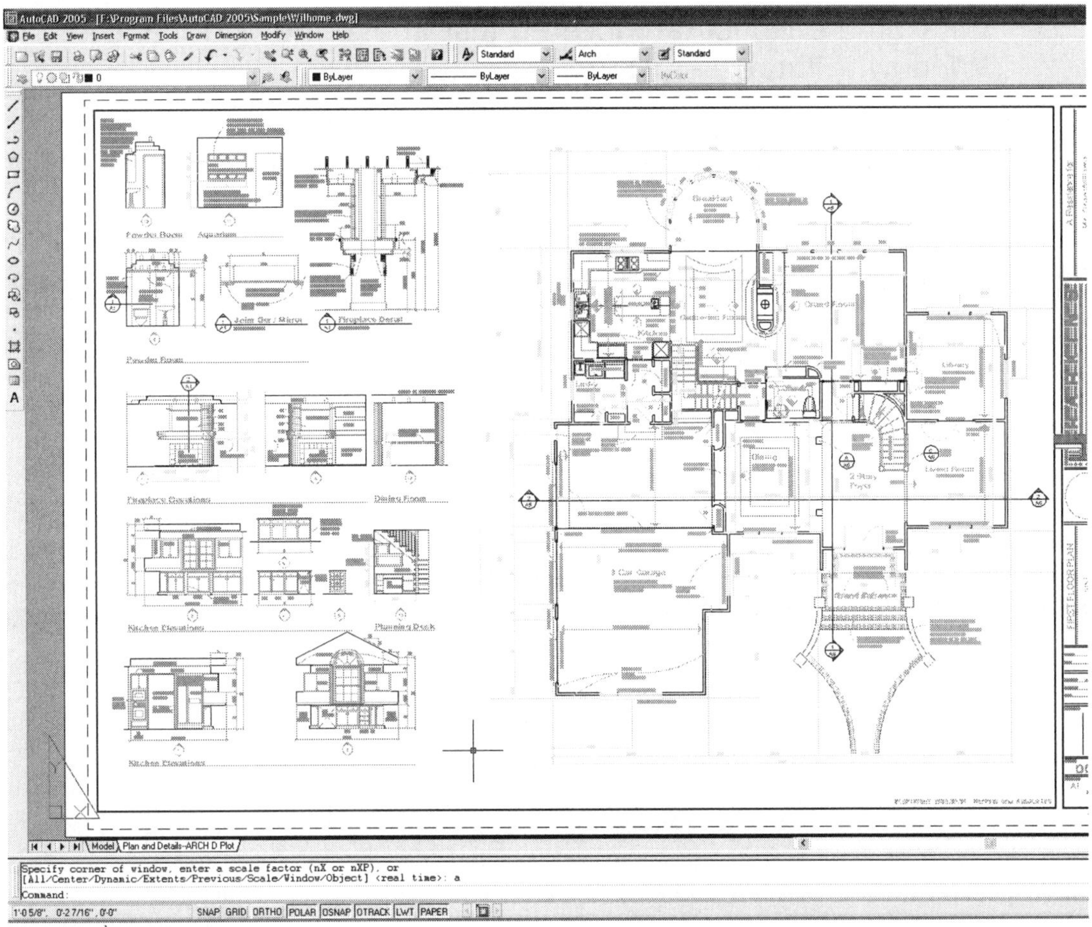

Figure 1-5.1 Wilhouse.dwg drawing

Switching to Model Space:

As briefly mentioned earlier, the *Layout View* tabs to the right of the *Model* tab are primarily for printing sheets with drawings and details composed on them.

The *Model* tab (i.e., Model Space) is really where all the drawing is done. Then the drawings are arranged in *Layout Views* on sheets (e.g., 8 ½" x 11" or 24" x 36") for printing. Finally, the Layout Views from multiple drawings can organized in the new Sheet Set Manager which allows you to print complete drawing sets (the Sheet Set Manager is covered in Lesson 8).

The *Wilhouse* drawing should have opened with the *"Plans and Details - ARCH D Plot" Layout View* tab set current.

> ***Note**: Layout View tabs can be named (or renamed) to anything you want, simply right-click on a tab and select Rename (exception – you cannot rename the Model tab).*

Next you will switch to *Model* space to practice Panning and Zooming.

3. Click on the Model tab, located just above the Command Window. (Figure 1-5.2)

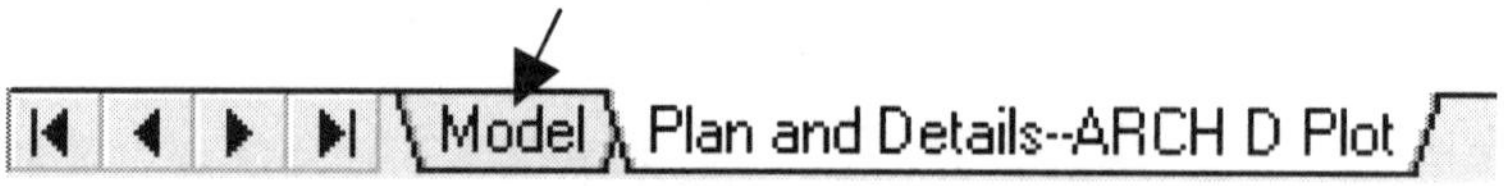

Figure 1-5.2 Layout View tabs– "Plan and Det..." tab set current

You are now in Model Space.

Using Zoom and Pan Tools:

You can access the zoom tools from the **Standard Toolbar**, the *View* pull-down menu and the *scroll wheel* on your mouse.

Standard Toolbar view icons (from left to right)
• Pan Realtime • Zoom Realtime • Zoom Window *(includes drop-down arrow for additional zoom tools – notice the small triangle)* • Zoom Previous

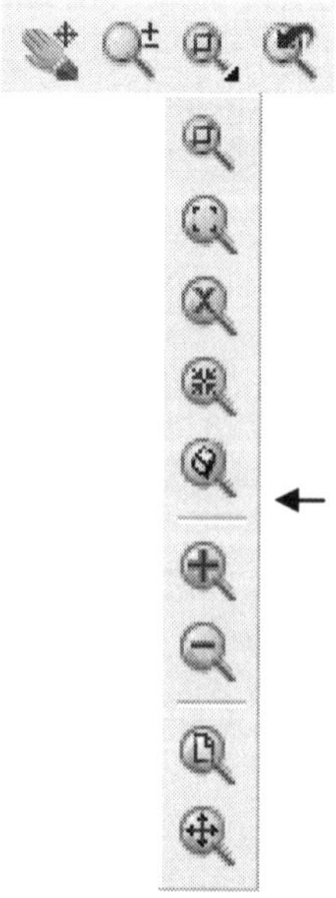

← Flyout toolbar from *Zoom Window* icon

Figure 1-5.3 View tools on the Standard Toolbar

Zoom In

1. Select the **Zoom Window** tool by clicking on its icon. (Figure 1-5.3)

2. Select a window over your floor plan. (Figure 1-5.4)

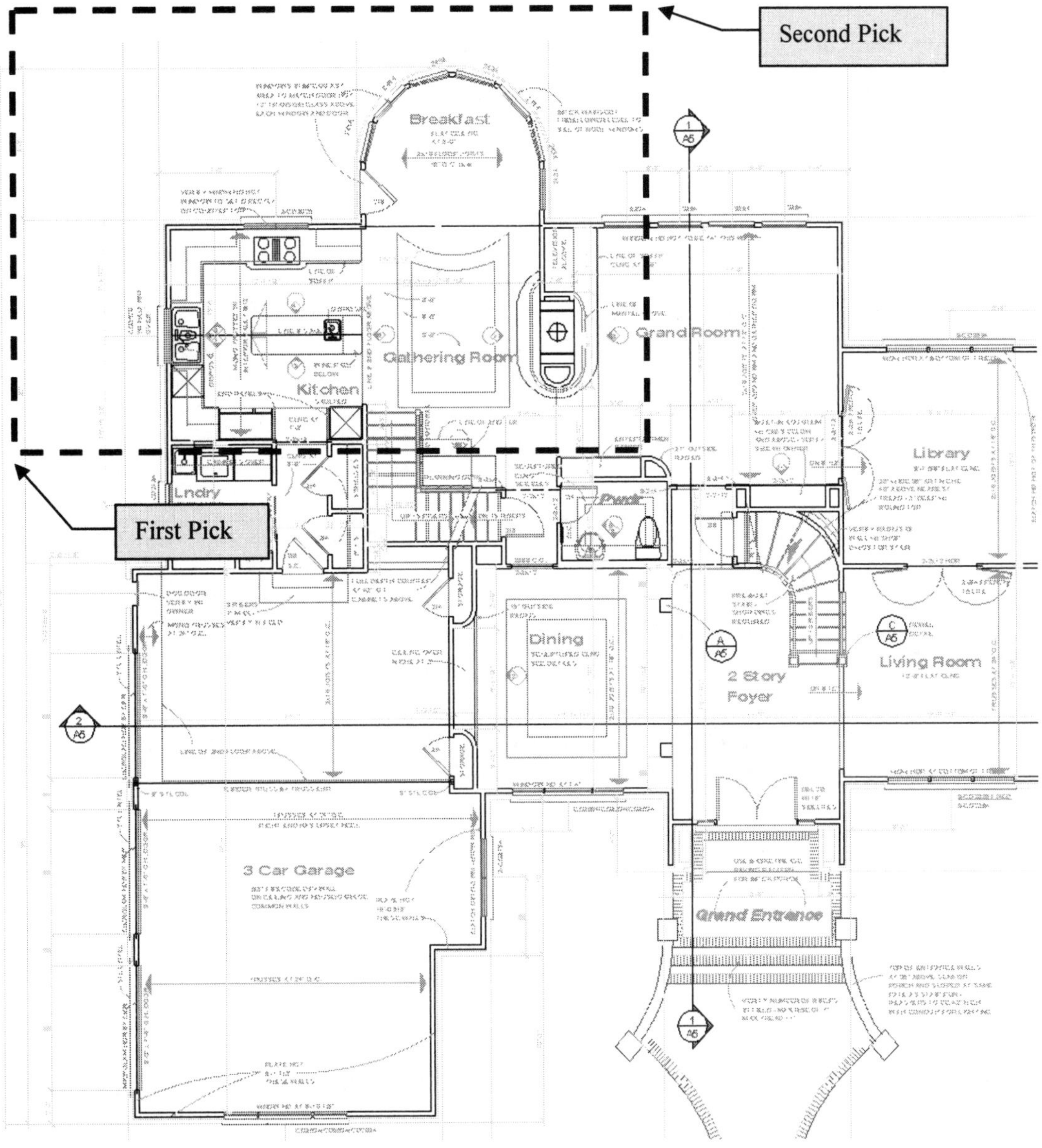

Figure 1-5.4 Zoom Window area

You should now be zoomed in to the specified area (Figure 1-5.5).

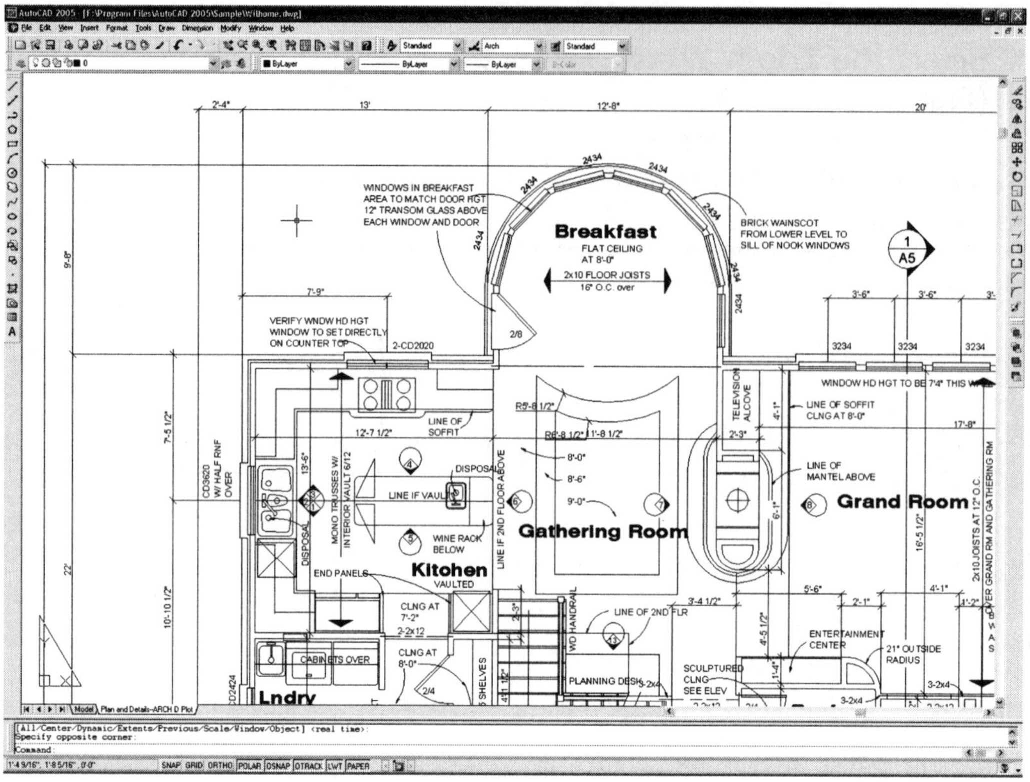

Figure 1-5.5 Zoom Window results

Zoom Previous 

3. Select the **Zoom Previous** tool by clicking on its icon on the Standard Toolbar. (Figure 1-5.3)

You should now be back where you started.

Zoom Extents (flyout toolbar) 

This tool is located on a hidden toolbar (called a flyout). Any icon, such as the *Zoom Window* icon (Figure 1-5.3), that contains a small black right-triangle in the lower right corner has a hidden flyout toolbar associated with it. To view the flyout you simply hold the mouse button down (left button) and then let go of the button when the cursor is over the icon (on the flyout) that you want.

4. On the *Zoom Window* icon press and hold the mouse button down, then release the mouse button over the **Zoom Extents** icon.

Take a minute and try the other zoom tools to see how they work. When finished, click **Zoom Extents** before moving on.

> **For Your Information:**
> Whenever this book refers to clicking the mouse button, it is always referring to the left button. Any other variation with be specifically instructed.
> For example: *Right* click on the OSNAP button on the Status Bar.

Pan Realtime 

The *Pan Realtime* tool allows you to perform a real-time pan in your drawing view.

Panning is similar to using the horizontal and vertical scroll bars next to the drawing window, except you drag the mouse on the screen and are able to go in both directions at the same time (i.e., at an angle)

Realtime means that you see the drawing "smoothly" slide across the screen as you move the mouse. On older versions you would pick two points and then AutoCAD would move the drawing instantly from point A to point B with no "smooth" transition between.

5. Click the **Pan Realtime** icon; this icon is located on the *Standard Toolbar* (Figure 1-5.3).

You should now notice a **Hand Symbol** in place of the typical Arrow Pointer. You can think of this hand as grabbing *Model Space* (when you hold down the mouse button) and moving it within the *Drawing Window*.

6. Try panning around in the *Wilhouse* drawing currently open on your computer; hold the mouse button down, drag the mouse, release the mouse button, drag again if you wish.

> **Be Aware:**
> You are not moving the drawing. You are just changing what part of the drawing you see in the drawing window.

7. When you are done *Panning* right-click anywhere in the *Drawing Window*, and then select **Exit** from the pop-up menu. (Figure 1-5.6)

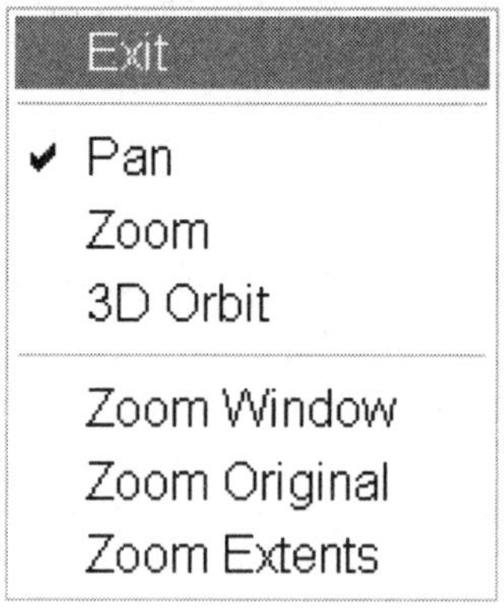

Figure 1-5.6 Pan Realtime right-click pop-up menu

Notice the other options you have in the pop-up menu shown in Figure 1-5.6. You can quickly toggle from Pan to Zoom, or Zoom Window, Original or Extents.

Using the Scroll wheel on the mouse

Using a mouse with a scroll wheel is highly recommended for AutoCAD users. You can seamlessly perform most of the commands covered in this lesson without typing a command or clicking on any icons. Learning to use the wheel is so straight forward and intuitive that the following paragraph should be all that is required for you to start using the wheel productively!

The scroll wheel on the mouse is one of the best improvements to the computer in recent years. In AutoCAD you can Pan and Zoom without even clicking a zoom icon. You simply **scroll the wheel to zoom** and **hold the wheel button down to pan**. This can be done while in another command (e.g., while drawing lines). Another nice feature is that the drawing zooms into the area near your cursor, rather than zooming only at the center of the drawing window like the Zoom In tool does. Finally, if you double-click on the wheel AutoCAD zooms the extents of the drawing. In this author's experience, the Microsoft mice seem to work best with AutoCAD.

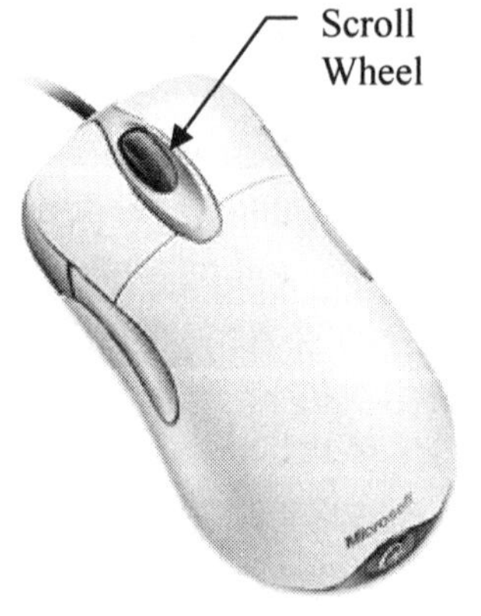

Figure 1-5.7 Microsoft's Optical IntelliMouse shown

Exercise 1-6:
Using the AutoCAD Help System

The AutoCAD Help System can be very useful when you understand how it works. This exercise will walk you through the Help System user interface.

This is a "project based" book, which is a book where you end up with a cohesive project, rather than a hundred drawings that have nothing to do with each other. Furthermore, only the commands necessary to complete a task are covered in depth.

Many commands, such as the Arc command, have several sub-commands. Rather than study every feature of a command, you will only study the essential parts so as not to overwhelm you with too much information. The book will occasionally make reference to the Help System so you can review a command more thoroughly if you are having problems.

This section (and book) will help you to be able to find answers to questions on your own. And with AutoCAD (as with architecture) there is so much to know, it's often better to now how to find the information than it is to remember ALL the information.

Open **AutoCAD 2005**

1. Select **Help** from the **Help** pull-down menu. Figure 1-6.1

You should now be in AutoCAD's Help System window (Figure 1-6.2). The next section walks through its various features.

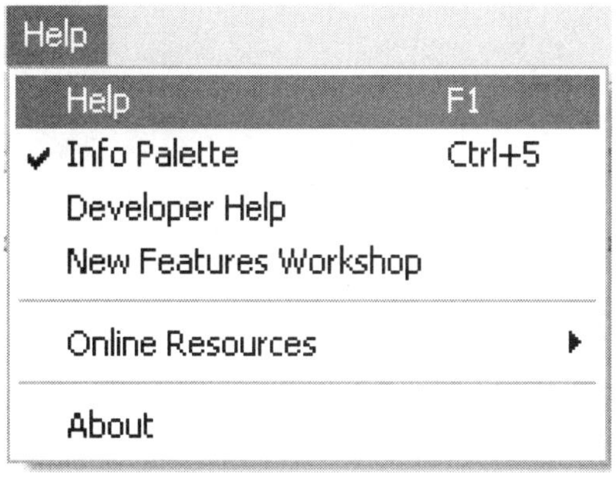

Figure 1-6.1 Help pull-down menu

> **Keyboard shortcuts:**
> Many commands in AutoCAD have a keyboard shortcut, which means you can press a key(s) on the keyboard instead of clicking an icon or a pull-down menu.
> **For example**: to start the line command (and you are not currently in another command), you can type the letter L and then Enter. You can find some of these keyboard shortcuts listed next to the command in the pull-down menu; notice F1 listed next to Help in the Help menu (Figure 1-15).
>
> Most advanced users employ a combination of keyboard and icon use.

Exploring the Help System user interface:

AutoCAD contains an extensive set of documentation on your computer's hard drive. This is basically your owner's manual; from this window you can research the "ins and outs" of the program.

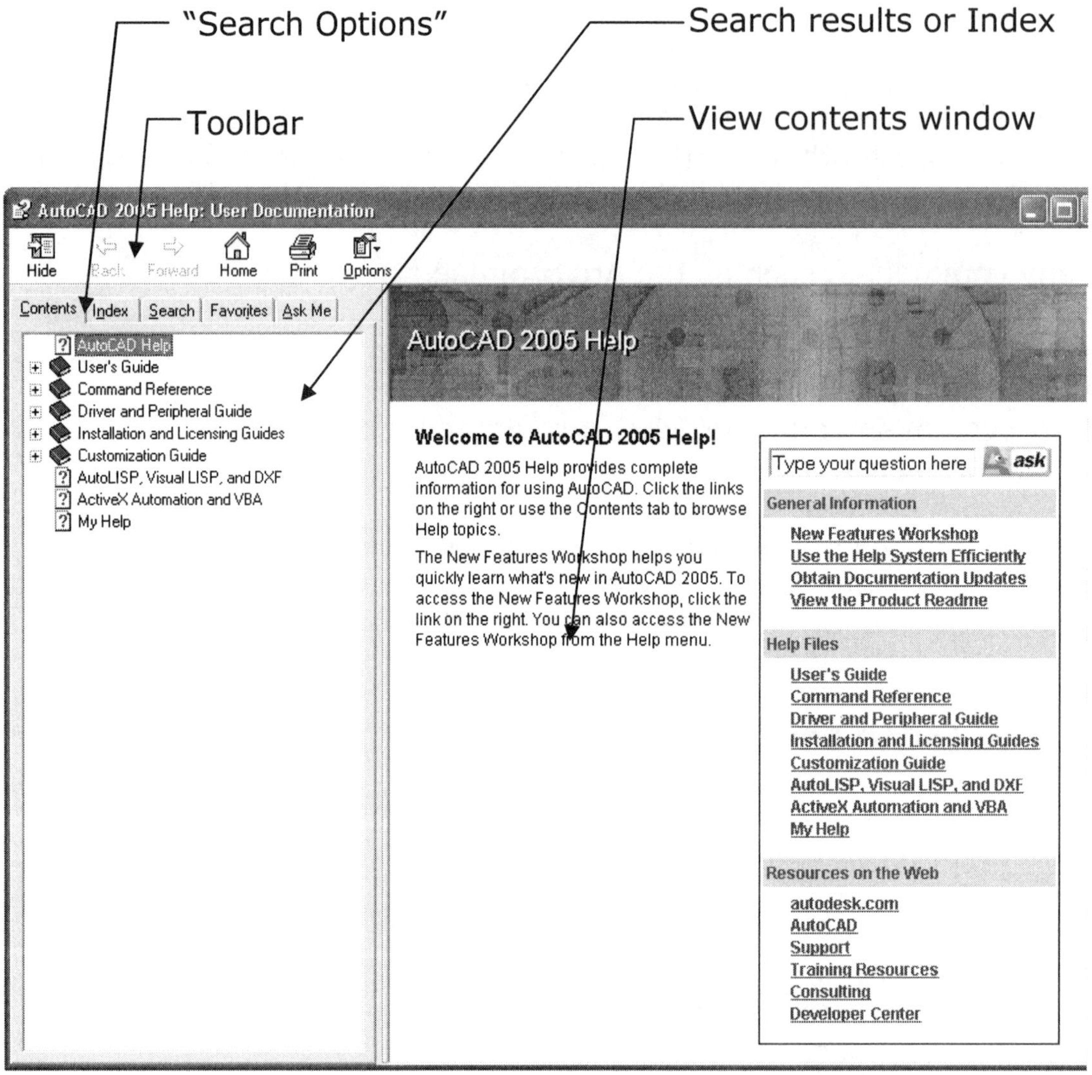

Figure 1-6.2 AutoCAD's Help System window

Expanding items in the index pane:

Whenever you see a **plus** symbol in a small box next to an item, that means it has sub-items available. To display the sub-items you click on the plus to "expand" the list.

When an item is "expanded", it will have a **minus** symbol next to it. Clicking on the minus symbol will "collapse" the list (i.e. make the sub-items disappear).

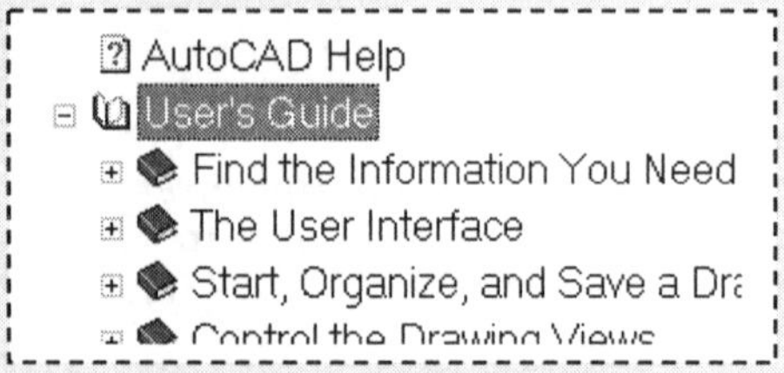

"expanded" item (ref. Figure 1-6.2)

"Search Options" Tabs:
These Tabs give you several ways to access the vast amount of information contained in the online documentation. The following is a brief overview of each Tab:

Contents: Lists the major topics (which used to be separate books that came with the program) and subtopics (the contents of those books).

You have to have a good idea of what you are looking for and where to look when using this Tab. (Figure 1-6.3)

Index: An extensive list of keywords, in alphabetical order, of all the commands and variables available in AutoCAD.

You can type a word in the text-box, just below the Tabs, and quickly jump to many of the items that relate to that word. (Figure 1-6.4)

Search: This tab allows you to type a word and search for all the entries that have that word in it.

With this option you get a large variety of options that relate to the item being researched. (Figure 1-6.5)

Favorites: Allows you to save a link to an item that you might need to access on a regular basis.

If you find yourself looking up a variable often (e.g., the variable that controls the precision of dimensions), this feature allows you to store it in an easy to find place.

Ask Me: Uses advanced search technology to find information in the documentation database by analyzing a question written in everyday language.

Allows the user to try searching for information by entering a question similar to a question you might ask someone if they where available to ask.
Figure 1-6.6

The Help System in action:

The various Tabs all access the same information; to show an example of this, and to study how each Tab works, you will use each search option to find the Circle command.

2. Click on the **Contents** tab.

3. Expand the following items: **User's Guide → Create and Modify Objects → Draw Geometric Objects → Draw Curved Objects.**

4. Select **Draw Circles** listed under *Draw Curved Objects.*

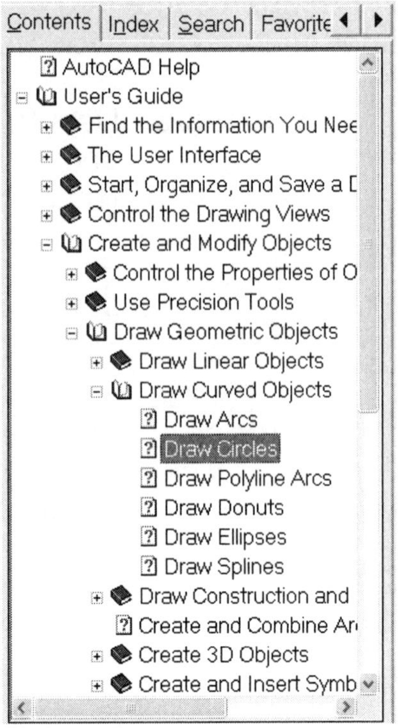

Figure 1-6.3 Help – Contents tab

You should now see (in the View Contents Window) the various ways in which you can create circles. Figure 1-6.3

5. Click on the **Index** tab.

6. Type **CIRCLE command** in the *find* text-box.

7. Select the *Topic* titled **Circle**, found in the **AutoCAD Command Reference** manual and then click **Display.** Figure 1-6.4a

8. Finally, select the **Concepts** tab in the "*View Contents Window*".

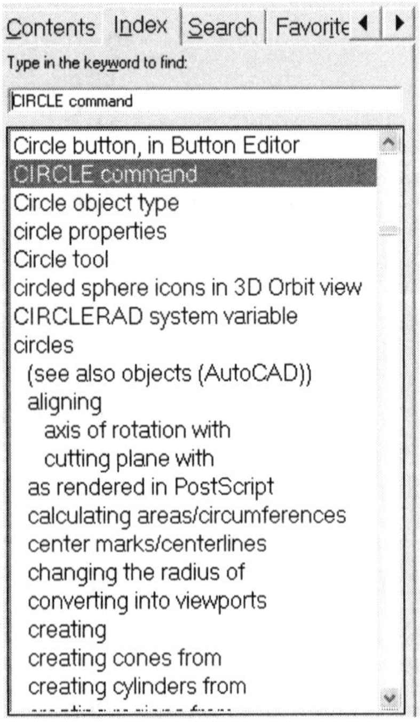

Figure 1-6.4 Help – Index tab

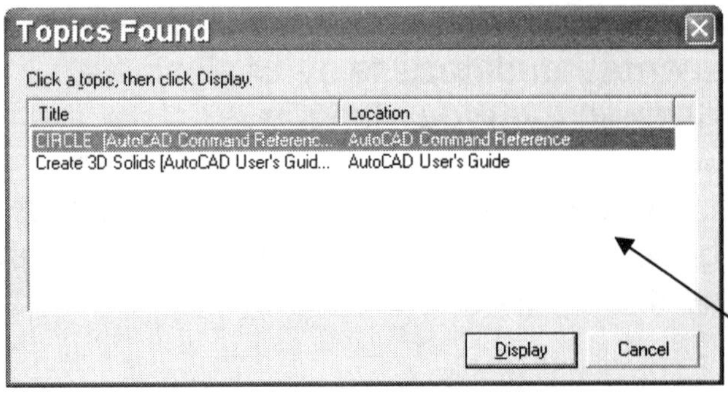

Figure 1-6.4a
Index tab – Topics Found

You should now see the same information on drawing Circles. Figure 1-6.4

9. Click on the **Search** tab.

10. Type **circle** in the search text-box.

11. Double-click the item that starts with Circle in the search results list.

12. Finally, select the **Concepts** tab in the *"View Contents Window"*.

You should now see the same information on drawing Circles. Figure 1-6.5

13. Click on the **Ask Me** tab.

14. Type "**how do I draw a circle**" in the *Ask* text-box.

15. Select the **Ask** button to submit the question.

16. Click **Draw Circles** from the search results list.

You should now see the same information on drawing Circles. Figure 1-6.6

You can quickly see for yourself how each option might be beneficial in different situations.

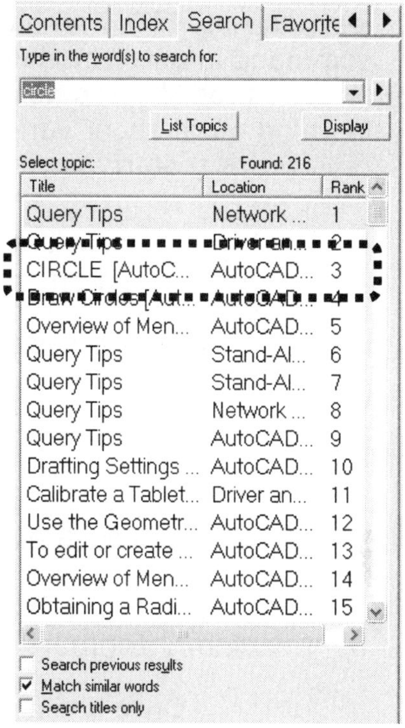

Figure 1-6.5 Help – Search tab

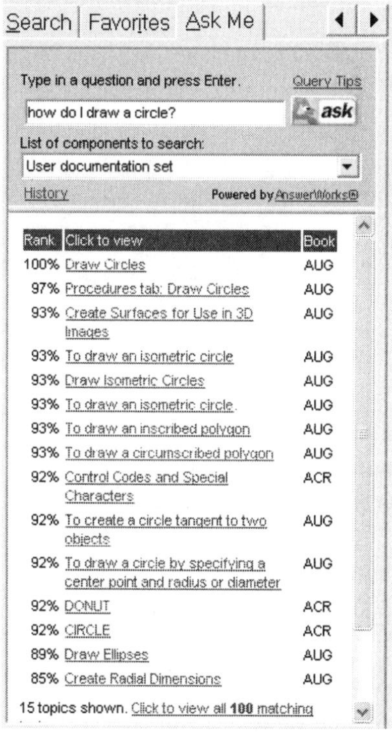

Figure 1-6.6 Help – Ask Me tab

One final note:
In the past, printed documentation contained several errors due to the fact that they were being generated while the software was still being developed. Now, with the online documentation and the internet, you can download updates. When you first load the Help System, select *"Obtain Documentation Updates"*. *(This requires a connection to the internet.)*

Using the Info Palette:

The Info Palette is a feature designed to help new (and experienced) users learn to AutoCAD. The palette changes its content relative to the current command in use. You should consider leaving this palette open while learning to use AutoCAD; it is not required for this book, but would be useful in learning more about various commands covered in this book. You will quickly review this feature now.

17. From the *Help* pull-down menu select **Info Palette** - *if it does not have a check mark next to it.* Figure 1-6.1

    The Info Palette is open when the same label has a check next to it in the Help pull-down menu. Figure 1-6.7

18. Click the **Circle** icon from the *Draw* toolbar.

    Notice the *Info Palette* content is updated to display links related to information on drawing circles. Figure 1-6.8

19. Press the **ESC** key and then click the **Erase** icon from the *Modify* toolbar.

    Once again you should notice the content update with information relating to the *Erase* command. Figure 1-6.9

    If you want the current information displayed to remain for awhile, you can "Lock" the *Info Palette*. When Locked, the content is not updated until the Palette is Unlocked. Notice the Lock icon in the upper right corner. Figure 1-6.9

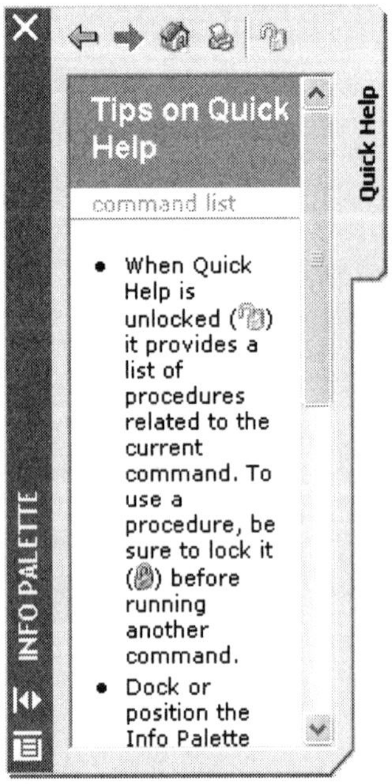

Figure 1-6.7 Info Palette

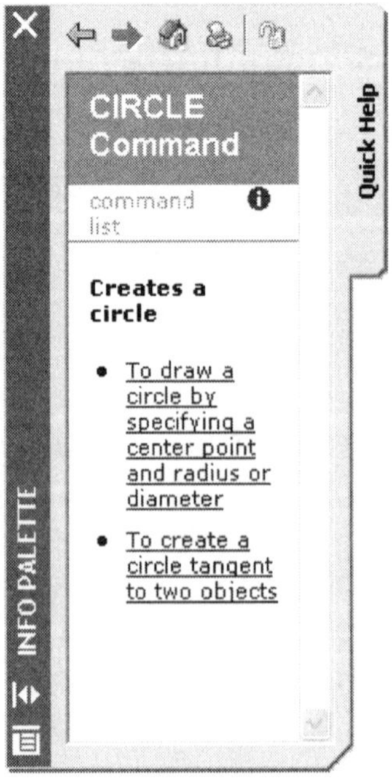

Figure 1-6.8 Info Palette

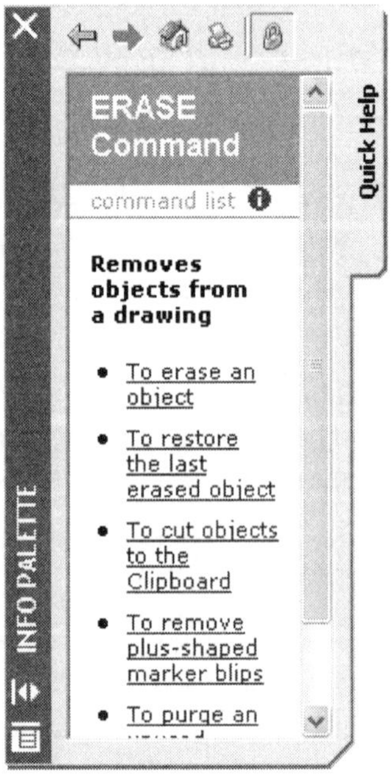

Figure 1-6.9 Info Palette

Self-Exam:

The following questions can be used as a way to check your knowledge of this lesson. The answers can be found at the bottom of this page.

1. The Modify Toolbar allows you to save your drawing file. (T/F)

2. You can zoom in and out using the wheel on a wheel mouse. (T/F)

3. AutoCAD is made specifically for architectural design. (T/F)

4. A ______________ file allows you to start your drawing with certain settings preset the way you like or need them.

5. In the AutoCAD user interface, the ____________ ____________ displays prompts for specific user input.

Review Questions:

The following questions may be assigned by your instructor as a way to assess your knowledge of this section. Your instructor has the answers to the review questions.

1. Many commands have keyboard shortcuts. (T/F)

2. AutoCAD does not provide much in the way of online documentation. (T/F)

3. The Drawings listed at the bottom of the Window pull-down menu allow you to see which Drawings are currently open. (T/F)

4. When you use the Pan tool you are actually moving the drawing, not just changing what part of the drawing you can see on the screen. (T/F)

5. To Close AutoCAD you simply click the red X in the upper right. (T/F)

6. The icon with the floppy disk image () allows you to

__________________ a drawing file.

7. An icon with a small black triangle in the lower right corner is called a

___________ ______ icon.

8. Use the ___________ _____________ tool to switch the view back to the one just prior to your last zoom command.

9. Holding the Scroll Wheel down initiates the _____________ command.

10. The Model Tab (on the layout view tabs bar) is where most of the actual drafting and design is done. (T/F)

Self-Exam Answers:
1 - F, **2** - T, **3** - F, **4** - Template, **5** – Command Window

Notes:

Lesson 2
Crash Course Introduction (the Basics)::

This lesson is meant to give you a brief introduction to a few of the most used commands. You will be walked through each drawing, in this lesson, step-by-step. The intent is for the user to get some of the basic concepts in mind before going through subsequent chapters.

Exercise 2-1:
Lines and Shapes

Drawing lines

The number one command in AutoCAD is the Line command. Lines in AutoCAD are extremely precise drawing elements. This means you can create very accurate drawings. Lines, or any drawn object, can be as precise as 8 decimal places (i.e., 24.999999999) or 1/256.

AutoCAD is a vector based program. That means each drawn object is stored in a numerical database. For example, a line is stored in the drawing's database as the X, Y, Z coordinates for its starting point and the X,Y,Z, coordinates for its endpoint. These coordinates are all relative to the drawings 0, 0, 0 position; called the **Origin**.

When a line needs to be displayed on the screen, AutoCAD reads the line's coordinates from the drawing database and displays a line between those two points on the screen. This means that the line will be very accurate at any scale or zoom magnification.

A raster based program, in contrast to vector based, is comprised of dots that infill a grid. The grid can vary in density, and is typically referred to as resolution (e.g., 600x800, 1600x1200, etc.). This file type is used by graphics programs that typically deal with photographs; such as Adobe Photoshop. There are two reasons this type of file is not appropriate for CAD programs:

1. A raster based line, for example, is composed of many dots on a grid (which also represents the line's width). When you zoom in (or magnify) the line, it starts to become pixilated, meaning you actually start to see each dot in the grid. In a vector file you can "infinitely" zoom in on a line and it will never become pixilated

because the program recalculates the line each time you zoom in.

2. A CAD program, such as AutoCAD, only needs to store the starting point and end point coordinates for each line; the dots needed to draw the line are calculated on the fly for the current screen resolution. Whereas a raster file has to store each dot that represents the full length and width of the line. This can vary from a few hundred dots to several thousand dots, depending on the resolution, for the same line.

The following graphic illustrates this point:

Vector vs. Raster lines

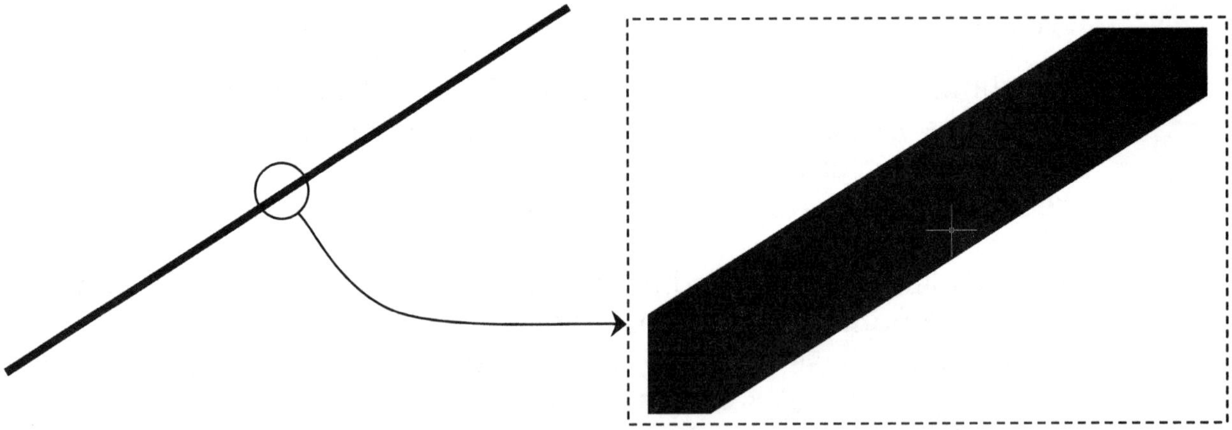

Figure 2-1.1 Vector Line Example
File Size: approx. 33kb

Figure 2-1.1a Vector Line Enlarged 1600%

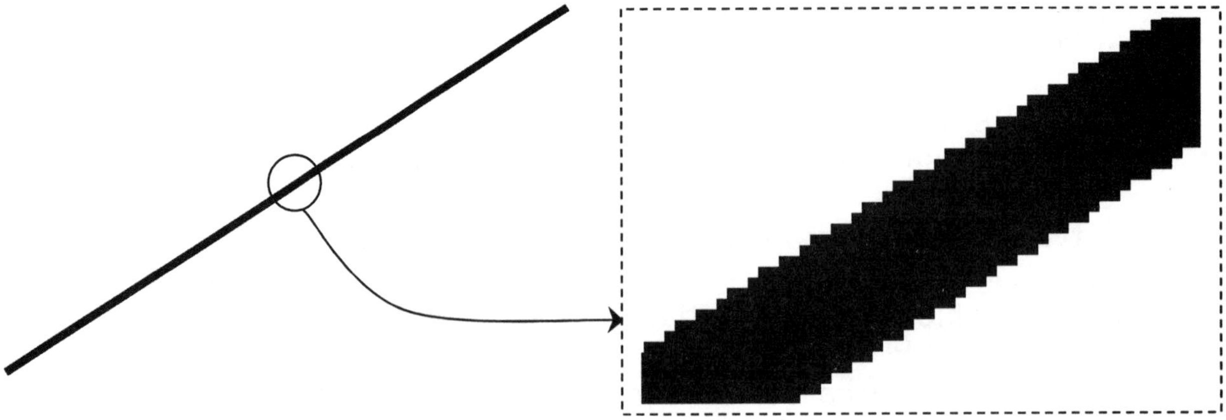

Figure 2-1.2 Raster Line Example
File Size: approx. 4.4MB

Figure 2-1.2a Raster Line Enlarged 1600%

The Line Command:

You will now study the Line command.

1. **Open** AutoCAD.

2. **Close** the empty drawing automatically opened by AutoCAD.

> **Warning:**
> The empty startup drawing that is opened by default when you start AutoCAD, does not have the various variables preset for architectural CAD use.
>
> So you should make sure you start with the correct template file whenever instructed to start a new drawing file in this book.

3. Select **New** from the *File* menu.

4. Use the following Template file to start your new drawing from: **Architectural Imperial.dwt** *(in the SheetSets sub-folder).*

Updating the Architectural Template file:

Before you start drawing you will set the drawing Units to Architectural, the default is Decimal. This is the type of setting that should be preset in a Template file. After making this change, you will save the file as a new template file for use in this book.

5. From the *Format* pull-down menu select **Units.**

6. Set the *Type* to **Architectural** and *Precision* to **0'-0 1/64".** (Figure 2-1.3)

7. Click **OK.**

8. From the *File* menu click **Save As.**

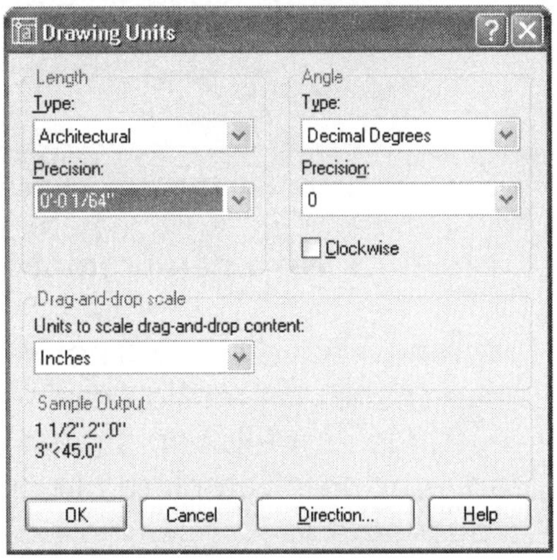

Figure 2-1.3 Drawing Units dialog

9. Change the *Files of Type* (near the bottom) to **AutoCAD Drawing Template (*.DWT).** Figure 2-1.4

You will notice that the folder location automatically updates to the AutoCAD template folder.

10. Switch to the **SheetSets** sub-folder.

11. Set the *File Name* to **Architectural Imperial 2.dwt.** (Figure 2-1.4) ***FYI:*** *This will be the template used to start new drawings in this book.*

12. Click **OK** and then click **OK** again to close *the Template Description* dialog.

13. Select **Close** from the *File* pull-down menu.

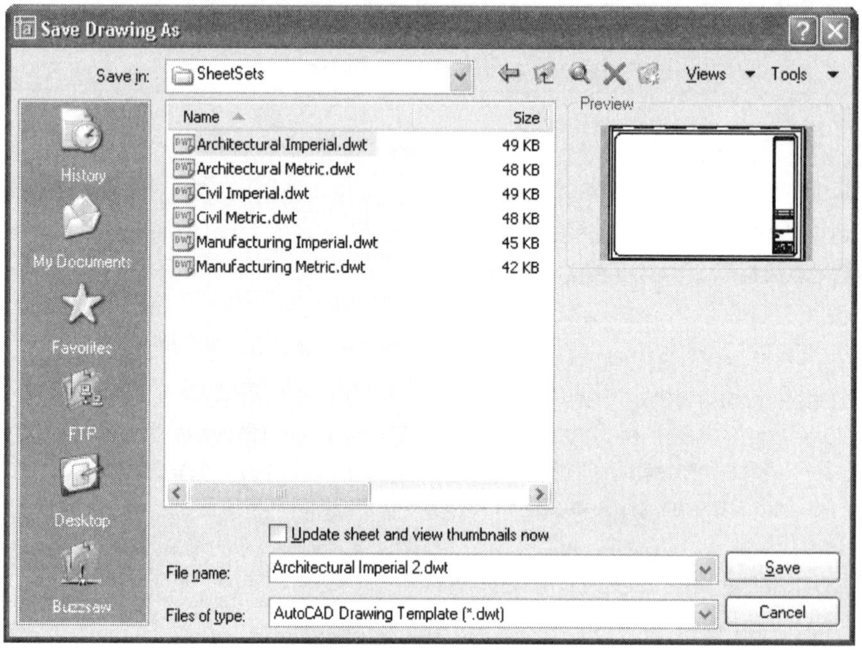

Figure 2-1.4 Save Drawing As dialog

14. Click **No** when prompted to save the drawing file.

You now have a new *Template* file with the *Units* set the way you like (need) them. You can use this technique to modify other settings as well. You should always start fresh from a template file so your new Template file does not have any drawings or other "baggage" in it.

15. Select **New** from the *File* menu.

16. Select your new Template file:
Architectural Imperial 2.dwt *(in the SheetSets sub-folder).*

17. Click on the **Model Tab** to switch to *Model Space* (which is where all the drawing is done as previously mentioned).

18. Select the **Line** command from the *Draw Toolbar.* 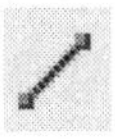

19. **Draw a line** from the lower left corner of the screen to the upper right corner of the screen (by simply clicking two points on the screen) *Note*: do not drag / hold your mouse button down; just click. (Figure 2-1.5)

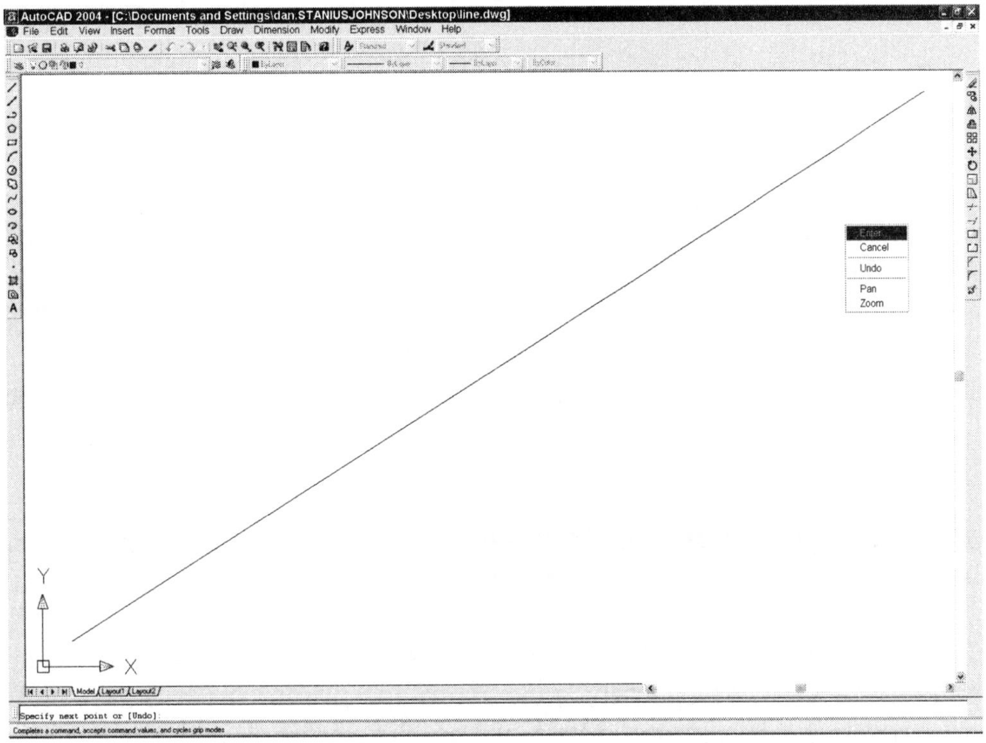

Figure 2-1.5 Your first line!

After clicking your second point, you should notice by looking at the Command Window, that the *Line* command is still active. You could continue to draw lines; with the last point picked becoming the first point for the next line segment. In this case you will end the line command per the following instructions.

20. After clicking your second point (i.e., the endpoint), **right-click** anywhere on the screen and select **Enter** from the pop-up menu. (Figure 2-1.6)

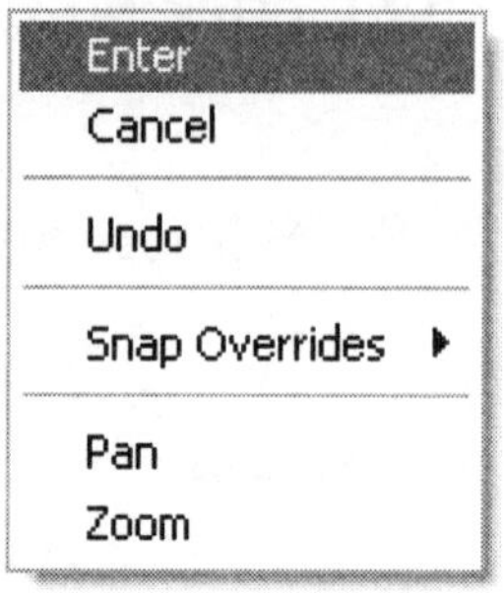

Figure 2-1.6 Right-click Menu; line command active

> **Did you make a mistake?**
> Whenever you make a mistake in AutoCAD you can use the **UNDO** command to revert to a previous drawing state. You can perform multiple UNDOs all the way to your previous *Save*.
>
> Similarly, if you press Undo a few too many times, you can use **REDO**

This constitutes your first line! However, as you are probably aware, it is not a very accurate line as far as length and angle are concerned.

Typically you need to provide information such as length and angle when drawing a line; you rarely pick arbitrary points on the screen like you did in the previous steps. Most of the time you also need to accurately pick your starting point (for example: how far one line is from another or picking the exact middle point on another line).

Having said that, however, the line you just drew still has precise numbers associated with its length and angle. In the next step you will use the Properties Palette to view the line's length and angle.

21. Select the **Properties Icon** from the Standard Toolbar (or press Ctrl + 1).

You now have the *Properties Palette* open on your screen. Notice that the text-box at the top says "No selection"; this is because no objects are selected yet. Figure 2-1.7

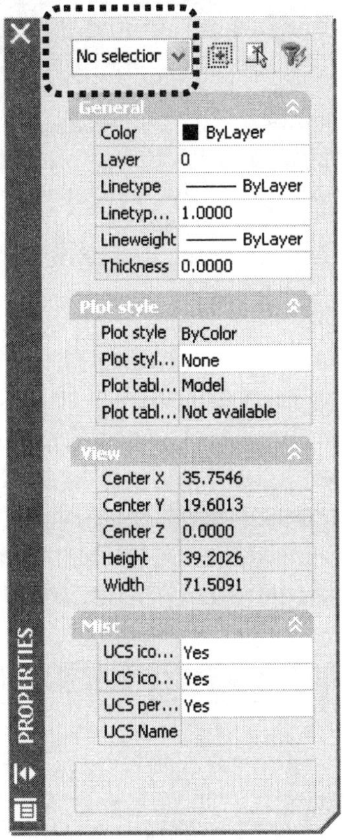

Figure 2-1.7 Properties Palette – No objects selected

Now that the *Properties Palette* is open, you can select the line to display its properties.

22. **Select the Line**: Hover the cursor over the line and click on it.

You should now see the line's properties. Notice the text-box at the top now indicates what type of object is selected. Figure 2-1.8

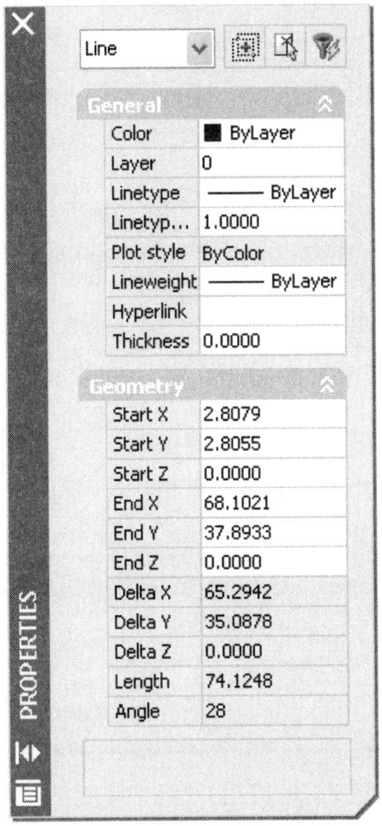

Figure 2-1.8 Properties Palette – Line selected

Notice the information displayed for the selected line:

- The X, Y and Z coordinates are listed, relative to the drawings origin (0,0,0), for both the start and end points.
- The line's Length and Angle are listed.
- Delta X and Delta Y; the Delta X is the horizontal distance between the start point and the end point.

The white areas are editable and the grey areas are not. You cannot edit the length, for example, because AutoCAD needs more info, like what direction to make the line longer.

Are your units and size correct?

If the properties on your computer are displaying the line's data in decimals instead of feet and inches (as shown in Figure 2-1.8), that means you did not change the Units to Architectural in the Format menu.

Similarly, if you're drawing window is not approx. 3'-2" x 2'-11" then you either started with the wrong template or the copy on your computer has been changed (if the later is the case, zoom in (or out) to correct the screen display.

At this point you should close the drawing and start this lesson over.

You should make one final observation about the line's properties and the current view: the Delta X and Delta Y represent the horizontal and vertical distances between the line's start and end points. This tells us that the drawing area, currently visible on the screen, is about 3'-2" across (horizontally) and 2'-11" up and down (vertically). That means that the largest item we can draw (and still see what we are doing) is something that is 3'-2" wide x 2'-11" tall. (See Figure 2-1.9.)

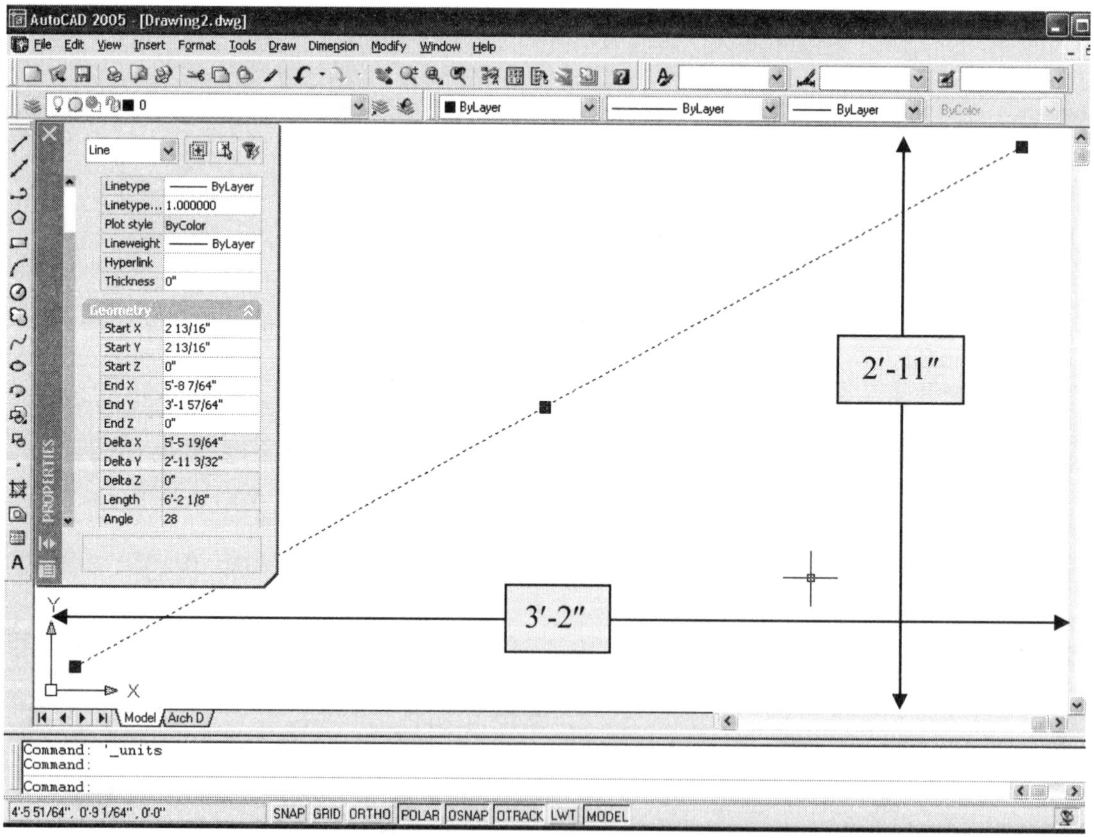

Figure 2-1.9 Visible area of current drawing

Even though your current view is showing a relatively small area, *Model Space* (where you do all your drafting and design) is actually an infinite drawing board.

In architectural CAD drafting, everything is drawn "real-world" size (or full-scale) ALWAYS! If you are drawing a building, you might draw a line for the exterior wall that is 600'-0" long. If you are drawing a window detail, you might draw a line that is 1/8" long. In either case you are entering that line's actual length.

You could, of course, have an 1/8" line and a 600'-0" line in the same drawing. Either line would be difficult to see at the current drawing magnification (i.e., 3'-2"x2'-11" area). So you would have to zoom in to see the 1/8" line and zoom out to see the 600'-0" line. You will try this next:

Draw a 1/8" line:

23. For now, **Close** the Properties Palette by clicking in the X in the upper corner of the palette

The next steps will walk you through drawing an 1/8" horizontal line. AutoCAD provides more than one way to do this. You will try one of them now.

You should understand that it is virtually impossible to draw a perfectly horizontal or vertical (or any precise angle) by visually picking points on the screen. You need AutoCAD's help!

24. On the *Status Bar*, make sure **Polar Tracking** is turned on. (Figure 2-1.10). *It should look like a button pushed in (i.e., ON).*

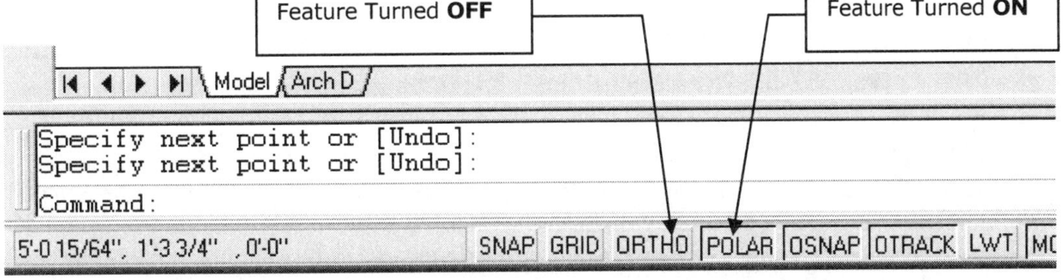

Figure 2-1.10 Status Bar – shown with Polar (i.e., Polar Tracking) turned on
TIP: *You can adjust the Polar settings by right-clicking on the button.*

25. Using the **Line** Command: Pick a point somewhere in the upper left corner of the *Drawing Window.*

26. Start moving the mouse towards the right, and generally horizontal until you see a dashed reference line (extending off the screen in the direction you want to draw the line) appear on the screen as in **Figure 2-1.8.**

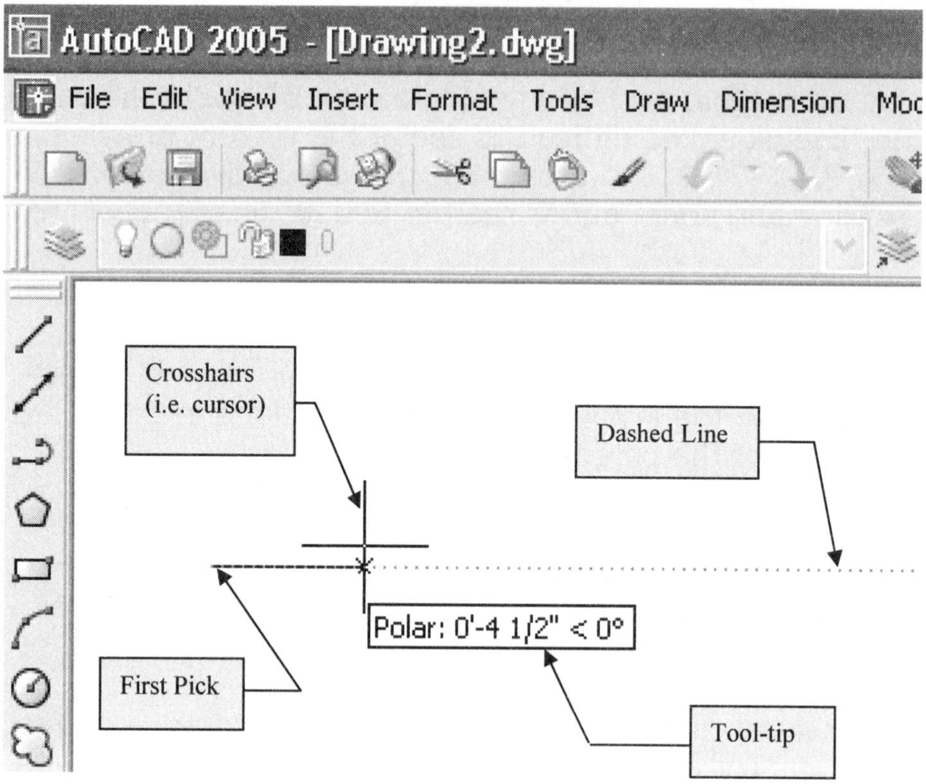

Figure 2-1.11 Drawing a line with the help of Polar Tracking
TIP: *Polar Tracking is active when you see the dashed line extending off the screen and the tool-tip.*

27. With the dashed line and *Tool-tip* visible on the screen, take your hand off the mouse (so you don't accidentally move it), and type: **1/8** and then press **Enter.**

TIP: *Notice you did not have to type the inch symbol; AutoCAD always assumes you mean inches unless you specify otherwise. A future lesson will review the input options in a little more detail.*

You have just drawn a line with a precise length and angle!

28. Use the **Properties Palette** to verify it was drawn correctly (similar to steps 21 and 22).

29. Use the **Zoom Window** tool to enlarge the view of the 1/8″ line.

30. Now use the **Zoom Extents** or **Zoom Previous** tools so that both lines are visible again.

Draw a 600′ line:

31. Select the **Line** icon and pick a point in the lower right corner of the *Drawing Window.*

32. Move the crosshairs (i.e., mouse) straight up from your first point so that *Polar Tracking* activates (Figure 2-1.12).

33. With the dashed line and tool-tip visible on the screen, take your hand off the mouse (so you don't accidentally move it), and type: **600′** and then press **Enter.**

TIP: Notice this time you had to type the foot symbol (′) or AutoCAD would have assumed you meant 600 inches, which is only 50′.

Figure 2-1.12 Drawing another line with the help of Polar Tracking

34. End the Line command *(right-click and select Enter).*

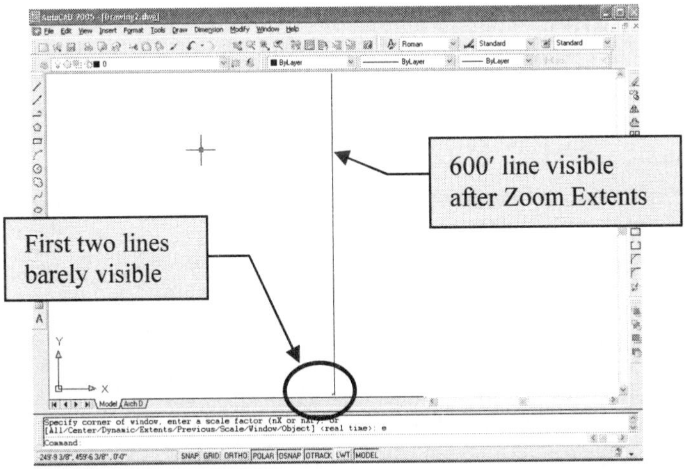

Figure 2-1.13 Drawing with three lines

Because the visible portion of the drawing area is only 2′-11″ tall (Figure 2-1.9), you obviously would not expect to see a 600′ line. You need the change the drawings magnification (i.e., zoom out) to see it.

35. Use **Zoom Extents** to see the entire drawing (Figure 2-1.13).

Drawing Shapes:

AutoCAD gives you the commands to draw common shapes like square/rectangles, circles, ellipses, polygons. These commands can be found on the Draw Toolbar. You will take a look at Rectangle and Circle now.

Rectangle:

36. Use **Zoom Previous** (or Zoom Window) to get back to the original view.

37. Select the **Rectangle** tool from the *Draw Toolbar.* 

    Notice the *Command Window* has the following prompt:
    Specify first corner point or [Chamfer/Elevation/Fillet/Thickness/Width]:

38. Pick your "**first corner point**" somewhere near the middle-bottom of the *Drawing Window*. Figure 2-1.14

    Notice the *Command Window* has the following prompt:
    Specify other corner point or [Dimensions]:

At this point you can pick a point on the screen, type a X,Y,Z coordinate, or use the sub-command "Dimensions".

39. Activate the sub-command "Dimensions" (this allows you to enter the size of the rectangle); Type **D** and then press **Enter.**

    You are now prompted to enter the length:
    Specify length for rectangles <0′-0″>:

40. Type **6.5** and then press **Enter** (this equals 6 ½″).

    You are now prompted to enter the width:
    Specify width for rectangles <0′-0″>:

41. Type **14** and then press **Enter** (this equals 1′-2″).

The last step is to select the position of rectangle relative to the start-point previously picked.

42. Move the cursor around the start-point in a circular fashion, notice the four positions in which the *Rectangle* is displayed; then click in the upper-right quadrant to complete the *Rectangle*. (Figure 2-1.14)

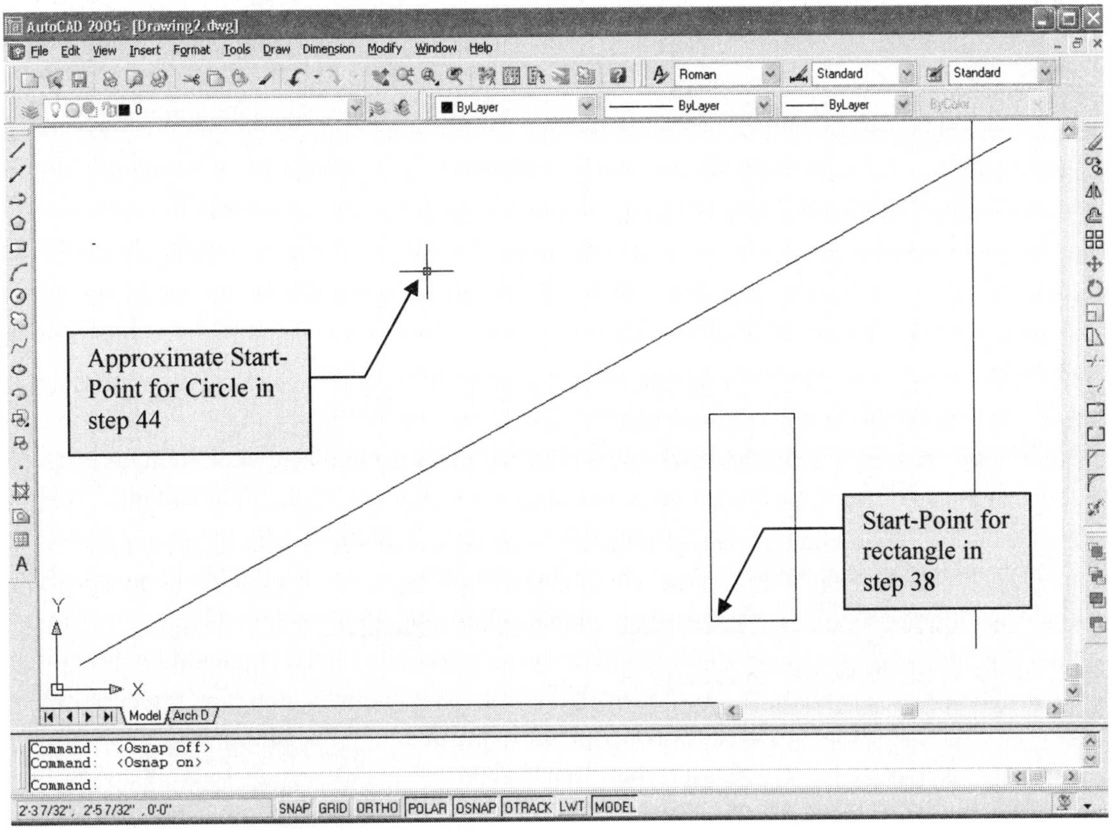

Figure 2-1.14 Drawing with Rectangle added

Circle:

43. Select the **Circle** tool from the *Draw Toolbar.* 

44. You are now prompted to pick the center point for the circle; pick a point approximately as shown in Figure 2-1.14.

You should now see the following prompt:

Specify radius of circle or [Diameter]:

Move your mouse around to see that you could arbitrarily pick a point on the screen to create a quick circle if needed, then proceed to step 45 where you will draw a circle with a radius of 6 5/8".

45. Type **6-5/8** and then press **Enter** (this equals 6 5/8"). (Figure 2-1.15)

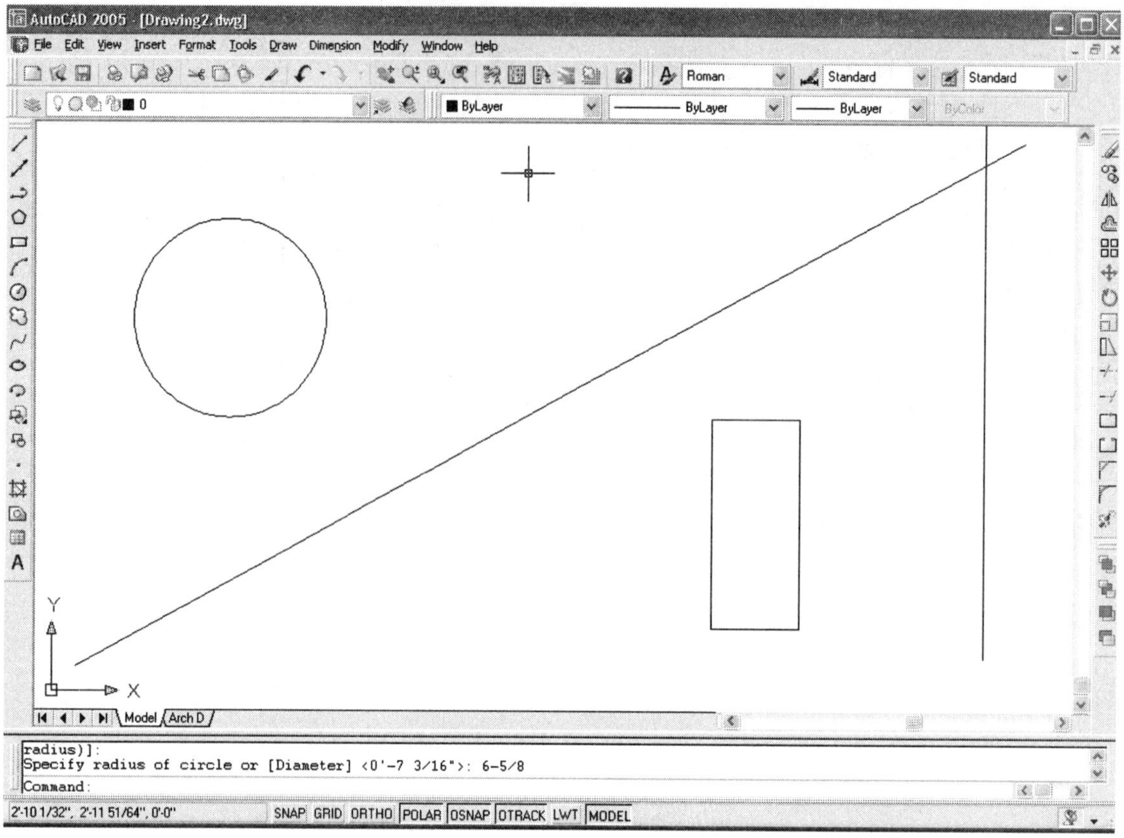

Figure 2-1.15 Drawing with Circle added

46. View the Properties for both the Circle and Rectangle.
    Notice: *See Figure 2-16 for the Circle's Properties; you can actually modify the Circle by entering a new Circumference or Area.*

47. **Save** your drawing as **ex2-1.dwg.**

> **Where should I save my files?**
> *You should create a folder to save these files into; typical a sub-folder in the My Documents folder. Your instructor may specify a location for your files.*

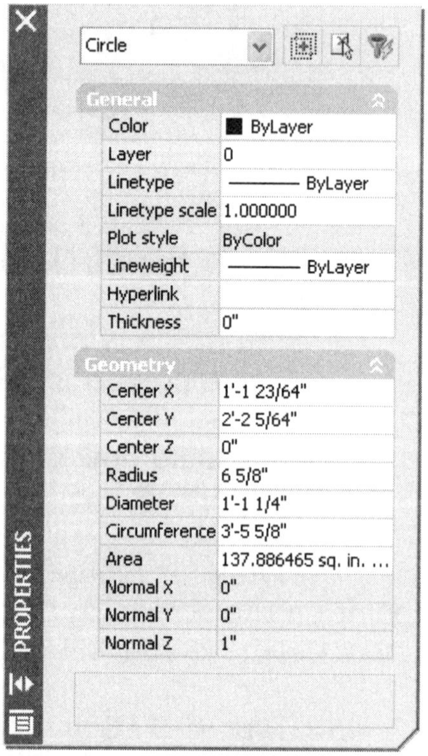

Figure 2-1.16 Properties for circle

Exercise 2-2:
Object Snaps

Object Snap is a tool that allows you to accurately pick a point on an object. For example, when drawing a line you can use Object Snap (osnap) to select, as the start-point, the endpoint or midpoint of another line.

This feature is absolutely critical to drawing accurate technical drawings. Using this feature allows you to be confident you are creating perfect intersections, corners, etc. Figure 2-2.1

Object Snaps Options:

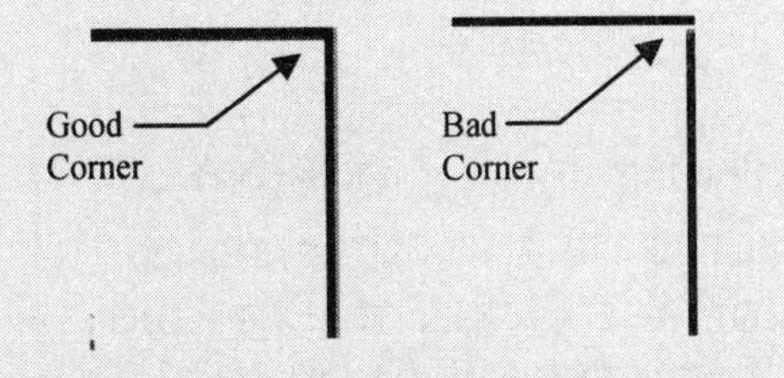

Figure 2-2.1 typical problem with Object Snap is not used

You can use *Object Snaps* in one of two ways.

- Using the *Running OSNAP* mode
- On an individual pick-point basis

Running *Osnap* mode is a feature that, when turned on, constantly scans the area near your crosshairs when AutoCAD is looking for user input. You can configure which types of points to look for.

Using an *Object Snap* for individual pick-points allows you to quickly select a particular point on an object. This option will also override the Running *Osnap* setting, which means you tell AutoCAD to just look for the endpoint on an object (for the next pick-point only) rather than the three or four types being scanned for by the Running *Osnap* feature.

Enabling Running Object Snaps:

To toggle *Object Snap* on and off you simply click the **OSNAP** button on the *Status Bar*.

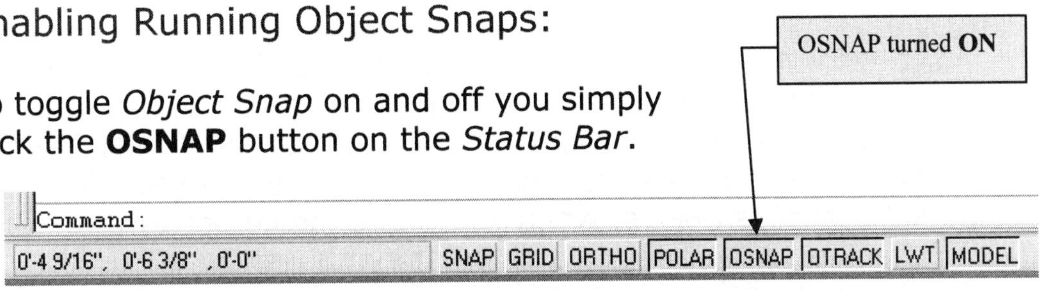

Figure 2-2.2 Status Bar – shown with OSNAP (Object Snap) turned on

Snap Symbols:

By now you should be well aware of the Object Snap Symbols that AutoCAD displays as you move your cursor about the drawing window (while you are in a command like Line and AutoCAD is awaiting your input or pick-point).

If you hold your cursor still for a moment, while a snap symbol is displayed, a tool tip will appear on the screen. However, when you become familiar with the snap symbols you can pick sooner (rather than waiting for the tool tip to display). Figure 2-2.3

The TAB key cycles through the available snaps near your cursor.

The keyboard shortcut turns off the other snaps for one pick. For example, if you type END on the keyboard while in the line command, AutoCAD will only look for an Endpoint for the next pick.

Finally, typing NON (none) turns all snaps off for one pick (assuming running OSNAP is enabled).

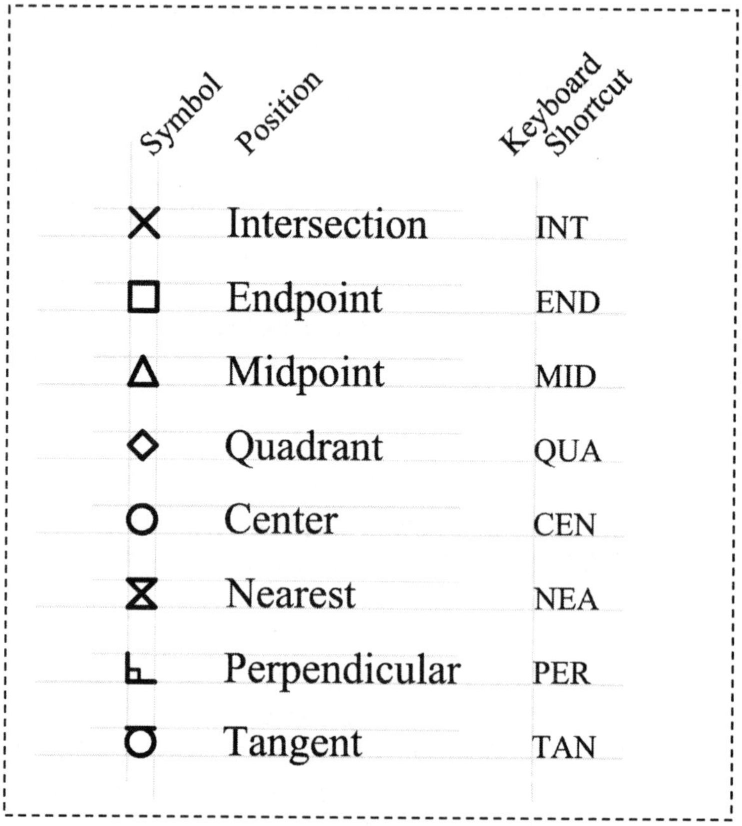

Figure 2-2.3 OSNAP symbols that are displayed on the screen when selecting a point.

Setting Object Snaps:

You can set AutoCAD to have just one or all Object Snaps running at the same time. Let's say you have Endpoint and Midpoint set to be running. While using the Line command, you move your cursor near an existing line. When the cursor is near the end of the line you will see the Endpoint symbol show up, when you move the cursor towards the middle of the line you will see the Midpoint symbol show up.

The next step shows you how to tell AutoCAD which Object Snaps you want it to look for.

First you need to ***Open*** the drawing from the previous Lesson.

1. **Open** drawing **ex2-1.dwg** (if not currently open).
2. Next, do a **Save-As** and name the drawing **ex2-2.dwg.**
3. Right-click on the *OSNAP* button on the *Status Bar* and select **Settings** from the pop-up menu. (Figure 2-2.4)

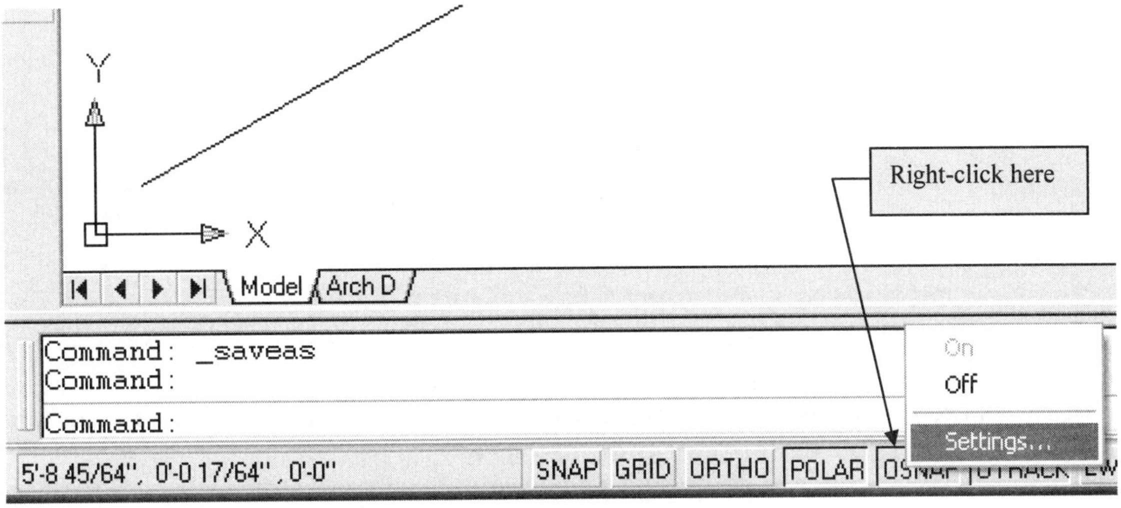

Figure 2-2.4 Right-click on OSNAP button located on the Status Bar

You are now in the **Drafting Settings** dialog box on the *Object Snaps* tab, compare to **Figure 2-2.5**.

4. Make sure only the following *Object Snaps* are checked:
   a. Endpoint
   b. Midpoint
   c. Center
   d. Intersection
   e. Perpendicular
5. Click **OK** to Close the dialog box.

> **FOR MORE INFORMATION...**
>
> For more on using Object Snaps, search AutoCAD's Help System for **Drafting Settings**.
>
> Then double-click the **Drafting Settings Dialog Box** and then select the **Object Snap** link within the article.

> **FYI...**
>
> The *Running Object Snaps* shown in Figure 2-2.5 are for AutoCAD in general, not just the current drawing.
>
> This is convenient; you don't have to adjust to your favorite settings for each drawing (existing or new).

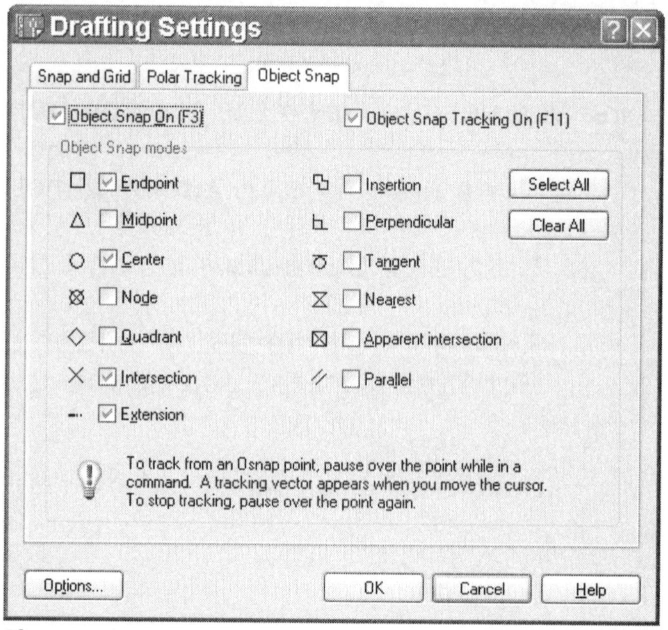

Figure 2-2.5 Object Snap tab on Drafting Settings dialog

Now that you have the *Running Object Snaps* set, you will give this feature a try.

6. Using the **Line** command, move your cursor to the lower-left portion of the diagonal line. (Figure 2-2.6)

7. Hover the cursor over the line's endpoint (without picking), when you see the *Endpoint Symbol* you can click to select that point.

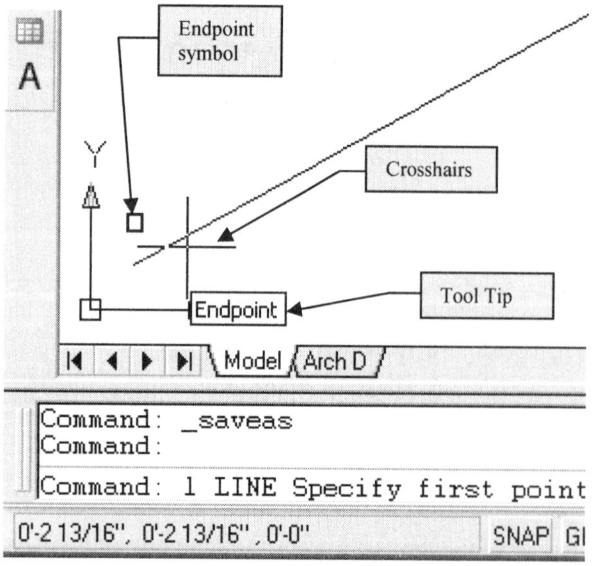

Figure 2-2.6 Endpoint OSNAP symbol visible

> **Just so you know...**
>
> It is important that you see the *OSNAP* symbol before clicking. Also, once you see the symbol you should be careful not to move the mouse too much.
>
> These steps will help to ensure accurate corners.

While still in the Line command you will draw additional lines using *OSNAP* to accurately select the line's *Endpoint*.

8. Draw the additional lines shown in **Figure 2-2.7** using the appropriate *Object Snap* (changing the Running Snap as required to select the required point).
    a. ***TIP #1*:** When using the Line command you can draw several line segments without having to end the Line command and then restart it for the next line segment. After picking the start and end points for a line, the end point automatically becomes the first point for the next line segment; this continues until your finish the Line command (i.e., right-click and select Enter).
    b. ***TIP #2*:** At any point, while the Line command is active, you can right-click on the OSNAP button on the Status Bar and adjust its settings. This will not cancel the line command.

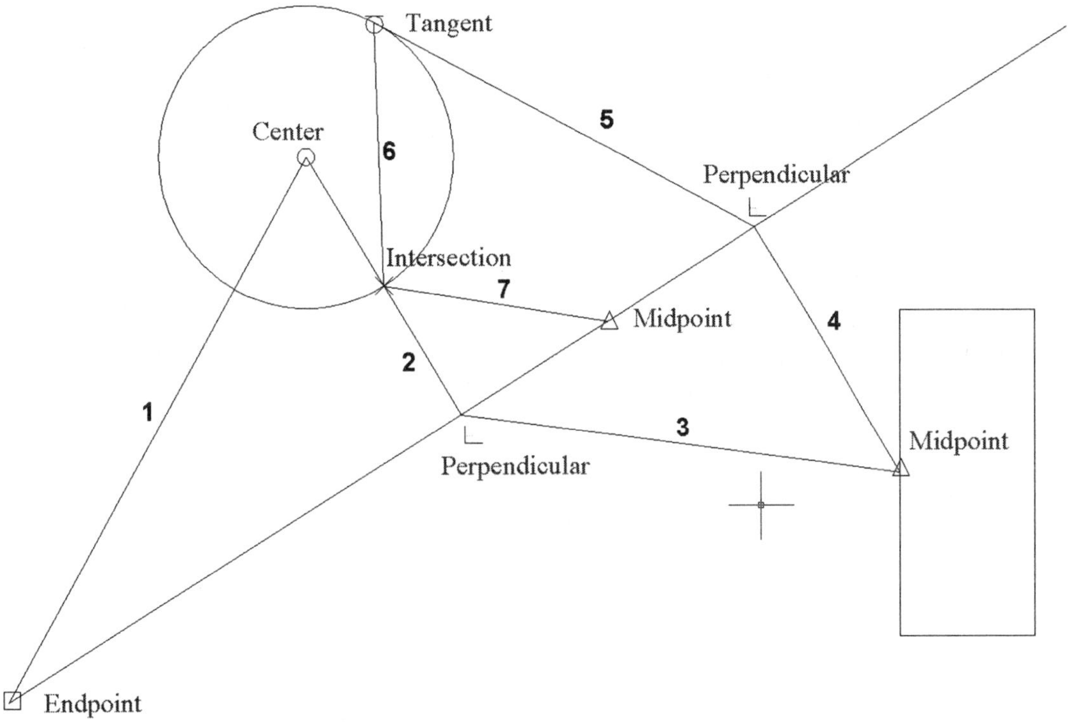

Figure 2-2.7 Several lines added using running OSNAPS. The numbers indicate the order the lines are to be drawn in.

9. **Save** your drawing.

> **This is an architectural example?**
>
> OK, this is not really an architectural example yet. However, the point here is to focus on the fundamental concepts and not architecture just yet.

Exercise 2-3:
Modify Tools

The Modify Tools are the most used in AutoCAD. Much time is spent tweaking designs and making code related revisions.

Example: Use the Draw tools (e.g., Lines, Circles, Rectangles) to initially draw the walls, doors, windows and furniture. Then use the Modify tools to *Stretch* a room so it is larger, *Mirror* a door so it swings in the direction of egress, and *Move* the furniture per the owner's instructions.

You will usually access the various Modify tools from the Modify Toolbar; you can also access them from the Modify Menu shown in Figure 2-3.1. (You can probably visualize what most of the commands do by their name.)

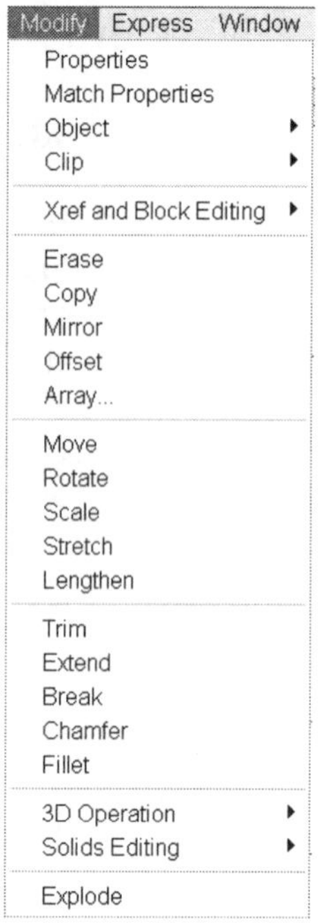

Figure 2-3.1 Modify menu

In this exercise you will get a brief overview of a few of the Modify tools, manipulating the tangled web of lines you have previously drawn.

1. **Open** drawing **ex2-2.dwg** from the previous lesson.

2. **Save-As ex2-3.dwg.**
   FYI: *You will notice in this book that instructions or commands that have already been covered will have less "step-by-step" instruction.*

Erase command:

It is no surprise that the Erase tool is a necessity, things change and mistakes are made. You can erase one entity at a time or several. Erasing entities is very easy; you select the Erase Icon, pick the objects to erase and then right-click (which equals pressing Enter on the keyboard). You will try this on two lines in your drawing.

3. Select **Erase.** 

4. [Notice the *Command Line* is prompting: **Select objects:**]
   Use the mouse to select the lines identified in **Figure 2-3.2**.
   TIP: *See the section below on Selecting Entities.*

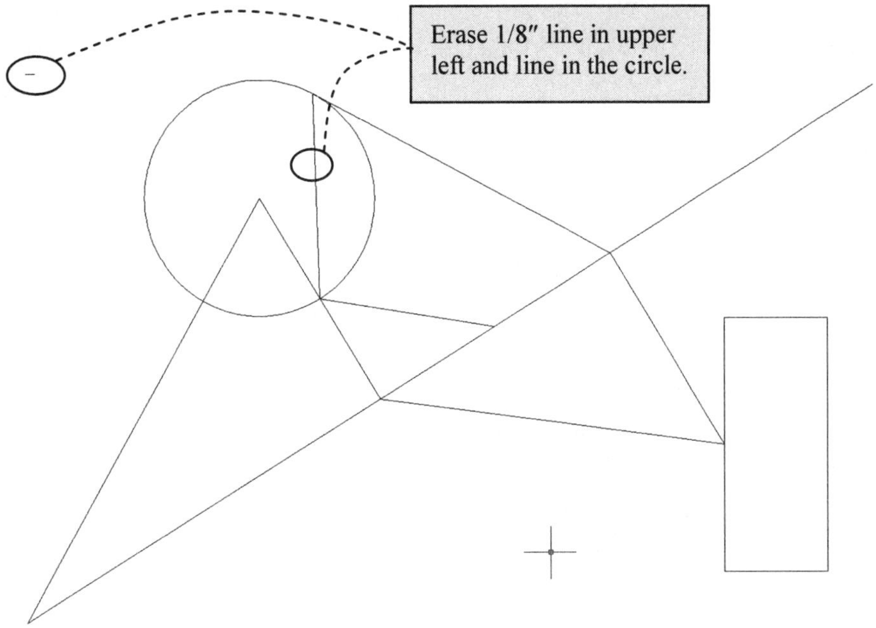

Figure 2-3.2 Lines to be erased

5. **Right-click** to complete the task.

Selecting entities:

At this time we will digress and take a quick look at the various techniques for selecting entities in AutoCAD. Most commands work the same when it comes to selecting entities. As mentioned before, you need to keep your eye on the *Command Line* so you know when AutoCAD is ready for you to select entities or provide other user input.

When selecting entities, you have two primary ways to select them:

- Individually select entities one at a time
- Select several entities at a time with a window

You can use one, or a combination of both, methods to select entities (when using the Copy command for example).

Individual Selections:
When prompted to select entities (to copy or erase, for example), simply move the cursor over the object and click. With most commands you repeat this process until you have selected all the entities you need – then you typically press Enter or right-click to tell AutoCAD you are done selecting.

Window Selections:
Similarly, when prompted to select entities, you can pick a Window around several entities to select them all at once. To select a window, rather than selecting an object as previously described, you select one corner of the window you wish to select (that is, you pick a point in "space"). Now as you move the mouse you will see a rectangle on the screen that represents the window you are selecting. When the Window encompasses the entities you wish to select – click the mouse.

You actually have two types of Windows you can select. One is called a **Window** and the other is called a **Crossing Window**.

Window:
This option allows you to select only the entities that are completely within the Window. Any lines that extend out of the Window are not selected.

Crossing Window:
This option allows you to select all the entities that are completely within the Window and any that extend outside the Window.

Using Window versus Crossing Window:
To select a *Window* you simply pick your two points from left to right (Figure 2-3.3a).

Conversely, to select a Crossing Window, you pick the two diagonal points of the window from right to left (Figure 2-3.3b).

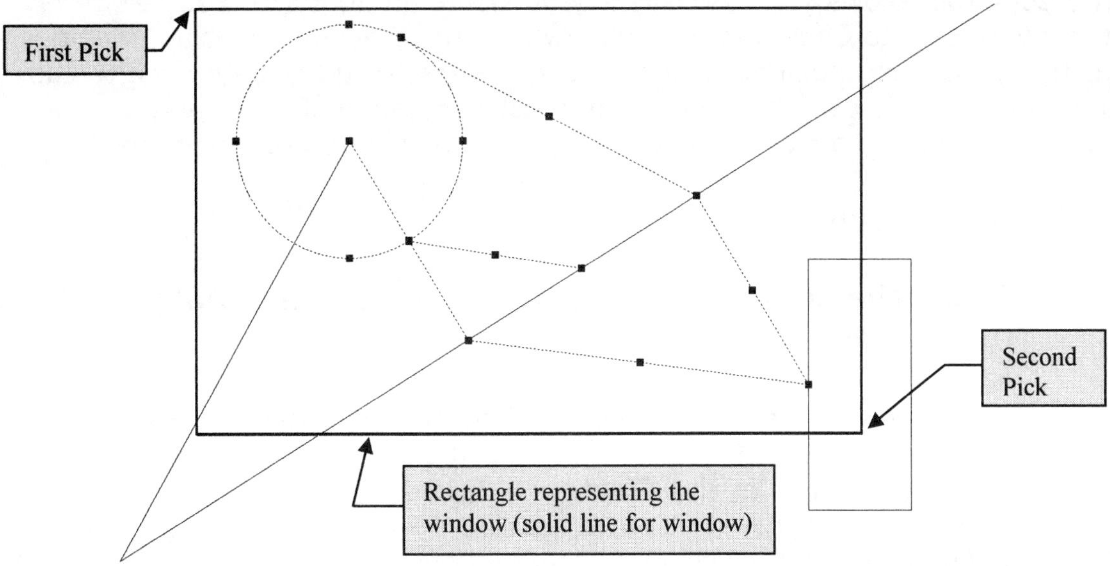

Figure 2-3.3a Lines selected using *Window;* only the lines within the window are selected.

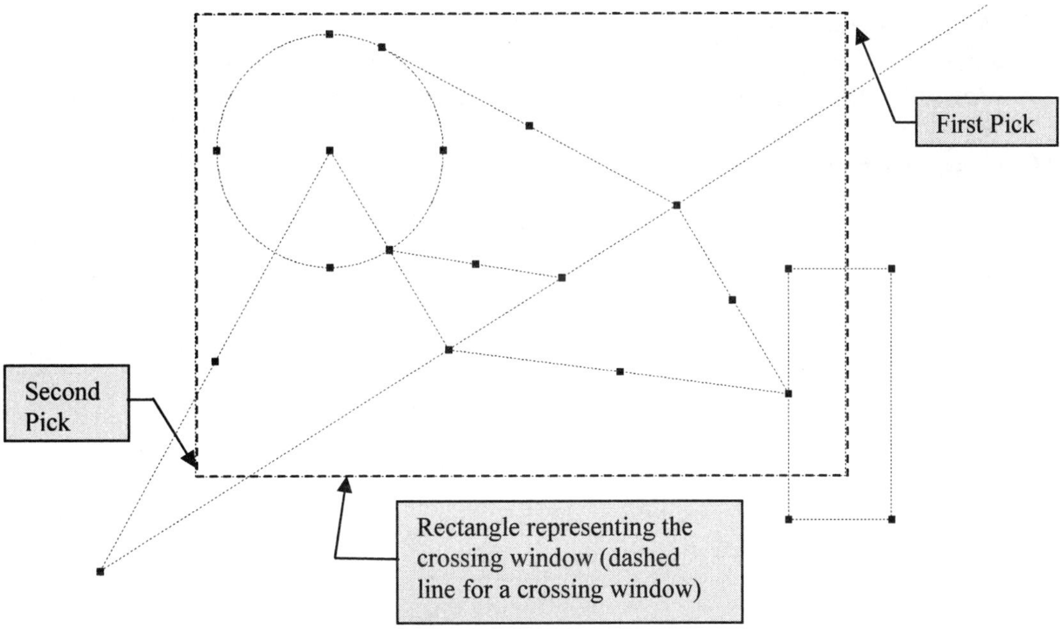

Figure 2-3.3b Lines selected using a *Crossing Window;* all lines are selected.

Copy command:

The Copy tool allows you to accurately duplicate an entity(s). You select the items you want to Copy and then pick two points that represent an imaginary vector (which provides both length and angle) defining the path used to copy the entity to; you can also type in the length and angle if there are no convenient points to pick in the drawing. You will try both methods next.

6. Select **Copy.** 

7. **Select the circle** and then **right-click** - *this tells AutoCAD that you are done selecting entities to copy.*

***Notice the prompt*:** **Specify base point or displacement, or [Multiple]:**

8. Pick the **Center** of the **Circle.** (Figure 2-3.4)
   FYI: *You actually have three different OSNAPS you can use here: Center, Endpoint and Intersection. All occur at the exact same point.*

Specify second point of displacement or <use first point as displacement>:

9. Pick the Endpoint of the angled line in the lower left corner. (See Figure 2-3.5.)
   FYI: *At this point you could continue copying the circle all over your drawing; AutoCAD will remain in copy mode until you press Esc or Enter*

10. Press **Enter.**

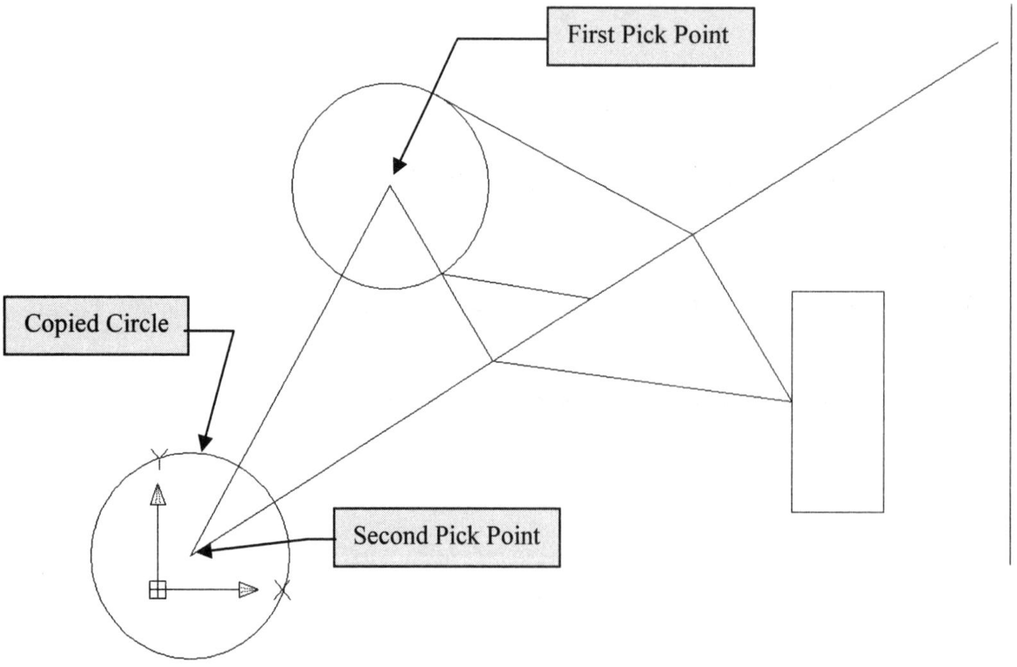

Figure 2-3.4 Copied circle; also indicates points selected

11. Select **Copy.** 

12. **Select the rectangle** and then **right-click.**

13. Pick an arbitrary point on the screen. *(In this scenario, it makes no difference where you pick; you will see why in a moment.)*

At this point you will type in the displacement data (i.e., distance and angle), rather than picking a second point on the screen.

14. In the *Command Window* type: **@18<45** and then press **Enter** twice or right-click. (See Figure 2-3.5.)

What does @18<45 mean?

When you need to Move or Copy something to a very specific location, you can type in the distance and angle from the original entity. This is very useful when you do not have any entities drawn that represent this distance and angle (e.g., Figure 2-3.4).

The **@** symbol tells AutoCAD that the distance and angle to follow are relative to the point just picked.

The **18** represents the distance, in this case 18 inches. Remember, if you do not specify feet or inches AutoCAD assumes inches. So in this example you would not have to press the extra key for the inch symbol; although 18″ would work.

Here are some other valid distances:

1′4	*equals* 1′-4″	16	*equals* 1′-4″
3′	*equals* 3′-0″	36	*equals* 3′-0″
0-3/4	*equals* 3/4″	.75	*equals* 3/4″
3-5/8	*equals* 3 5/8″	1′3-5/8″	*equals* 1′-3 5/8″

The **<** symbol tells AutoCAD the next number is the angle.

The 45 represents the angle (or direction) the entities will be Moved or Copied in.

Here are some angles and a graphical representation of its direction:

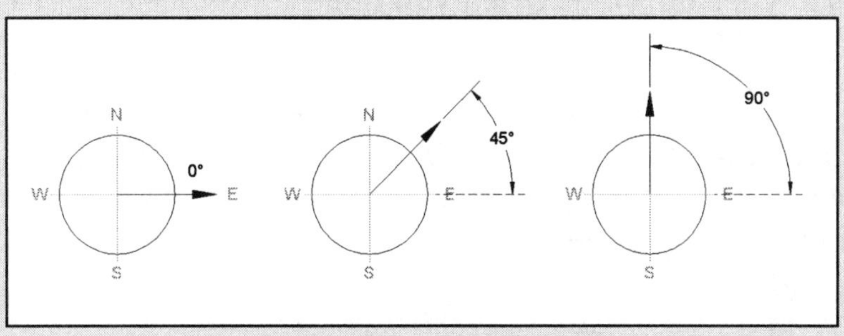

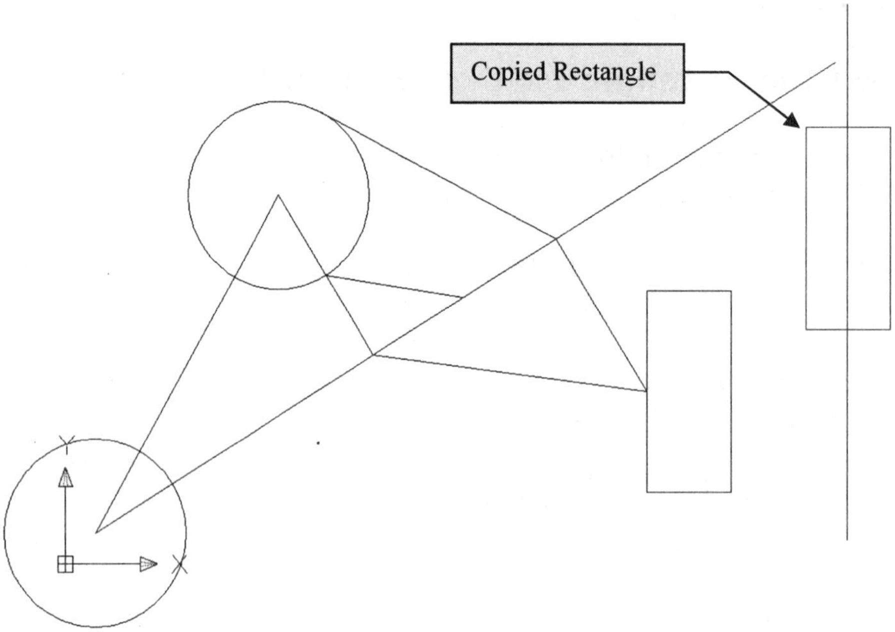

Figure 2-3.5 Copied rectangle. Dashed line represents the distance and angle of displacement.

Note: your drawing may look a little different than this one because your drawing is not totally to scale.

Move command:

The Move command works exactly like the Copy command except, of course, you move the entities rather than copy them. Given the similarity to the previous command covered, the Move command will not be covered here. You are encouraged to try it yourself. Use the Undo command to get back to the drawing shown in Figure 2-3.5 before proceeding.

Rotate command:

With the Rotate command, you can arbitrarily or accurately rotate one or more entities in your drawing. When you need to Rotate accurately, you can pick points that define the angle (assuming points exist in the drawing to pick) or you can type a specific angle. The architectural template you are using in this book has the degrees "type" set to decimal. Other types are available such as Deg/Min/Sec and Radians, but architects typically use decimal angles unless drawing a site plan from a surveyor's drawing that has angles listed in another format.

15. Select **Rotate.** 

16. **Select the rectangle** you just copied and then **right-click** - *this tells AutoCAD that you are done selecting entities to rotate.*
    You are now prompted: **Specify base point:**
    This is the point about which the rotation will occur.

17. Pick the *Midpoint* of the vertical line on the left side of the rectangle. **(Figure 2-3.6)**

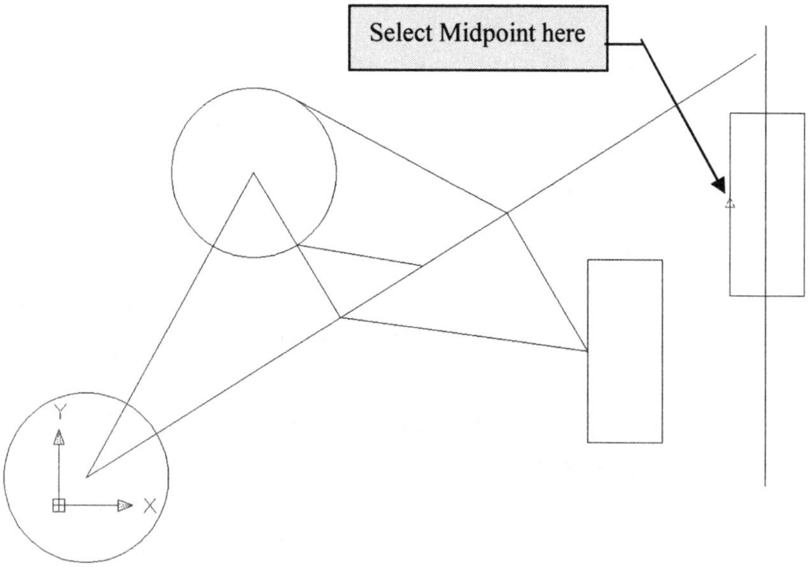

Figure 2-3.6 Rotate command. First Step - Select midpoint of vertical line on left.

You are now prompted: **Specify rotation angle or [Reference]:**

18. Type **90** and then press **Enter.**

Similar to the rotation examples recently discussed, the previous step just rotated the rectangle 90 degrees counter-clockwise. (Figure 2-3.7)

19. Select the **Undo** command.

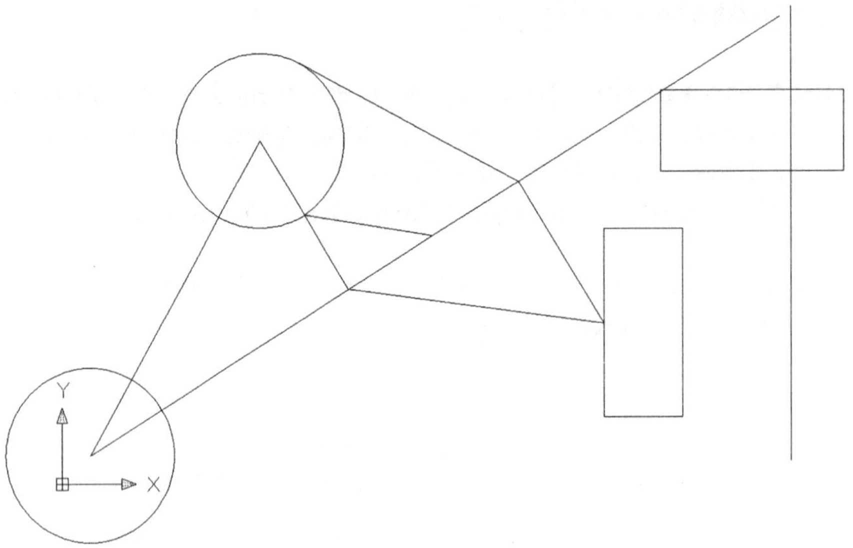

Figure 2-3.7 Rotate command – Rectangle rotated

Now you will do the same thing, except with a different angle. A negative angle rotates the entities in a clockwise direction.

20. Use the **Rotate** command, **select the rectangle** and then **pick the same Midpoint** as in step 17.

21. This time, for the *Rotation Angle,* type **-45** and **Enter.**

Notice, now, that the rectangle rotated 45 degrees in the clockwise direction. (Figure 2-3.8)

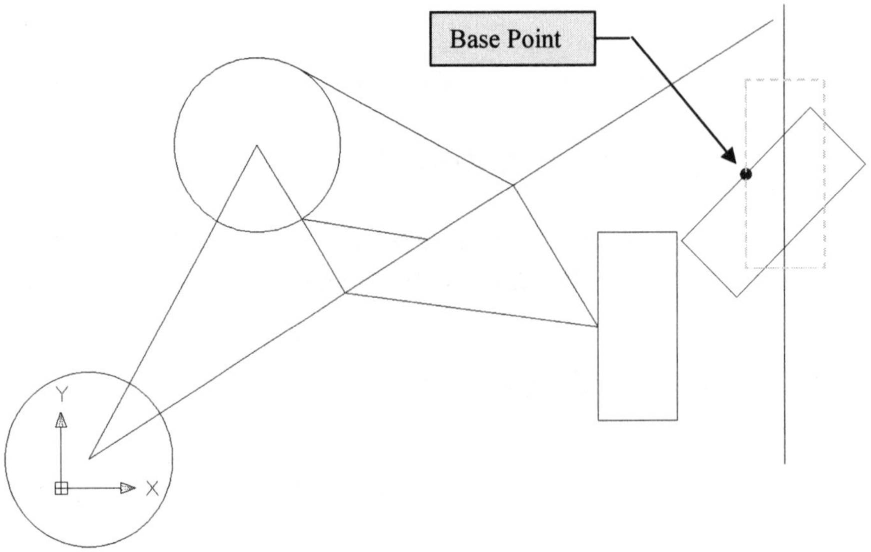

Figure 2-3.8 Rectangle rotated. Dashed rectangle represents original position.

Scale command:

The Scale command has steps similar to the Rotate command. First, select what you want to scale and then specify the base point. Then, instead of entering a rotation angle, enter a scale factor (e.g., 2 or .5; where 2 would be twice the original size and .5 would be half the original size).

Next you will use the Scale command to adjust the size of the circle near the bottom.

Before you scale the circle, you should use the **Properties Dialog** box to note the **diameter** of the circle. After scaling the circle, you will refer back to the Properties Dialog to note the change. This step is meant to teach you how to verify the accuracy and dimensions of entities in AutoCAD.
TIP: *You can double-click on most objects to view its properties.*

22. Select **Scale.** 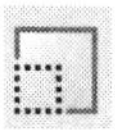

23. **Select the circle** (the one at the bottom) and then **right-click.**

You are now prompted: **Specify base point:**
This is the point about which the entity (or entities) will be scaled.

24. Pick the center of the circle. *(In this case you can use one of three Osnaps: Center, Endpoint or Intersection.)*

You are now prompted: **Specify scale factor or [Reference]:**

25. Type **.5** and press **Enter.**

Now use the **Properties Dialog** to note the change in the size of the circle, from 6 5/8" to 3 5/16" radius. A Scale Factor of .5 reduces the entities to half their original scale. (Figure 2-3.9)

Selecting the correct base point:
You need to select the appropriate Base Point, for both the Scale and Rotate commands, to get the results desired. A few examples are shown in Figure 2-3.10. The dashed line indicates the original position of the entity being modified. The black dot indicates the base point selected.

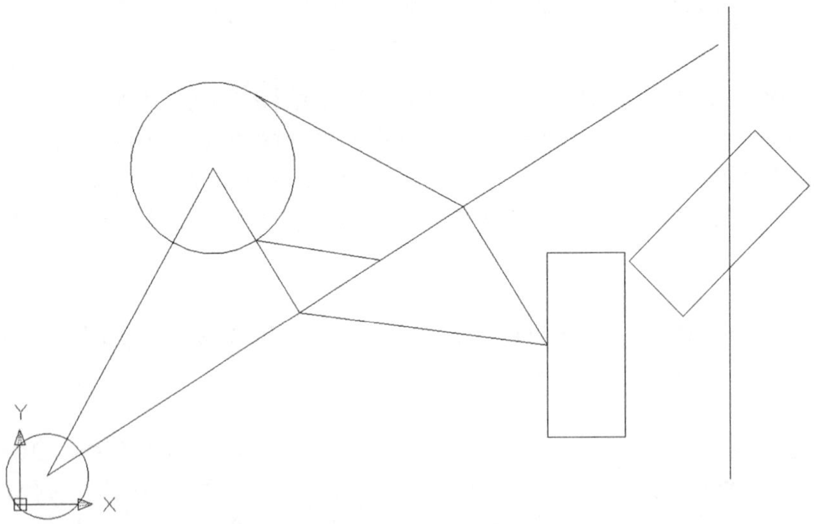

Figure 2-3.9 Scaled circle. Notice it is half the size of the other circle.

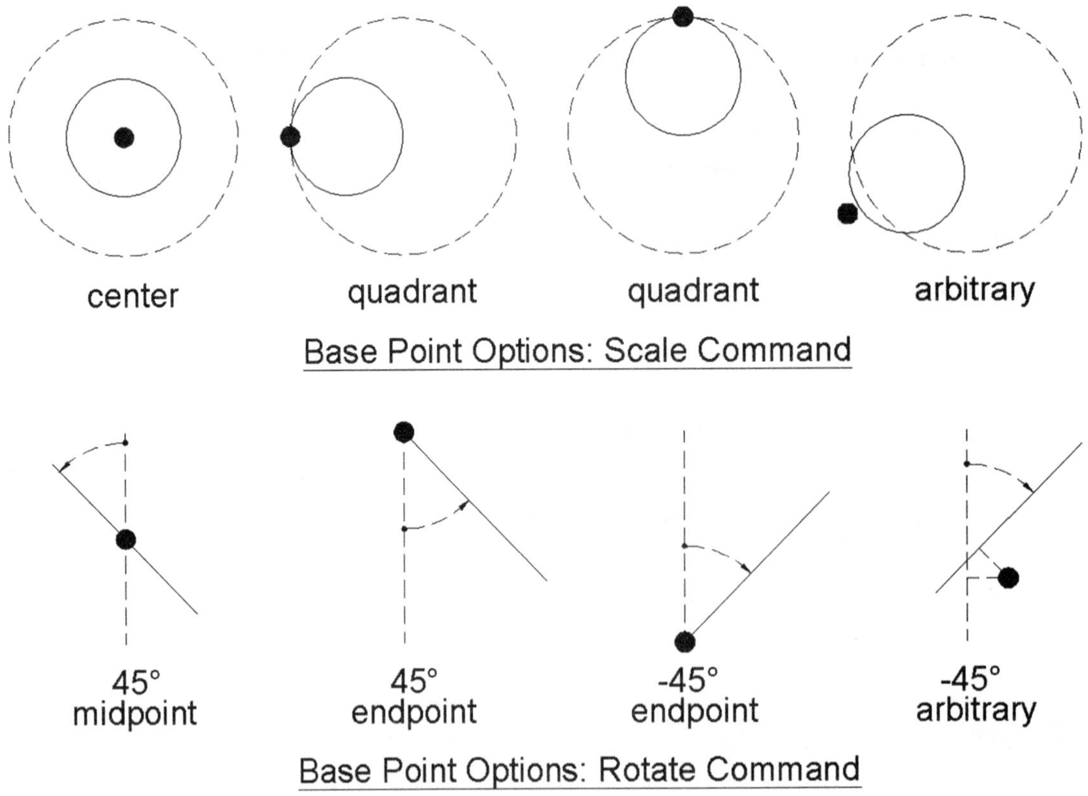

Figure 2-3.10 Base Point Options. The various results when different base points are selected.

This will conclude the brief tour of the Modify toolbar.

As you surely noticed, the Modify Toolbar has a few other icons that have not been investigated yet. Most of these will be cover later in this book.

26. Save your drawing (your drawing should already be named: **ex2-3.dwg** per step number 2 above).

Images courtesy of LHB
www.LHBcorp.com

Carter Residence

Exercise 2-4:
Annotations

Annotations (text; notes) allow the designer / drafter to accurately describe the drawing. You will take a quick look at this feature now.

Annotations:

Adding annotations to a drawing can be as essential as the drawing itself. Often the notes (i.e., annotations) describe something about a part of the drawings that would be difficult to discern from the drawing alone.

For example, a wall framing drawing showing a bolt may not indicate, graphically, how many bolts are needed or at what spacing. The note might say *"5/8" anchor bolt at 24" O.C."*

Next you will add text to your drawing"

1. **Open** drawing **ex2-3.dwg** from the previous lesson.
2. **Save-As ex2-4.dwg.**
3. **Zoom Extents** if required, to see the entire drawing.
4. Select the **Multiline Text** (referred to as *Mtext*). 

Notice the current *Command Prompt*; you are given the current *Text Style* (covered more thoroughly later in the book) and the current *Text Height*. You are also prompted to **specify first corner**. Basically you are specifying a window (or box) that will contain the text, which is easily adjusted later as well. Figure 2-4.1

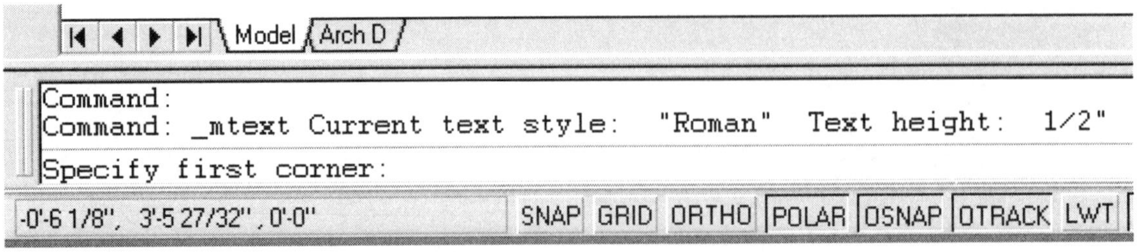

Figure 2-4.1 Command prompt for Mtext command

5. Pick your first point and then your second point to define a box as shown in **Figure 2-4.2**
   TIP*: You rarely click and drag your mouse button in AutoCAD; mostly you click and release the mouse button and then position the cursor at the second location and then click again.*

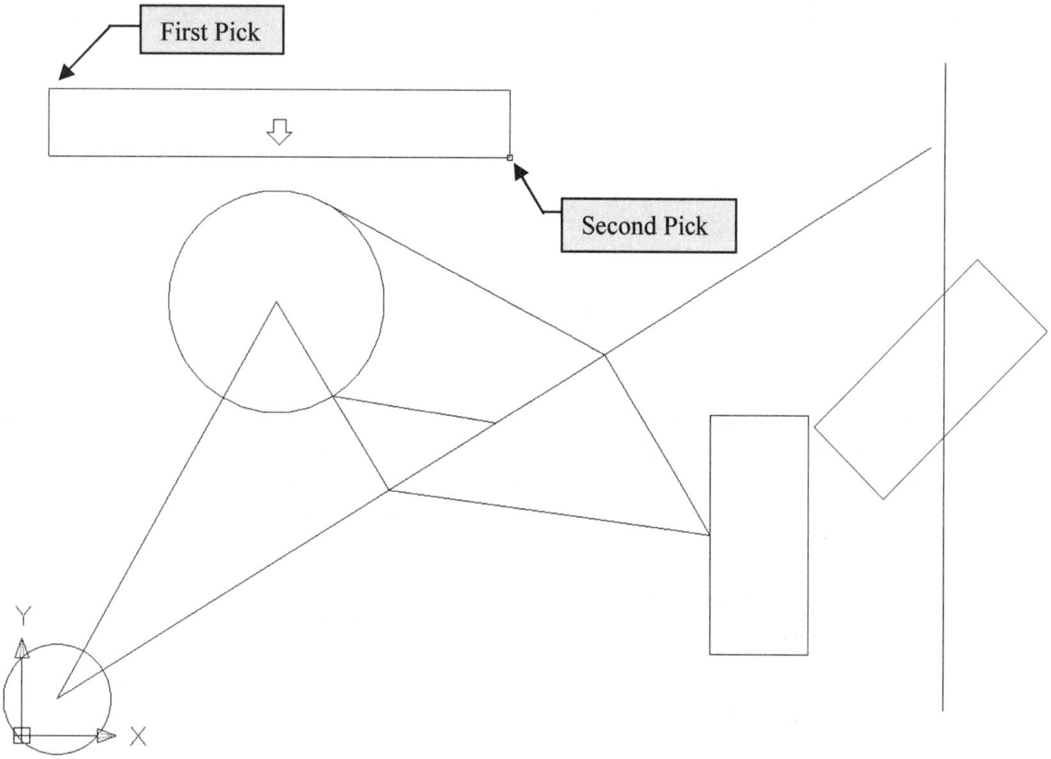

Figure 2-4.2 Mtext; defining the window that contains the text (first point picked; picking second)

You can now enter text in the *Mtext* window. This window will not be visible when you are done typing. The *Mtext* tool is similar to text editors like MS Word or WordPerfect; you can make text bold, italic, centered, underlined, etc.

Next you will enter some text.

6. In the *Mtext Editor* you will type the following text (Figure 2-4.3): **Learning AutoCAD 2005 is fun!**

> **TIP!**
> In the *Mtext* editor you can right-click to see a pop-up menu that gives you access to several tools like Select All and Find and Replace. See image to the right for an example.

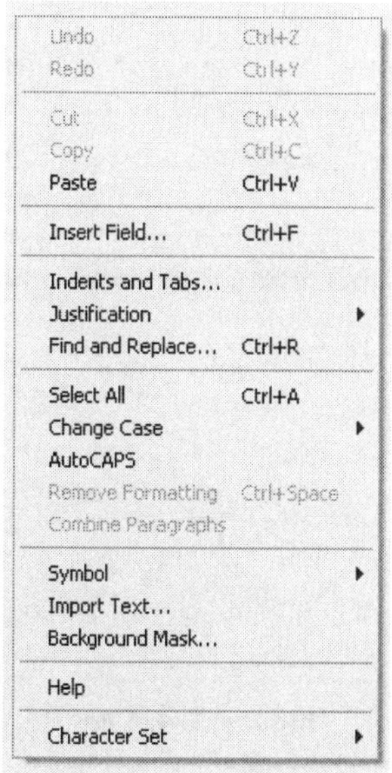

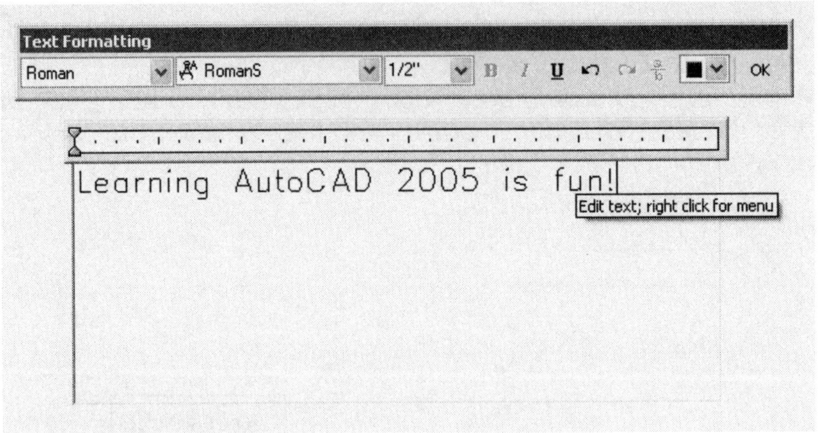

Figure 2-4.3 Mtext; text typed in text editor window, Text Formatting toolbar displayed

7. When finished typing text, click the **OK** button on the floating Text Formatting toolbar shown in Figure 2-4.3 above.
   TIP: *If you ever want to cancel the Mtext window without typing text, you can simply press the Escape button on the keyboard.*

Your text should look similar to Figure 2-4.3. Text can be Moved and Rotated with the tools on the *Modify Toolbar*.

8. **Save** your drawing.

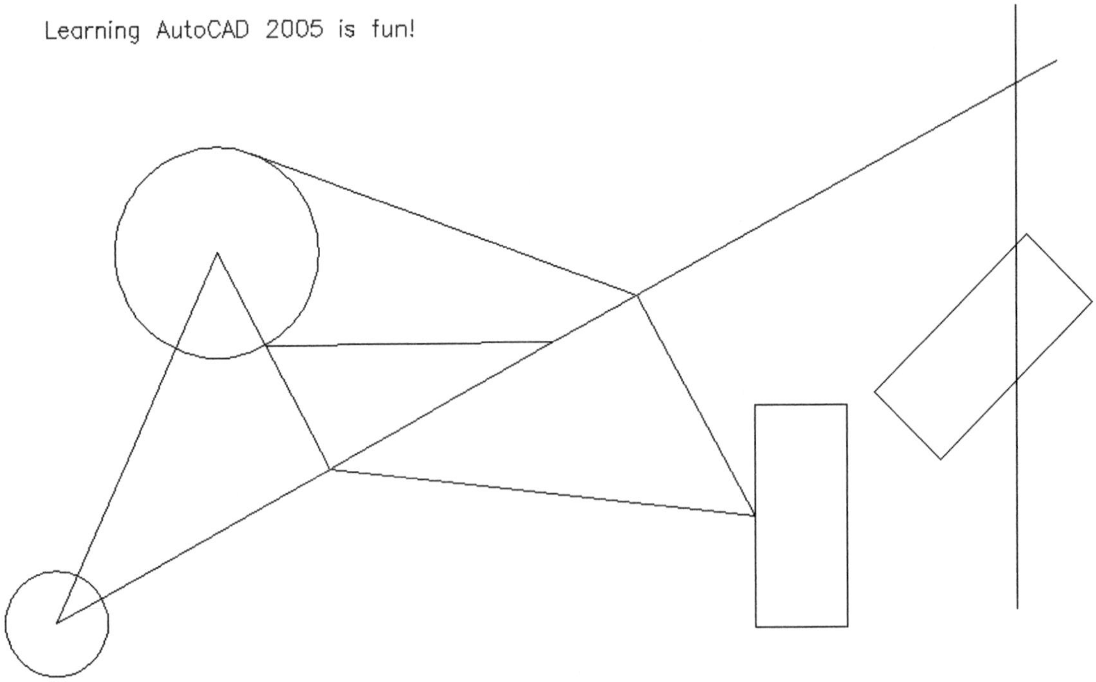

Figure 2-4.4 Mtext; final results of text entered

Exercise 2-5:
Printing

The final exercise in this lesson will cover another essential feature in CAD, which is printing. Printing takes some time to fully understand. Printing will be covered more thoroughly later in this book (Lesson 8).

Print Room in a large architectural firm

Image courtesy of BWBR Architects
www.bwbr.com

In this exercise you will print to an 8 ½" x 11" piece of paper with the drawing filling the screen.

1. Open drawing **ex2-4.dwg.**

2. Use the Zoom tools if required to display the portion of drawing shown in Figure 2-4.4.

3. Select the **Plot** icon (called print in other programs). You are now in the Plot Dialog box. This is where you tell

AutoCAD what printer or plotter to use, what scale and what size paper to name a few examples. (Figure 2-5.1)

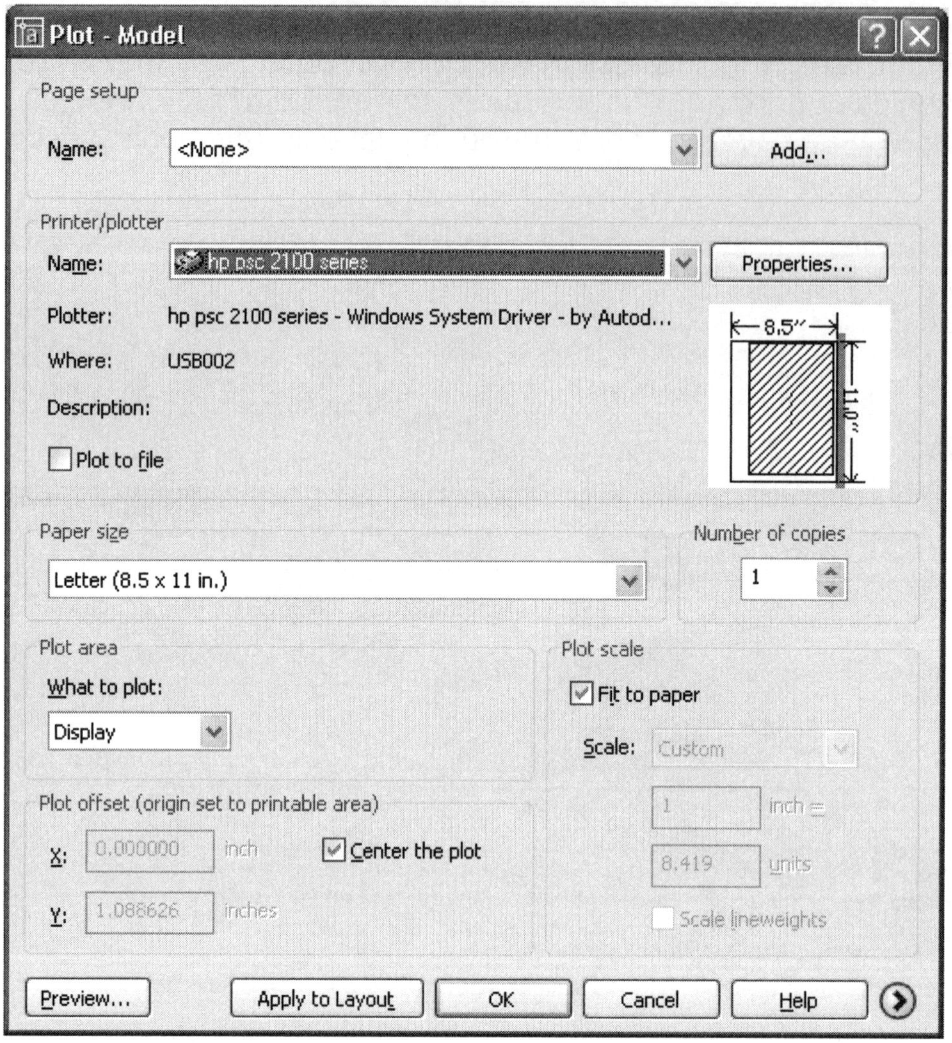

Figure 2-5.1 Plot Dialog Box; basic options

4. Make the following adjustments: (Figure 2-5.1)
    a. Select a **Printer** you have access to
    b. Paper size: **Letter (8.5 x 11 in.)**
    c. What to plot: **Display**
    d. Center the plot: *checked*
    e. Plot scale: **Fit to paper** *checked*

Additional settings are available, but are hidden because they are not used as often. You will take a quick look at this before plotting.

5. Click the "more options" arrow in the lower right corner of the *Plot* dialog box. (Figure 2-5.1)

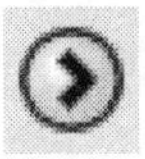

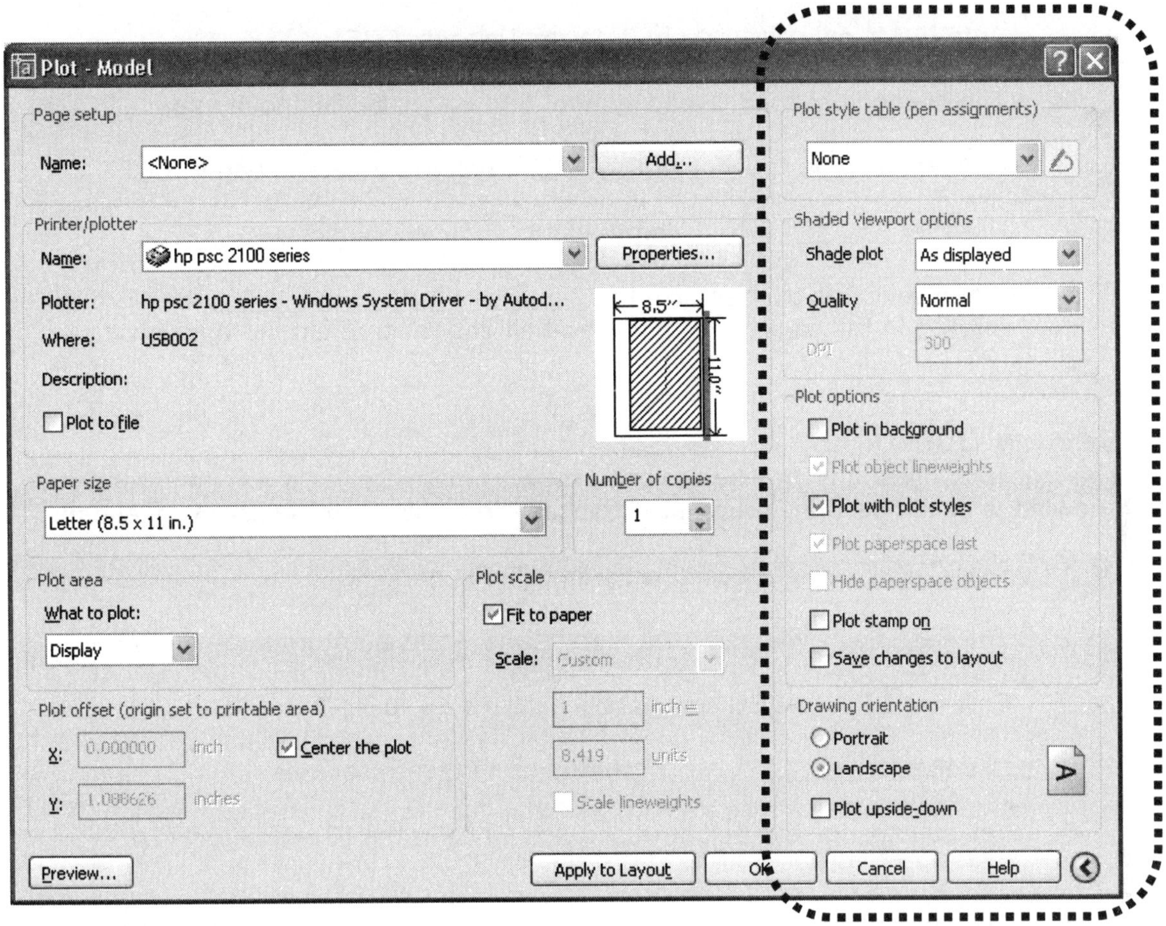

Figure 2-5.2 Plot Dialog Box; basic + more options shown

6. The only setting you need to verify is that *Drawing Orientation* is set to **Landscape.**

7. Click **OK** to send the plot (print).

USING PREVIEW...

Before you click OK, it is a good idea to click the *Preview* button first. This will show how your drawing will look on the size paper selected.

Doing a *Preview* first will save time and paper.

Self-Exam:

The following questions can be used as a way to check your knowledge of this lesson. The answers can be found at the bottom of this page.

1. AutoCAD is only accurate to 3 decimal places. (T/F)
2. The diamond shaped Osnap symbol represents the Midpoint snap. (T/F)
3. "Full Preview" in the Plot Dialog WILL save you time and paper. (T/F)
4. Use the ______________ command to duplicate objects.
5. When selecting entities, use the ____________ ____________ to select all the entities in the selection window and all entities that extend through it.

Review Questions:

The following questions may be assigned by your instructor as a way to assess your knowledge of this section. Your instructor has the answers to the review questions.

1. AutoCAD is a raster based program. (T/F)
2. The Base Point you select for Rotate and Scale is not important. (T/F)
3. Entering 16 for a distance, actually means 16'-0" to AutoCAD. (T/F)
4. Use the _________________ command to create squares.
5. You can change the height of the text while in the Mtext editor. (T/F)
6. Selecting this icon () allows you to _______________ one or more entities in a drawing.
7. What is the name of the Template file you are to use when creating a new Drawing in this book? ____
8. With the Rotate command, typing 45 for the degrees prompt, rotates the entities in the __________________________ direction; whereas -45 rotates the entities in the ______________________________ direction.
9. List all the Osnap points available on a circle (ex. Line: endpoint, midpoint, nearest) ____.
10. The OSNAP button on the Status Bar must be "pushed in" (i.e., on) to automatically and accurately select snap points while drawing. (T/F)

Self-Exam Answers:
1 - F, **2** - F, **3** - T, **4** - Copy, **5** – Crossing Window

Lesson 3
Drawing Architectural Objects (Draw & Modify)::

This lesson is meant to give you practice drawing in AutoCAD. While doing so, you will become familiar with the various shapes and sizes of the more common symbols used in a residential set of drawings.

Each drawing will be created in its own drawing file. The drawings (i.e., symbols) will be used later to automate drafting.

For some of the symbols to be drawn, you will have step-by-step instruction and / or a study on a particular command that would be useful in the creation of that object. Other symbols to be drawn are for practice by way of repetition and do not provide step-by-step instruction.

Do NOT draw the dimensions, they are for reference only.

Exercise 3-1:
Rectilinear Objects

Overview

All the objects you will draw in this exercise consist entirely of straight lines, either orthogonal or angular.

As previously mentioned, all the objects MUST BE drawn in SEPERATE drawing files. Each object will have a specific name provided, which is to be used to name the drawing file. All files should be saved in your personal folder created for this course.

Each object drawn will have the lower left corner located at the origin (0,0,0). This will be discussed further in a moment.

Each new drawing created for this course should be done using the **Architectural Imperial 2.dwt** template file.

You probably don't know anything about AutoCAD Layers yet, or if you are somewhat familiar with them, ALL entities drawn in Exercises 1 and 2 should be drawn on the default Layer, that is, Layer 0 (zero). So just make sure the Layer Toolbar displays Layer 0 similar to the Layers Toolbar shown on page 1-5.

filename: **Bookcase.dwg**

This is a simple rectangle that represents the size of a bookcase.

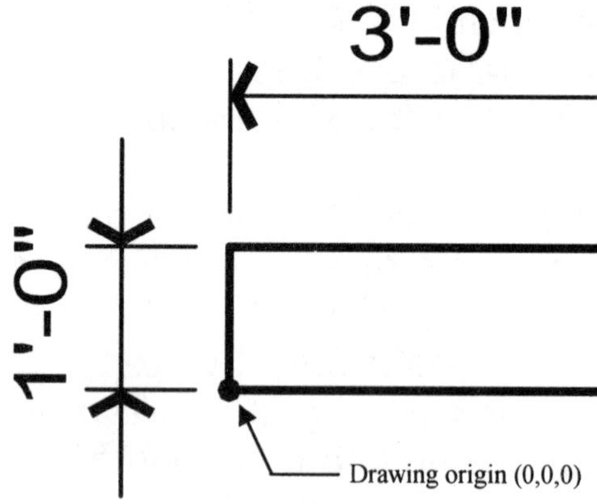

1. **Open** a new drawing.
2. Select the **Rectangle** command.
3. For the first point, enter **0,0.**
   NOTE: *When entering an x,y,z coordinate, AutoCAD assumes Z equals 0 if you only enter X and Y values.*
4. At the **Specify Other Point** prompt, type **D** and **Enter.**
5. Enter **3'** for the length and **1'** for the width.
6. Position the cursor so the bookcase is displayed up and to the right of the drawing Origin (i.e., 0,0) and **click.**

That's it!

7. **Save** you drawing per the name listed above.

filename: **Coffee Table.dwg**

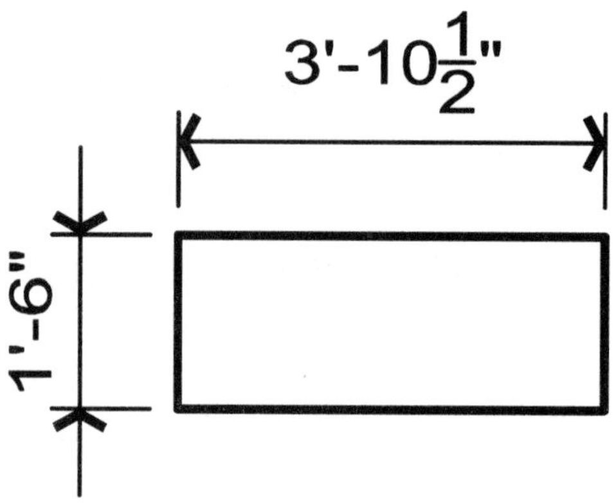

8. Similar to the steps listed above, plus the suggestions mentioned below, create the coffee table shown to the left.

<u>Entering fractions</u>: the 3'-10 ½" can be entered in one of three ways.

- 3'10.5 — *Notice there is no space between the feet and inches*
- 3'10-1/2 — *Note the dash location; it separates the inches: whole - fraction*
- 46.5 — *This is all in inches; that is 3'- 10 ½" = 46.5"*

filename: **desk-1.dwg**

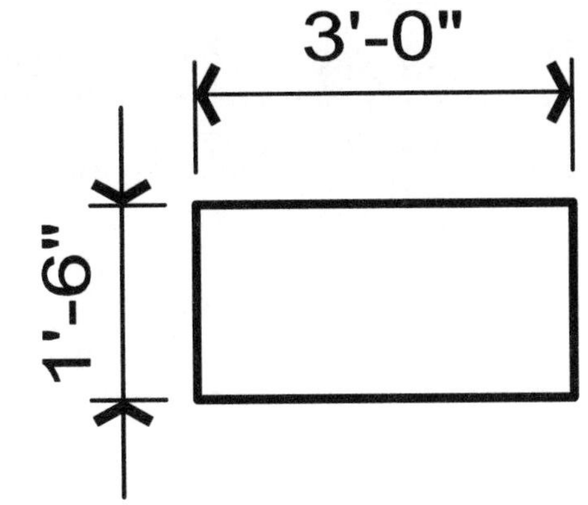

9. Draw the Desk in its own file, similar to the steps outlined above.

10. After completing *desk-1.dwg*, select **Save-As** from the *File* pull-down menu.

11. Enter **Night Table.dwg** for the name and then click **Save.**

filename: **Night Table.dwg**

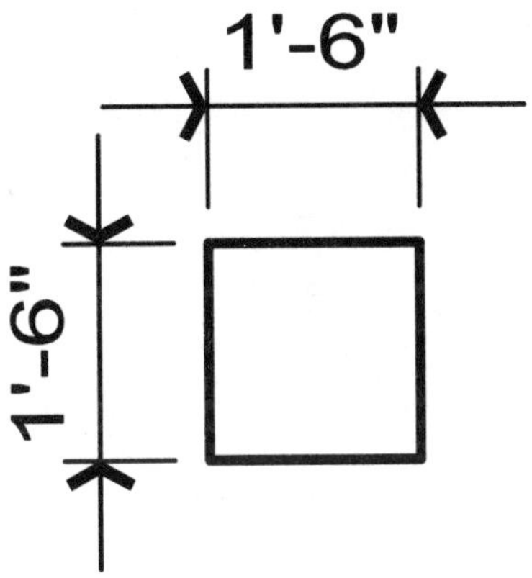

Obviously you could draw this quickly per the previous examples. However, you will take a look at the Stretch command now.

You will use the Stretch command to stretch the 3′-0″ wide desk down to a 1′-6″ wide night table; we don't want to move the lower left corner which aligns with the Origin.

12. Select **Stretch** from the *Modify Toolbar* .

13. Select a **Crossing-Window** as shown in **Figure 3-1.1.**
    TIP: *Refer back to page 2-20 for more on crossing-windows.*

14. Make sure **Polar Tracking** is turned on (Tip: Status Bar).

15. Move your cursor to the left, with the Polar Tracking locking into the horizontal position, as shown in Figure 3-1.2.

16. Type **1′6** in the *Command Window* and press **Enter.**

17. **Save** your drawing.

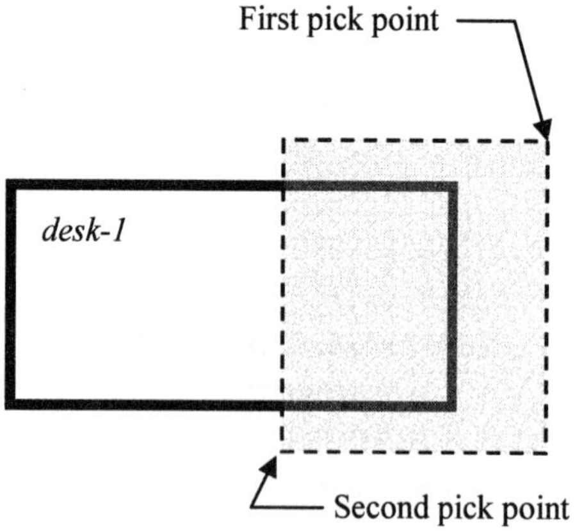

Figure 3-1.1 Stretch Command – crossing-window selection shown

Which objects get stretched and which objects don't?

When you select a portion of drawing to be stretched, like the example to the left, some entities are stretched while others are moved.

Notice in the example to the left (Figure 3-1.1), the two horizontal lines are stretched, whereas the vertical line simply moves 1'-6" to the left.

<u>You can think of it this way:</u>
Any lines that pass thru the crossing-window are stretched.
Any lines that are completely within the crossing-window are moved.

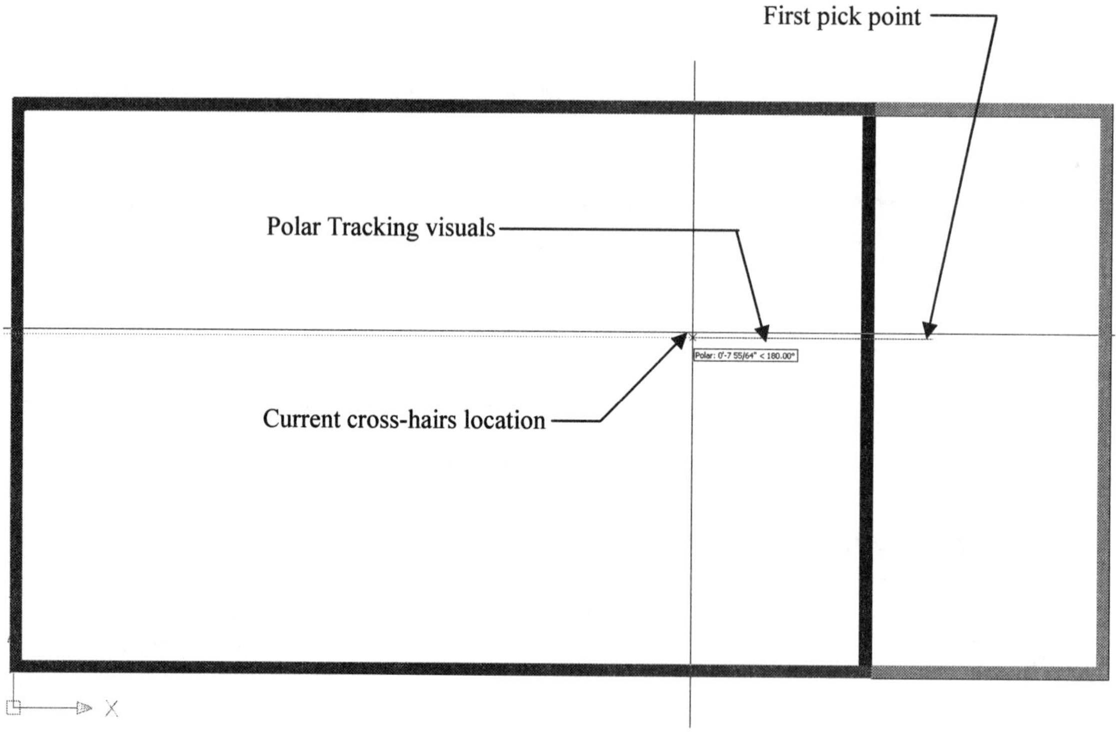

Figure 3-1.2 Stretch Command – Stretch in progress; first point picked

filename: **dresser-1.dwg**

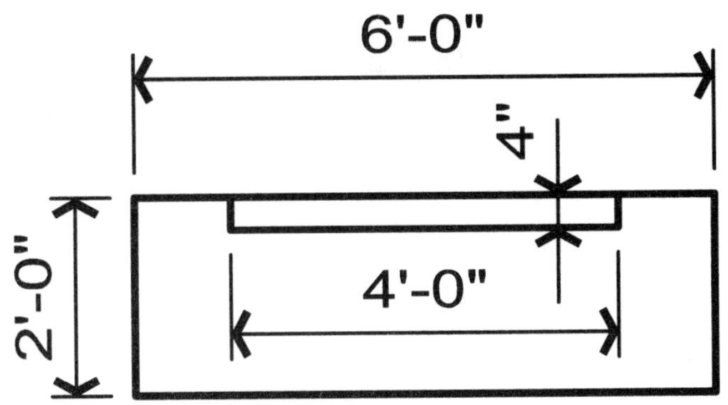

18. Draw the Dresser using the following tip:
    TIP: *Simply draw two rectangles. Make sure the large rectangle is at the Origin. Move the smaller rectangle into place using the Move command and Osnaps.*

filename: **dresser-2.dwg**

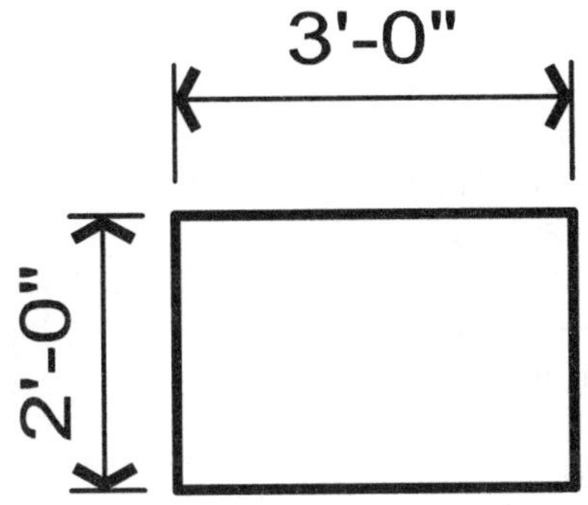

19. Draw this smaller dresser.

filename: **desk-2.dwg**

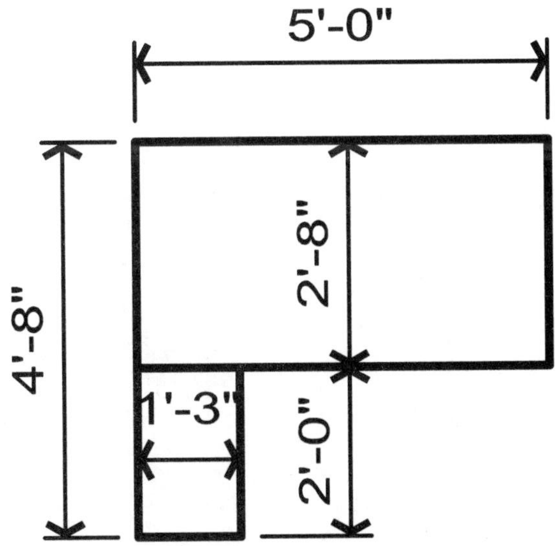

20. Draw this desk in the same way you drew dresser-1 (i.e., two rectangles). Make sure the lower-left is at the Origin!

filename: **file cabinet.dwg**

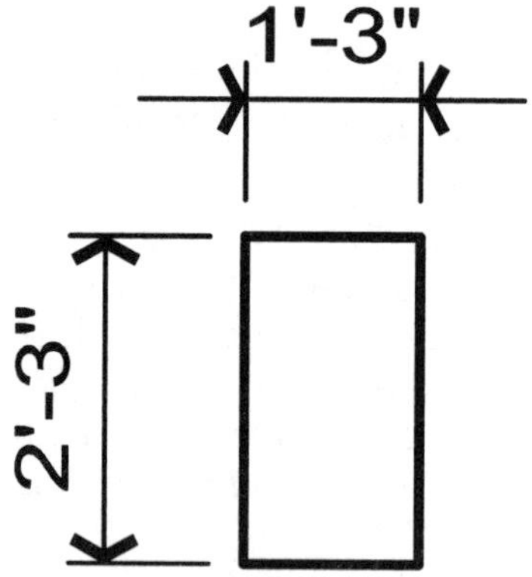

21. Draw this file cabinet.

filename: **chair-1.dwg**

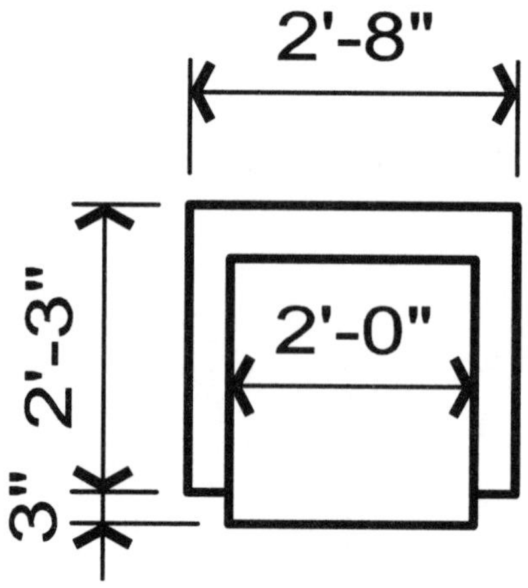

22. Draw this chair per the following tips:

> Draw the 2'x2' square first, and then draw three (temporary) rectangles as shown to the right. If necessary, move them into place w/ Move and Osnaps. Next, draw a line for the arms and backrest and then delete the three temporary rectangles.

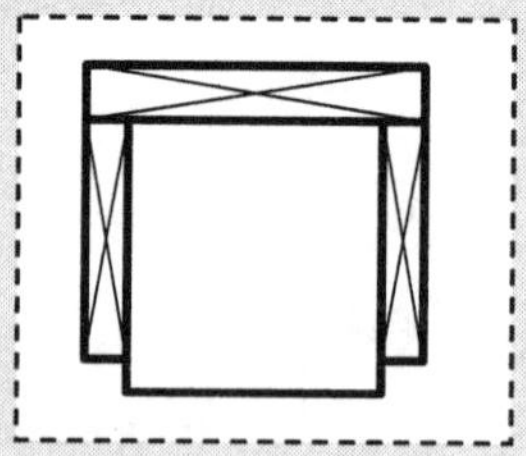

filename: **sofa.dwg**

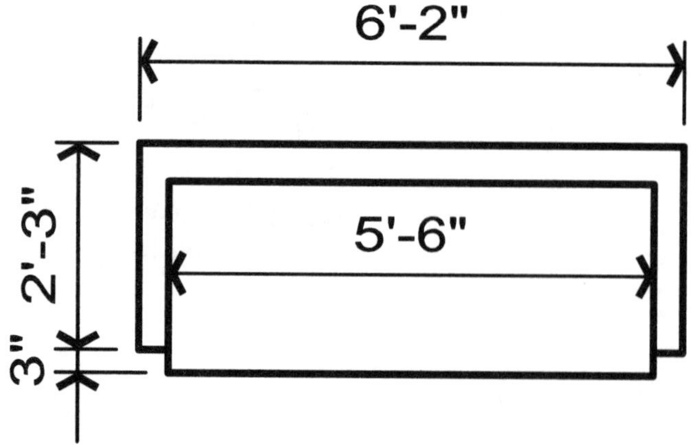

23. Do a Save-As from the chair-1 file and stretch to create the sofa.

filename: **bed-double.dwg**

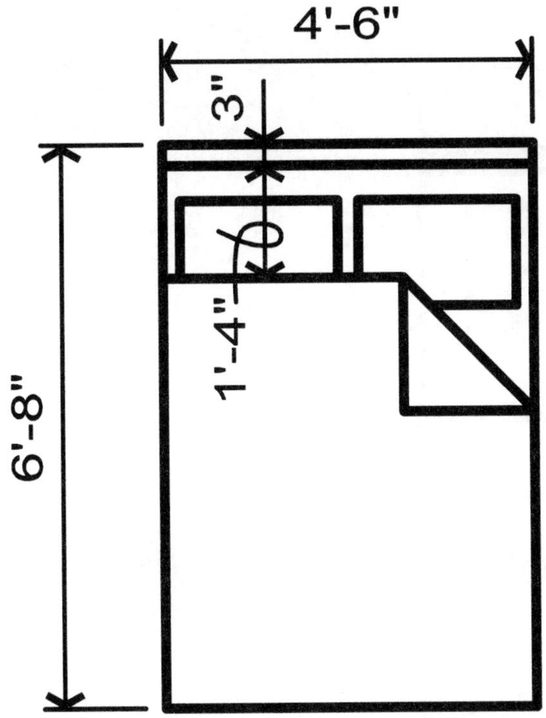

24. Draw the following three beds using lines and rectangles, the exact size of items not dimensioned is not important. Use Stretch to create the two larger beds.

filename: **bed-queen.dwg**

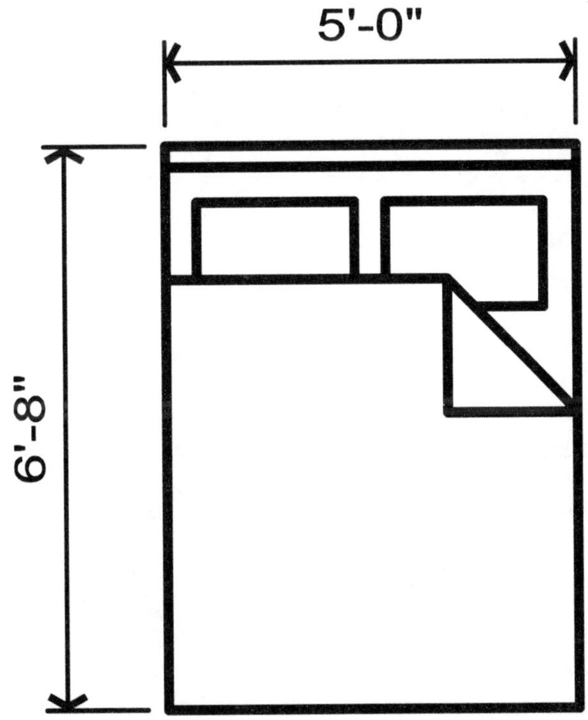

Image courtesy of Stanius Johnson Architects
Daniel's Construction, Amery WI. Photo by Robert Aho
www.staniusjohnson.com

filename: **bed-king.dwg**

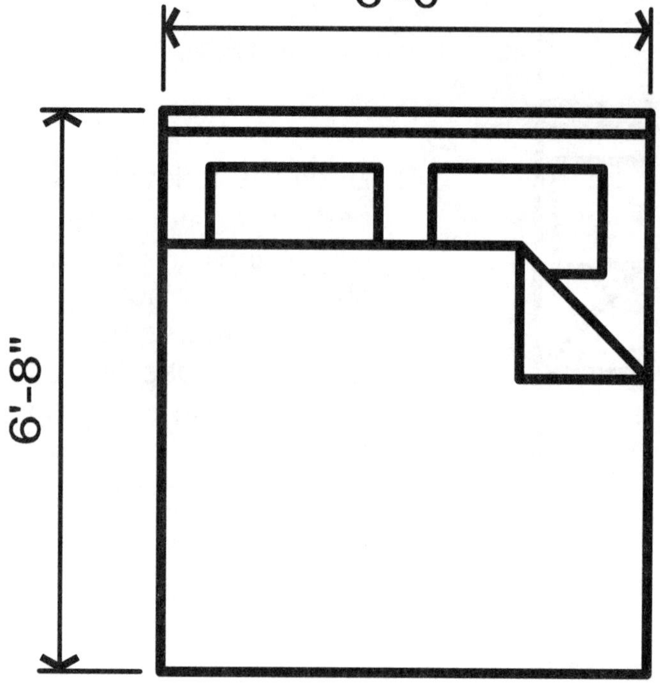

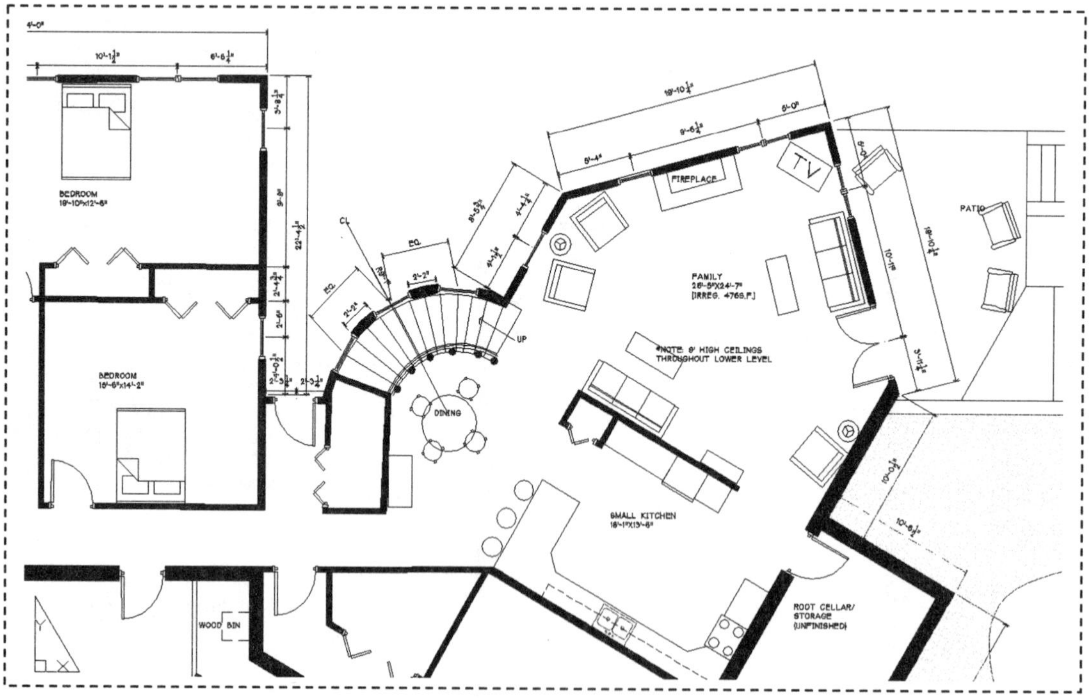

Figure 3-1.3 Floor Plan example using similar furniture to those drawn in this exercise.

Image courtesy of Stanius Johnson Architects
www.staniusjohnson.com

Exercise 3-2:
Objects with Curves

Similar to the previous exercise, you will draw several shapes; this time the shapes will have curves in them.

You will look at the various commands that allow you to create curves, like Arc, Circle and Fillet.

Again, you will not draw the dimensions as they are for reference only. Each drawing should be drawn in its own drawing file; save the drawing with the filename provided.

One more thing about layers, they all occupy the same space. Layers are similar to a stack of transparencies in that you can slip one out of the stack (i.e., turn a Layer off). However, in AutoCAD, all the transparencies in the stack would occupy the space as if there were only one and not a stack (whereas 20 transparencies would be 10 times thicker than a stack of two transparencies → 2 x 10 = 20).

Finally, the black dot on each of the drawings below is for reference only. This dot represents the location of the Drawing Origin (0,0).

filename: **laundry-sink.dwg**

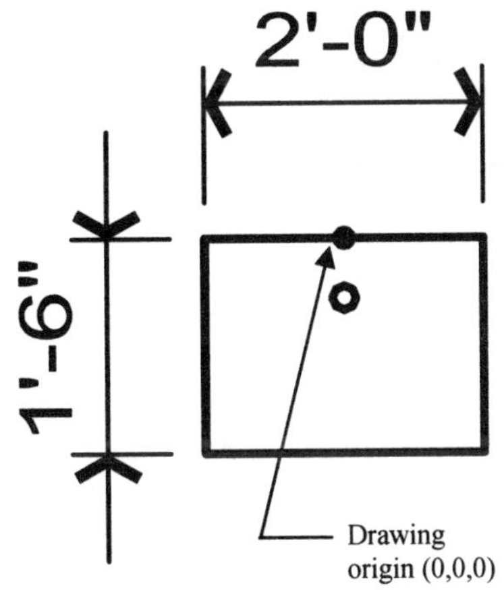

This is a simple rectangle that represents the size of a laundry sink, with a circle that represents the drain.

1. **Open** a new drawing.

2. Select the **Rectangle** command.

3. Enter the *Dimensions* shown.

4. Use the **Move** command to position the Rectangle relative to the *Origin*: Pick the **Move** icon, select the rectangle, pick the midpoint of the top horizontal line for the first point, and then type **0,0** for the second point, and then press **Enter**.

Next you will draw a circle for the drain. The drain needs to be centered left and right, and 5" from the top edge. The following steps will show you one way in which to do this.

5. Pick the **Circle** icon.

6. Type **0,0** to locate the center point of the Circle.
   (This is the midpoint of the top edge of your rectangle.)

7. Type **1** for the radius and press **Enter.**
   (This creates a 2" diameter circle.)

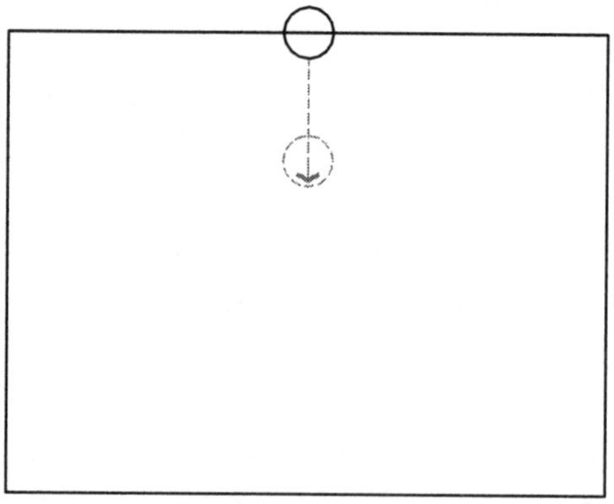

Figure 3-2.1 Creating a circle and moving it into place.

Next you will use the Move command to reposition the circle.

8. Select the **Move** icon.

9. Pick the circle. *(Press Enter to tell AutoCAD you are done selecting entities to move.)*

10. For your **First point of displacement**, pick anywhere in the *Drawing Window*; in this example the first point is irrelevant.

11. For your **Second point of displacement**, enter **@5<-90.**
    (See page 2-23 for an explanation on this. Notice it is the same for the Copy command.)

12. If you haven't already done so, press **Enter** to complete the move operation. (Figure 3-2.1)

13. **Save** the file per the name listed above.

REMEMBER:
The black dot shown on the previous page represents the *Drawing Origin* and is not to be drawn. This may be a little confusing on the Laundry Sink example because you drew a circle at that same location. But, if you recall, you *Moved* the circle (as apposed to *Copying* it). So the circle should not be there anymore.

filename: **dryer.dwg**

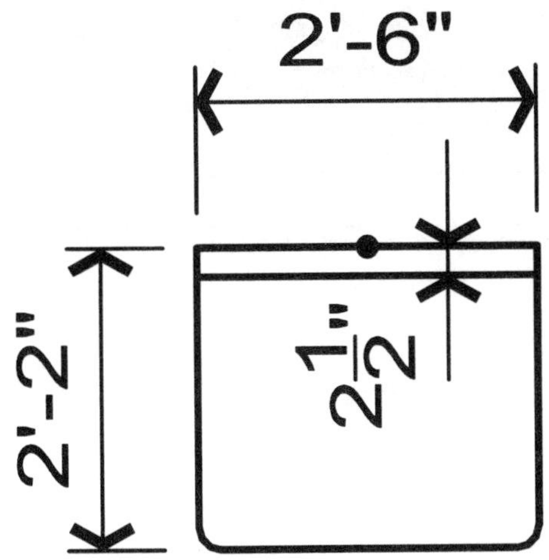

Here you will draw a dryer with rounded front corners. This, like all the other symbols in this lesson, is a plan view symbol (i.e., as viewed from the top).

14. Draw a 30"x26" Rectangle.

15. **Move** the rectangle into place as described in the previous drawing (laundry sink).

Next you will draw the line that is 2 ½" from the back of the dryer.

16. Select the **Line** icon.

17. Pick the start and end points per Figure 3-2.2.

18. Select the **Move** icon.

19. Select the line you just drew.
    ***TIP**: The line was drawn directly on top of the rectangle so you will not actually see a separate line. However, by selecting the area the line was drawn, you will select the line rather than the rectangle. This is because the line was drawn last.*

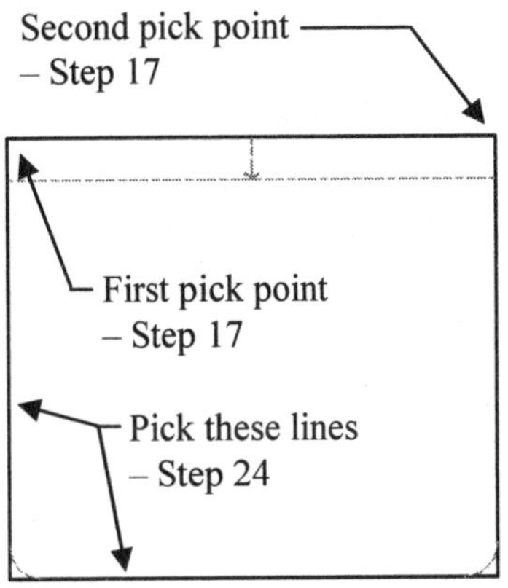

Figure 3-2.2 Drawing a line

Notice that you did not have to tell AutoCAD (by entering a number) how long the line needed to be. Instead, you picked two points that you knew were 30" apart. Next you will move the line into its correct location.

20. Use **Step 11** in this exercise as an example for correctly moving the line into position.

Next you will round the front corners of the dryer.

21. Select the **FILLET** icon from the *Modify Toolbar* .

Notice the prompts in the Command Window (Figure 3-2.3). The Radius is set to zero; you will need to change that to 2".

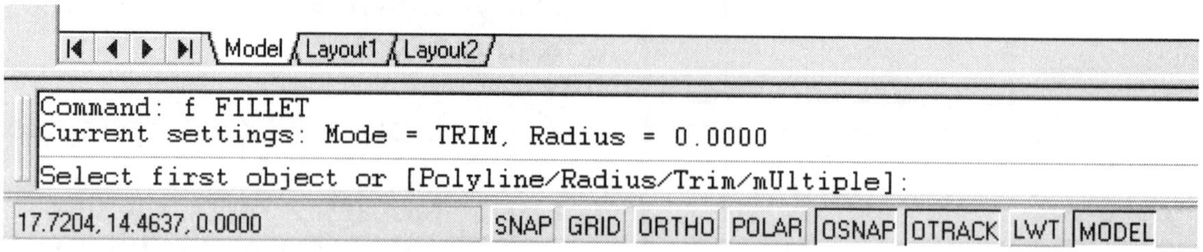

Figure 3-2.3 Fillet Command – command window prompts after initiating the command

22. Type **R** and then **Enter.** *(This runs the sub-command Radius.)*

23. Type **2** and then **Enter.**

Next you will select the two lines, whose intersection you want filleted.

24. Select the vertical line on the left and then select the horizontal line on the bottom (front). See Figure 3-2.2.

25. Repeat the previous step to **Fillet** the other corner.

26. **Save** your drawing.

filename: **Washer.dwg**

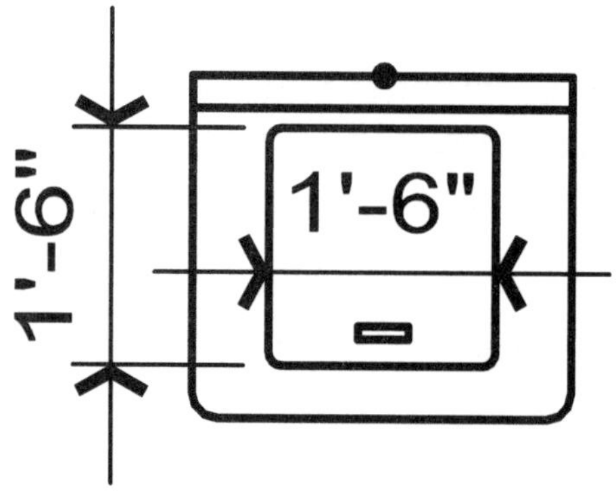

This drawing is identical to the dryer except for the door added to the top. You can open the dryer drawing and do a *Save-As* to get a jump start on this drawing.

To draw the door you will use the **Offset** command on the *Modify Toolbar*.

The **Offset** command is easy to use. To use it you…

- Enter the *Distance* you want to offset a line
- Select the line you want to offset
- Pick which side of the line you want to Offset to

27. Select the **Offset** icon on the *Modify Toolbar.*

28. Type **4** and then press **Enter.**

29. Select the rectangle (that represents the perimeter of the washer) as the line you wish to offset.

30. Pick anywhere inside the rectangle.

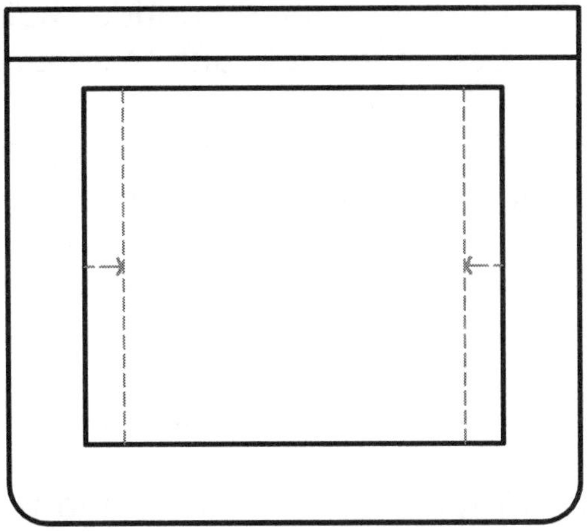

Figure 3-2.4 Outer rectangle offset inward 4" Note that the dashed lines are the location of the "door" after it is stretched in Step 31

Picking within the rectangle caused the rectangle to offset towards the inside. You are encouraged to Undo at this point and see what happens when you click on the outside of the rectangle. Obviously the rectangle will offset to the outside of the existing rectangle. When finished experimenting with the Offset command, make sure to restore the proper rectangle per step 30 above.

Next you will stretch the rectangle to adjust its width.

31. Use the **Stretch** techniques previously covered to stretch the right side of the inner rectangle **2"** to the left. (Figure 3-2.4)

32. Repeat the previous steps to **Stretch** the left side **2"** to the right. (Figure 3-2.4)

You should now have a properly sized door (1'-6" x 1'-6").

You should occasionally double check your dimensions; it is easy to accidentally type the wrong distance. Next you will verify the door is the correct size using the Dimension tool (there are other ways to do this, but we will focus on a command you already know).

33. Use the **Linear** command from the *Dimension* pull-down menu to draw the two dimensions shown for the washer drawing on page 3-12.
    TIP: *Make sure you use the Osnaps to accurately pick the points you are dimensioning to.*

34. Once you have verified that your drawing is correct you can **Erase** the two dimensions.

Next you will Fillet the corners of the door. AutoCAD provides a sub-command for Fillet that will round all the corners at once. You will try this option now. *(**NOTE**: This option only works on closed polylines, which is what the rectangle command creates. If you simply drew the rectangle with individual lines you would have to fillet each corner separately.)*

35. Select the **Fillet** icon and set the radius to **1".**

36. Type **P** (for Polyline) and press **Enter.** (Figure 3-2.3)

37. Select the door [rectangle] and pick somewhere within the door [rectangle].

All four corners should now be rounded off.

38. Draw a small 4"x1" rectangle to represent the door handle; draw it anywhere. Using *Osnaps*, move it to the midpoint of the bottom door edge, and then move the handle 2" up.

39. Save your drawing (make sure the name is Washer).

filename: **Range.dwg**

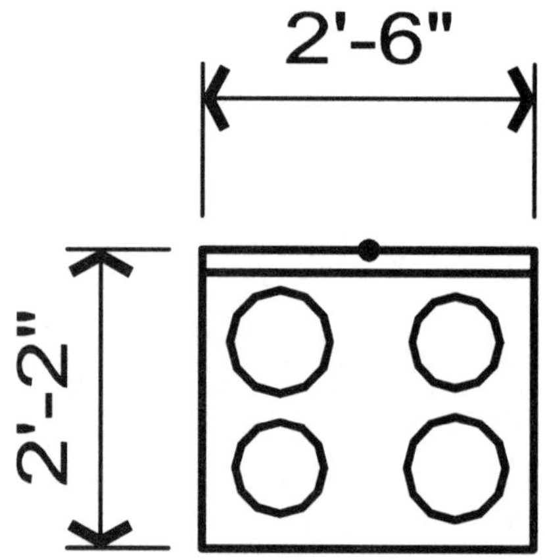

Now you will draw a kitchen Range with four circles that represent the burners.

In this exercise you will have to draw temporary lines (called construction lines) to create reference points needed to accurately locate the circles. Once the circles have been drawn the construction lines can be erased.

40. Draw the range with a 2″ control panel at the back. Refer to the steps described to draw the dryer, if necessary.

41. Draw the four construction lines shown in Figure 3-2.5. (They do not need to be dashed lines.)

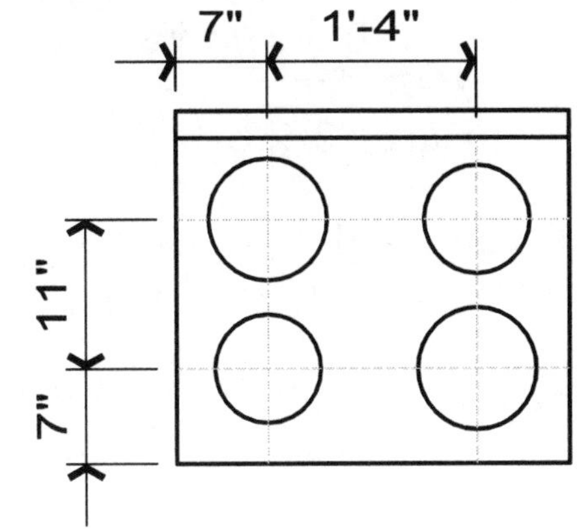

Figure 3-2.5 Range with four temporary construction lines (shown dashed)

42. Draw two 9 ½″ circles and two 7 ½″ circles using the intersection of the construction lines to locate the center of the circles. Figure 3-2.5

43. Erase the four construction lines.

44. Save your drawing.

filename: **Chair-2.dwg**

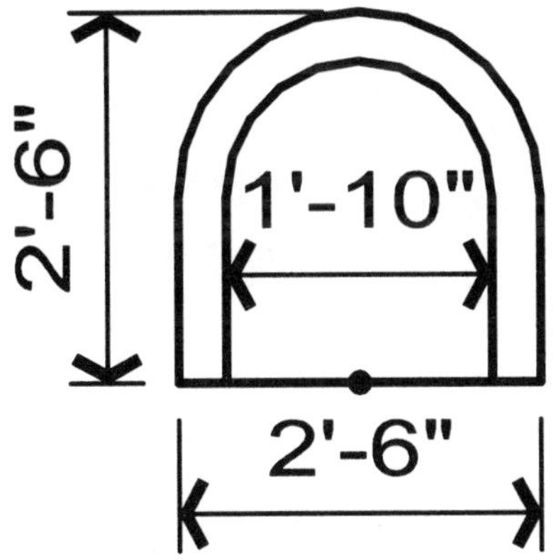

Now you will draw another chair. You will use the *Line* and *Offset* commands as well as the *Arc* command.

First you will draw the three straight lines at the perimeter.

45. First draw the **2′-6″** line across the bottom. Use one of the following methods to accurately position the line relative to the drawing Origin (0,0).

a. Drawing the line, type 0,0 for your first point and then type 2′-6″ (with Polar tracking on; to the right). Finally, move the line 1′-3″ to the left (this will position the line such that your 2′-6″ line's midpoint is at the origin).

b. Anywhere in the drawing, draw a horizontal line 2′-6″ long. Now use the Move command. Pick the midpoint of the line for the first point and type 0,0 for the second point.

46. Using *Polar Tracking* (or *Ortho*) draw two vertical lines **1'-3"** long. Figure 3-2.6

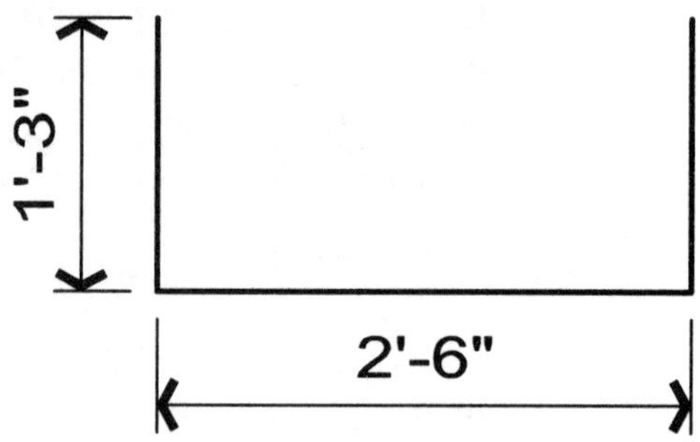

Figure 3-2.6 Three lines drawn for Chair-2

Next you will draw an Arc to complete the perimeter of the chair.

47. Select the **Arc** icon from the *Shapes Toolbar.* 

    Notice you are prompted to **Specify the start point of arc.**

48. Pick the upper *Endpoint* of the vertical line on the right. (See Figure 3-2.7.)

    You are now prompted in the Command Window:
    Specify second point of arc or [Center/End]:

49. Type **E** and press **Enter**; this allows you to specify the arc's endpoint next.

50. Pick the upper *Endpoint* of the vertical line on the left for the arc's Endpoint. (See Figure 3-2.7.)

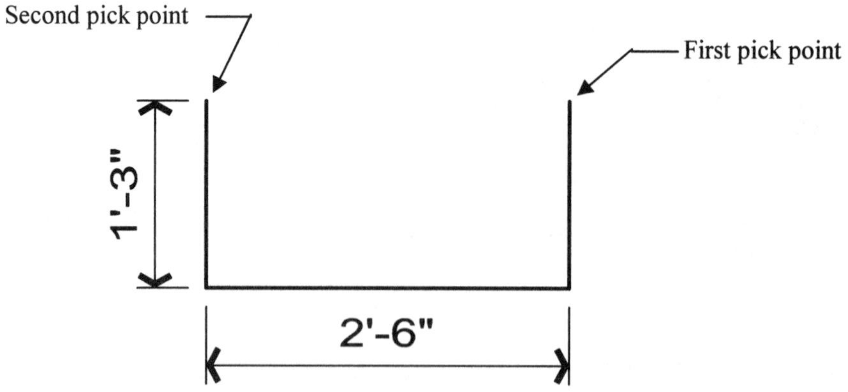

Figure 3-2.7 Pick points for arc command

Finally you are prompted:
Specify center point of arc or [Angle/Direction/Radius]:

51. Type **R** (for Radius) and **Enter.**

52. Type **1′-3″** and **Enter.**

You have now completed the perimeter of the chair. If the arc is in the wrong position you may have picked your points in the wrong order.

53. Use the **Offset** command to offset the arc and two vertical lines the required distance.

Notice that because you drew the perimeter with individual lines, the entire outline did not offset like the rectangle did. This would work if you turned these lines into polylines (which will be covered later in the book).

54. Save your drawing.

filename: **Love-Seat.dwg**

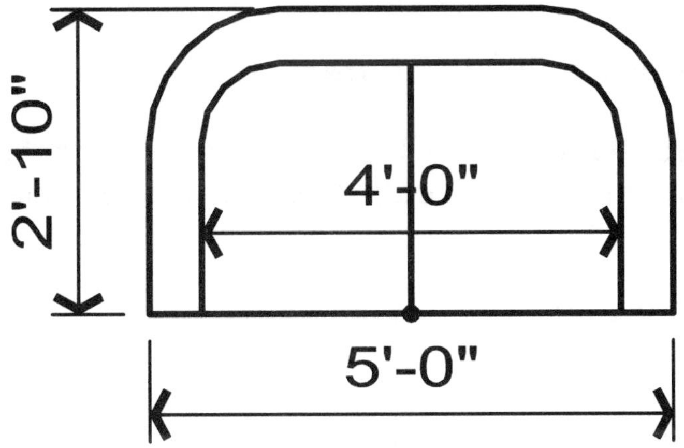

You should be able to draw this Love Seat without any further instruction. You can do so using a combination of the following commands:

- Line
- Fillet
- Offset
- Move

TIP:
When starting the Love Seat drawing above, you might initially get the idea to draw a 2′-6″ line from the Origin to the right and then another 2′-6″ line from the Origin to the left. This would give the appearance of a 5′-0″ line with the center at 0,0.
Typically that should be avoided. Anything that looks like one line should actually be only one line in AutoCAD. It is considered sloppy drafting when you have several smaller lines makeup one line or several overlapping lines.

filename: **Tub.dwg**

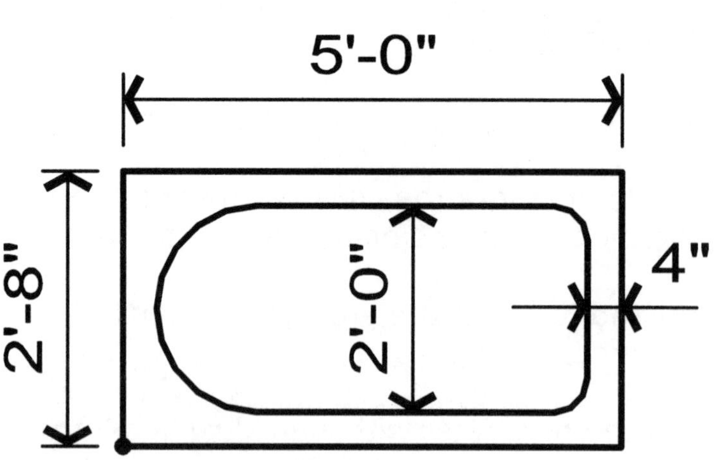

Now you will draw a bath tub. You will use several commands previously covered. You will also be introduced to another command called Explode. This command allows you to turn a polyline (e.g., rectangles) into individual lines.

55. **Draw** the rectangle.

56. **Offset** the rectangle inward **4".**

Next you will use the Explode command to change the smaller rectangle from a *Polyline* to individual lines so you can edit them separately.

57. Select the **Explode** icon on the *Modify Toolbar.* 

58. **Pick** the smaller rectangle and then **Enter.**

Select one of the lines to see that only one line is selected, rather than the entire rectangle (i.e., all four lines). Press Escape to unselect the line and proceed to the next step.

59. **Erase** the vertical line on the left. Figure 3-2.8

60. **Stretch** the two horizontal lines 1'-0" to the right. Figure 3-2.8

61. Draw an **Arc** with a **1'-0"** radius.

62. **Fillet** the two corners to have a **4"** radius.

63. **Save.**

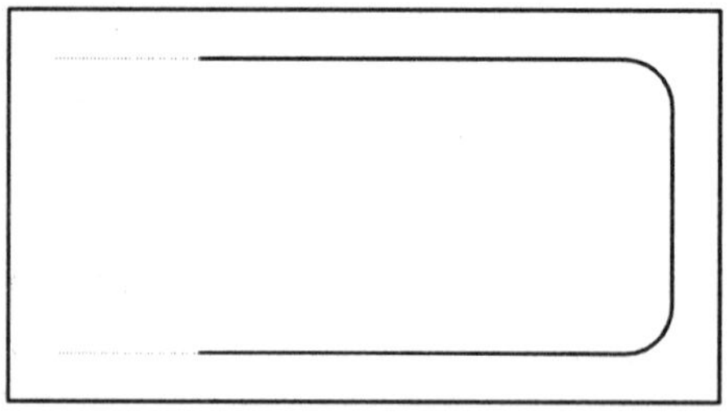

Figure 3-2.8 Horiz. Lines stretched 1'-0" to the right

filename: **Lav-1.dwg**

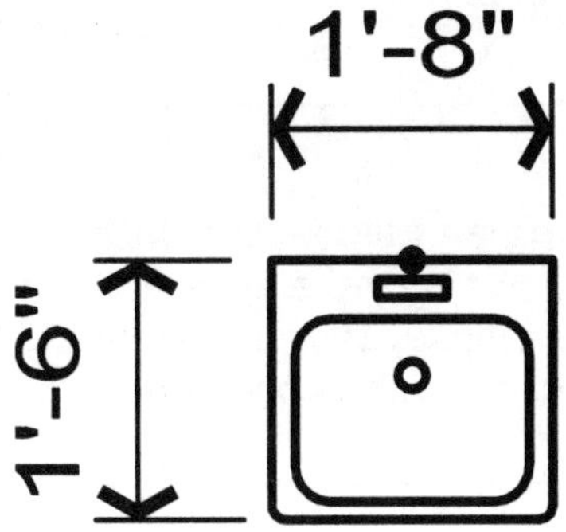

Draw this lavatory per the following specifications:

- Larger arcs shown shall have a 2 ½″ radius.
- Smaller arcs shown shall have a 1″ radius.
- Sides and Front of sink to have 1 ½″ space (offset).
- Back to have 4″ space (offset).
- Small rectangle to be 4 ½″ x 1″ and 1 ½″ away from the back.
- 2″ Dia. Drain 8″ from Origin.

filename: **Lav-2.dwg**

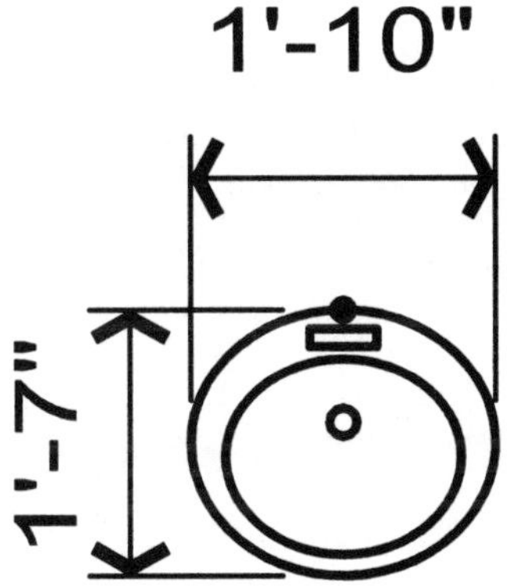

Next you will draw another lavatory. This time you will use the *Ellipse* Command.

64. Open a new drawing.

65. Select the **Ellipse** icon on the *Shapes Toolbar.* 

First you will specify the vertical axis for the ellipse.

66. Type **0,0** for the axis endpoint.

67. With **Polar Tracking** (or Ortho) turned on, point the cursor straight down (i.e., vertical in the negative direction) and then type **1'7**, press **Enter.**

Now you need to specify the horizontal axis of the ellipse.

68. Again, with **Polar Tracking** on, position the cursor towards the right until is snaps to the horizontal plane and then type **11** and then **Enter.** ***NOTE:*** *11" is half the width; 1'-10"*

> ## Problems?
> If you are having problems, it may be that you are using an Ellipse icon with preset sub-options like defaulting to define the centerpoint of the ellipse first. That icon will actually have a dot shown in the center of the ellipse. If you are having a problem similar to this press Escape and then type Ellipse on the command prompt.

That's all it takes to draw an ellipse!

69. **Offset** the ellipse inward **2 ½".** (Figure 3-2.9)

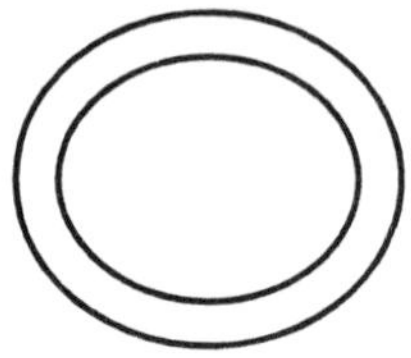

Figure 3-2.9 Ellipse offset inward 2 ½"

70. **Move** the inner ellipse downward (towards the front of the sink) **1".**

Next you need to draw the faucet and drain. As it turns out, the faucet and drain for Lav-1.dwg are in the same position relative to the Origin. So to save time you will Copy/Paste these items from the Lav-1.dwg drawing into the Lav-2.dwg drawing.

71. **Open Lav-1.dwg.**

72. From the **Edit** pull-down menu, select **Copy with Base Point.**

73. Type **0,0** and then **Enter.**

74. Select the faucet (i.e., the small rectangle) and the 2" drain; then press **Enter.**

75. **Close** the **Lav-1.dwg.**

76. In the **Lav-2.dwg** drawing, select **Paste** from the **Edit** pull-down menu.

77. Type **0,0** for the insertion point.

You should now have the faucet and drain correctly positioned in your Lav-2.dwg drawing.

78. Save your drawing.

filename: **Sink-1.dwg**

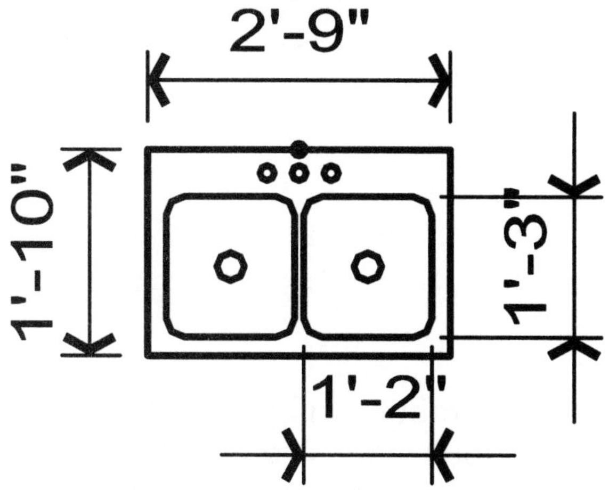

Draw this lavatory per the following specifications:

- 2″ space (i.e., offset) at sides and front.
- 3″ Dia. Circles centered in sinks.
- 2″ rad. for Fillets.
- 1 ½″ Dia. at faucet spaces; 3 ½″ apart.

filename: **Water-closet.dwg**

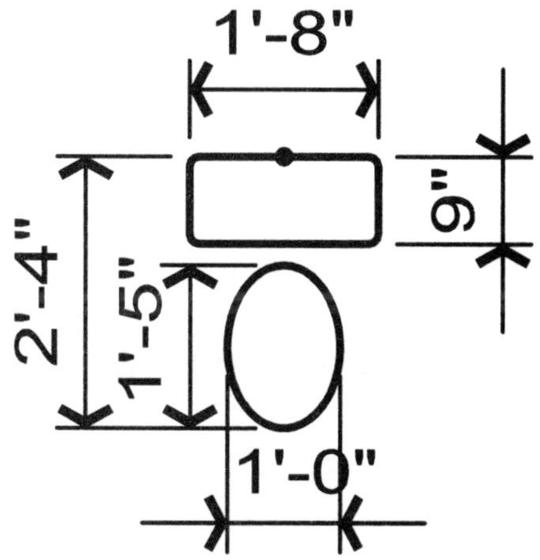

You should be able to draw this symbol without any help.

***TIP*:** Draw a construction line from the Origin straight down 11″ (2′-4″ – 1′-5″ = 11″). This will give you a point to pick when drawing the ellipse.

***NOTE*:** You could also start the ellipse command and type 0,-11 for the first point. These are coordinates relative to the Origin.

filename: **Tree.dwg**

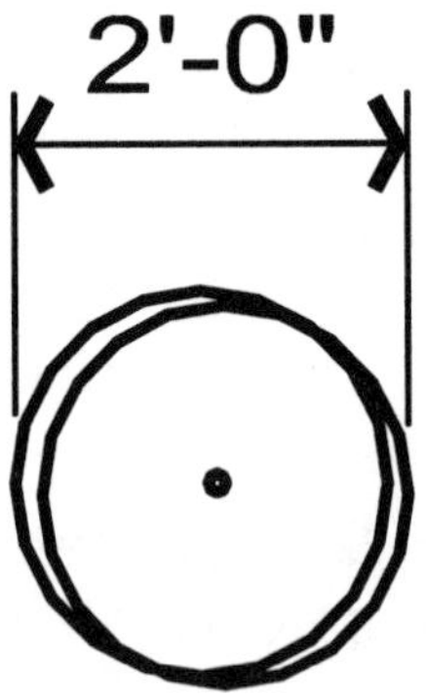

79. Draw one large circle and then copy it similar to this drawing.

80. Draw one small circle (1"Dia.) with the center at the Origin.

81. Save to Tree.dwg.

filename: **Door-36.dwg**

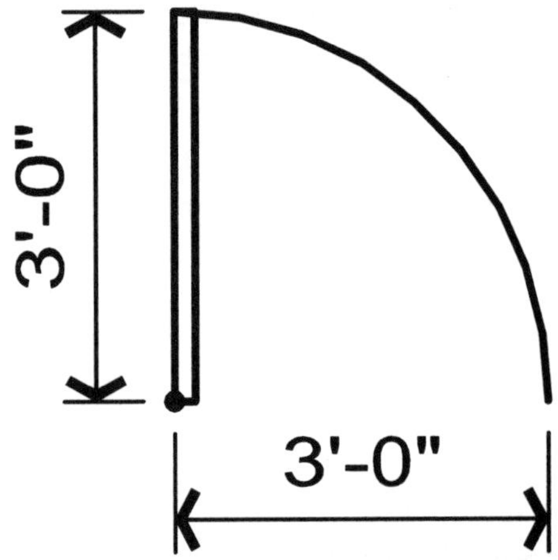

This symbol is used to show a door in a floor plan. The arc represents the path of the door as it opens and shuts.

A symbol like this, 90 degrees open, helps to avoid the door conflicting with something in the house (e.g., cabinets or toilet)

82. Draw a **2" x 3'-0" rectangle.**

83. Draw an Arc with a 3'-0" radius. Instead of picking points, enter the following coordinates: start point at **3',0** and its end point **0,3'.** ***(Remember:*** *These points are relative to 0,0.)*

filename: **Door-30.dwg**

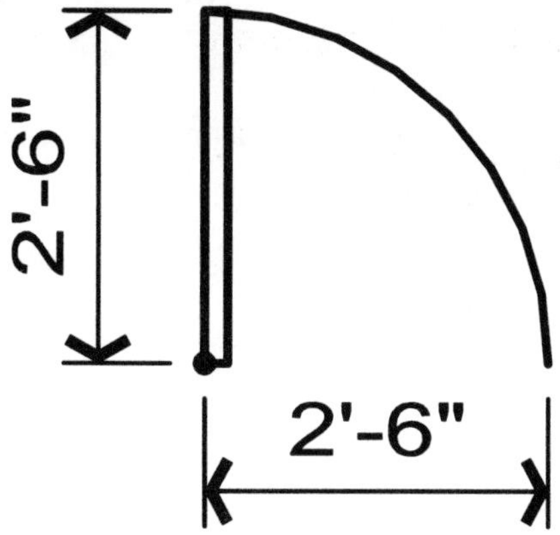

Using the previous two steps as an example, draw this smaller door.

Note: A door's thickness does not usually change, so leave it at 2".

filename: **Door2-36.dwg**

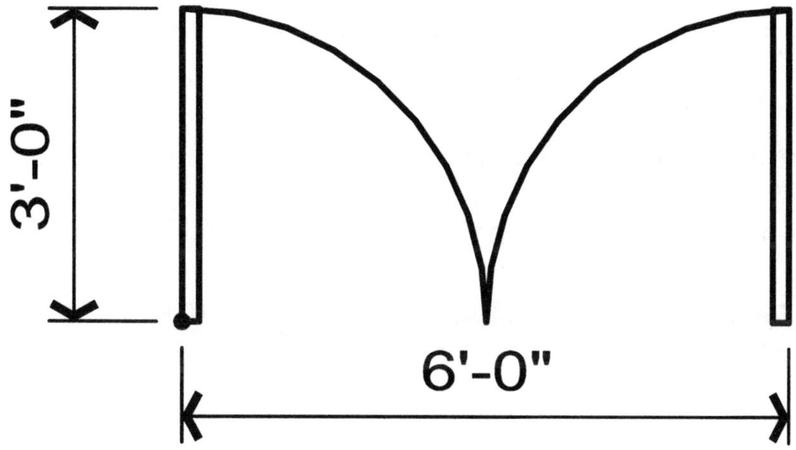

Here you will use a previous drawing and the Mirror command to quickly create this drawing showing a pair of doors in a single opening.

84. **Open** drawing **Door-36.dwg.**

85. **Save-As** to drawing **Door2-36.dwg.**

Next you will mirror both the rectangle and the arc.

86. Pick the **Mirror** icon from the *Modify Toolbar.* 

87. Select the rectangle and arc, and then press Enter.

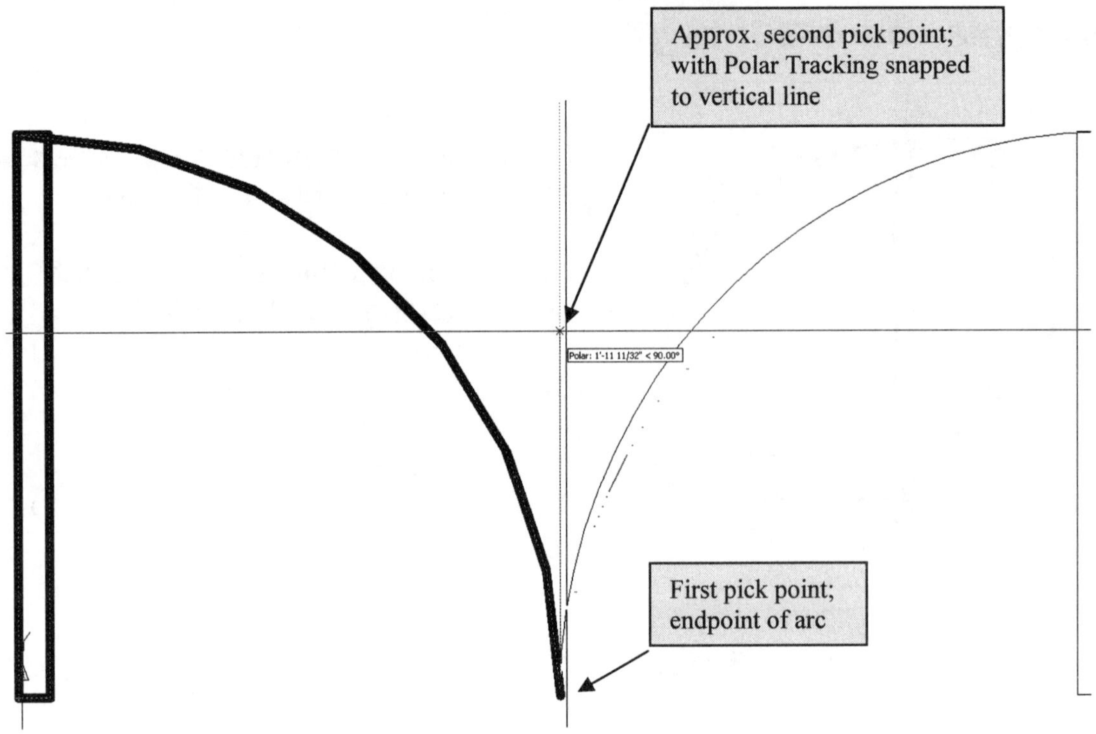

Figure 3-2.10 Mirror command; door being mirrored, first point picked, in process of picking second

Notice the current prompt: **Specify first point of mirror line:**

88. Pick the two points described in Figure 3-2.10.

Basically, you drew an imaginary line that is a plane about which to mirror the selected entities.

Notice the prompt: **Delete source objects? [Yes/No] <N>:**

You do not want the original door to be deleted here so.

89. Type **N** and press **Enter.**

90. **Save** your drawing.

filename: **clg-fan-1.dwg**

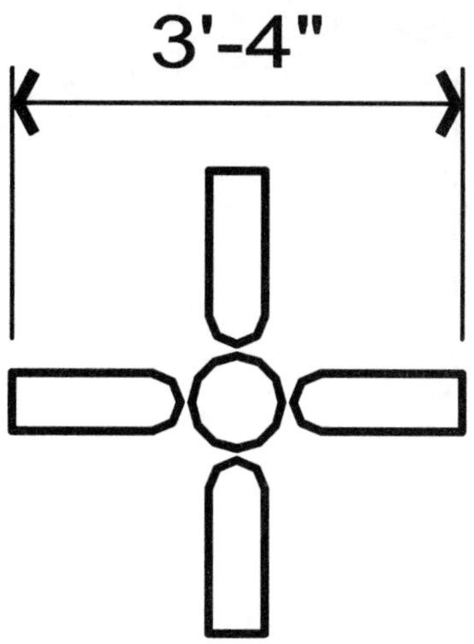

You will use the Array command while drawing this ceiling fan.

The Array command can be used to array entities in a rectangular pattern (e.g., columns on a grid) or in a polar pattern (i.e., in a circular pattern).

You will use the polar array to rotate and copy the fan blade all in one step!

91. Start a new drawing and create the portion of drawing shown in Figure 3-2.11. *(The drawing origin should be the center of the circle.)*

92. Type **Array** and press **Enter.**

You are now in the Array dialog box where you can select the entities to be arrayed. Specify the type (e.g., polar or rectangular), and the number and spacing (or angle). See Figure 3-2.12.

93. To see the correct options, you need to select **Polar Array.**

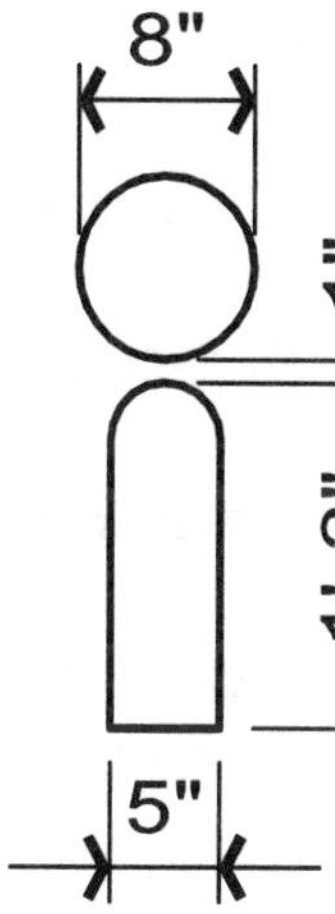

Figure 3-2.11
Dimensions for first part of fan to be drawn

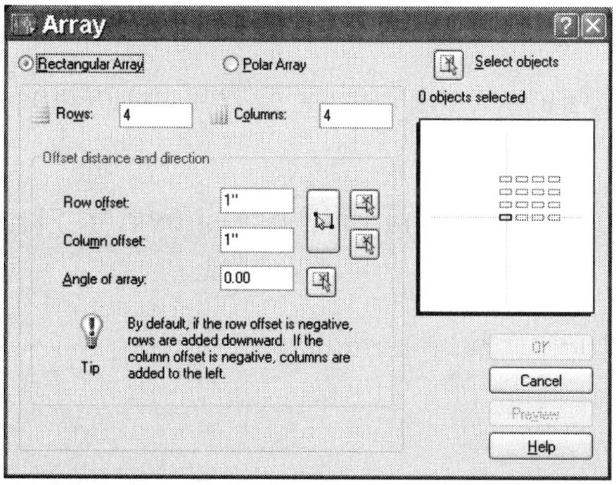

Figure 3-2.12
Array dialog box with default options selected

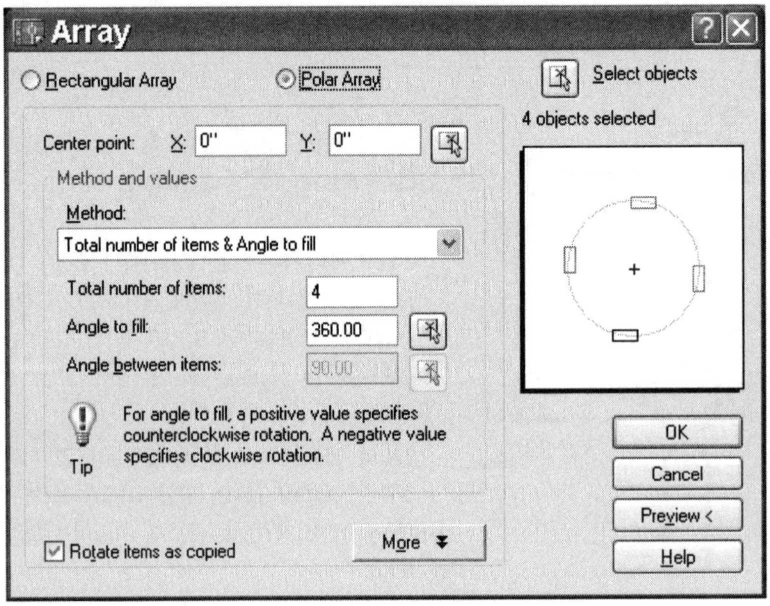

Figure 3-2.13
Array dialog box with correct options selected for this example

Next you will tell AutoCAD which entities you would like to array.

94. Click the button next to the **Select objects** label.

95. Select the entities at make up the fan blade.

96. Press **Enter** *(to indicate you are done selecting)*.

Now you will specify the *Center Point* about which the fan blade will be rotated (which is the drawing origin and the center of the circle).

97. Click the button to the right of the *Center Point* label.

98. Using the *Center Osnap*, **select** the center of the circle, and then **Enter.**

99. Make sure the remaining settings match those shown in Figure 3-2.13.

100. Select **OK** to complete the array.

101. **Save** your drawing.

filename: **clg-fan-2.dwg**

Use the previous example to draw this ceiling fan. Notice the overall size is different.

filename: **HC-symbol.dwg**

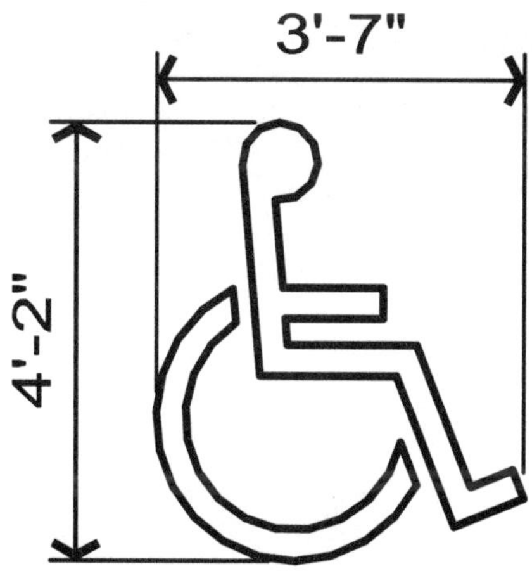

You may have some trouble drawing this symbol at this point. However, this will make you reflect on many of the commands you have covered thus far in this book (e.g., line, rotate, offset, arc).

The distance between parallel lines should be 3 ½".

All other dimensions can be approximated so that your drawing looks as close to this one as possible.

Exercise 3-3:
Using Layers

Using Layers in AutoCAD helps to separate different types of data. Mostly, you will use Layers to make things visible or invisible, and to control lineweights.

In a Floor Plan, for example, you will draw all the walls on one Layer and the Doors on another Layer. You will also draw items such as windows, stairs, furniture, appliances, etc. each on its own Layer.

Many architectural firms have an Office Standard when it comes to Layers. This means that everyone in the firm uses the same Layer name (e.g., A-WALL) to draw walls on, for example.

Example

To see a quick example of how layers work you will open the *Wilhome* drawing again and adjust some of the layer settings and then notice the effect those changes have on the drawing.

1. **Open** the *Wilhome.dwg* located in the C:\Program Files\AutoCAD 2005\Sample folder.

2. Switch to the **Model** Tab.

3. Select the **Layer Properties Manager** from the *Layer Toolbar.* 

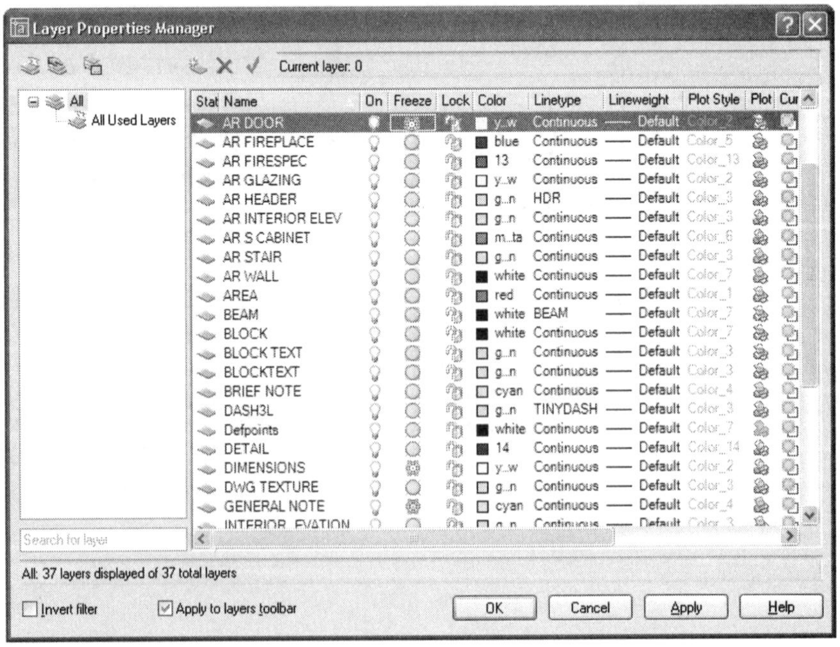

Figure 3-3.1
Layer Properties Manager; three layers set to frozen (step 4)

You are now in the *Layer Properties Manager* where you can adjust the visibility and properties such as lineweight and linetype of the entities on a particular layer.

All drawings have a *Layer* named 0 (i.e., zero). You can add as many layers as you wish in a drawing file. Notice in **Figure 3-3.1** that the *Wilhome* drawing has several *Layers*. Many of the *Layer Names* are descriptive enough for you to tell what information is drawn on each layer.

Next you will Freeze (i.e., turn off the visibility of) three Layers.

4. In the column labeled "**Freeze**" click the *Sun* symbol (which will change the symbol to a B&W *Sun*) for the following *Layers (see Figure 3-3.1)*:
    - **AR DOOR**
    - **DIMENSIONS**
    - **GENERAL NOTE**

> **TIP:**
>
> The "Freeze" column may not display the full label; instead you will see a portion of the label (e.g. Freez) which means the column is not wide enough to display the full label.
>
> You can, if you wish, stretch the column wider with your mouse.
>
> You simply place the cursor between two labels and drag the mouse. This is helpful when the Layer names are long as well.

5. Click **OK** to apply the Layer modifications. Do not click the "X" in the upper right corner of the *Layer Properties Manager* as that will close the dialog box without applying the modifications (which is the same as clicking *Cancel*).

***FYI**: You do not have to click the Apply button unless you want to commit your changes before closing the dialog. For example, if you want to rename a Layer from A-Wall to A-Wall-Demo and then create a new Layer named A-Wall, you would have to "apply" the rename before you could create the A-Wall layer (you cannot have two layers with the same name).*

Notice the changes to the *Wilhome* drawing. Compare Figure 1-5.5 to Figure 3-3.2. The dimensions, doors and annotation are no longer visible. However, they still exist in the drawing file.

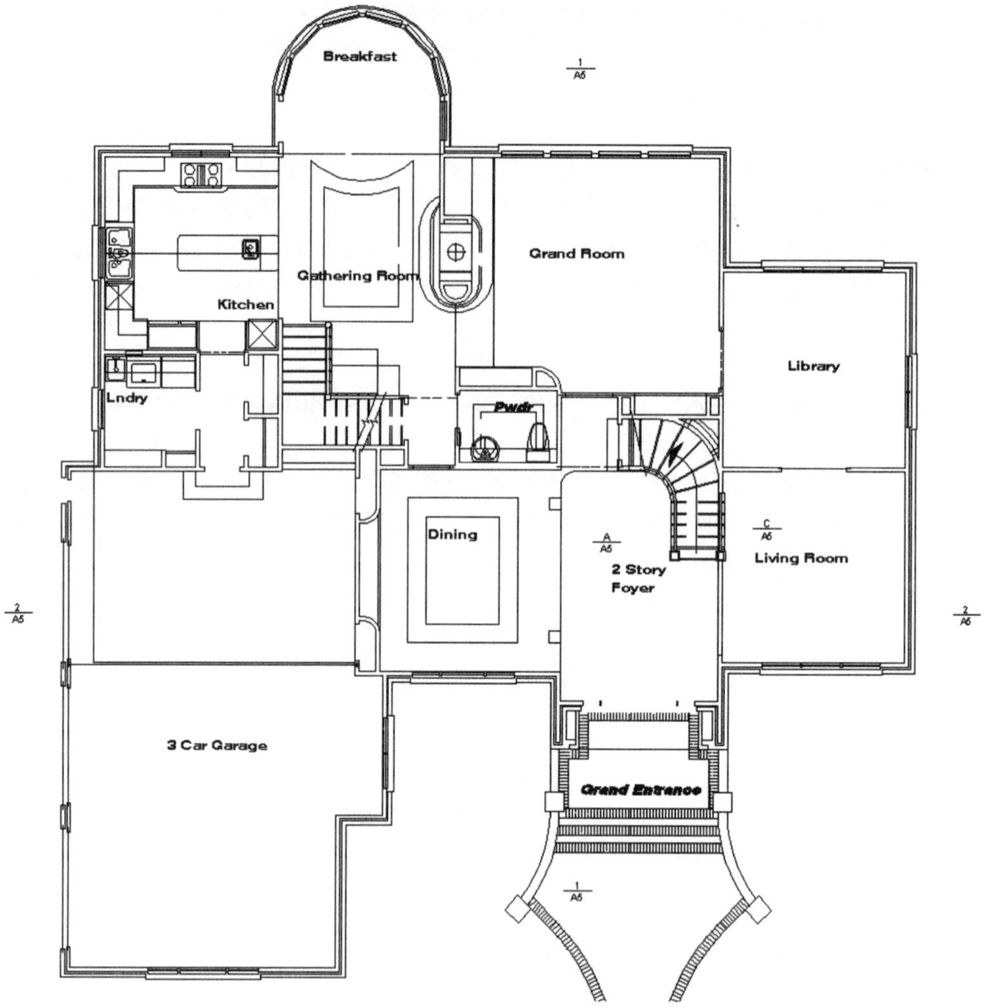

Figure 3-3.2
Wilhome sample drawing with layers frozen

Next you will change the color of a layer to see the effect it has on the current drawing.

6. **Open** the **Layer Properties Manager** again.

7. Locate the *Layer* named **AR WALL**, and then in its Color column, **select the color** listed for this Layer (which should be white).

You are now in the *Select Color* dialog box. (Figure 3-3.3)

8. Select color **Blue** (color #5) – shown selected in **Figure 3-3.3.**

9. Click **OK** to exit the *Color Selector* and then click **OK** again to close the *Layer Properties Manager.*

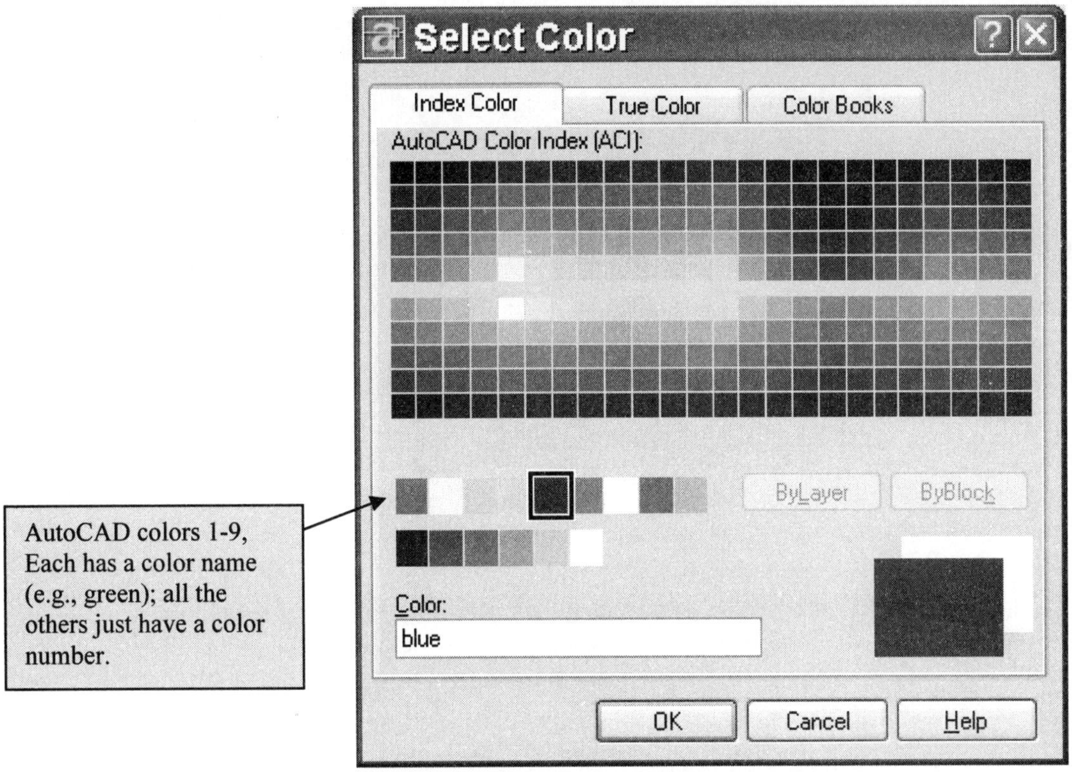

Figure 3-3.3
Select Color dialog box *(part of the Layer Properties Manager)*

10. **Exit** the *Wilhome* drawing <u>without</u> saving any changes.

Now you will open a new drawing and walk through the basics steps of creating and using *Layers* in a drawing.

Creating Layers

11. **Open** a new drawing.

12. **Open** the *Layer Properties Manager.*

13. Click the **New** button. 

A new row has been added to the list; by default you are immediately positioned to enter the *Layer* name.

14. Type the word **Circle** and then press **Enter.**

15. Repeat steps 13 and 14 to create the following layers:

    i. **Lines**
    ii. **Rectangles**
    iii. **Text**

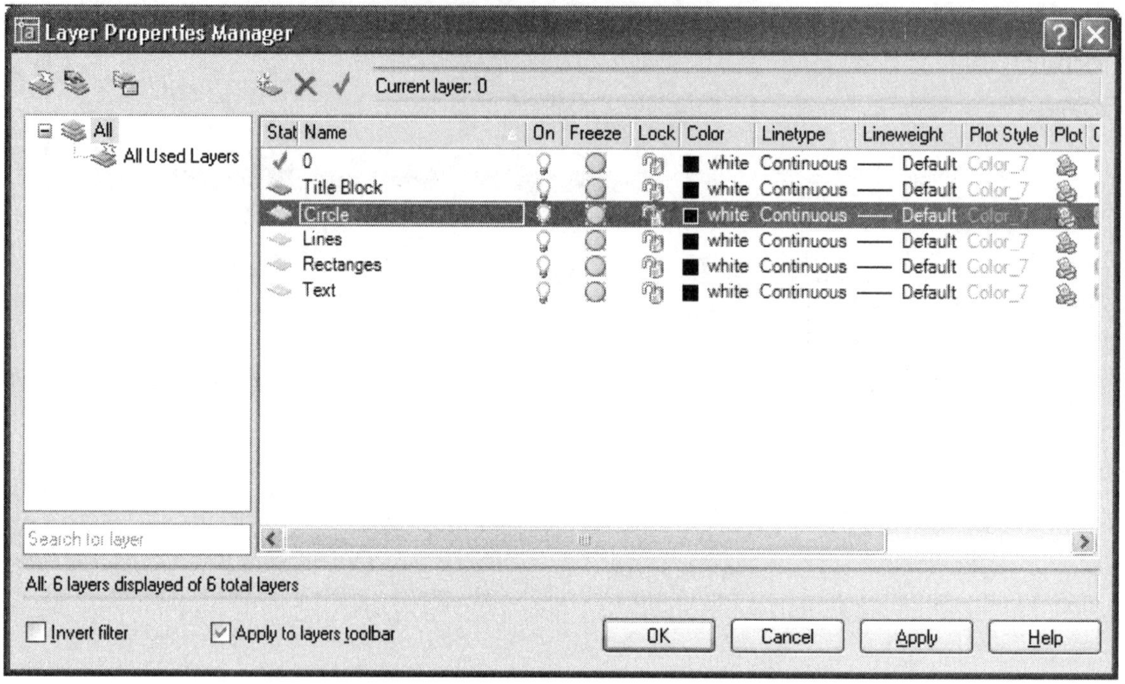

Figure 3-3.4
Layer Properties Manager; with 4 layers created

Next you will assign a new color to three of the new Layers.

16. Set the Layer colors as follows:

    i. **Circles** Green *(color #3)*
    ii. **Rectangles** Red *(color #1)*
    iii. **Text** Cyan *(color #4)*

17. Click **OK** to close the *Layer Properties Manager* and apply the changes.

You now have four new layers, each with a different color.
Figure 3-3.4

***FYI:** The Layer named "Title Block" is from your template file. Additional Layers can be added to template files to reduce new drawing setup steps.*

Drawing on Layers

Now that you have layers you will learn how to draw on different Layers. The easiest method is to set a Layer Current, and then all entities drawn after that will automatically be placed on that layer (i.e., the current layer).

Looking at Figure 3-3.4, notice directly above the Name column is the drawings Current Layer (which is set to 0).

AutoCAD provides a few different ways to change the *Current Layer*. One is in *the Layer Properties Manager* (Figure 3-3.4). You simply click on the Layer Name you want to set to current and then click the *Current* button. Another method is described next.

You can quickly set the *Current Layer* via the *Layers* Toolbar (Figure 3-3.5); this is a dynamic toolbar. The toolbar will change its display per the following three scenarios:

- No entities in the current drawing are selected (no grips visible).
  - The Current Layer is displayed.
- One or more entities selected which are on the same Layer.
  - Displays which layer the selected entities are on.
- A group of entities selected which are on two or more Layers.
  - Display is blank to indicate multiple layers.

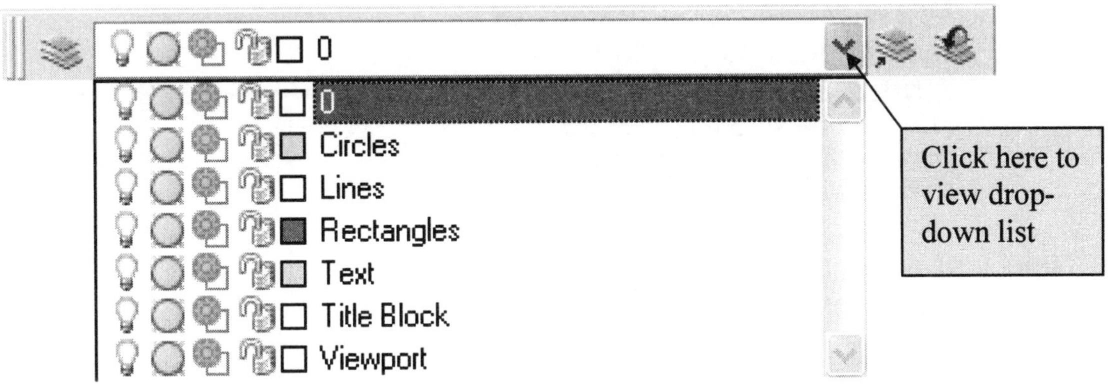

Figure 3-3.5
Layers Toolbar; figure shows layer drop-down list in the dropped-down position

So, to change the *Current Layer*, you click the down arrow to the right of the display in the Layers Toolbar to view the drop-down list (which lists all the Layers in the current drawing). Next, you click on the name of the Layer you want to be current and that's it! *This only works if nothing is selected; otherwise you are changing which Layer the selected entities are on.*

Next you will change the *Current Layer* to Rectangle so when you draw rectangles they will automatically be drawn on the rectangle Layer.

18. Press the **Esc** key twice on the keyboard. This ensures that no entities are selected.

19. Click the **Down-Arrow** on the *Layers Toolbar.* (Figure 3-3.5)

20. Move the cursor over the layer named Rectangle and click.

The rectangle Layer is now set current which means that anything drawn from now on (until the current layer is changed again) will be drawn on the rectangle Layer.

Be aware that the layer name in no way implies that only rectangles can be drawn on the rectangle Layer. That is the intention and the drafter's responsibility to make sure only rectangles go on the rectangles layer. *Note that we could rename the Circle Layer to Ellipse and it would have no effect on the circles previously drawn on that Layer.*

21. **Draw a Rectangle** that is **28"** wide and **48"** tall (*with the lower left corner at the Origin*).

22. **Draw** two more rectangles per the dimensions provided in **Figure 3-3.6.** *(This can be accomplished using a combination of the following commands: Offset, Stretch and Move.)*

Next you will draw several lines; so you will need to change the *Current Layer.*

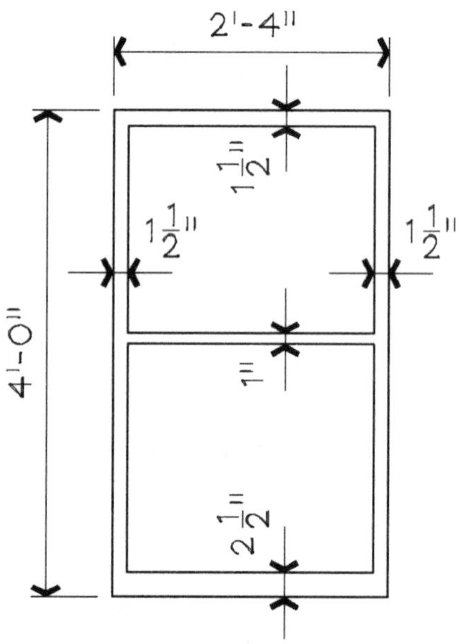

Figure 3-3.6
Three Rectangles drawn

23. Making sure no entities are selected; use the *Layers Toolbar* to make **Lines** the *Current Layer.*

24. Using the dimensions provided in **Figure 3-3.7**, draw the vertical lines shown.
(*This can be achieved using either the Move or Offset commands.*)

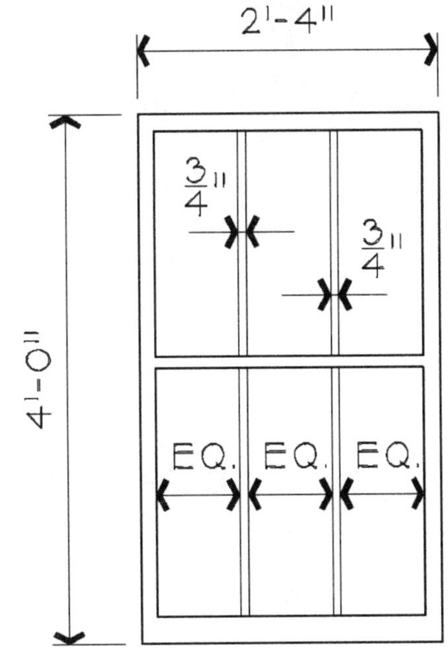

You may have already figured out what you are drawing; it is a double-hung window in elevation view.

You have two more lines to draw.

25. **Draw** the two short horizontal lines shown in Figure 3-3.8.
(The lines are near each side towards the middle; compare with Figure 3-3.7.)

Figure 3-3.7
Eight vertical lines drawn

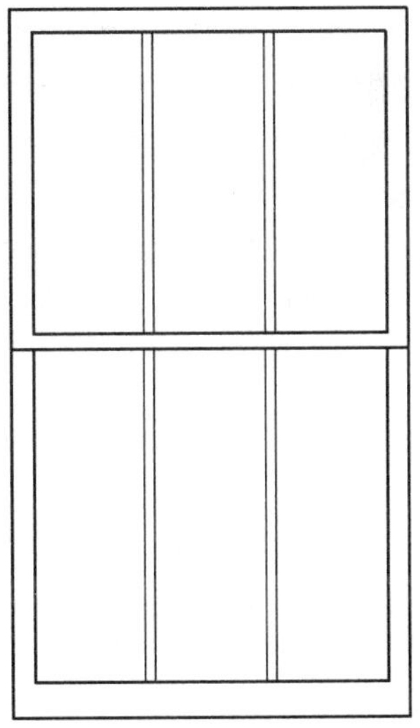

26. Use the **Mtext** command to enter the text: "**Double-Hung Window**" directly below the window. Make the text 2 ¼" high.
Figure 3-3.9

Figure 3-3.8
Two short horizontal lines drawn (cf. Figure 3-3.7)

Oops

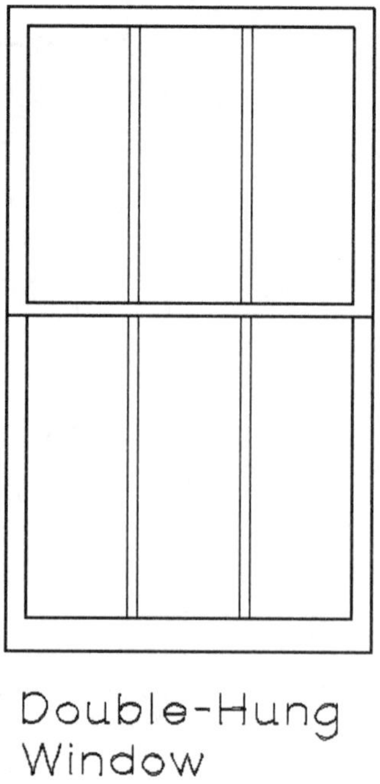

Figure 3-3.9 Text added

If you were following the directions step by step, you missed a step. You forgot to change the Current Layer to Text.

You should notice one visual clue that the text is on the wrong Layer; it's the same color as the lines previously drawn (White). If the text were on the correct Layer it would be Cyan (the color you assigned to the text layer).

Next you will take a quick look at how to change which layer an entity is on.

Moving entities from one Layer to another

Remember, when nothing is selected the Layers Toolbar shows the Current Layer and when something is selected it shows which Layer the selected entity is on.

27. **Select the text**, make sure nothing is selected (*press Esc key*) and click on the text.
    (Notice the Layer Toolbar is indicating that the text is on the Lines Layer.)

28. From the *Drop-Down* list, on the *Layer Toolbar*, select **Text.**

Notice now, with the text still selected, the *Layer Toolbar* indicates that the text is on the Text layer (Figure 3-3.10).

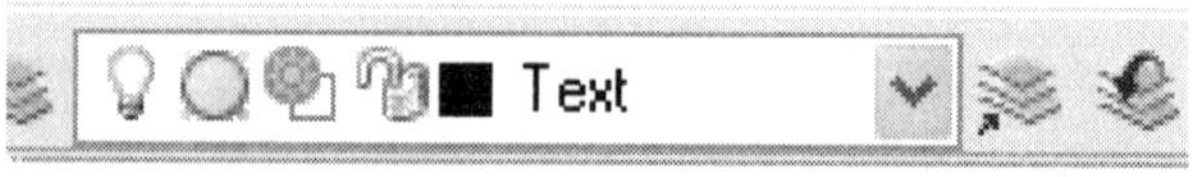

Figure 3-3.10 Text currently selected

29. Now press the **Esc** key to unselect the text.

Notice the *Layer Toolbar* is now showing the Current Layer again. Try selecting and unselecting the various entities in your drawing to see the *Layer Toolbar* change.

30. Make the circle Layer current and then draw a large circle around the window / text, similar to Figure 3-3.11.

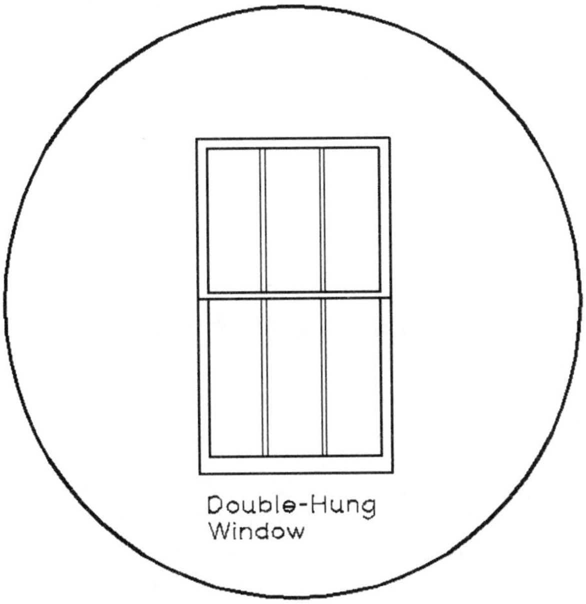

Figure 3-3.11 Circle added

One more look at controlling Layer visibility

Before concluding this chapter you will take one more look at *Freezing* and *Thawing* Layers, this time using your own drawing.

31. **Freeze** the Lines layer *(via Layer Properties Manager)*.

Notice the lines all disappear from the screen.

32. **Thaw** the Lines layer.

33. **Freeze** the Circle layer.

You should have received a message stating that AutoCAD "Cannot freeze the current layer" (Figure 3-3.12). To freeze the Circle layer you would have to set another layer as current first.

Figure 3-3.12 AutoCAD message

34. Set the Rectangles layer as current.

35. Now *Freeze* the Circle layer.

Try a few more variations on the Freeze/Thaw scenarios before proceeding to the next step.

36. Make sure all Layers are turned On and Thawed.

37. **Print** the drawing showing all entities (including the circle).

38. **Delete** the Circle and text.

39. **Save** the drawing as Window.dwg.

What's the difference between Freeze and Off?

On the surface there is no difference between Freeze and Off when it comes to controlling Layer visibility. If you Freeze a Layer its contents are not displayed; the same is true when you turn a Layer Off.

The difference has to do with display memory. When a Layer is Frozen the information required to display it onscreen is not loaded into your graphics card's memory. On the other hand, when a Layer is only turned Off, all the information required to display the entities on that Layer are loaded into your graphics card's memory.

<u>The Pro's and Con's:</u>
The main benefit to turning a Layer Off rather than Freezing it is:

> When you turn a Layer back on it will instantly display (without a regeneration)
> [negative: slower panning and zooming on large / complex drawings]

The benefit to Freezing a Layer rather than turning it Off:

> Faster Panning and Zooming without the extra baggage required in the graphics card
> [negative: requires a time consuming Regen whenever a Layer is Thawed]

<u>Recommended use:</u>
Freeze the following Layers in your drawing if:

> The Layer will typically "never" be on in the current drawing (e.g. doors and furniture in a reflected ceiling plan)

Turn a Layer Off in your drawing if:

> The Layer is generally always on but you want to make it invisible for a short period of time (e.g. hiding the Text and Dimension layers to print a "clean" floor plan).

When using this method you can confidently select all the layers in the *Layer Properties Manager* and turn them all On without worrying about making a Layer show up that shouldn't.

Self-Exam:

The following questions can be used as a way to check your knowledge of this lesson. The answers can be found at the bottom of this page.

1. There is no difference between Freeze and Off. (T/F)
2. A drawing's Origin is 0,0. (T/F)
3. Construction lines are useful drawing aids. (T/F)
4. Use the ______________ command to an oval shape.
5. When you want to make a previously drawn rectangle wider you would use the _______________ command.

Review Questions:

The following questions may be assigned by your instructor as a way to assess your knowledge of this section. Your instructor has the answers to the review questions.

1. Use the Offset command to quickly create a parallel line(s). (T/F)
2. The Explode command will reduce a polyline (e.g., rectangle) to individual lines. (T/F)
3. With the stretch command, lines completely within the crossing-window are actually only moved, not stretched. (T/F)
4. You have to select entities and a center point when using polar Array (T/F)
5. Occasionally you need to draw an object and then move it into place to accurately locate it. (T/F)
6. Selecting this icon (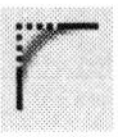) allows you to ____________ two intersecting lines.
7. Fill in the blanks; draw a line 3'-4" long and straight up: @____ < _____
8. Use the _______________ command to create a reverse image.
9. You can use either ___________ or _____________ in the Layer Properties Manager to control the visibility of a Layer.
10. When no entities are selected, the Layer Toolbar displays the ________ layer.

Self-Exam Answers:
1 - F, **2** - T, **3** - T, **4** - Ellipse, **5** – Stretch

Notes:

Lesson 4
Residential Project: FLOOR PLANS::

In this lesson you will jump right in and get started drawing your floor plans for the residential project. Throughout the lesson you will be introduced to a few new commands and you will study common methods used to draw floor plans.

Exercise 4-1:
Walls

Introduction

Two lines, a certain distance apart, represent the walls in a floor plan. In AutoCAD these walls are drawn on a layer named A-WALL. The distance between the two lines is the same as the actual thickness of the wall (or very close to it); wall thicknesses are usually rounded off to the nearest ¼".

The following is an overview of how walls are typically dimensioned in a floor plan. This information is intended to help you understand the dimensions you will see in the exercises, as well as prepare you for the point when you dimension your plans.

Stud walls (wood or metal) are typically dimensioned to the center of the walls. This is one of the reasons the walls do not need to be the exact thickness. Here are a few reasons why you should dimension to the center of the stud rather than to the face of the gypsum board:

- The contractor is laying out the walls in a large "empty" area. The most useful dimension is to the center of the stud; that is where they will make a mark on the floor. If the dimension was to the face of the gypsum board, the contractor would have to stop and calculate the center of the stud, which is not always the center of the wall thickness (e.g., a stud wall with 1 layer of gypsum board on one side and 2 layers of gypsum board over resilient channels on the other side).

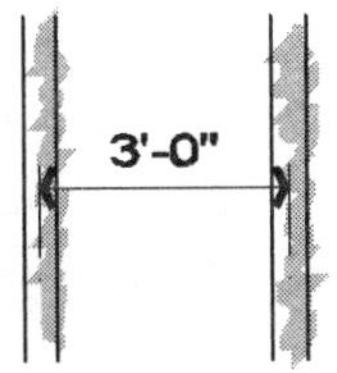

Dimension Example
- Two Stud Walls

- The extra dimensions (text and arrows) indicating the thickness of the walls would take up an excessive amount of room on the floor plans; space that would be better used by notes.

Occasionally you should dimension to the face of a wall rather than the center. Here's one example:

- When indicating design intent or building code requirements, you should reference the exact points/surfaces. For example, if you have uncommonly large trim around a door opening, you may want a dimension from the edge of the door to the face of the adjacent wall. Another example would be the width of a hallway; if you want a particular width you would dimension between the two faces of the wall and add the text "clear" below the dimension to make it known, without question, that the dimension is not to the center of the wall.

Dimensions for masonry and foundation walls:

- Foundation and masonry walls are dimensioned to the nominal face and not the center. These types of walls are modular (e.g., 8"x8"x16") so it is helpful, for both designer and builder, to have dimensions that relate to the masonry wall's "coursing".

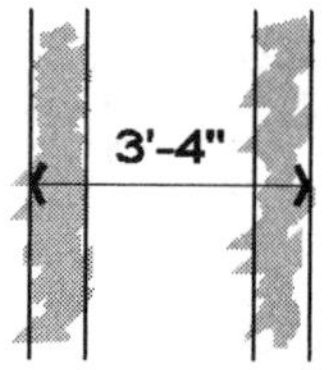

Dimension Example - Two masonry Walls

Dimensions from a stud wall to a masonry wall:

- The rules above apply for each side of the dimension line. For example: a dimension for the exterior foundation wall to an interior stud wall would be from the exterior face of the foundation wall to the center of the stud on the stud wall.

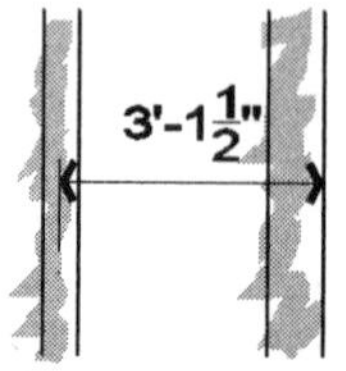

Dimension Example - stud to masonry

Contos Residence

Image courtesy of Anderson Architects
Alan H. Anderson, Architect, Duluth, MN

Overview of the plans you will be drawing

The following sketches will give you an idea of the floor plans you will draw in this lesson.

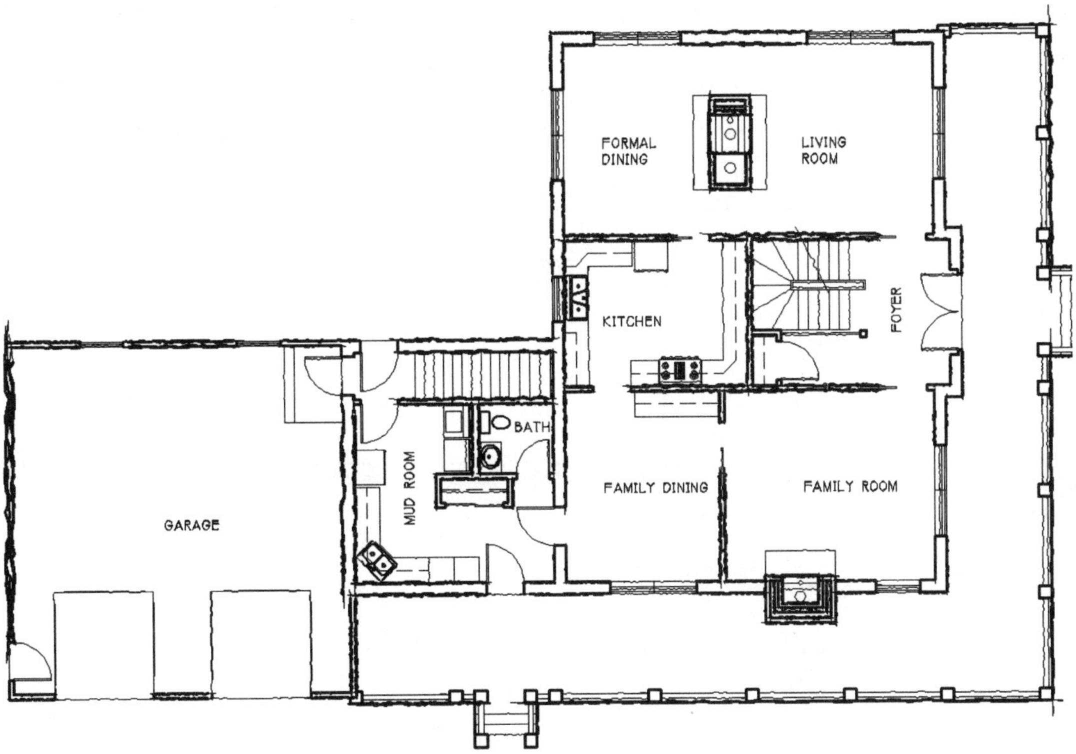

Figure 4-1.1 Sketch - First Floor Plan

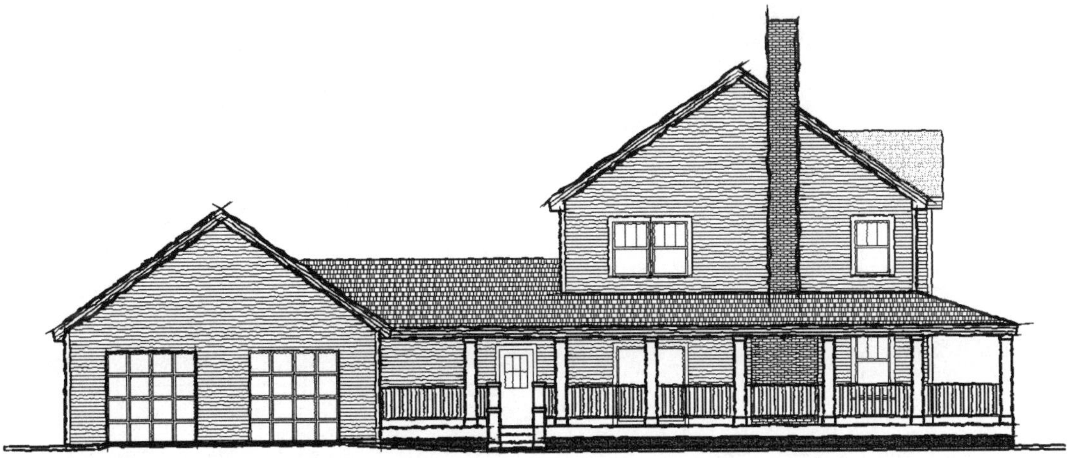

Figure 4-1.2 Sketch – South Elevation

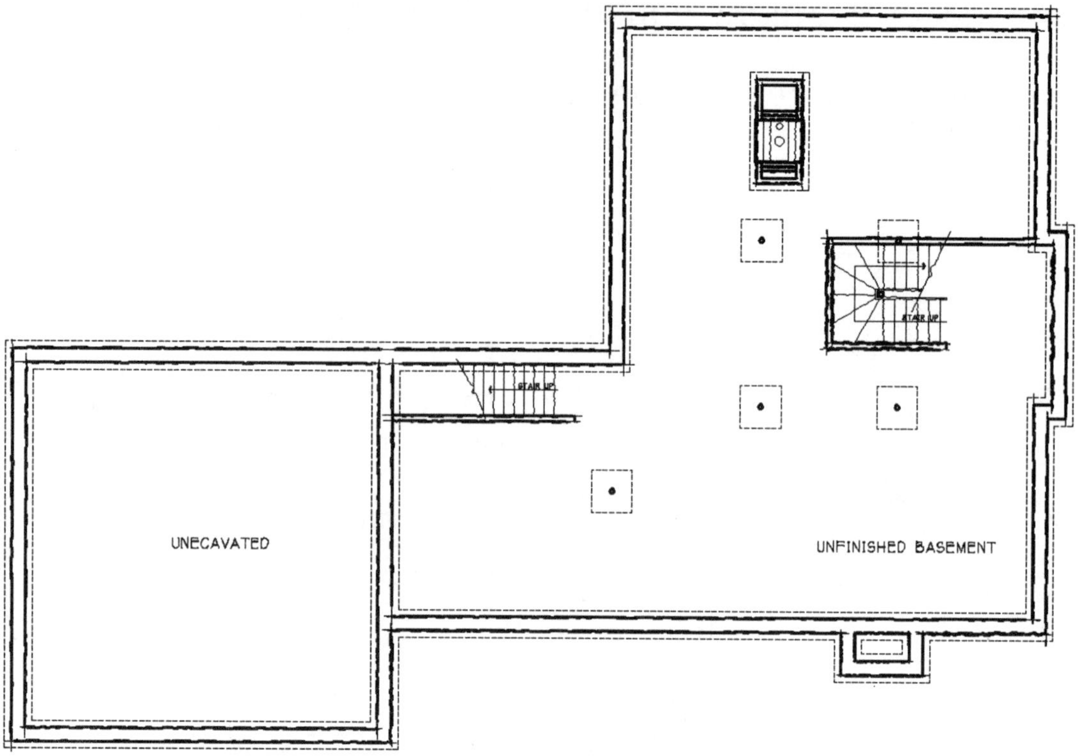

Figure 4-1.3 Sketch - Basement Floor Plan

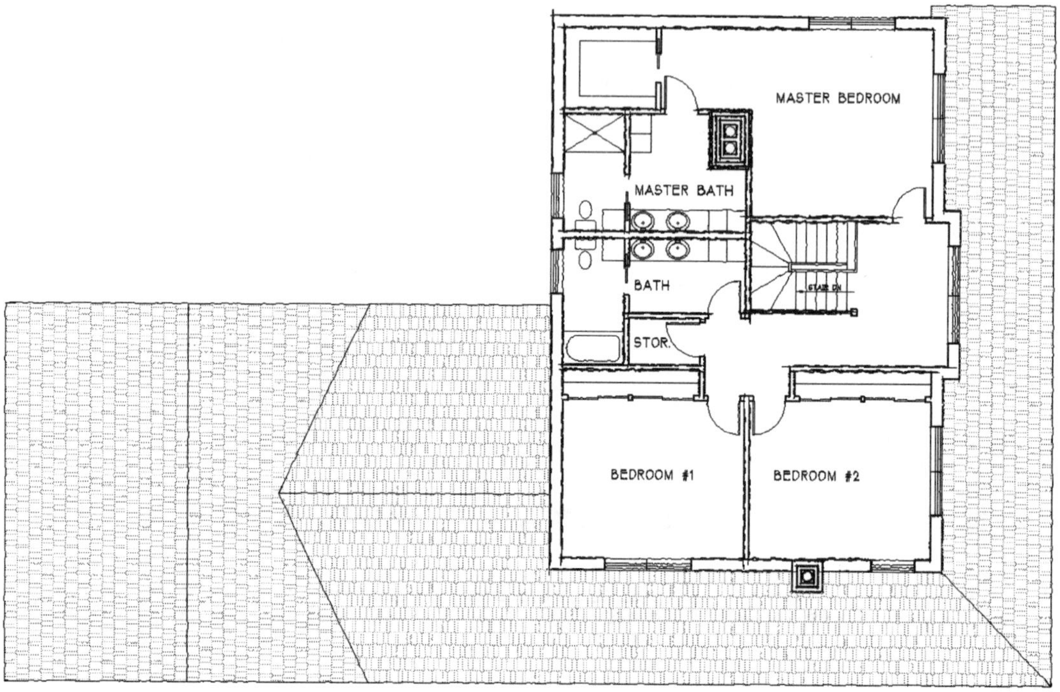

Figure 4-1.4 Sketch - Second Floor Plan

Getting started

In this exercise you will draw just the walls for all three floor plans. Similar to the exercises in lesson 3, you will draw each floor plan in a separate drawing.

Additionally, each drawing will have a common origin; this will make it easy to copy/paste and overlay the plans to make sure things lineup from floor to floor. You will use the upper left corner of the two-story portion of the residence as the origin.

Drawing walls involves extensive use of just a handful of commands, most of which you already know how to use. The most typical commands used in drawing walls are:

- Line
- Offset
- Stretch
- Trim
- Extend

The last two commands, Trim and Extend, have not been covered yet. You will study these commands in this exercise.

You will now start drawing the basement floor plan walls.

1. Start a new drawing named **Flr-B.dwg.**
   Don't forget to use the correct template: "Architectural, English units - Named Plot Styles".

2. Switch to *Model Space* if necessary.

3. Create the layer **A-WALL** *(Color: White; Linetype: Continuous).*

4. Draw the lines shown in **Figure 4-1.5** with either *Ortho* or *Polar Tracking* turned on.

   a. TIP for drawing the first line: enter 0,0 for first point and then enter @24'<-90 *(See page 2-23 for more info).*

   b. You do not need to draw the dimensions yet.

All the dimensions shown in the foundation perimeter drawing (Figure 4-1.5) relate to masonry coursing. See the tip on the next page.

5. Use the **Distance** command to double check your dimensions before moving on. Now is the time to make corrections *(located on the Inquiry Toolbar).*

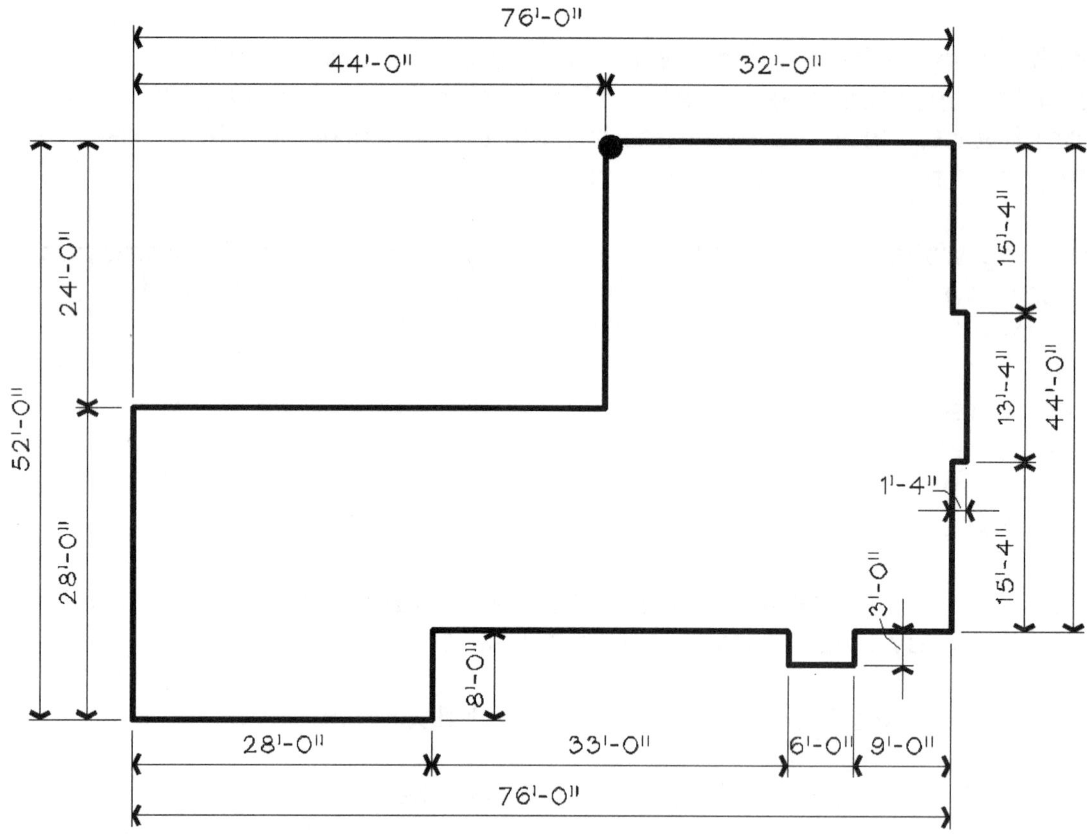

Figure 4-1.5 Foundation perimeter - Basement Floor Plan
The black dot represent the Origin (i.e., 0,0)

TIP:
Concrete blocks come in various widths, and most are 16″ long and 8″ high. When drawing plans there is a simple rule to keep in mind to make sure you are designing walls to coursing. This applies to wall lengths and openings within CMU walls.

Dimension rules for CMU coursing in floor plans:

- *e*′-0″ or *e*′-8″ where *e* is any even number (e.g., 6′-0″ or 24′-8″)
- *o*′-4″ where *o* is any odd number (e.g., 5′-4″)

The foundation walls consist of 12″ thick concrete blocks, so you will use the offset command to quickly create the interior side of the wall.

6. Use the **Offset** command to offset the lines previously drawn toward the center of the structure **12″** (Figure 4-1.6).

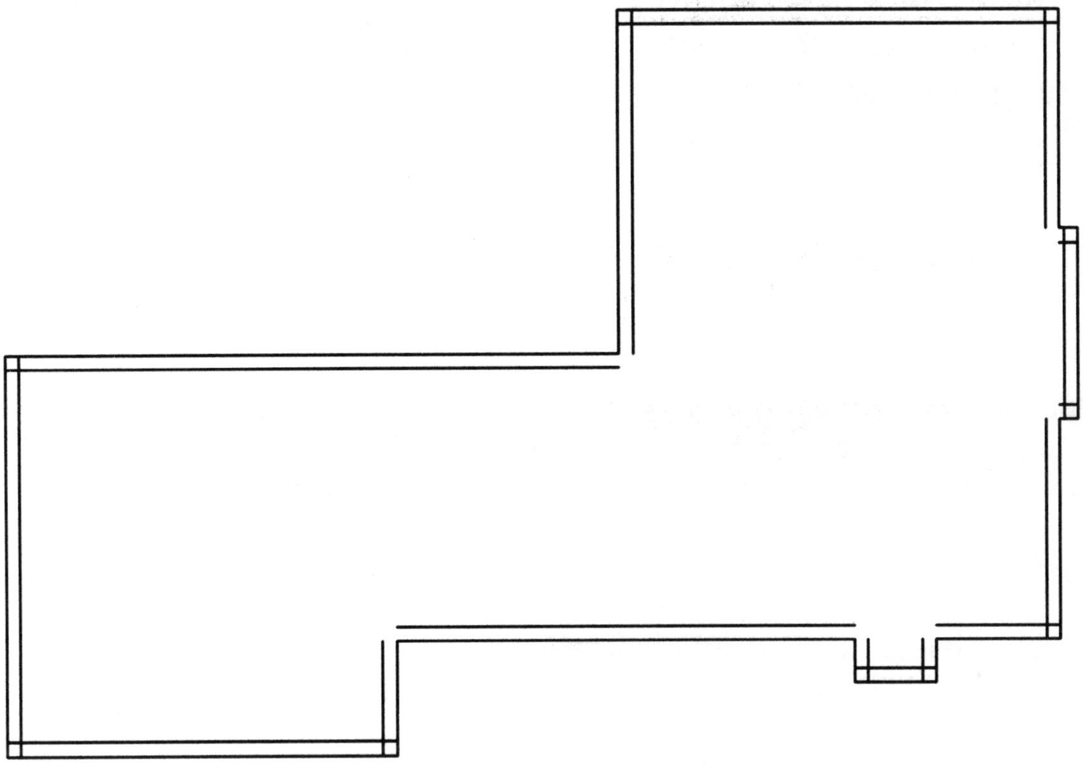

Figure 4-1.6 Preliminary Foundation perimeter - Basement Floor Plan

Notice in the figure above that the *Offset* command simply offsets a line of the same length as the original line. Thus, at inside corners the lines are too long and outside corners the lines are not long enough.

If you recall, from the previous Lesson, the Rectangle command creates what is called a "closed polyline". If you had used the Polyline command to draw the perimeter the entire outline would have offset with perfect corners. You would then have to explode the polyline(s) in order to create the interior walls.

7. Use the **Fillet** command with the radius set to **0** (i.e., zero) to clean up all the corners. Do not Fillet the corner identified in Figure 4-1.7.

You should now have exterior walls with all but one "cleaned-up" corner.

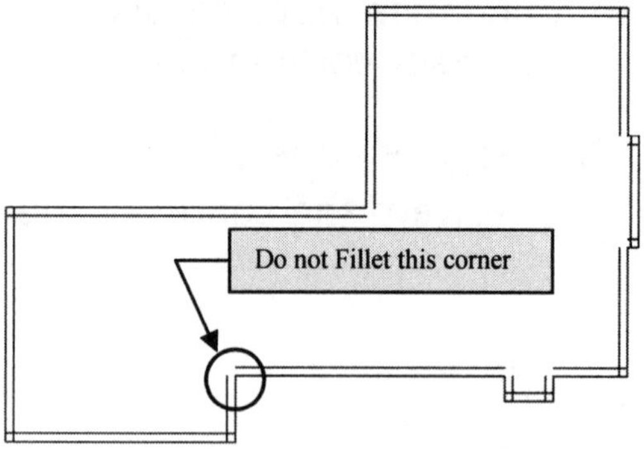

Figure 4-1.7 Do not *Fillet* this corner
Basement Floor Plan

Using the Extend command

You will use both *Extend* and *Trim* to complete the other major masonry wall in the basement. Both commands are located on the Modify Toolbar; hover your cursor over the icon to view its tool tip which displays the command name.

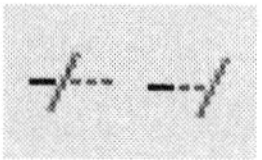

Trim **Extend**

8. Select the **Extend** command.

You are now prompted to **Select boundary edges...**
This is what you want to extend too.

9. Pick the horizontal line identified in Figure 4-1.8.

10. Press **Enter** to tell AutoCAD you are done selecting.

You are now prompted to **Select object to extend...**

11. Pick the short vertical line identified in Figure 4-1.8.

12. Press **Enter** to complete the line extension.

TIP:
When selecting a line to extend, AutoCAD is aware of which side of the line's midpoint you select. This is because you can extend a line in both directions (assuming you selected lines to extend to <i.e., boundary edges> on each side). In the example above, you need to select the portion of the vertical line that is closest to the horizontal line.

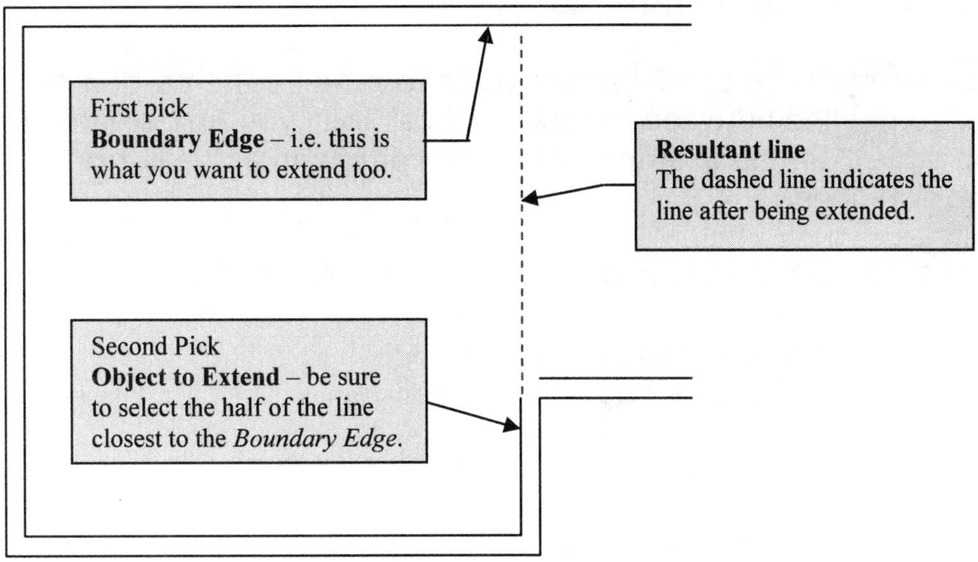

Figure 4-1.8 Using the Extend command to extend a line

You will now draw the other line representing the 12" concrete block wall between the basement and the unexcavated area below the garage. You have several ways in which you can draw this line. One is to offset the line you just extended to the right 12" and then Fillet the bottom corner, the following steps represent another option:

13. Draw a vertical **Line** from the Endpoint below to the Perpendicular point above (see Figure 4-1.9).

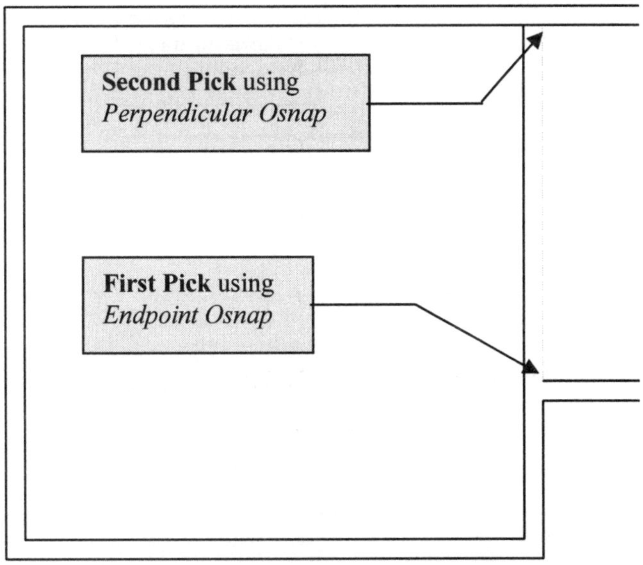

Figure 4-1.9 Drawing a line

Using the Trim command

Now you will use the Trim command to remove the portion of horizontal line between the two vertical lines you just created (at the top edge). In this example, the Trim command actually breaks one line into two lines.

14. Select the **Trim** icon from the *Modify Toolbar.*

You are prompted to **Select cutting edges...**
These are the lines you want to trim too.

15. Select the two vertical lines you just drew.

16. Press **Enter** (or right-click) to tell AutoCAD you are finished selecting cutting edges.

You are now prompted to **Select object to Trim...**
This is the portion of line you want to go away.

17. **Select** the portion of horizontal line between the two vertical lines and then press **Enter.**

The horizontal line is now trimmed (see Figure 4.1-10).

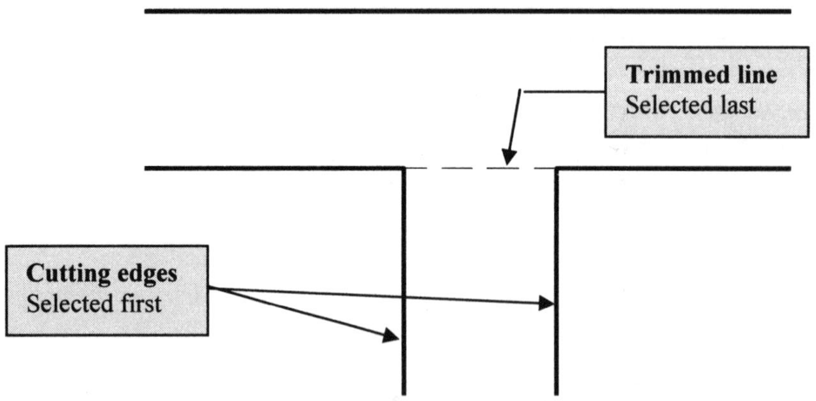

Figure 4-1.10 Trimming a line

FYI:
In the previous example of the Trim command, if you had only selected one of the vertical lines, the entire portion of the horizontal line would be erased depending on which side of the vertical line you selected to trim.

Next you will complete the foundation wall at the south (towards the bottom) fireplace.

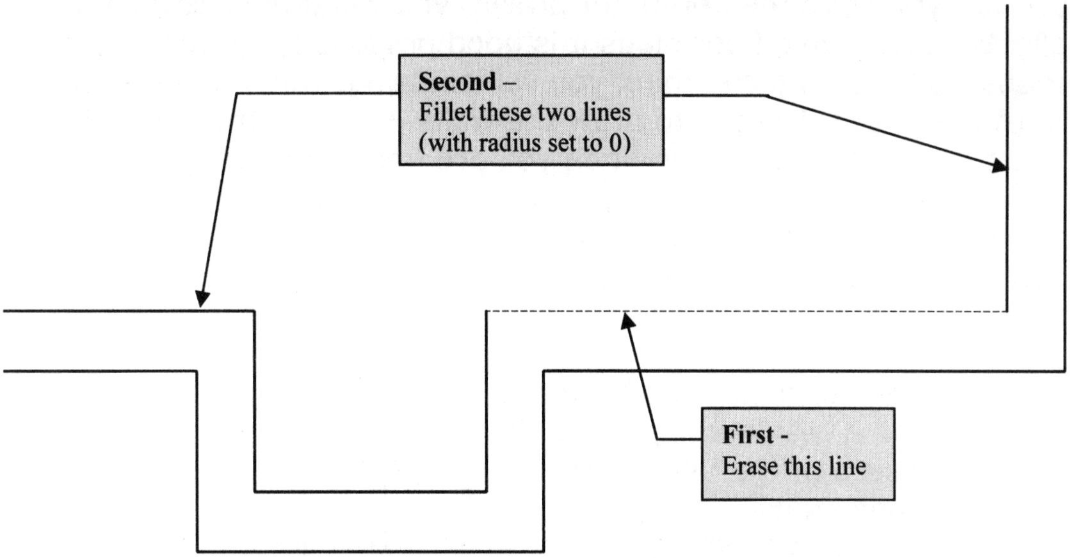

Figure 4-1.11 Creating and modifying walls

18. Modify the drawing as shown in **Figure 4.1-11**
19. Modify drawing as shown in **Figure 4.1-12**

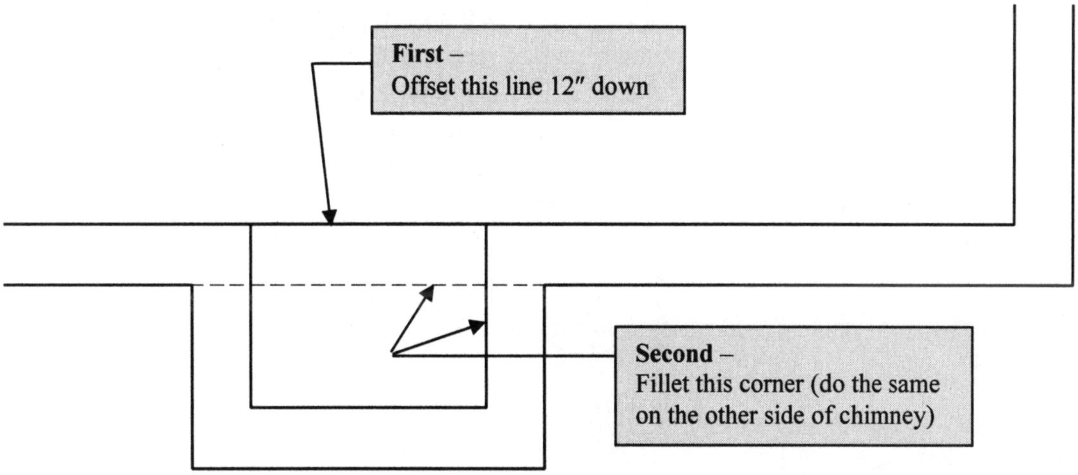

Figure 4-1.12 Creating and modifying walls

Drawing the interior walls

Now that you have the perimeter drawn, you will draw a few interior walls. When drawing floor plans it is good practice to sketch out the various wall systems you think you will be using; this will help you determine what thickness to draw the walls. Drawing the walls at the correct thickness helps later when you are fine-tuning things.

The exterior walls in the basement are simply 12" concrete block so we did not need to sketch it.

Take a moment to think about the basic interior wall in a residential project. It typically consists of the following:

- 2x4 wood studs
  (actual size is 1 ½" x 3 ½")
- 5/8" gypsum board
  (1/2" is often used to save money)

The wall system described above is sketched to the right (Figure 4-1.13).

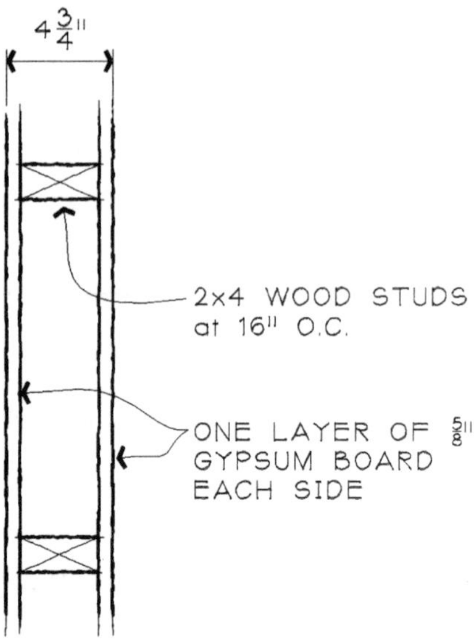

Figure 4-1.13
Sketch – Plan view of interior wall system

All your interior walls should be drawn **4 ¾"** for each floor. The exterior walls will be different for the upper floors (the concrete block does not go up to the roof); you will sketch it when you get to drawing the main level floor plan.

Image courtesy of
Stanius Johnson Architects
Daniel's Construction, Amery WI.
Photo by Robert Aho
www.staniusjohnson.com

You will now draw the interior walls to complete the walls for the basement floor plan.

20. Draw the interior walls shown in **Figure 4-1.14** using the line command. *(The dimensions shown are not to the center here, for your convenience in drafting the walls.)*

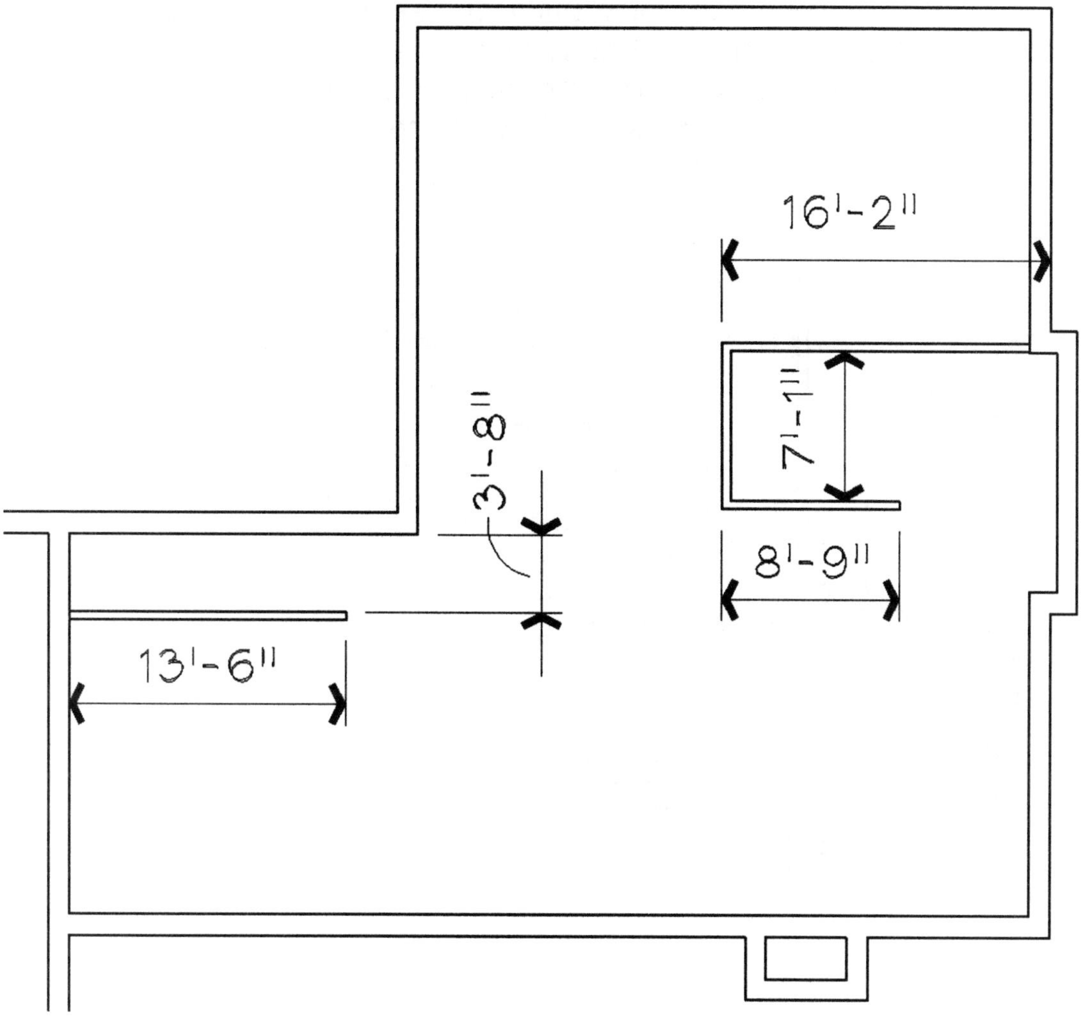

Figure 4-1.14 Interior walls to be drawn

Notice (in Figure 4-1.14) where one wall system meets another, the lines are not trimmed. This helps to delineate the extents of each wall. You would, however, trim the lines between two stud walls of varying thickness.

Drawing the Main Level Floor Plan

Before starting the main level floor plan you will sketch the exterior wall system (see Figure 4-1.15). Notice the exterior sheathing and siding are out past the face of the concrete block foundation wall. Even though the outside face of the exterior wall is technically not aligned with the outside face of the foundation wall below, you will ignore the thickness of the sheathing and siding in plan view. This allows you to draw the outside of the exterior walls in the same position as the outside face of the foundation wall below. This makes it easier to draft and for the contractor to read the dimensions on the blue prints. All the contractor needs to know is the face of the exterior 2x4 is flush with the face of the foundation wall below.

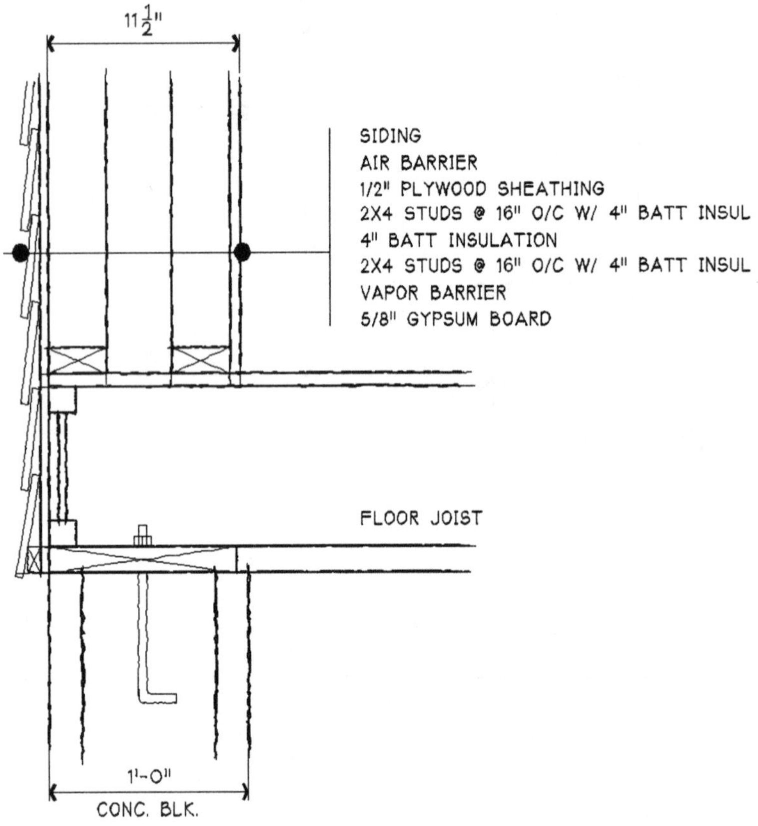

Figure 4-1.15 Sketch - Exterior wall in section view

This wall system will be studied more closely later in the book. However, a brief explanation will be provided. This is a super-insulated wall design. Not only does the wall have a high R-value due to the amount of insulation, the double stud wall does not transmit cold from the exterior face to the interior face like a traditional single 2x6 stud wall would.

21. Start a new drawing named **Flr-1.dwg**

22. Using the **11 ½"** exterior wall dimension shown in Figure 4-1.15, draw the exterior walls shown in Figure 4-1.16.
*(**NOTE**: The garage will not be heated so the walls do not need to be super-insulated; draw these walls at 4 ¾" thick.)*

23. Be sure the Origin is in the same relative position as the basement floor plan. If it is not, use the *Move* command to move the First floor plan into its correct position.

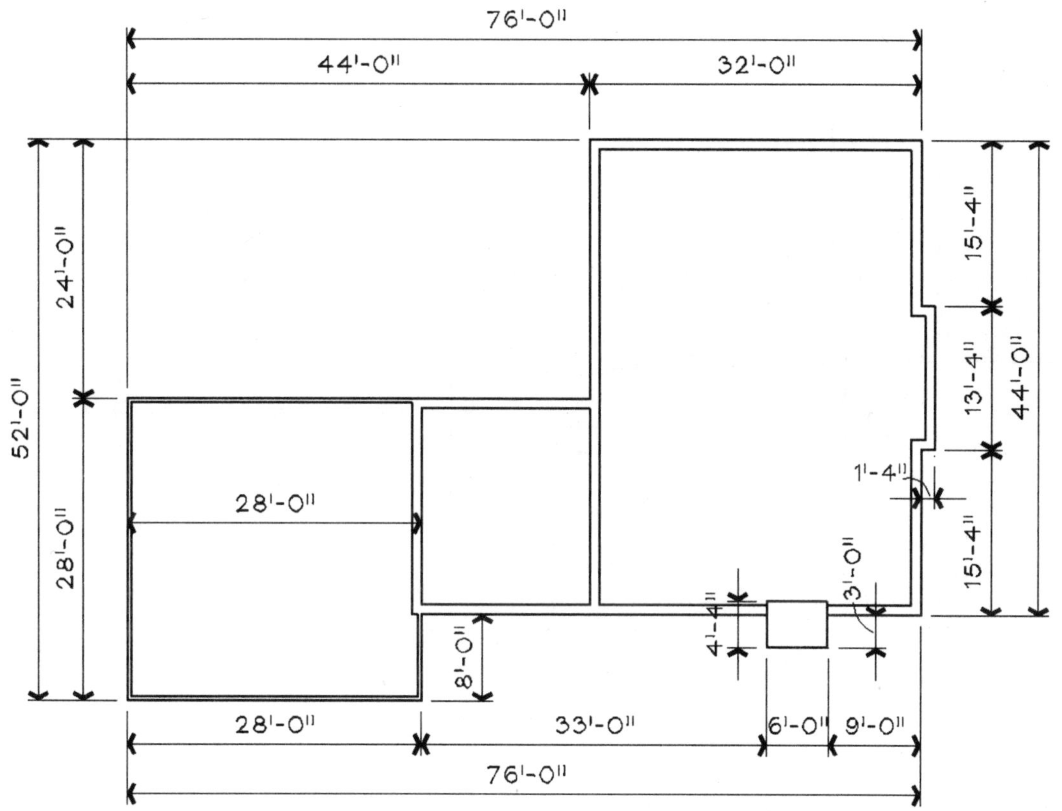

Figure 4-1.16 Exterior walls - First floor plan

Notice, with the exception of two added dimensions, all the dimensions given in Figure 4-1.16 are the same as those given for the basement floor plan. (See Figure 4-1.5.)

Now you will draw the interior walls.

24. Draw the interior walls shown in **Figure 4-1.17**, keeping the following in mind:

    a. Remember to use the **4 ¾"** dimension from Figure 4-1.13.
    b. Again, the dimensions shown are to the face of the walls.
    c. Trim all intersections except at the southern fireplace.
    d. The two major horizontal interior walls are to align with the inside face of the exterior wall as shown.

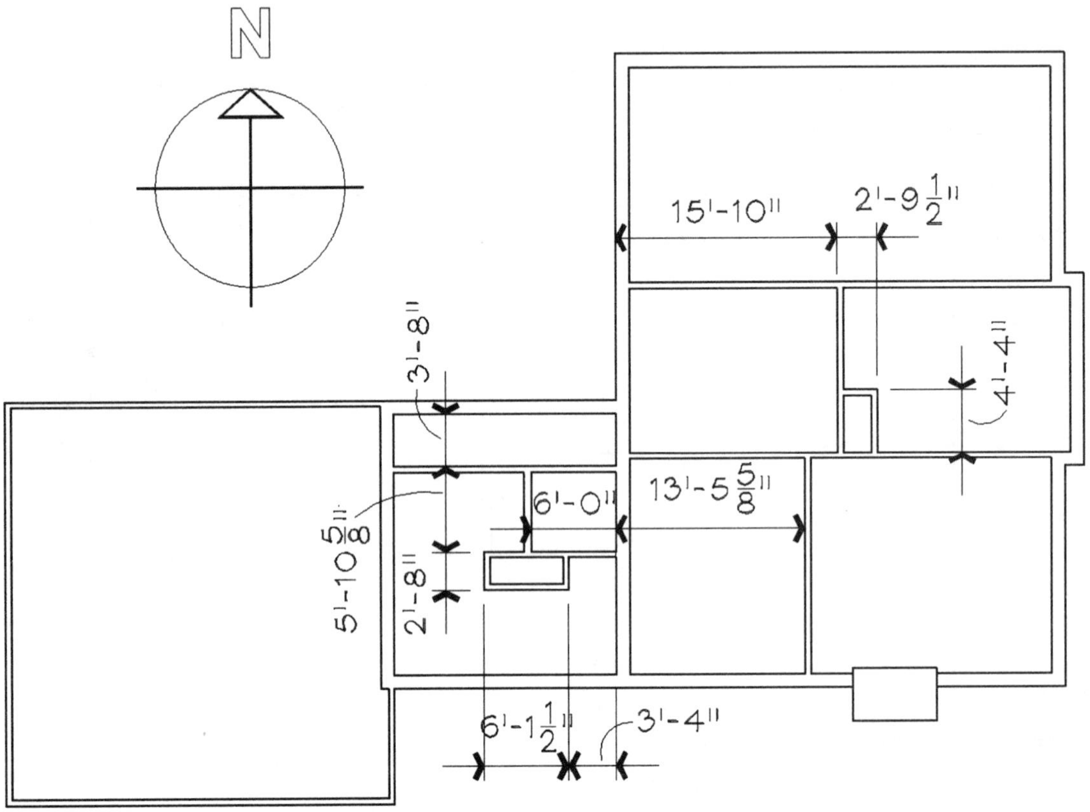

Figure 4-1.17 Interior walls – First floor plan

FYI: *Unless there are unusual circumstances, north is always up on architectural plan drawings (i.e., floor plans, site plans, etc.).*

This completes the First floor plan walls.

Drawing the Second Level Floor Plan

Here you will use the same wall thicknesses previously identified.

Exterior Walls: 11 ½″
Interior Walls: 4 ¾″

25. Start a new drawing named **Flr-2.dwg.**

26. Using the same relative *Origin*, Draw the Second floor exterior walls shown in **Figure 4-1.18.**

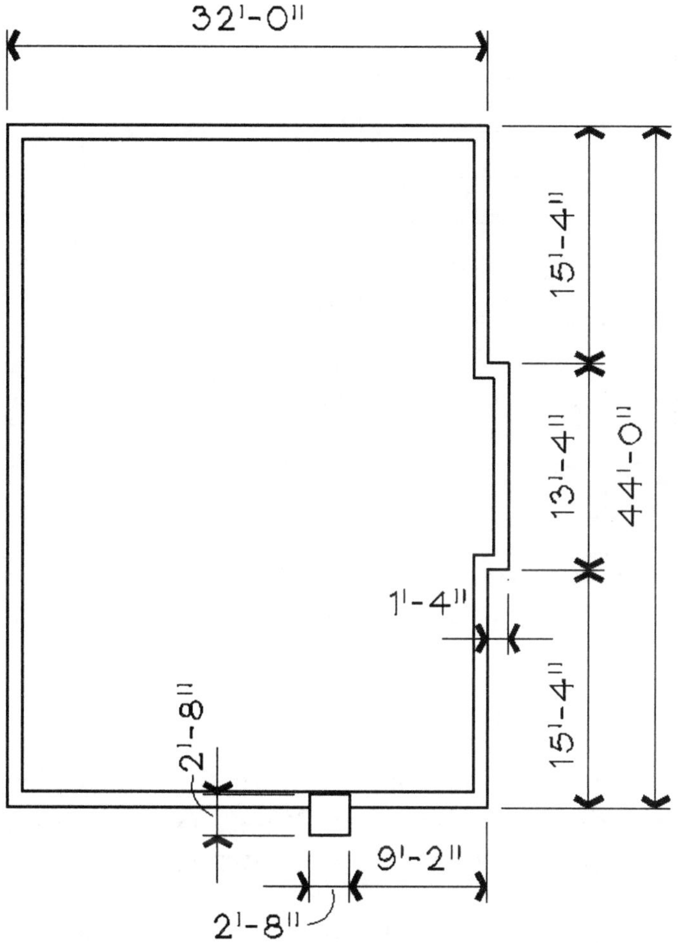

Figure 4-1.18 Exterior walls – Second floor plan

27. Draw the interior walls shown in **Figure 4-1.19.**

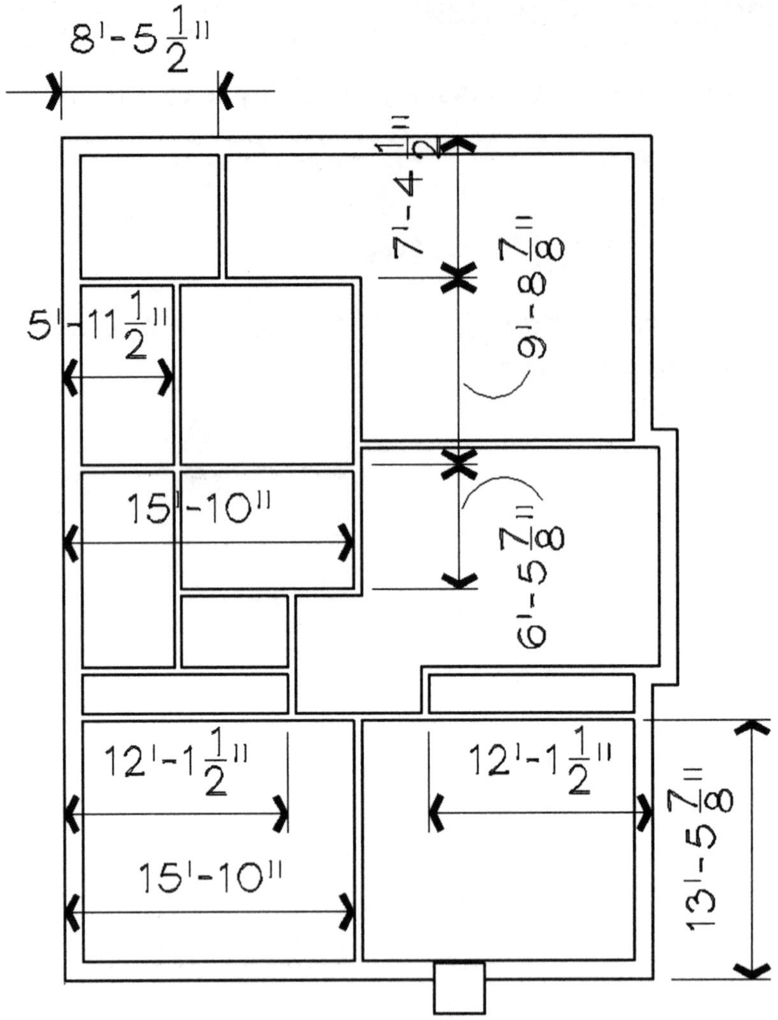

Figure 4-1.19 Interior walls – Second floor plan

28. **Save** your floor plan drawings.

This concludes the exercise on drawing walls for your floor plans. You should now have a good working knowledge of *Offset*, *Trim*, *Extend* as well as using the *Distance* command to verify your drawings.

In the next exercise you will use Offset, Extend and Trim to locate and create door openings in the walls. Additionally, you will learn how to insert pre-drawn symbols (called blocks) into your drawing. In this case you will insert the door symbols previously drawn in Lesson 3.

Exercise 4-2:
Doors

Now that you have drawn the walls, you will add some doors. This involves locating where the door opening will be in the wall and then trimming the wall lines to create the opening. Finally, you insert a door symbol that indicates which side the hinges are on and the direction the door opens.

New doors are typically shown open 90 degrees in floor plans, which helps to avoid conflicts such as the door hitting an adjacent base cabinet. Additionally, to make it clear graphically, existing doors are shown open only 45 degrees.

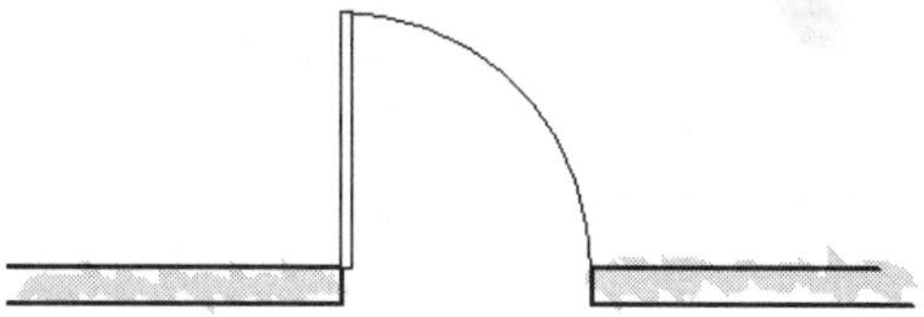

Door symbol Example – New Door drawn with 90 degree swing

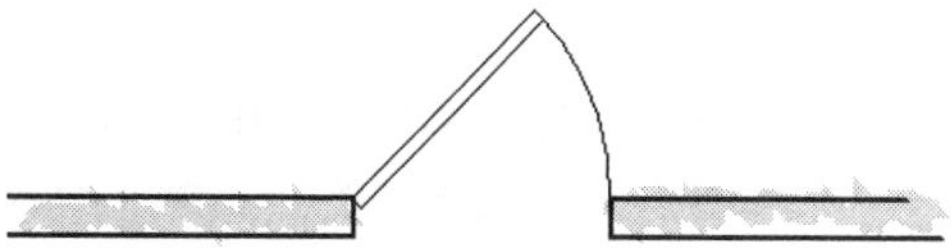

Door symbol Example – Existing Door shown with 45 degree swing

One of the most powerful features of any CAD program is its ability to reuse previously drawn content. With AutoCAD you can insert entire drawing files as symbols into your drawing. Most of the individual drawings you drew in Lesson 3 will be inserted as symbols (AutoCAD calls them blocks), into the three floor plans.

For those new to drafting, you may find this comparison between CAD and hand-drafting interesting: When hand-drafting, one uses a straightedge or a plastic template that has doors and other often used symbols to trace.

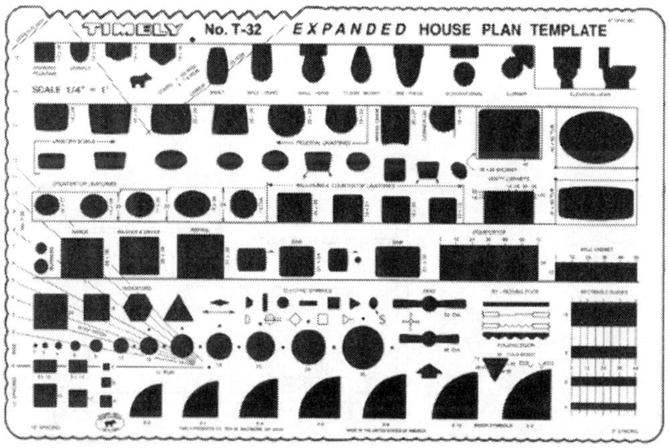

Hand Drafting Template – Plastic template with holes representing common residential shapes (at ¼" – 1'-0") *Image used by permission, Timely Templates www.timelytemplates.com*

Doors in stud walls are dimensioned to the center of the door opening. On the other hand, and similar to dimensioning masonry walls, doors in masonry walls are dimensioned to the face (see example below).

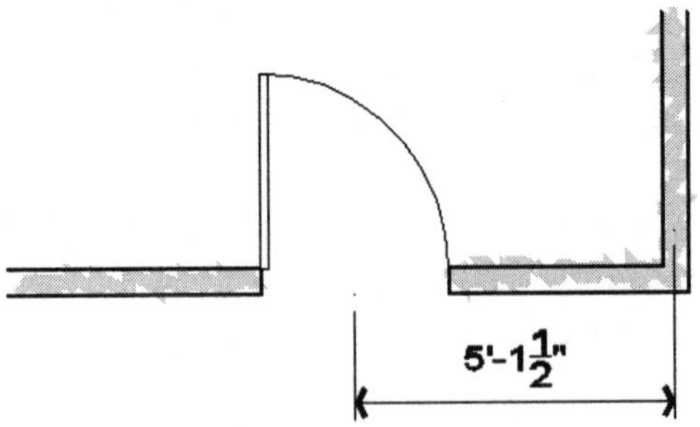

Door Dimension Example – Dimension to the center of the door opening

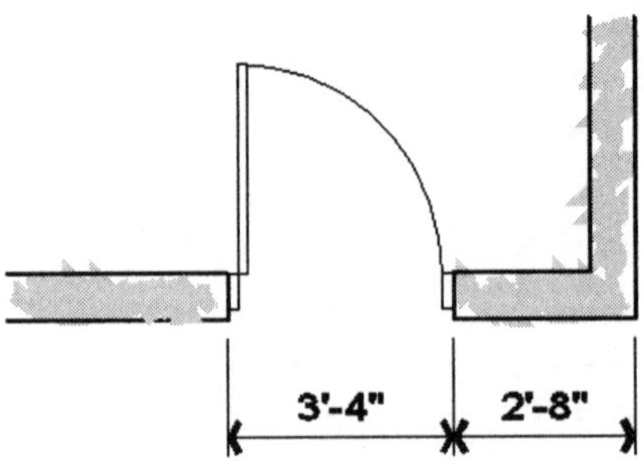

Door Dimension Example – Dimension the opening size & location

Placing a door usually involves the following commands:
Offset, Extend, Trim, and Insert.

Getting started

First you will locate all the openings in the plans. This includes trimming the wall lines.

1. Open your **Flr-1.dwg** drawing file.

2. **Zoom** into the area shown in **Figure 4-2.1.**

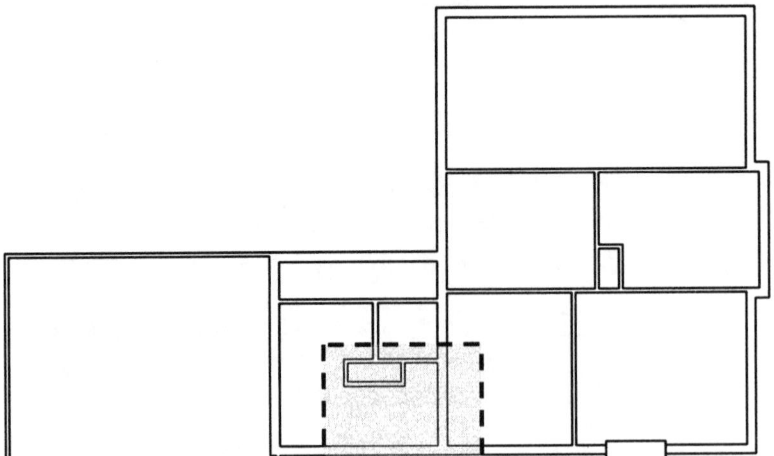

Figure 4-2.1 Zoom into area shown

3. **Offset** the vertical line **2'-6"** to the west (to the left) as shown in **Figure 4-2.2.**

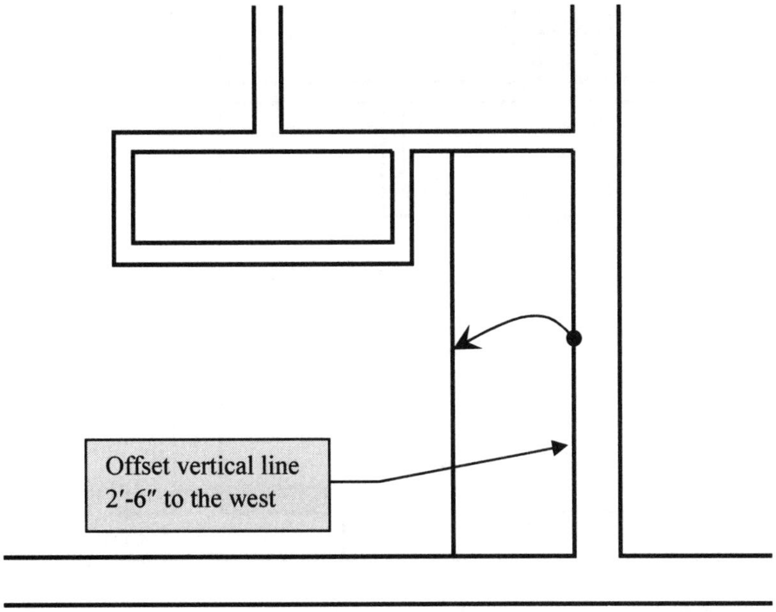

Figure 4-2.2 Offset vertical line 2'-6"

4. **Extend** the new line south, to the outside face of the exterior wall (Figure 4-2.3).

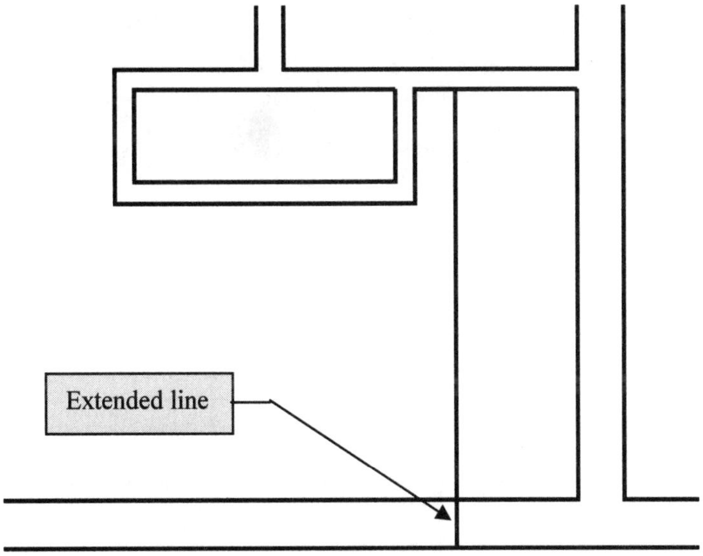

Figure 4-2.3 Extend new line south

5. Now **Trim** the line so its length equals the depth of the wall (Figure 4-2.4).

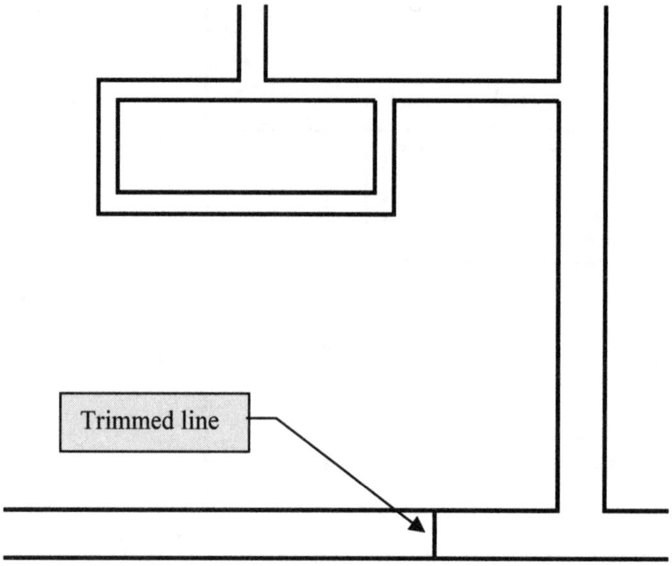

Figure 4-2.4 Trim the new vertical line

Next you will offset the new line; the offset distance will be the width of the door.

If your line located the center of the door opening you would offset it each direction, with the offset distance being half the width of the door opening. Then you would delete the center line.

6. **Offset** the line **3'-0"** to the west. (Figure 4-2.5)

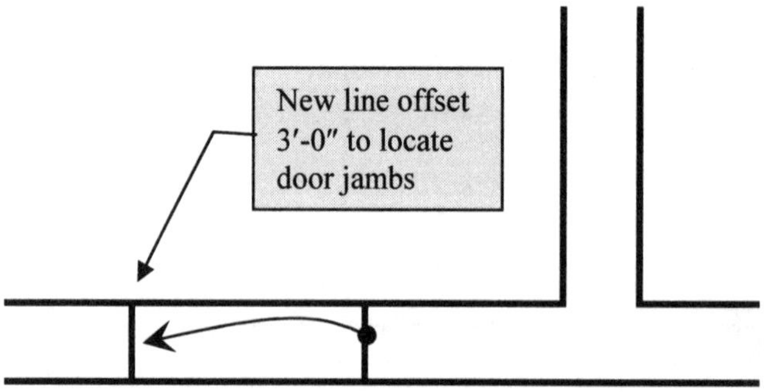

Figure 4-2.5 Offset to define the door opening

Finally, you will use Trim to remove the wall lines within the door opening.

7. **Trim** the wall lines within the door opening. (Figure 4-2.6)

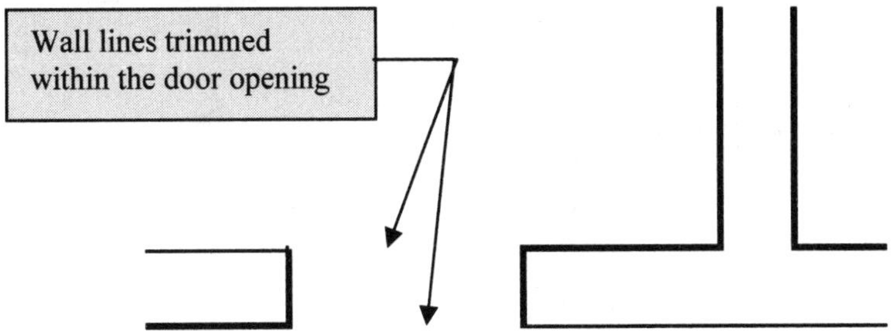

Figure 4-2.6 Trim the wall lines within the door opening

That completes the steps necessary to accurately locate a door opening in a wall. Next you will create the rest of the openings for both the first and second floors (the basement has no doors).

> **What layer do the new jamb lines go on?**
> The two vertical lines (jamb lines) just drawn go on the same layer as the wall.

Locate and size the remaining openings:

8. Using the following four drawings (Figures 4-2.7,8,9,10), create the door openings for the first and second floors

9. Be sure to Save often to avoid losing work in the event you have a power outage or the AutoCAD program crashes

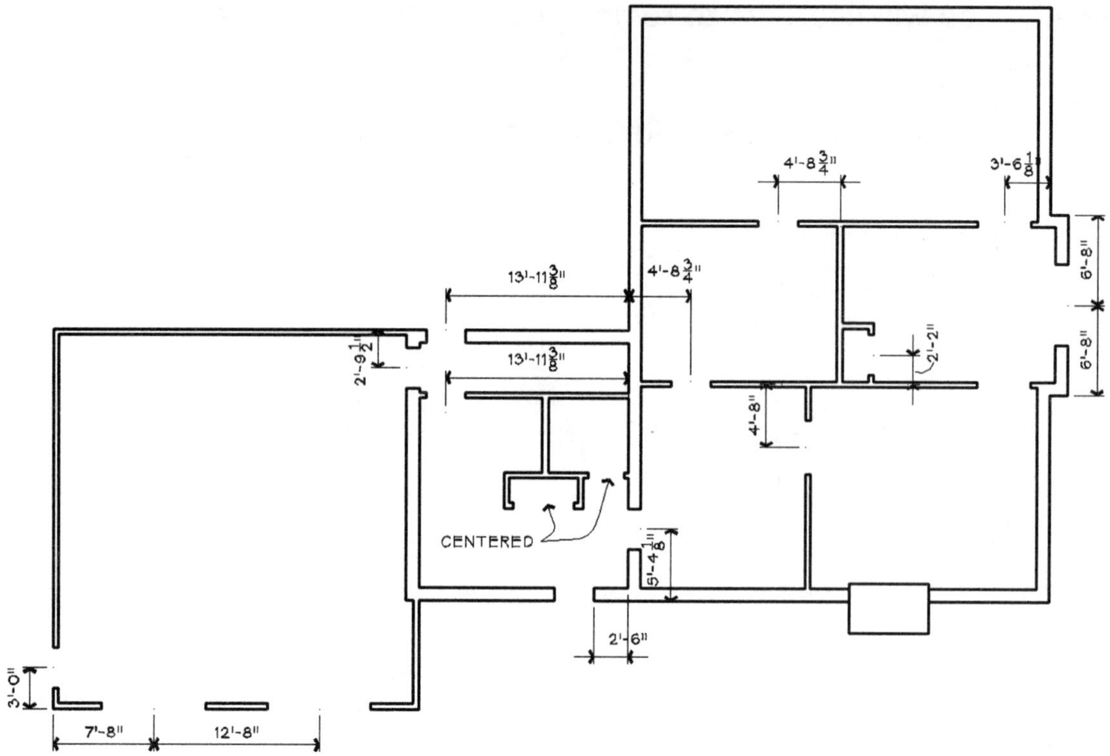

Figure 4-2.7 Door opening; First floor

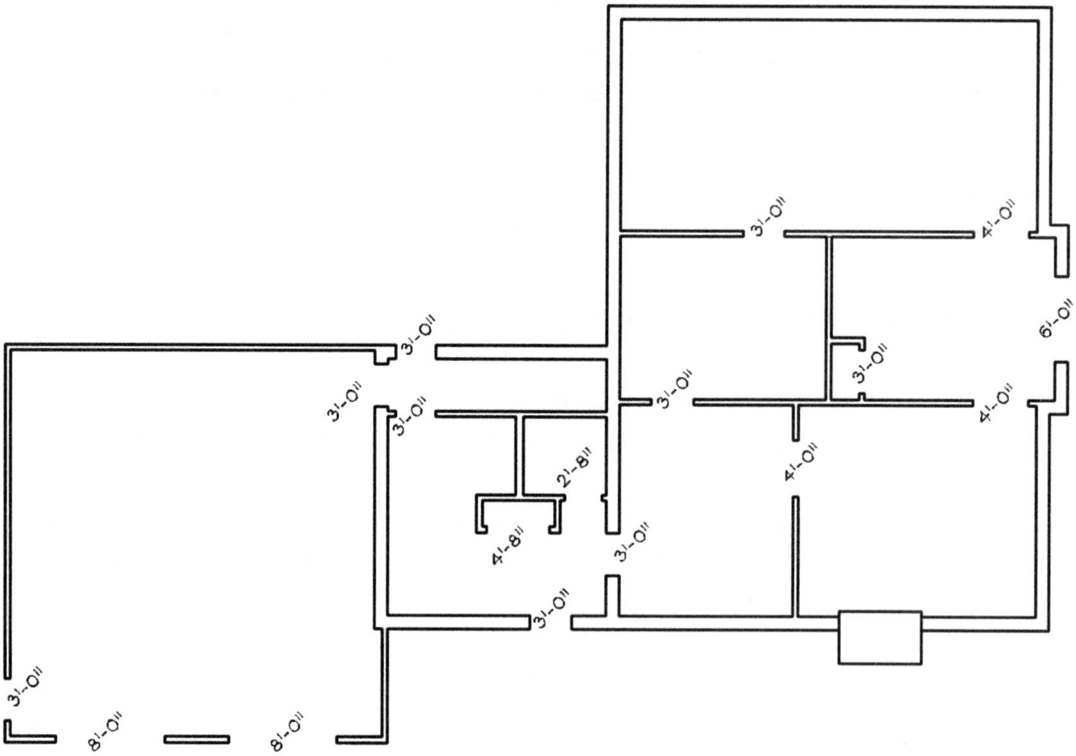

Figure 4-2.8 Door/opening sizes; First floor

4

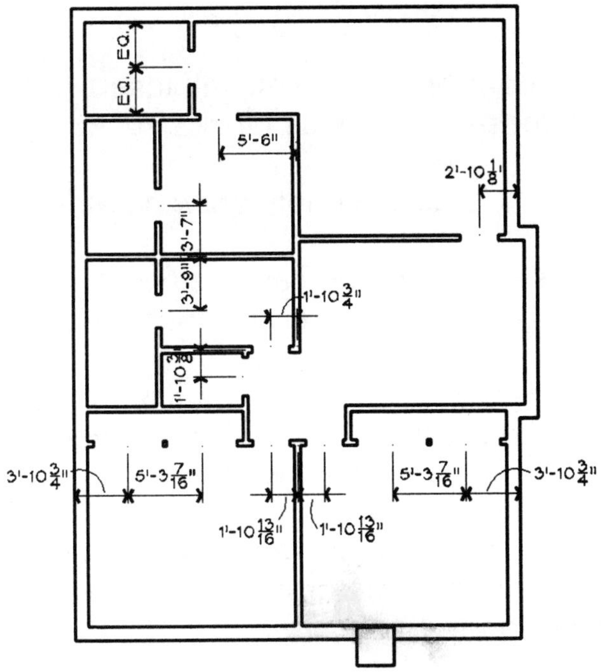

Figure 4-2.9 Door locations; Second floor

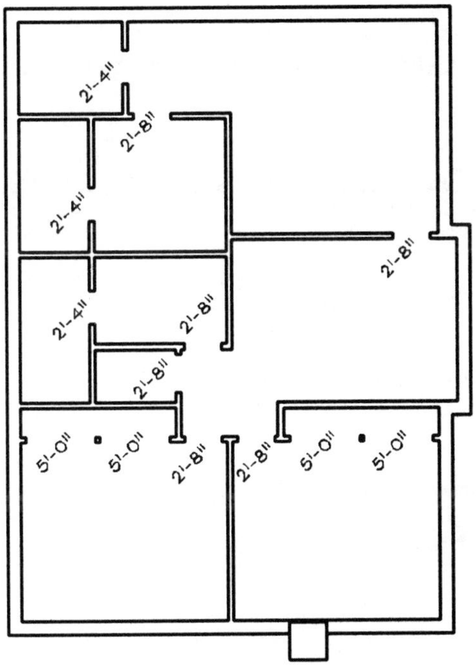

Figure 4-2.10 Door/opening sizes; Second floor
- angled number represents size of opening

Inserting the door symbols (aka Blocks):

Now that you have created all the door openings you will insert the door symbols. AutoCAD refers to these symbols as blocks.

Blocks have several advantages compared to simply drawing individual lines for everything.

- A Block contains a group of entities so you can easily move it without having to meticulously select each entity that makes up the symbol.
- Blocks can also be redefined, meaning that you can add or remove the amount of detail in a block. When it's redefined, all the instances of that block in the current drawing are automatically updated.
- Blocks can consist of an entire drawing located on your hard drive. Thus, they can be used in multiple drawings as needed.
- Blocks help reduce the drawing file size.

You will insert the door blocks you created in the previous lesson. You may occasionally need to *Rotate* and *Mirror* the *Block* once it is inserted. Additionally, you will need to create additional blocks as needed throughout this book.

Door *Blocks* go on their own *Layer* called A-DOOR. Next you will set this up.

10. Create a Layer named **A-DOOR** and set its color to **Yellow** (Color #2).

11. Set the **A-DOOR** Layer to be the **Current** Layer.

12. Select **Block...** from the **Insert** pull-down menu.

You are now in the *Insert* dialog (Figure 4-2.11), which allows you to insert blocks that already exist in the current drawing and other drawings located on your hard drive.

13. Click the **Browse...** button.

14. Browse to the location where you saved the **Door-36** drawing created in the previous chapter.

15. Click **Open.**

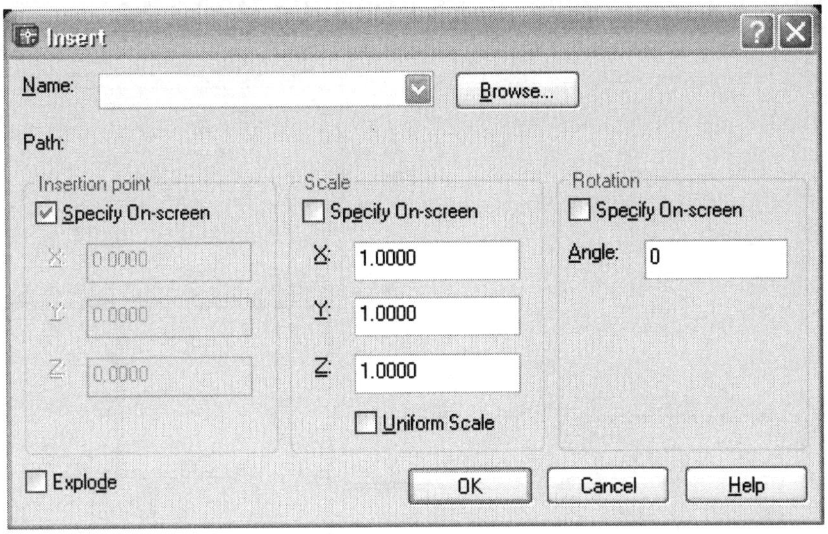

Figure 4-2.11 Insert dialog; allows you to insert blocks into the current drawing

16. **Insert** the **Door-36** drawing using *Osnaps* to accurately position the door block within the opening. Insert the doors as shown in Figure 4-2.12. ***TIP:*** *Use Rotate and Mirror (previously covered) as required to indicate the required swing.*

Notice the block insertion point?

Notice that the hinge side of the door block is attached to the center of the cross-hairs. This relates to the drawing Origin (0,0) of the Door-36 drawing file.

If the drawing Origin had been located on the latch side of the door in drawing Door-36, the latch side of the door would have been attached to the cross-hairs during insert.

You may have noticed that you have not created a 2'-8" wide door yet. Simply follow the steps outlined in the previous chapter, creating the door symbol in a separate drawing file.

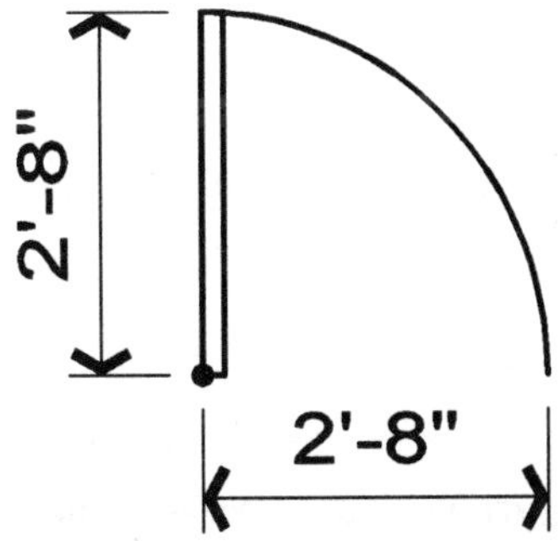

17. Create the 32" wide door drawing; name the file **Door-32.**

18. Insert the 2′-8″ wide doors using the **Door-32** file.

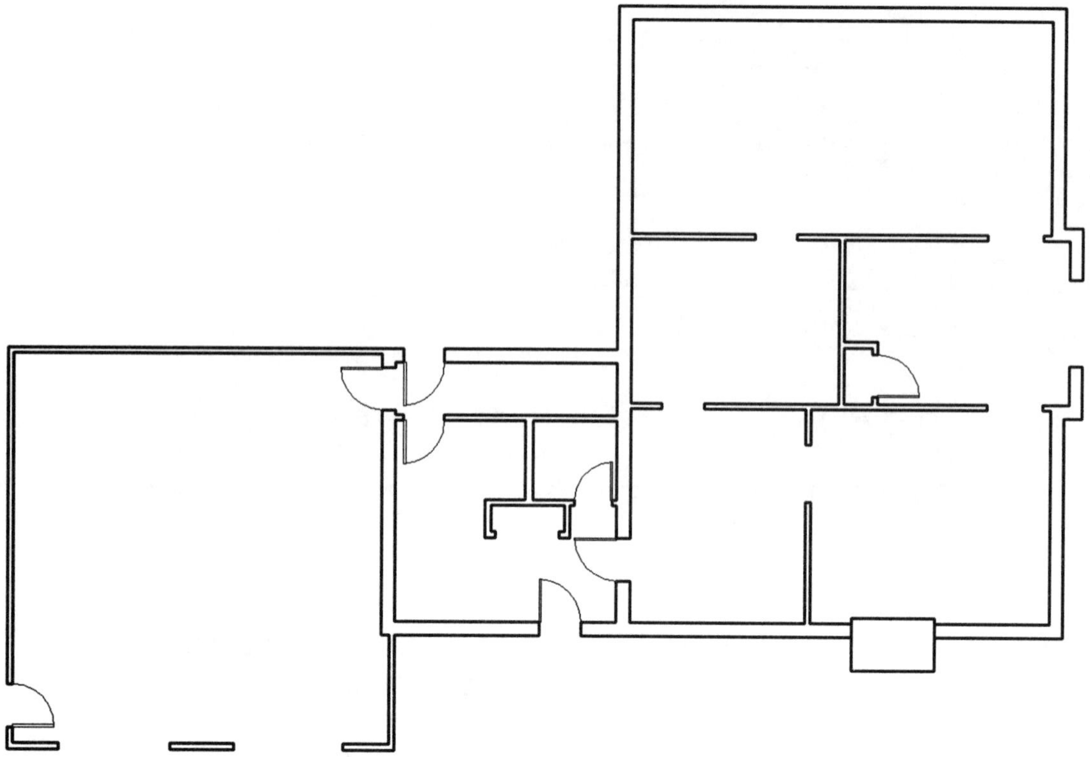

Figure 4-2.12 Door-36 and Door-32 blocks inserted; First floor

19. Insert the **Door2-36** drawing file as a block at the main entry as shown in **Figure 4-2.13.**

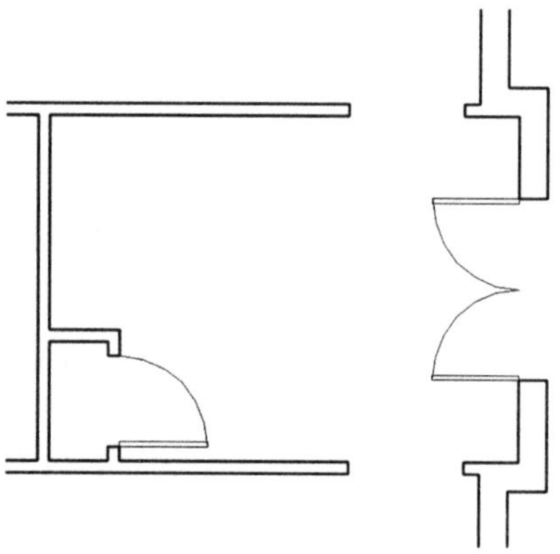

Figure 4-2.13 Door2-36 added

Next you will insert the doors on the second floor.

20. **Save Flr-1.dwg** and **Open** the Second floor drawing file **Flr-2.dwg.**

21. Insert the doors for the Second floor as shown in **Figure 4-2.14.**
__NOTE:__ On the Second floor all swing doors are 32″ wide doors.

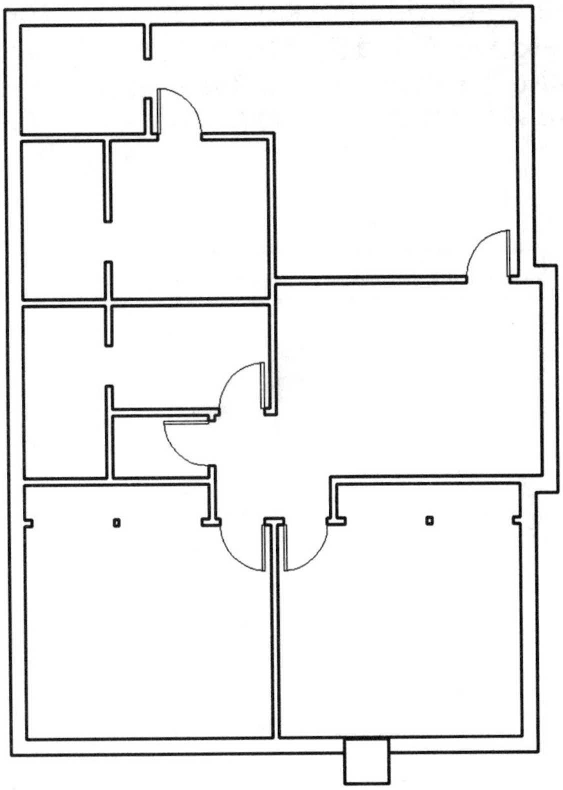

Figure 4-2.14 Door-32 blocks inserted; Second floor

Sliding pocket doors:

Sliding pocket doors are doors that slide into the wall rather than swinging open into a room. This type of door is convenient when the door will be open most of the time and you do not want, or have room for, an open door. On the other hand, if the door will be used often, like the door from the hallway into the bath room, you should use a swinging door for ease of use and long-term durability.

One important thing to keep in mind when designing a room with a sliding door: the entire width of the door is in the wall when the door is fully open. That means you need space in the wall next to the door that equals the width of the door plus a few inches depending on the manufacturer (this includes plumbing and electrical that might be in the wall).

Next you will create the 2'-4" and 4'-0" wide Sliding Pocket Doors.

22. **Open** a new drawing file and name it **Pocket-28.dwg.**

23. **Create** the 2'-4" wide Pocket Door (show the door 2" thick) shown in **Figure 4-2.15.** *TIP: Do not draw the dimensions or the black dot. Also, the dashed lines in the figure below represent a wall. Finally, make sure everything is on layer zero (i.e., 0).*

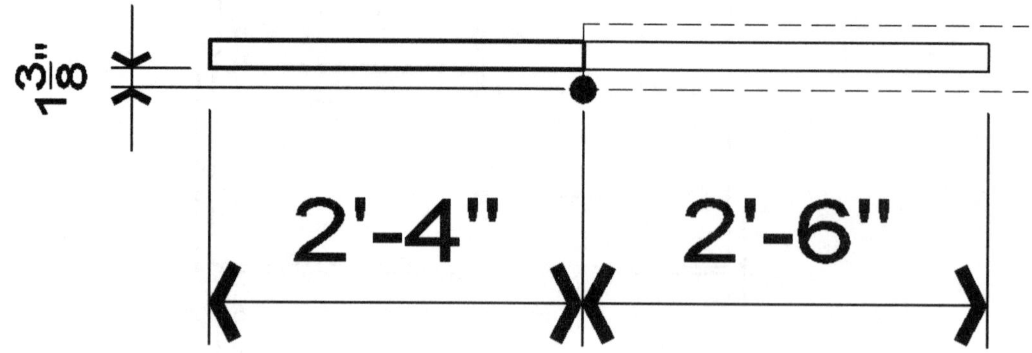

Figure 4-2.15 Pocket-28; First and Second floor

This block (pocket-28) will show the door in the fully closed position; you can adjust this to be partially open if you prefer.

24. **Insert** the 2'-4" wide Pocket door in the three locations shown in Figure 4-2.16 (make sure the current layer is set to A-DOOR before inserting the blocks; also, you may need to stretch the opening location a little so the pocket door fits in the wall).

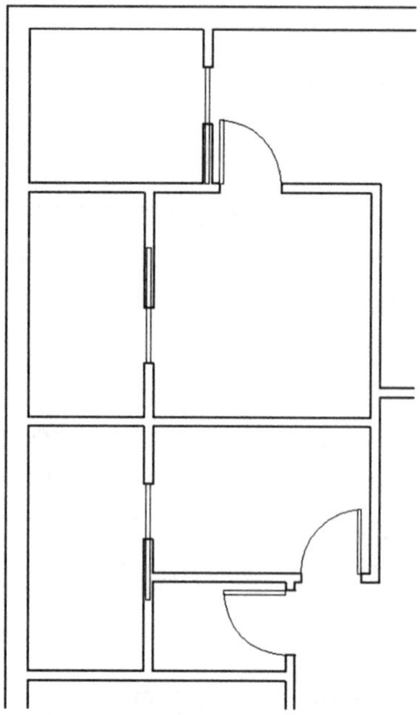

Figure 4-2.16 Pocket-28; three locations; Second floor

25. Do a **Save-As** to save the Pocket-28 to a file named **Door-48.**

26. Use the **Stretch** command to create the 48" pocket door.

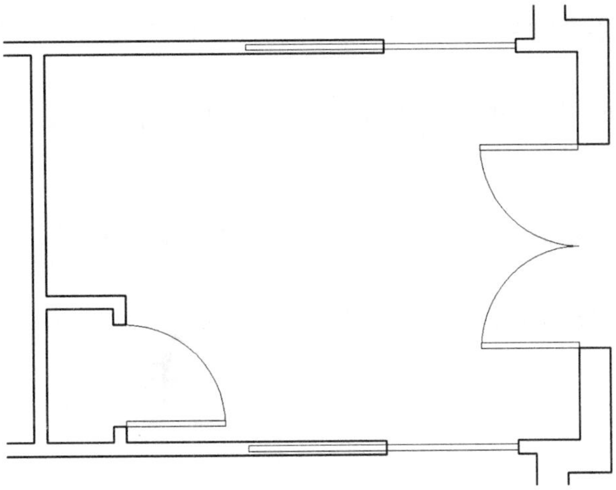

Figure 4-2.17 Pocket-48; two locations; First floor

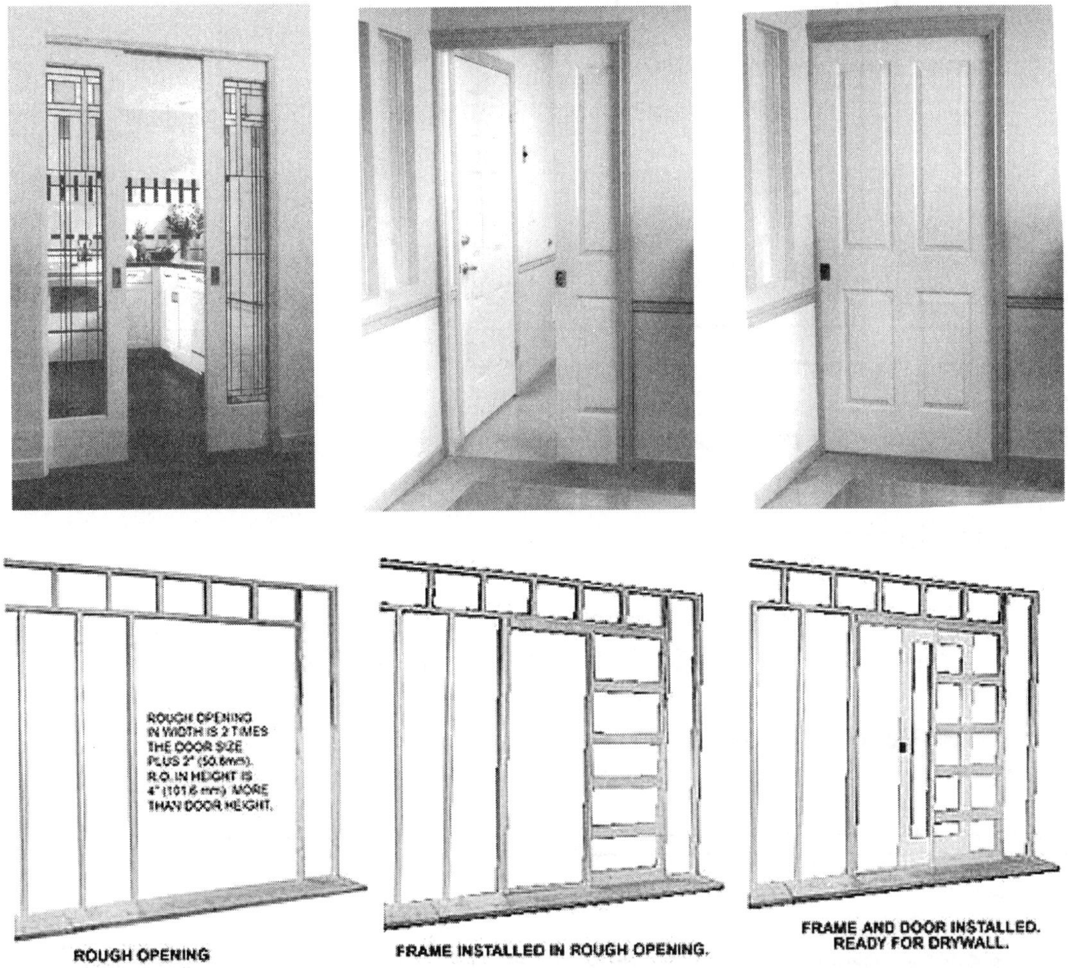

POCKET DOOR EXAMPLES – Double door and Single door photos (top); Installation illustration (bottom); *Images used by permission, KrisTrack www.kristrack.com*

Drawing closet doors:

These doors will be drawn right in the Flr-1 and Flr-2 drawings (on layer A-DOOR).

27. **Draw** two rectangles, each 1 ½" thick, per Figure 4-2.18.

28. Do the same on Second floor; 4 closet openings total.

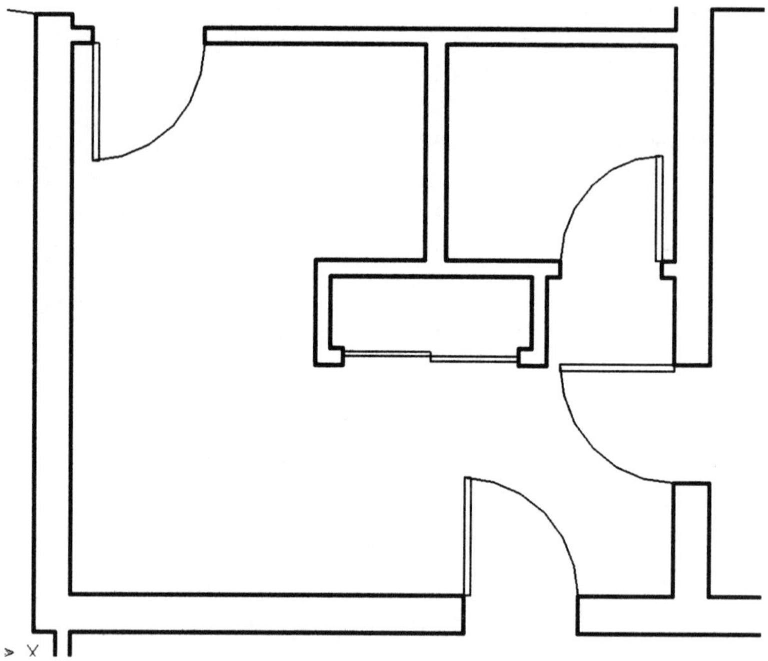

Figure 4-2.18 Closet door added; First floor

Garage doors:

29. Similar to the closet doors, you will simply draw a rectangle (place on layer A-DOOR), see Figure 4-2.19.

30. **Save** your drawings.

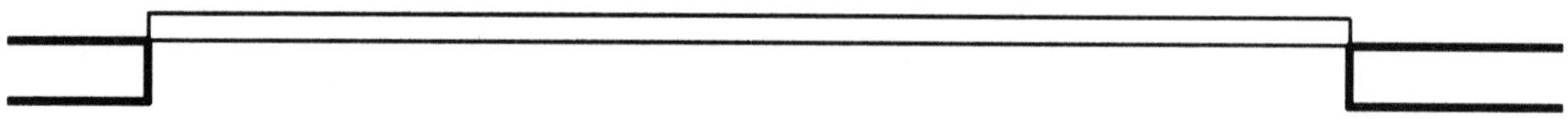

Figure 4-2.19 Garage door added; 2" thick door shown

Exercise 4-3:
Windows

In this exercise you will add exterior windows to your plans. This is similar to placing doors, discussed in the previous exercise.

One difference between drawing doors and windows is that windows are drawn on two separate layers:

A-GLAZ	The window frame and glass (aka glazing) are drawn on this layer.
A-GLAZ-SILL	The sill lines are drawn on this layer (This represents the portion of wall that continues below the window).

Lineweights:

The primary reason that two *Layers* are use is to control lineweights. The thickness of a line (i.e., lineweight) is commonly controlled by which *Layer* it is on. One benefit to this is that you can adjust the lineweight setting in one location and all the lines on that *Layer* are updated.

When thinking about how lineweights relate to a window in plan, you need to consider whether the line is in section or elevation.

The diagrams below show the different components that make up a window in plan view.

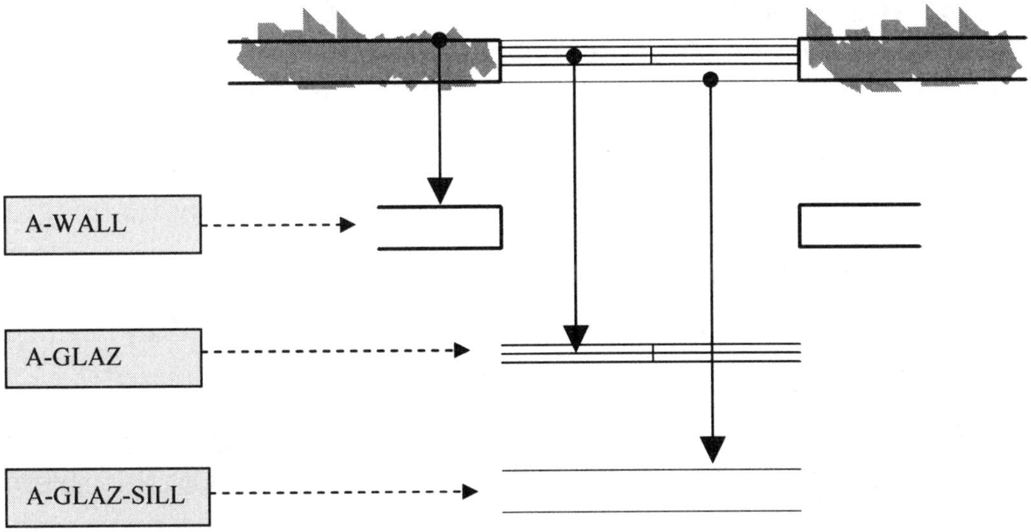

Window Opening Example Components / Layers for a window

You can think of floor plans as cutaways of the 3D building. The cutting plane is usually about 4' – 5' above the floor level. Notice in the following illustration that the wall is in section but the window sill is not. The sill is technically in elevation – while looking down.

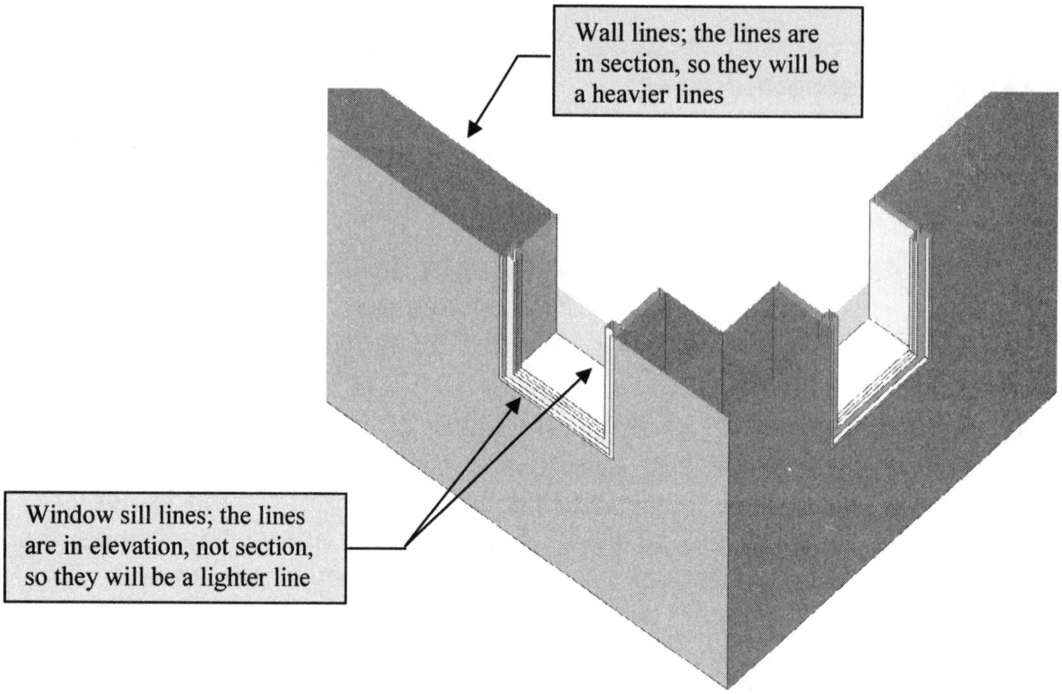

Figure 4-3.1 Window Isometric; floor plan cutting plane

Drawing the windows:

The windows could be blocks, similar to the doors, but you will simply draw lines to create the windows in this exercise. Again, the advantages of blocks are that you can pick any part of a block and the entire thing will highlight; you can also redefine a block and all occurrences of it in the current drawing will automatically be updated.

1. Create the openings in your exterior walls the same way you created the door openings (Figure 4-3.3, 4-3.4, 4-3.5):
   a. the [wider] double windows are **6'-8"**
   b. the single windows are **3'-2"**
   c. the basement windows are as dimensioned in plan
   d. see the *extra credit* option towards the end of this exercise

2. Create the following *Layers*:
   A-GLAZ (color Yellow); **A-GLAZ-SILL** (color Red)

3. Draw the "window lines" per the example shown in Figure 4-3.2; draw a line in the center of the window for the double wide windows. *(This indicates two window frames mulled together.)*

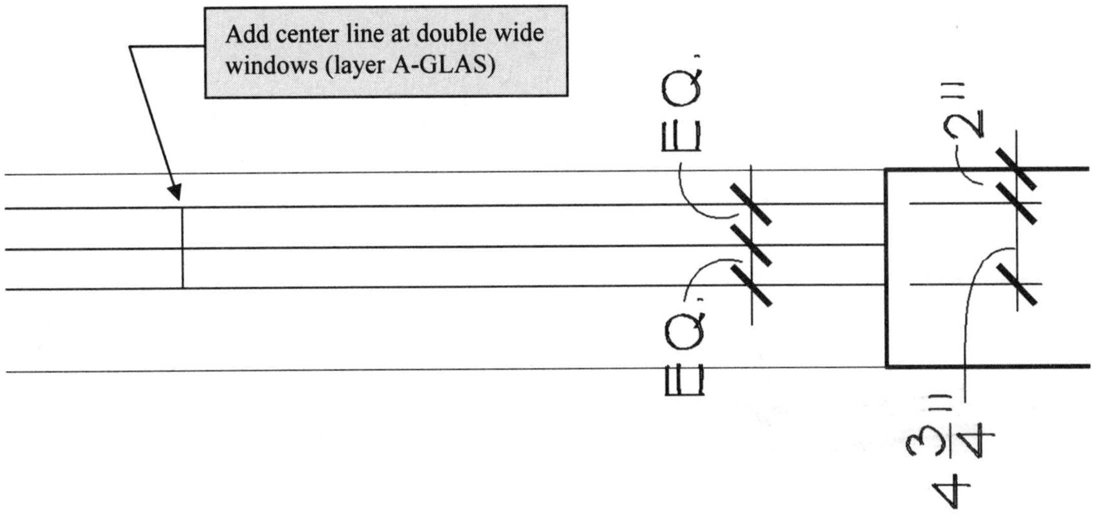

Figure 4-3.2 Window Lines; note that EQ. is an abbreviation Equal

4. **Save** your drawings.

> **Note:**
> When the walls are not as thick as our super-insulated walls, you simply draw two sill lines (like normal) and one line centered on the wall for the glass. So you would have three lines total (rather than the five lines shown above.
>
> **This is how you should draw the windows in the garage walls.**

Window Example; Exterior sheathing still needs to be cut out

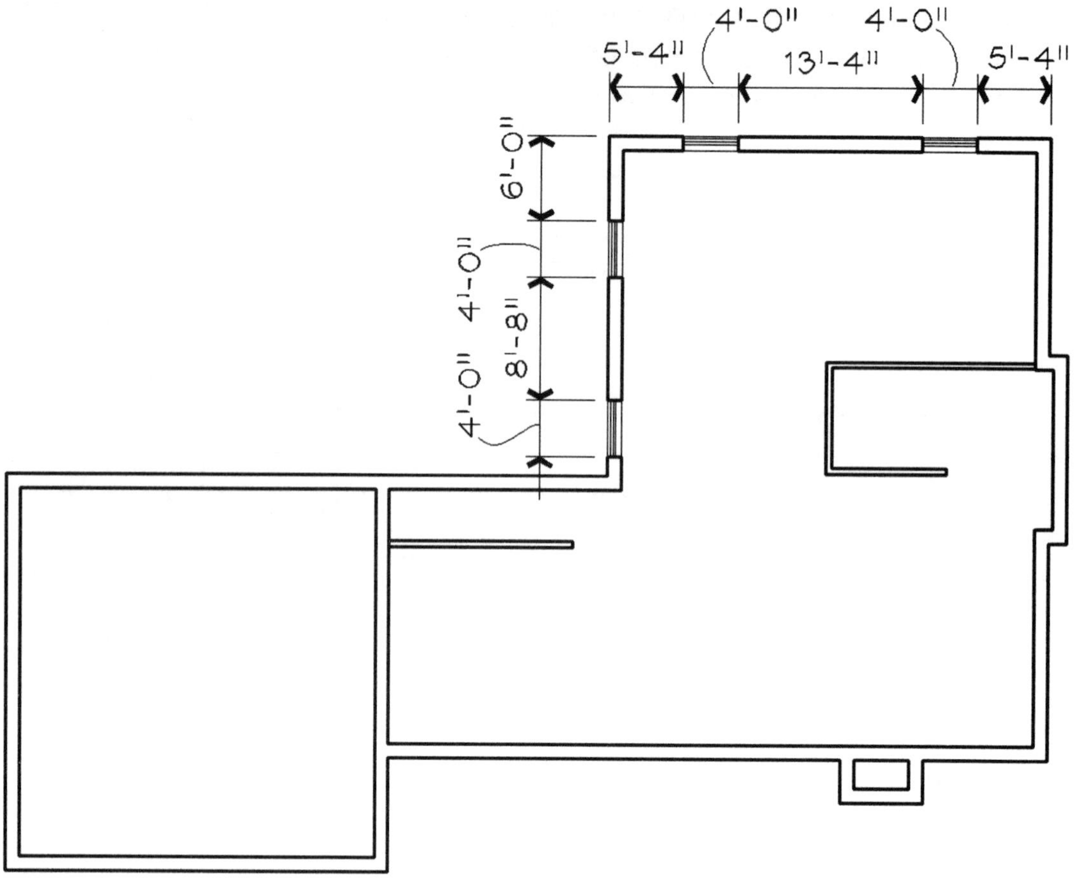

Figure 4-3.3 Window Locations; Basement floor

Window dimensions in masonry walls?

Dimensioning windows in masonry openings is similar to dimensioning doors (discussed in the previous exercise).

The mason laying the block typically has nothing to do with the windows; they just want to know how big to make the opening and how far it is from the previous opening.

On the other hand, the carpenter typically builds the walls and installs the windows. Additionally, dimensioning windows to the center is beneficial because the window manufacturer used to draw the details may not be the one used in the project. Window sizes can vary from manufacturer to manufacturer.

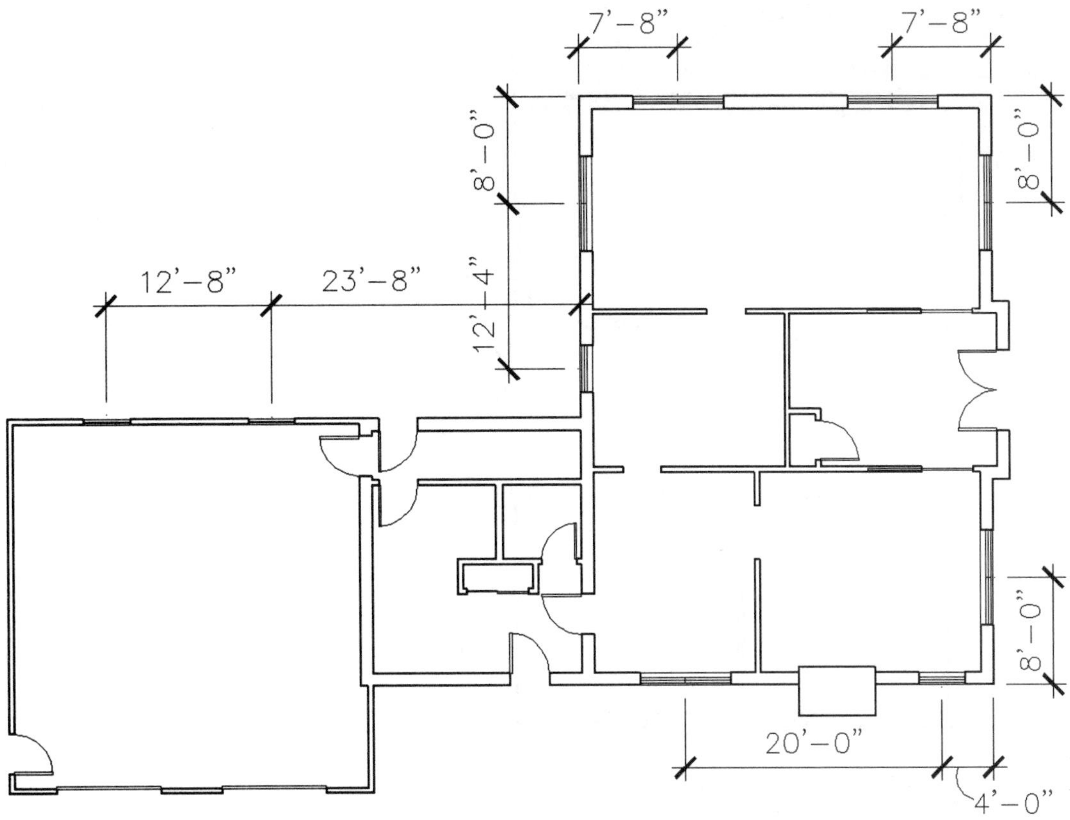

Figure 4-3.4 Window Locations; First floor

Double Window Example
Two Double-Hung windows

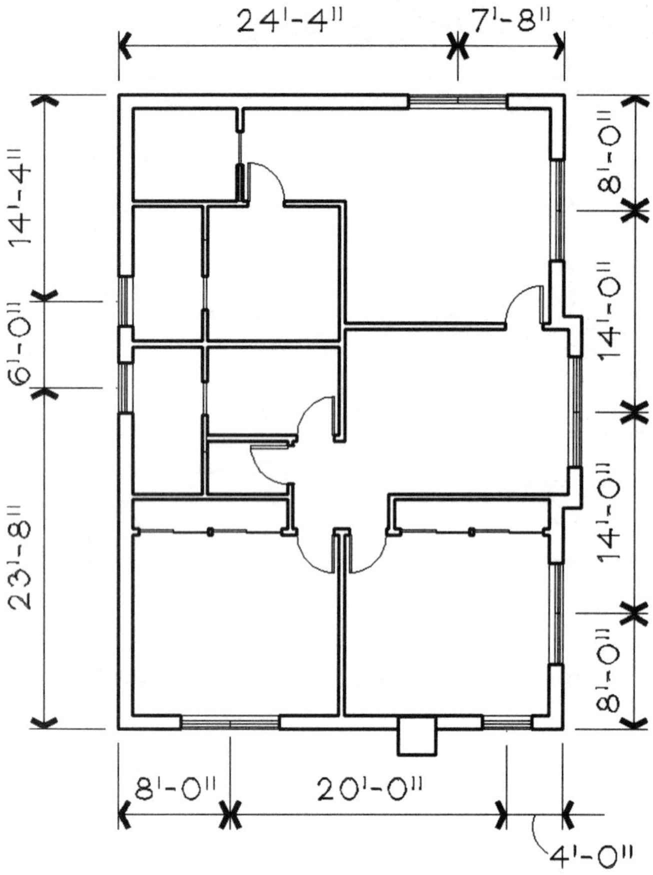

Figure 4-3.5 Window Locations; Second floor

Software offered by window manufacturers?

Some window manufacturers offer software to insert their windows into your AutoCAD floor plans. One such manufacturer's program, offered free via the internet, is Marvin Windows and Doors.

The program is called **Marvin Design System** (MDS) and can be downloaded via the following URL: **http://architect.marvin.com**

If you are taking this course for credit, your instructor may offer extra credit if you use this program to insert your windows into the floor plans.

NOTE: *In a classroom lab setting you need to make sure you have permission to install software!*

Exercise 4-4:
Annotation and Dimensions

As previously mentioned in Lesson 2, annotations (text; notes) and Dimensions allow the designer / drafter to accurately describe the drawing.

To complete this lesson you will add room names and dimensions to your floor plans.

Room Names:

Now you will add the room names to the floor plans.

1. **Open** your floor plan drawings.

2. Create the *Layer* **A-ANNO-TEXT** (color 4) and set it *Current.*

3. Using the **Multiline Text** command, create **9" Arial** type text in the center of the floor plan that reads: "UNFINISHED BASEMENT". See Figures 4-4.1 and 4-4.2.
   __Tip__: Refer back to exercise 2-4 for more on MText.

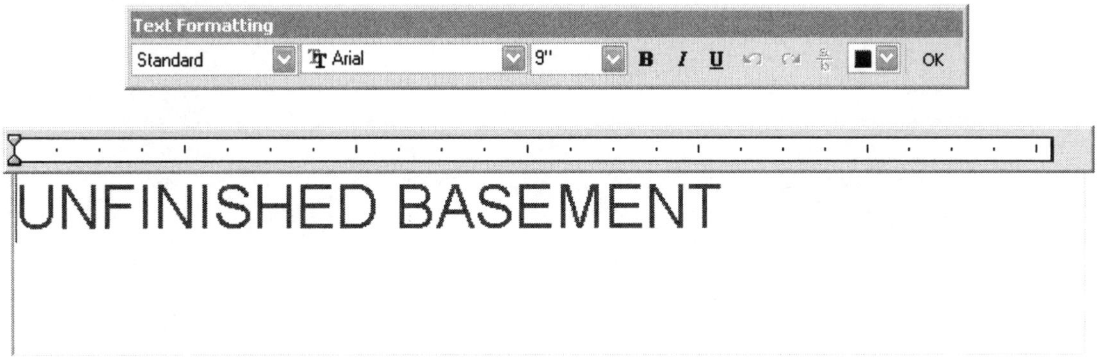

Figure 4-4.1 Mtext command; 9" high Arial text

4. Looking at **Figures 4-4.3** and **4-4.4**, add the room names to the first and Second floors; remember to create the appropriate text layer.

> **Tip:**
> Double click on MText to edit it in the MText editor.

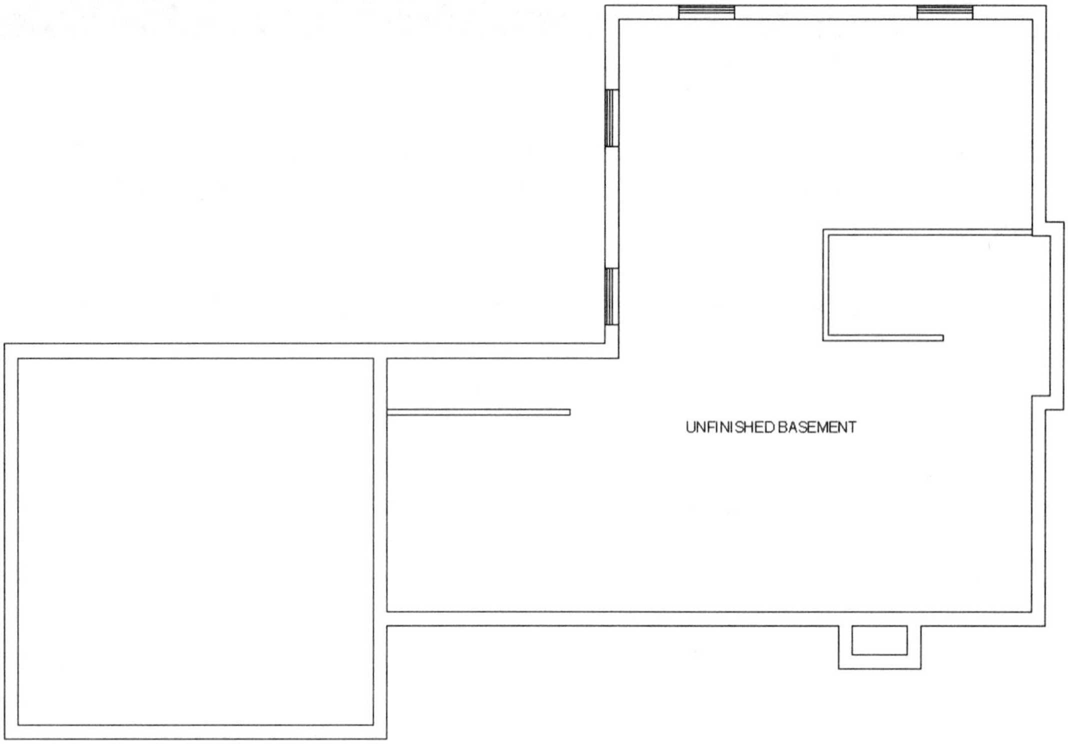

Figure 4-4.2 Text added; Basement floor plan

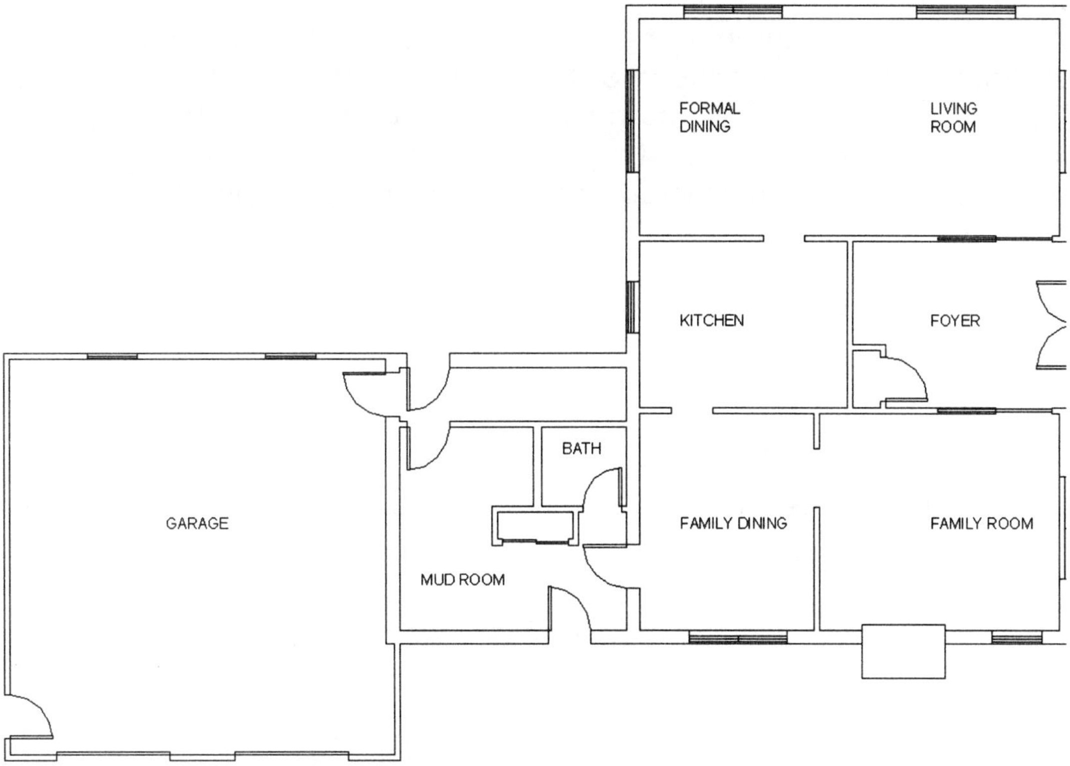

Figure 4-4.3 Text added; First floor plan

> **UPPERCASE vs. Lowercase text:**
>
> Text, on architectural drawings, is typically all uppercase. The lowercase letters can be hard to read, especially when they overlap lines or the printer made the strokes of the letters to thick.
>
> One exception might be a large body of general notes that are off to the side of the plans.

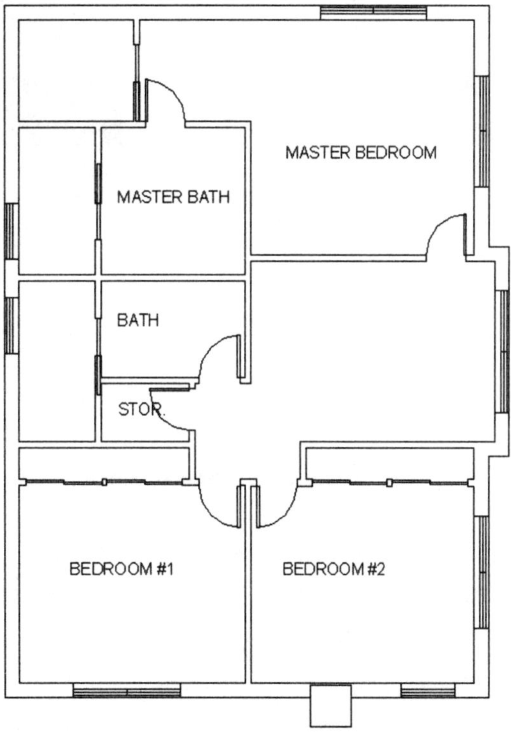

Figure 4-4.4 Text added; Second floor plan

Dimensions:

A floor plan has all the major elements dimensioned on them. It is not desirable to leave the location of these major components to be scaled off the blue prints; in fact, many larger residential projects and most commercial projects, the contract prohibits the contractor to scale the drawings. (They are instructed to request the information from the Architect.)

Next you will dimension all the Walls, Doors and Windows on the exterior walls.

5. Create the Layer **A-ANNO-DIMS** (color 30) and set it *Current*

6. In the **Flr-B** drawing, click **Dimensions → Style...** (Figure 4-4.5)

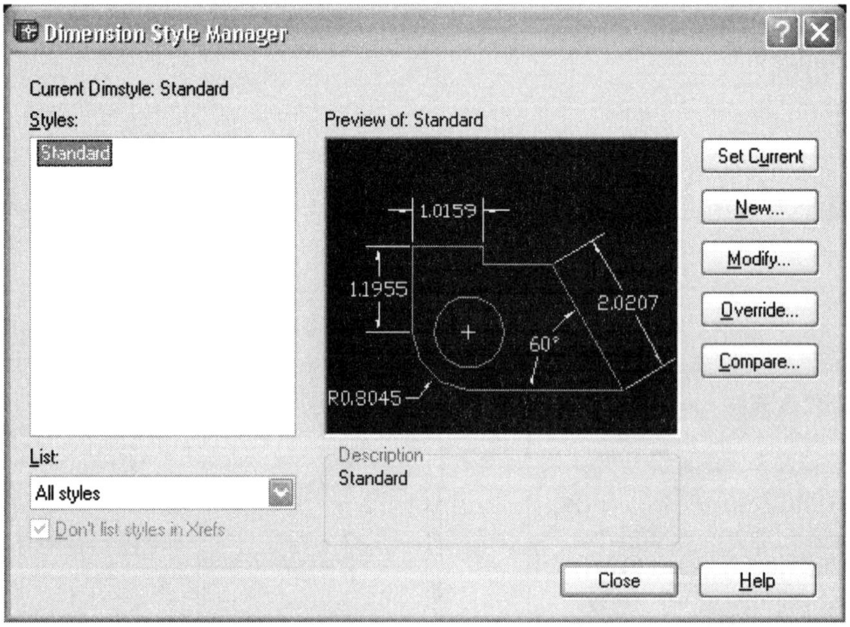

Figure 4-4.5 Dimension Style Manager; Standard style selected

7. Click the style **Standard** (on left), and then click **Modify...**

You are now in the dialog box that allows you to control how the dimensions look when you draw them. You will adjust a few of these settings (Figure 4-4.6).

8. Make the changes identified with a star (★) in Figures 4-4.6, 4-4.7, 4-4.8, 4-4.9

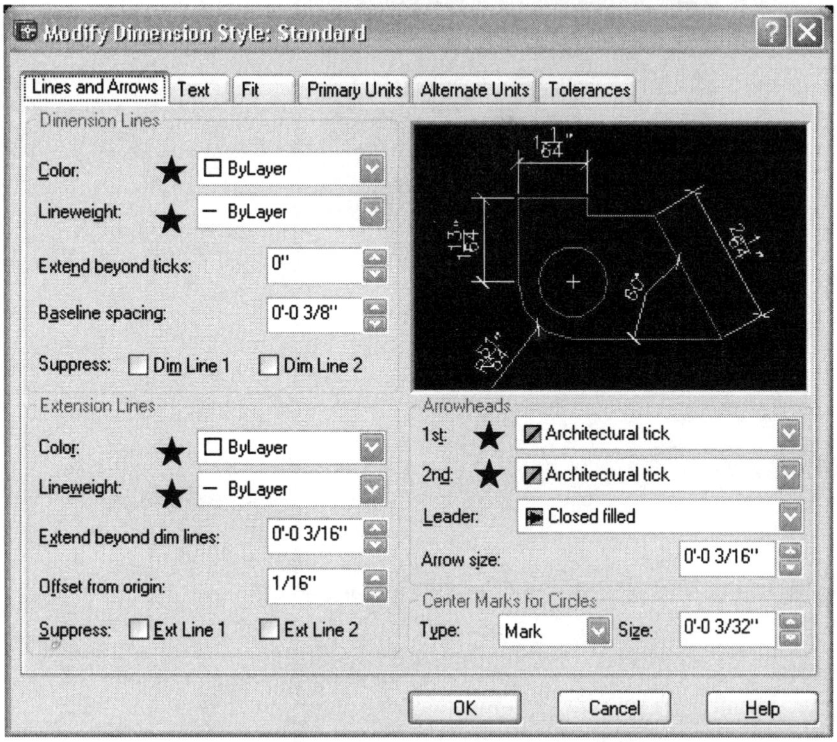

Figure 4-4.6
Modify Dimension Style;
Lines and Arrows tab

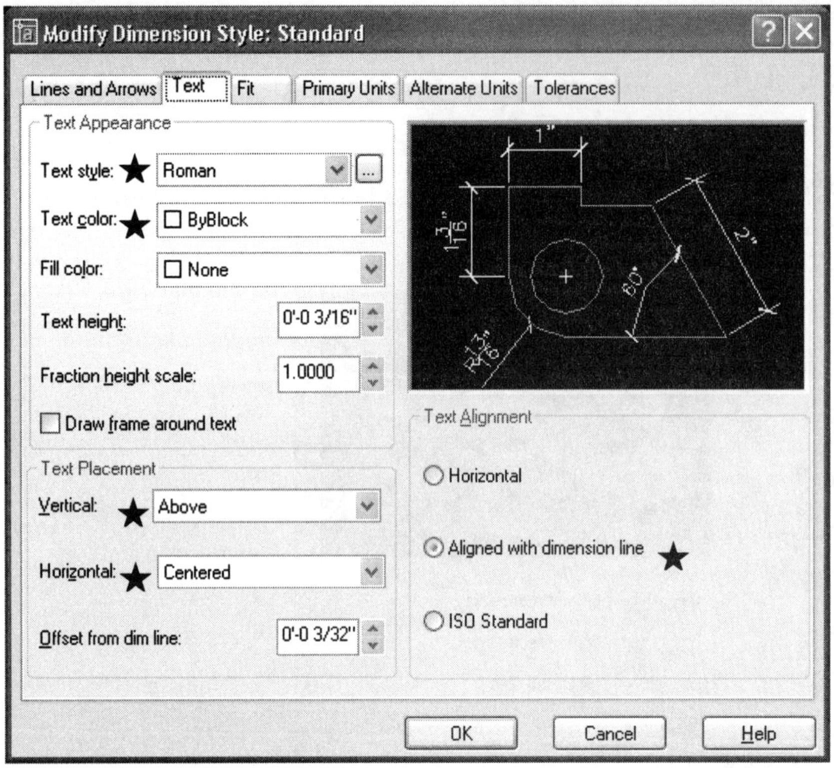

Figure 4-4.7
Modify Dimension Style;
Text tab

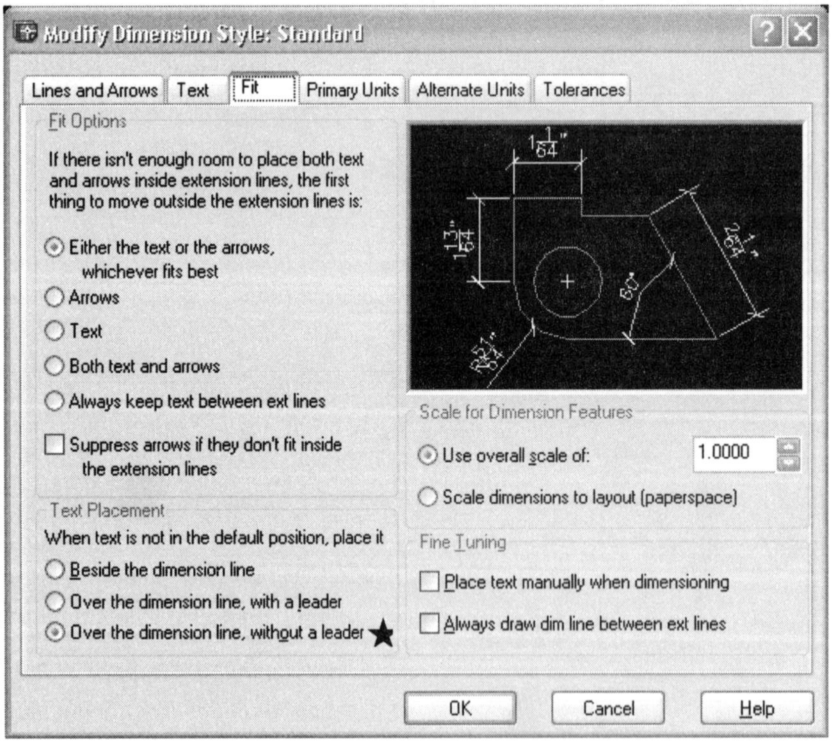

Figure 4-4.8
Modify Dimension Style;
Fit tab

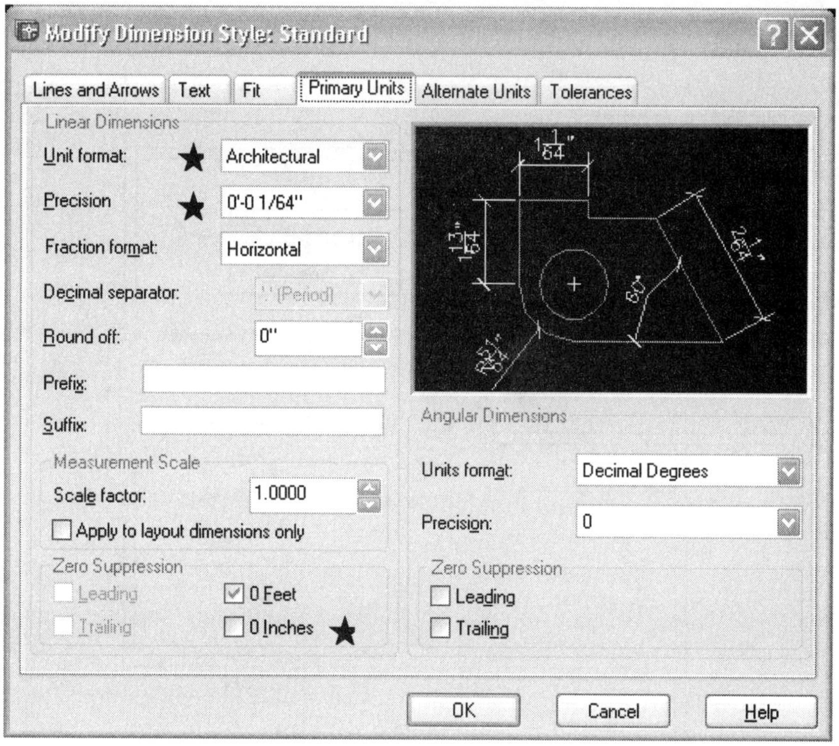

Figure 4-4.9
Modify Dimension Style;
Primary Units tab

9. Click the **OK** button.

10. Click **Close** to exit the *Dimension Style Manager.*

Many of the changes you just made are self-explanatory by the description and the preview images which changes as you adjust the settings.

11. From the **Dimension** menu select **Linear.**

12. Draw the dimension shown in **Figure 4-4.10**.
(Your dimension will not look like the one in Figure 4-4.10 yet.)

Notice your text and ticks do not show up. Looking back at the "Modify Dimension Style" images, you will see the text and arrow sizes are each set to 3/16". This is the size you want the text to be on the plotted sheet, but you are drawing in Model Space where everything is drawn full scale, so your 3/16" text is much smaller than your 12" foundation walls. If you zoom way in on your dimension line you will see the text and ticks; give it a try. You do not change the height in the previous dialog boxes, rather, you adjust an AutoCAD variable (which is a multiplier for all the sizes in the dimension style).

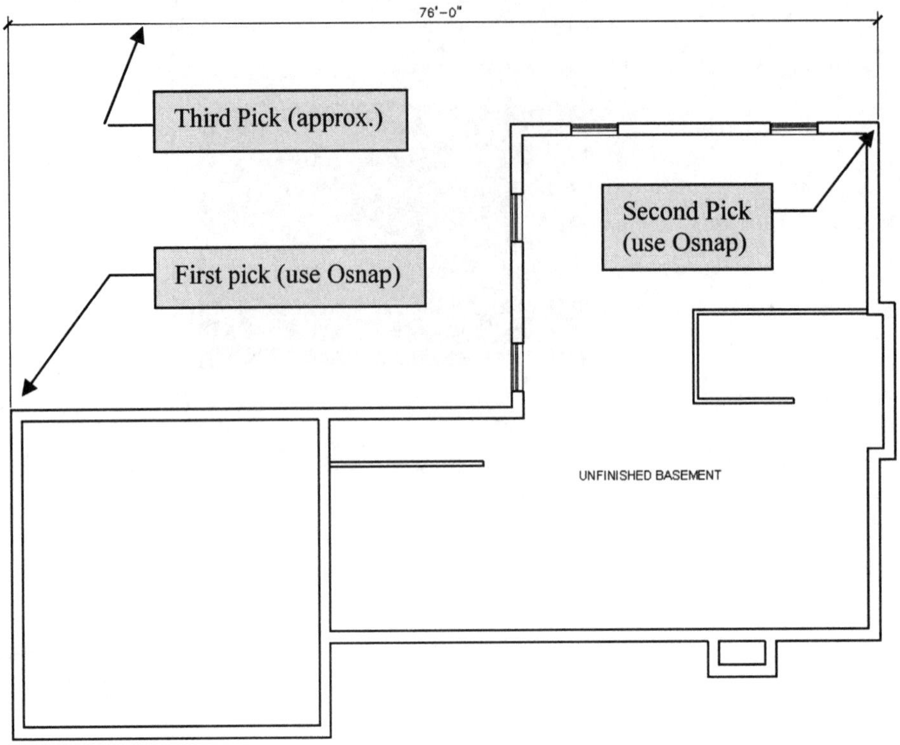

Figure 4-4.10 Dimension Added; Basement floor plan

13. At the *Command Prompt* type **DIMSCALE** and press **Enter.**

You are now shown the current *DIMSCALE* setting and prompted to enter a new value. The value you enter here depends on what scale you plan on printing your floor plan at. We plan on printing ours at 1/4″ = 1′-0″ so you will enter 48. The following chart shows you the value for other scales:

Full	1		1″ = 10′-0″	120
1/16″ = 1′-0″	192		1″ = 20′-0″	240
3/32″ = 1′-0″	128		1″ = 30′-0″	360
1/8″ = 1′-0″	96		1″ = 40′-0″	480
3/16″ = 1′-0″	64		1″ = 50′-0″	600
1/4″ = 1′-0″	48		1″ = 60′-0″	720
3/8″ = 1′-0″	32		1″ = 100′-0″	1200
1/2″ = 1′-0″	24			
3/4″ = 1′-0″	16			
1″ = 1′-0″	12			
1 ½″ = 1′-0″	8			
3″ = 1′-0″	4			

Figure 4-4.11 Various settings for AutoCAD variable DIMSCALE

14. Type **48** and press **Enter.**

15. Now erase the dimension you just drew and draw it again.

Your dimension should look like the one in Figure 4-4.10 now. The *DIMSCALE* variable multiplied many of the settings in your dimension style by 48. Thus, for the text and arrows, 48 x 3/16" = 4.5".

This applies to annotation as well. All your notes typed with Mtext should be 4.5" high (for a ¼" print out). FYI, the room names are larger so they stand out more.

16. Complete the dimensioning of the exterior (for each floor plan) per the following figures. (Figures 4-4.12, 4-4.13, 4-4.14)
    TIP: *#1 Make sure you draw on the correct layer.*
    #2 Use Osnap to accurately pick points to dimension too.
    #3 When creating a string of dimensions, use Osnap for the third pick to make sure the dimensions line up perfectly.

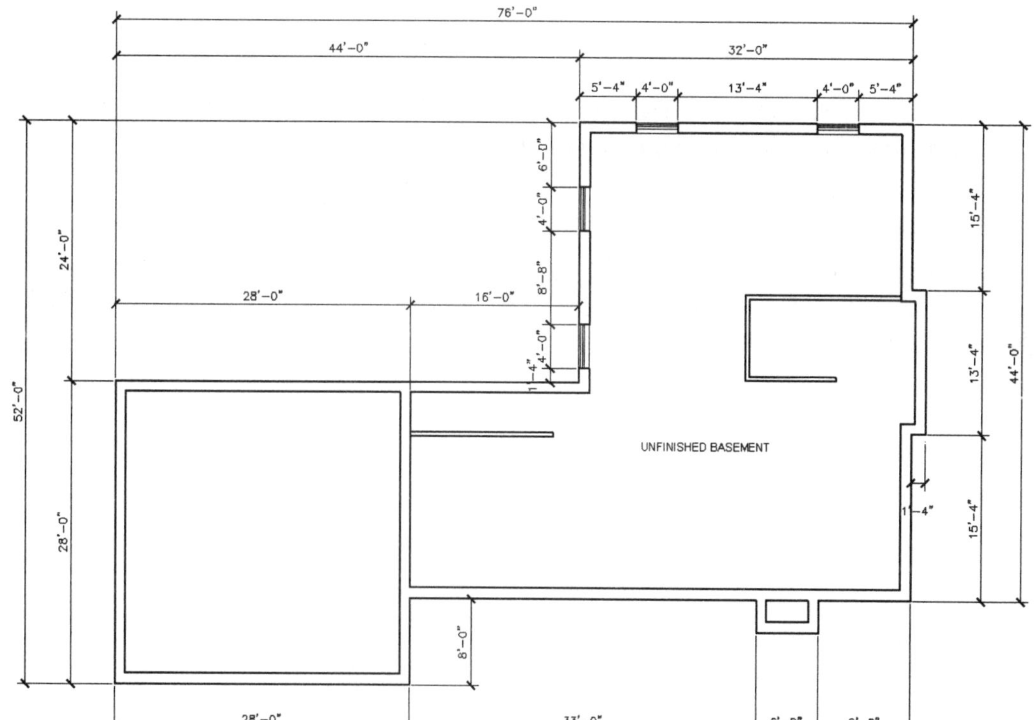

Figure 4-4.12 Dimensions added; Basement floor plan

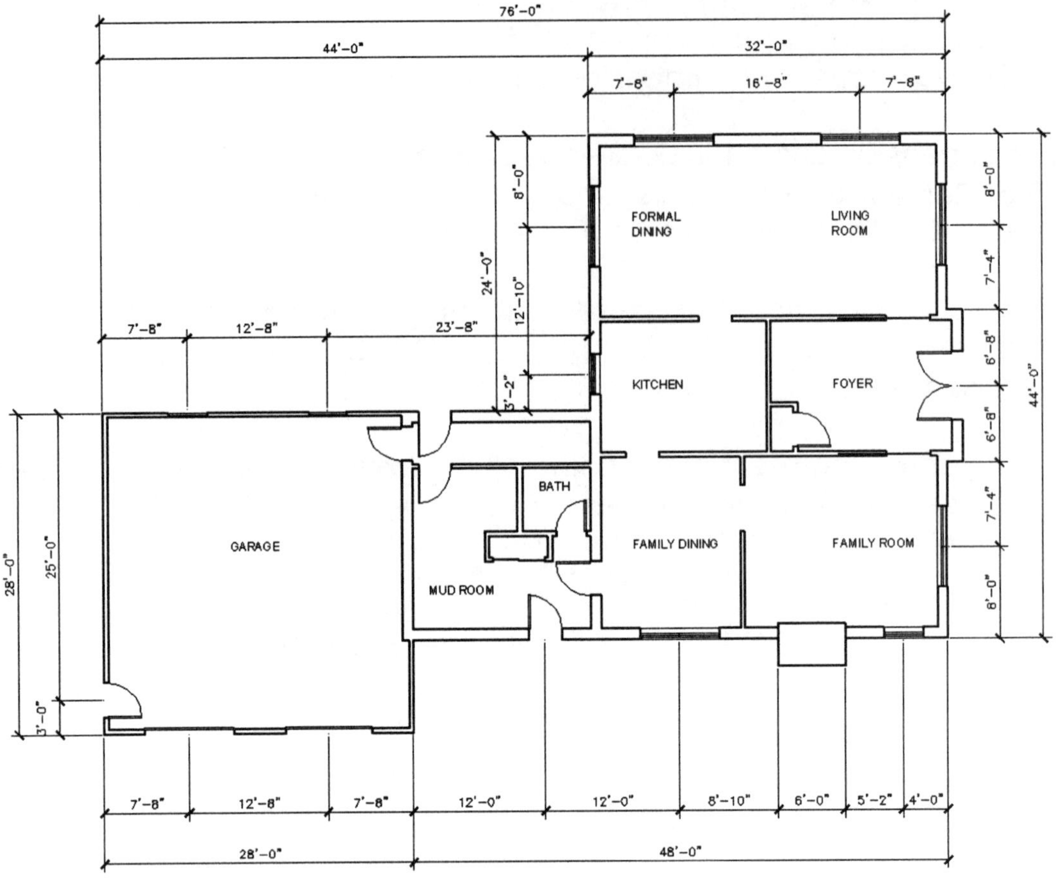

Figure 4-4.13 Dimensions added; First floor plan

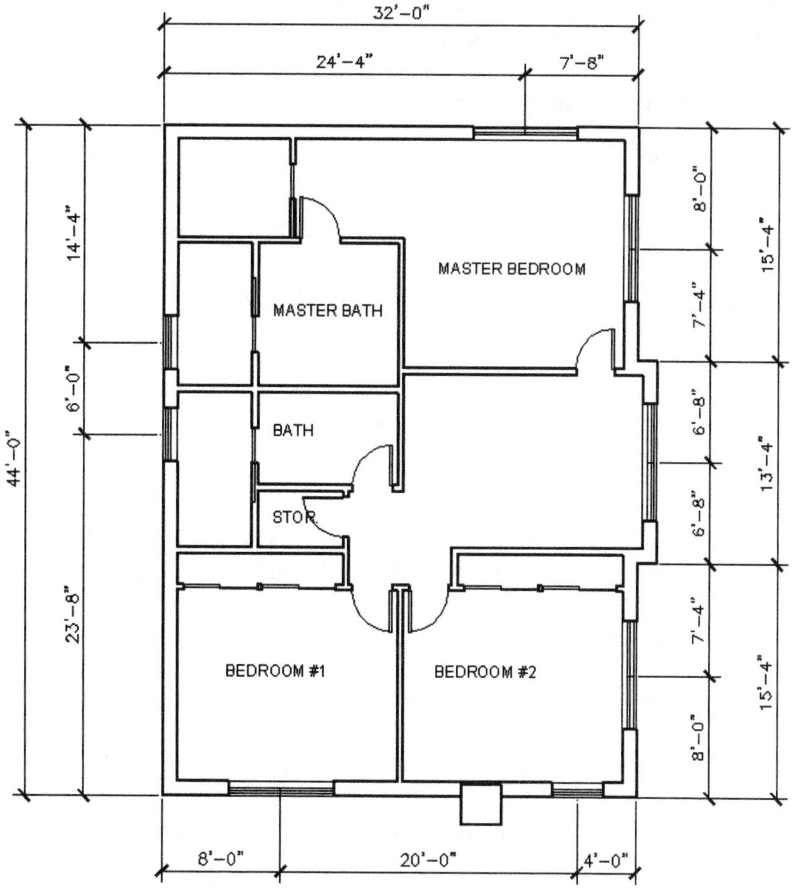

Figure 4-4.14 Dimensions added; second floor plan

17. **Save** your drawings.

18. **Print** each floor plan "**scaled to fit**" on **8 ½ x 11** paper; refer back to exercise 2-5 for an overview on printing.
__TIP__: If you use the Print Display option, per ex2-5, you will need to position the floor plan as large as possible on in the Drawing Window. You may want to try using the Plot Window option at this point, so you can tell AutoCAD exactly what you want to print.

This concludes the "Floor Plans" exercise. Next you will develop the exterior elevations while taking a look at additional AutoCAD features like *Bhatch* (which fills an area with a pattern) and *Grip Editing* (which allows you to manipulate lines without using AutoCAD commands).

Self-Exam:

The following questions can be used as a way to check your knowledge of this lesson. The answers can be found at the bottom of this page.

1. Offset is very useful for drawing floor plans. (T/F)

2. You dimension to the center of masonry walls. (T/F)

3. It does not matter which half of the line you pick when using extend. (T/F)

4. Use the ______________ command remove a portion of line between two crossing lines.

5. All walls go on the ________________ layer.

Review Questions:

The following questions may be assigned by your instructor as a way to assess your knowledge of this section. Your instructor has the answers to the review questions.

1. Text on architectural drawings is typically uppercase. (T/F)

2. The A-GLAZ-SILL layer is meant to be a lighter line. (T/F)

3. It does not matter which layer dimensions are drawn on. (T/F)

4. Use the ________________ variable to control dimension text size.

5. You cannot Mirror a block; like your door blocks. (T/F)

6. These icons (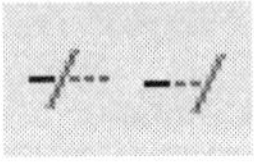) allow you to ________________ and to ________________ respectively.

7. For masonry coursing, what are the two options; 6'- ____" and 6'- _____"

8. In plan view, a door open 90 degrees is a ______________ door; and a door open 45 degrees is a ____________________________ door.

9. What *Layer* do jamb lines go on? ______________________________.

10. When Inserting a drawing as a block, the insertion point for the block is the same as the drawing origin (i.e., 0,0) it was created in. (T/F)

Self-Exam Answers:
1 - T, **2** - F, **3** - F, **4** - Trim, **5** – A-WALL

Additional Tasks:

Task 4-1 (Fireplace – north)

Draw all the lines shown on Layer A-WALL. Copy / Paste this line work from the Basement floor plan to the First floor plan.

Commands used: Offset, Trim, Extend, Fillet, Layer Manager, Circle

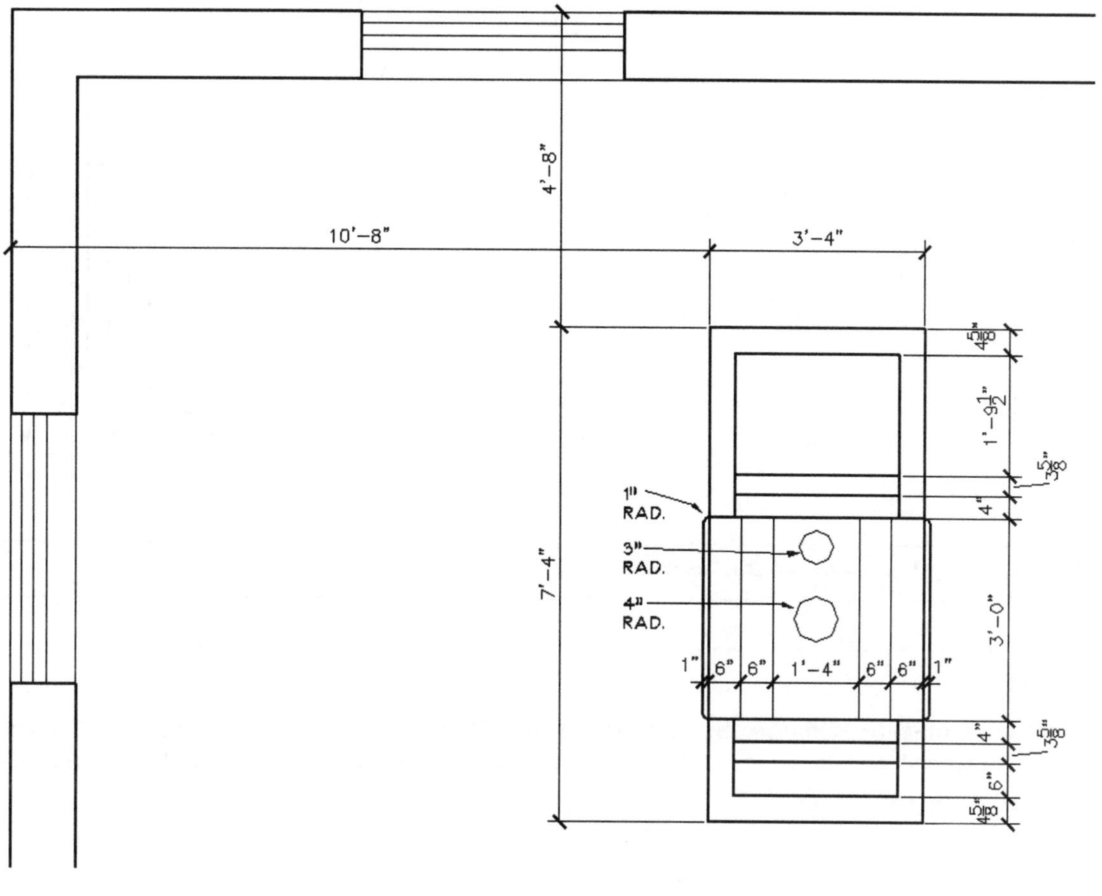

Task 4-1 (1) Fireplace (north); Basement floor plan view (First floor is similar).

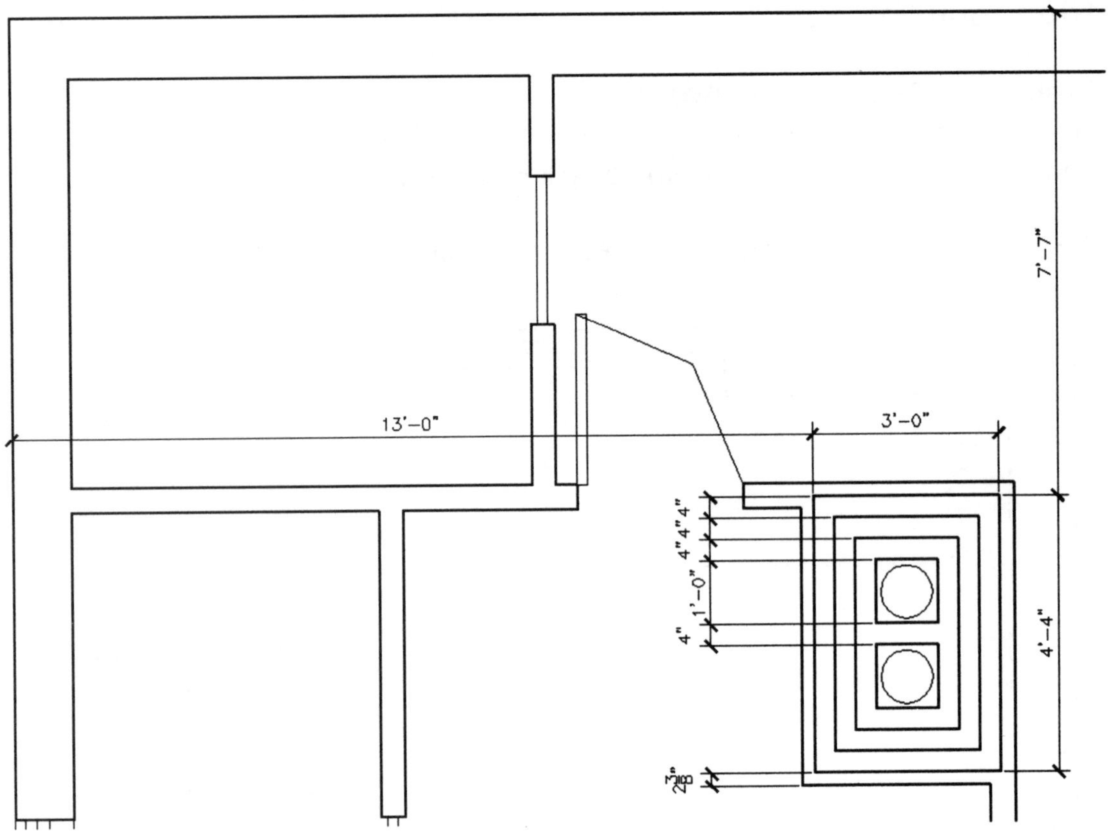

Task 4-1 (2) Fireplace (north); Second floor plan view.

TIP:

If you right-click while in the *Leader* command, you can select *Settings*. This gives control over various options; (see image below). This tip is meant to be helpful for completing Task 4-2.

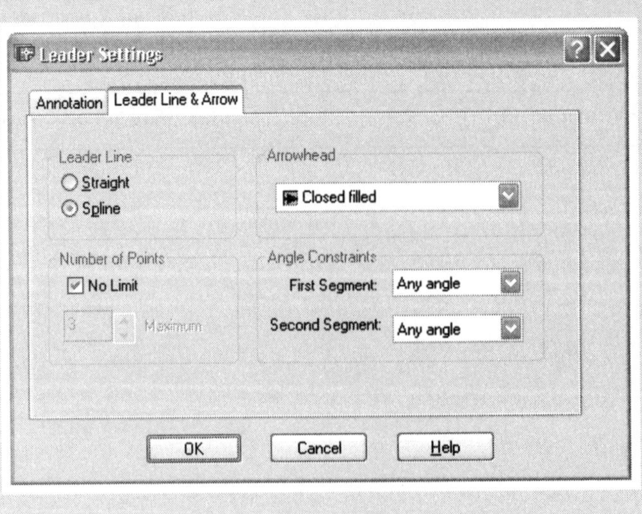

Task 4-2 (Main Stairway)
Draw all the lines shown on Layer A-FLOR-VERT (color Yellow). Copy / Paste this line work from the Basement floor plan to the First floor plan and then modify for that condition. Handrail lines are 1 ½" apart. You can use the Array (polar) to create the angled lines (or rotate – 90 degrees divided by 3). The line with the arrow has not been covered yet but is very simple: pick Leader from the Dimension menu and draw the lines, starting at the arrow end.

Draw the text on layer A-ANNO-TEXT (color 4).

The angled line that trims off part of the stair indicates where the stairs pass through the imaginary cutting plane for the floor plan; draw these lines on the A-FLOR-VERT layer (color 2).

Approximate the line work not dimensioned; TYP. Means typical (i.e., they are all the same dimension).

Commands used: Line, Offset, Trim, Extend, Fillet, Layer Manager, Array, Leader, Mtext

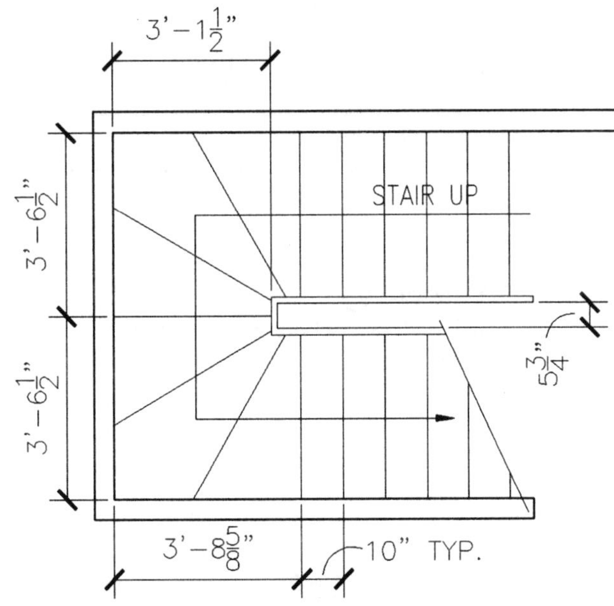

Task 4-2 (1) Main Stair; Basement floor plan view.

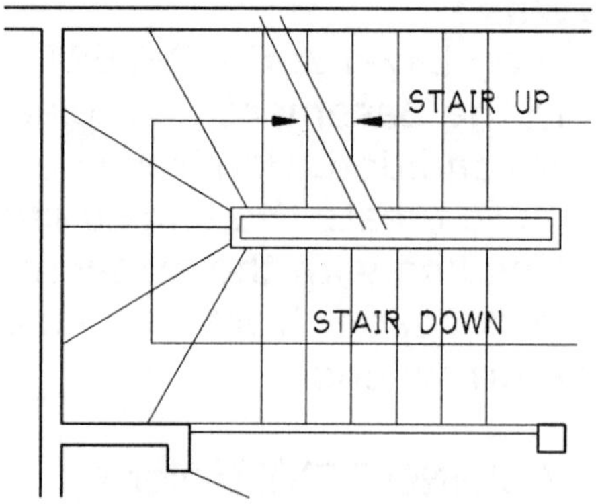

Task 4-2 (2) Main Stair; First floor plan view.

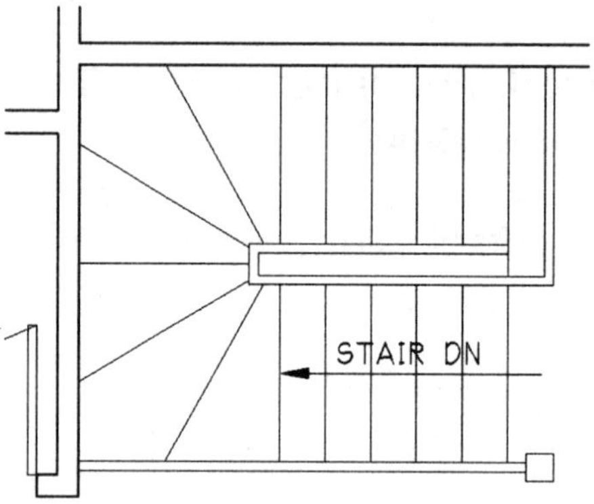

Task 4-2 (3) Main Stair; Second floor plan view.

Task 4-3 (Secondary Stairway)

Similar to the previous Task, draw this stairway.

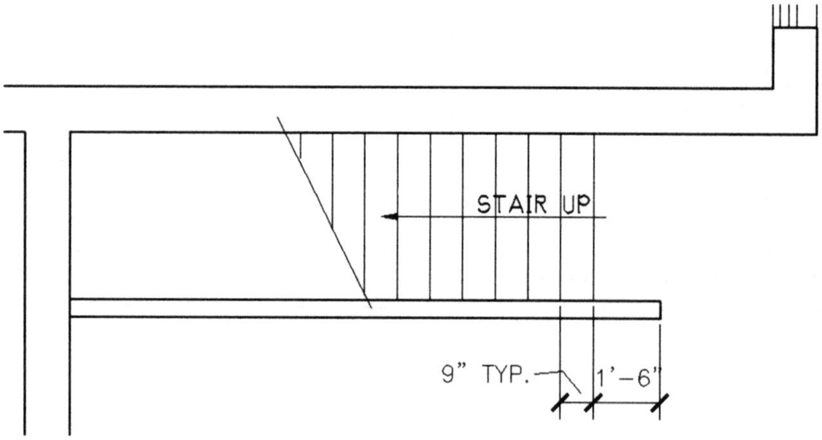

Task 4-3 (1) Secondary Stair; Basement floor plan view.

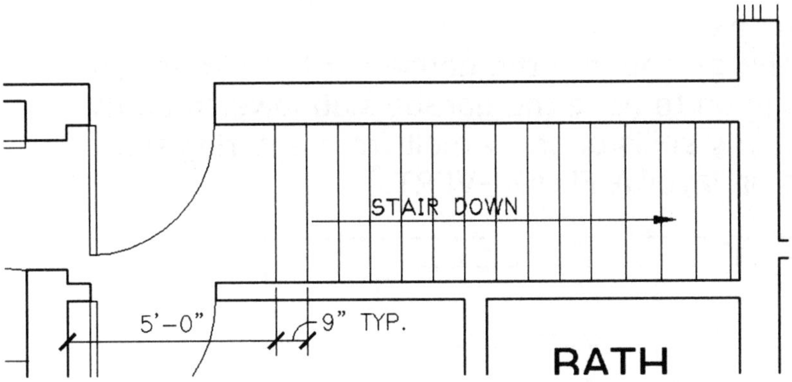

Task 4-3 (2) Secondary Stair; First floor plan view.

Task 4-4 (Porch)

Draw the porch per the dimensions shown.

Draw the large columns (12"x12") and outside lines on layer A-WALL and the railings and steps on layer A-FLOR-VERT.

You do not need to draw the dimensions (unless instructed otherwise).

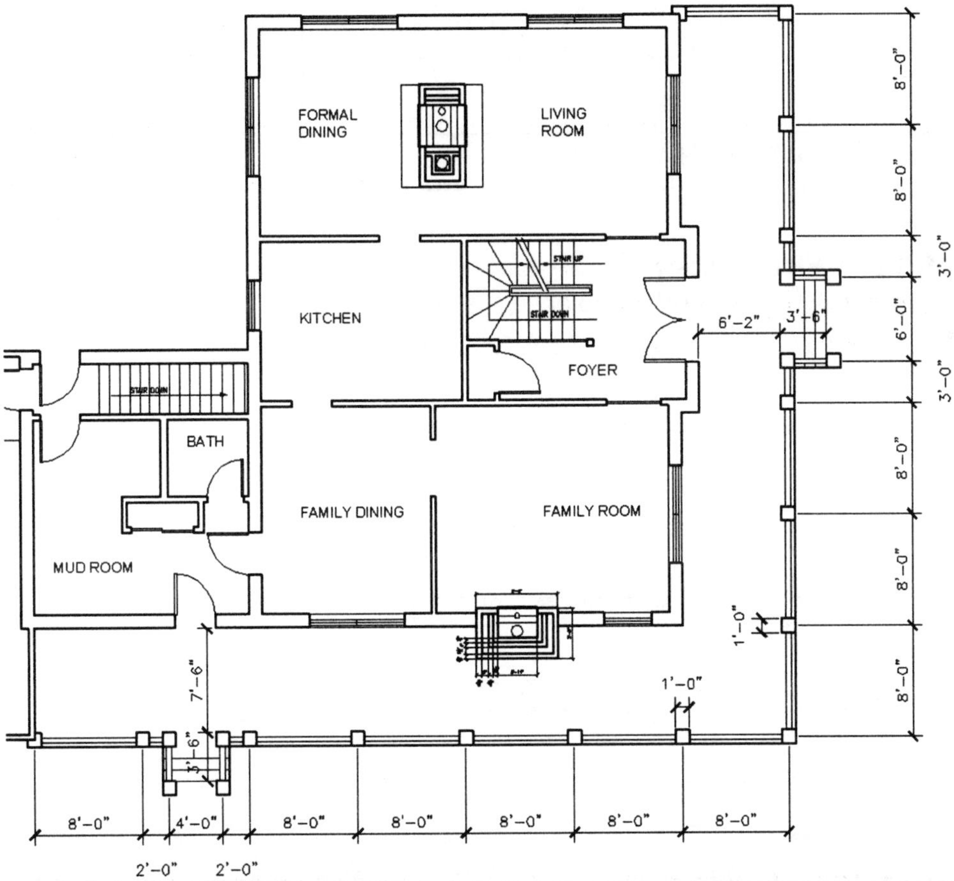

Task 4-4 Porch; First floor plan

Task 4-5 (Garage Steps)

Draw the steps from the garage into the house per the dimensions shown. Note: It is common to have the garage slab lower than the house floor to prevent any spills or snow melt from entering the house. Draw the lines on layer A-FLOOR-VERT.

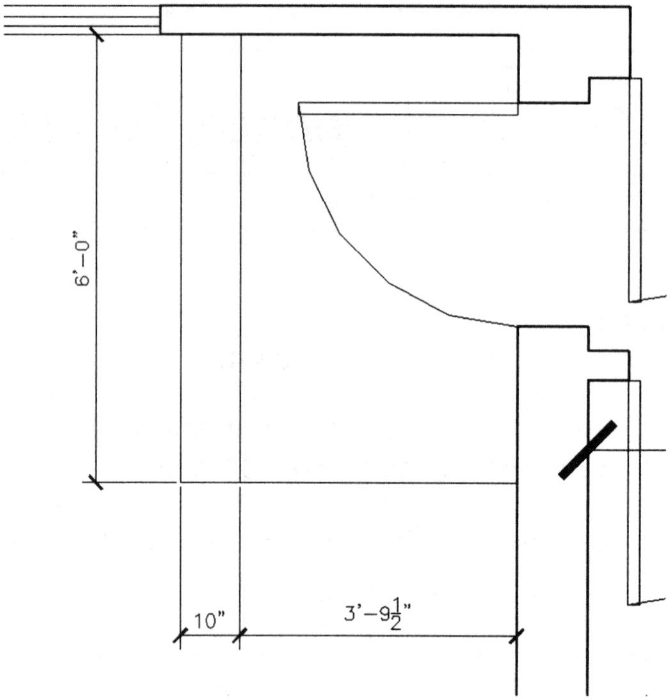

Task 4-5 Garage Steps; First floor plan

Task 4-6 (South Fireplace)

Add the following detail to the south fireplace (similar to Task 4-1).

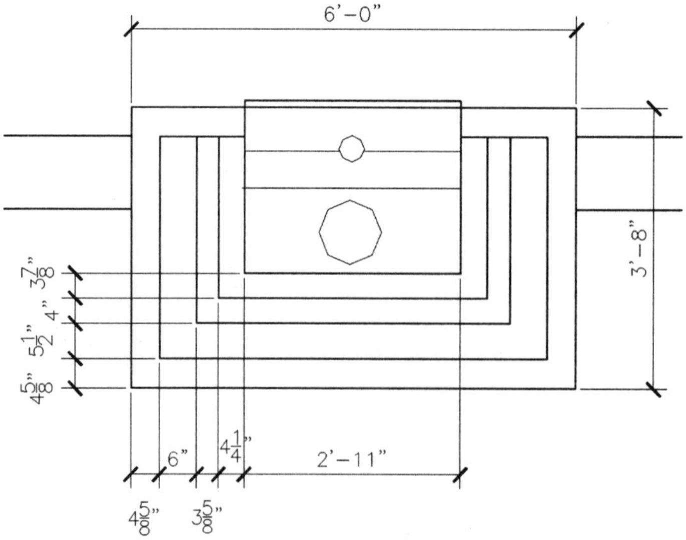

Task 4-6 Fireplace (south); First floor plan

Lesson 5
Residential Project: EXTERIOR ELEVATIONS::

In this lesson you will draw the exterior elevations based on the floor plans previously drawn. You will also take a look at a few new commands and tools like grip editing.

Exercise 5-1:
Elevation Outlines

Introduction

When designing a residence, one needs to be sensitive to the massing and proportions of each elevation and the various elements within. The exterior elevations are the drawings used to develop the outward aesthetic of the structure. Too often this is not given enough thought and time, thus resulting in harsh, unappealing homes with vast amounts of siding and awkward sized and positioned windows.

In this section you will look at blocking out the exterior elevations based on information previously drawn in the floor plans. The vertical dimensions will be given to you (which will also be used to draw your sections).

You will start a new drawing to draw all four elevations in. Each elevation will align horizontally; which aids in aligning windows, doors, roof edges, etc.

South Elevation (Figure 5-1.1)

1. Create a new drawing named **Exterior Elevations.dwg.**

First you will draw the outline for the garage.

2. Looking at your printed out, dimensioned, floor plans (on page 4-6), notice that the garage is 28'-0" wide.

3. Draw a horizontal line **28'-0"** long.

4. Draw a vertical line **9'-6 1/2"** tall at each end of the horizontal line previously drawn. (Figure 5-1.3)

Figure 5-1.1 Completed South Elevation to be drawn in this lesson

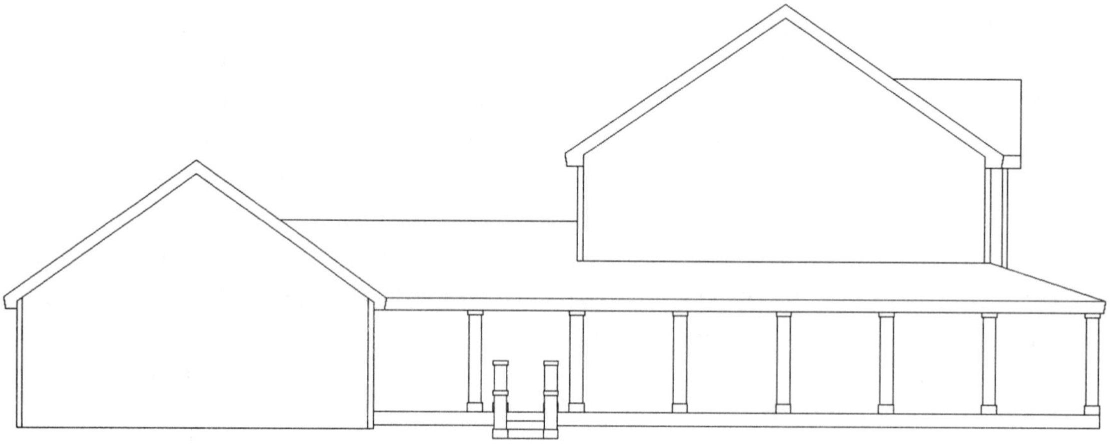

Figure 5-1.2 Outline of South Elevation to be drawn in this exercise

Figure 5-1.3 Garage elevation; first three lines

Next you will draw the angled line representing the sloped roof edge. This roof has an 8/12 pitch. That means that for every 12" horizontally, the roof drops (or rises) 8".

The easiest way to draw this line is to draw temporary lines per the description above and then draw an angled line that connects the dots; you will do this in the following steps:

5. At the top of the vertical line on the left, draw a horizontal line 12" long towards the right. (Figure 5-1.4)

6. Now draw a vertical line 8" long. (Figure 5-1.4)

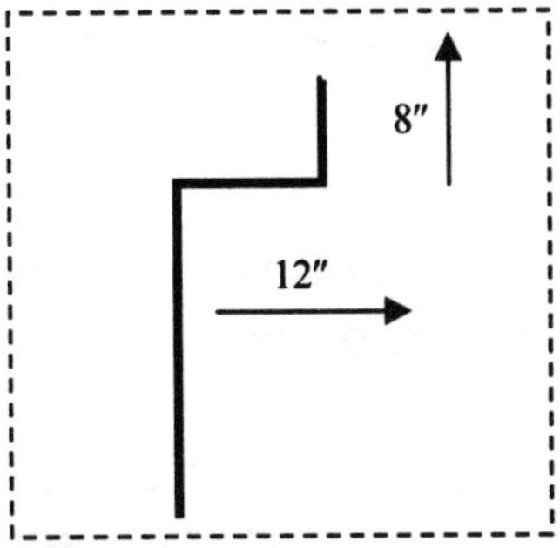

Figure 5-1.4
Temporary lines used to create roof edge (left side)

7. Draw the angled line using the endpoints of the temporary lines as snap points. (Figure 5-1.5)

Figure 5-1.5
Angled line drawn using Osnaps

8. **Erase** the temporary lines. (Figure 5-1.6)

9. **Mirror** the angled line, using the Midpoint of the 28'-0" horizontal line. (Figure 5-1.7)

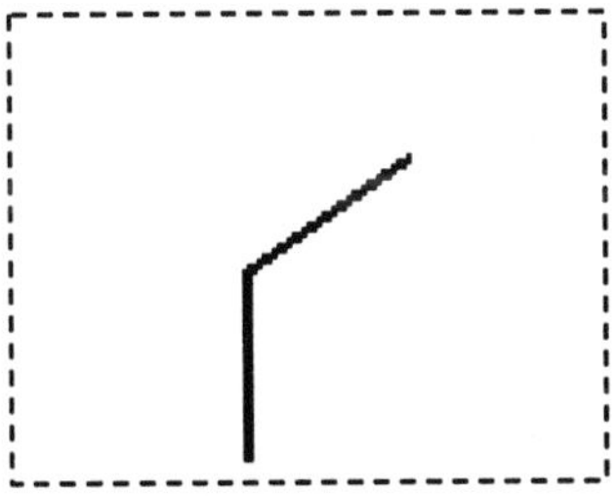

Figure 5-1.6
Temporary lines erased

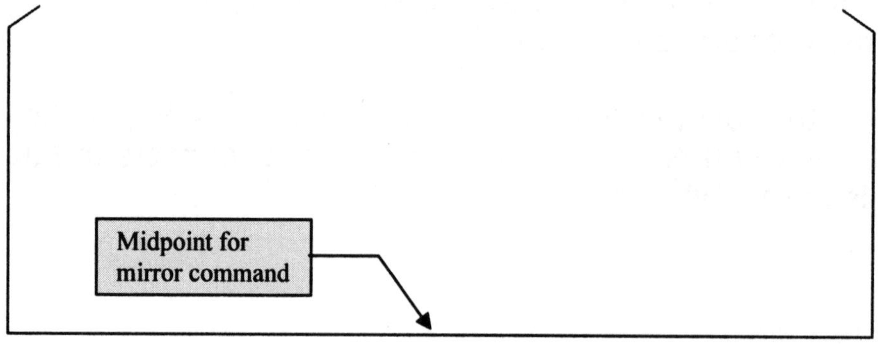

Figure 5-1.7 Garage elevation; angled line mirrored

You will now use the Fillet command to extend the two angled lines up to the peak.

10. Select the **Fillet** command. Make sure the Radius is set to **0"**, and then select the two angled lines. (Figure 5-1.8)

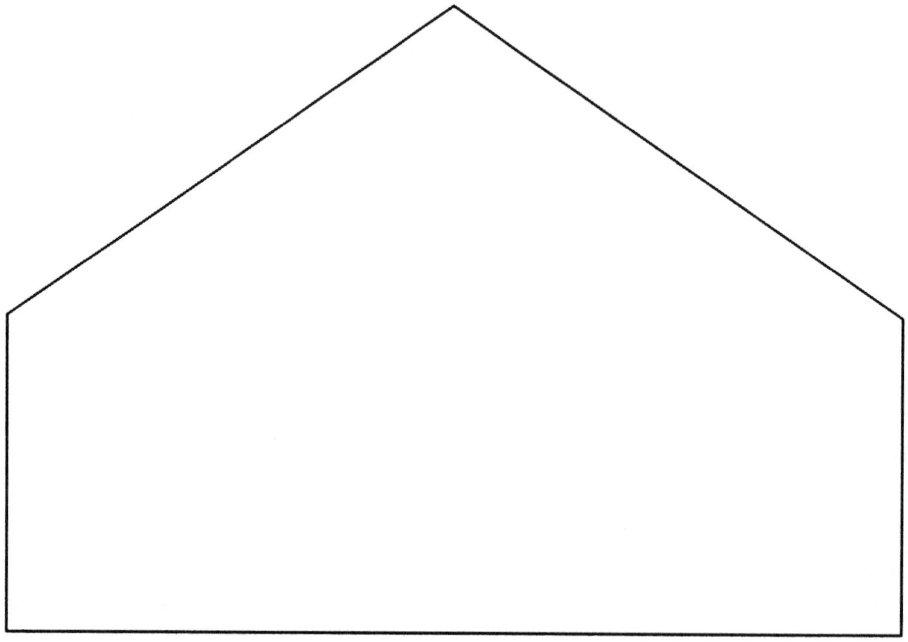

Figure 5-1.8 Garage elevation; roof line completed

Next you will Offset your two vertical lines inward. These lines will represent the vertical trim boards that the siding dies into.

11. **Offset** the two vertical lines **5 ½"** inward. (Figure 5-1.9)

12. Use the **Extend** command to extend the trim lines up to the angled lines.

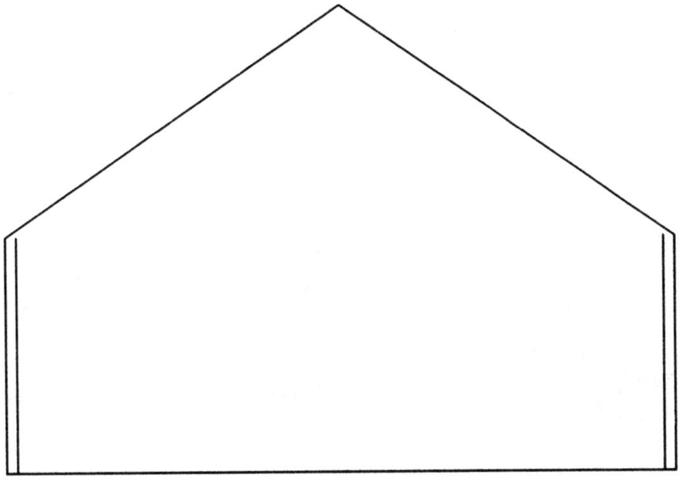

Figure 5-1.9 Garage elevation; corner trim

13. **Offset** the two roof lines outward **10 ½".** (Figure 5-1.10)

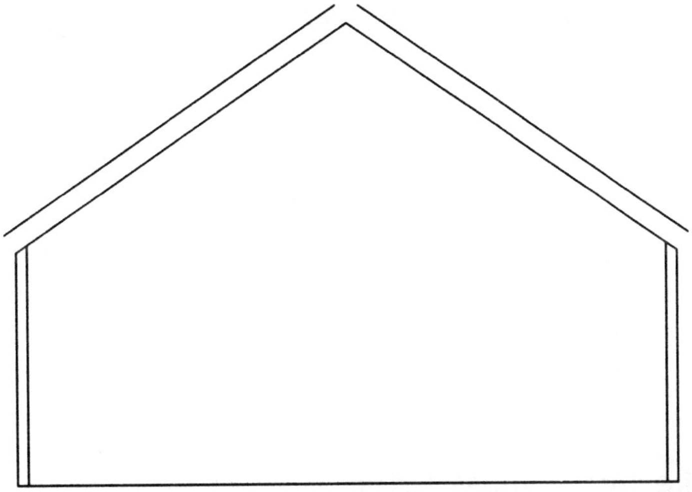

Figure 5-1.10 Garage elevation; fascia lines

14. Fillet the two new lines to form the ridge at the top.

Next you will develop the overhang. It is sometimes helpful to sketch the roof edge detail (you will draft it later in this book) so you can draw it correctly and not have to go back and tweak the elevations later. Figure 5-1.11 is our sketch, showing a total of 10 ½" for the fascia and a 1'-0" overhang.

Next you will draw the roof edge in your elevation.

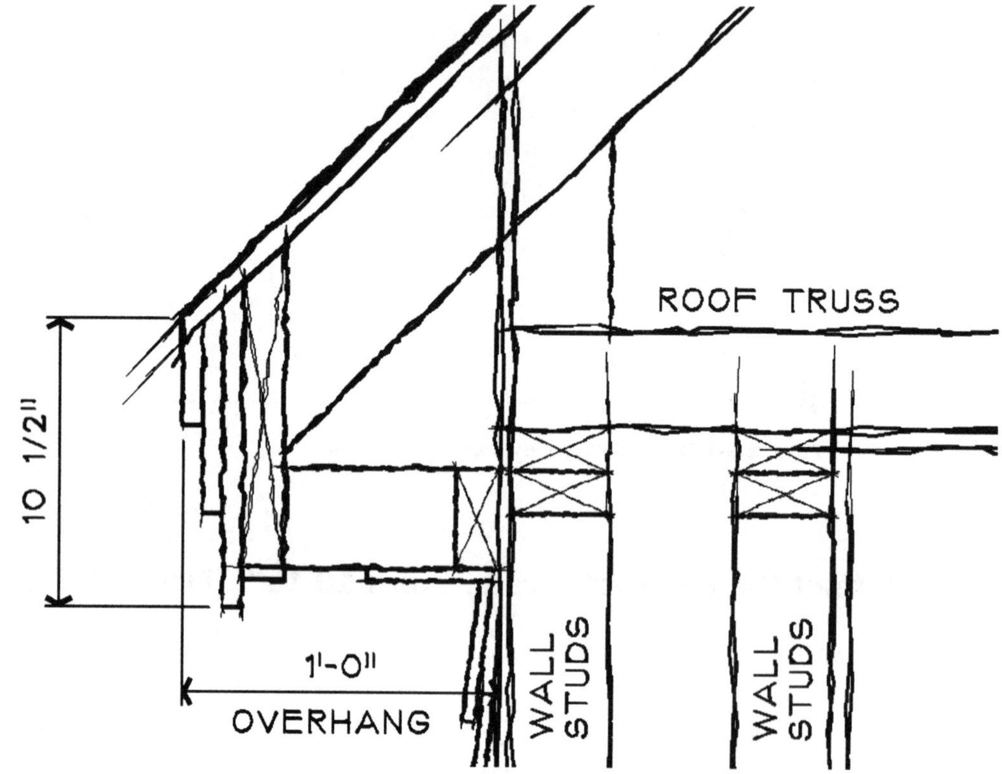

Figure 5-1.11 Typical Roof edge; similar condition at garage

15. Draw the roof edge profile as shown in **Figure 5-1.12**.

    a. Draw the temporary line (shown dashed in Figure 5-1.12) and offset it down 5 7/8", and then delete the temporary line.

    b. Make sure you use Ortho or Polar Tracking to assure horizontal and vertical lines.

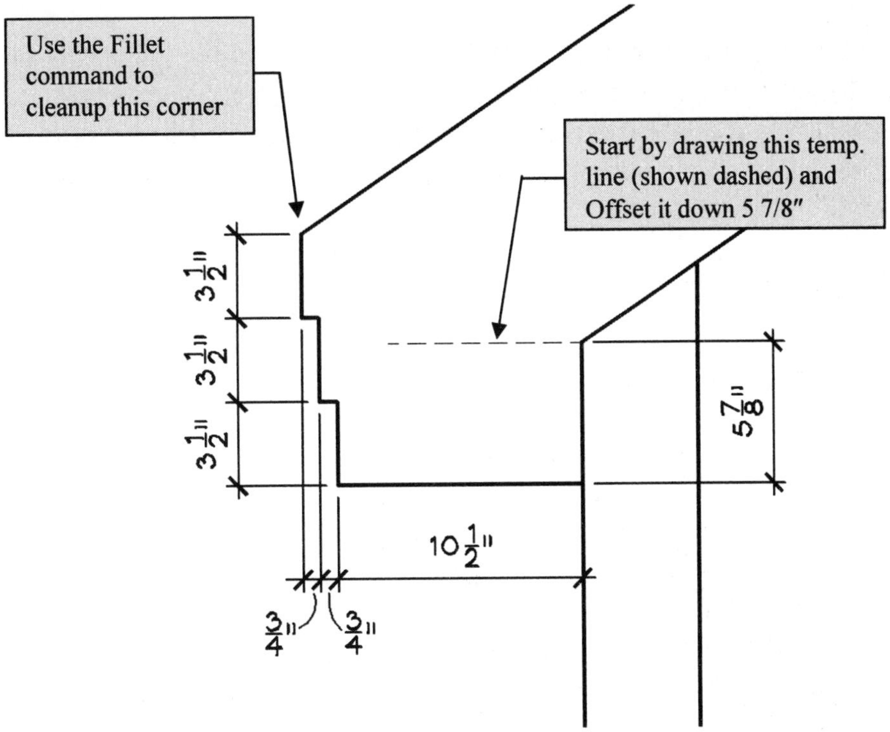

Figure 5-1.12 Typical Roof edge profile

16. Use the **Mirror** command to mirror the roof edge to the other side of the garage.

This completes the outline of the garage. Next you will work on the house.

Referring to your dimensioned plans (or page 4-6) notice the overall dimension is 76'-0" and the garage takes up 28'-0" of that dimension. So the remaining portion to be drawn is 48'-0".

17. Draw a line **48'-0"** to the right. (Figure 5-1.13)

The first floor of the house is higher than the garage floor (to keep the snowmelt from getting into the house for us northerners!), so you need to move this line up; recall the steps drawn in Task 4-5.

18. **Offset** the 48'-0" line up **1'-4".** (Figure 5-1.14)

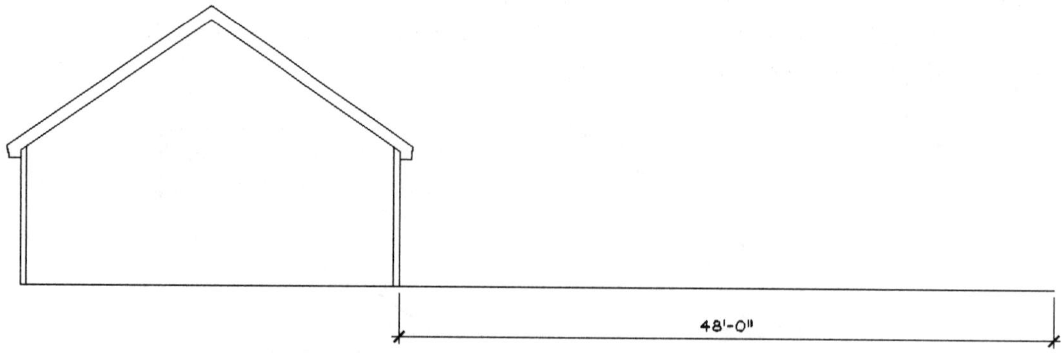

Figure 5-1.13 48′-0″ line drawn to the right

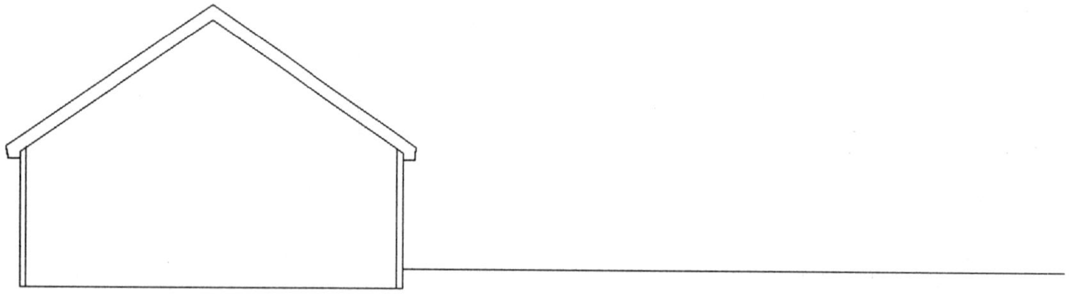

Figure 5-1.14 48′-0″ line offset up 1′-4″

19. Draw two vertical lines 19′- 1 5/8″ long and 32′-0″ apart; note the two story portion of the building is 32′-0″ wide on your dimensioned plans.

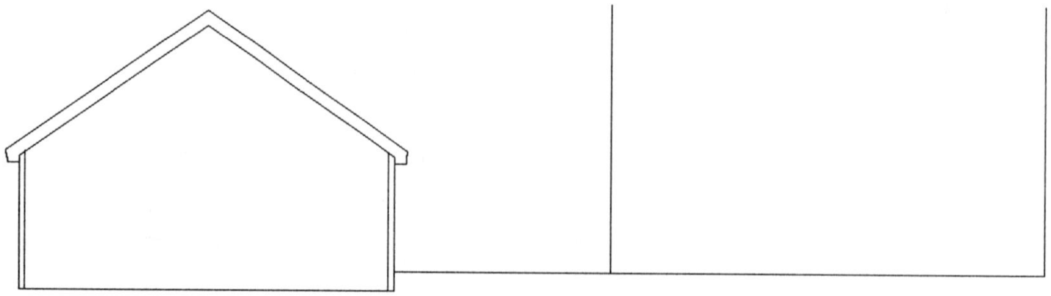

Figure 5-1.15 Vertical lines 32′-0″ apart; 19′- 1 5/8″ long lines

20. The vertical trim, roof edge and pitch are the same as the garage, so follow the same steps to complete the roof as shown in **Figure 5-1.16**.

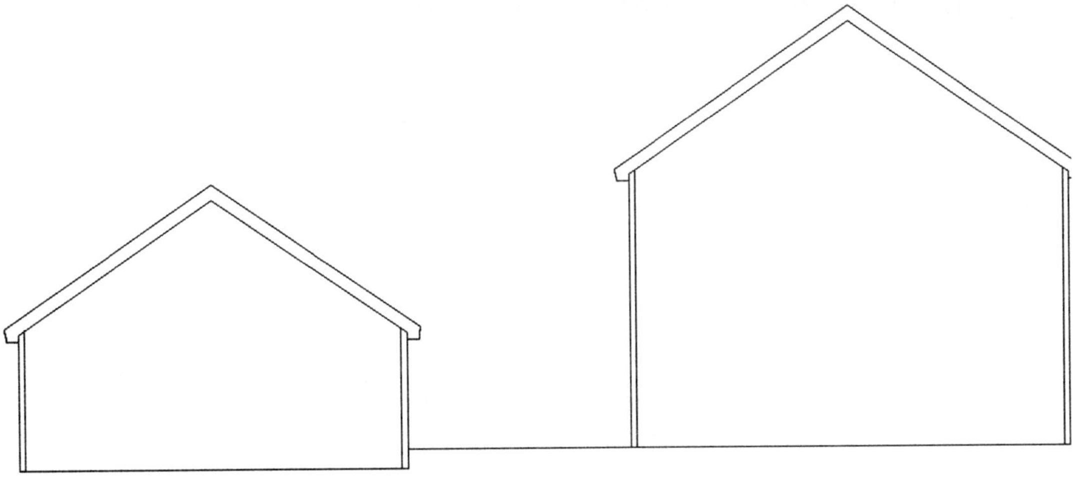

Figure 5-1.16 Roof outline added to two story portion of house

21. **Offset** the first floor line **12'-5 9/16"** up to establish the ridge line; extend and trim as required. (Figure 5-1.17)
TIP: Knowing the building is 20'-0" wide below the portion of roof in question, you could draw a section through this area to calculate the height of the ridge line (this roof and the porch only have a 4/12 pitch).

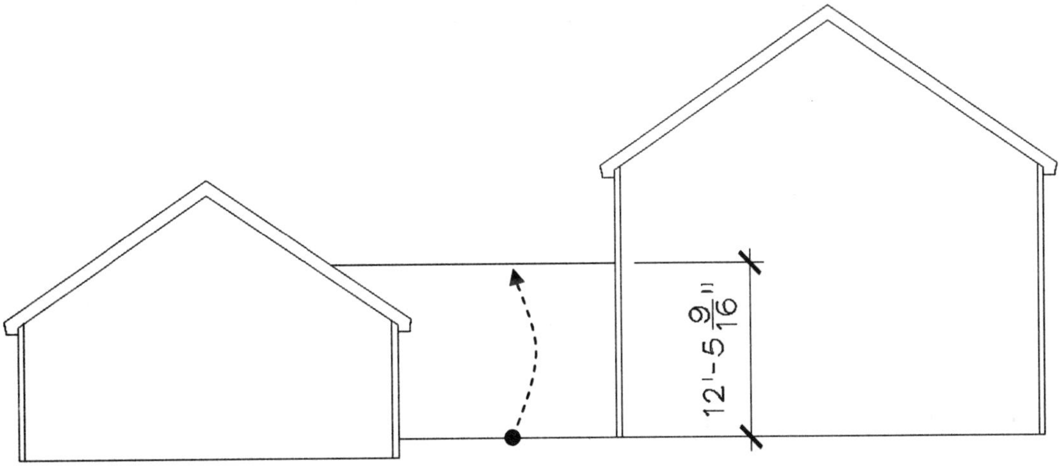

Figure 5-1.17 South Elevation; added roof ridge line

Taking a look back at Figure 5-1.2 you will notice that the fascia of the porch roof aligns with the garage roof. Therefore you can draw horizontal lines extending from the endpoints of the garage roof edge.

22. Draw two horizontal lines as shown in **Figure 5-1.18**, the length does not matter at this time.

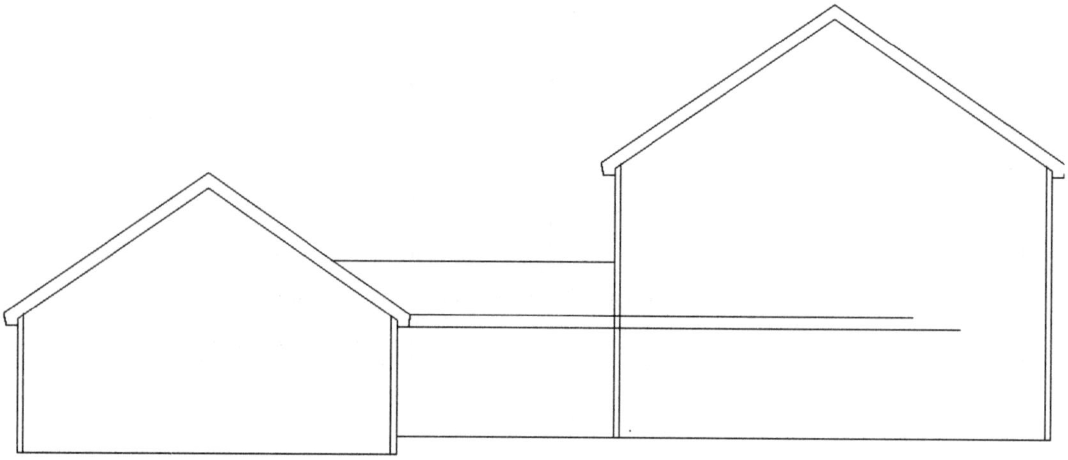

Figure 5-1.18 South Elevation

23. Draw an **8'-6"** line as shown in Figure 5-1.19.

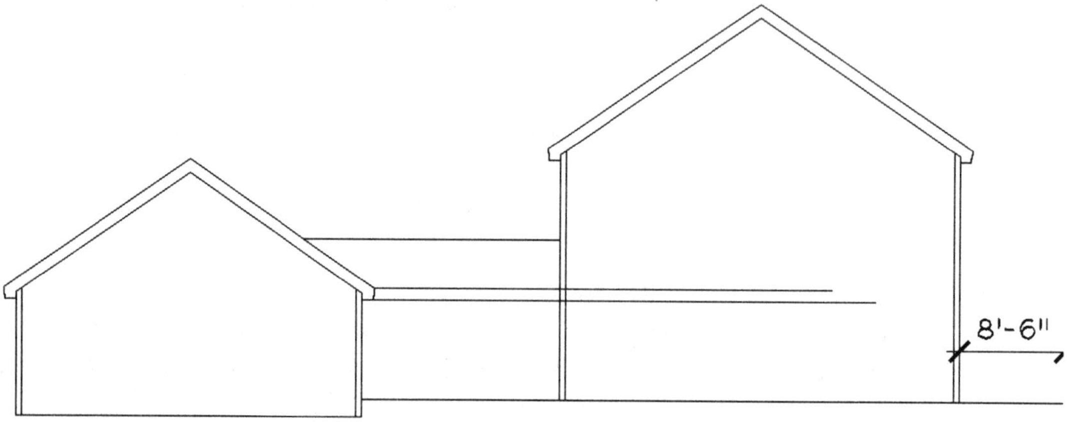

Figure 5-1.19 South Elevation

24. At the edge of the 8'-6" line just drawn, you will draw one of the porch columns per the dimensions shown in Figure 5-1.20.

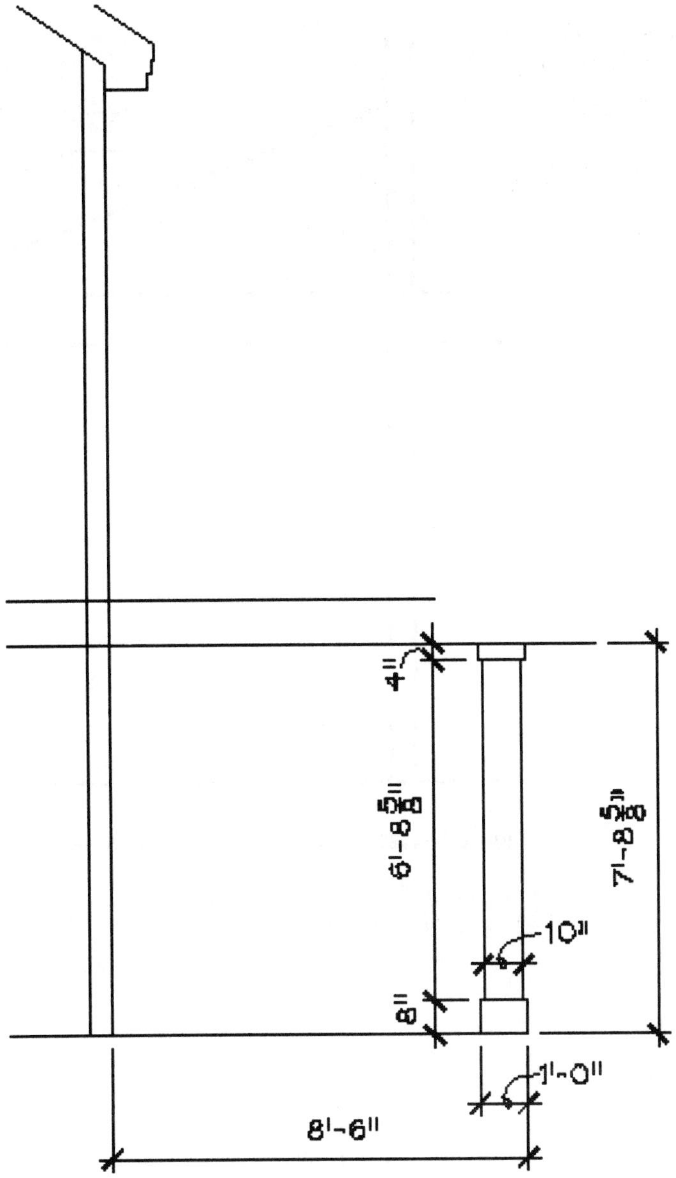

Figure 5-1.20 South Elevation; porch column

25. Using the same roof edge profile, draw the porch roof with a **4/12** pitch as shown in **Figure 5-1.21**. Extend the sloped roof line up to the face of the building as shown.

26. Draw the horizontal line where the porch roof meets the wall, and then trim the vertical lines to the new horizontal line as shown in **Figure 5-1.22**.

27. Draw the rest of the columns; locate them using the floor plan dimension previously provided (or use the Xref described next).

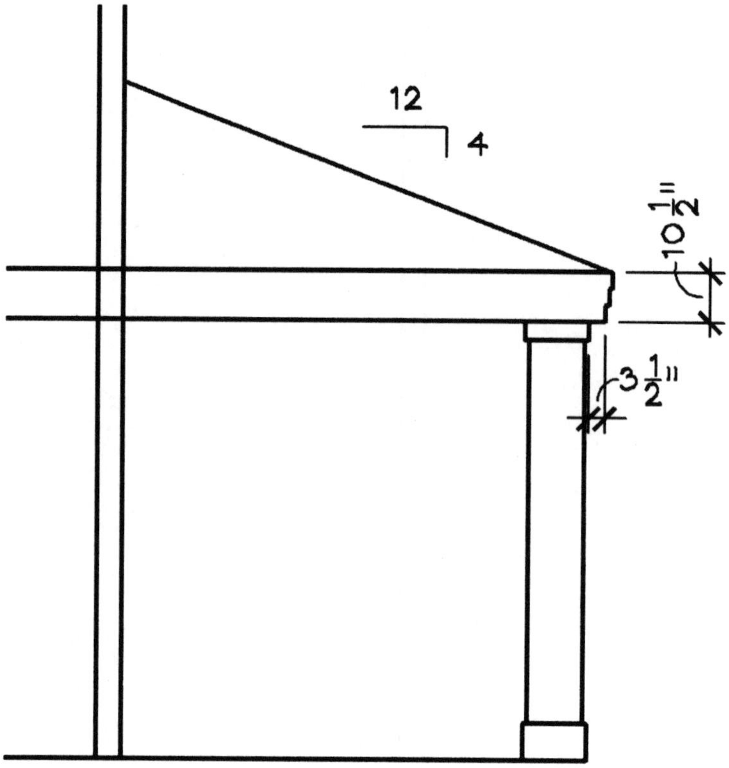

Figure 5-1.21 South Elevation; porch roof

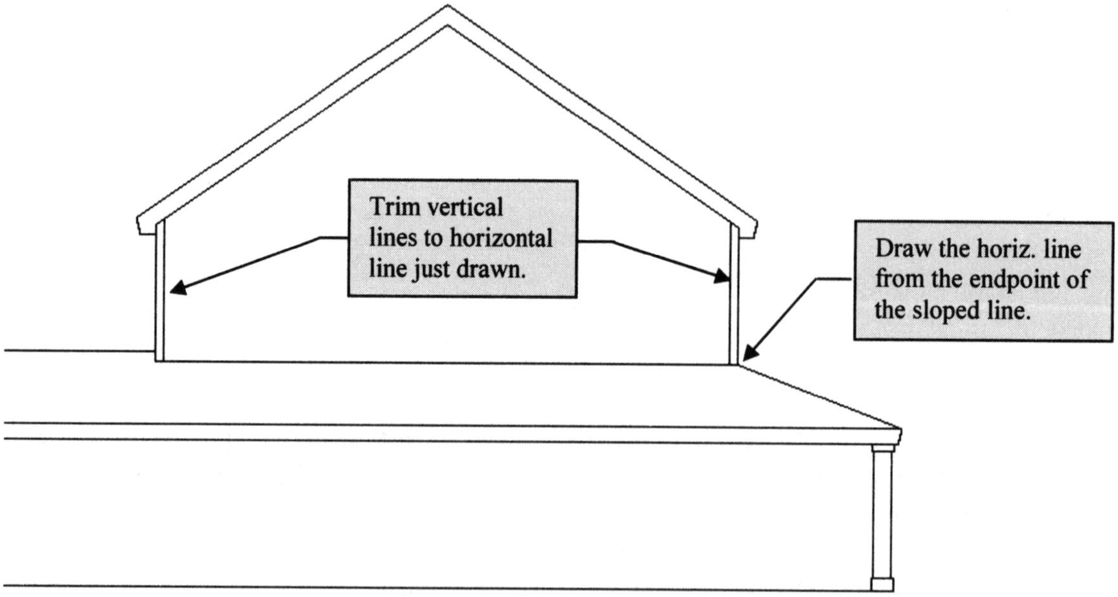

Figure 5-1.22 South Elevation; porch roof

External References

We will digress for a moment and take a look at *External References.* Basically, this is a way to bring another drawing into the current drawing. AutoCAD remembers where the file is located on the computers hard drive and reloads it every time the drawing is opened. This saves disk space and assures the referenced drawing stays current.

You will use *External Reference* (Xref) to bring in a floor plan so you can project lines off of it, which can speed the elevation process. When you are done you will use the *Xref Manager* to detach the drawing.

28. In the *"exterior elevations.dwg"* file select **External Reference** from the **Insert** menu.

29. Browse to the location of your **flr1.dwg** file and then select **Open.** (Figure 5-1.23)

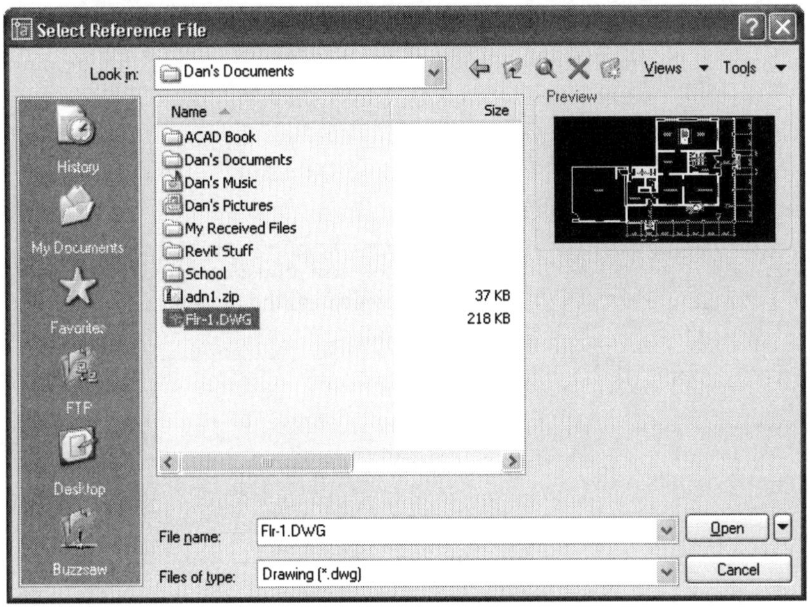

Figure 5-1.23 Insert External Reference (browse)

30. Next, check **specify on-screen** under *Insertion Point* and then click **OK.** (Figure 5-1.24)

31. Pick a point to the upper left of your elevation for an Insertion Point.

32. **Rotate** the floor per **Figure 5-1.25**.

33. You can now use the floor plan and elevation to project temporary lines to quickly block out the new elevation (West).

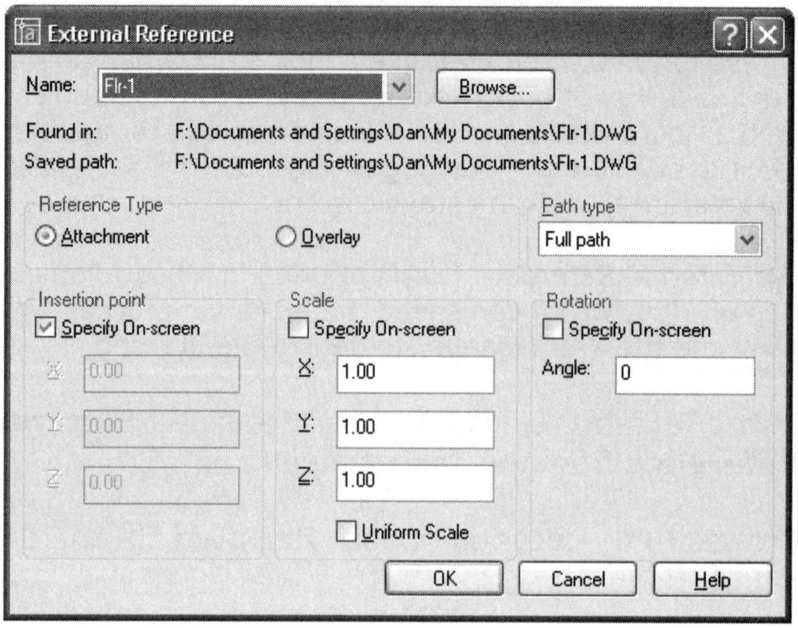

Figure 5-1.24 Insert External Reference dialog

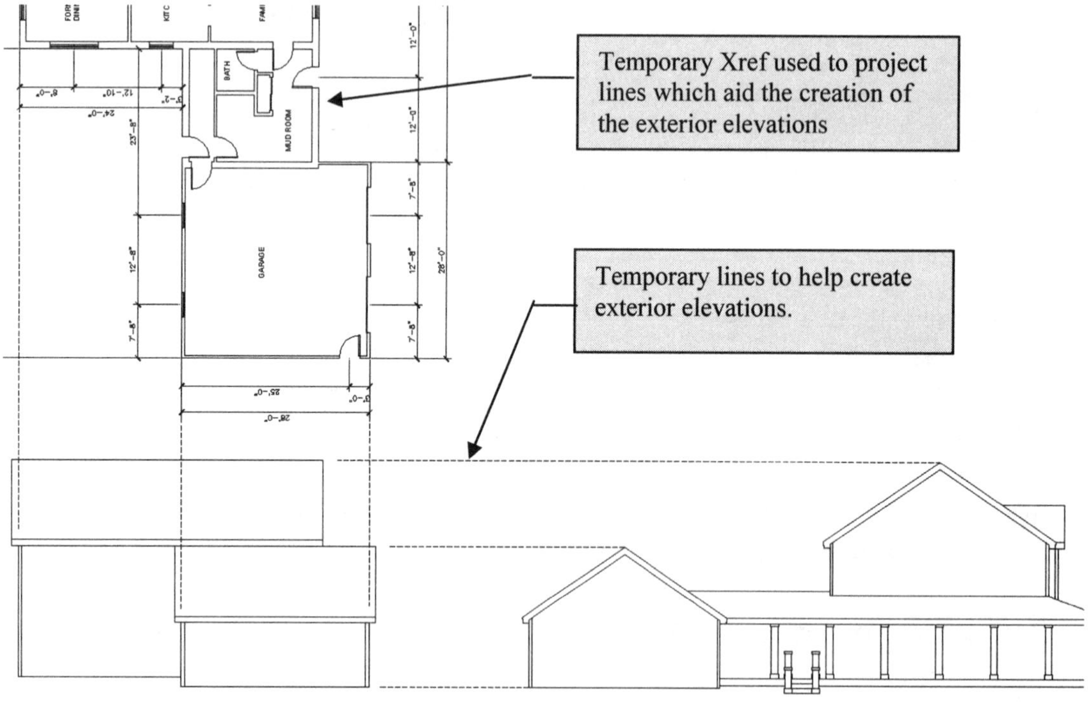

Figure 5-1.25 Inserted External Reference; rotated flr1 drawing

When you are finished using the External Reference (Xref) you can easily detach it from your drawing.

34. Select **Xref Manager** from the **Insert** menu.

35. Make sure **Flr1** is selected under *Reference Name* list and then click the **Detach** button and then click **OK.** Figure 5-1.26

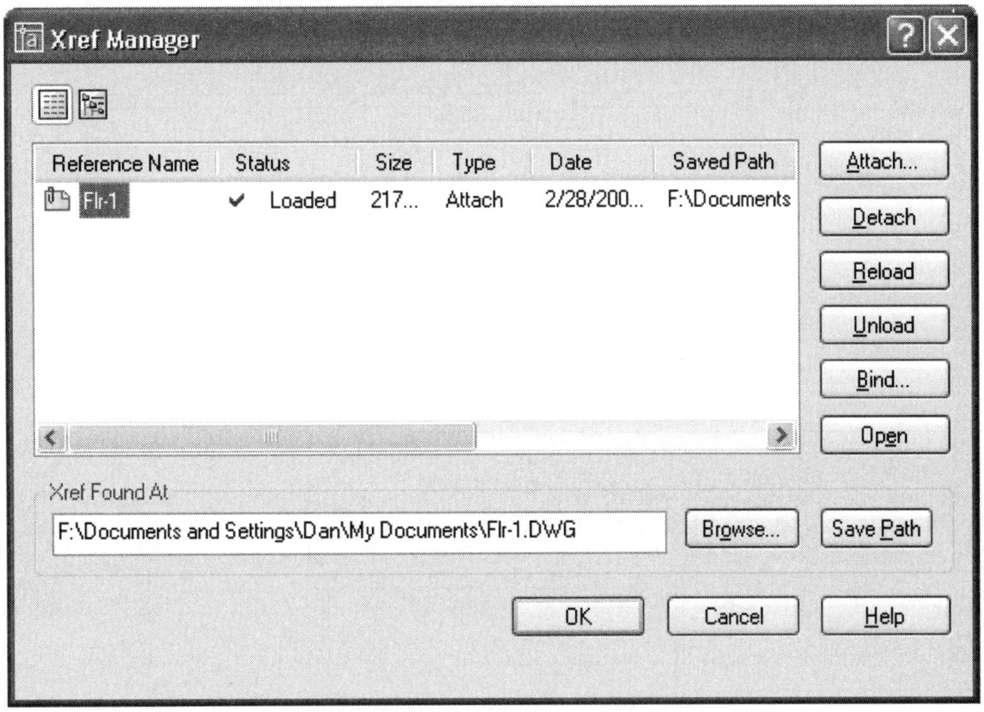

Figure 5-1.26 Xref Manager

Finishing the exterior elevation outlines

You should now have enough information to complete the outlines of the remaining exterior elevations.

36. Using the dimensions from the floor plans and the portion of elevation previously drawn, complete the outline of the four elevations per Figures 5-1.27, 5-1.28, 5-1.29 and 5-1.30.

37. **Save** your drawing.

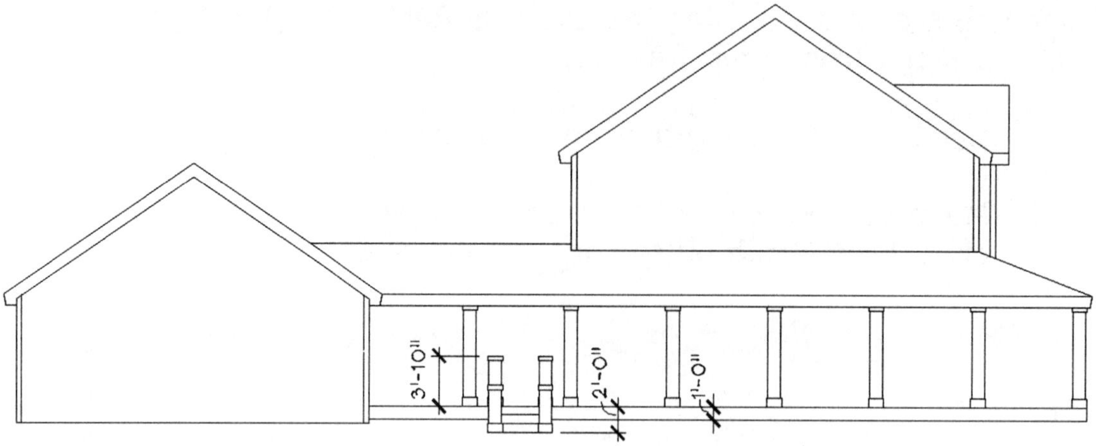

Figure 5-1.27 South elevation

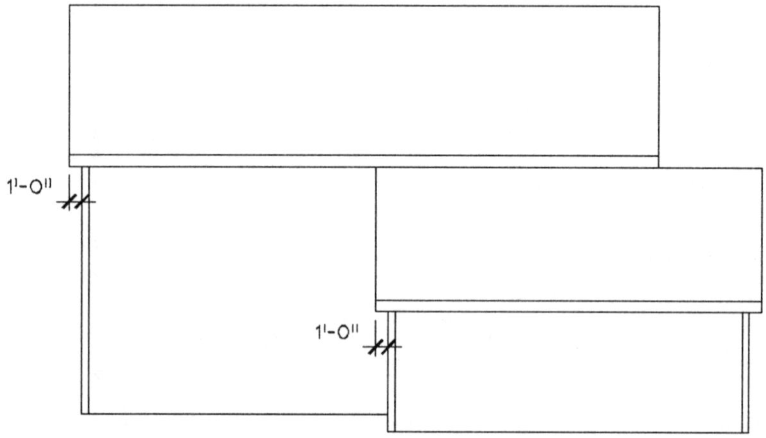

Figure 5-1.28 West elevation

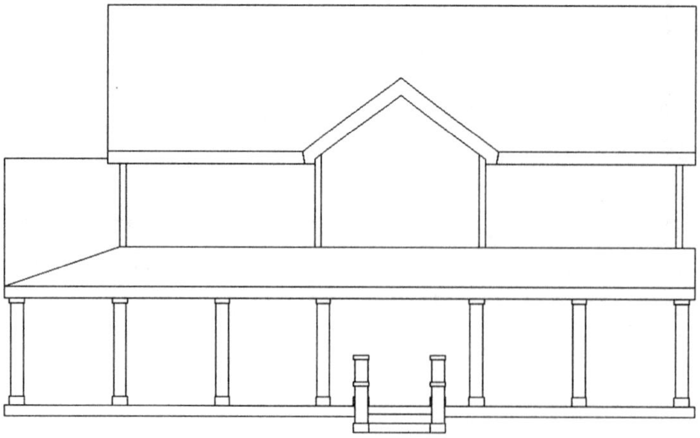

Figure 5-1.29 East elevation

FIND THE MISSING ELEMENT!

Comparing this elevation with the floor plan and other elevations, find the portion of elevation that is missing from Figure 5-1.30; add it to your elevation to correct the problem.

When drawing elevations, you need to thoroughly scan the plans and elevations to make sure you get everything.

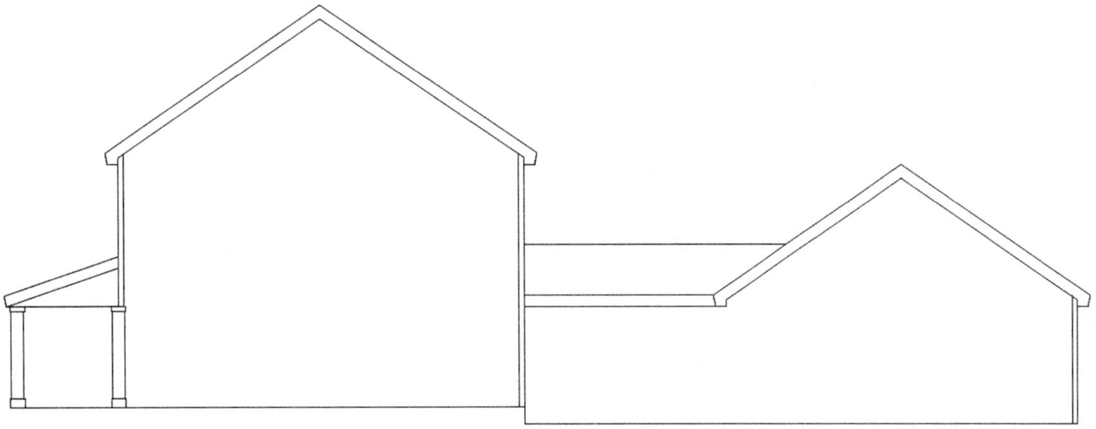

Figure 5-1.30 North elevation

Image courtesy of Anderson Architects
Alan H. Anderson, Architect, Duluth, MN
Interior Design, Steven W. Sanborn, A.I.A., Santa Rosa, CA

Exercise 5-2:
Windows

In this section you will add the windows to the exterior elevations. You will also study the Block feature a little more.

Drawings the Windows:

First, you will draw each window type in a separate drawing, similar to the drawing completed in Exercise 3-3.

1. Open a new drawing.

2. On *Layer* 0 (zero), draw the window shown in **Figure 5-2.1**.

    a. Set the bottom middle as the Origin.

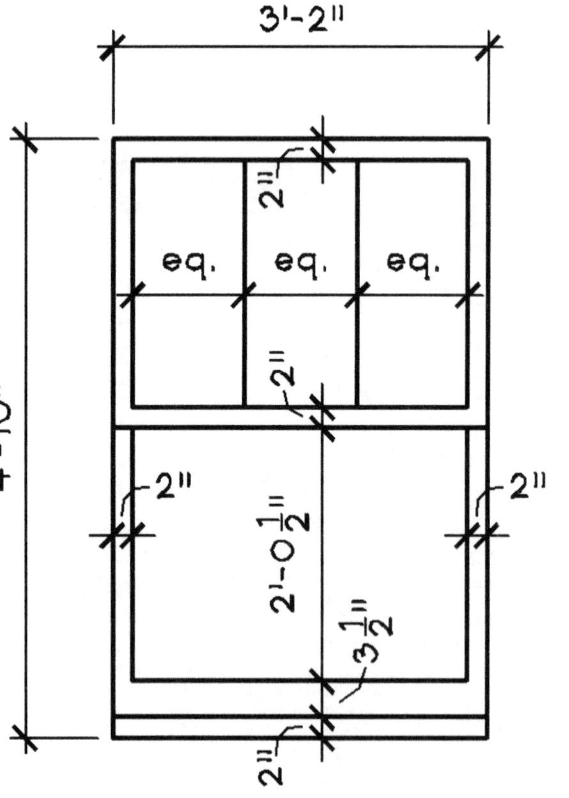

Figure 5-2.1 Window-1 drawing

Carter Residence *Image courtesy of LHB www.LHBcorp.com*

3. Save the window drawing as **Window-1.dwg.**

4. Save-As to a drawing named **Window-2.dwg.**

5. Create the window shown in **Figure 5-2.2**.
__NOTE:__ It is the same size as the window previously drawn so you can copy it over to create the second window.

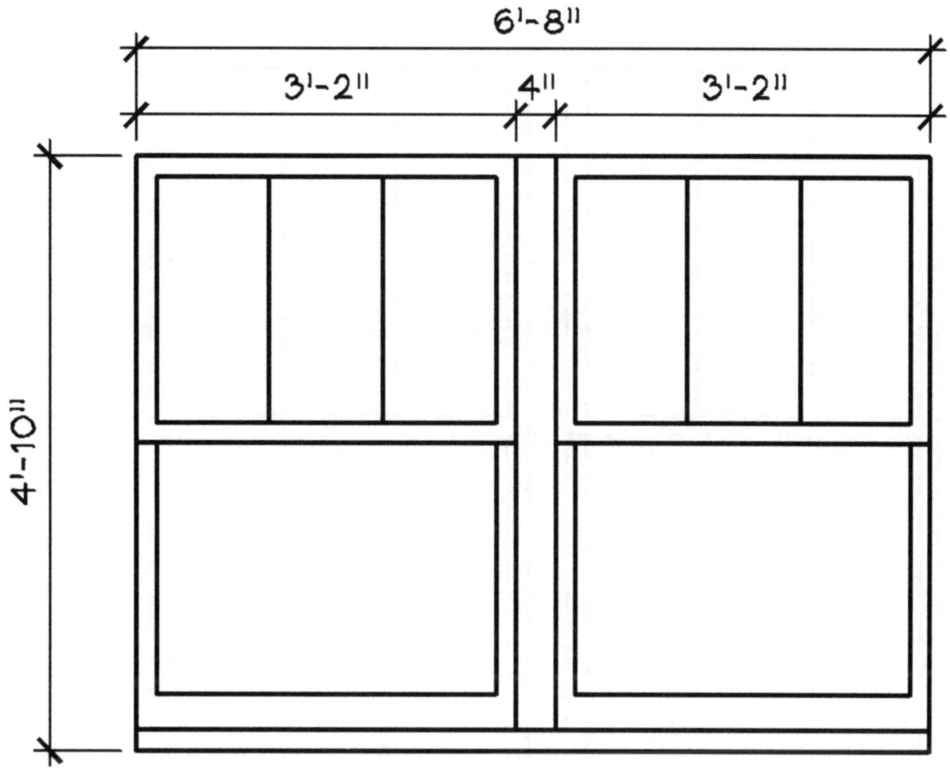

Figure 5-2.2 Window-2 drawing

6. **Save** your drawing (as Window-2.dwg).

The third window type is similar to window-2 except taller. The next steps will have you save a copy and stretch the window to the correct size.

7. **Save-As** to a drawing named **Window-3.dwg.**

8. Use the **Stretch** command to quickly create the window shown in **Figure 5-2.3**.

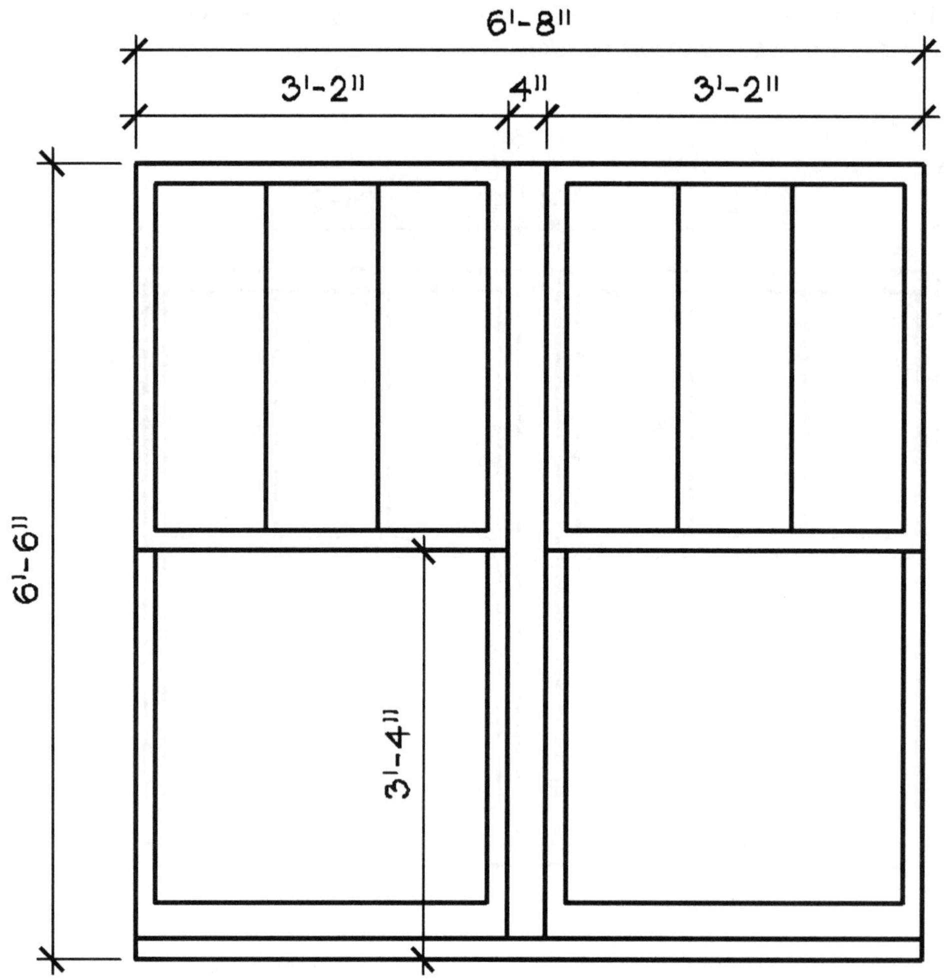

Figure 5-2.3 Window-3 drawing

9. **Save** your drawing.

10. **Save-As** to a drawing named **Window-4.dwg.**

11. *Erase* one of the windows and use *Fillet* to create the window shown in **Figure 5-2.4**.

You may recall in Exercise 3-3 that the vertical lines in the upper sash where more detailed in that you drew two lines; whereas, here you only drew one.

Detail such as this is either added or removed depending on what scale the drawing will be printed as. Lower detail, like the window above is more appropriate for smaller scale prints; like 1/8" = 1'-0" or ¼" = 1'-0". Higher detail would be better on larger scale details; like ½" = 1'-0" or ¾" = 1'-0".

Too much detail on a smaller scale print usually produces a drawing where the lines run together, creating what looks like a really heavy line.

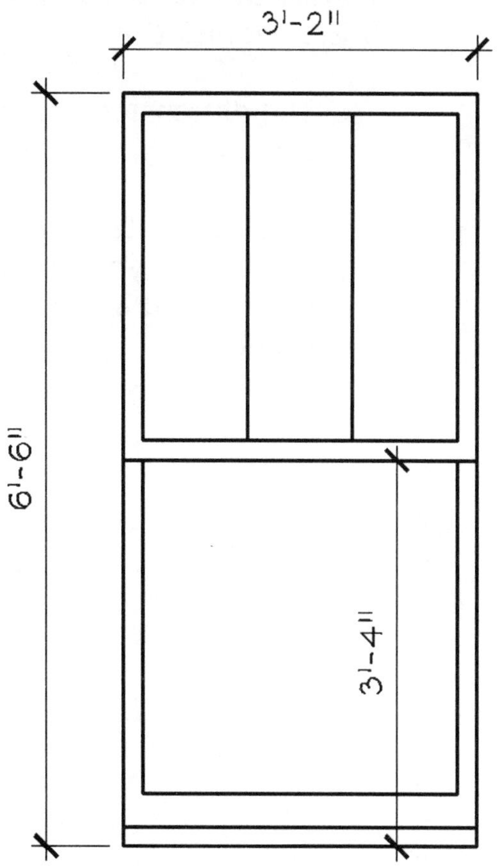

Figure 5-2.4 Window-4 drawing

Now that you have created the various window types, you will insert them into the exterior elevations; the same way you inserted the door symbols into the floor plans.

12. **Open** the **Exterior Elevations** drawing.

13. Create a new *Layer* named **Windows** and set it to color Yellow; you will place the window blocks on this *Layer.*

14. From the **Insert** pull-down menu select **Block.**

15. *Browse* to the location where you saved the **Window-1** drawing.

16. **Insert** the **Window-1** block into the location shown in Figure 5-2.5; noting the following:

    a. The dimension shown is from the garage floor to the window sill.

    b. The horizontal dimension is to be derived from the plans; make sure you use the center of the window as a snap point if you are using an Xref'ed floor plan to locate the windows.

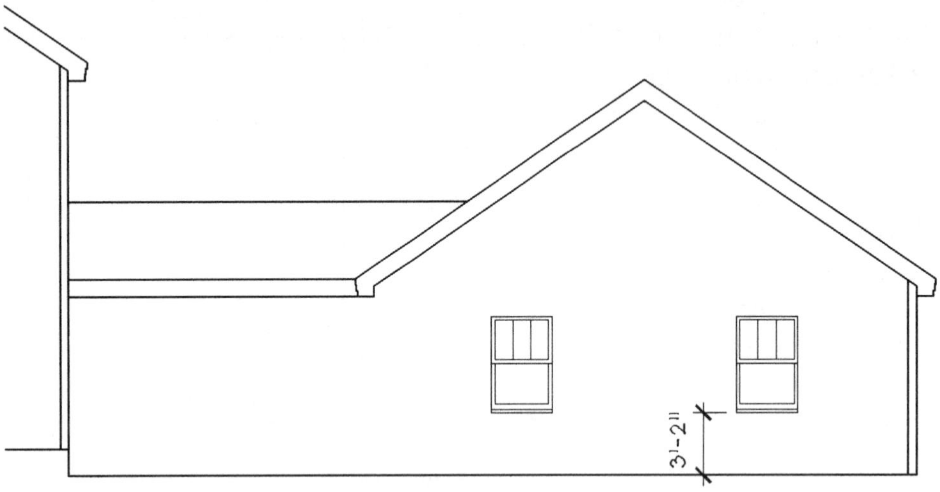

Figure 5-2.5 Window-1 block inserted - North elevation

Once a block (an external drawing in this case) has been inserted into your drawing you can copy it around to additional locations; you do not have to use the Insert command every time.

17. **Insert** instances of **Window-1, Window-2, Window-3** and **Window-4** as blocks per **Figure 5-2.6**.

    a. Do not worry about the windows overlapping the porch roof and columns right now; you will adjust this later.

    b. Make sure you insert the window blocks on the *Layer* named **Windows.**

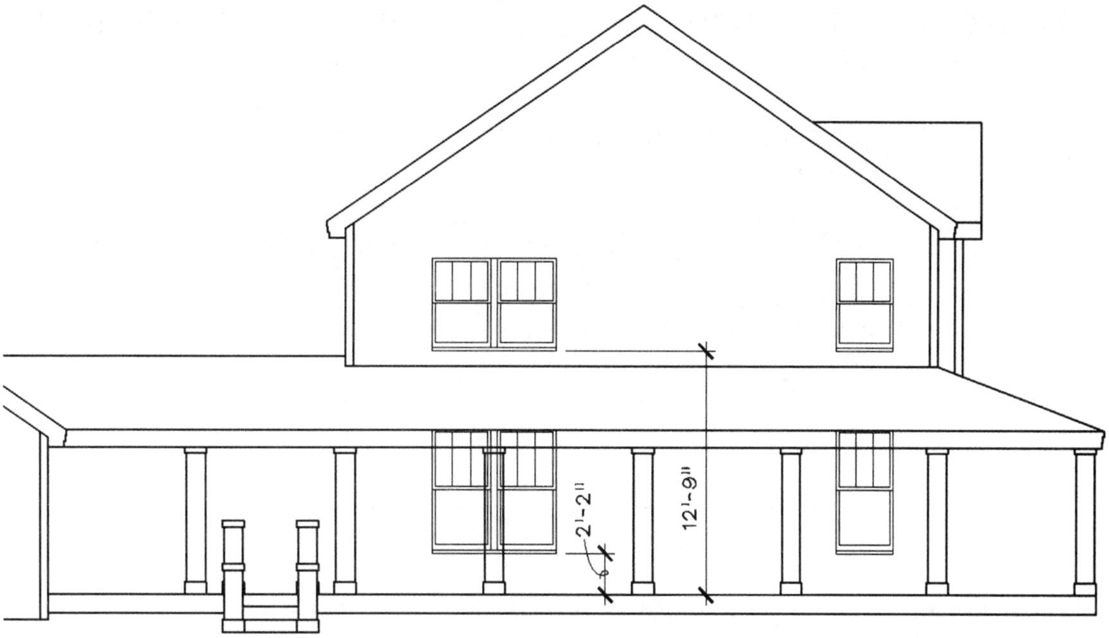

Figure 5-2.6 Window blocks inserted - South elevation

18. Using the sill-height dimensions and procedures previously described, insert the remaining windows based on the window locations shown in the plan. (Figures 5-2.7a, b, *and* c)

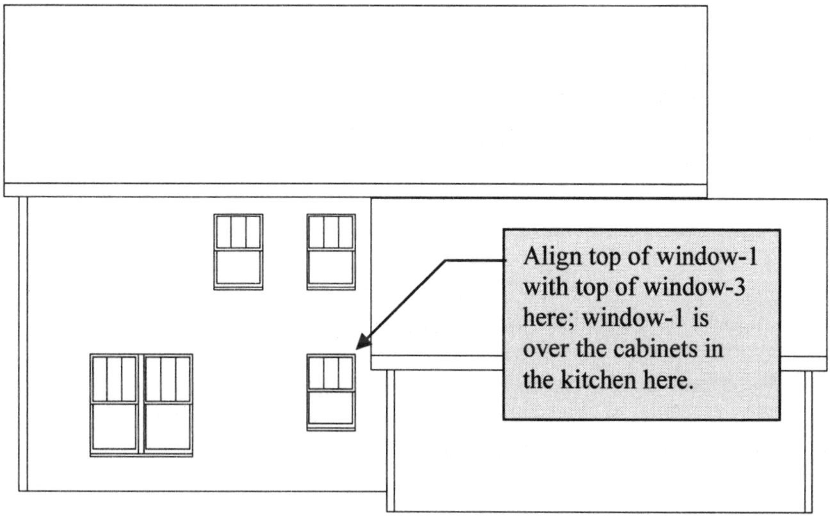

Figure 5-2.7a Window blocks inserted - West elevation

Figure 5-2.7b Window blocks inserted - East elevation

Figure 5-2.7c Window blocks inserted - North elevation

Advantages of using blocks:

In addition to the window being one object when it is a block, which is easy to pick and move around, you can also make changes which instantly apply to all instances of the block in a particular drawing.

Next you will modify the block by adding trim, which is part of the siding. You will do this before adjusting the windows that are behind the porch roof and columns.

> **When should I use a block?**
> Anytime something is repetitive and exactly the same (or with few variations like your windows in elevation), you should use a block. This makes the drawing size smaller and any changes much quicker.

19. **Open** each of the four window type drawings and add a **5" wide trim board** to three sides and extend the sill lines as shown in **Figure 5-2.8**.

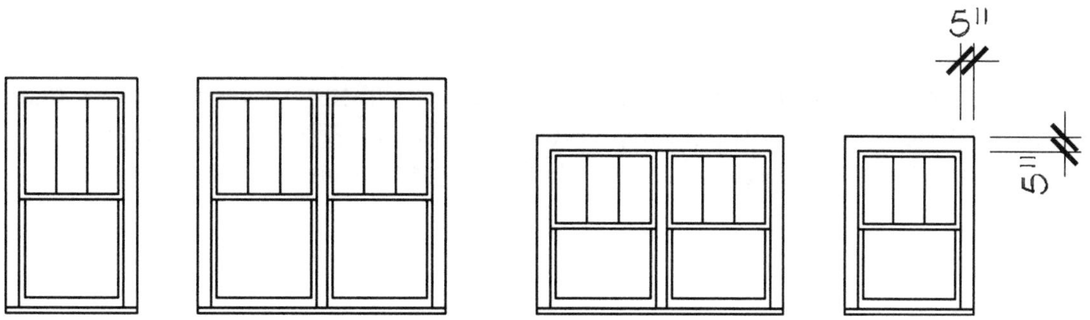

Figure 5-2.8 Revised windows (siding trim added)

20. **Save** each of the four window type drawings (Window-1.dwg, window-2.dwg, window-3.dwg, window-4.dwg).

21. In the *Exterior Elevations* drawing, **Zoom In** on the south elevation.

Notice the window elevations are as they were when you originally inserted them. After the next step they will all automatically update.

22. Per steps previously outlined (starting with step 14), insert the four window types again; note the following:

    a. When you are prompted to re-define the *Block*, click **YES**. (Figure 5-2.9)
    b. When you are at the final stage, where you are prompted to pick a point on the screen to insert the block, you can press the Esc key; this cancels the insert, but not before updating the block definition in the current drawing.
    c. Or, you can insert the window blocks off to one side and delete them.

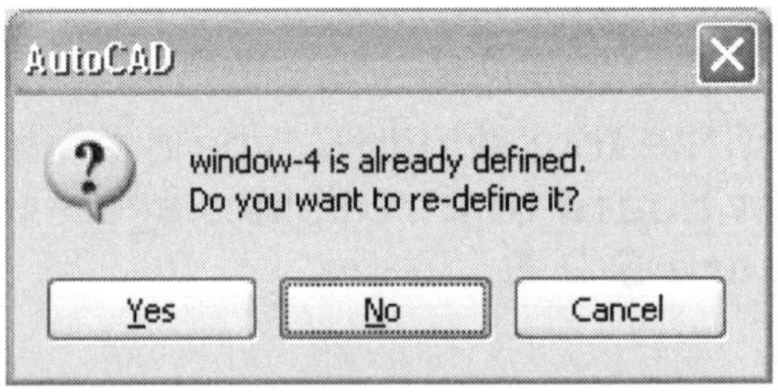

Figure 5-2.9 Re-define block prompt

You should review the south elevation again; notice the windows have been all updated automatically (Figure 5-2.10)! The other three elevations are updated also. This feature can save a lot of time.

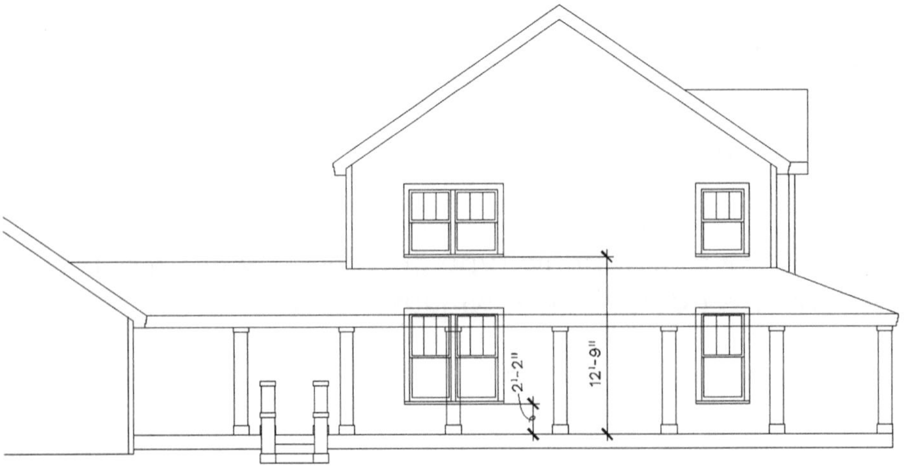

Figure 5-2.10
Re-defined blocks in South elevation

Exploding blocks:

The *Explode* command allows you to reduce a *Block* to its basic components (i.e., lines, arcs, text, etc.). Only the blocks selected are exploded. And, even if you *Explode* all the instances of a particular *Block* in a drawing, the definition of the *Block* will still existing in the drawing; this allows you to insert the *Block* without having to browse to the original drawings on your hard drive (i.e., C drive).

Next you will *Explode* the *Blocks* at the porch and trim the portion of window covered by the porch roof and columns.

23. Select the **Explode** icon from the *Modify* toolbar. 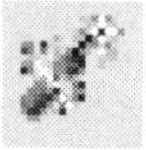

24. Select the two windows on the south elevation and the two windows on the east elevation that are covered by the porch roof.

The four windows are now exploded to there original lines. Next you will trim the windows so you only see the lines that are not obstructed from sight by another building element.

25. **Trim** and **Erase** the window lines as shown in **Figures 5-2.11 and 5-2.12**.

Figure 5-2.11 Exploded windows (original lines trimmed and erased); East elevation

Figure 5-2.12 Exploded windows (original lines trimmed and erased); South elevation

After exploding the blocks you should have noticed that the lines changed color (from yellow to white). If you recall, you created the window on Layer 0 in the original drawings and placed the window blocks on the Windows layer in the *Exterior Elevations* drawing. When a block is exploded, you get the original line-work on the original layers.

So, to clean house, you need to move the exploded window lines to the Windows layer.

26. Revise the drawing so the exploded windows are on the **Windows** *Layer.*

Exercise 5-3:
Doors

In this exercise you will add exterior doors to your plans. In the process you will take a quick look at using a feature called "Grip Edit".

1. **Open** "exterior elevations.dwg" drawing file.

2. Create a new *Layer* named **Doors**; set the color to *Green.*

The elevations, as a whole, do not have more that two instances of any door; plus two of the doors need to be trimmed because they are behind other architectural elements.

Thus it is not beneficial, in this case, to create blocks of each door. So you will draw each door type in-place and then copy the entities to the second location (if applicable).

3. On the Doors Layer, draw the door shown in **Figure 5-3.1** on the east elevations.

The door / frame elevation shown in Figure 5-3.1 represents two doors that are mostly glass and a glass transom above the doors that aligns with the tall windows on either side (not shown in Figure 5-3.1).

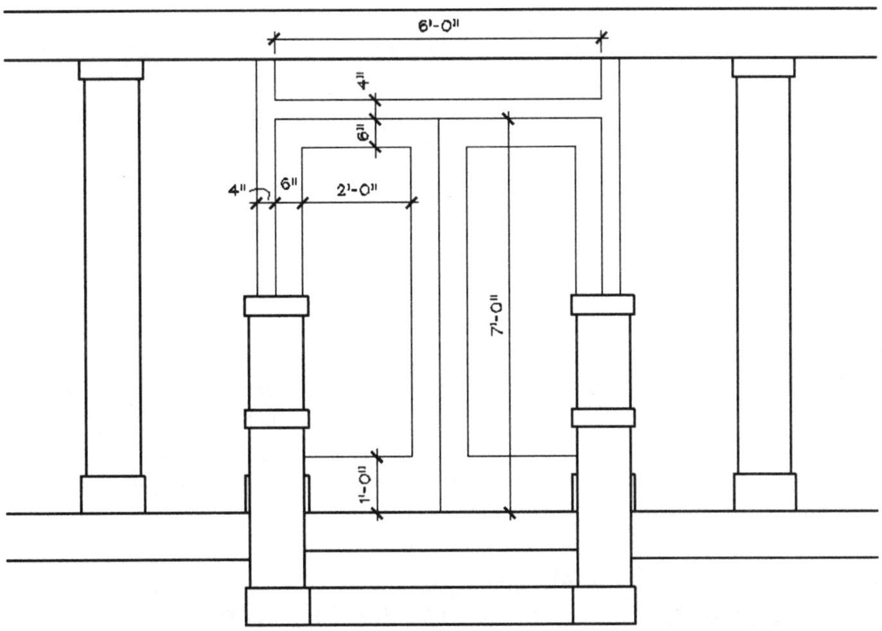

Figure 5-3.1 Door elevation; East elevation

Notice that the double doors you just drew correspond to the double doors you drew in the first floor plan.

4. Draw the portion of door shown in **Figure 5-3.2** on the west elevation (door into garage); you will draw more of the door in subsequent steps.

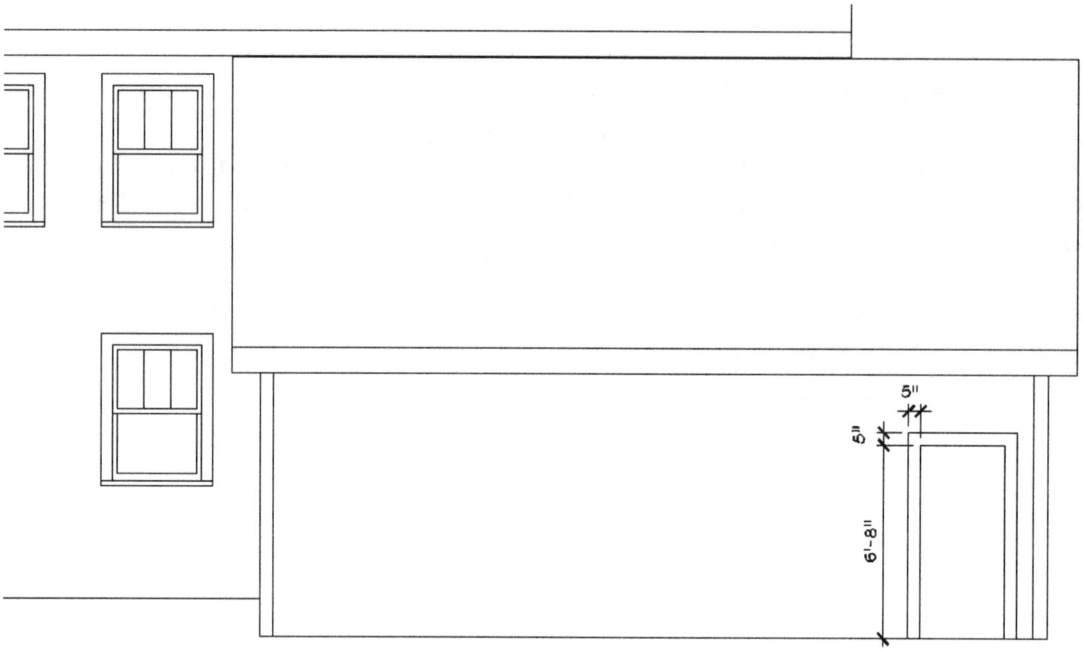

Figure 5-3.2 Partial door elevation; West elevation

Residential Door sizes!

Doors come in many shapes and sizes.

Thickness: 1 3/8", 1 3/4" and 2 1/4"

The 1 3/8" door is most often used in residential construction and the 2 ¼" door is typically only used on exterior doors for high-end projects – i.e., big budget.

Size: range from 1'-0" x 6'-8" to 4'-0" x 9'-0"

The height of a residential door is usually 6'-8". This writer recently worked on a project where 7'-0" high doors were specified. The contractor was so used to the standard 6'-8" dimension; he framed all the exterior openings at 6'-8". To top it off, the exterior walls where concrete (ICF system), so the openings could not be modified. Thus, 6'-8" doors were used.

You can find more information on the internet; two examples are
algomahardwoods.com and madawaska-doors.com
(wood veneer door mfr.) *(custom solid wood door mfr.)*

5. (**NOTE:** Do not jump ahead here; follow the next few steps closely!) Using the **Offset** command, offset the previously drawn lines inward, as shown in **Figure 5-3.3**.

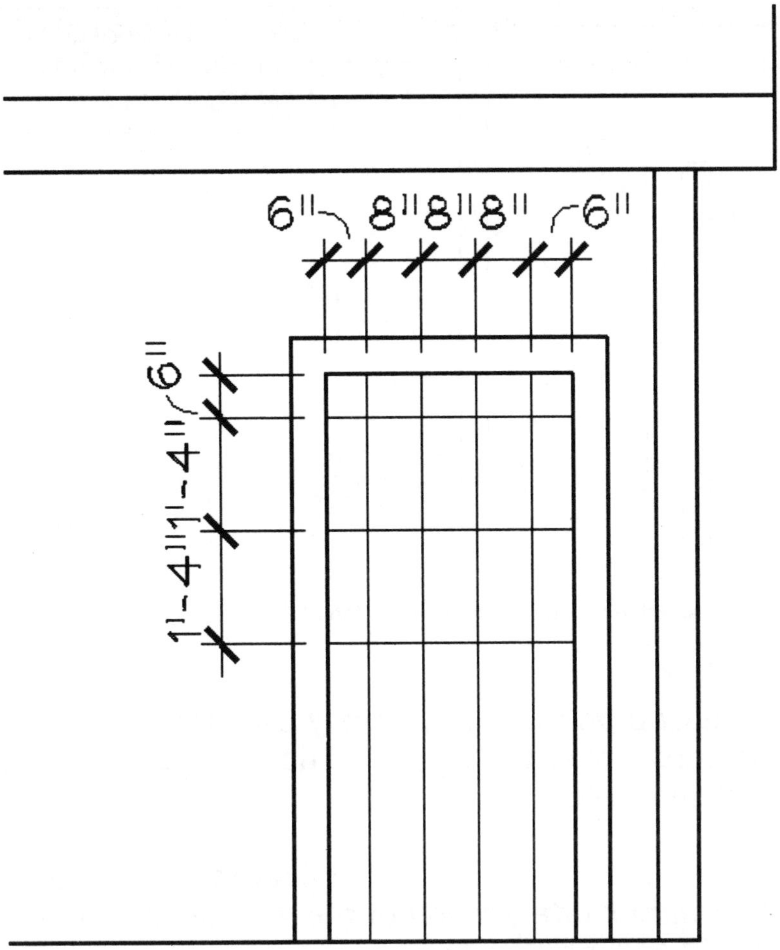

Figure 5-3.3 Door elevation with lines offset; West elevation

Using the Grip Edit feature:

Next you will use the *Grip Edit* feature to modify the lines to represent the window in the door panel.

Grip Edit allows you to modify lines without having to activate a command first. Basically you select a line, then select one or more of the visible grips and then reposition the grips by selecting another point.

6. Without any commands active, select the horizontal line shown in **Figure 5-3.4**.

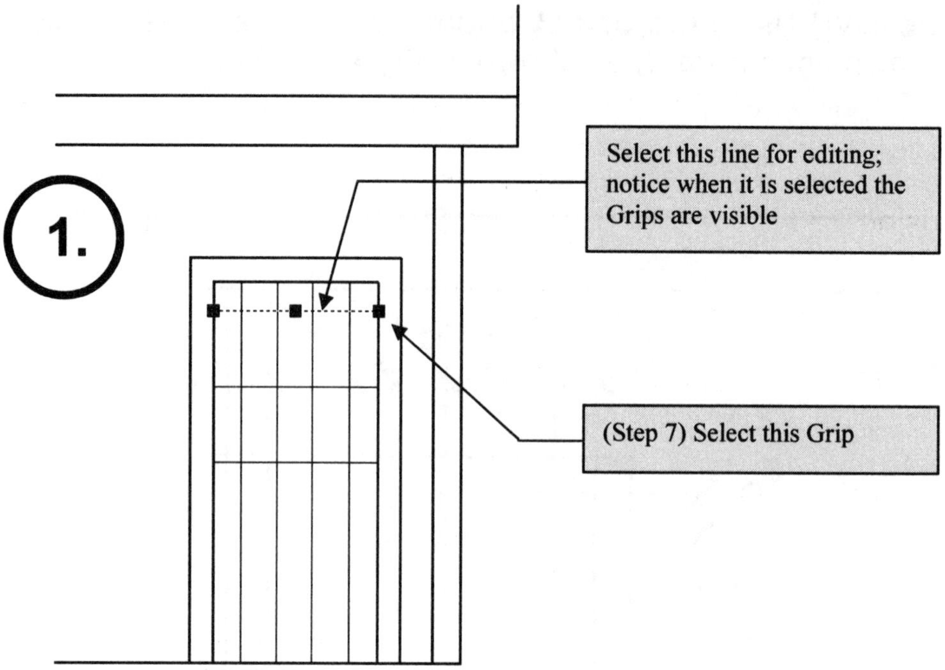

Figure 5-3.4 Line selected for editing; West elevation

7. Select the *Grip* on the right; simply click the mouse button with the cursor over the *Grip*, you do not drag the mouse button. Figure 5-3.4

8. Move the mouse to the left. Using **Osnaps**, select either *Perpendicular* or *Intersection* of the vertical line shown in **Figure 5-3.5a** and **5-3.5b**.

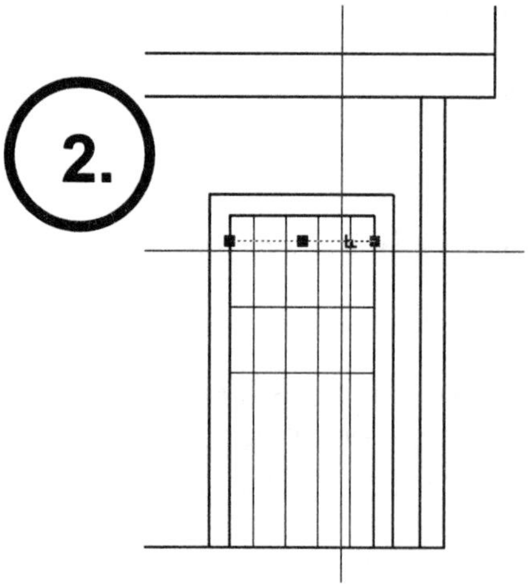

Figure 5-3.5a Perpendicular snap

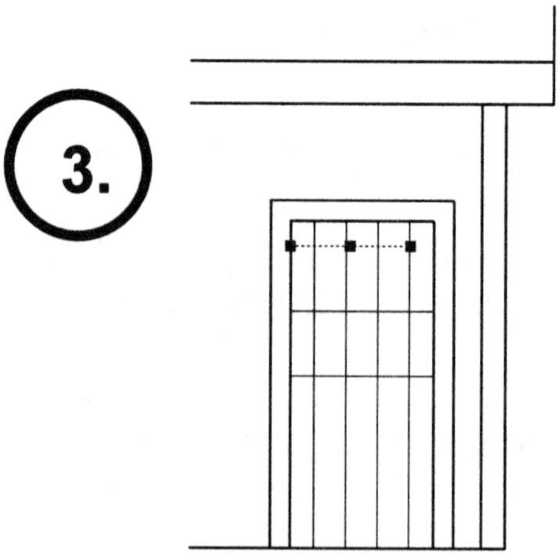

Figure 5-3.5b Relocated snap

9. Finally, press the **Esc** (i.e., escape) key, on the keyboard, to clear the grips (and unselect the horizontal line).

Essentially, you just trimmed a line without using the Trim command.

10. Using the same technique just described, modify the lines using grips to look like **Figure 5-3.6**.

AutoCAD also allows you to select more than one Grip at a time. You will try this next to adjust the bottom of the (4) vertical lines.

11. Select the (4) vertical lines; you can click each line individually or use a crossing window *(by clicking right to left).*

12. Holding the **Shift** key, **click** each of the lower Grips on the (4) vertical lines; the selected grips will turn red.

13. Releasing the **Shift** key, click the lower right grip.
    Remember: *Do not drag the mouse, i.e., hold the mouse button down continuously.*
    Figure 5-3.7

Figure 5-3.6
Lines modified with grips

14. Moving the mouse straight up, use the *Endpoint Osnap* to accurately select the lower horizontal line.

Your door is now complete and should look like **Figure 5-3.8**.

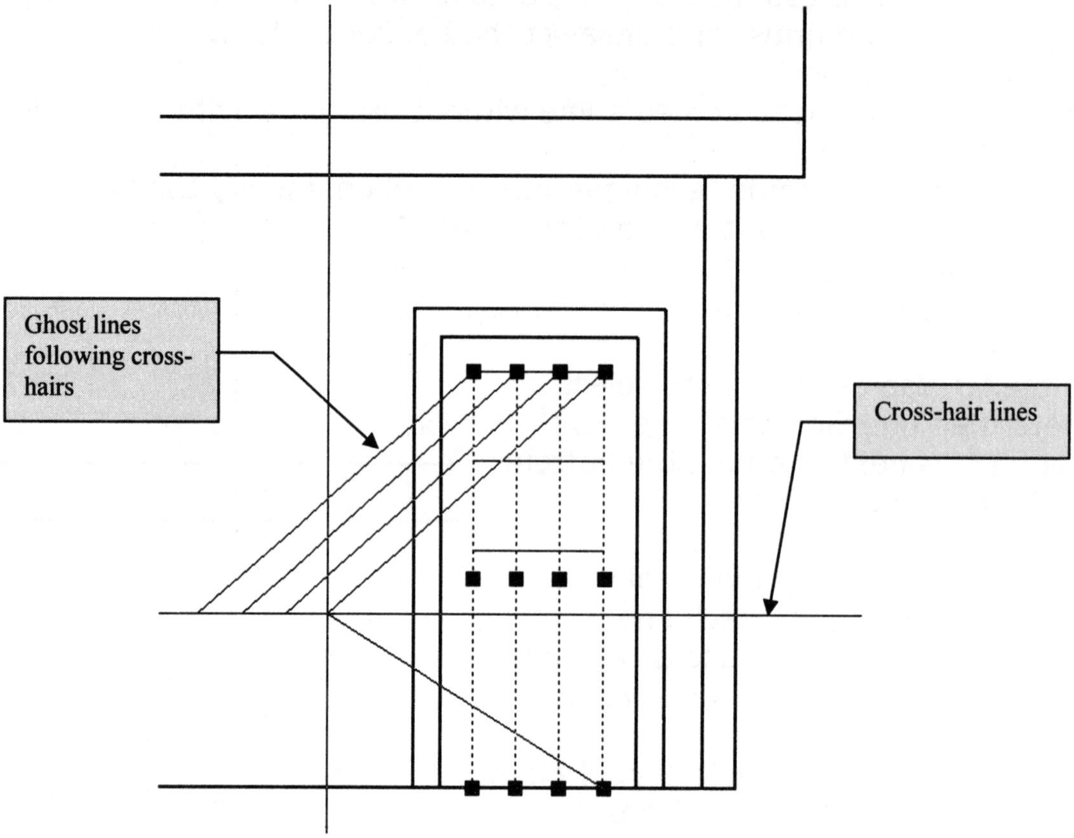

Figure 5-3.7 Modifying multiple grips at once

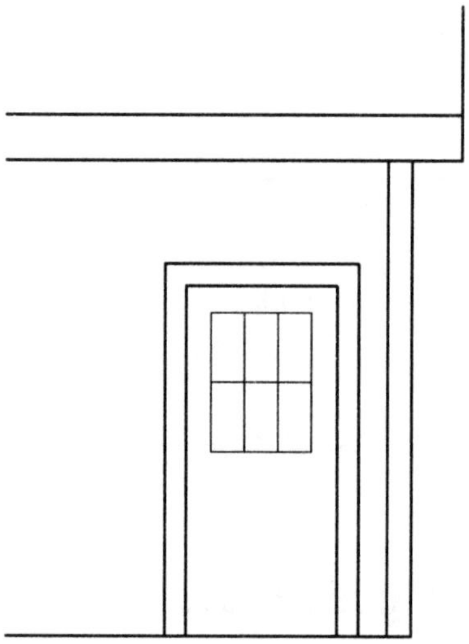

Figure 5-3.8 Completed door elevation

Before moving on, here are a few additional comments on the Grip Edit command that you may want to investigate further on your own.

- You select the middle Grip to move the entity.
- If you select a grip and then right-click, you get additional modification options. (Figure 5-3.9)
- The grip that is selected is, by default, the base point for the Mirror command.

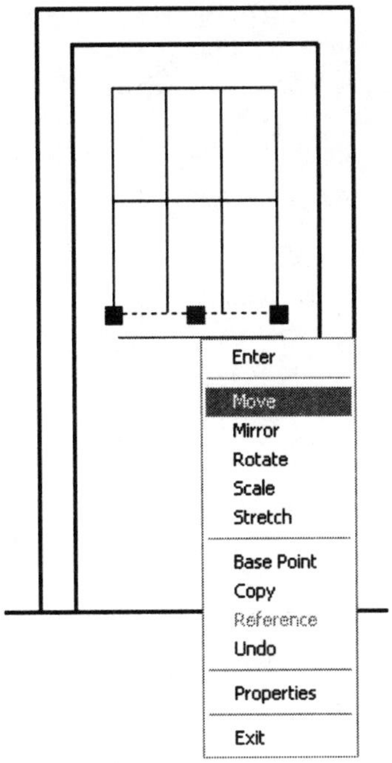

Figure 5-3.9
Right-click with grip selected

15. **Copy** the door just created to the other two locations (per the floor plans) – also make sure the doors are placed in the correct floor elevation (see **Figures 5-3.10 and 5-3.11**).

Figure 5-3.10 Door added and trimmed - South elevation

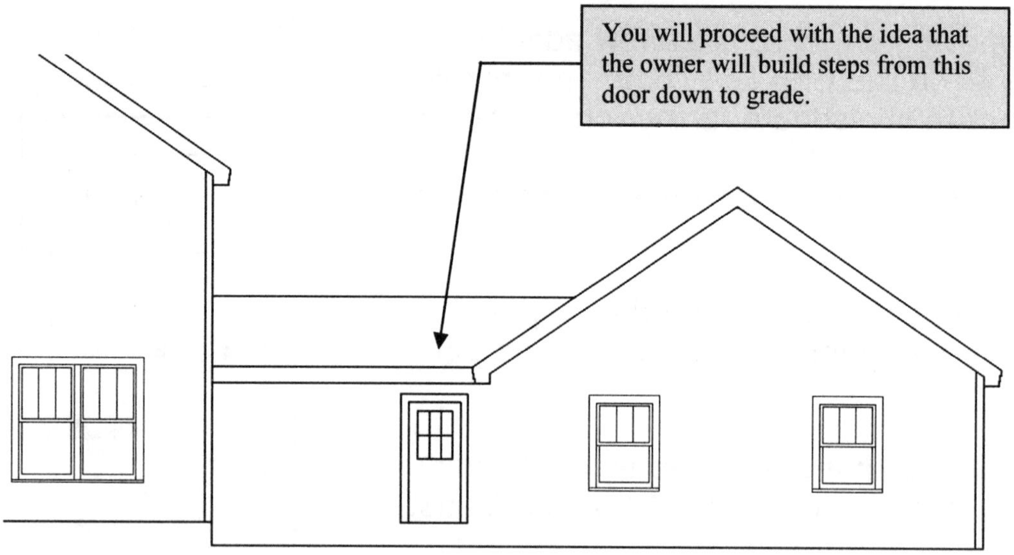

Figure 5-3.11 Door added - North elevation

Garage Doors:

16. Draw the **garage door** shown in **Figure 5-3.12**;
    a. All panels are to be equally spaced.
    b. Copy door to other location.
    c. Save your drawing!

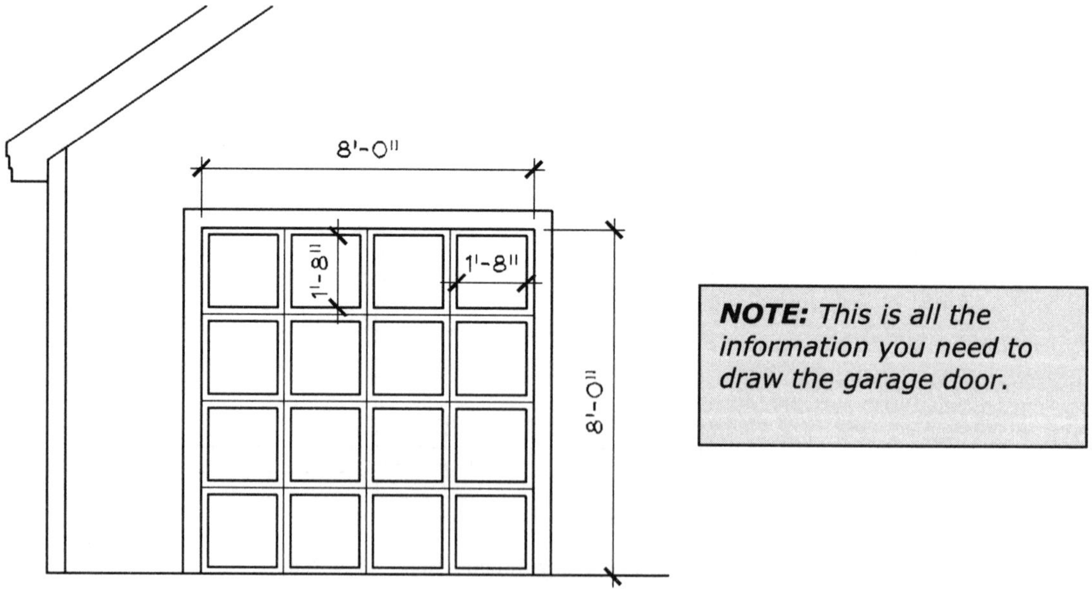

Figure 5-3.12 Garage Door

Exercise 5-4:
Chimney, Railing and Siding

In this exercise you will draw the chimneys, the railing at the porch and the siding and brick patterns.

Chimney:

1. Open your **Exterior Elevations** drawing.

2. Draw two vertical lines at the first floor that represent the width of the fireplace; refer to the first floor plan for location and width.

3. Draw the upper portion of the chimney as shown in Figure 5-4.1 (with the 2′-8″ portion centered on the first floor lines):
   a. Trim the fascia as shown.
   b. You will finish the bottom / porch roof intersection next.

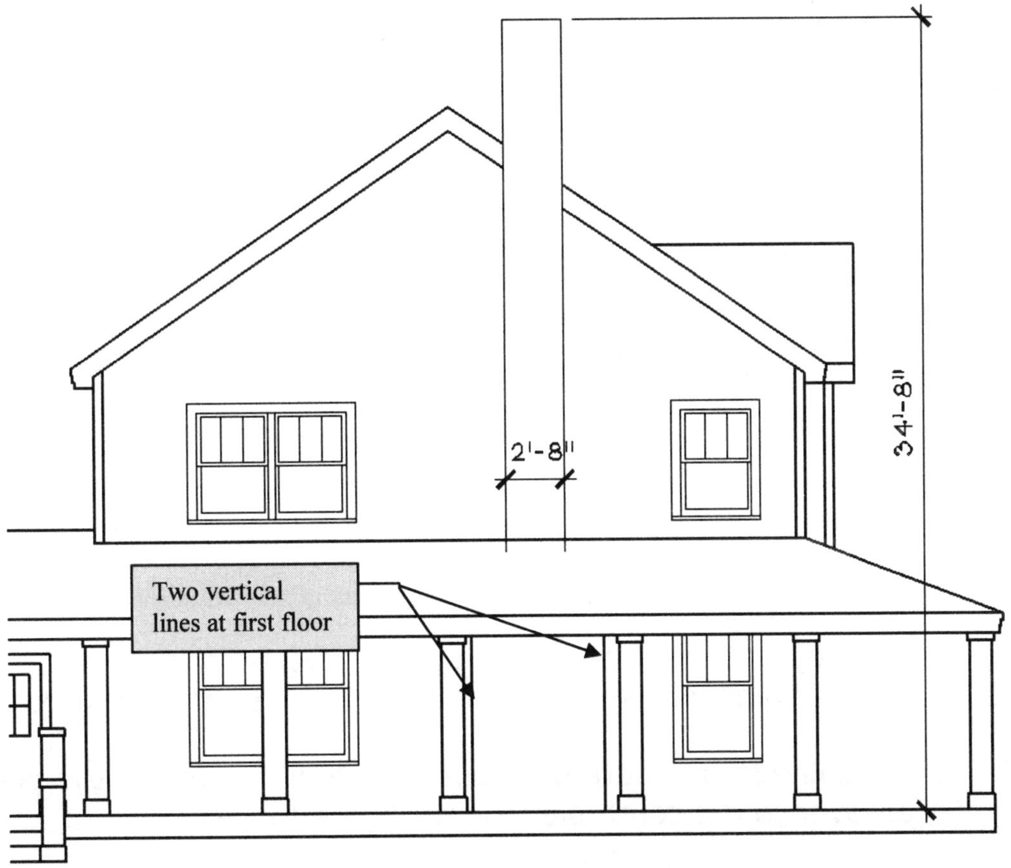

Figure 5-4.1 Chimney - South elevation

Next you will draw the side view of the chimney. Once you are done with this view you will be able to complete the front view.

4. One the east elevation, draw the chimney as shown in Figure 5-4.2.

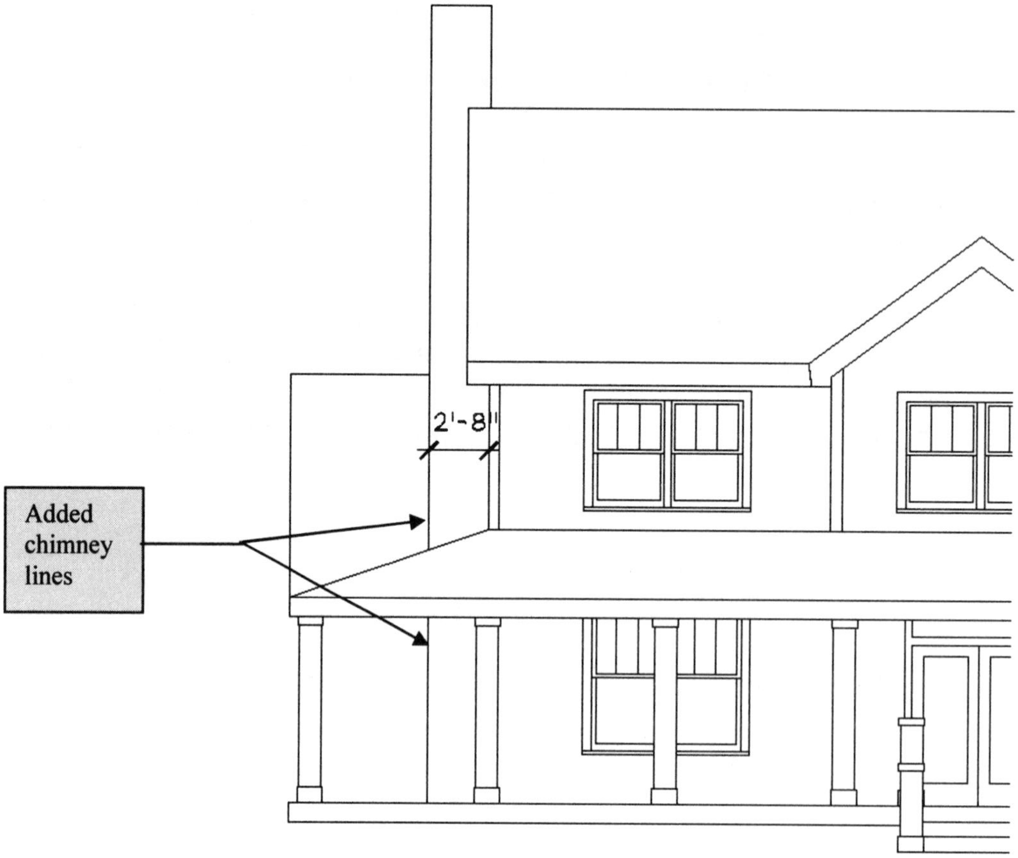

Figure 5-4.2 Chimney – East elevation

Now you can project a line from this elevation over to the south elevation to determine where the chimney intersects the porch roof.

5. Draw a line from where the upper chimney intersects the porch roof, over to the south elevation. (Figure 5-4.3)

Notice how the side view of the chimney helps determine where the chimney intersects the porch roof in the front view of the chimney.

Figure 5-4.3 Chimney - South elevation
FYI: *This technique is called Orthographic Projection.*

6. Complete the chimney as shown in Figure 5-4.4.

Figure 5-4.4 Chimney - South elevation

7. Zoom into the top of the chimney and draw a concrete chimney cap shown in Figure 5-4.5.

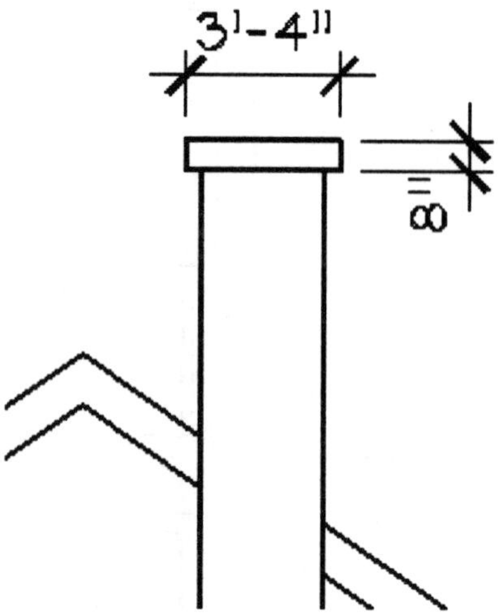

Figure 5-4.5 Chimney Cap

8. Copy the chimney cap to the other elevation.

9. Draw the chimney in the other two elevations. (Figures 5-4.6 and 5-4.7)

Figure 5-4.6 Chimney - West elevation

Figure 5-4.7 Chimney - North elevation

You will draw the other chimney later.

Chimney Caps!

You can buy prefabricated chimney caps in all shapes and sizes. Here are a couple web sites that sell / make them:

http://www.ejmcopper.com/chimneycaps.html
http://classiccopper.com/store
http://chimneycapdesign.com/

Porch Railing:

10. Create a *Layer* named **Railing** (color Red).
11. **Zoom** into to porch on North Elevation.
12. Draw the railing shown in Figure 5-4.8.

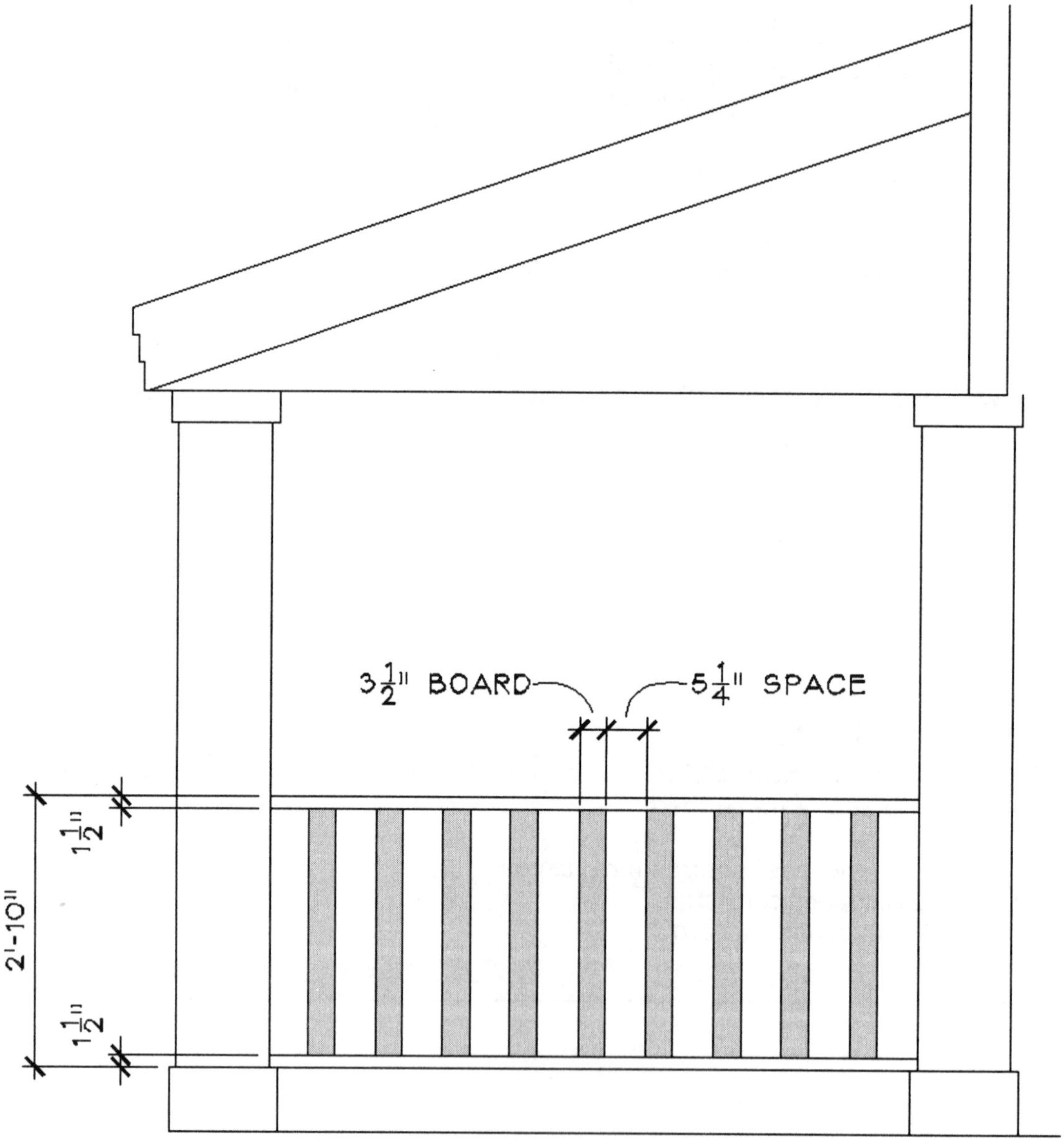

Figure 5-4.8 Railing - North elevation; shading added for clarity

13. Draw the rest of the railings on the other elevations. (Figures 5-4.9, 5-4.10)

Figure 5-4.9 Railing - East elevation

Figure 5-4.10 Railing - South elevation

14. **Trim** any lines that extend behind the 3 ½″ boards or the 1 ½″ top and bottom rail. (Figures 5-4.9 and 5-4.10)

Using the Hatch command:

The tool used in AutoCAD to draw patterns, such as bricks, siding and shingles, is called *Boundary Hatch*. This tool allows you to quickly fill an enclosed area with one of many predefined patterns. You will use this feature to add the shingles, siding and bricks to your elevations.

First you will draw the roof shingles.

15. **Zoom** in to the East Elevation.

16. Create a *Layer* called **Shingles**, color Blue.

17. You can start the **Hatch** command in one of the following ways:
    a. Click the Hatch icon on the *Draw* toolbar. 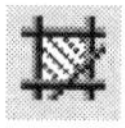
    b. Select Hatch from the *Draw* pull-down menu.
    c. Type bhatch at the *Command Prompt.*

You should now see the Boundary Hatch dialog. (Figure 5-4.11)

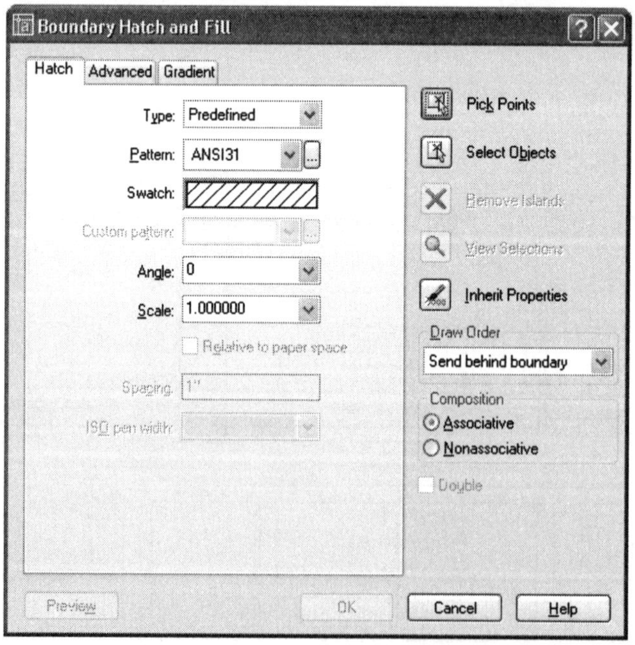

Figure 5-4.11 Boundary Hatch (also called Bhatch)

18. Click the down-arrow next to the Pattern name and select **AR-RSHKE.**

TIP: *If you do not know the name of the pattern you want, you click the "…" button next to the name drop-down; then you are able to select from several thumbnail images.*

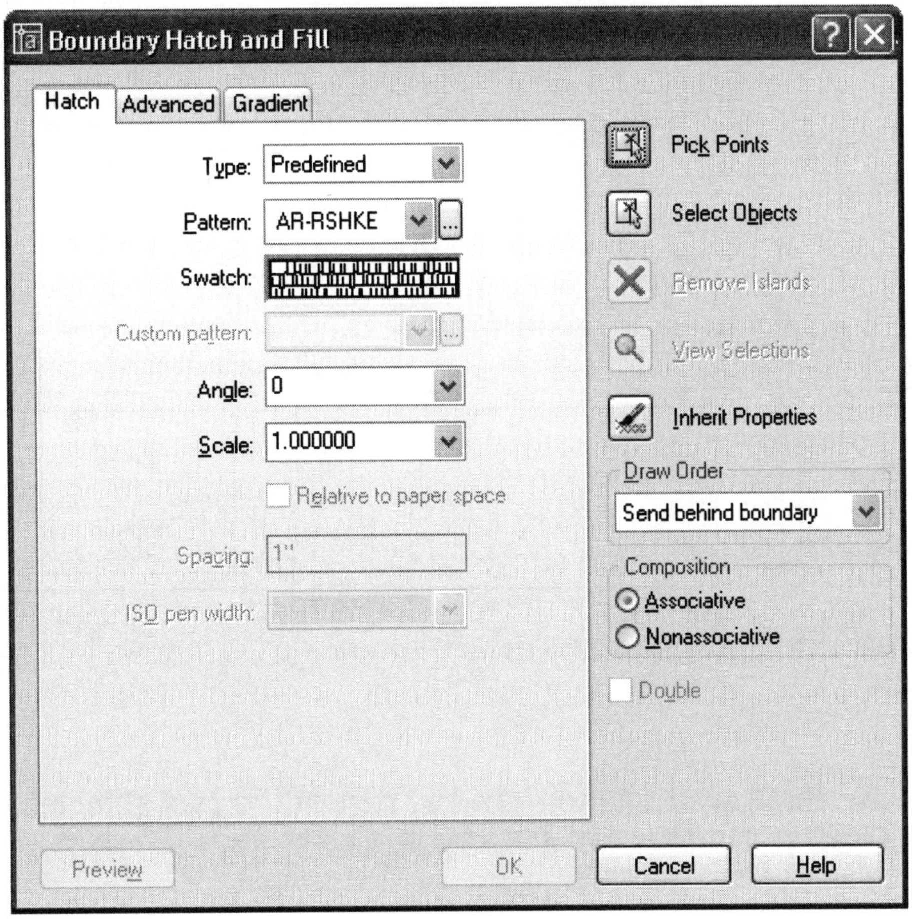

Figure 5-4.12 Boundary Hatch; pattern selected

Next you will pick a point in the drawing that is completely enclosed.

19. Click the **Pick Points** button.

20. Click anywhere in the roof, see **Figure 5-4.13**.

21. After picking an area, **right-click** and select **OK.**

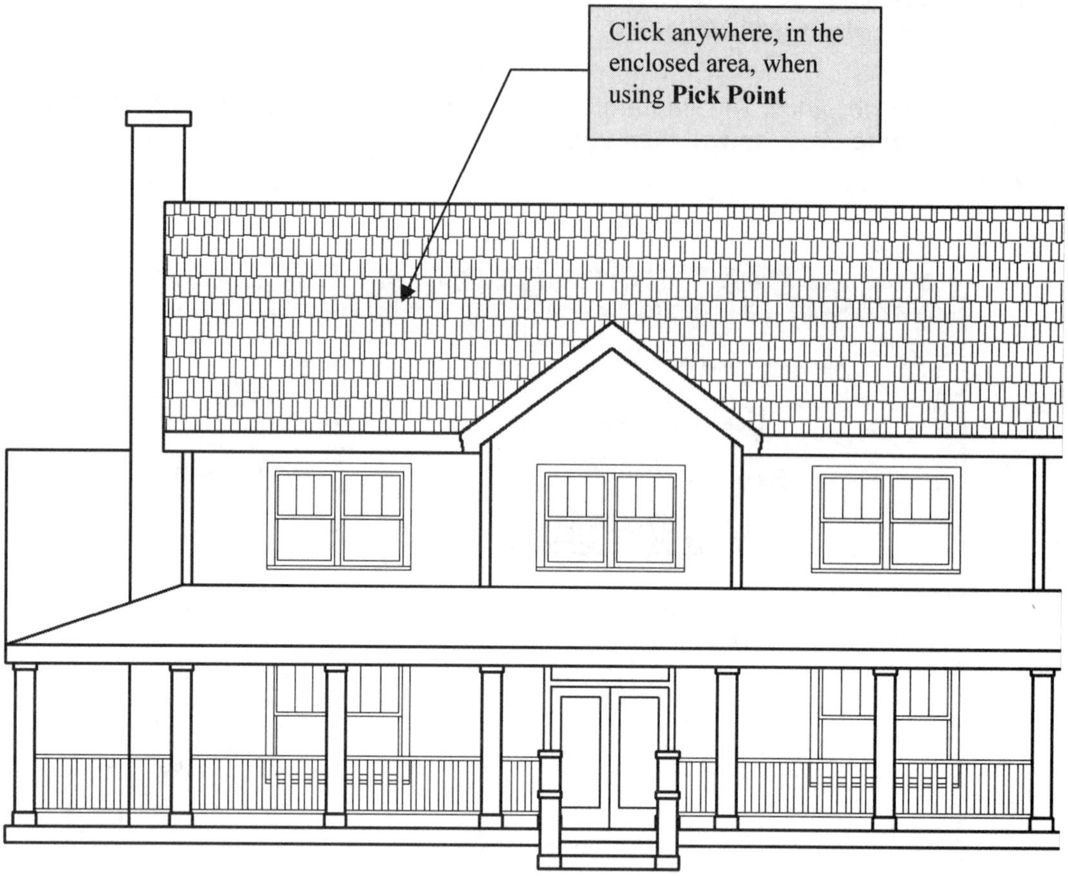

Figure 5-4.13 Boundary Hatch; one enclosed section hatched

22. Use the **Hatch** tool to draw the rest of the roof shingles.
    TIP: *Only hatch one area at a time; it is easier later when you have to re-hatch an area due to a change.*
    (See Figures 5-4.17 – 19.)

Next you will draw the brick at the chimney.

23. Use the **Hatch** tool to draw the brick at the chimney:
    a. Do not draw the brick pattern behind the railing; this would create too much clutter.
    b. Use the pattern named: **AR-BRSTD.**
    c. See fully hatched **Figures 5-4.17 – 19.**
    d. Create on *Layer* named **Brick.**

Finally you will draw the siding; this will be a little different.

24. Create a *Layer* named **Siding**, color Blue.

25. Initiate the **Hatch** command.

26. Select **User Defined** next to *Type.*

27. Next to *Spacing* enter **4** (this means the lines will be 4" apart). See Figure 5-4.14.

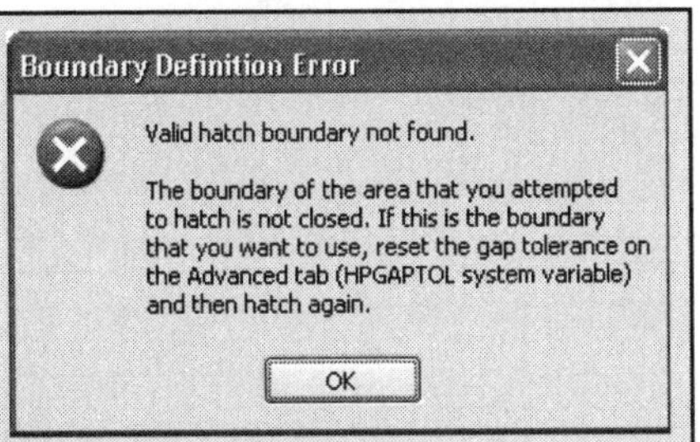

TIP:
If you use the "Pick Points" button and click in an area that is not closed, you will get this error message.
It may not be obvious where the opening is in the area you wish to hatch. You need to zoom in on each intersection and corner to find the opening. Finally, you ""close" the opening with a line of trim.

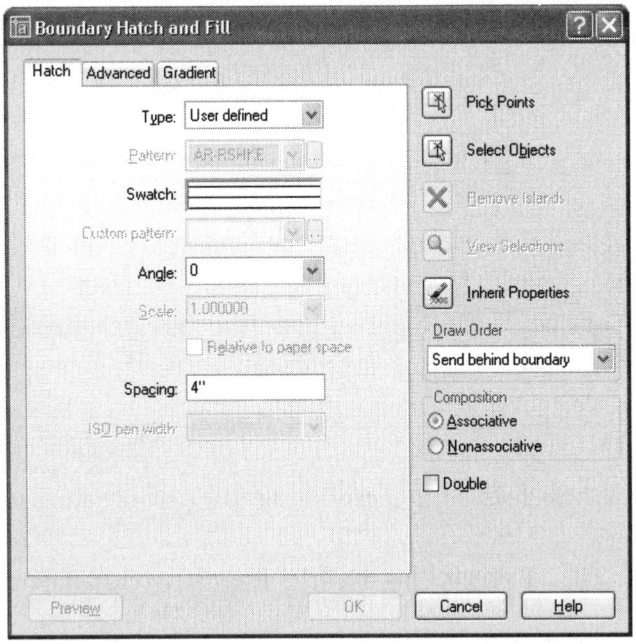

Figure 5-4.14 Boundary Hatch; User Defined pattern

28. Zoom into the west elevation and use the **Pick Points** button to select one area at a time to hatch with the siding pattern (see Figure 5-4.15).

Notice (in Figure 5-4.15) the hatching is visible with in portions of the window block. AutoCAD does not do a good job hatching around blocks with several lines in it, like your window block. Next you take a look at resolving this problem.

Figure 5-4.15 Boundary Hatch; User Defined pattern used to draw 4" siding

29. **Erase** the siding hatch around the windows.

30. Draw three lines that extend from within the window to out past the building. (Figure 5-4.16)

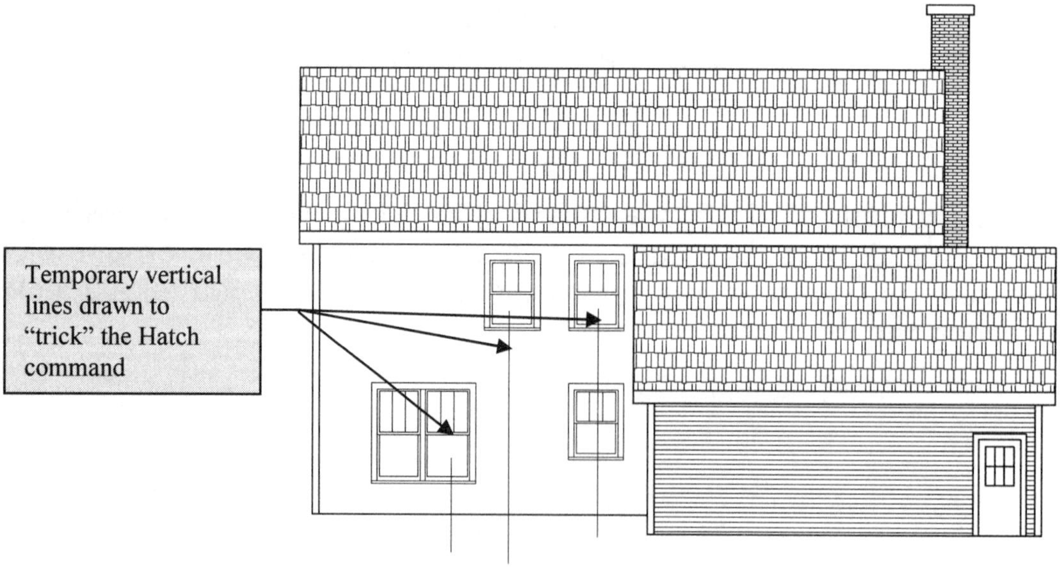

Figure 5-4.16 Vertical lines drawn to "trick" the hatch command

31. Now use the **Hatch** command to draw the siding in that area again. (Figure 5-4.17)

Figure 5-4.17 Vertical lines drawn to "trick" the hatch command

Notice the Hatch does not extend into the block anymore.

32. **Erase** the three temporary vertical lines.

33. Use this technique to draw the rest of the siding; hatching one area at a time (see Figures 5-4.18 – 19).

TIP!
You can double-click on a hatch pattern to display the Hatch dialog box. This dialog is the same as the one used in creating the hatch pattern. Here you can change the pattern or adjust the scale and / or spacing.

Figure 5-4.18 Hatching complete - East elevation

Figure 5-4.19 Hatching complete - North elevation

Figure 5-4.20 Hatching complete - South elevation

Figure 5-4.21 Hatching complete - West elevation

Self-Exam:

The following questions can be used as a way to check your knowledge of this lesson. The answers can be found at the bottom of this page.

1. You do not need to create a block if the item to be drawn only exists once in the drawing. (T/F)

2. You can use Grip Edit to adjust the length of a line. (T/F)

3. Use the Hatch command to draw the brick pattern in elevation. (T/F)

4. When drawing the exterior elevations, the horizontal location for the windows and doors came from the ____________________ drawings.

5. All doors go on the ______________ layer.

Review Questions:

The following questions may be assigned by your instructor as a way to assess your knowledge of this section. Your instructor has the answers to the review questions.

1. The Hatch command does not have very many patterns to select from. (T/F)

2. Redefining a Block causes all instances to automatically update. (T/F)

3. You can project lines from another elevation and from the plans to locate where the chimney intersects the sloping roof below it – also referred to as orthographic projection. (T/F)

4. Name the command that links a drawing to the current drawing:

   ______________ ________________.

5. You can double-click on a hatched area to edit its properties. (T/F)

6. This icon (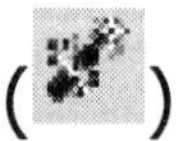) allows you to ___________________ a block.

7. A 6/12 pitch means; for every 12"__________ the roof rises 6"__________

8. Name the Hatch pattern used to draw the brick ___________________

9. What is the most often used door thickness? _____________________.

10. You should use a Block when something in the drawing is repetitive and exactly the same. (T/F)

Self-Exam Answers:
1 - T, **2** - T, **3** - T, **4** – Floor Plan, **5** – DOORS

Additional Tasks:

Task 5-1 (Grade Line)

Draw the grade lines shown in the images below.

Create a layer named **Grade** and set its color to Magenta.

Use the **Polyline** command via this icon on the Draw toolbar: 

After picking your first point, type **W** for width; enter **4"** (for both the starting width and end width).
Alternatively, you can draw the polyline and then adjust the width afterwards using the Pedit command.

Draw the grade as close as possible to that shown below. Extend the lines at the corners of the building down to the grade line.

All grade lines should be at the same vertical location for common corners on each of the two elevations showing that corner.

Commands used: Polyline, Pedit, Layer Manager

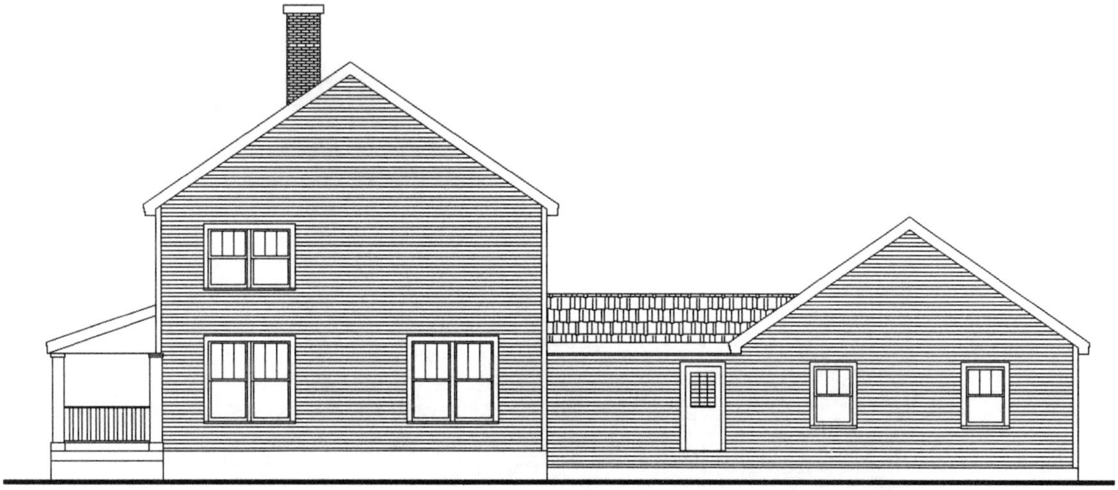

Task 5-1 (1) North Elevation with grade line added; grade line is approx. 2'-6" below porch floor

Task 5-1 (2) East Elevation with grade line added; grade line is approx. 2′-6″ below porch floor

Task 5-1 (3) South Elevation with grade line added; grade line is approx. 2′-6″ below porch floor

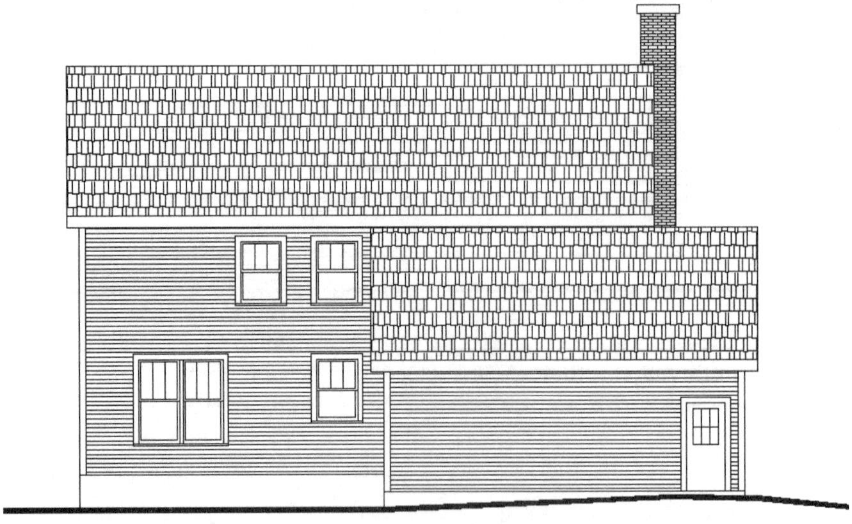

Task 5-1 (4) West Elevation with grade line added

Task 5-2 (Draw the other Chimney)
Draw the other chimney based on reference lines from the floor plan and other elevations. Draw as much as you can in each elevation and then use orthographic projection to complete the task.

Draw the same chimney cap and use the same hatch pattern used to draw the first chimney.

Commands used: Line, Trim, Extend, Hatch

Task 5-2 (1) South Elevation with other chimney added

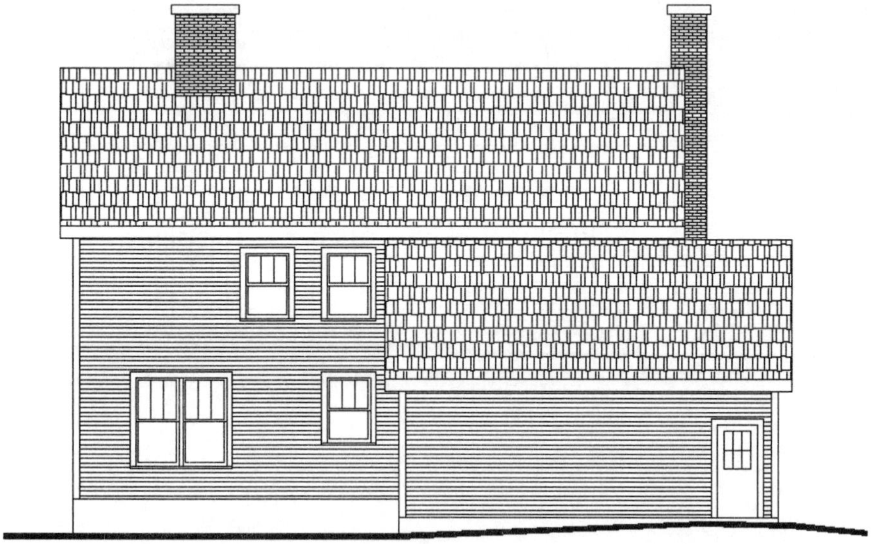

Task 5-2 (2) West Elevation with other chimney added

Task 5-3 (Print content from a web site)

Using your internet web browser, print one page of information from one of the web sites mentioned in Lesson 5.

ONLY HAND IN ONE PAGE.

Task 5-4 (Adding foundation lines)

First you will draw the lines and then adjust the lines so they look dashed.

FYI: Dashed lines typically represent lines that are hidden from view but are still helpful to show.

1. Create a *layer* named **Foundation**, set its color to Red.

2. Draw the lines as shown below (4 images), and then proceed to Step 3 for instruction on making the lines dashed.

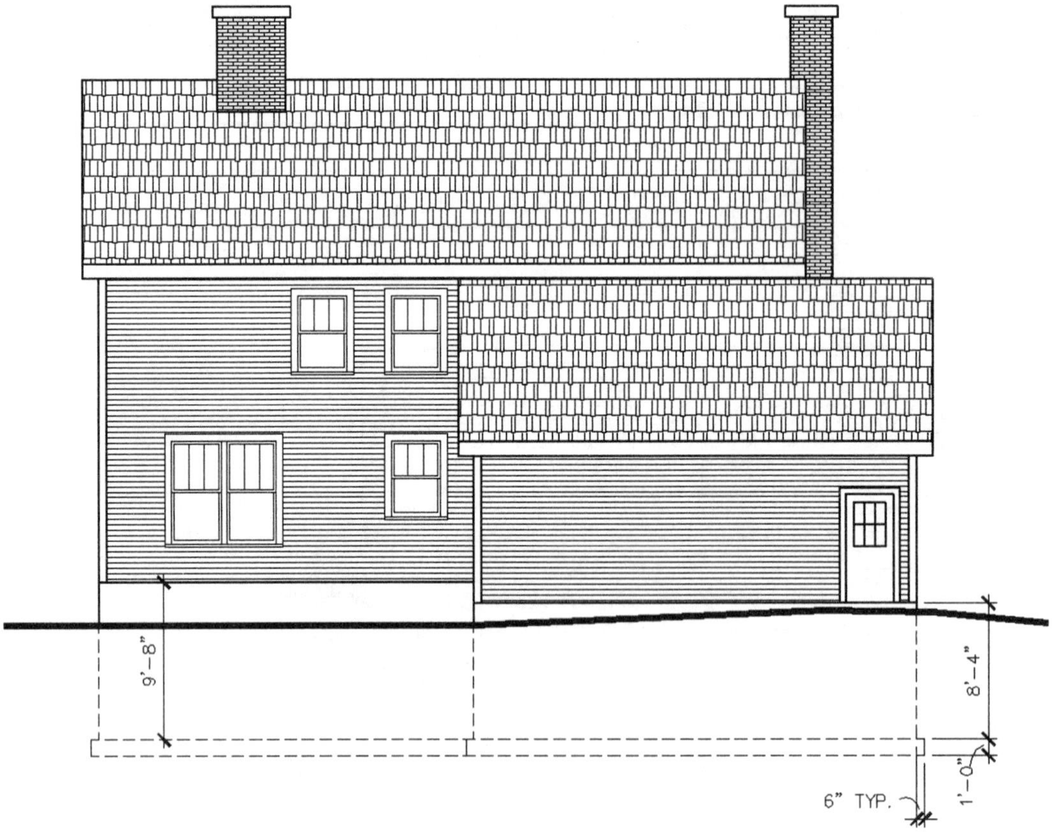

Task 5-4 (1) West Elevation with foundation lines added

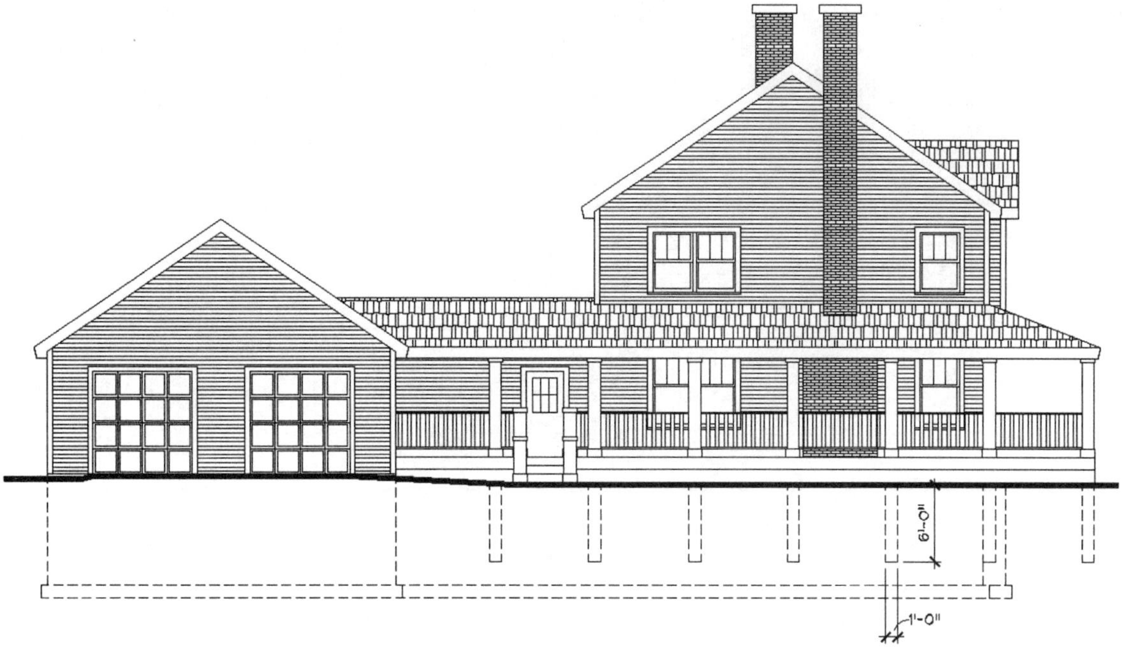

Task 5-4 (2) South Elevation with foundation lines added

Task 5-4 (3) East Elevation with foundation lines added

Task 5-4 (4) North Elevation with foundation lines added

Creating dashed lines:

3. Open the **Layer Manager.**

4. In the **Foundation** (layer name) row, click the linetype name (which should be Continuous at the moment).

You are now in the Select Linetype dialog.

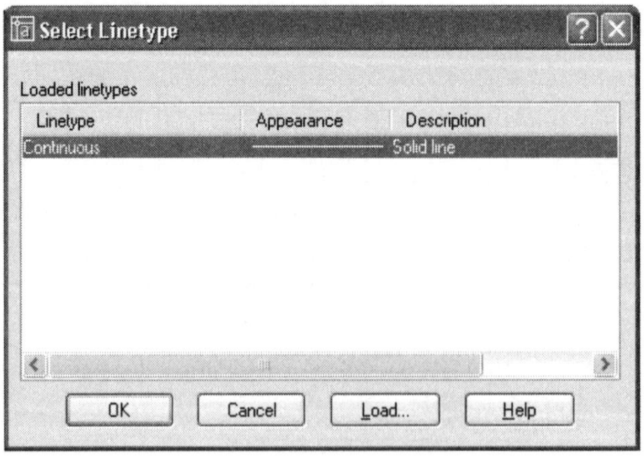

You will notice that the current drawing only has one lineweight loaded. Next you will Load another linetype into the current drawing.

5. Click the **Load...** button.

You are now in the Load or Reload Linetypes dialog.

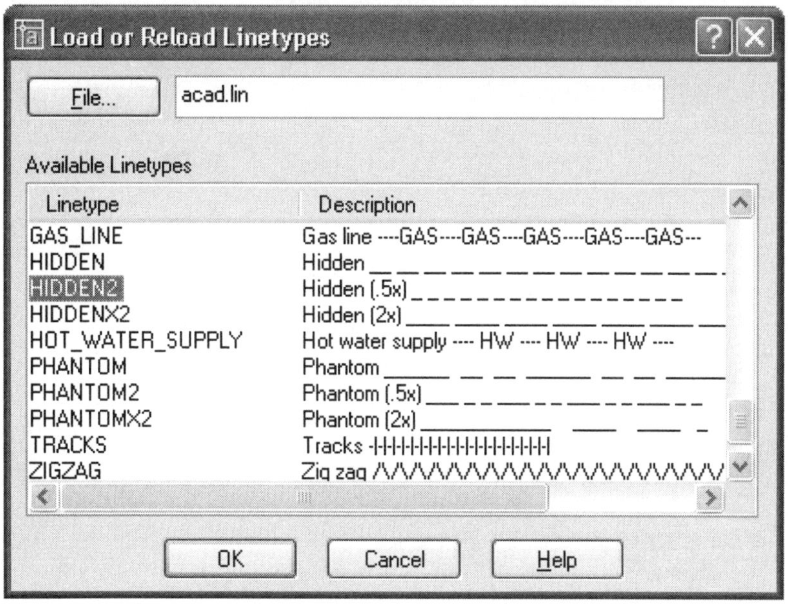

6. Scroll down to the **HIDDEN2** linetype; select it and click **OK.**

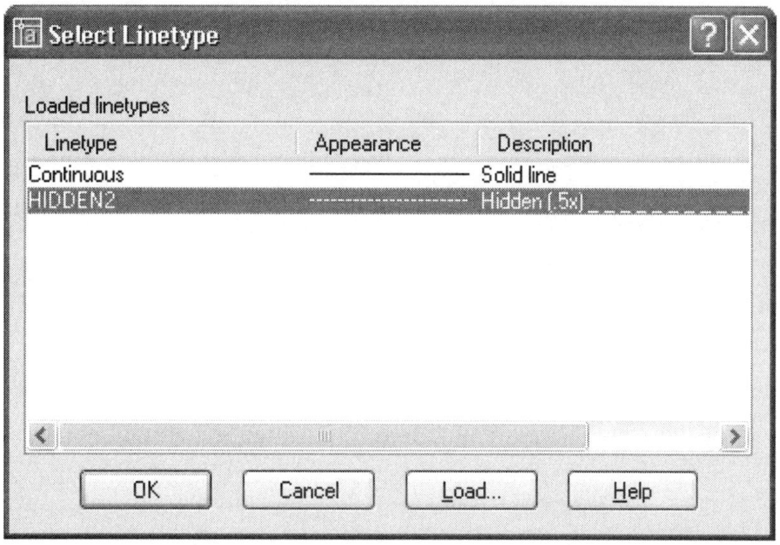

7. Select **HIDDEN2** and click **OK.**

8. Click **OK** to close the *Layer Manager.*

9. Type **LTSCALE** and **Enter**, then type **48** and then **ENTER.**

10. Type **REGEN** and then **Enter.**

Notes:

Lesson 6
Residential Project: SECTIONS::

In this lesson you will create simple building and wall sections. A section helps the builder understand how the structure is to be constructed; it also shows the vertical relationships, such as floor and ceiling locations.

Exercise 6-1:
Building Sections

Introduction

Building sections show an overall section thru the structure.

The building sections are typically the same scale as the exterior elevations.

Because the building section generally has the same outline as one of the exterior elevations, you can copy the elevation and use it as a starting point for you building section.

You will do this next.

Building Section Outline

1. **Open** your drawing named **Exterior Elevations.dwg.**

2. **Save-As** to a drawing file named **Building Section.dwg.**

3. **Zoom-In** on the South elevation. Figure 6-1.1

4. *Erase* and *Trim* all inner lines to create an outline of the building as shown in **Figure 6-1.2.**

Figure 6-1.1 South elevation drawn in previous lesson

Typical Non-Plan Layers

Non-plan drawings typically have a handful of Layers whose names represent the thickness of the lines drawn on that Layer. These drawings do not need the same level of control as floor plans so the Layering system is simplified (e.g., you would never need to freeze a layer that contained the steel beams).

The general concept with lineweights is this:

Things in Section	Lines should be heavy
Things in elevation	Lines should be a middle-of-the-road (medium) lineweight
Hatch patterns	These are the lightest lines

5. Create the following Layers:

a. **G-Detl-Hevy**	White	Heavy lines
b. **G-Detl-Medm**	Green	Medium lines
c. **G-Detl-Lite**	Red	Light lines

6. Modify the remaining lines (in Figure 6-1.2) to the Layers just created (i.e., change the outline to G-Detl-Hevy, the shingle hatch to G-Detl-Lite, etc.).

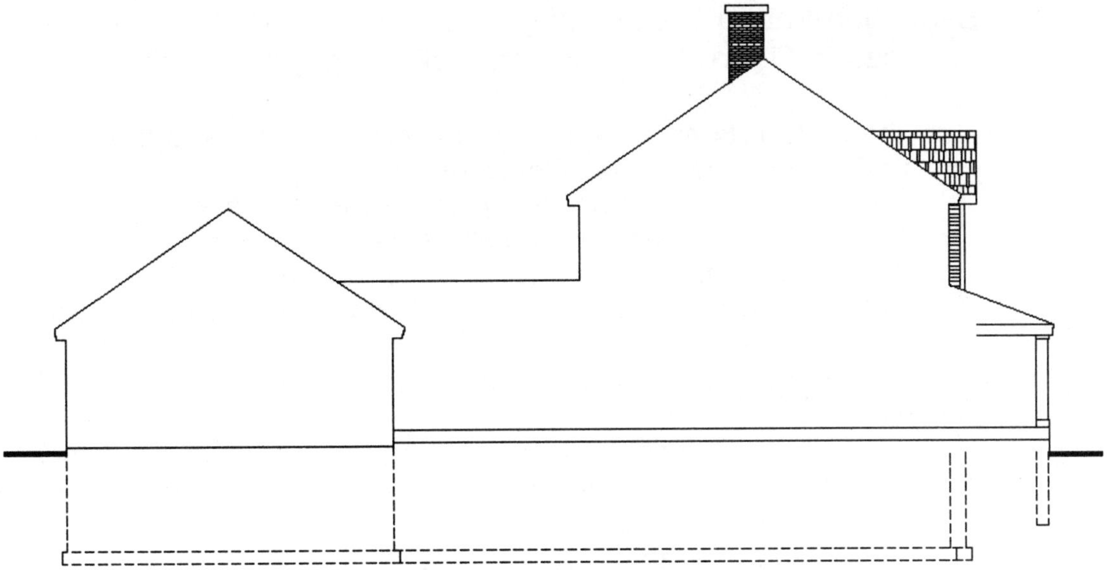

Figure 6-1.2 Modified South Elevation; outline to start building section

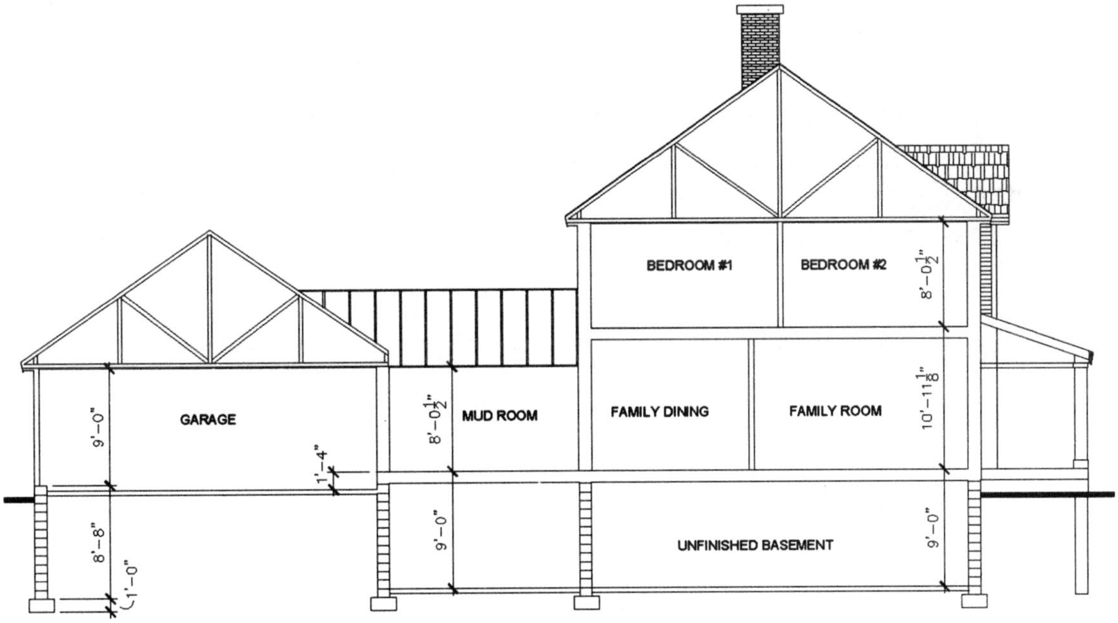

Figure 6-1.3 Building Section

7. Begin generating the building section based on the information provided in Figure 6-1.3 and the following guidelines:

   a. The wall thicknesses and locations are to be derived from the Xref'ed floor plans (See Figure 6-1.4)
   NOTE: *The heavy dashed line represents the section location.*
   b. The first and second floor thickness is 11".
   c. The two trusses (shown in elevation) have equally spaced vertical members with the diagonals drawn last (all 2x4 framing – i.e., 3 ½").
   d. Trusses shown over Mud Room are 2x4's (i.e., 1 ½") at 2'-0" o.c.
   e. The horizontal lines in the foundation wall are 8" apart; which represents the individual concrete masonry units (CMU).
   f. Draw the dimensions shown.
   g. The garage / basement slab is 5" thick.
   h. Add the room labels (you can copy them from the floor plans).
   i. Extend the truss lines into the overhang/fascia area (simple).

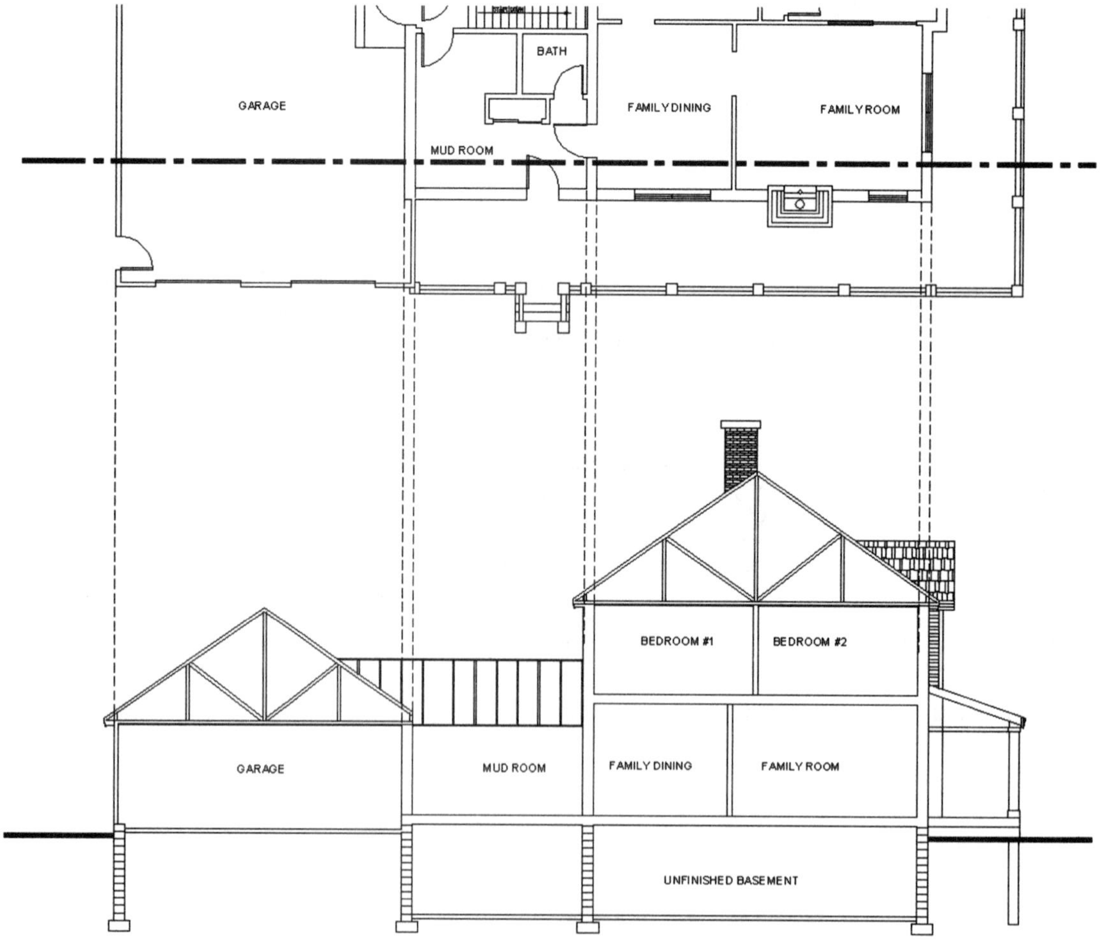

Figure 6-1.4 Building Section; with Xref'ed plan and temp. reference lines

Exercise 6-2:
Typical Wall Section

Introduction

Wall sections are similar to building sections in that they show how a building is constructed and the vertical relationships (e.g., floor-to-floor heights). The difference between a wall section and a building section is implied by their names; a wall section is just one wall in section; a building section is a section though the entire building. Wall sections are also drawn at a larger scale than building sections.

On smaller projects, where the building section can be drawn larger, you may not need a wall section because everything can be clearly drawn and noted on the building sections.

The wall sections are typically as large as possible, so that it will still fit on the sheet. Occasionally a large repetitious area will removed with break lines to allow the section to be larger (see Figure 6-2.1).

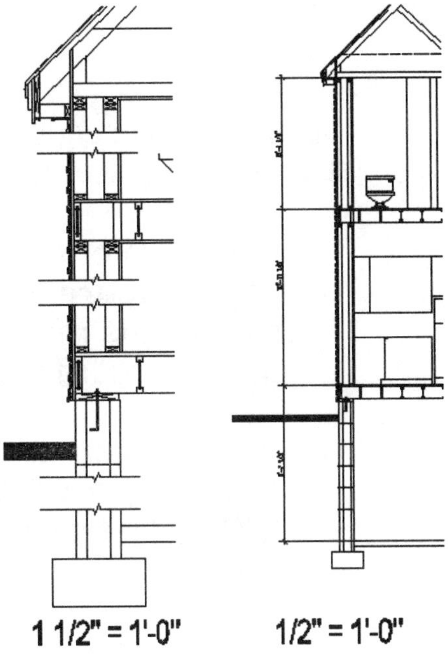

Figure 6-2.1 Wall section with break lines and section with out. Note that section with break lines is larger.

Wall sections are usually started after the building sections have been substantially developed. You can use the linework from the building section to start your wall section.

You will do this next.

Wall Section Linework

1. **Open** your drawing named **Building Section.dwg.**

2. **Save-As** to a drawing file named **Wall Section.dwg.**

3. *Erase* and *Trim* portions of the building section so it looks similar to the ½" = 1'-0" wall section shown in Figure 6-2.1. *Tip: draw a temporary vertical line to trim too.*

4. Use the same *Layers* as Exercise 6-1.

You are now ready to begin developing the wall section. Your section will look similar to Figure 6-2.2. You will use the information in the enlarged details, Figures 6-2.3 and 6-2.4, to draw the wall section.

5. Draw the wall section shown in **Figure 6-2.2** per the following information:

   a. Use the information in the roof edge detail (**Figure 6-2.3**) to draw items such as the roof sheathing and gypsum board the correct size.

   b. Use the information in the rim joist detail (**Figure 6-2.4**) to draw the joist, siding, floor sheathing and sill plate.

   c. Draw the second floor rim joist condition based on the information provided in the similar condition identified in item b above (Figure 6-2.4).

   d. Do not add any notes or dimensions at this time.

6. **Save** your drawing.

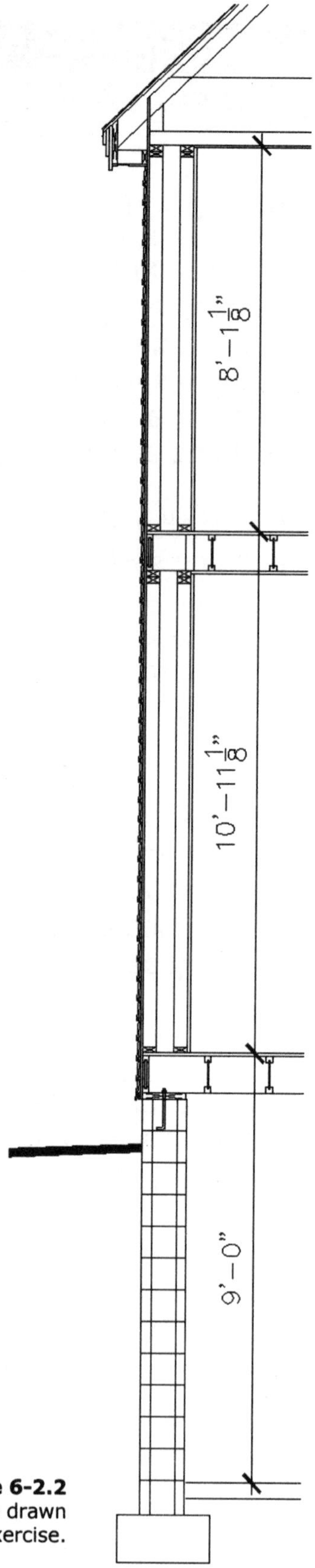

Figure 6-2.2
Wall section to be drawn in this exercise.

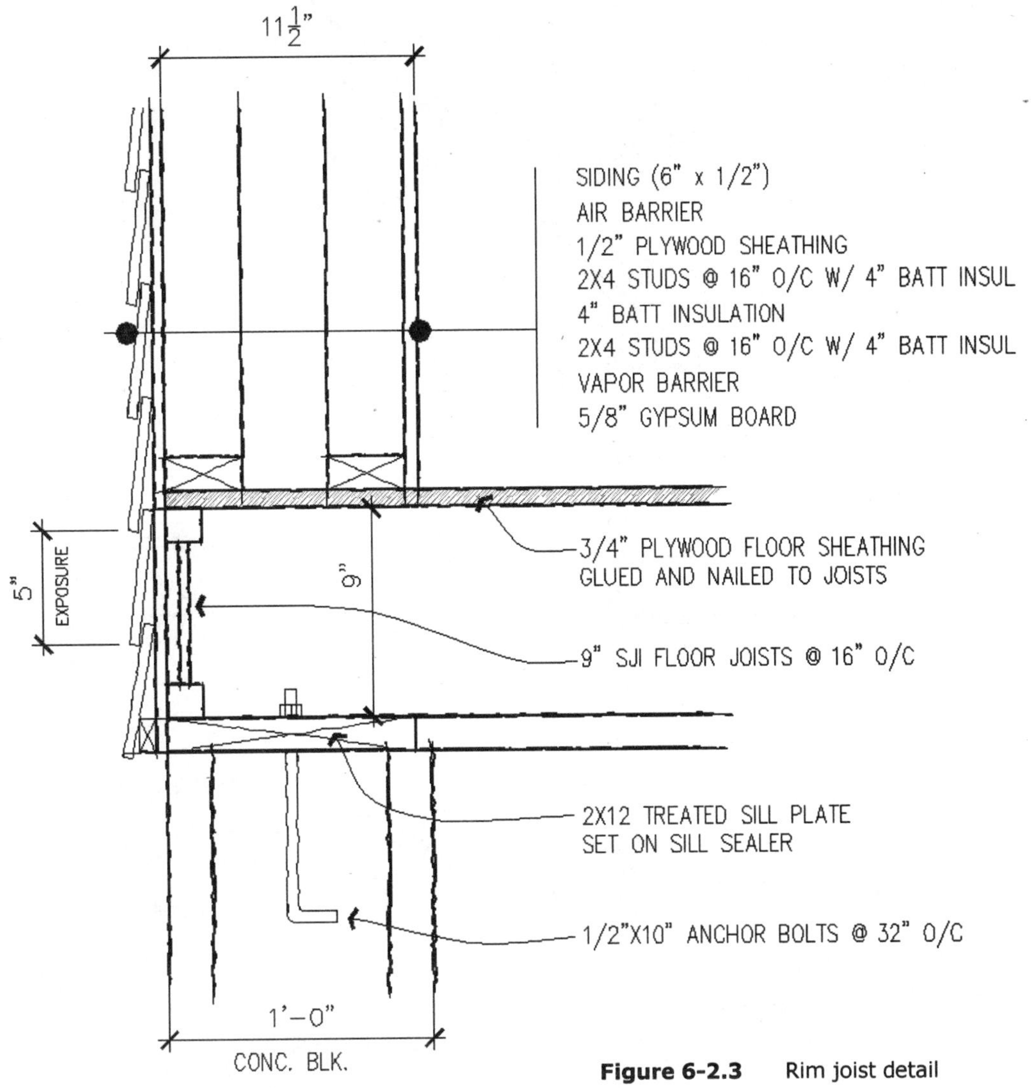

Figure 6-2.3 Rim joist detail

Notes on the rim joist sketch

The 2x12 sill plate creates a flat surface for the joists to sit on and be nailed too. The sill plate is set on a foam sill sealer that fills the voids between the irregular concrete block and the smooth wood; which helps to decrease air infiltration. The L-shaped anchor bolts are set in grout and help hold the sill plate down (with a nut and washer on top).

The first siding board rests on a "starter strip" which places the board at the correct angle (which matches the other boards above).

The air barrier goes on just before the siding; it helps to reduce air infiltration into the building. Air barriers allow moisture pass through - this is not a vapor barrier.

The vapor barrier goes just behind the finish (on the warm side of the wall). This prevents moisture from condensing within the wall. Avoid double vapor barriers as the moisture cannot escape and creates mold. This is why air barriers are not a vapor barrier.

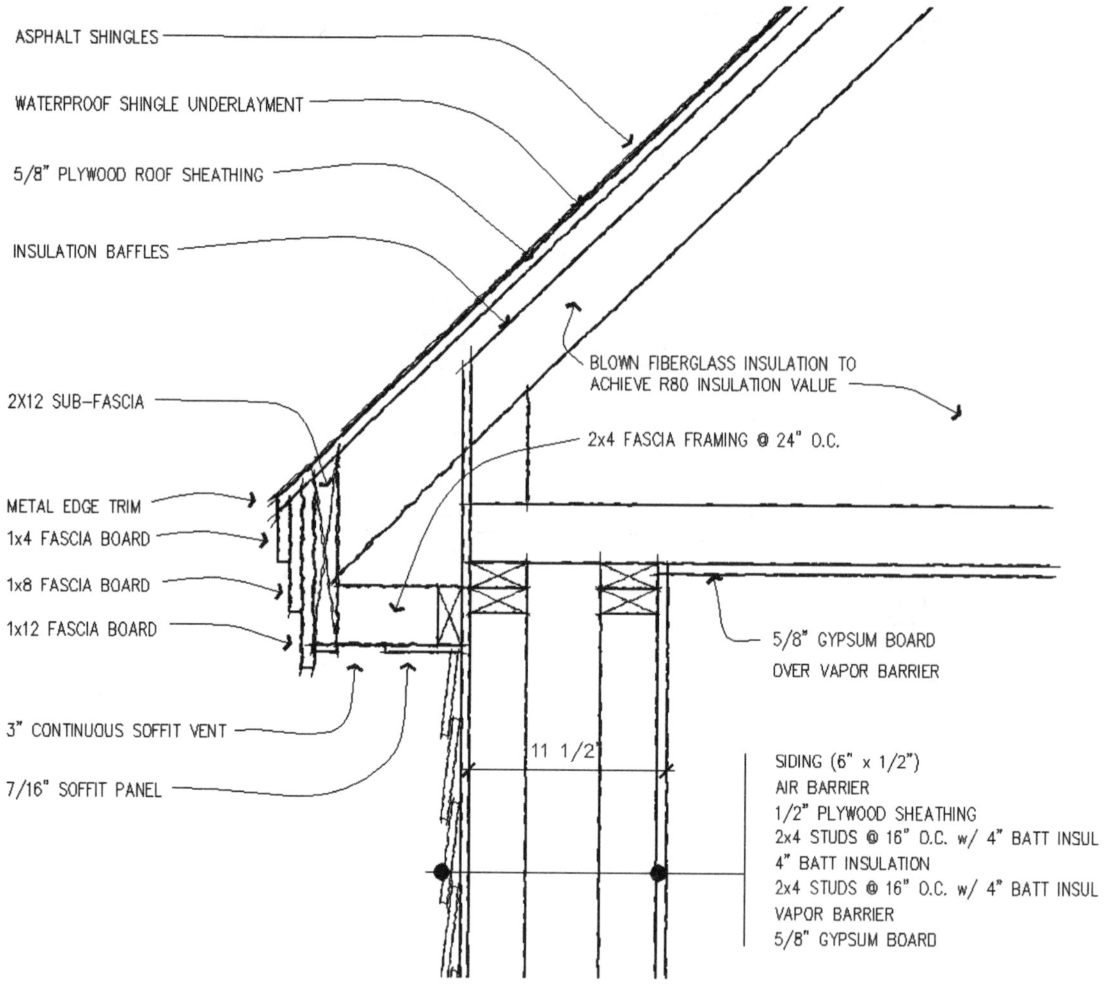

Figure 6-2.4 Roof edge detail

Notes on the roof edge sketch

The "waterproof shingle underlayment" (i.e., Ice and Water Shield) is required on overhangs and valleys in colder climates. This helps prevent melted snow, which freezes at overhangs and then backs up under the shingles, from leaking though the roof sheathing. This product is occasionally applied over the entire roof in place of felt to create a second layer of waterproofing on the roof.

The insulation baffles are thin panels attached between the trusses. The baffles maintain an air space between the roof sheathing and the blown insulation.

The soffit vent allows outside air into the attic space. This helps the attic space to maintain the same outside air temperature, which reduces the possibility of condensation at the shingles / sheathing plane.

Similar to the wall condition, the vapor barriers go just behind the finish (on the warm side of the ceiling) – between the truss and the gypsum board in this case.

Exercise 6-3: Adding Annotation to Wall Section

In this exercise you will add notes and dimensions to your wall section

1. **Open** "wall section.dwg" drawing file.

2. Create a new *Layer* named **G-Anno-Text**; set the color to *Cyan.*

You have to determine what scale you will be printing the section at before adding notes and dimensions. The largest scale that will fit on a 24"x36" sheet is ½" = 1'-0". Looking back to Figure 4-4.11, on page 4-46, you can get the multiplier for the text. Then you take the multiplier x the desired [printed] text height (3/16") to get the "model space" text height. Remember, in "model space" you are drawing text on top of a full scale wall section, so the text needs to be scaled up proportionally.

Thus: 8 x 3/16" = 1 1/2"

So all the text for any 1 1/2" = 1'-0" drawing should be **1 ½"** high.

> **Tip:**
> You may want to stop and spend a few minutes to figure out what the text height should be for each scale and add another column with that information to Figure 4-4.11 (on page 4-46) for quick reference in the future.

You can change this in the text editor, but AutoCAD also has a variable that can be adjusted for the text height. You will try this next.

3. At the *Command Prompt* type **textsize** and then press **Enter.**

4. Type **1.5** (or 1-1/2) and then press **Enter.**

The default text size is now set to 1 ½".

Finally, before you begin adding notes and dimensions, you need to set the *Dimscale* variable (discussed in exercise 4-4); this will make sure the dimensions and arrows on your *Leaders* are the correct size.

5. At the *Command Prompt* type **dimscale** and them press **Enter.**

6. Type **8** and then press **Enter.**

Next you will use the *Mtext* command and the *Leader* command to add notes to your wall section.

The *Leader* command has the ability to add the text as the final step in drawing the *Leader* (which is the default setting). However, this makes it difficult to properly align the notes. Thus, it is recommended that you add the notes first, using the *Mtext* command, and then add the *Leaders* (with the text option turned off; see tip on page 4-53).

One method for aligning the text, as required in the next step, is to use the Mtext command to add the first note, and then use the copy command (with Ortho on) to create the remaining notes.

Once you have all the notes (or at least most) added you can draw the Leaders.

7. Add the notes shown in **Figure 6-3.1**:
   a. Use the **Mtext** command.
   b. Place all text on layer **G-Anno-Text.**
   c. All text to be aligned as shown.
   d. The *Leaders* will be added in the next step.
   e. If the notes on Figure 6-3.1 are difficult to read you can look at Figures 6-2.3 and 6-2.4 for the same notes.

8. Now draw the **Leaders** (make sure the current layer is set to G-Anno-Text - See **Figure 6-3.2.**

9. Add the four dimensions shown in Figure 6-3.3; draw them on *Layer* **G-Anno-Dims** (color 30).

10. **Save** your drawing.

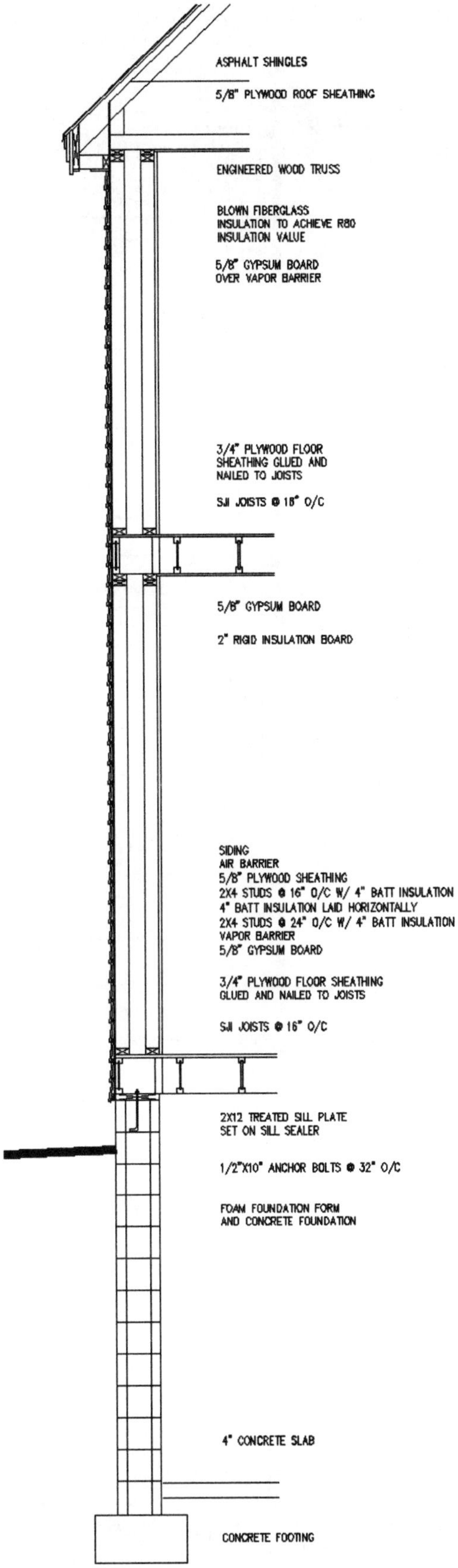

Figure 6-3.1 Notes added

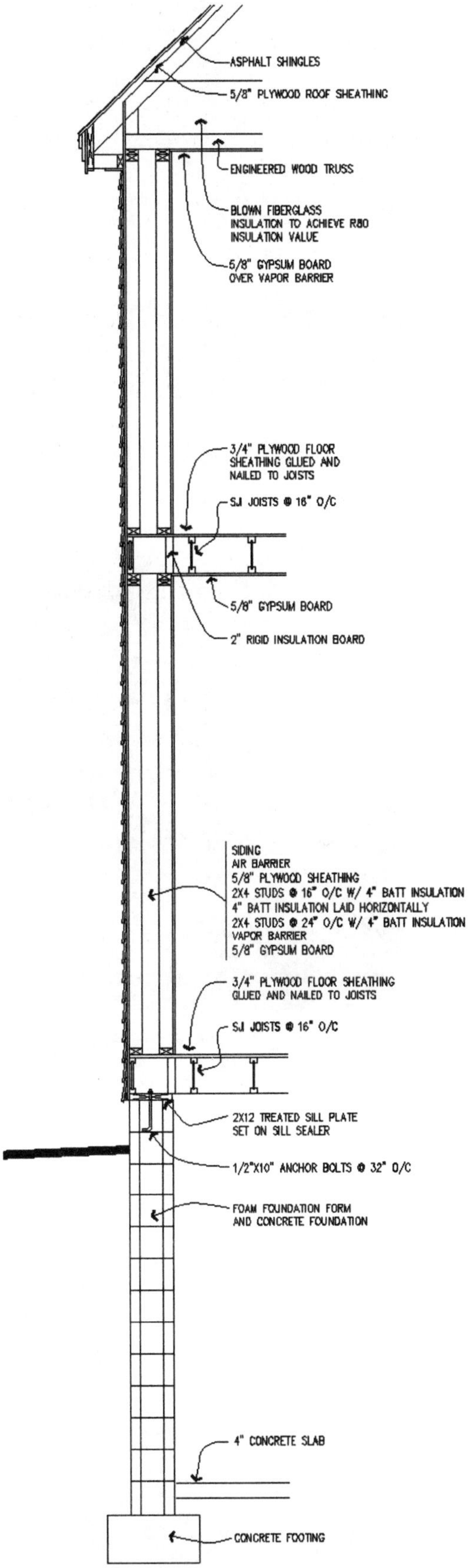

Figure 6-3.2 Leaders added

Image courtesy of Anderson Architects
Alan H. Anderson, Architect, Duluth, MN
Interior Design, Steven W. Sanborn,
A.I.A., Santa Rosa, CA

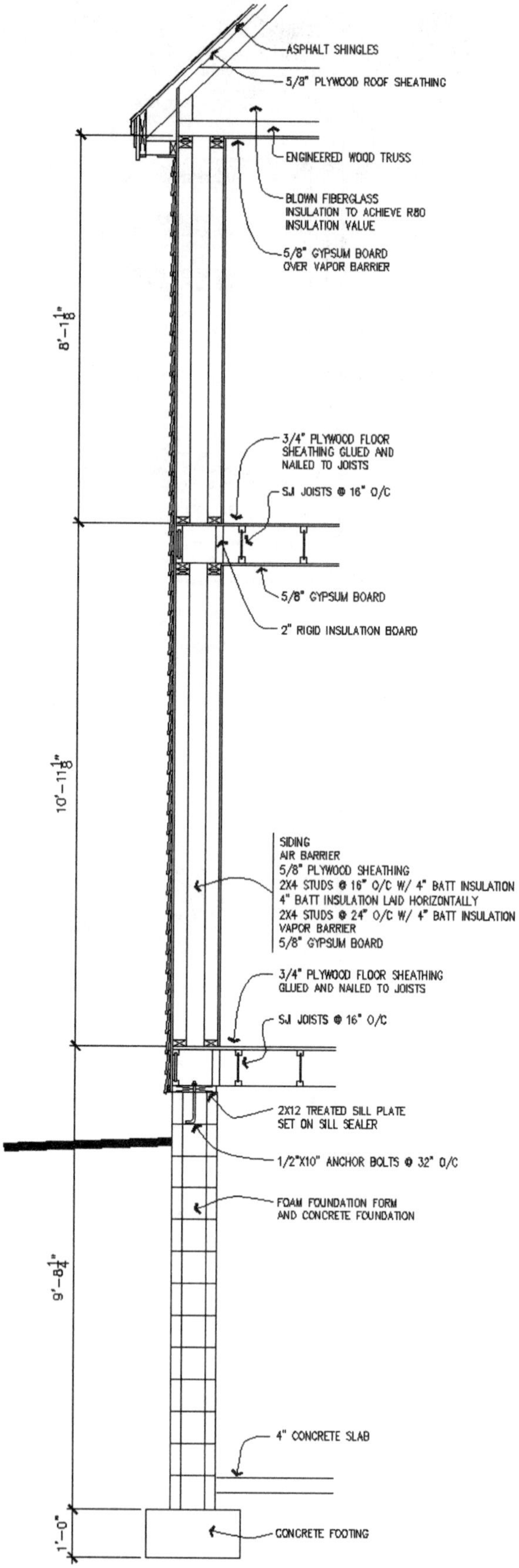

Figure 6-3.3 Dimensions added

Exercise 6-4:
Stair Section

In this exercise you will draw and dimension a simple stair section.

1. **Open** "building section.dwg" drawing file.

You will draw a simple profile of a stair in this exercise. Unless the stair is very complex or unique in some way, you do not need to draw a large scale section because contractors build stairs regularly and lumber yards sell standard treads and risers that simplify the construction process.

Next you will add dimensions to document the number of risers/treads and their size.

First you will use an Xref'ed first floor plan to locate the first riser.

2. Align the first floor plan with your building section and extend a line from the top riser (in plan) to the building section. Figure 6-4.1

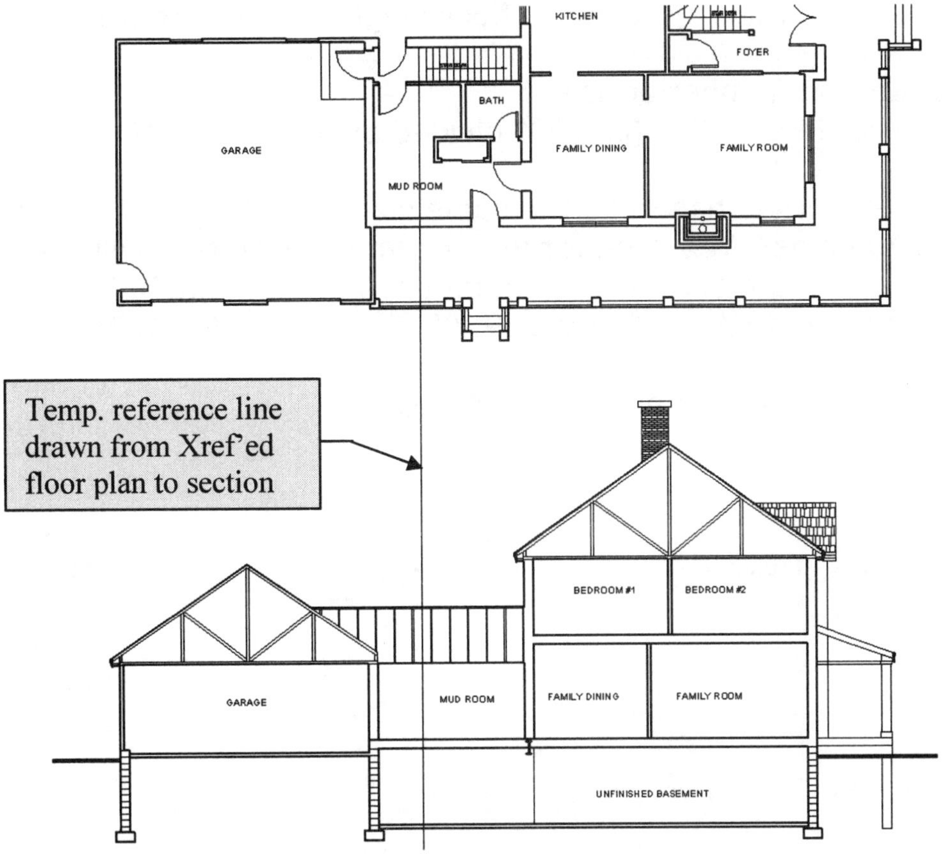

Figure 6-4.1 Building section with line extended from plan to locate top riser

Calculate Tread / Riser Size

The Riser is typically calculated to be as large as building codes will allow. Occasionally a grand stair will have a smaller riser to create a more elegant stair.

Similarly, the Tread is usually designed to be as small as allowable by building codes.

The largest riser and shortest tread creates the steepest stair allowed. This takes up less floor space (see **Figure 6-4.2**). A stairway that is too steep is uncomfortable and unsafe.

Building codes vary by location; for this exercise you will use 7" (max.) for the risers and 9" (min.) for the treads.

Codes usually require that each tread be the same size, likewise with risers.

Calculate the number and size of the risers:

Given:
Risers: **7"** max.   Floor to floor height: **9'-0"** (from ex. 6-1)

Calculate the number of risers:
9'-0" divided by 7" (or 109" divided by 7") = 15.429

Seeing as each riser has to be the same size, we will have to round off to a whole number. You cannot round down because that will make the riser larger than the allowed maximum (9'-0" / 15 = 7.2"). Therefore you have to round up to 16. Thus: 9'-0" divided by 16 = 6.75

So you need **16** risers that are **6 3/4"** each.

Figure 6-4.2 Stair rise / run comparison

Drawing the Tread / Riser profile

Next you will use the Array command to create several lines appropriately spaced.

3. Use the **Array** command to "copy" the top concrete slab line up to create the tread lines (see **Figure 6-4.3**).

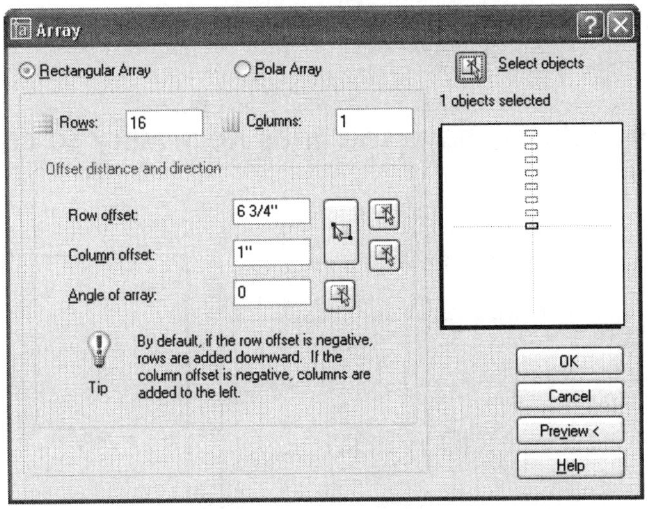

Figure 6-4.3 Array dialog box (set to array the horizontal Slab line upward)

You should now have horizontal lines like Figure 6-4.4.

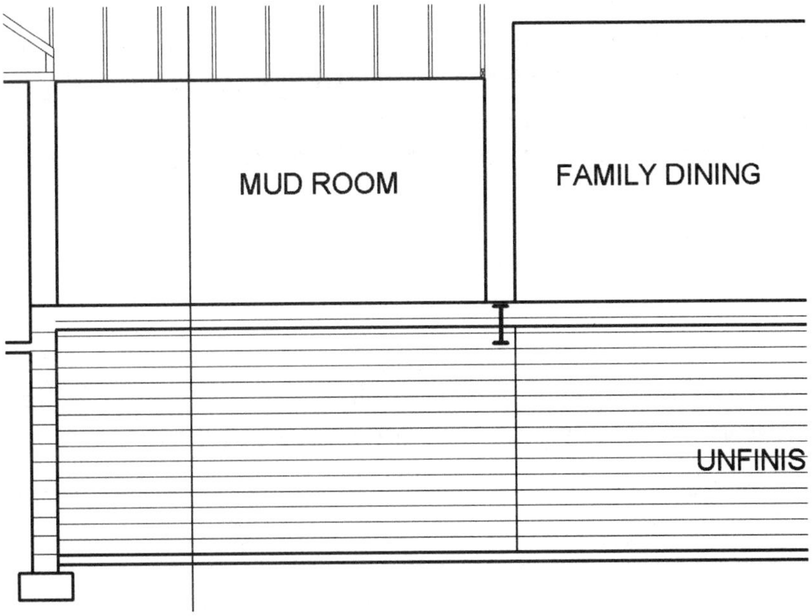

Figure 6-4.4 Horizontal lines arrayed to create stair profile

Notice that if you set the *Row Offset* to 8" in the *Array* command, you could have drawn the concrete block in elevation (on the foundation wall beyond).

Next you will array the vertical line to create the stair riser lines.

4. Array the vertical line to the right:
   a. Columns: **16**
   b. Column offset: **9"**

Your drawing should now have the lines necessary to create the stair profile (see Figure 6-4.5).

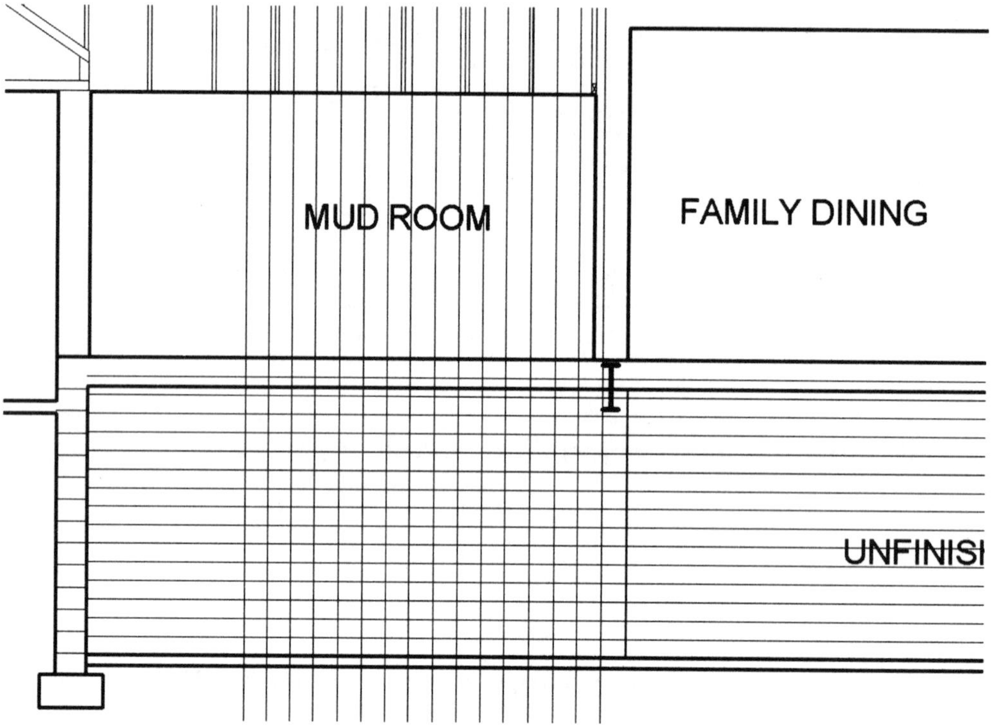

Figure 6-4.5 Vertical lines arrayed to create stair profile

5. **Save** your drawing at this time (just in case).

Finally' you need to use the Trim command to clean up the linework so it looks like a stair. The following image has the stair profile superimposed over the current linework to help you understand the task at hand (Figure 6-4.6).

6. Use the **Trim** command to create the stair profile shown in **Figure 6-4.6.**

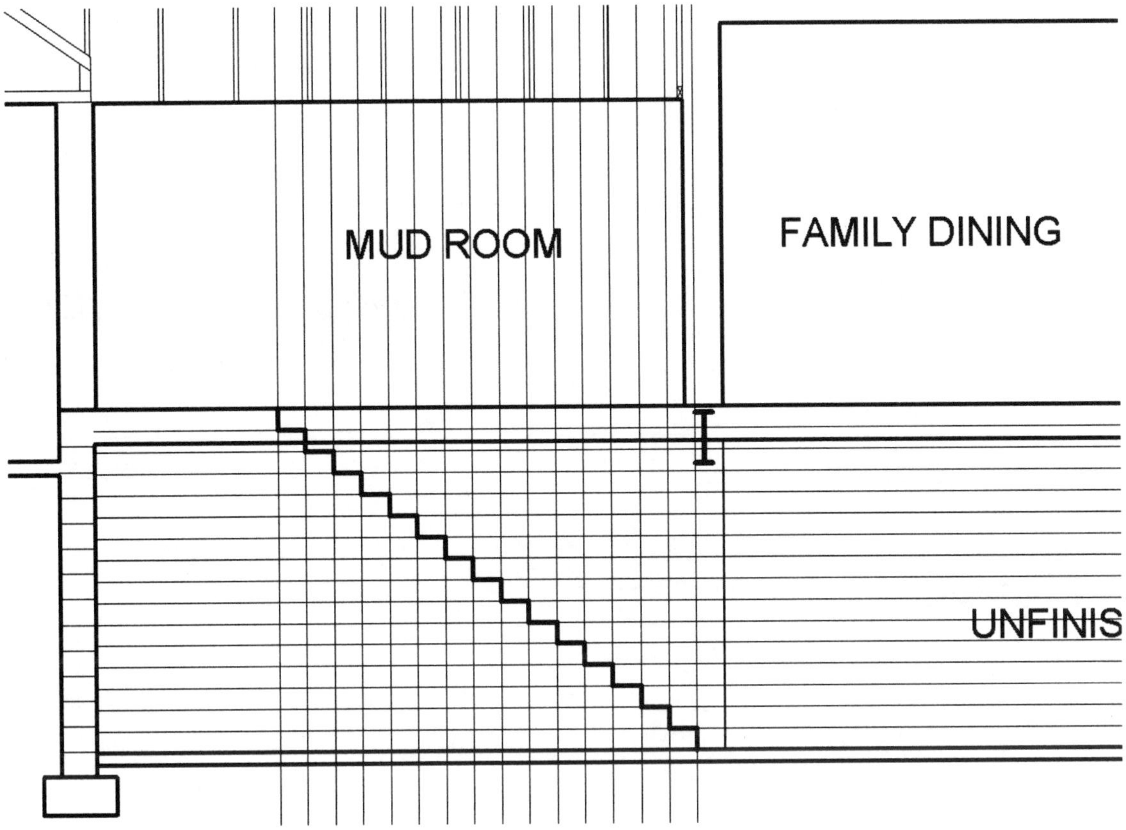

Figure 6-4.6 Vertical and Horizontal lines with desired stair profile superimposed

7. Modify the first floor lines to show the "hole" in the floor for the stair (see Figure 6-4.7).

Stair annotation and Dimensions:

To complete this exercise you will create a note and two dimensions.

8. Add the **Text** and **Leader** shown in Figure 6-4.7:
   a. Set **Dimscale** to **48** (this is for a ¼" drawing).
   b. The **text height** should be **4.5"** (again, for a ¼" drawing).
   c. Text should read: **WOOD STAIR WITH THREE 2x12 STINGERS AND A WALL MOUNTED HANDRAIL**

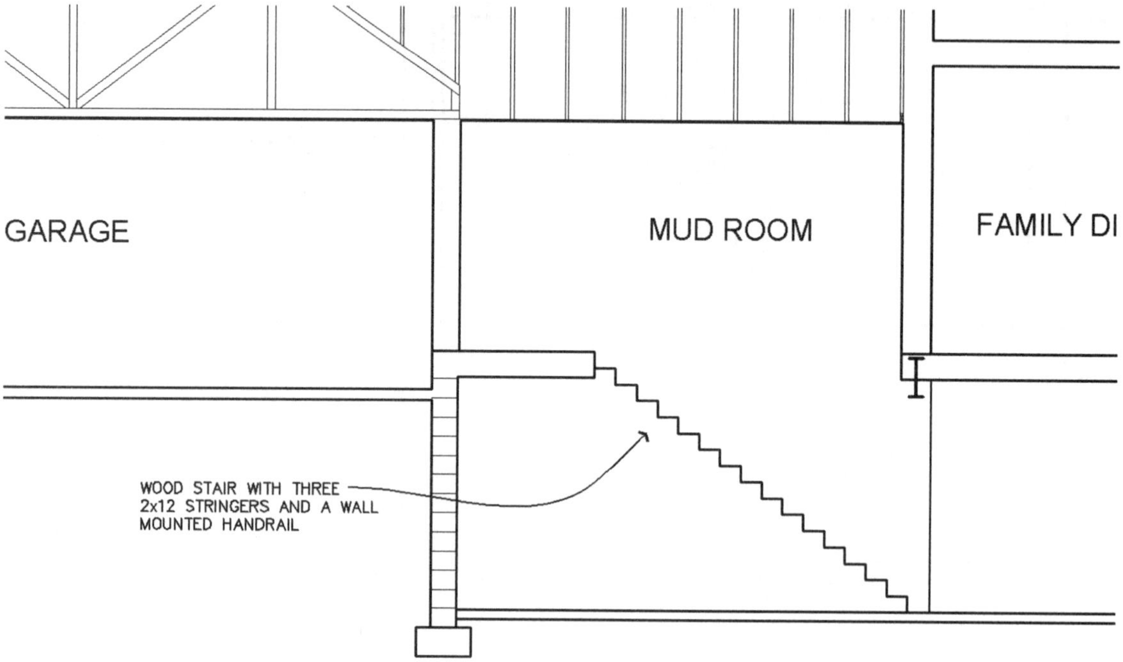

Figure 6-4.7 Annotation added to section

Next you will add dimensions to you stair and learn how to add additional text to the dimension line.

9. Add a horizontal and vertical dimension (linear), as shown in Figure 6-4.8.

Next you will modify the dimension line text.

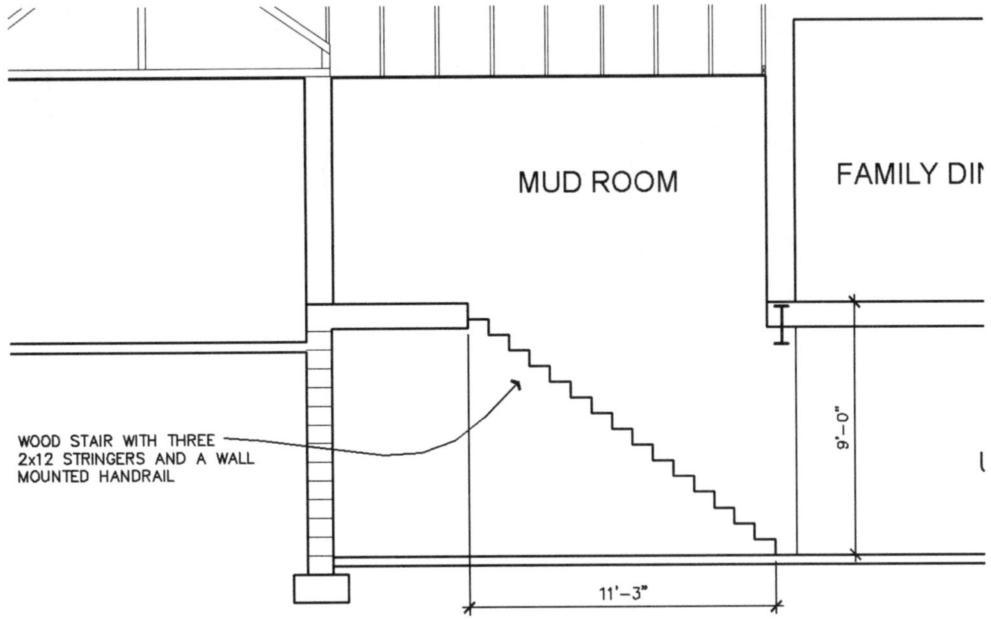

Figure 6-4.8 Two dimensions added to section

10. Select the horizontal dimension line.

11. Right-click and select **Properties.**

12. Locate the *Text Override* field and enter the following:
 15T. @ 9" = <>

Note: the line just typed means the stair has 15 treads that are 9"; all added together you get 11'-3". The <> symbol tells AutoCAD to insert the current dimension (try stretching the dimension to see the number change).

13. Similarly, modify the vertical dimension to read:
 16R. @ 6 3/4" = <>
 (See Figure 6-4.10)

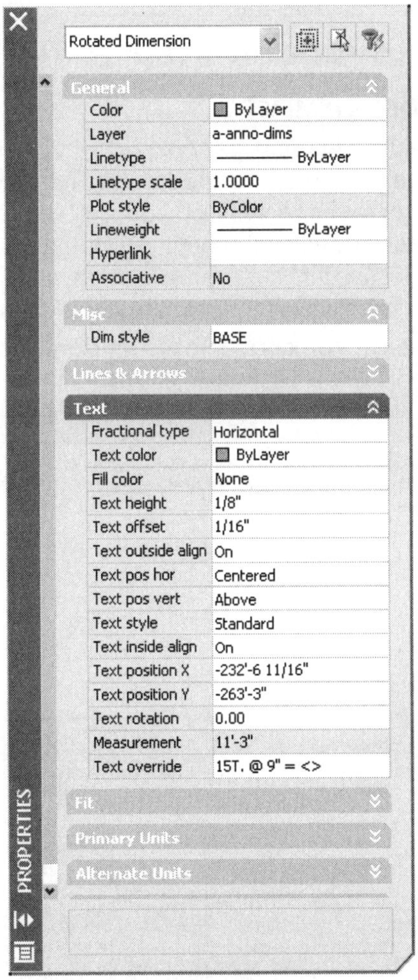

Figure 6-4.9 Properties; horizontal dimension selected

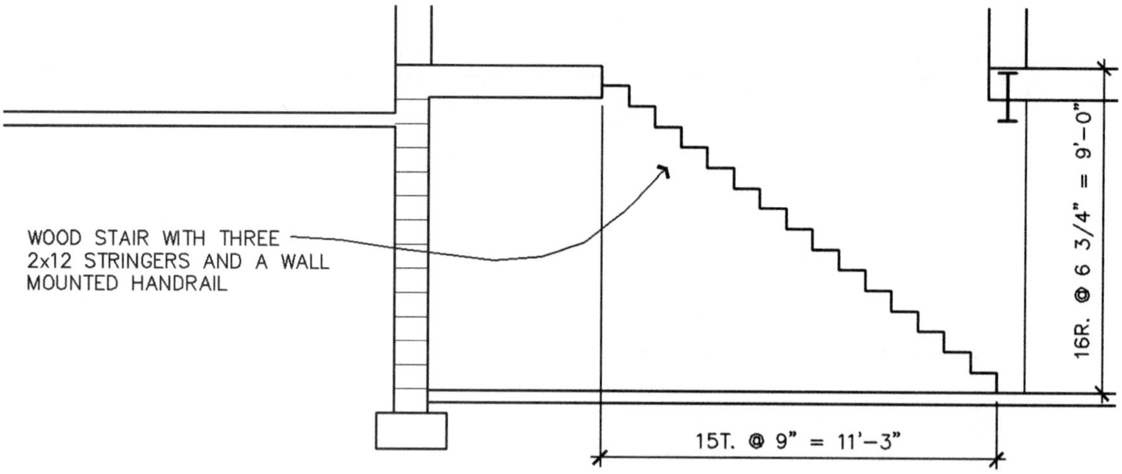

Figure 6-4.10 Stair with modified dimensions

14. **Save** your drawing

Advanced stair tools in other CAD programs:

AutoCAD is a general drafting program that does not have any tools specifically for designing stairs. However, architectural specific CAD programs have advanced stair tools available. *Autodesk Architectural Desktop 2004*, for example, has a stair tool that can create several stair styles all based on predefined rules (e.g., max. riser). When done drawing the stair you can even view it in 3D.

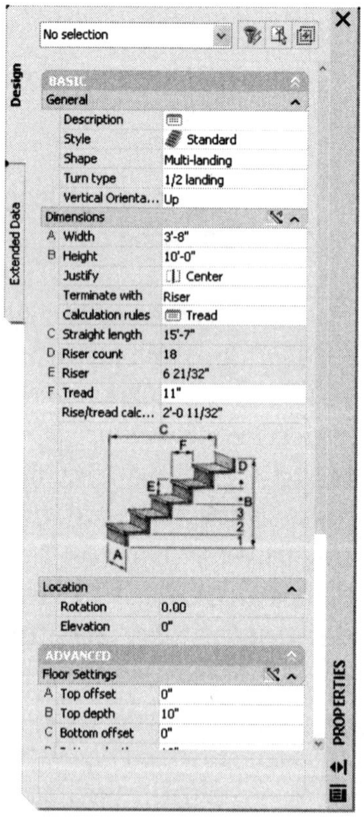

ADT Properties dialog for stair tool

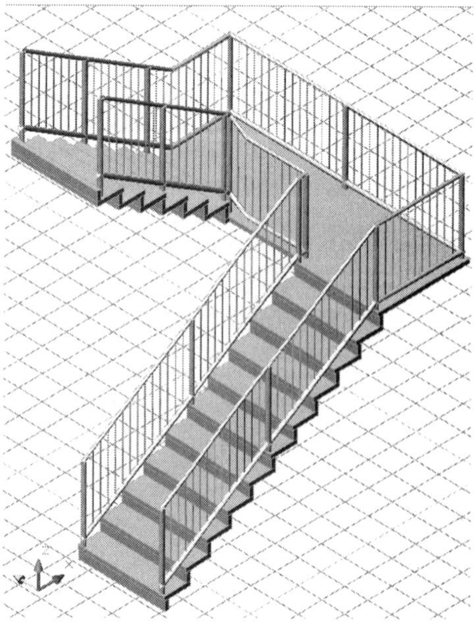

Example stair drawn with ADT 2004

Self-Exam:

The following questions can be used as a way to check your knowledge of this lesson. The answers can be found at the bottom of this page.

1. The Layer name in non-plan drawings relates to the thickness of lines on that Layer. (T/F)
2. You can Xref the plans to locate interior walls in your building sections. (T/F)
3. You should know what scale a wall section will be printed at before adding text and dimensions so its size is correct. (T/F)
4. What is the variable that controls the size of dimensions? ______________.
5. The Leader command can also add text. (T/F)

Review Questions:

The following questions may be assigned by your instructor as a way to assess your knowledge of this section. Your instructor has the answers to the review questions.

1. A vapor barrier is installed on the cold side of a wall. (T/F)
2. A wall section is typically as large as possible and still fit on the sheet. (T/F)
3. Lineweights help drawings to be more readable. (T/F)
4. Name the three non-plan Layers created in this Lesson:

   ________________ ________________ ________________.

5. A Sill Sealer helps to reduce air infiltration into a building. (T/F)
6. Name the variable that sets the default text height ________________.
7. What command creates an arrow with a line behind it? ________________.
8. What size text would you use for a ½″ = 1′-0″ drawing ________________.
9. What Layer should text go on is section drawings? ________________.
10. Things in section are the lightest lines in a drawing. (T/F)

Self-Exam Answers:
1 - T, **2** - T, **3** - T, **4** – Dimscale, **5** – T

Additional Tasks:

Task 6-1 Additional Building Sections

Draw additional building sections, using the exterior elevations as a starting point (similar to exercise 6-1).

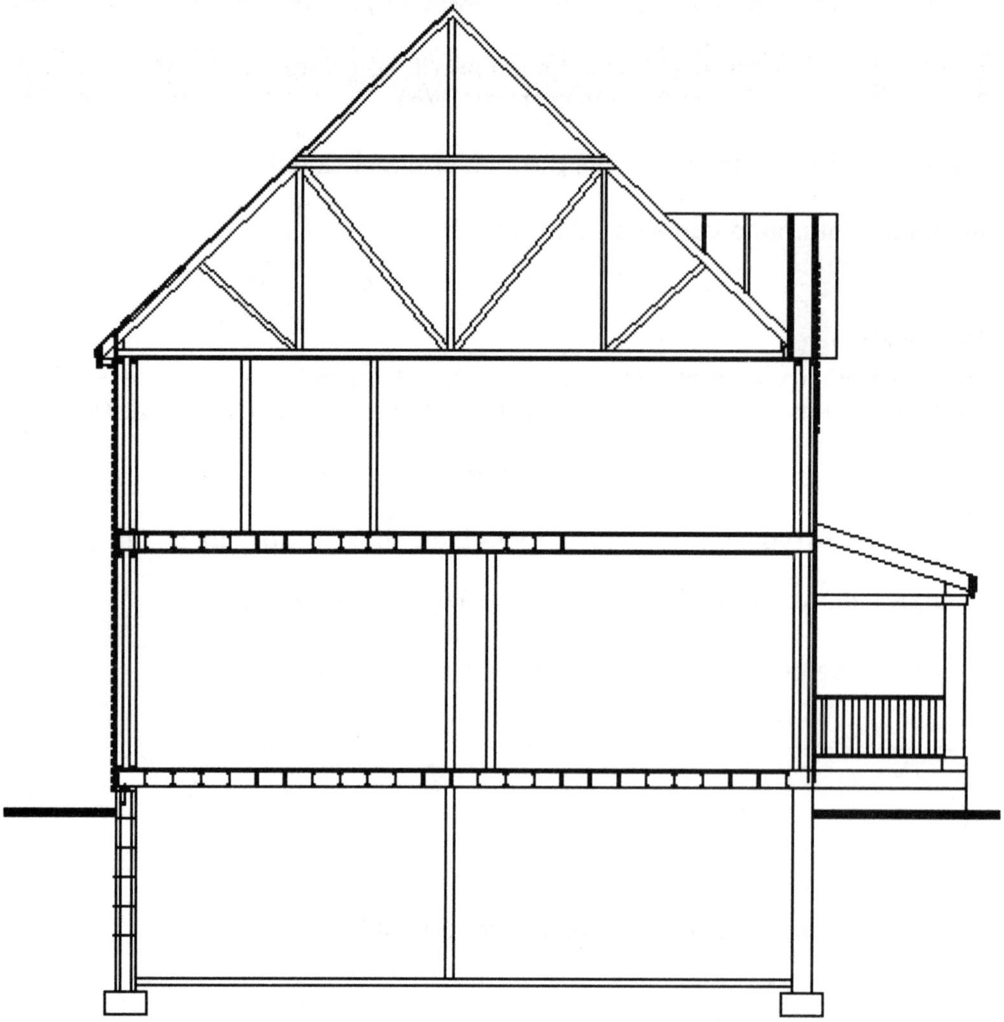

Task 6-1 (1) Building Section (section centered on front door / dormer)

Task 6-2 Wall Section at Garage

Draw a wall section at the garage (similar to exercise 6-2).
Tip: Remember the exterior garage walls only have one 2x4 wall.

Task 6-3 Hatch Wall Sections

Per your instructor's direction, add hatching to your section (e.g., concrete block, concrete footing and batt insulation).

Lesson 7
Residential Project: Plan Layout & Elevations::

In this lesson you will further develop the floor plans and create interior elevations. You will add plumbing fixtures to the bathrooms and add furniture to the plans.

Exercise 7-1:
Bathroom Layout

Introduction

In this exercise you will layout the bathroom fixtures. This typically involves thinking about where the plumbing is coming from and how it will get to each fixture without conflicting or compromising the design; also things like circulation and door swings should be considered.

Like your floor plan, all fixtures are drawn (or inserted) into Model Space at full scale.

1. **Open** your second floor plan drawing **Flr-2.dwg.**

2. **Zoom** in to the bathroom area shown in **Figure 7-1.1.**

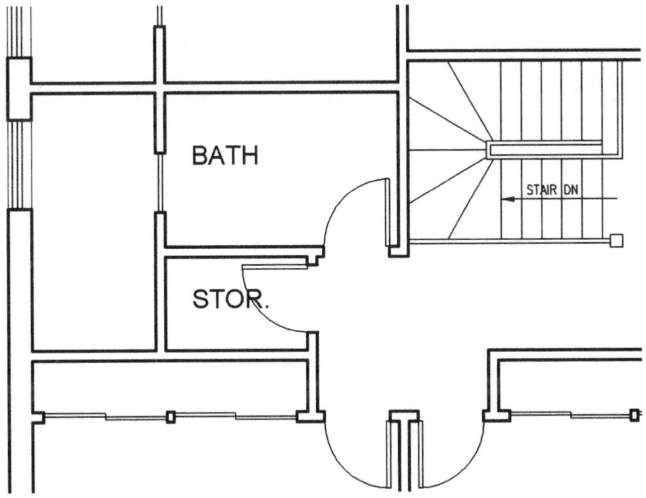

Figure 7-1.1 Second floor plan; zoomed into bathroom area

The first plumbing fixture you will insert is the tub, but first you will double check your wall locations to make sure it will fit. If you refer back to the tub you drew in Lesson 3 (page 3-18), you will notice the tub is 5'-0" long. This is a standard size for a tub.

3. Use the **Distance** command (or draw a dimension and then erase it) to verify you have exactly **5'-0"** between the exterior wall and the interior wall as show in Figure 7-1.2.

   a. If you do not have exactly 5'-0", use the Stretch command to adjust the interior wall.

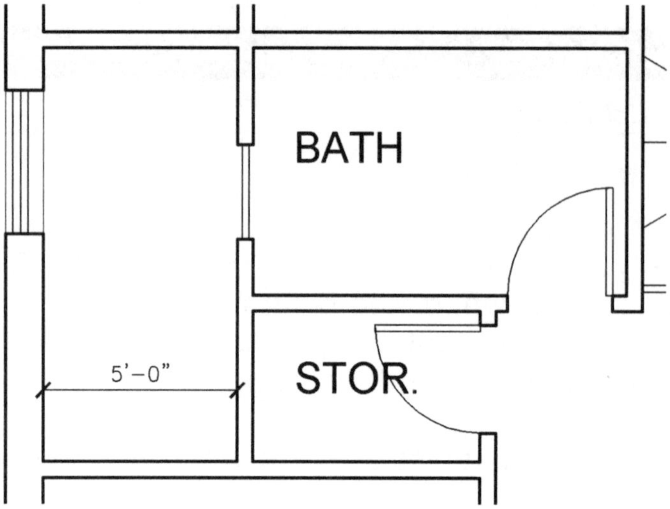

Figure 7-1.2 Second floor bathroom; verify wall locations

As you have already seen, when you insert an external drawing file, like you are about to do with the Tub drawing, it comes in as a *Block* (i.e., a named group of entities). The *block* will be inserted on the current *Layer*.

You can easily change the *Layer* by selecting the *Block* and then picking the desired Layer from the *Layer Control* drop-down list on your toolbar.

However, in anticipation of the fact that we will be inserting several plumbing fixtures, you will create a Layer and set it current before inserting the blocks.

4. Create a *Layer* named **A-Flor-Pfix**, set its color to **Green.**

5. Set the A-Flor-Pfix *Layer* to be the **Current Layer.**

6. Use the **Insert** command to insert the **Tub.dwg** file you previously created (Figure 7-1.3).

   a. Make sure you use *Osnaps* to accurately pick the corner of the wall.

   b. The more rounded side of the tub is the back, the other side is where the faucet / piping is; make sure the faucet is on the interior wall as shown in Figure 7-1.3.

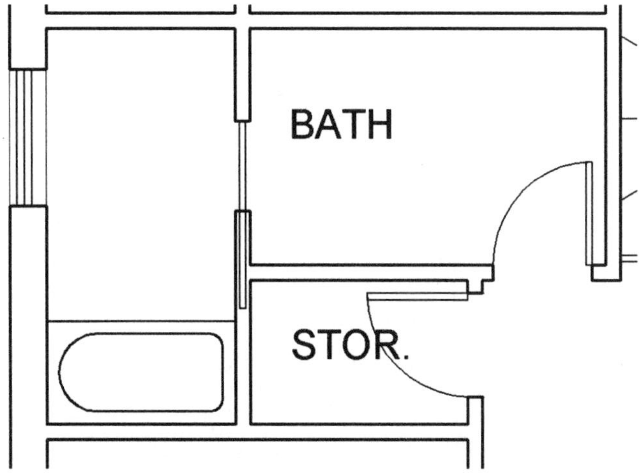

Figure 7-1.3 Second floor bathroom; tub block added

Fixture locations in cold climate regions

As you know, whether you live in a cold climate or not, water expands when it freezes. When this happens in a pipe, the pipe bursts under the extreme pressure exerted by the expanding water/ice. The problem is further compounded by the fact that the pipe is usually buried in the wall behind cement board and ceramic tile.

Therefore, when ever possible, you should avoid placing plumbing fixtures on an exterior wall in cold climates (at least the faucet / piping side in the case of a tub).

The problem usually only occurs when the heating system fails and the residents don't notice the problem right away, are on vacation or the property is vacant. However, the problem can still occur during extreme weather condition (e.g., -40-60 degrees F).

If you must place the fixtures on an exterior wall you should build a second wall in front of the insulated exterior wall and provide grilles at the top and bottom of the wall to allow the warm room air to enter the wall cavity.

7. Use the **Insert** command to insert the **Toilet.dwg** file you previously created (Figure 7-1.5).

    a. Insert a toilet at a corner of the room (see Figure 7-1.4); this puts the fixture in a known location, which then can be moved.

    b. Locate the fixture 18" away from the side wall; also, move the toilet so there is 1" between the fixture and the back wall. (Figure 7-1.5)

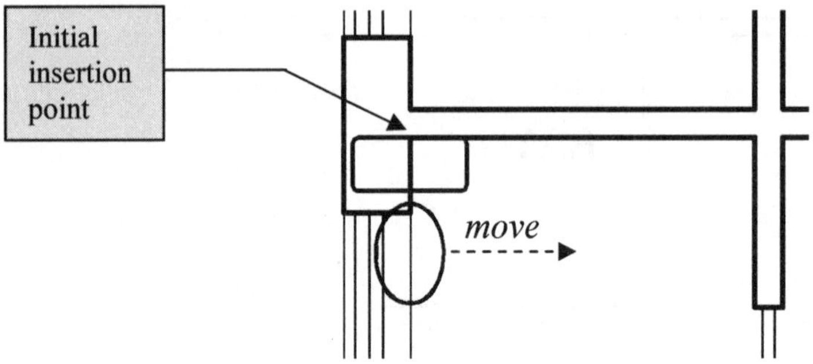

Figure 7-1.4 Second floor bathroom; toilet block inserted with osnap

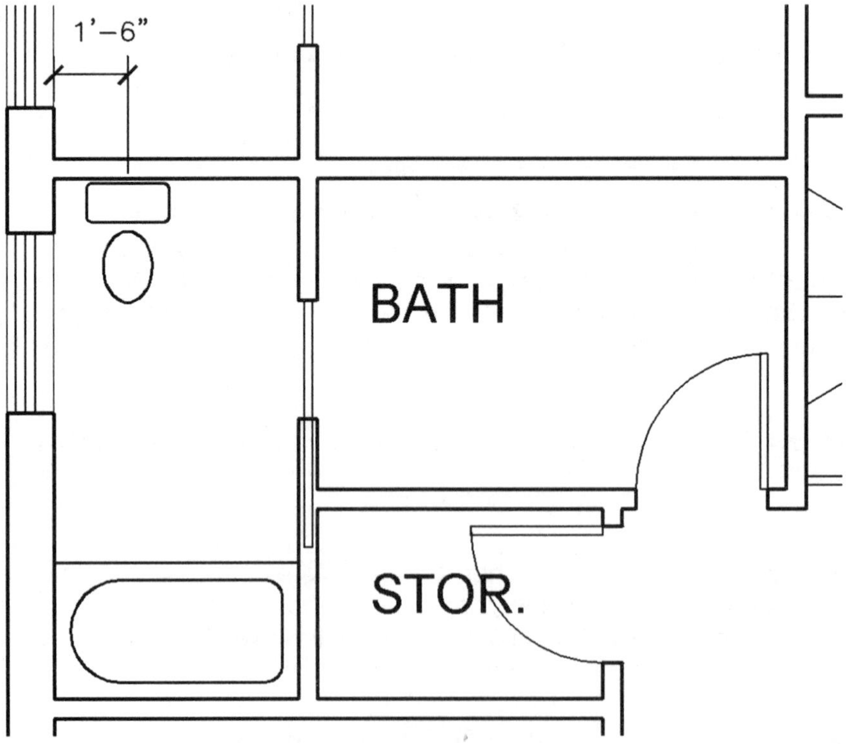

Figure 7-1.5 Second floor bathroom; toilet block moved into place

Next, you will add two sinks to the plans. The sinks are in base cabinets, so you will draw the lines that represent the cabinet first.

Also, remember that in floor plans you should separate each building element onto different Layers; this helps to have better control over visibility and lineweights of those elements. So, you will create a Layer to draw the base cabinets on as follows:

Name	Color	Linetype	Descriptions
A-Flor-Case-L	Yellow	Continuous	Base cabinets
A-Flor-Case-U	Red	Hidden2	Wall cabinets

8. Create the two layers described above.

Now you will draw the countertop/vanity. The top is typically 21" deep.

9. Draw the base cabinets, on *Layer* **A-Flor-Case-L**, as shown in **Figure 7-1.6**
   TIP: *Offset the wall lines to create the countertop in plan and then use trim to clean up the lines; finally, change the lines to the correct layer.*

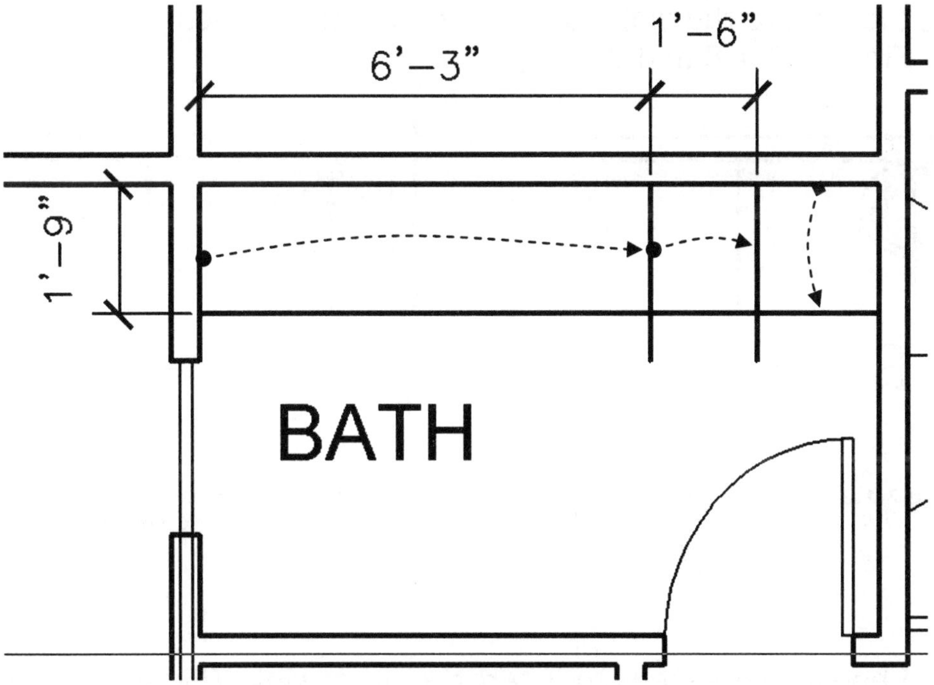

Figure 7-1.6 Second floor bathroom; offset wall lines to create vanity/countertop

10. **Offset** the wall line as shown in Figure 7-1.7; these lines will be erased after the sinks have been inserted.

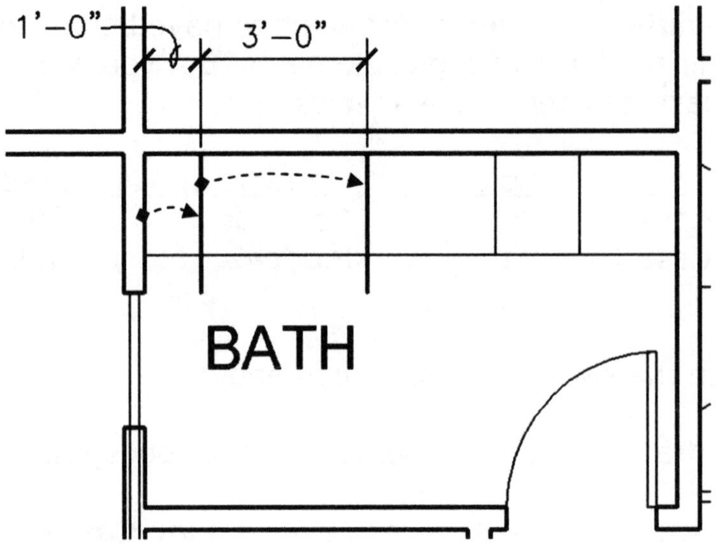

Figure 7-1.7 Second floor bathroom; offset wall lines to help locate sinks

11. **Insert** the **Lav-2** drawing file, previously created, using the *Insert* command (or Block command from the Insert menu); then move the sink down **1"** with Ortho turned on. (See Figures 7-1.8 and 7-1.9.)

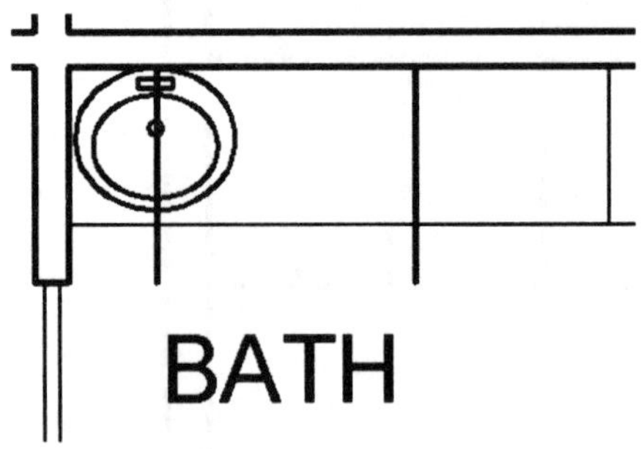

Figure 7-1.8 Second floor bathroom; sink inserted at intersection of temp. line and wall

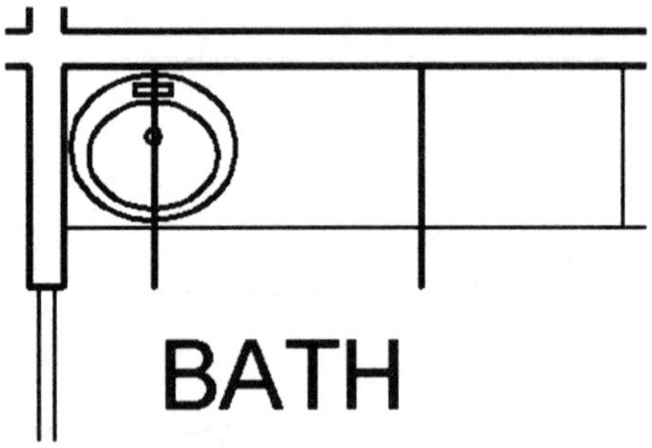

Figure 7-1.9 Second floor bathroom; sink moved 1" out from wall

12. Repeat these steps to insert the other sink. (Figure 7-1.10)

13. **Erase** the temporary lines. (Figure 7-1.10)

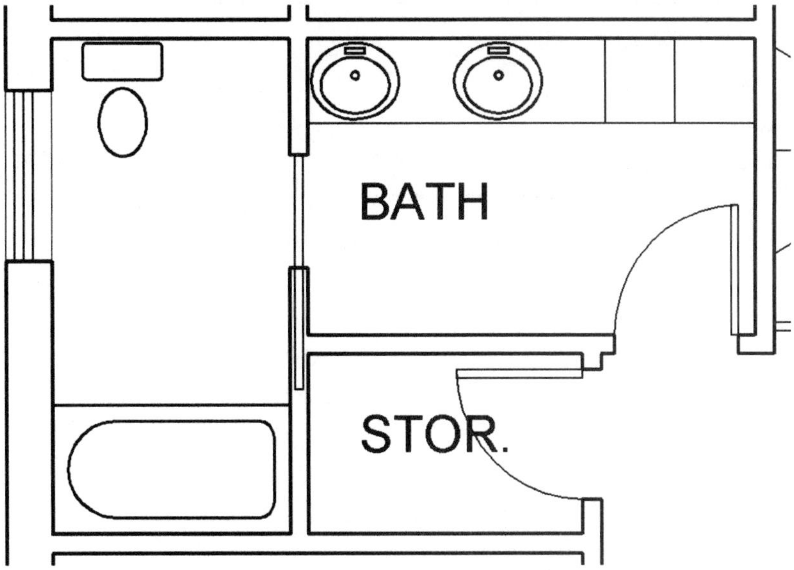

Figure 7-1.10 Second floor bathroom; with tub, toilet and sinks added

This completes the bathroom layout.

In the next exercise you will draw the interior elevation of the cabinets. (FYI, you will see why the sinks are spaced the way they are.)

Image courtesy of Anderson Architects
Alan H. Anderson, Architect, Duluth, MN
Interior Design, Steven W. Sanborn, A.I.A., Santa Rosa, CA

Exercise 7-2:
Bathroom Elevation

Introduction

The purpose of interior elevations is to show information that is not easily described on a floor plan. For example, you can show how high a countertop is, how tall a door is or the layout of wall and base cabinets.

Floor plans typically have horizontal dimensions and interior elevations typically have all the vertical dimensions. However, interior elevations are usually drawn larger than the floor plan (1/4" = 1'-0" floor plans and ½" = 1'-0" interior elevation); so you may have additional horizontal dimensions that would be hard to read on a smaller plan.

In this exercise you will draw the interior elevation for the bathroom. You will use an *Xref* of the floor plan to get started and learn how to use a feature called *DesignCenter* to insert blocks contained in other drawings.

1. **Open** AutoCAD.

2. Start a new drawing named **Bathroom Elevation.**

3. **Xref** your second floor plan (**Flr-2**) into the drawing.

Next you will use a feature called Xclip, which allows you to crop an Xref. This will allow you to position the bathroom area close to your interior elevation drawing.

4. **Zoom Extents**, so you can see the entire drawing.

5. Zoom into the bathroom area. (Figure 7-2.1)

6. At the *Command Prompt* type **XC** and then **Enter.**

7. **Select** the Xref'ed floor plan and then press **Enter** three times.

8. Click twice to select a window as shown in **Figure 7-2.1.**

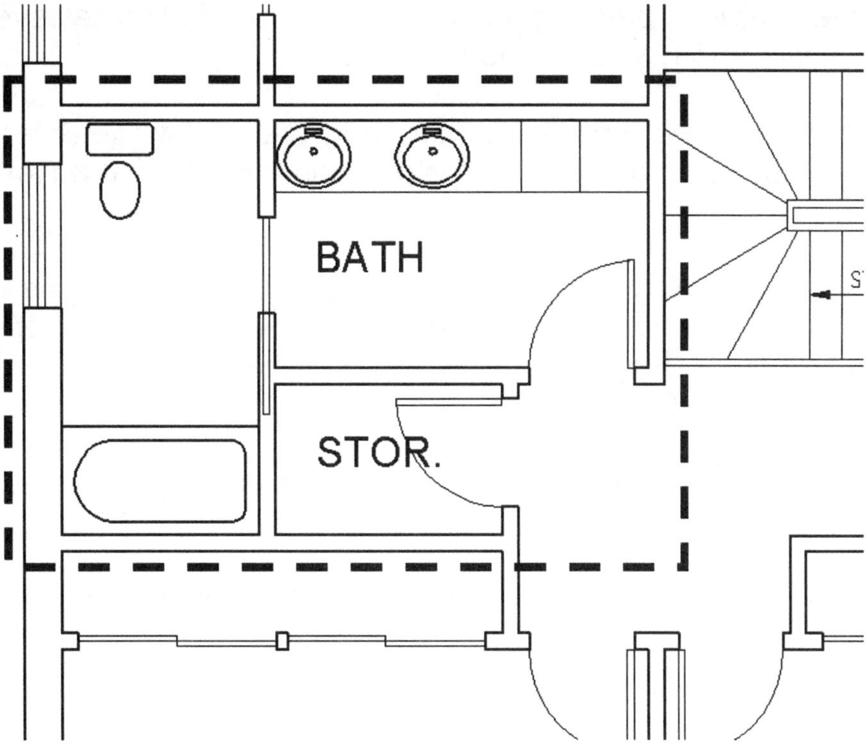

Figure 7-2.1 Second floor plan; bathroom area to select for Xclip

More about Xclip

This section is meant to give you a little more information about the Xclip command.

Removing an Xclip from an Xref

Type Xclip and then select the Xref and then type D (for the Delete sub-command) and then press Enter. You will now see the entire Xref again.

Irregular shaped clips

You can either create the outline before using the Xclip command or after.

If you create it before, you need to create a Polyline; you can even use Pedit to smooth (spline) the outline. Once the Polyline is created you enter the XC command, select the Xref, and then press enter twice. Now enter S for the "select polyline" sub-command. Finally, select your Polyline and you are done.

Or, you can also follow the prompts and create the outline within Xclip command. However, you cannot get a smooth outline like you can with the method previously described.

You can experiment with the other sub-command features by looking at the prompts at the command prompt while the Xclip command is active.

Now that the Xref is in place you can use it to quickly locate several lines in your elevation; you will do this next.

9. Arbitrarily draw a horizontal line and then draw the 8 vertical lines (snapping to the *Xref* for position), as shown in Figure 7-2.2.

Looking back at the Wall Section from exercise 6-3 you can see the 8'-1 1/8" dimension represents the floor to truss bearing height. If you subtract ½" for the ceiling gypsum board, you have the ceiling height for your elevation' 8'-0 5/8".

10. **Offset** the horizontal line **8'-0 5/8"** upward. (Figure 7-2.3)
    TIP: *Type 8'0-5/8 at the command prompt.*

11. **Trim/Extend** the wall lines to the horizontal floor and ceiling lines. (Figure 7-2.3)

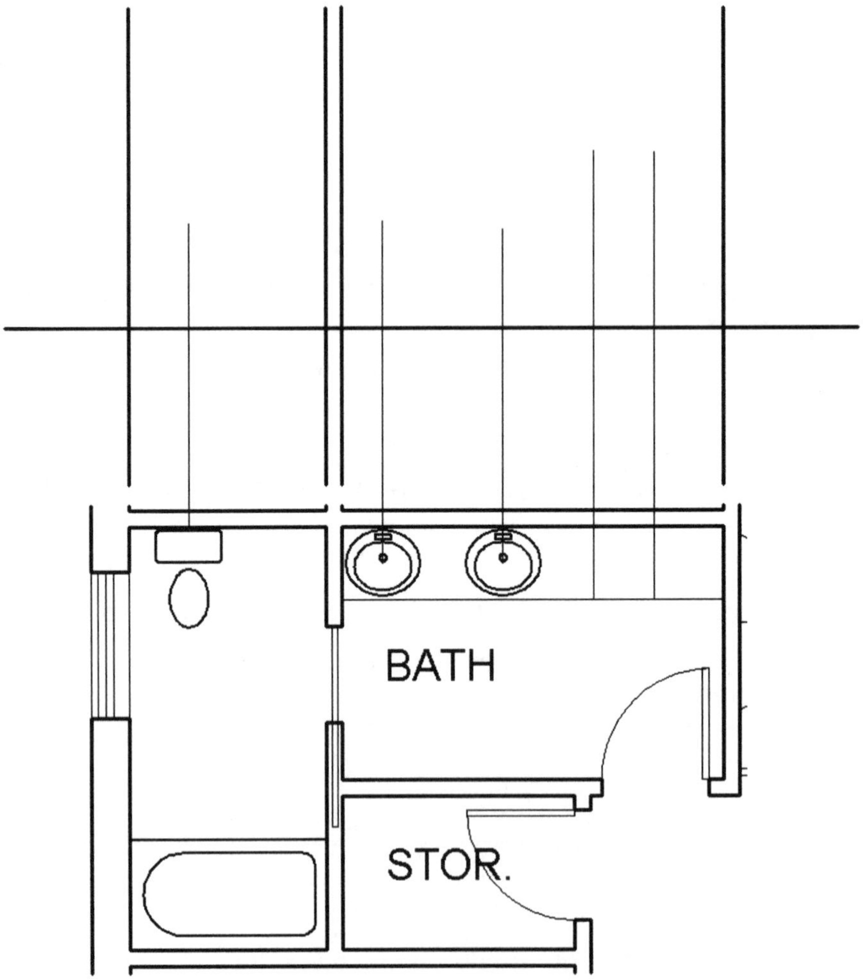

Figure 7-2.2 Interior Elevation: lines extended from Xref

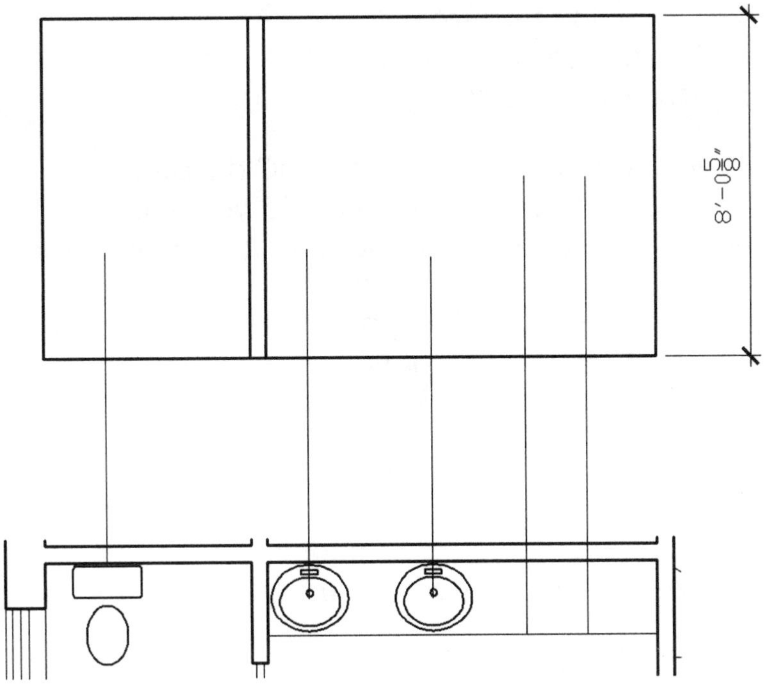

Figure 7-2.3 Interior elevation: lines trimmed and extended

Using AutoCAD DesignCenter

AutoCAD DesignCenter (DC) allows you to quickly access drawings (whether currently open or not), and drag items such as Blocks, Linetypes, Layer definitions, etc. into the current drawing. You will use the DC to insert a toilet in elevation from a preinstalled sample drawing (a file that comes with the AutoCAD software).

12. From the *Standard Toolbar* select the **DesignCenter** icon (shown to the left).

You should now see the dialog box shown in **Figure 7-2.4**. This is the default view.

If you only see the vertical title bar shown to the left of Figure 7-2.4, then it is set to *Auto-Hide*. Simply hover your cursor over the title bar and the full image will show. This feature is meant to save space on your screen (i.e., larger drawing window).

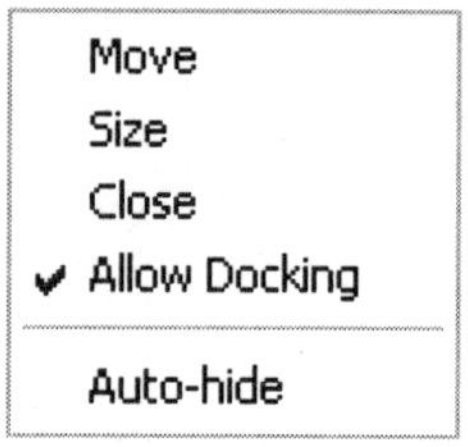

To disable the Auto-Hide feature:
Right-click on the title bar and uncheck the Auto-Hide option (see right-click menu to right).

Similar to the Properties dialog box, the DC dialog is modeless. That means it can be open while you are drawing (whereas the Layer dialog box must be closed before you can continue drawing). TIP: If you are running a dual screen system you can drag both the properties dialog and the DC dialog over to the second screen so you have the convenience of having them open without sacrificing valuable drawing area.

Also on the title-bar right-click options is the ability to *Allow Docking*. If this is checked, the dialog will snap to the side of the AutoCAD window (similar to a toolbar). Some people prefer this option so it does not cover the drawing window in an awkward fashion.

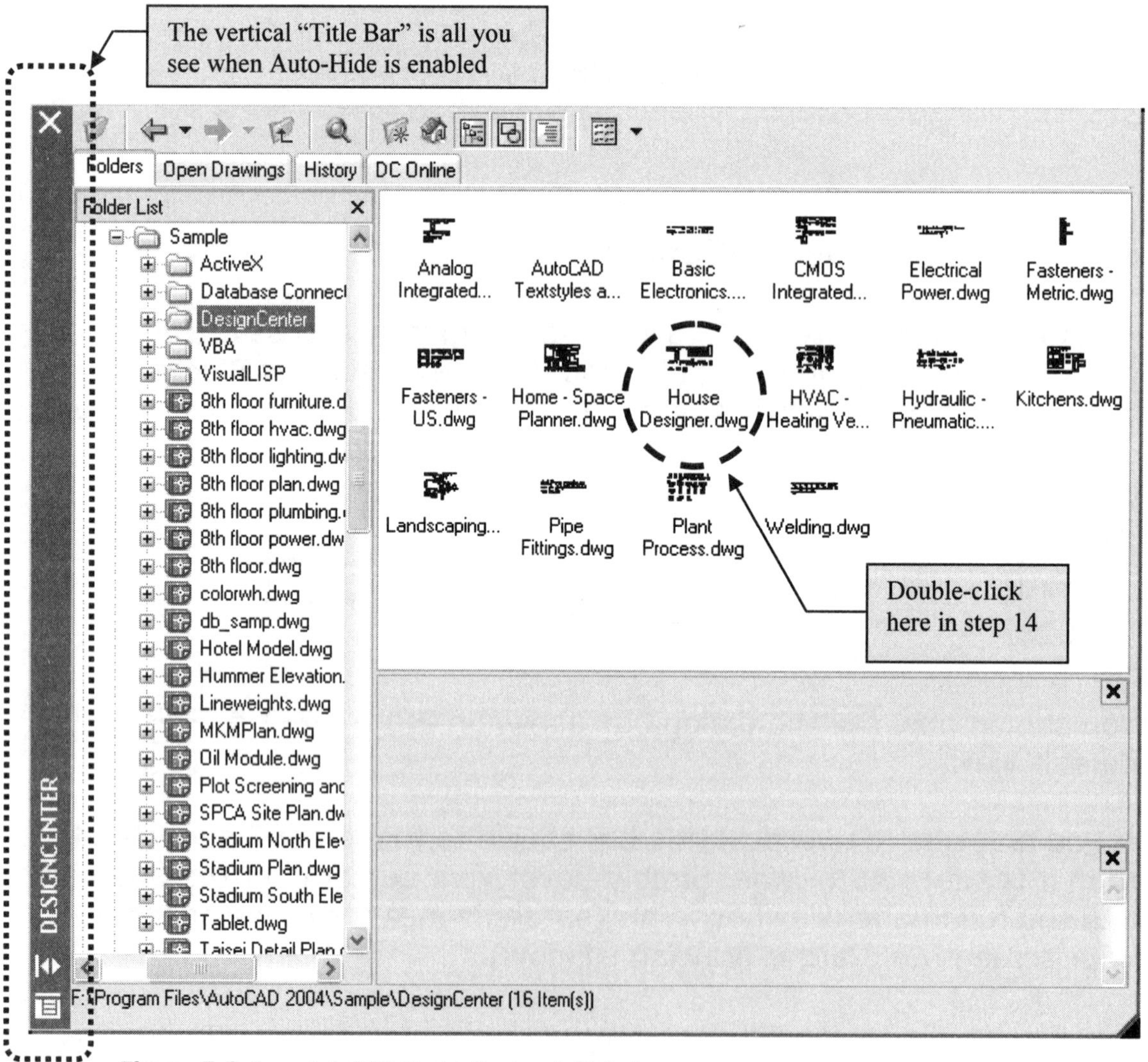

Figure 7-2.4 AutoCAD DesignCenter; initial view

13. First, verify you are in the correct area in DC:
    a. Click on the **Folders** tab.
    b. In the *Folder List* pane, browse to the following folder: C:\Program Files\AutoCAD 2005\Sample\DesignCenter.
    ***TIP:** You may have to scroll horizontally and vertically to see everything – or stretch the Folder List pane bigger.*
    c. Your DC should look like Figure 7-2.4.

14. In the right pane double-click **House Designer.DWG.**

You can now see the various categories of information you have access too (see Figure 7-2.5). Notice that the selected drawing file is highlighted on the left, in the *Folder List* pane.

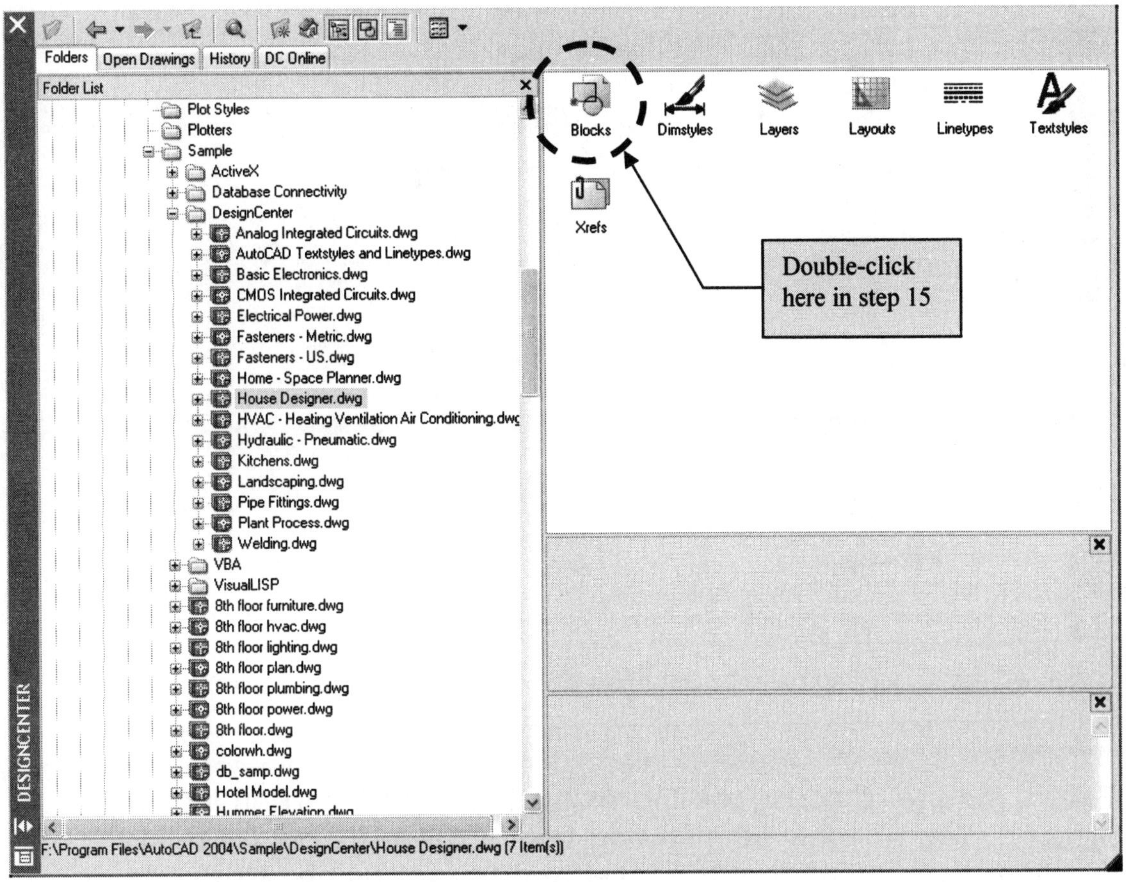

Figure 7-2.5 AutoCAD DesignCenter; *house designer* sample file selected

15. Double-click on the **Blocks** icon in the right pane.

You can now see a thumbnail image of all the *Blocks* within the *House Designer* sample drawing file.

TIP: *If you do not see thumbnail images, click the View icon and select Large icons.*

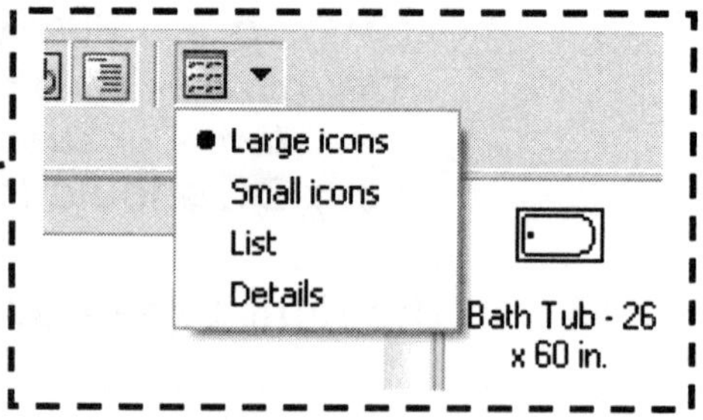

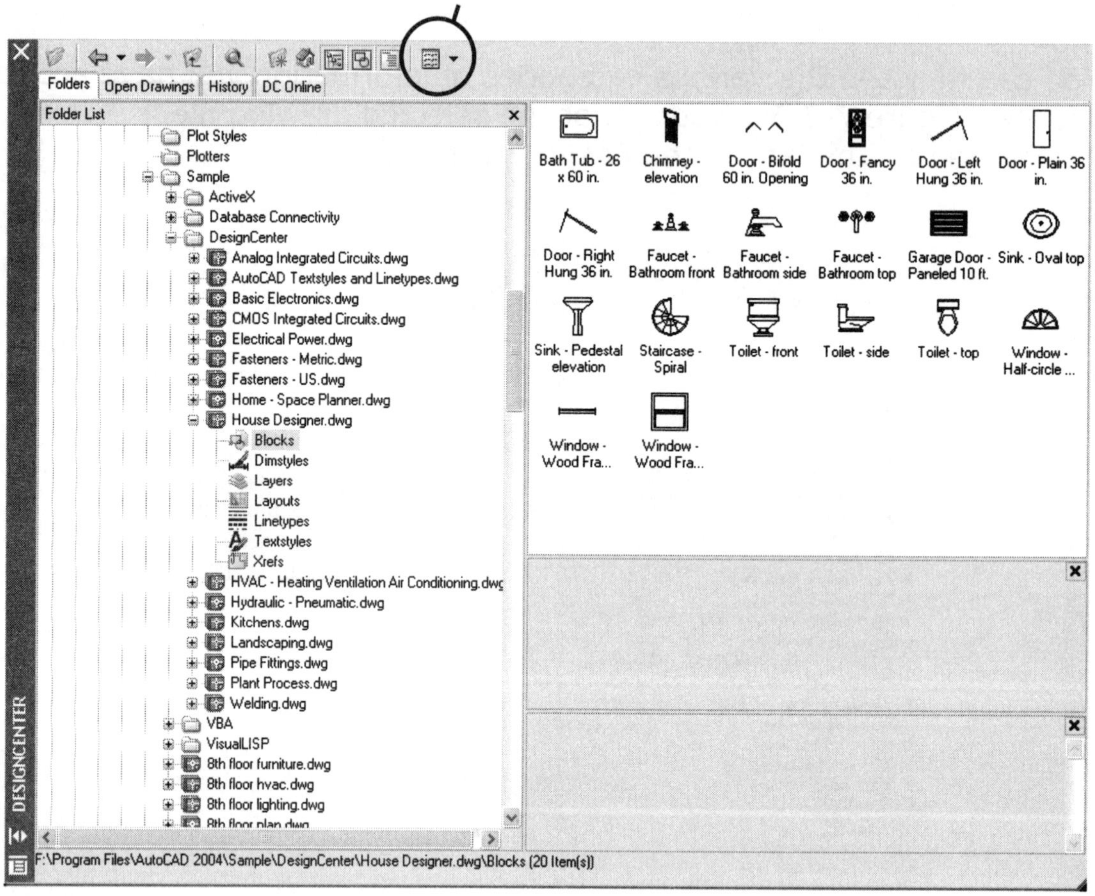

Figure 7-2.6 AutoCAD DesignCenter; blocks within the *house designer* sample file

Take a minute to notice the *Blocks* available for insertion into your drawing. You will only be inserting two of these *Blocks* for this drawing: the elevation of the toilet and the elevation of the Faucet.

16. Double-click on the **Toilet – front** block.

You are now in the standard *Insert Block* dialog box with the *Toilet – front* block selected.

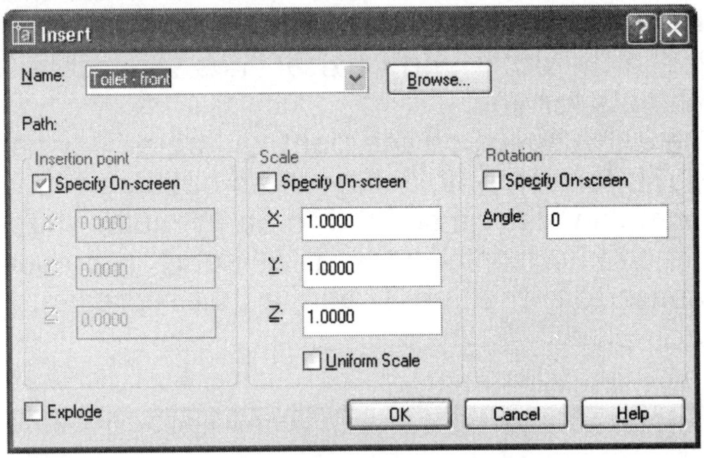

Figure 7-2.7 Insert dialog; initiated from DC

17. Click **OK.**

18. Using *Osnaps*, select the **intersection** of the floor line and the temporary vertical line projected from the toilet in the Xref'ed floor plan. (Figure 7-2.8)

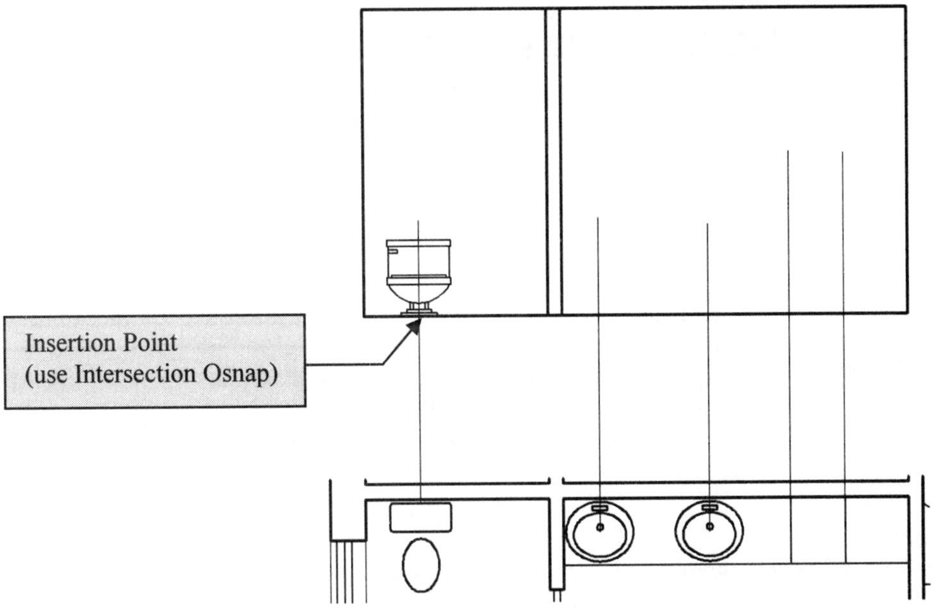

Figure 7-2.8 Bathroom elevation; toilet block inserted

Now you will draw the cabinets.

19. Draw the countertop and cabinets shown in Figure 7-2.9:
    a. You do not have to draw the dimensions.
    b. Notice that the two vertical lines from the sink are centered on their respective cabinets.
    c. Notice the other two vertical lines will locate the tall cabinets for you.
    d. The extra space on the right will be a filler panel; this allows for some flexibility when building the walls; the filler panel can also be scribed to an irregular shaped wall.
    e. The two horizontal lines, 1 ½" apart, represent the countertop; the line 3" above that represents the backsplash.

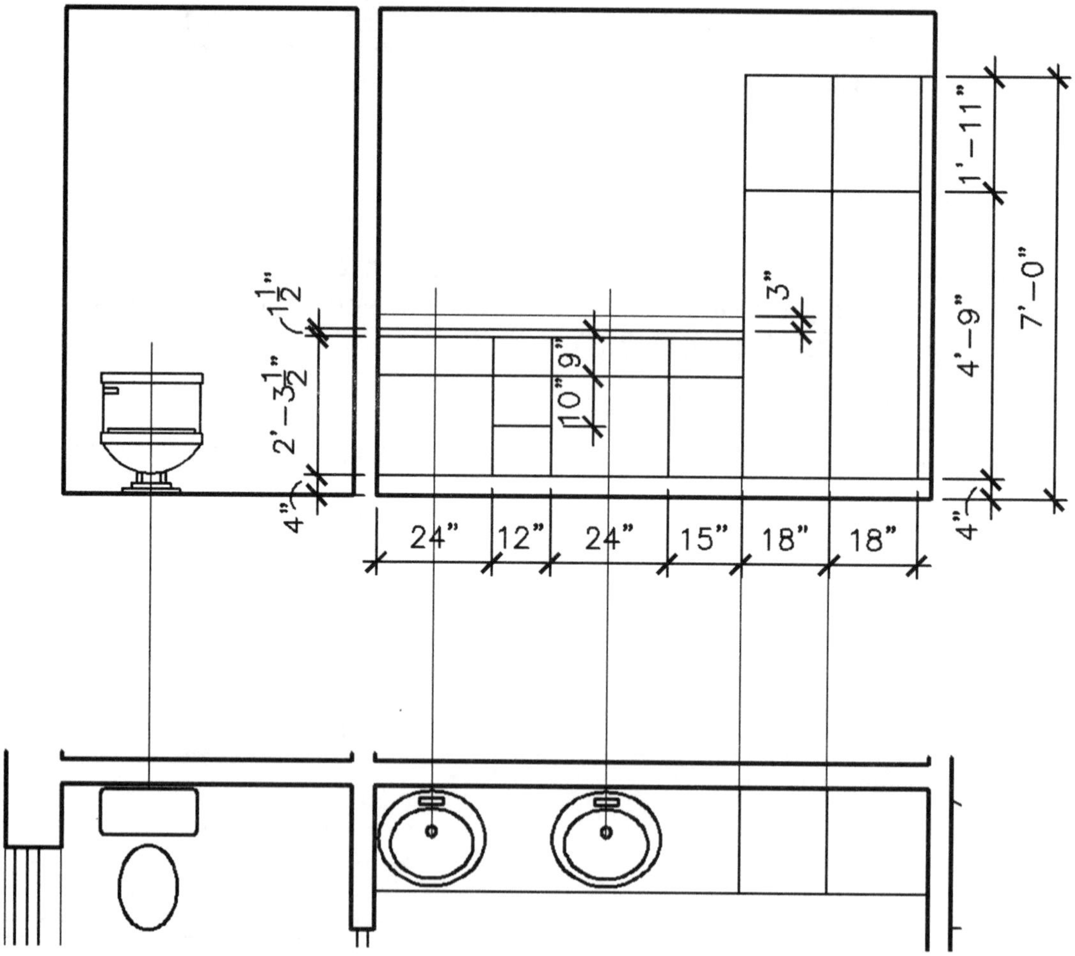

Figure 7-2.9 Bathroom Elevation; countertop and cabinet outlines

Next you will add more detail to the cabinets and draw the remaining elements required for this exercise.

20. Draw the remaining elements shown in Figure 7-2.10
    a. The mirrors are 2′-0″ wide and 2′-6″ tall, centered on the sink below.
    b. The vanity lights above the mirror are the same width as the mirror and 6″ tall; draw the rest to look like drawing.
    c. Use *DesignCenter* to *Insert* the **Faucet – Bathroom front** *Block* from the *Home Designer* drawing.
    d. Use dimensions in drawing below (you do not have to draw the dimensions at this time).

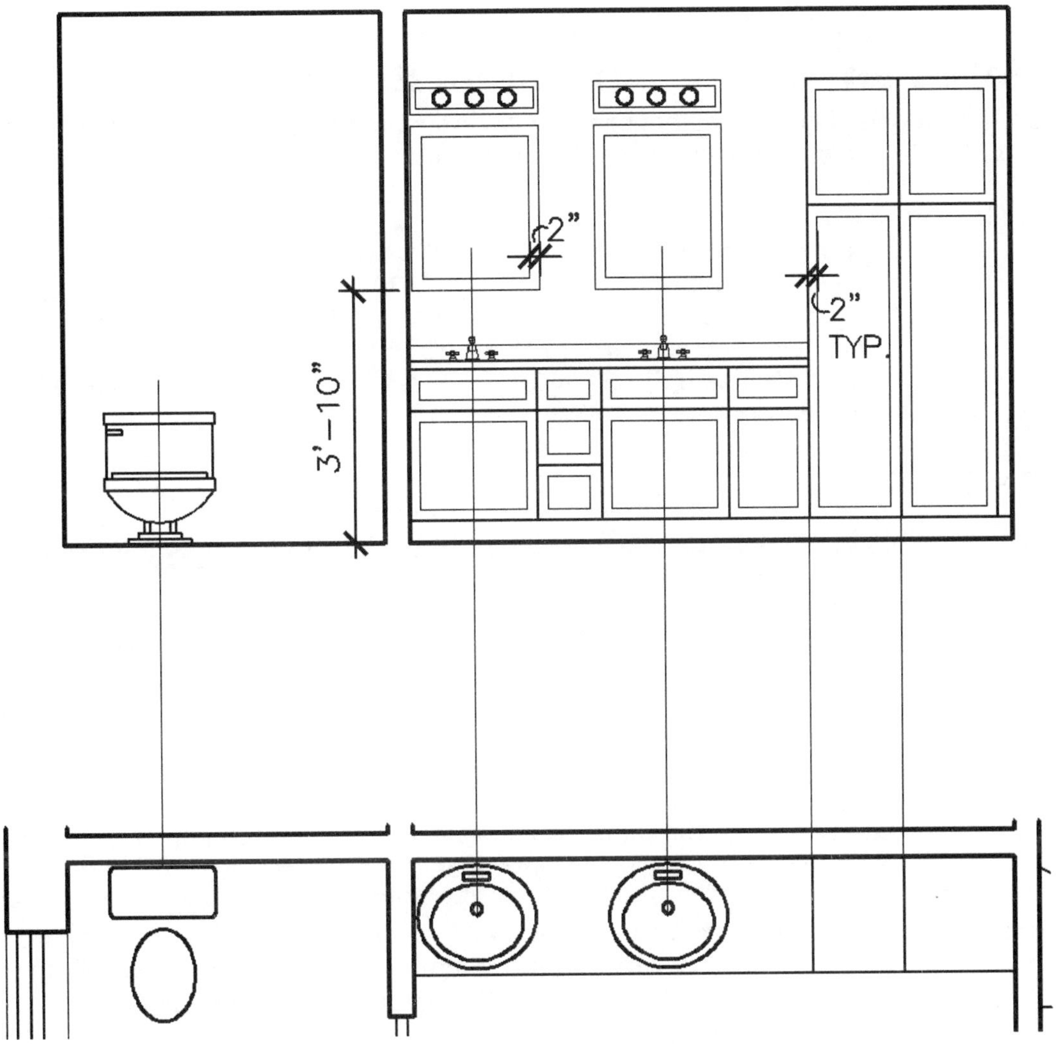

Figure 7-2.10 Bathroom Elevation; remaining elements to be drawn

Depending on the project you could add much more detail to the elevation.

For example, you could add:

- electrical outlets and switches to make sure they end up where you want them;
- the ceramic tile pattern and indicate the accent tile pattern as well;
- the location of the pulls on the cabinets;
- towel bars that might be in this particular elevation;
- the toilet paper holder – especially if it is recessed in a tiled wall.

Notes on cabinet sizes and design

Bathroom and kitchen cabinets come in several standard sizes. They usually start at 12″ wide and increase in size by 3″ increments.

In kitchens,

- Wall cabinets are typically 12″ deep
- Wall cabinet heights: 18″, 24″, 30″. 36″, 42″
- Base cabinets are 24″ deep with a 25″ deep countertop
- Base cabinets are 36″ high (to the top of the countertop)
- Cabinets up to 24″ wide have 1 door; 27″ – 48″ wide have 2 doors

In bathrooms,

- Vanity cabinets are typically 21″ deep
- Vanity cabinets are 33″ (or 36″) high (to top of countertop).

The internet is loaded with information on designing kitchens, a few examples to get you started are:

www.kohler.com Major plumbing fixture manufacturer; web site is packed with kitchen and bath design information.

www.merilatt.com *National Cabinet Manufacturer*; full line of cabinets including details and specifications.

www.superkitchens.com *Valuable Design Information*; planning and products overview, including the National Kitchen and Bath Associations "40 guidelines of kitchen planning".

www.homedepot.com *Construction Superstore*; Kitchen and Bath interactive design tool and miscellaneous product information

http://doityourself.com/kitchen/

You will now complete the elevation by adding notes and dimensions.

21. **Erase** the temporary vertical guidelines.

22. Type **XR** (to enter the Xref manager) and **Detach** the *Flr-2* Xref from the *Bathroom Elevation* drawing.

23. Using **Mtext**, add the notes shown in **Figure 7-2.11.**
    TIP: *Make sure the notes and leaders go on Layer A-ANNO-TEXT.*

24. Using the **Linear** Dimension tool, add the dimensions shown in Figure 7-2.11.
    TIP: *Make sure the dimensions go on Layer A-ANNO-DIMS.*

25. **Save** your **Bathroom Elevation** drawing.

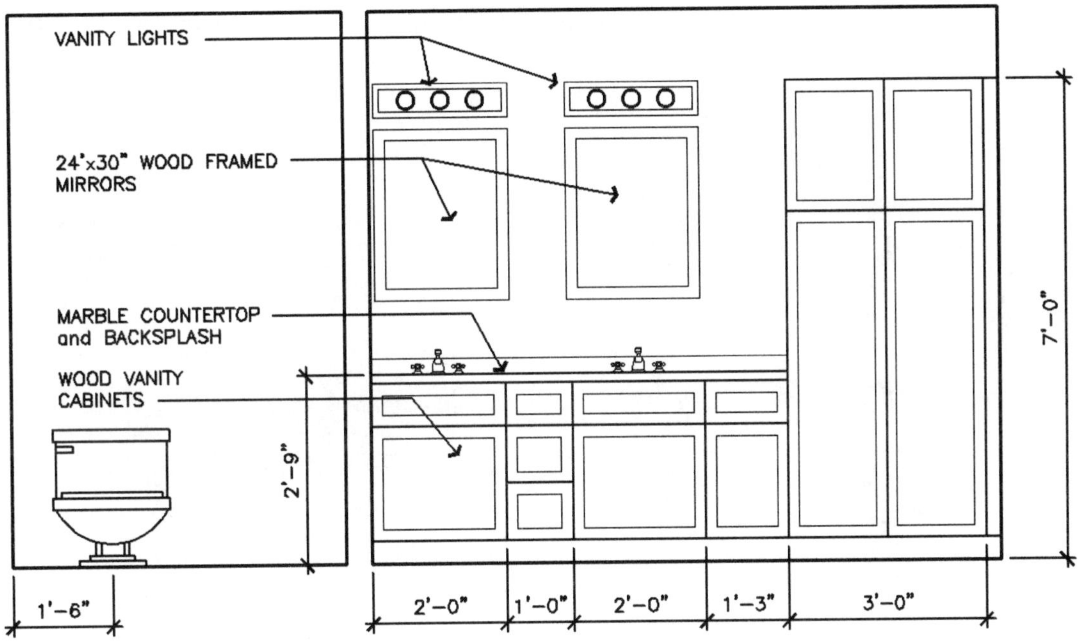

Figure 7-2.11 Bathroom Elevation; notes and dimensions added

Don't forget about lineweights:

Don't forget to draw your lines on the different non-plan layers (previously discussed on page 6-2) based on how heavy the linework should be. For interior elevations:

- **Heaviest Lines**: The outline of the room should be the heaviest line.
- **Medium Lines**: Objects out from the wall, like cabinets, should be the next heaviest.
- **Lightest Lines**: Any lines on the wall (e.g., the mirror) should be the lightest lines
- **Light Gray Lines**: Hatch patterns for ceramic tile or brick joints should be a light and gray line so it is not too intense. (This has not been covered yet.)

The actual implementation of lineweights will be covered in Lesson 8.

Carter Residence

Image courtesy of LHB
www.LHBcorp.com

Exercise 7-3:
Adding Furnishings to your Floor Plans

In this exercise you will add Blocks that represent various furnishings. Laying out furniture helps both you and the client to verify that your floor plan design is functional. You will see that blocks are available from several sources; this is in addition to the ones you drew at the beginning of this book.

First you will start with the Master Bedroom.

1. **Open** "Flr-2" drawing file.

2. Create a *Layer* named **A-FURN**, color set to **Red.**

3. Set the **A-FURN** *Layer* current.

4. Zoom into the Mater Bedroom area.

Next, you will insert a few of the symbols you created in Lesson 3.

5. **Insert** the following *Blocks*, created in Lesson 3 (Figure 7-3.1):
   a. **Bed-king**
   b. **Night-stand**
   c. **Dresser-1**
   d. **Chair-2**

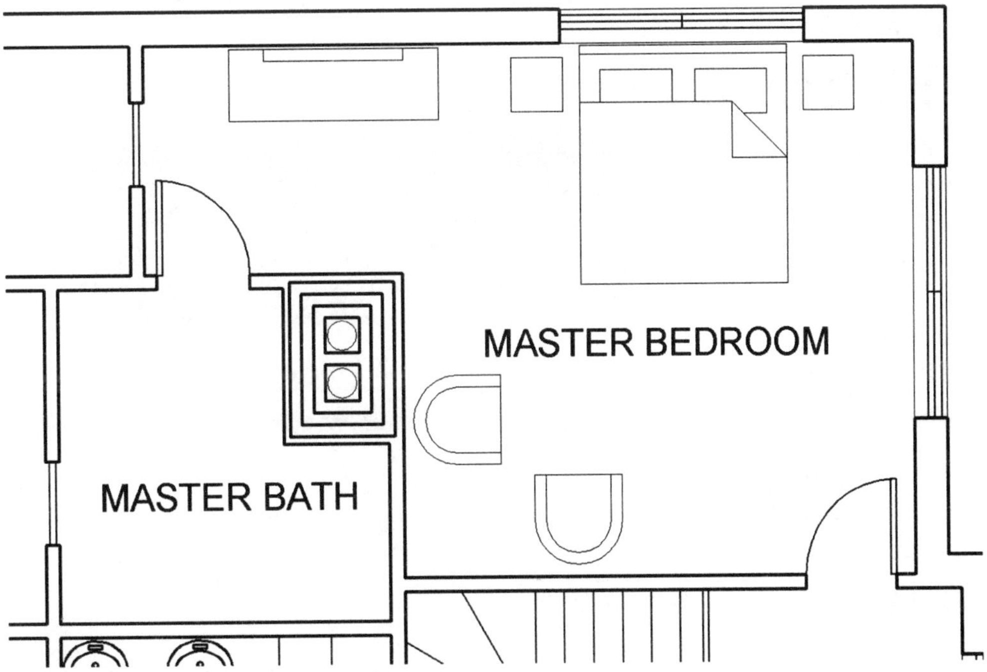

Figure 7-3.1 Master Bedroom; *Blocks* inserted

Now you will use *DesignCenter* to insert a *Block* located in a sample drawing file that was installed with AutoCAD.

6. Similar to Exercise 7-2, use *DesignCenter* to browse to the sample drawing file named **Home – Space Planner.dwg.** (Figure 7-3.2)

7. Insert **Plant - Rubber or Philodendron** from the *Blocks* category. (Figure 7-3.3)

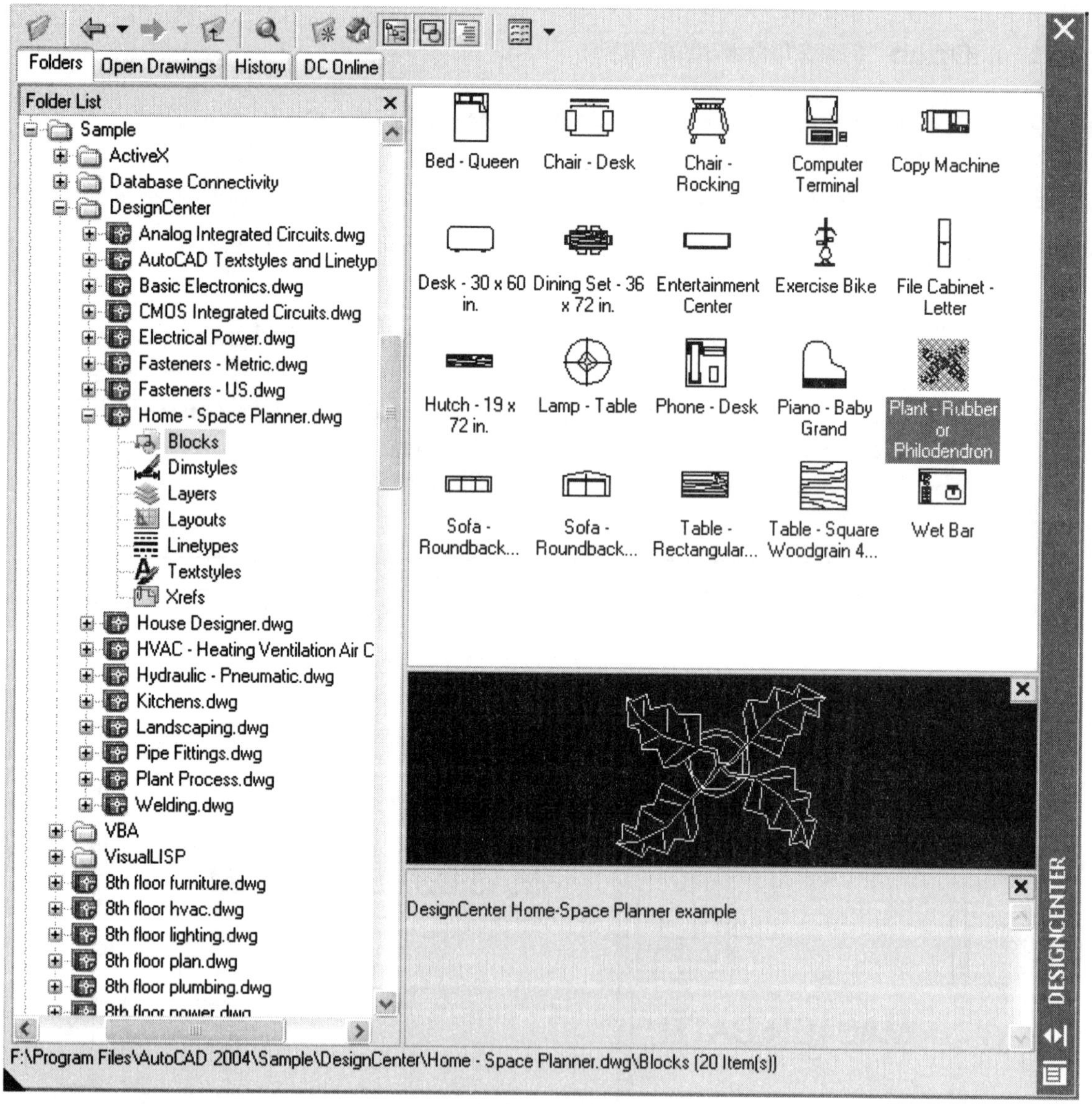

Figure 7-3.2 DesignCenter; *Blocks* to insert

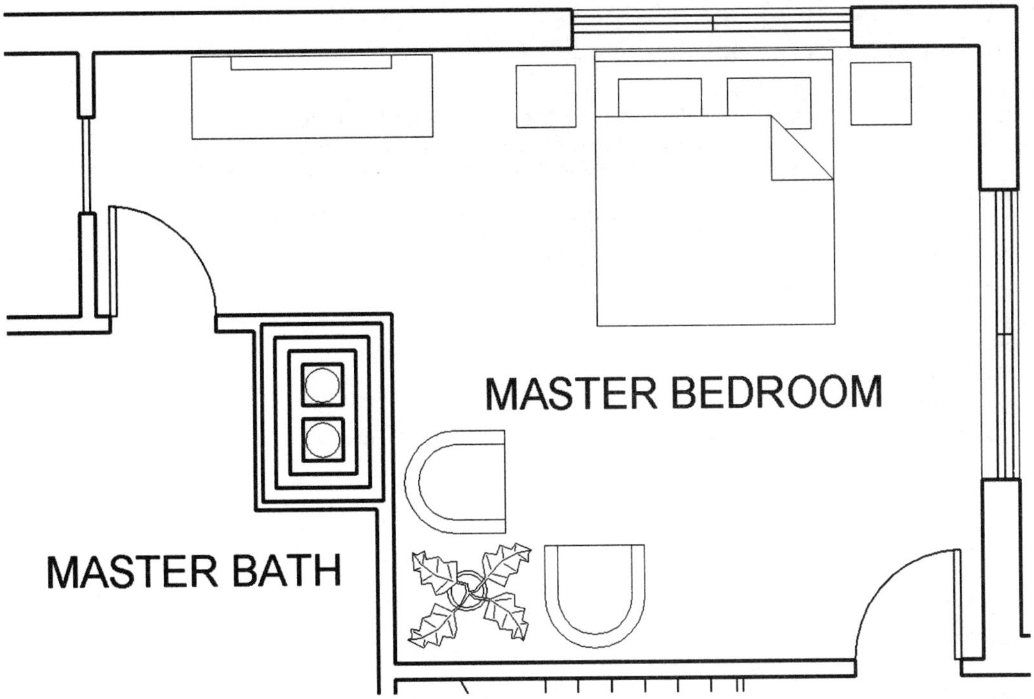

Figure 7-3.3 Master Bedroom; plant *Block inserted between chairs*

Additional content resources

In addition to the design content you have drawn and that found in DesignCenter, you can acquire additional content from other sources. Below are but a few examples.

DesignCenter	click the DC Online tab (Figure 7-3.4)
Sweets Online:	www.sweets.com
CAD Block Exchange Network	www.cben.net
AutoCAD Blocks	http://www.autocadblock.com/
AutoCAD Block Library	http://www.cadmonkey.com/blocks.htm
Wood Panel Systems	http://www.newenglandclassic.com
Fireplaces	http://www.firespaces.com

Many manufacturers have CAD blocks on their web sites for download or will mail you a CD if you ask them.

Warning!
Keep in mind that some of the symbols available on the internet, or else where, may not be accurate for a number of possible reasons. You should very the size and accuracy of important symbols!

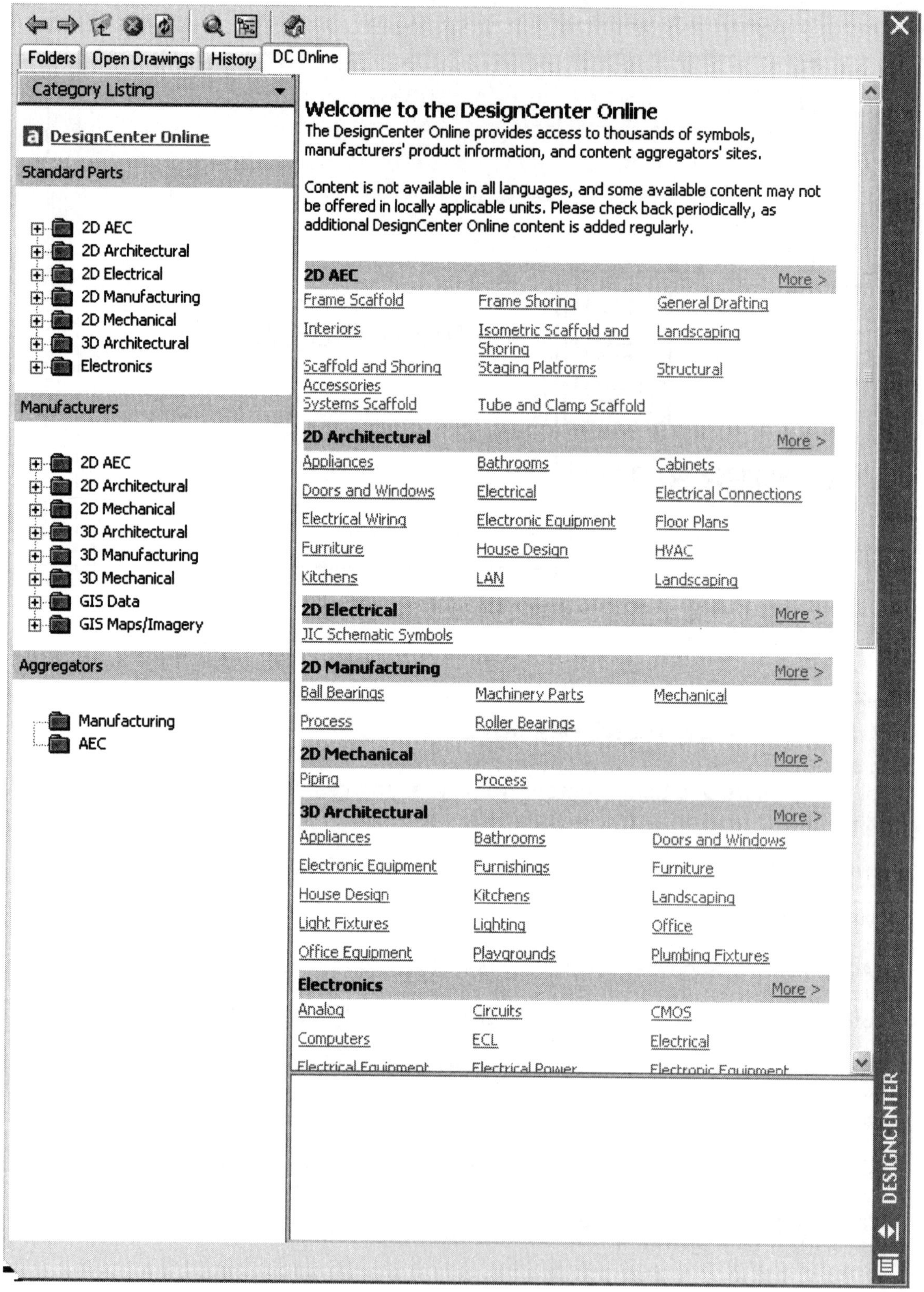

Figure 7-3.4 DesignCenter; DC Online tab current

Walk-In closet:

It is helpful to draw as much information as possible to better understand the complete design concept and make sure everything is coordinated. Drawing the clothes racks, for example, will show which walls are open and be more accessible for an electric outlet. You will do this simple task next.

8. **Zoom** into the walk-in closet.

9. **Offset** both the south and west wall lines into the room **12".** (Figure 7-3.5)

10. **Trim** the two new lines and change them to *Layer* **A-FURN.** (Figure 7-3.5)

Next you will draw lines to represent hanging cloths.

11. Draw a line **18"** long (on *Layer* A-FURN) and randomly copy and rotate it as shown in Figure 7-3.6.

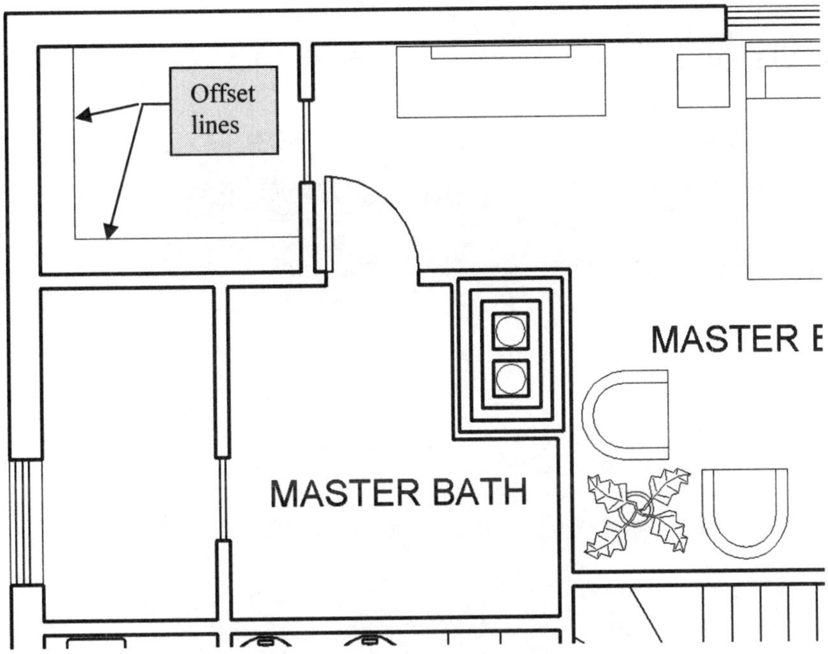

Figure 7-3.5 Master Bedroom Walk-in Closet; lines offset for hanging rod

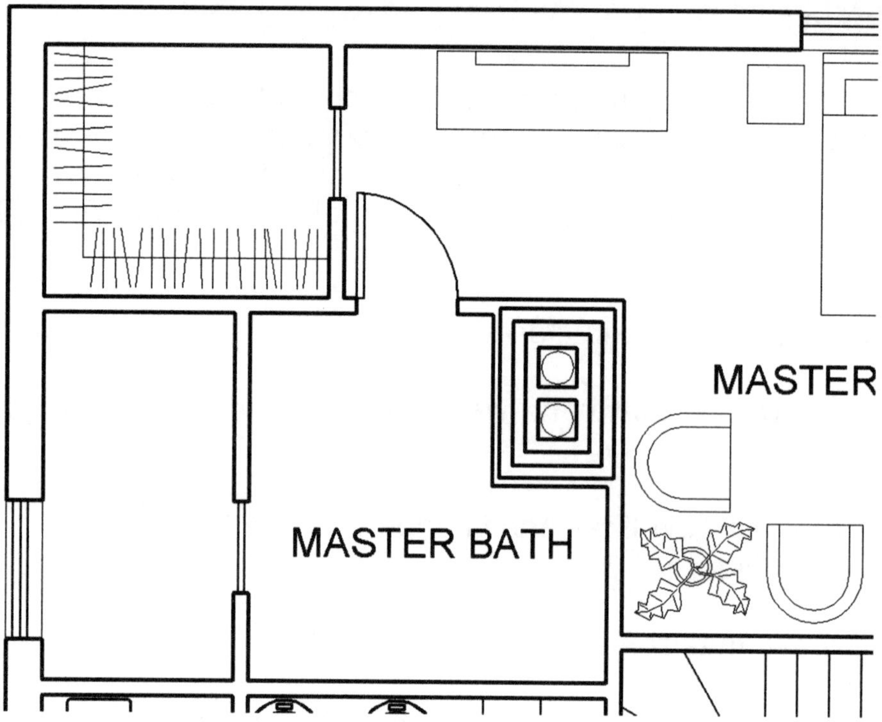

Figure 7-3.6 Master Bedroom Walk-in Closet; lines (i.e., hangers) added

That completes the Master Bedroom layout.

12. **Save** your drawing.

Image courtesy of Anderson Architects
Alan H. Anderson, Architect, Duluth, MN
Interior Design, Steven W. Sanborn, A.I.A., Santa Rosa, CA

Exercise 7-4:
Using Tool Palettes

Tool Palettes are a feature introduced in the previous version (AutoCAD 2004) which helps to organize content (blocks) and frequently used hatch patterns. First you will explore the standard, out-of-the-box, Tool Palettes. After looking at the Tools provided you will learn how to customize the Tool Palettes.

Overview of the "out-of-the-box" Tool Palettes:

First you will open one of your floor plans, so it will be ready to test the Tools on the Palette.

1. **Open** "Flr-2" drawing file.
2. Click the **Tool Palette** icon ( ) if the *Palette* is not currently displayed; the *Tool Palette* icon toggles the visibility on and off.

The initial view of the *Tool Palette* should look like **Figure 7-4.1**. Notice, down one side, are *Tabs*, similar to file folder tabs, which allow you to organize different groups of hatches, content and commands. The current *Tab* should be the one labeled "**Sample office project**".

TIP: If you only see the Title Bar show up when toggling the Tool Palettes icon, simply hover your cursor over the Title Bar and the Palettes will display. This is caused by a feature called "Auto-Hide", which will be covered shortly.

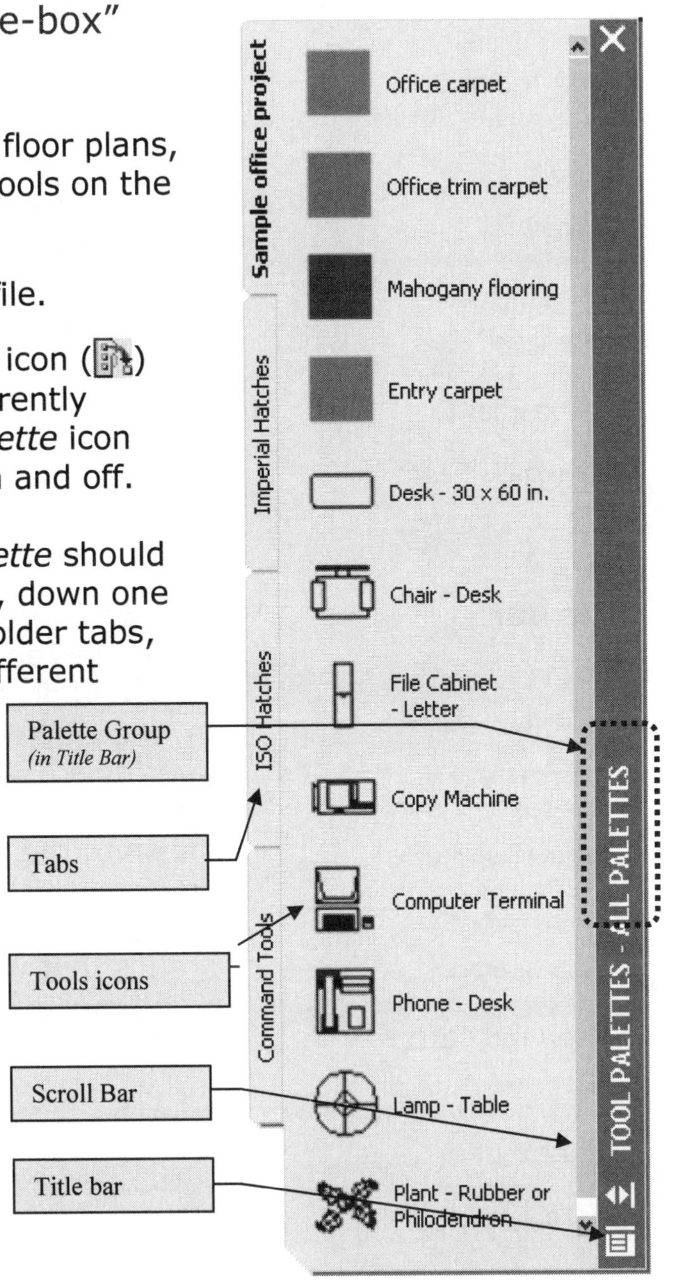

Figure 7-4.1 Tool Palettes; Sample office project tab

Tabs:

Used to organize *Blocks*, *Hatch Patterns* and *Commands* that are used regularly. You can add new *Tabs* as well as rename and reposition existing *Tabs*.

- Move Up
- Move Down
- New Tool Palette
- Rename Tool Palette

Right-click menu

Tools icons:

You can store *Blocks*, *Hatch* patterns and commands on *Palettes*. Each *Icon* has various settings to control, such as the scale and layer *Blocks* are inserted. Similarly, you can control properties like *Hatch* Pattern Scale and Color. These predefined properties will be covered next.

- Cut
- Copy
- Delete Tool
- Rename
- Properties...

Right-click menu

Title Bar:

This is the area you select when you want to move the *Tool Palettes* Window on the screen (click and drag). When *Auto-Hide* is turned on, the *Title Bar* is all you see when the *Tool Palettes* are open. Auto-Hide and other options are set via the right-click menu shown to the left. When you have Palette Groups (which are several Palette Tabs), you can toggle between them via the list of Groups that would be displayed at the bottom of the menu (currently your drawing only has the default Group: *All Palettes*)

- Move
- Size
- Close
- ✔ Allow Docking
- Auto-hide
- Transparency...
- New Tool Palette
- Rename
- Customize...
- ✔ All Palettes

Right-click menu

Inserting a Block from a Tool Palette:

Now you will practice inserting a Block from the Tool Palette; you will insert a lamp on each night table in the master bedroom.

3. Zoom into the master bedroom. (Figure 7-4.2)

4. From the *Sample Office Project* tab on the *Tool Palettes*, click (not drag) on the **Lamp – Table** icon.

5. Click near the center of the night table on the right side of the bed. (Figure 7-4.2)

6. Repeat steps 4 and 5 to place a lamp on the other night table.

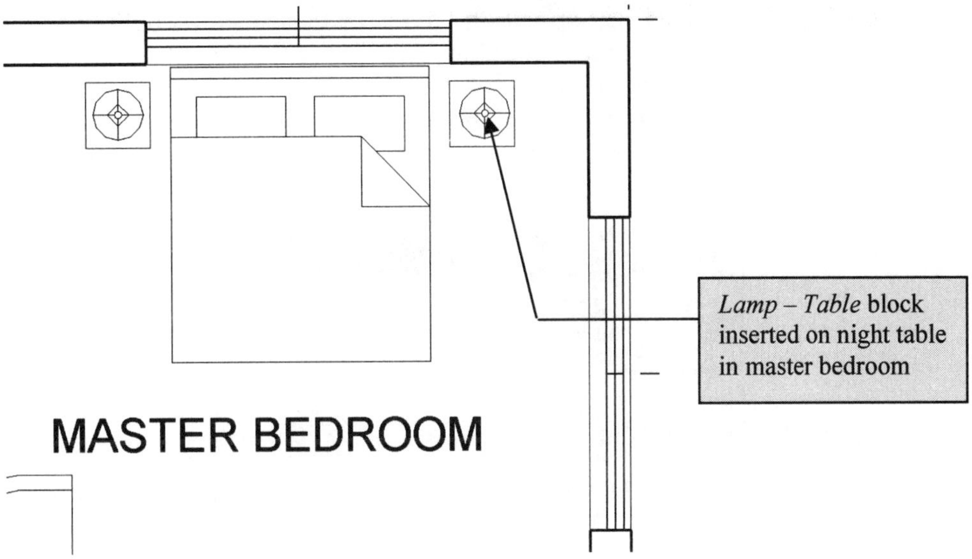

Figure 7-4.2
Second Floor Plan; Lamp – Table block inserted on night tables

Notice when you clicked the *Tool Palette* icon, you did not see the standard *Insert* dialog (Figure 4-2.11)? This is because all the settings you are normally prompted for from the *Insert* dialog have been pre-assigned to each *Block* stored in a *Palette*. You will explore these settings next.

7. Right-click on the **Lamp – Table** icon. (Figure 7-4.1)

8. Select **Properties...** from the pop-up menu.

Take a minute to observe some of the settings available for the selected tool (Lamp –Table). The main settings are:

Source file: AutoCAD imports the block from an external drawing file; so the file must always exist in the location specified.

Scale: This is set to 1 for "real-world" items like furniture and fixtures; they are drawn actual size and don't need to be scaled. However, annotation symbols (e.g.,, detail bubble) need to be scaled relative to intended plot scale.

Color: This should almost always be set to "ByLayer", which means the Layer the block is inserted on controls the color of the Block (assuming the lines in the Block were drawn on layer zero).

Layer: When set to "use current", the block is inserted on the current Layer; just like the standard Insert Block command. However, unlike the standard Insert Block command, you can pre-specify a Layer for the Block to be inserted on. So in the example below, you know the Block should always be inserted on the A-Furn layer. Simply setting the Layer property to A-Furn assures you that it will always be inserted on the correct Layer, regardless of the Current Layer setting.

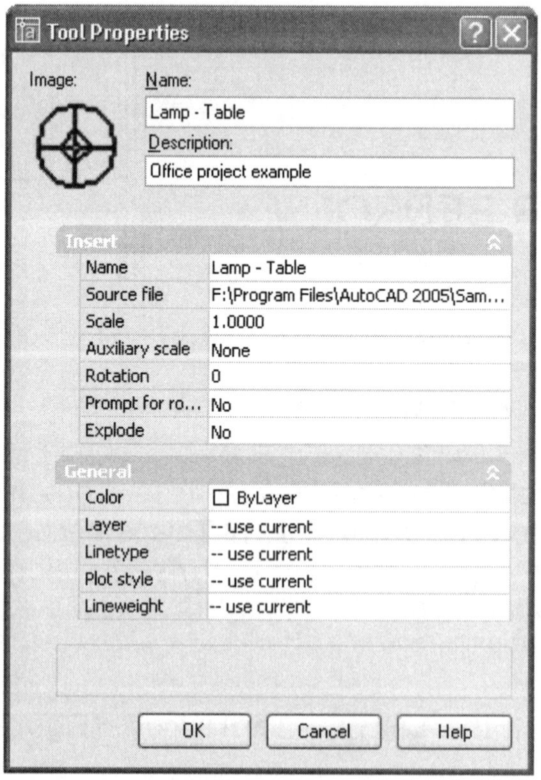

Figure 7-4.3
Tool Properties; Lamp – Table tool

Using a Hatch Tool on the Tool Palettes:

Next you will use one of the standard Solid Hatch patterns predefined on the *Sample Office Project* tab.

You will be using the Solid Hatch tool to fill in the walls, which will make them stand out more when printed. You should be aware that the name associated with a Hatch Tool is only meant to help you remember the specific settings (e.g., pattern, scale, color) associated with that icon. It does not really matter that you will be using a tool that has been described as a floor finish to fill in your floor plan walls.

The first thing you will do is create a separate Layer for the wall fill pattern to go on; this will allow you to freeze it when you do not want it to show.

9. Create a Layer named **A-Wall-Patt**; leave the color set to 7 (white). ***NOTE:** Do **NOT** set this Layer to be current!*

To show how you can predefine the *Layer*, you will adjust the *Layer* setting for one of the *Hatch* Tools before filling the walls.

10. Right-click on the **Mahogany flooring** icon; located on the *Sample Office Project* tab on the *Tool Palettes.*

11. Select **Properties.**

12. Click on the word "use current" next to the Layer Property (this will cause a down-arrow to show up on the right).

13. Click the down-arrow to display the list of *Layers* in your drawing.

14. Select **A-Wall-Patt** and then select **OK** (Figure 7-4.4).
TIP: The layer will not show up in the list if it has not been previously created.

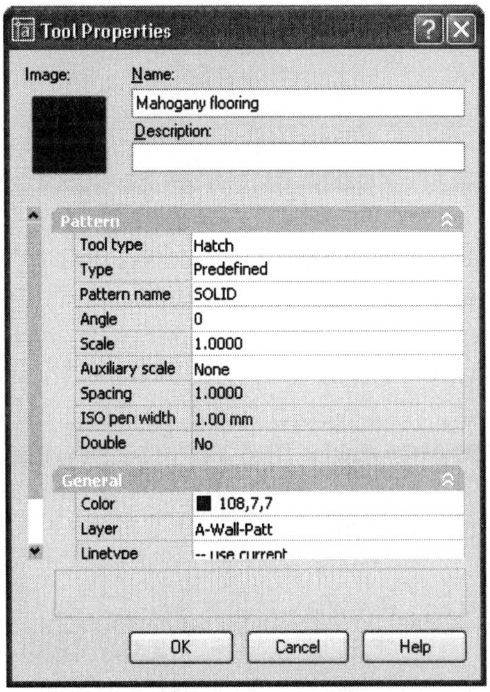

Figure 7-4.4
Tool Properties; Mahogany flooring tool

Now you are ready to fill a section of wall with the hatch tool.

15. Click the **Mahogany flooring** icon. (Figure 7-4.1)

16. Click within the wall area in the upper-right corner of the master bedroom. (Figure 7-4.5)
    TIP: If you get the error "Valid hatch boundary not found", you should zoom in on all corner- and end-points to verify they are truly connected; AutoCAD needs to find a "perfectly" closed area in order to draw a hatch pattern.

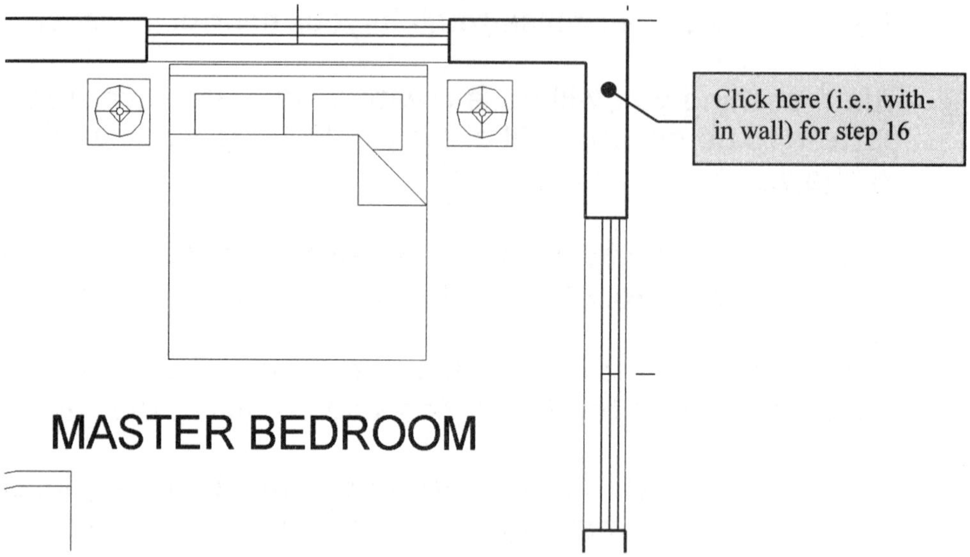

Figure 7-4.5
Second Floor Plan; area to click to specify area to be hatched

17. **Zoom Extents** to see the entire plan.

The selected portion of wall is now *Hatched* (Figure 7-4.6). It is good practice to only Hatch one or two closed areas at a time. If you were to Hatch all the walls, for the entire floor, at one time, you would have to do it all over again to accommodate one change. Whereas, you would only need to redo the fill pattern directly adjacent to the change.

18. Repeat steps 15-17 to *Hatch* the rest of the walls **on each floor**.

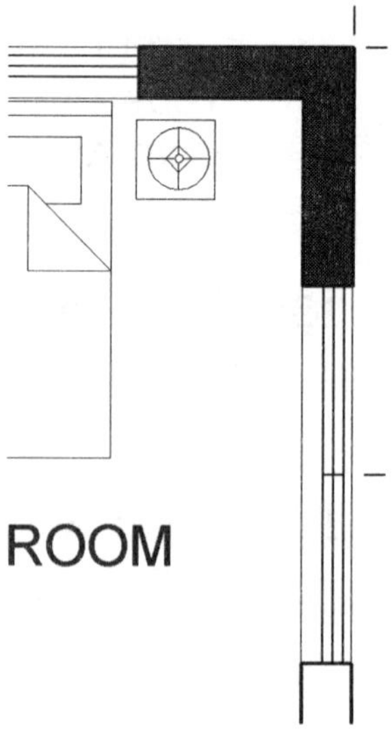

Figure 7-4.6
Portion of wall hatched

All your walls should now be Hatched. (Figure 7-4.7)

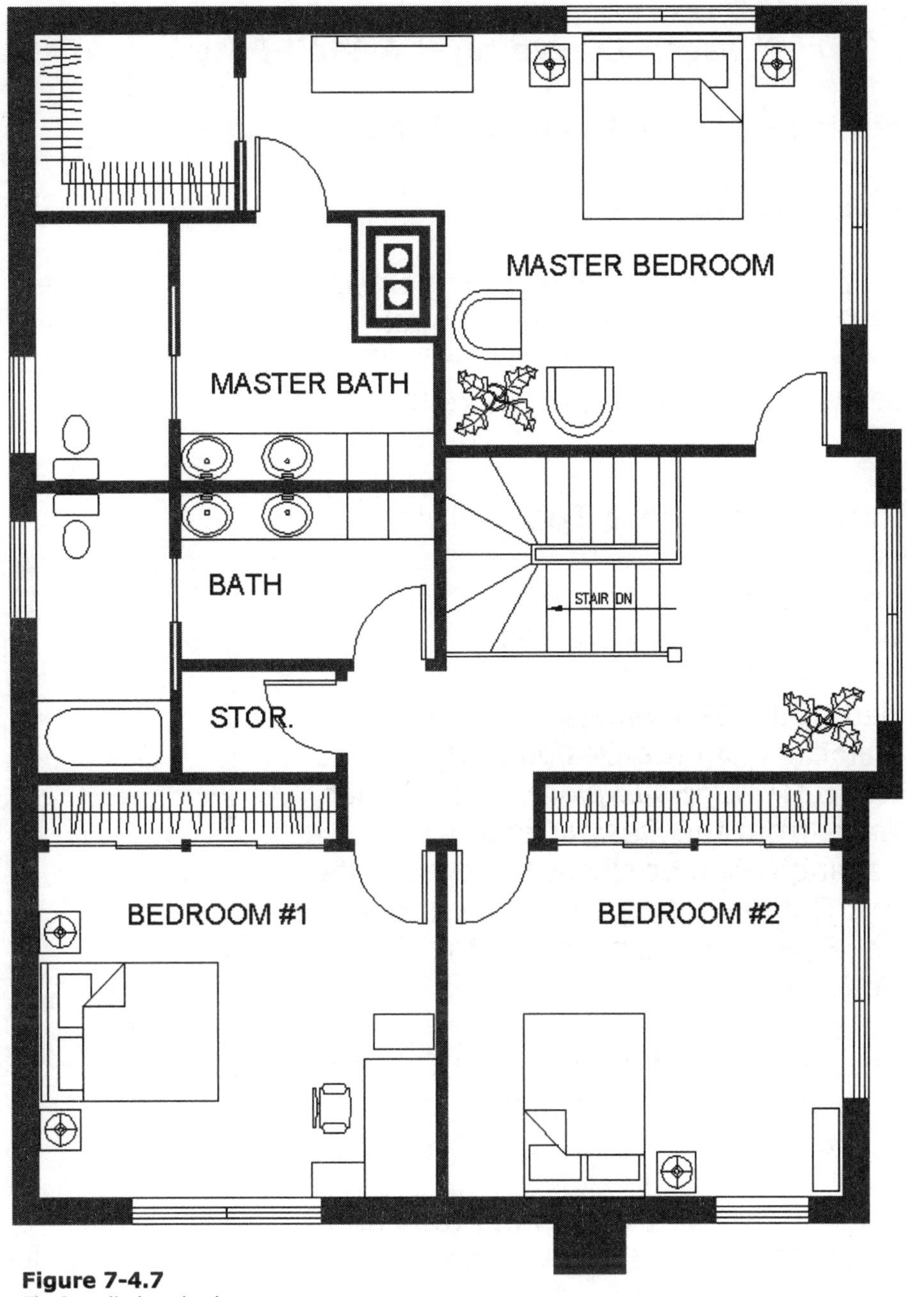

Figure 7-4.7
Flr-2 walls hatched

Notice how the floor plan reads more clearly with the walls hatched; there is no question where a wall starts and ends.

Next you verify the Solid Hatch was drawn on the correct Layer (even though that Layer was not set current when drawing the Hatch).

19. In the *Layer Manager*, **Freeze** *Layer* **A-Wall-Patt.**

All the wall hatching should no longer be visible.

20. **Thaw** Layer **A-Wall-Patt.**

You should also notice that the color for the *Solid Hatch* has been set *ByEntity* rather than *ByLayer*. So, even though the A-Wall-Patt *Layer* has its color set to 7, the *Solid Hatch* is set to True Color 108,7,7 per the color property in the *Tool Properties (see Figure 7-4.4)*.

Adding custom content to a Tool Palette:

Now you will create a custom Tab and add some of the blocks you have previously created.

Content is added to the *Tool Palettes* by "dragging and dropping" blocks from the *DesignCenter, Drawing Window or Windows Explorer*. So, similar to inserting *Blocks* from the *DesignCenter*, you browse to a drawing (open or closed) and open its Blocks category. Then you drag the desired *Block* to the *Tool Palette*. Finally you can specify the scale, Layer, etc. if desired.

First you will create a custom *Tool Palette* Tab; this creates a storage area for your frequently used symbols (i.e., *Blocks*)

21. Right-click on one of the existing tabs and select **New Tool Palette** from the pop-up menu (see page 7-28).

22. Enter the tab name: **My Symbols** in the area provided.

You now have a custom Tab ready to hold your Blocks or hatch patterns. (See Figure 7-4.8)

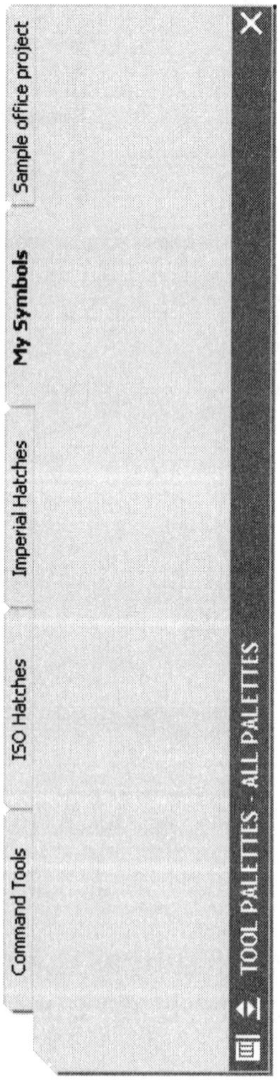

Figure 7-4.8
New Tool Palette tab

Make sure your Flr-2 drawing is open before proceeding.

23. Open the **DesignCenter** palette.

24. Click on the **Open Drawings** Tab.

25. Expand the Flr-2 drawing to view its categories (i.e., click the plus symbol) – *if necessary.*

26. Select the **Blocks** category. (Figure 7-4.9)

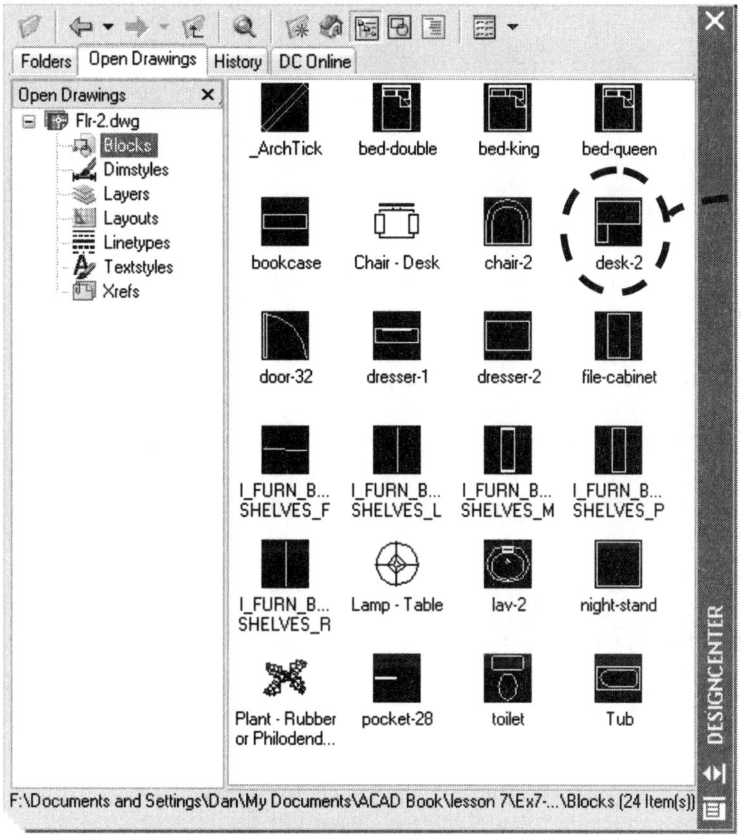

Figure 7-4.9
DesignCenter; Open Drawings Tab - Flr-2\Blocks selected

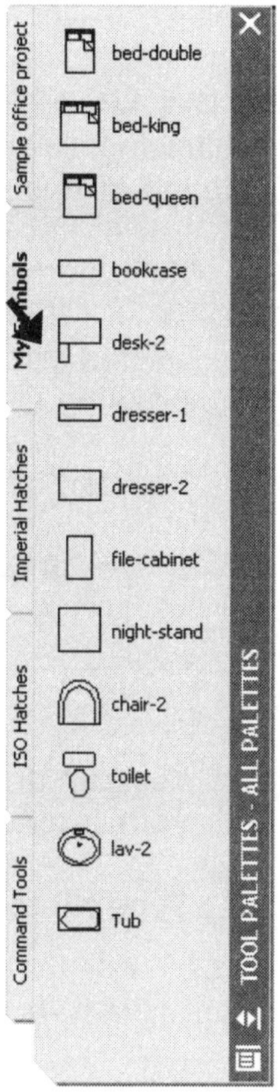

Figure 7-4.10
Custom content added to Tool Palette

27. Drag your *Blocks* (the ones you created) from *DesignCenter* to the "My Symbols" *Tool Palette.* (Figure 7-4.10)

28. Set the *Layer* to **A-Furn** (cf. 7-4.4) for each furniture symbol and A-Flor-Pfix for each plumbing fixture.

29. Save your **Flr-2** drawing.

Self-Exam:

The following questions can be used as a way to check your knowledge of this lesson. The answers can be found at the bottom of this page.

1. Base cabinets should be placed on the layer A-Flor-Case-L. (T/F)

2. Interior elevations are typically drawn at ½″ = 1′-0″ (T/F)

3. You can use an irregular shaped polyline to Xclip an external reference. (T/F)

4. What is the text height for a ½″ = 1′-0″ drawing? ________________.

5. DesignCenter's *DC Online* tab only has a handful of blocks available. (T/F)

Review Questions:

The following questions may be assigned by your instructor as a way to assess your knowledge of this section. Your instructor has the answers to the review questions.

1. Xclip permanently deletes all the clips lines. (T/F)

2. In this lesson you used DesignCenter to insert blocks contained within other drawing files. (T/F)

3. You can offset wall lines to quickly create a temporary reference line. (T/F)

4. In DesignCenter, to access drawings on your hard drive, you must have the

   ______________ tab selected (one of the four tabs near the top of DC).

5. You can draw lines from your Xclip'ed floor plan to position walls and fixtures in your interior elevation. (T/F)

6. Type XR to open the __________________ __________________.

7. This icon (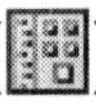) allows you to open __________________________.

8. All furniture should be drawn on layer __________________________.

9. All blocks (symbols) downloaded off the Internet are 100% accurate. (T/F)

10. DesignCenter must be closed, similar to the Layer dialog, before you can continue drawing in AutoCAD. (T/F)

Self-Exam Answers:
1 - T, **2** - T, **3** - T, **4** – 2 ¼", **5** – F

Additional Tasks:

Task 7-1 Toilet room plan layouts

Using the techniques learned in this lesson, add the plumbing fixtures to the two remaining toilet rooms. Refer back to Figures 4-1.1 and 4-1.4 for the fixture locations.

Task 7-2 Toilet room elevations

Using the techniques learned in this lesson, draw the interior elevations for the wall with the toilet and sink; for the plans drawn in the previous task (Task 7-1).

Task 7-3 Furniture layout

Using the techniques learned in this lesson, place furniture symbols throughout the house. Use your own ideas for this task. Imagine it was your house and decide where you would put the couch, the chair, the television, etc. Create new blocks for any symbols you may need but cannot find.

Image courtesy of
Stanius Johnson Architects
Daniel's Construction, Amery WI.
Photo by Robert Aho
www.staniusjohnson.com

Notes:

Lesson 8
Residential Project: Site Plan::

This lesson will introduce you to the basic site plan drafting concepts. First you will draw the existing site conditions from a survey. Secondly, you will draw the building footprint, driveway and walks on the site. Finally, you will draw new contours indicating finished grade and drainage for the site.

Exercise 8-1:
Draw existing survey

Introduction:

The first thing you typically do when preparing a site plan is draw the existing site conditions. A survey crew will gather the site data and then draw a site plan indicating the location of any buildings, trees, paved surfaces as well as contours describing the shape of the land.

Ideally, you would get an AutoCAD file from the surveyor which would allow you to pretty much start drawing the new conditions. One thing to understand, in this case, is that you will usually have to adjust the scale (i.e., size) of the drawing. The reason is that surveyors use one AutoCAD unit as a foot whereas architects use one AutoCAD unit as an inch. Therefore, if you where to list the distance of a line (from a survey drawing) that is 48′ in a drawing (with its units set to architectural), you will get 4′-0″ (see the following chart):

Drawing	Line	Units	Length	Adjustment
Survey	48 Acad units	Decimal	48′	n/a
Site Plan	48 Acad units	Architectural	48″=4′	48x12=576″=48′

Thus, you scale the survey drawing up 12 times to make it the correct scale in your site plan file (or any file that has the units set to architectural).

If you do not get an AutoCAD file of the survey you will have to draw it from the blueprint provided. This can be more challenging than reproducing an existing floor plan drawing because of the curved lines; curved lines are more difficult to create. In this lesson you will draw a site survey from a "hardcopy only" drawing.

Create Layers:

The first thing you will do is create the required *Layers*.

1. Create the following *Layers*:

	Layer Name	*Color*	*Linetype*
a.	C-ANNO-TEXT	YELLOW	CONTINUOUS
b.	C-PROP	MAGENTA	PHANTOM2
c.	C-TOPO	YELLOW	HIDDEN2
d.	C-TREE	CYAN	CONTINUOUS
e.	C-WATR	CYAN	CONTINUOUS

Draw the Property Lines:

Now you will draw the property line. This will involve entering decimal feet for lengths and degrees-minutes-seconds for angles.

2. On the correct *Layer*, draw the property line shown in Figure 8-1.1. Note the following:

   a. <u>Entering the length 134.6254'</u>
   You can directly enter the decimal foot property line lengths listed. Consider a similar example; when drawing a line you can enter 1'6" or you can enter 1.5'. In either case AutoCAD will draw the line the same length.

   b. <u>Entering the angle 101°56'</u>
   Entering angles by inputting Degrees-Minutes-Seconds requires a particular format: 101d56' (for this example). If you are in the line command you can enter the following to draw the line the correct length/angle, @122.653456'<78d4'. If you need to dimension angles using this format you would change the *Units* from the *Format* menu, change it to Deg/Min/Sec.

3. Set the *Ltscale* to **240**; this should make the property lines appear as a type of dashed line (Phantom2).

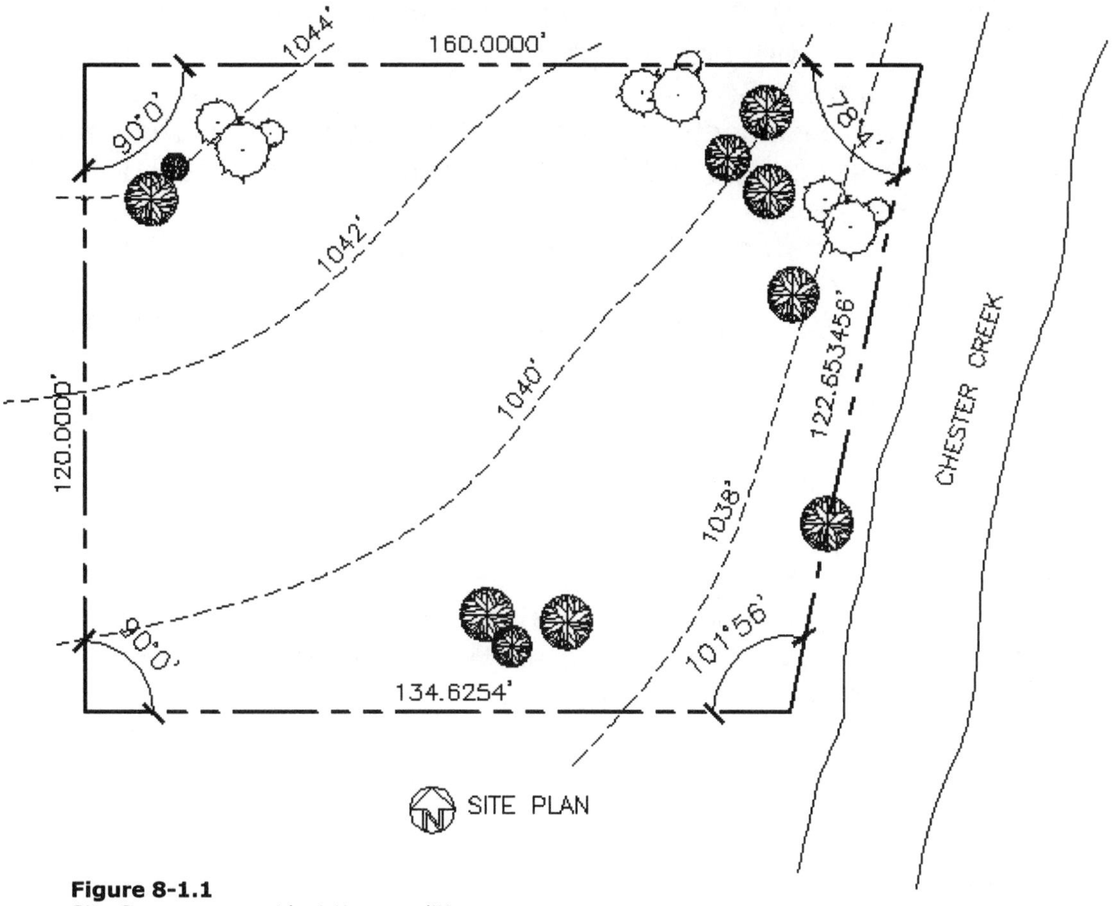

Figure 8-1.1
Site Survey; current/existing conditions

Drawing the contours:

You have a few options for getting the contours into your cad file. One is to scan the drawing and place it in AutoCAD at the correct scale; then you can draw/trace over the image. The second involves using a grid to approximately transfer the curved contour lines from the "hard copy" to the drawing file; you will try this next.

Normally you would hand draw a 10'-0" x 10'-0" grid on a blueprint of the survey using an engineer's scale and a parallel bar or drafting board. However, this step will not be necessary for this tutorial; the grid is already added in Figure 8-1.3.

4. Using the **Pline** command (i.e., polyline), draw the contours on the correct Layer per the comments below:
   a. Use the site plan with the 10'-0" x 10'-0" gird overlay in Figure 8-1.3.
   b. *See next page for continuation*.

c. Draw a 10'-0" x 10'-0" grid overlay on your site plan; aligned with orthographic property lines as shown in Figure 8-1.3.
d. Draw each contour; using the various locations the contour crosses the 10' x 10' grid as a reference (Figure 8-1.2). For example:
    i. Draw one contour at a time, following and noting where the line intersects the grid.
    ii. You only need to pick points where the contour line intersects a grid line; you will smooth out the line in a later step.
    iii. Notice that the contours cross exactly at some of the grid intersections; these are the easiest points to locate.
    iv. All other intersections can be approximated to be ¼, ½ or ¾ distance between two grid lines.
e. You want to be as accurate as possible, but it is not necessary to be as accurate as you need to be when drawing the floor plans.

5. Select all the contours; then, from the *Properties* palette, set the Linetype Generation to **Enabled.**

FYI: *This setting makes the dashes consistent in your dashed lines. When this feature is disabled, dashes are calculated for each line segment in the polyline; many of which may not be large enough to show a dash at all; making portions of the line look continuous.*

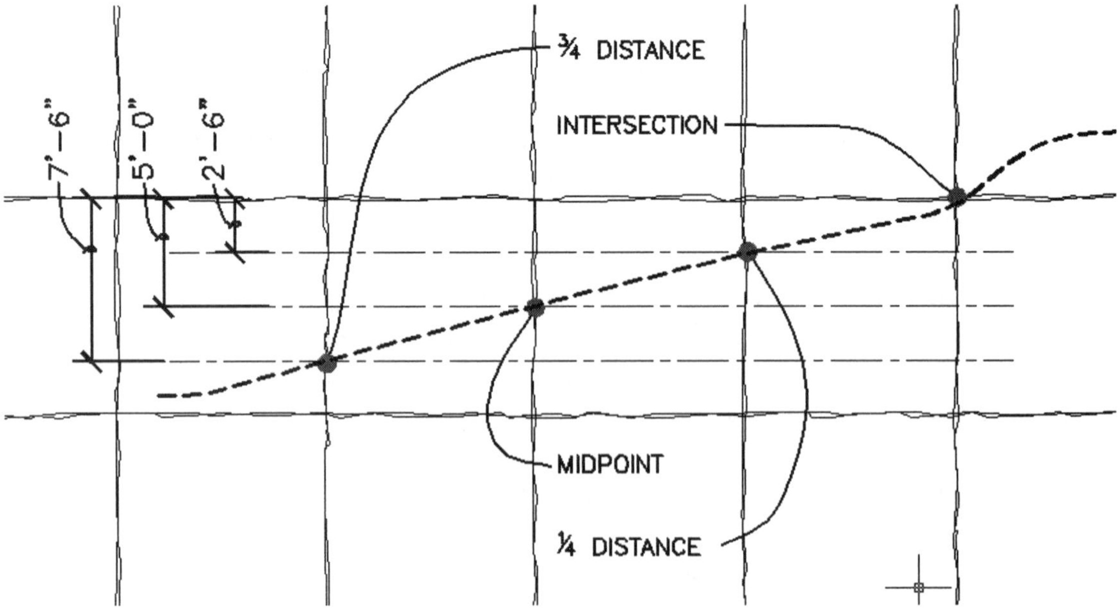

Figure 8-1.2
Contour layout explanation; the image above shows the four primary points the counter line crosses the vertical grid lines, the same process is used on horizontal grid lines

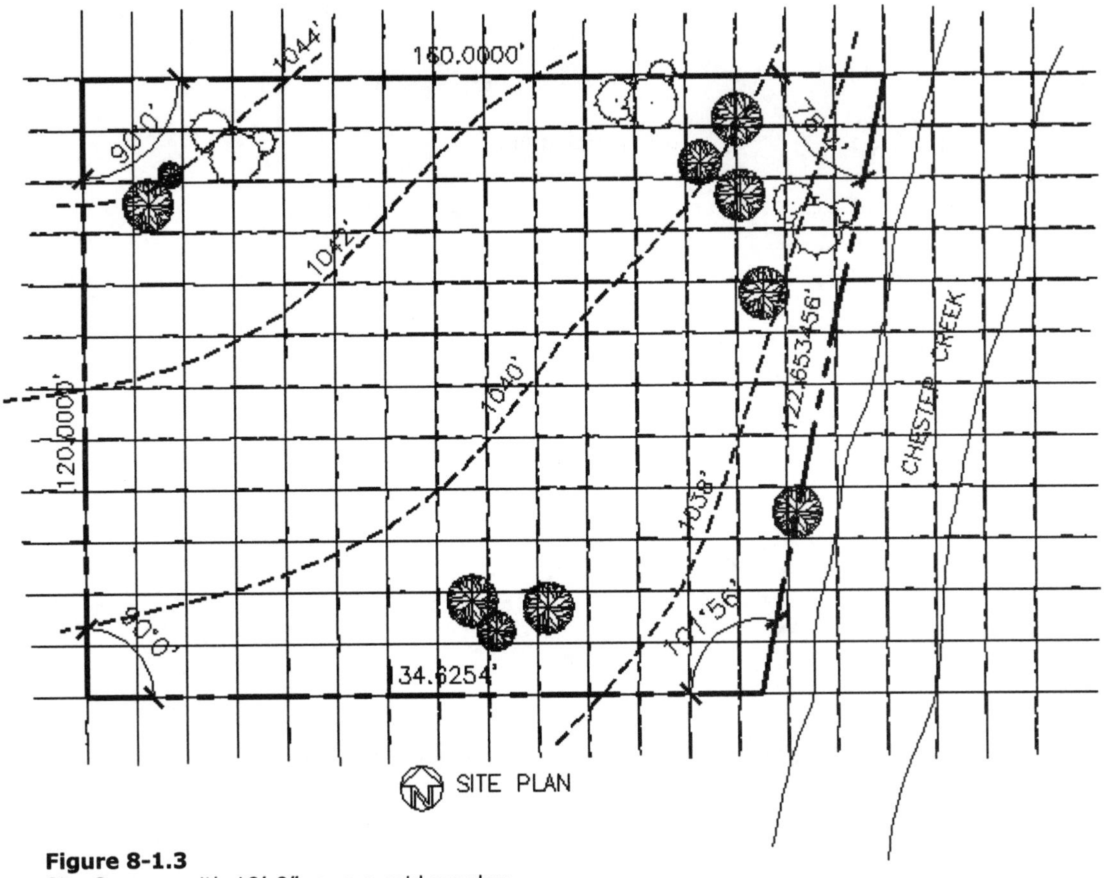

Figure 8-1.3
Site Survey; with 10'-0" square grid overlay

Smoothing the segmented contours:

Now you will use the *Pedit* (a.k.a., Polyline-Edit) command to smooth out the segmented contour lines. If you recall, you used the *Pedit* command to adjust the width of the grade line (which was a polyline) on your exterior elevations. Another sub-feature of the *Pedit* command is to smooth out a segmented *Pline*. The *Pedit* command has two methods available for smoothing a line; *Spline* and *Fit*.

You can see the effect each option has on a polyline in Figure 8-1.4. The top figure indicates the original "segmented" polyline where the dots represent the points you picked while drawing the *Pline*. The second (or middle) image shows what happens when you use the *Spline* option of *Pedit*. Finally the bottom image shows how the *Fit* option modifies a *Pline*.

Seeing as the points you pick to create the polyline (i.e., contour) are defining the path, you will want to use the *Fit* option on your contours.

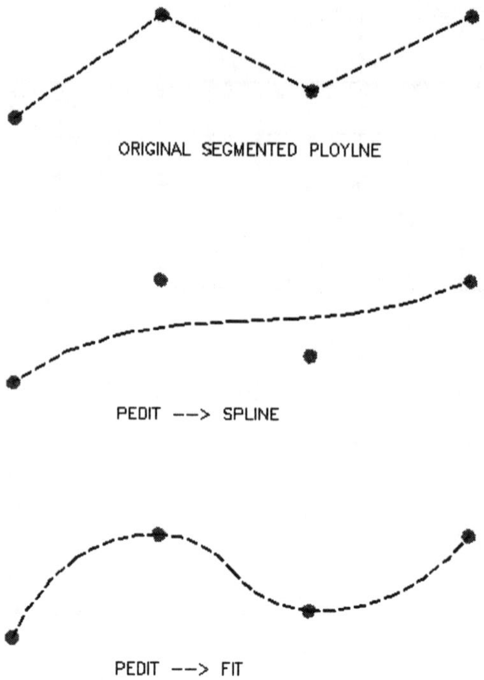

Figure 8-1.4
PEDIT Options; compare results of Pedit:Spline and Pedit:Fit

6. Type **Pedit**, press **Enter**, and then select one of the contour lines.

You now see the following in the *Command Window*:
Enter an option [Close/Join/Width/Edit vertex/Fit/Spline/Decurve/Ltype gen/Undo]:

7. Type **F** and then press **Enter.**

The line is now smoothed and you get the same prompt as before, which would allow you to further modify the polyline if necessary.

8. Press **Enter** to complete the *Pedit* command.

9. Repeat the previous three steps to smooth out each contour line.

10. Using the information just covered, draw the creek
    a. Draw the lines on *Layer* A-WATR.
    b. Smooth the lines using *Pedit.*

Adding the trees and north arrow:

Once again, thanks to one of AutoCAD's sample drawings you have access to the pre-drawn trees and north arrow shown in Figure 8-1.1. You will place these items next.

11. Using **DesignCenter** (and steps previously covered in this book), browse to the folder shown in Figure 8-1.5.

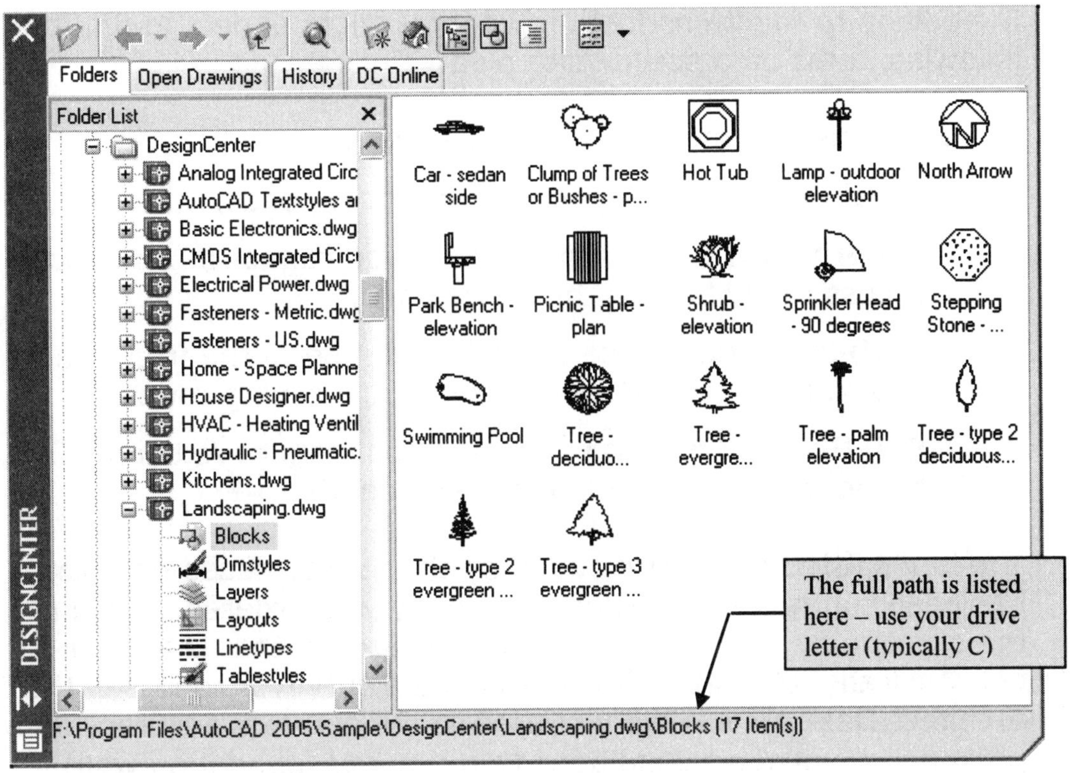

Figure 8-1.5
DESIGNCENTER; landscape blocks available via the sample files

12. Drag and drop "Clump of Trees or Bushes – plan" and "Tree – deciduous plan" into your site plan; the trees should automatically be placed on the correct *Layer*: C-Tree.

13. Copy the blocks around the drawing using Figure 8-1.3 as a reference for quantity and location.

    ***TIP**: You can (and should) scale and rotate the tree blocks so they don't all look the same and thus will better account for current conditions.*

14. Insert the North Arrow drawing from the DesignCenter as well.

15. Draw all the text shown in Figure 8-1.1, including the contour elevation labels, property line lengths and the creek label (all of which should be on the C-ANNO-TEXT layer).
    a. Make the text 3'-0" high.
    b. Rotate the text to align with the contours and property lines.

In addition to the items just drawn, you might expect to find the following items on a survey/site plan:

- **Utilities** - water, gas, storm, sewer cable, etc.
- **Land Features** - exposed ledge rock, ponds, etc.
- **Easements/Covenants** - areas you cannot build on so access to utilities can be maintained.
- **Setbacks** - how close a building can be to the front, back and side property lines based on local zoning codes.
- **Soil Boring Locations** - where soil tests have been done to the determine footing size and depth.

The items listed above are added by the survey based on what has been contracted for when the survey was ordered. If you (or the client) only paid for property line locations, that is all you get! Typically, the client directly pays the surveyor to lessen the Architect/Designer's liability related to the survey's accuracy and potential of unknown conditions (e.g., buried foundation wall).

You now have the existing site plan drawn and ready for you to place the new elements such as the building, walks, driveway, etc.

Exercise 8-2:
Add House, Driveway and walks

Introduction:

This exercise locates the outline of the building on the site as well as the driveway and sidewalk.

First you will create the appropriate Layers.

1.

Layer Name	*Color*	*Linetype*
a. C-BLDG	WHITE	CONTINUOUS
b. C-BLDG-PATT	254	CONTINUOUS
c. C-BLDG-PRCH	YELLOW	CONTINUOUS
d. C-WALK	RED	CONTINUOUS
e. C-ROAD	RED	CONTINUOUS

Now you will temporarily Xref in your first floor plan so you can draw an outline of your building and see where the doors are.

2. **Xref** your first floor plan (flr1.dwg) into the site drawing.

3. Move the Xref'ed floor plan so it is in the proper position, as shown in Figure 8-2.1

4. **Freeze** the dimension *Layer* in the floor plan Xref:

    a. When you Xref a drawing, all the visible *Layers* in that drawing are also visible in the Xref; you can freeze some *Layers* in the Xref if you wish.
    b. Each *Layer* in the Xref'ed drawing shows up in the *Layer Properties Manager*; each with the Xref's filename as a prefix.
    c. So, to freeze the Xref's dimension *Layer*, you will freeze the *Layer* named **Flr1|A-Anno-Dims.**

Next you will draw a polyline around the perimeter of the building.

5. On the **C-BLDG** Layer, draw a **Pline** around the perimeter of your building.

    a. Do not draw the outline around the porch, just the building.
    b. Use AutoCAD's Osnaps to accurately draw the outline.

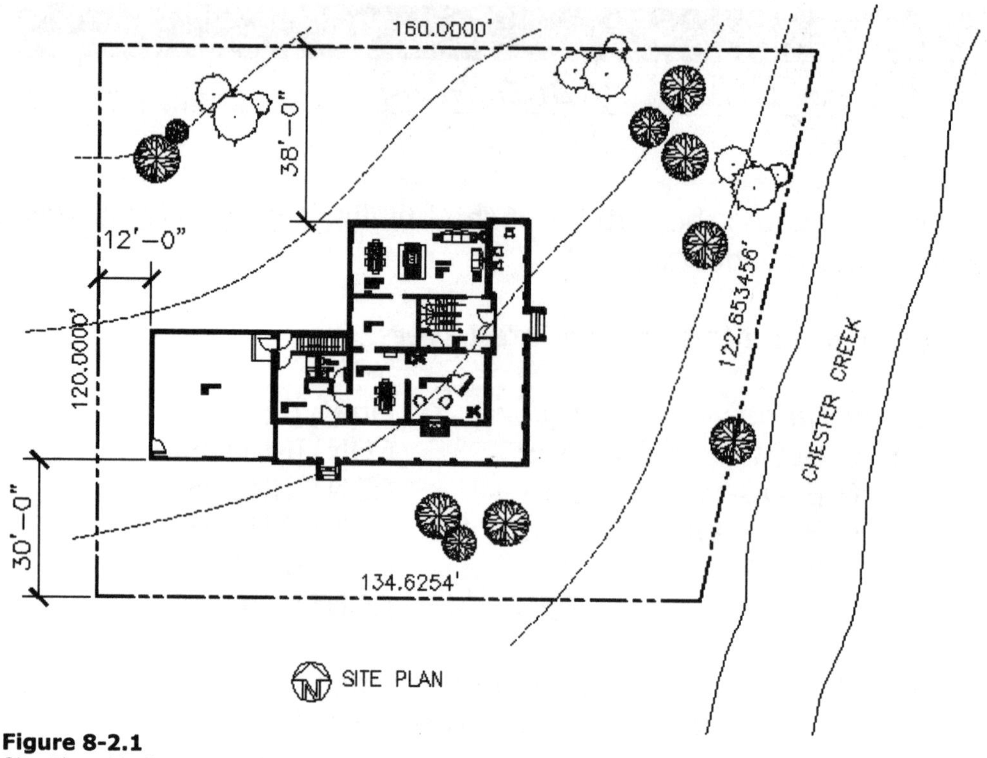

Figure 8-2.1
Site Plan; Xref positioned in proper location

6. Draw a **Pline** along the exterior side of the porch (C-Bldg-PRCH).

7. Add the dimensions shown in Figure 8-2.1; on *Layer* C-Anno-Dims.

   TIP: *Make sure your dimscale is set to 240.*

8. Draw a 22'-0" wide driveway centered on the garage doors; on *Layer* C-Road.

   TIP: *Draw a line from the midpoint of the wall between the two garage doors and then offset the line 11'-0" each way.*

9. Now draw a 5'-0" wide sidewalk as shown in Figure 8-2.3; on *Layer* C-Walk.

   TIP: *Draw one side of the sidewalk, using Fillet and then offset the lines 5'-0" to create the other side of the side walk.*

Next you will Unload (not detach) the Xref. By Unloading the Xref, you can quickly reload it without having to browse for it, position it and adjust the layers. This is handy for verifying, occasionally, that your building outline is still up to date.

10. In the *Xref Manager*, **Unload** the Flr1 drawing. (Figure 8-2.2)

11. Click **OK** to close the *Xref Manager*.

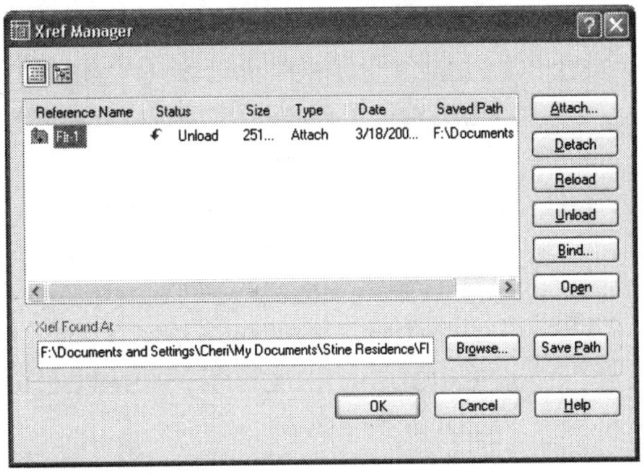

Figure 8-2.2
Xref Manager; Flr1 drawing unloaded

Your drawing should now look like Figure 8-2.3.

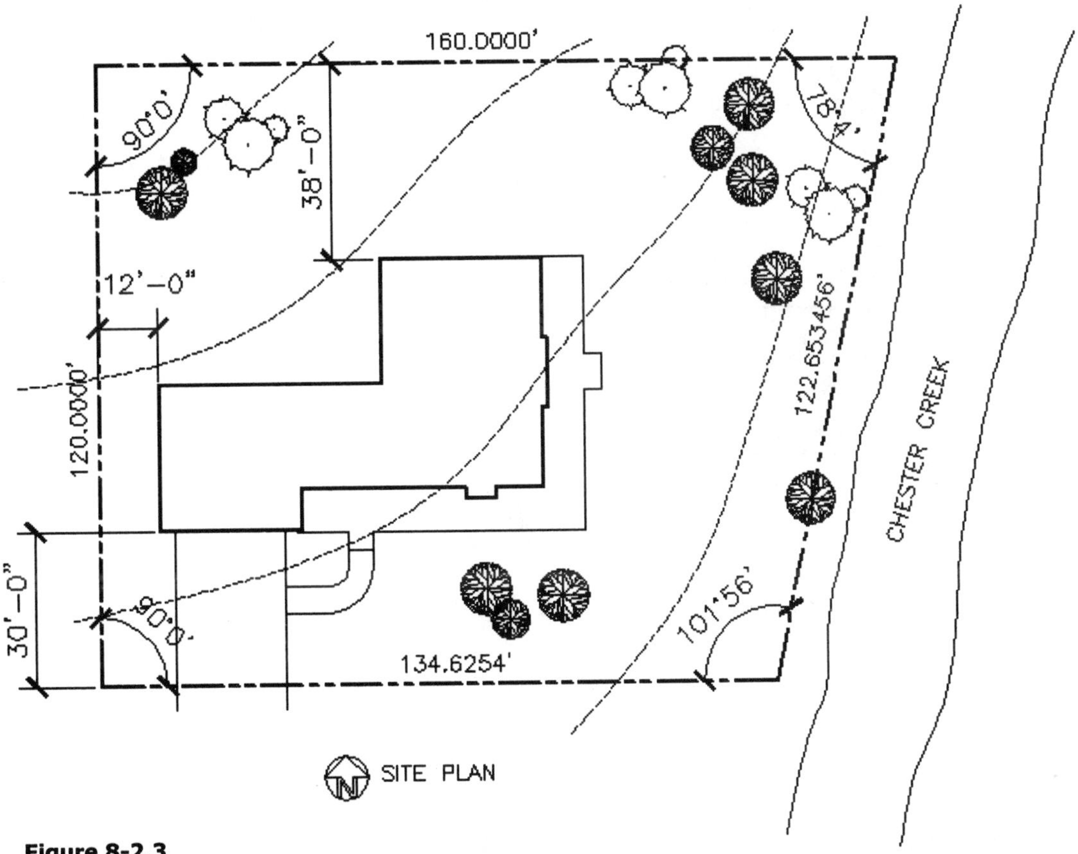

Figure 8-2.3
Site Plan; Building outline and paved areas added

Next you will fill the building foot print with a solid shade to help it stand out.

12. Using *Bhatch*, add a *Solid* hatch pattern to the building foot print on *Layer* A-Bldg-Patt.

13. Draw a 20'-0" x 16'-0" patio on the back inside corner of the residence (see Figure 8-2.4).

14. Use the Hatch (i.e., Bhatch) pattern "**GRAVEL**" at a scale of **48** as a symbol for stone pavers in the patio.

15. From the *Landscaping* sample drawing (discussed in the previous exercise), insert the picnic table; rotate as shown in Figure 8-2.4.

16. Save your drawing as **ex8-2.dwg.**

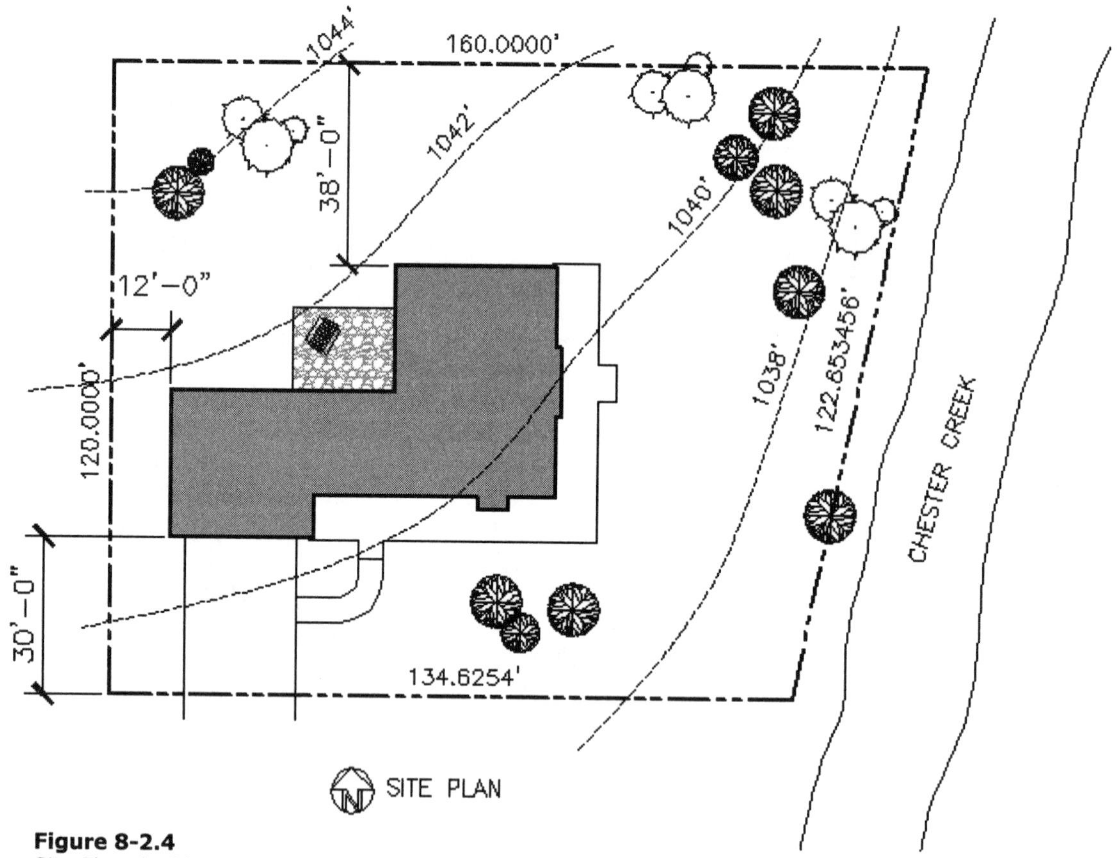

Figure 8-2.4
Site Plan; building fill and patio added

Exercise 8-3:
Layout new contours

Introduction:

In this lesson you will add new contours and take a quick look at drawing a cross section of the grade along a line.

The finished grade of the site needs to be modified primarily to handle site drainage. The drainage, as currently shown in Figure 8-2.4, would dump quite a bit of surface runoff (i.e., rainwater) into the back inside corner of the residence.

To indicate modified grading, new contours are added to the site plan. These contours show the contractor the final finished grade and intended drainage for the site.

New contours are shown with solid (i.e., continuous) lines:

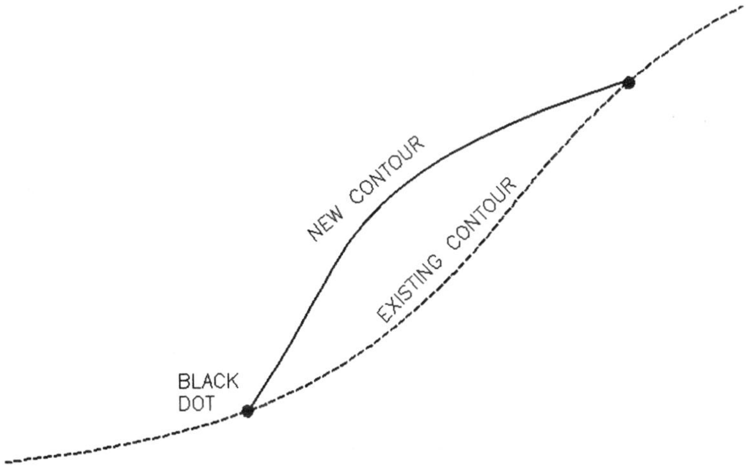

Figure 8-3.1
New Contour; new contour solid, existing contour dashed

As a contour with a smaller number (i.e., lower elevation) gets closer to a contour with a larger number (i.e., higher elevation), the contractor has to remove earth:

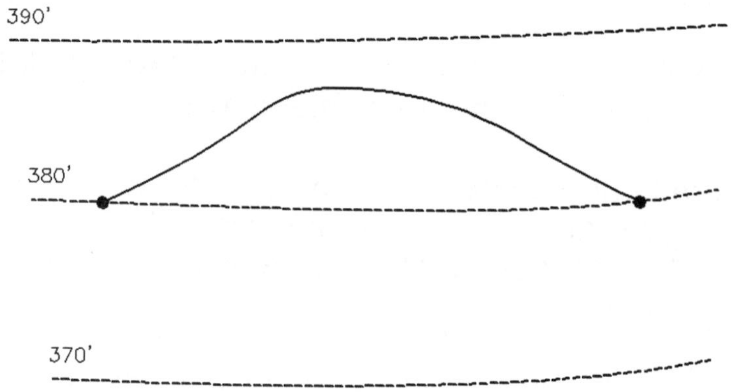

Figure 8-3.2
Earth Cut Example
Imagine the new contour extending straight into the existing hillside and coming back out to reconnect with the existing contour, all the earth above that line needs to be removed!

Conversely, when a higher contour is moved closer to a lower contour, the contractor has to add earth:

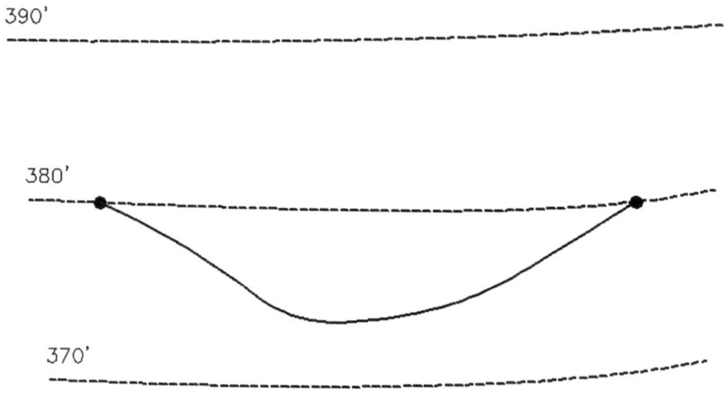

Figure 8-3.3
Earth Fill Example
Now imagine the new contour extending straight out into the air above the existing hillside and coming back to reconnect with the existing contour, earth needs to be added below the line to support it!

Now you will draw new contours on your site plan.

1. Create a *Layer* named **C-Topo-Neww.**
   a. Linetype: **Continuous**
   b. Color: **Green**

   ***FYI:** It looks like a mistake, but the strict National CAD Standards require four characters in their standard Layer naming conventions.*

You do not need to be extremely accurate when drawing the new contours in the next step; just try to get it as close as possible.

2. Draw the **new contours** shown in Figure 8-3.4.
   a. Use the Pline command to draw the lines.
   b. Use Pedit → Spline to smooth out the contours.
   c. Use the Nearest Snap to accurately attach your new contour with the existing contour.

3. Use the **Donut** command to create the black dots at the start and end points of each new contour line. (Figure 8-3.4)
   a. Set the inside radius to **0".**
   b. Set the outside radius to **24".**
   c. Draw the Donut on Layer **A-Topo-Neww.**

4. Use the **Leader** command to draw the "drainage flow" lines. (Figure 8-3.4)
   a. Start the Leader command and then type S for settings; select Spline, no limit, no mtext.
   b. Place the Leader on the **C-Anno-Text** Layer.
   c. Set the leader linetype to **Center2** (by entitiy).

5. Add the text "DRAINAGE FLOW" (as shown in Figure 8-3.4).

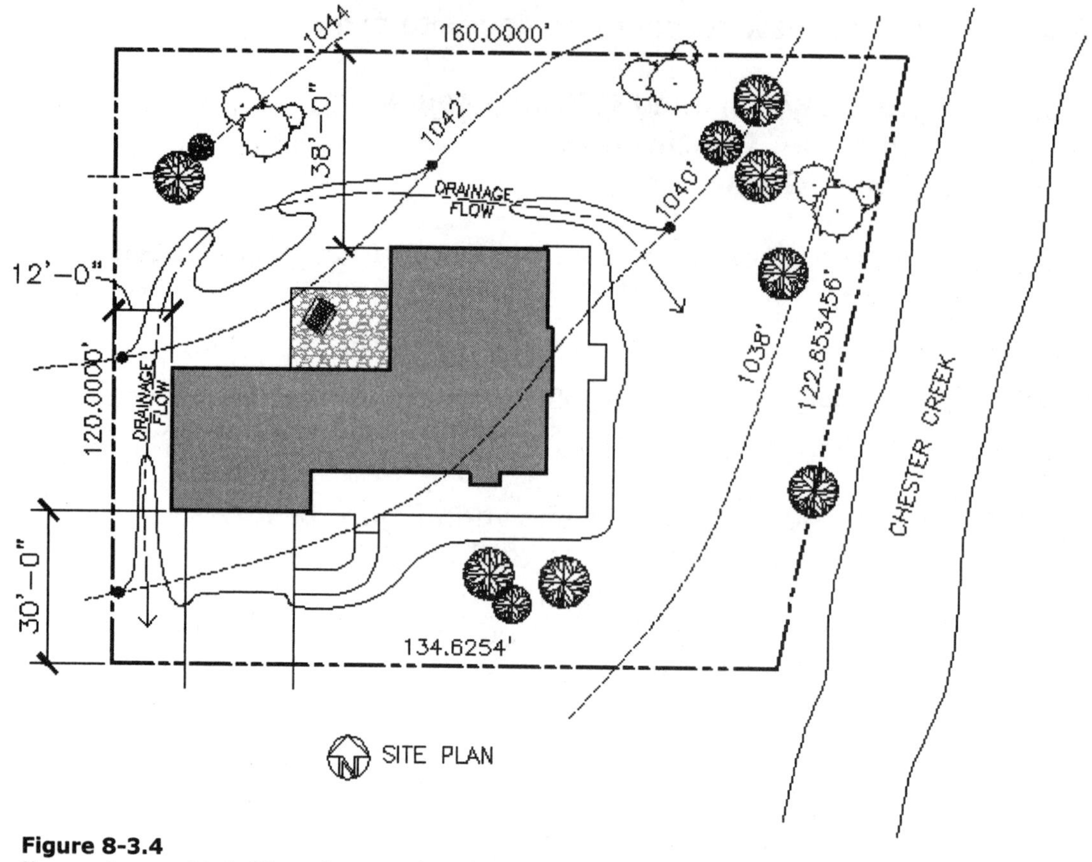

Figure 8-3.4
New contours added; Plines drawn and smoothed out with the Pedit command

Notice in the image above that the contour line 1040' cuts into the earth near each end of the new contour line and requires fill to be added in between.

The new contour lines reach up toward the higher contour where it intersects the drainage flow line. This creates a swale (not unlike a river, but more subtle of course) that "directs" water around the building.

A spot elevation should be called out in the back inside corner. The elevation should be high enough to allow any rainwater that falls in that area to flow away from the building.

Drawing a grade profile:

Now you will take a look at drawing a grade profile. A grade profile is analogous to drawing a building section; you are showing what the land looks like in a section view.

This profile, in this example, will show both the new and existing profiles. This could then be used to calculate the amount of cut and fill required on the site. It can also be used to determine the floor elevation of the building relative to the finished grade.

In this example you will draw a line generally perpendicular to the slope of the site. The first thing you will do is draw a line on the site plan that indicates where the profile is to be cut.

6. Draw a line on your site plan, approximately perpendicular to the contour lines as shown in Figure 8-3.5.

7. At this point you may want to temporarily copy your entire site plan off to one side so you can rotate it, making the section line aligned with the drawing window. (Figure 8-3.5)

   TIP: *The most accurate way to rotate the drawing is to use Rotate and then the Reference sub-command; first you pick your base point, and then R for reference, and then you pick one end of the section line and then the other end. Finally, you type 0 (or 180) and press enter. See AutoCAD's help system for more on this feature.*

8. In the closest available empty drawing area below the section line, draw 6 horizontal lines spaced 2'-0" apart. (Figure 8-3.5)

   FYI: *This spacing corresponds to the vertical distance between the contours.*

9. Project a vertical line down from the location where each contour intersects the section line. (Figure 8-3.5)

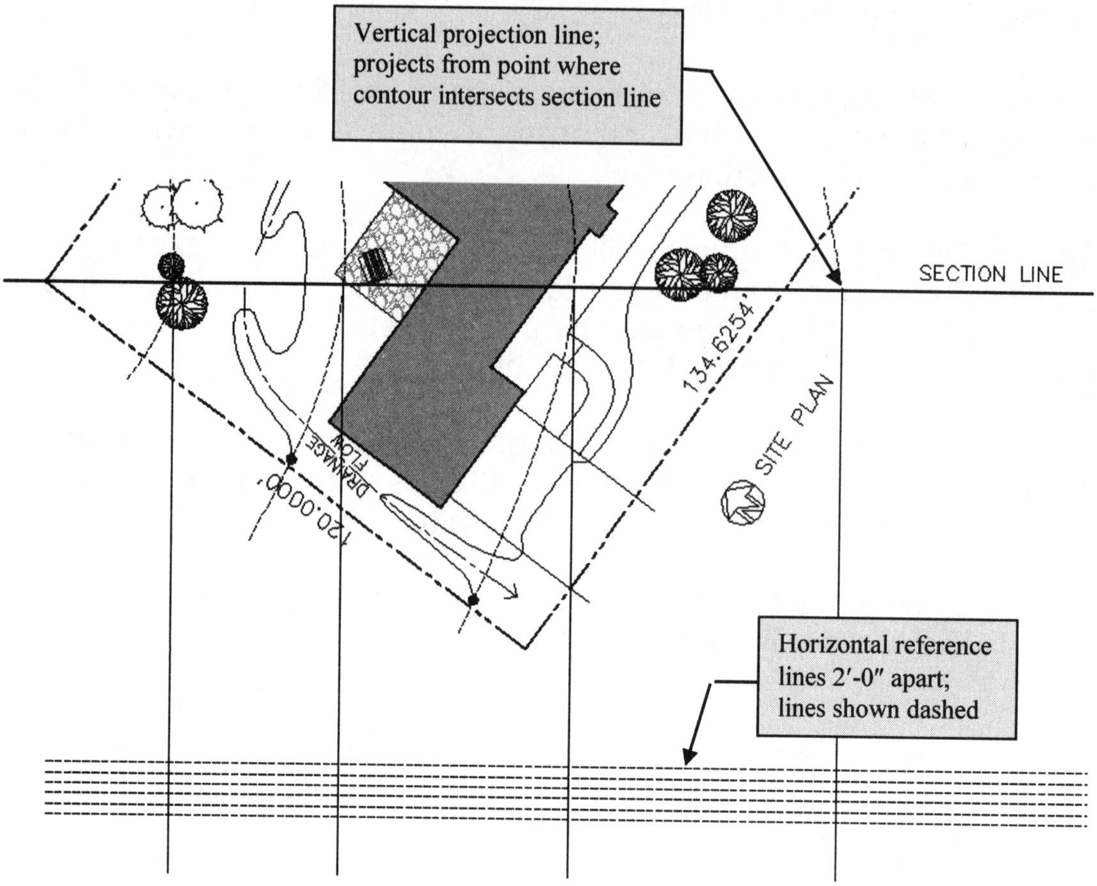

Figure 8-3.5
Reference lines for profile; copy of site plan rotated so section line is orthogonal

Now you simply play connect-the-dots to create the grade profile. (Figure 8-3.6)

10. Draw a Pline, picking the points where the vertical projection lines intersect the horizontal reference lines.

11. Use the **Fit** feature of *Pedit* to smooth out the line. (Figure 8-3.6)

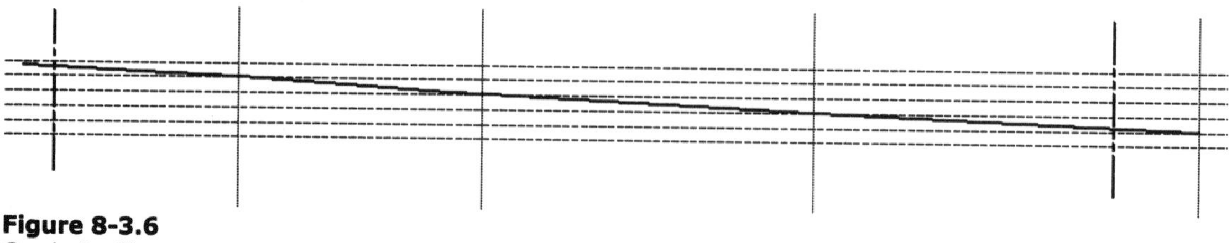

Figure 8-3.6
Grade Profile; property lines also added for context

12. You can now erase the vertical projection lines.

13. Use the same technique just covered to draw the new grade profile; then overlay the two to see the variation.
FYI: This section does not show a significant amount off cut and fill.

The sample image shown below indicates how a profile looks with both new and existing profiles. This image can be used to estimate the amount of cut and fill required for the project. The ideal situation is to have equal amounts of each to avoid buying fill or paying to haul extra fill away.

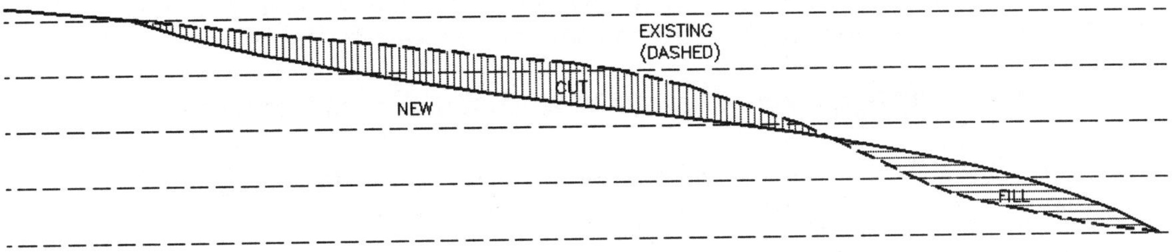

Figure 8-3.7
Sample Grade Profile; sample profile with both new and existing shown (existing shown dashed)

14. **Save** your drawing.

Self-Exam:

The following questions can be used as a way to check your knowledge of this lesson. The answers can be found at the bottom of this page.

1. You can use the Donut command to draw solid dots. (T/F)
2. You can "unload" an Xref and then quickly "reload" it later. (T/F)
3. You typically have to scale a survey drawing (drawn with Decimal units) down 12 times to work with Architectural units. (T/F)
4. You draw new contours on this Layer: ______________________
5. New contour lines which are "continuous" and existing are "dashed". (T/F)

Review Questions:

The following questions may be assigned by your instructor as a way to assess your knowledge of this section. Your instructor has the answers to the review questions.

1. A grade profile can help to calculate the amount of cut and fill required. (T/F)
2. Scaling and rotating the tree blocks as they are inserted helps to make the drawing look more natural (less like a cookie-cutter). (T/F)
3. A swale helps to direct to flow of surface runoff on a site. (T/F)
4. With the Pedut command, the ______________ sub-command makes a smoothed-out polyline that maintains the points you picked to draw the

   contour; whereas the ________________ sub-command allows the polyline to deviate from your original points.
5. Layers associated with an Xref have what as a name prefix? ____________
6. You need to set what property of a polyline to "enabled" to make the dashes

   consistent: ________________
7. When a "lower" (e.g., 1060') contour is rerouted to move closer to a "high" (e.g., 1065') contour, the contractor would have ______________ earth.
8. After picking your first point, type the "command window" instructions to draw a line 321.125' long with an angle of 43°12' (ccw off the horizontal):

   @__________<____________.
9. To draw a solid black dot with a 24" diameter you would use the Donut command with the "inside radius" set to 0" and the "outside radius" set to 12. (T/F)
10. What Layer does the building outline go on? __________________

Self-Exam Answers:
1 - T, **2** - T, **3** - F, **4** – c-topo-neww, **5** – T

Additional Tasks:

Task 8-1 Add items to the Site Plan:

Add additional items to the site plan, such as new trees and landscaping (labeling them as such). You can search the internet for pre-drawn blocks. Also add notes for the new road and sidewalk (e.g., backtop driveway; concrete sidewalk).

Task 8-2 Draw another grade profile:

Draw a grade profile that general follow one of the swales; this will be a more dramatic cut and fill profile.

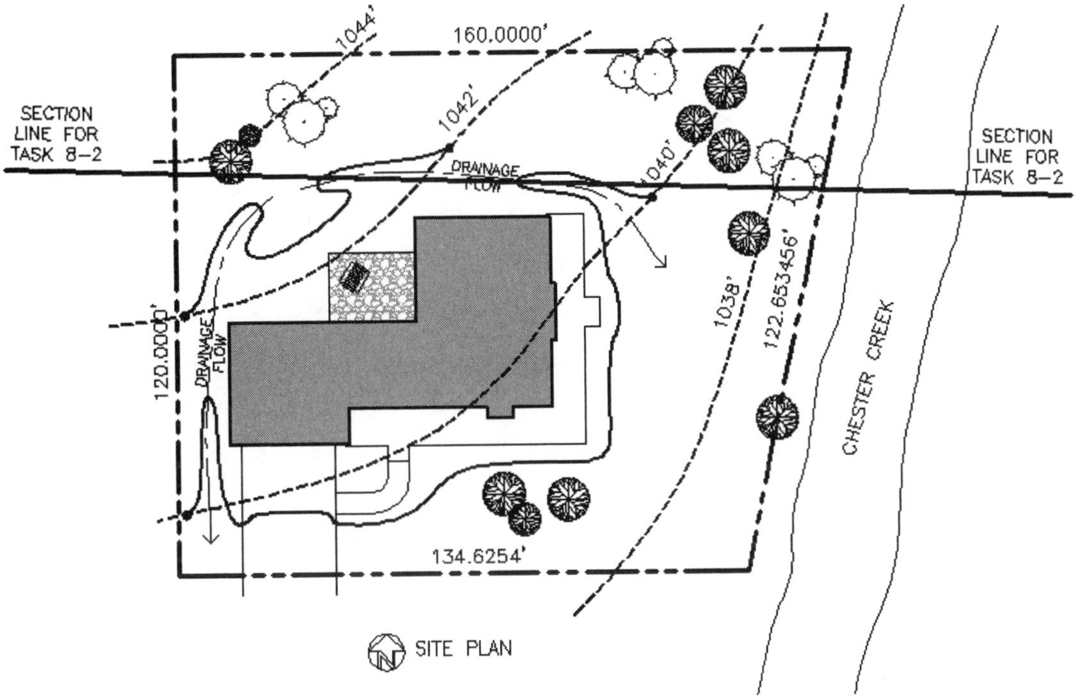

Task 8-3 Update the grade profile for each exterior elevation:

You can draw a grade profile at each side of the building and then superimpose that profile on your exterior elevations to accurately describe how the grade engages the buildings perimeter.

Notes:

Lesson 9
Residential Project: Schedules & Sheet Setup::

In this lesson you will learn to use the new Table feature to create schedules in AutoCAD. You will also explore how drawings are setup on sheets so they can be plotted with a professional look and fashion.

Exercise 9-1:
Room Finish Schedule

Introduction:

A Room Finish Schedule indicates what finish the walls, ceiling and floors get in each room. This information is typically organized in a grid of rows and columns, where each row represents a room and each column represents a surface to be finished. AutoCAD 2005 has a new feature, called Tables, that is designed to accommodate this type of data (i.e., schedules).

Most rooms have both a name and a number to facilitate accurate identification on plans and schedules. Numbers are not always required on residential projects; however, it is typically done for consistency. Using a number is necessary when you have multiple rooms with the same name. In your plan, for example, you have multiple bathrooms and bedrooms. On large commercial projects, a floor plan might have 30-40 rooms all labeled "office", so it is easy to see how important numbers are.

The first step is to add the room numbers to your floor plans.

1. **Open** your **Flr-1** drawing.

2. Add the room numbers:
   a. Double-click on each room name.
   b. Click the cursor at the end of the room name.
   c. Press Enter to start a new line.
   d. Type the room numbers shown in Figure 9-1.1.

   FYI: *Having the room name and number in the same mtext object helps to keep them aligned. It also makes moving them easier as you only have to worry about selecting one object, not two.*

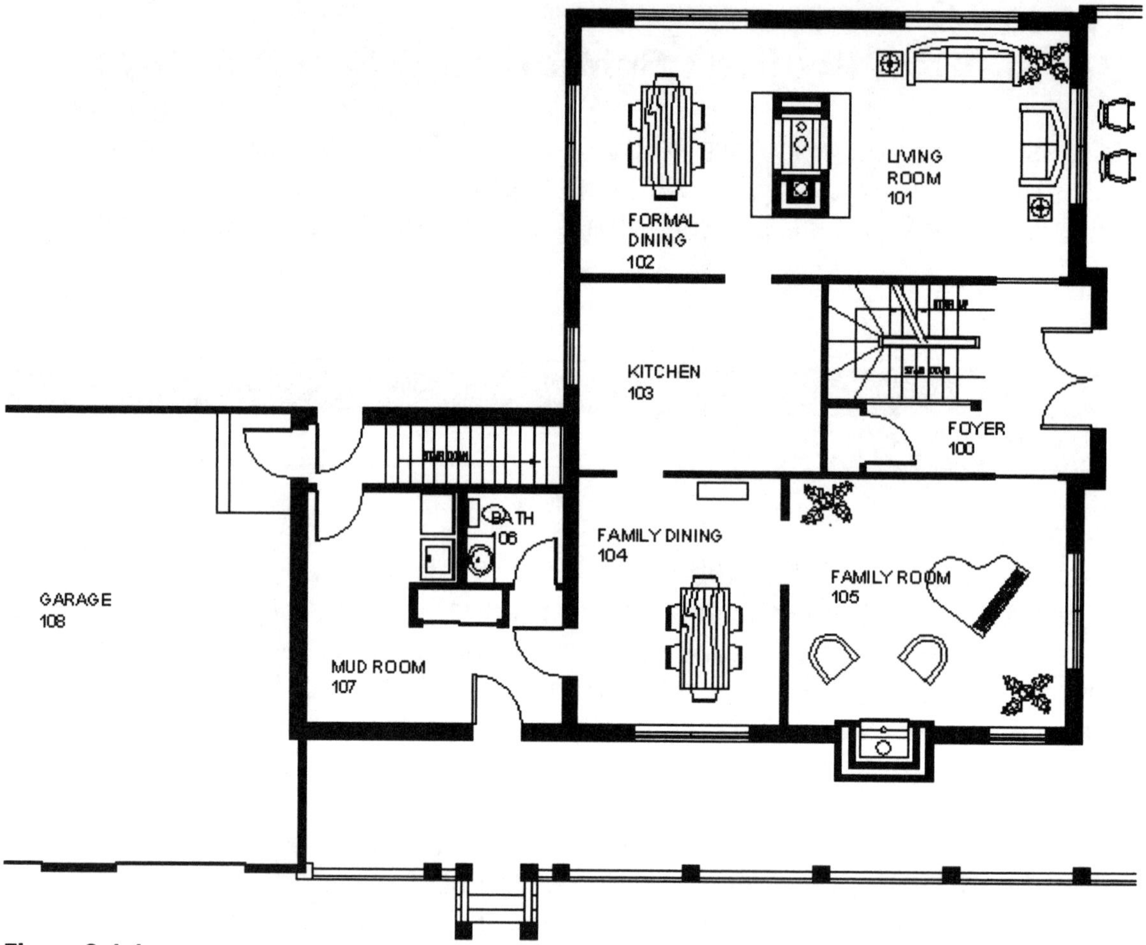

Figure 9-1.1
First floor plan; room numbers added

3. **Open** your **Flr-2** drawing.

4. Add the room numbers per Figure 9-1.2.

5. **Open** your **Flr-B** drawing.

6. Add the number **001** below the room name (i.e., UNFINISHED BASEMENT).

7. **Save** your floor plan drawings.

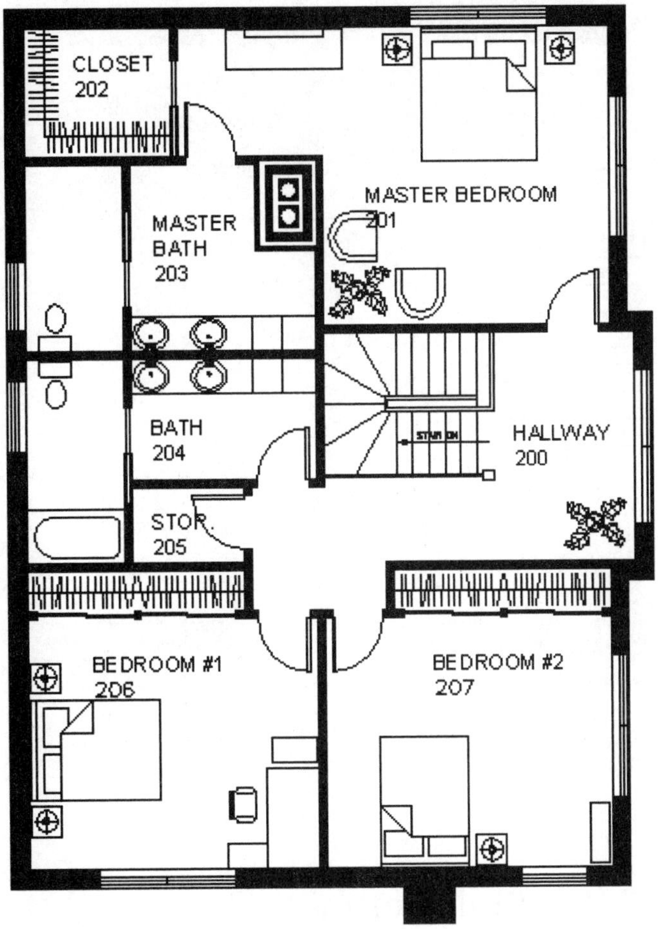

Figure 9-1.2
Second floor plan; room numbers added

Creating a Table:

8. Create a new drawing, using **Architectural Imperial 2.dwt** as your template file *(select File → New).*

9. Click the **Table** icon from the *Draw* Toolbar. 

You are now in the *Insert Table* dialog box (Figure 9-1.3). At this point you could create a table using the Standard table style; if other styles existed, you could select one of them as well. You will create a Table using the Standard style.

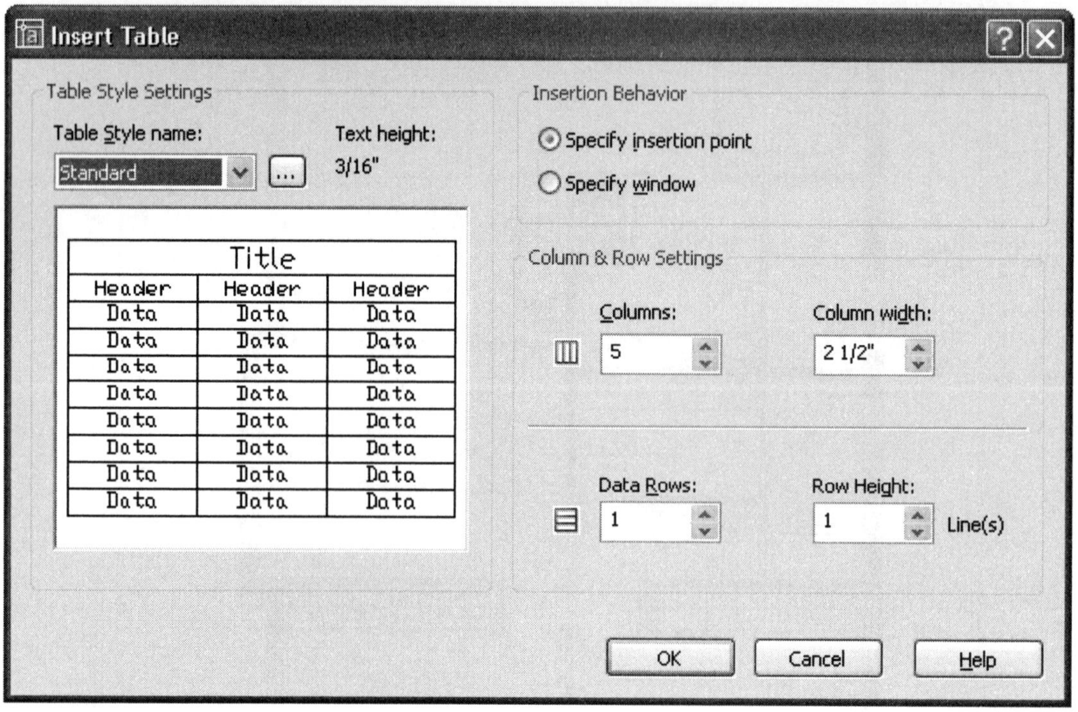

Figure 9-1.3
Insert Table dialog; initial view

Adjusting the Table Style settings:

The first thing you will do is adjust the *Standard* Table Style. As you can see in Figure 9-1.3, the *Text Height* is 3/16". You will adjust the *Text Height* to a smaller size as well as change the Font Style.

10. Click on the *Table Style* Settings button.  (See Figure 9-1.3)

11. Click the **Modify...** button *(to Modify the Standard table style).*

12. Make the changes shown in **Figure 9-1.4** to the **Data tab.**

13. Make the changes shown in **Figure 9-1.5** to the **Column Heads tab.**

14. Make the changes shown in **Figure 9-1.6** to the **Title tab.**

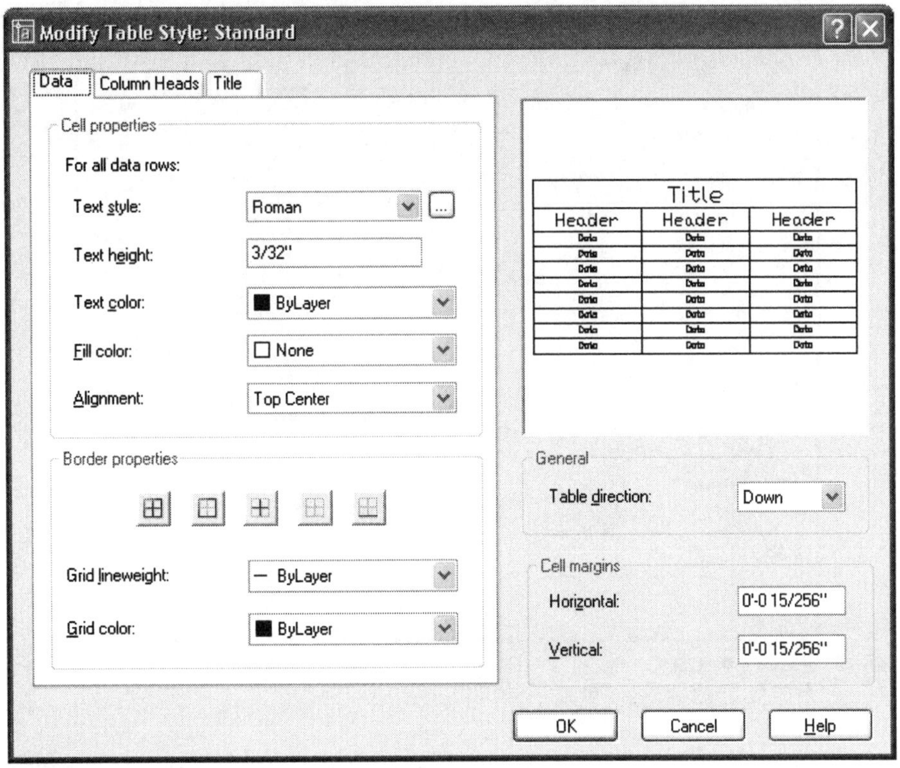

Figure 9-1.4
Modify Table Style dialog; Data tab

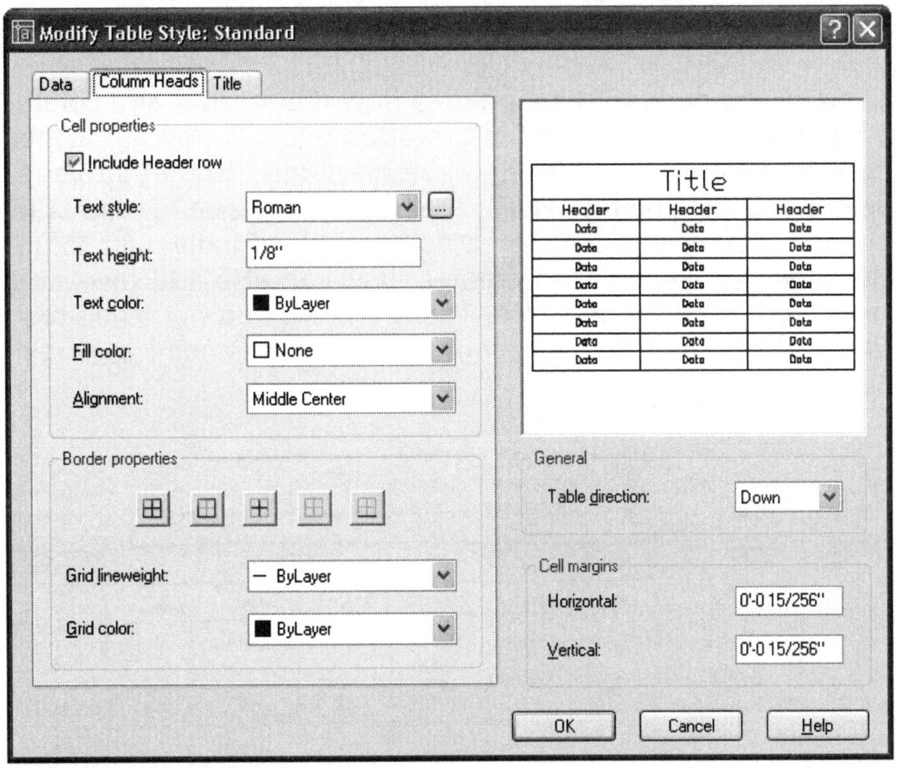

Figure 9-1.5
Modify Table Style dialog; Column Heads tab

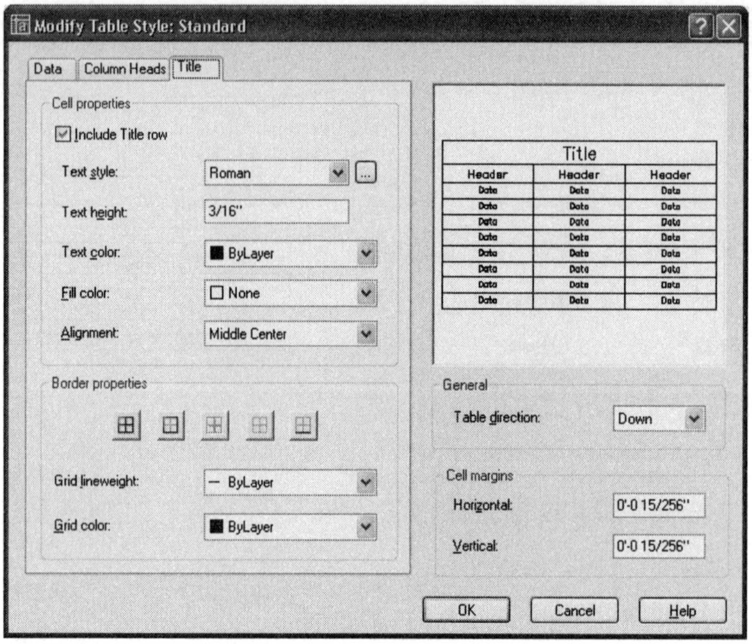

Figure 9-1.6
Modify Table Style dialog; Title tab

15. Click **OK** to close the *Modify Table Style* dialog.

16. Click **Close** to exit the *Table Style* manager and return to the *Insert Table* dialog.

At this point you need to have an idea how many rows and columns you need. You can sketch out what information you will need to display in the schedule (see Figure 9-1.7 for an example). You also need to specify the row height and the column width; this will be the size for the standard row/column. You will be able to adjust the size of individual columns/ rows once the Table has been created. You can also add rows and/or columns after creating the Table. Therefore, you do not to be too concerned about forgetting a row or column at this point as it can easily be added later.

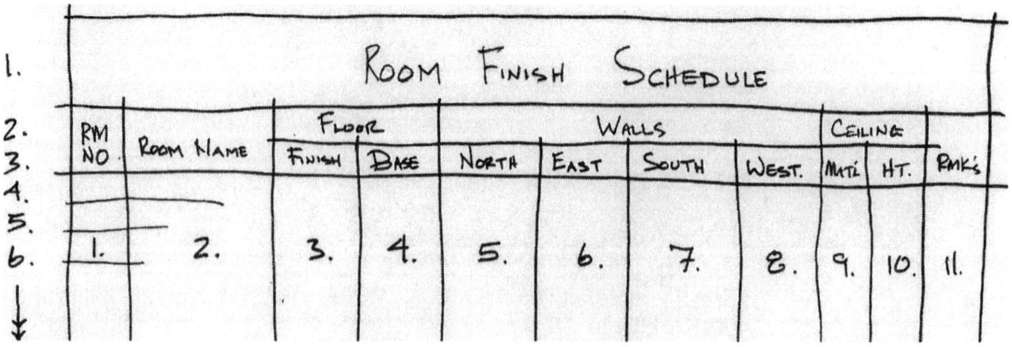

Figure 9-1.7
Preliminary Room Finish Schedule Sketch

Based on the sketch above, you will create a quick Table that has 11 columns and 6 rows. You will make additional adjustments later.

17. Make the following adjustments to the *Insert Table* dialog:

    a. Columns: **11**

    b. Column Width: **1"**

    c. Rows: **6**

    d. *Leave everything else at the default.* (Figure 9-1.3)

18. Click **OK** to insert the *Table.*

At this point you will see the specified Table attached to your cross-hairs so you can visually place it.

19. Move your cursor so the entire *Table* is visible and centered on the screen and click the mouse to place it.

You are now automatically prompted for the title of the table.

20. For the Table title, type "**ROOM FINISH SCHEDULE**" (Figure 9-1.8) *TIP: Just start typing; no need to click anywhere.*

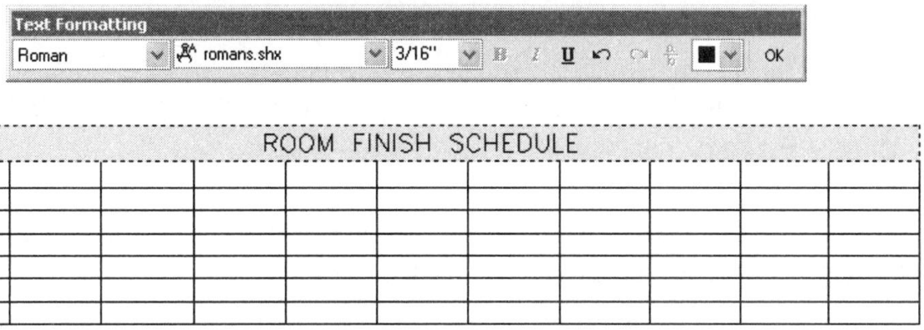

Figure 9-1.8
Inserted Table; entering table title text

21. Click **OK** on the *Text Formatting* toolbar.

You now have a Table created in your drawing. Next you will adjust the width of the columns to match the sketch.

22. Select a column to adjust its width per the following:
    a. Click and drag the mouse from the lowest cell to the highest cell (or visa versa).
    b. See Figure 9-1.9.

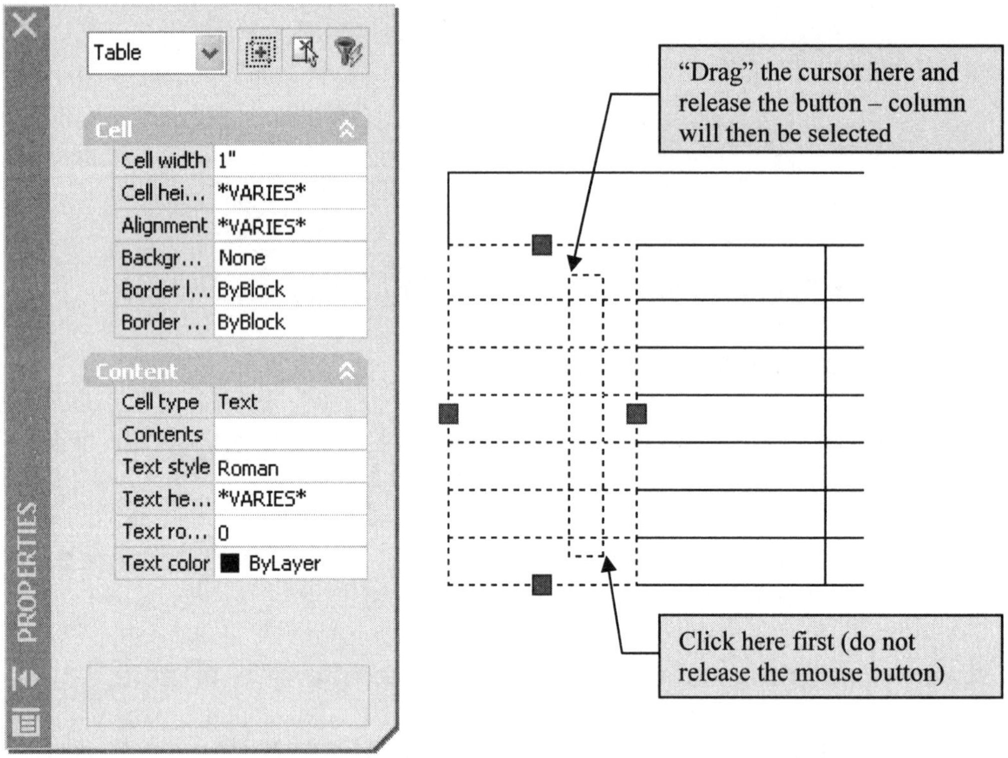

Figure 9-1.9
Table and its Properties;
column selected (selected cells properties displayed)

23. In the *Properties Palette*, change the *Cell width* to **.5"** and then press **Enter.**

The Table column has now been updated to display the *column width* per your specifications (Figure 9-1.10).

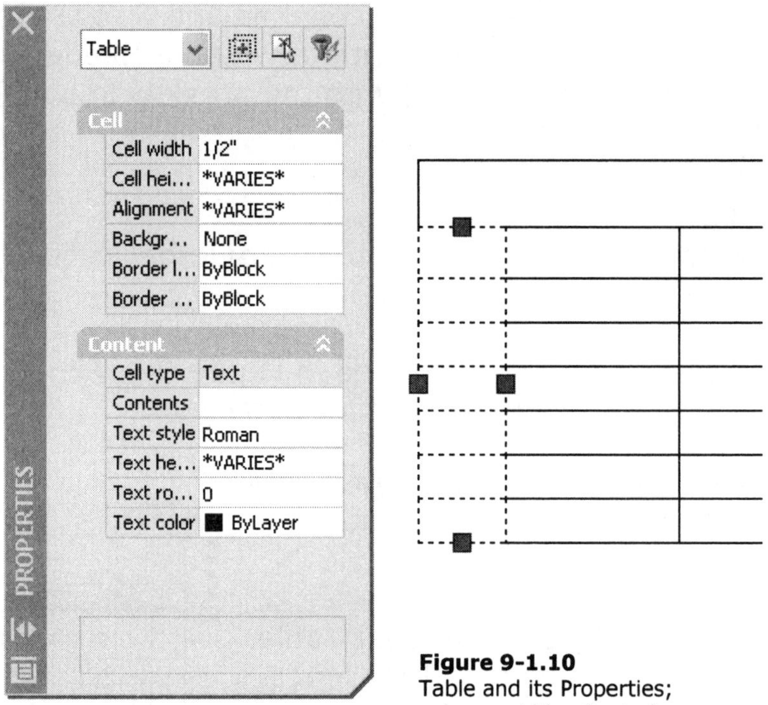

Figure 9-1.10
Table and its Properties; column width adjusted

24. Press **Esc** to Deselect the column.

25. Adjust the remaining column widths per the following information (Figure 9-1.11):

    a. Column 2 (room name): **2"**
    b. Columns 3 – 10: **1"**
    c. Column 11 (remarks): **2"**

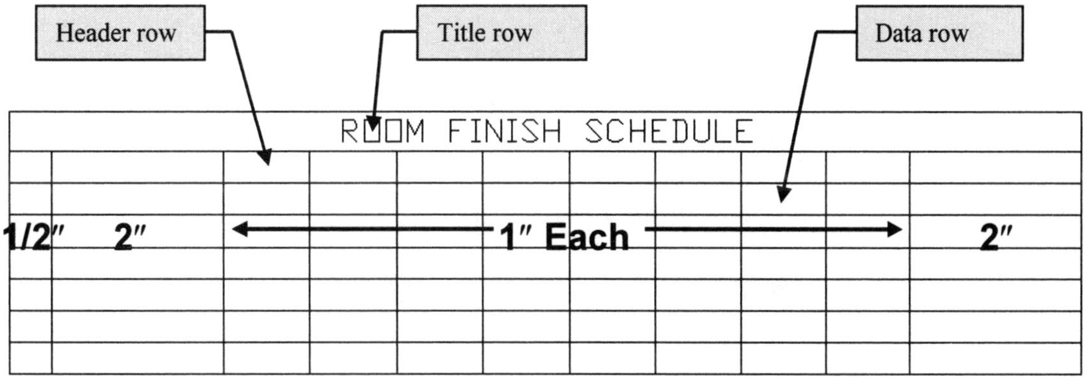

Figure 9-1.11
Table; all column widths adjusted

As you will recall, you specified 11 columns and 6 rows. In addition to that, a Table automatically has a Title row and a Header row. Compare the image above (Figure 9-1.11) with the preview image in Figure 9-1.3.

Merge Cells:

Next you will merge cells together to create larger cells within the Table.

26. Select the two cells identified in Figure 9-1.12.
__FYI:__ This is where the room number label goes.

27. Right-click and select **Merge Cells** → **All** from the pop-up menu. (Figure 9-1.13)

You now have a merged cell in your Table! Take a moment to notice the other commands listed on the pop-up menu in Figure 9-1.13.

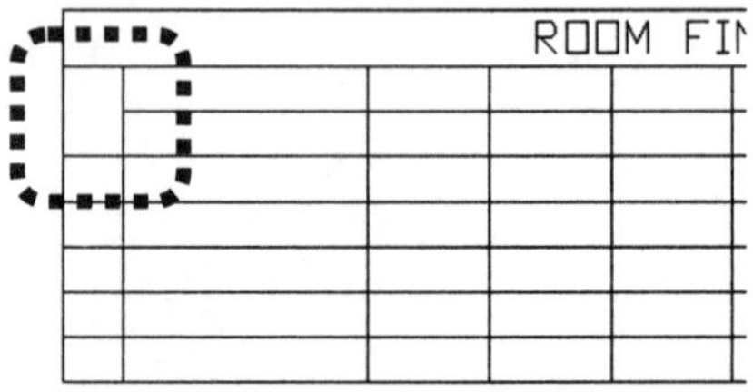

Figure 9-1.12
Table; two cells merged together

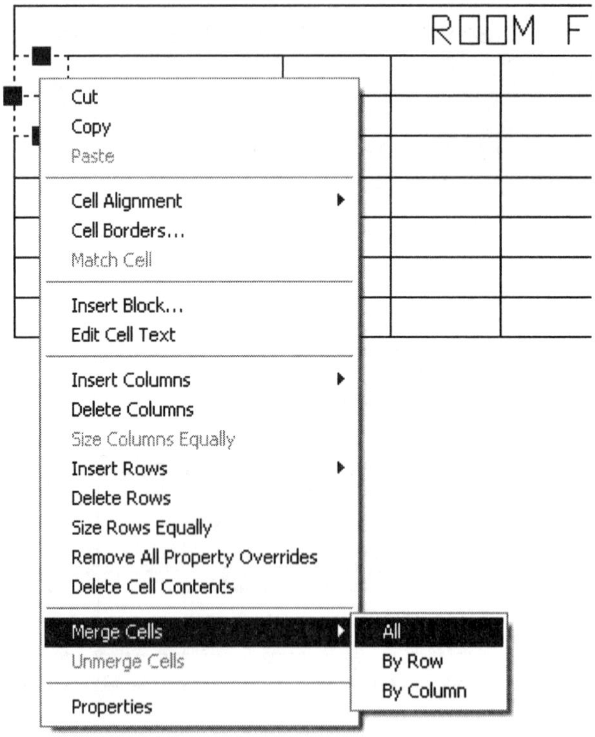

Figure 9-1.13
Merge Cells; two cells selected and then right-click

28. Use the **Merge Cells** feature to make your table look like the one in Figure 9-1.14.

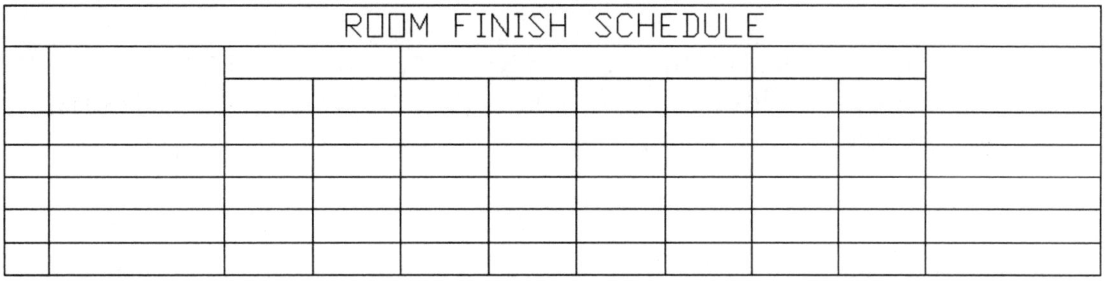

Figure 9-1.14
Merge Cells; several cells merged

Inserting additional rows:

Before adding data to the table, you will insert additional rows. A few too many will be added so you can learn to delete rows later.

29. Right-click in any *Data* cell and select **Insert Rows → Below.** (Figure 9-1.15)

30. Repeat the previous step until you have **20** *Data* rows.

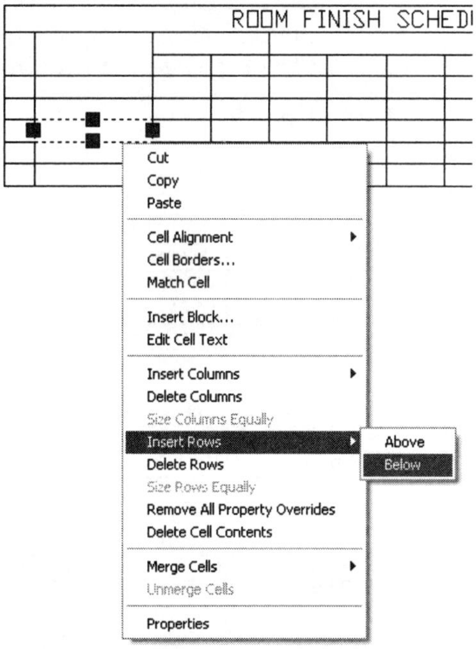

Figure 9-1.15
Insert rows; creates extra data lines

Adding column header labels:

Now you will add the labels that indicate what information is in each column within the schedule (table).

31. Double-click within each *Header* cell and type the label per the sketch in Figure 9-1.4; see Figure 9-1.16 for the finished product.

Adding data to cells:

It is very easy to add data to your *Table*; you simply double click in a cell and type. Next you will add the data to your table.

32. Looking at Figure 9-1.16, enter the data into your Table.

    TIP: *After you double-click in a cell, you can use the Tab and Arrow keys to move between cells.*

    TIP: *You can Copy/Paste multiple cells; click and drag to select the Cells to Copy, and then press Ctrl+C (copy to Windows Clipboard), and then click and drag to select the Cells to Paste too, and then press Ctrl+V (paste from Windows Clipboard).*

ROOM FINISH SCHEDULE									
RM NO	ROOM NAME	FLOOR		WALLS				CEILING	
		FINISH	BASE	NORTH	EAST	SOUTH	WEST	MAT'L	HEGIHT
001	BASEMENT	SEALED	N/A	CMU	CMU	CMU	CMU	EXP.	–
100	FOYER	Q.T.	Q.T.	WOOD PNL	WOOD PNL	WOOD PNL	WOOD PNL	GYP BD	8'–6"
101	LIVING ROOM	WOOD	WOOD	GYP BD	GYP BD	GYP BD	GYP BD	GYP BD	8'–6"
102	FORMAL DINING	WOOD	WOOD	GYP BD	GYP BD	GYP BD	GYP BD	GYP BD	8'–6"
103	KITCHEN	Q.T.	Q.T.	GYP BD	GYP BD	GYP BD	GYP BD	GYP BD	8'–6"
104	FAMILY DINING	CARPET	WOOD	GYP BD	GYP BD	GYP BD	GYP BD	GYP BD	8'–6"
105	FAMILY ROOM	VINYL	WOOD	GYP BD	GYP BD	GYP BD	GYP BD	GYP BD	8'–6"
106	BATH	MARBLE	MARBLE	C.T.	C.T.	C.T.	C.T.	GYP. BD.	8'–6"
107	MUD ROOM	Q.T.	Q.T.	GYP BD	GYP BD	GYP BD	GYP BD	GYP BD	8'–6"
108	GARAGE	SEALED	–	GYP. BD.	GYP BD	GYP BD	GYP BD	GYP BD	8'–6"
200	HALLWAY	WOOD	WOOD	GYP BD	GYP BD	GYP BD	GYP BD	GYP BD	8'–0"
201	MASTER BEDROOM	WOOD	WOOD	GYP BD	GYP BD	GYP BD	GYP BD	GYP BD	8'–0"
202	CLOSET	WOOD	WOOD	GYP BD	GYP BD	GYP BD	GYP BD	GYP BD	8'–0"
203	MASTER BATH	MARBLE	MARBLE	C.T.	C.T.	C.T.	C.T.	GYP. BD.	8'–0"
204	BATH	C.T.	C.T.	C.T.	C.T.	C.T.	C.T.	GYP. BD.	8'–0"
205	STORAGE	WOOD	–	GYP BD	GYP BD	GYP BD	GYP BD	GYP BD	8'–0"
206	BEDROOM #1	CARPET	WOOD	GYP BD	GYP BD	GYP BD	GYP BD	GYP BD	8'–0"
207	BEDROOM #2	CARPET	WOOD	GYP BD	GYP BD	GYP BD	GYP BD	GYP BD	8'–0"

Figure 9-1.16
Room Finish Schedule; with data entered

Deleting rows:

Next you will delete one of the extra rows. The following technique works the same way for columns as well.

33. Click within the Cell directly below BEDROOM #2.

34. **Right-click** and select **Delete Rows** from the pop-up menu. (Figure 9-1.17)

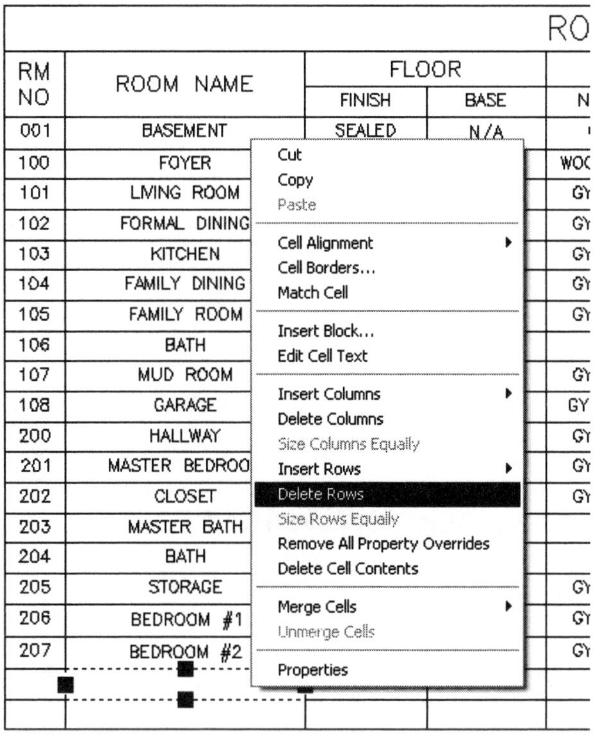

Figure 9-1.17
Room Finish Schedule; deleting a row

Making the table title text bold:

Finally, you will change the font for the *Table Title* (i.e., Room Finish Schedule) to Arial Black, which is a distinctive bold font. To do this you will need to create a new AutoCAD *Font Style* and then modify the *Table Style* to use the new *Font Style*.

35. From the *Format* menu select **Font Style...**

You are now in the Text Style dialog where you manage AutoCAD Text Styles. ***FYI:*** *AutoCAD Text Styles allow you to predefine several settings for a particular type of note or label. Additionally, like other "styles" in AutoCAD, if you change a style setting (e.g., the Width Factor), all the text of that style will update automatically.*

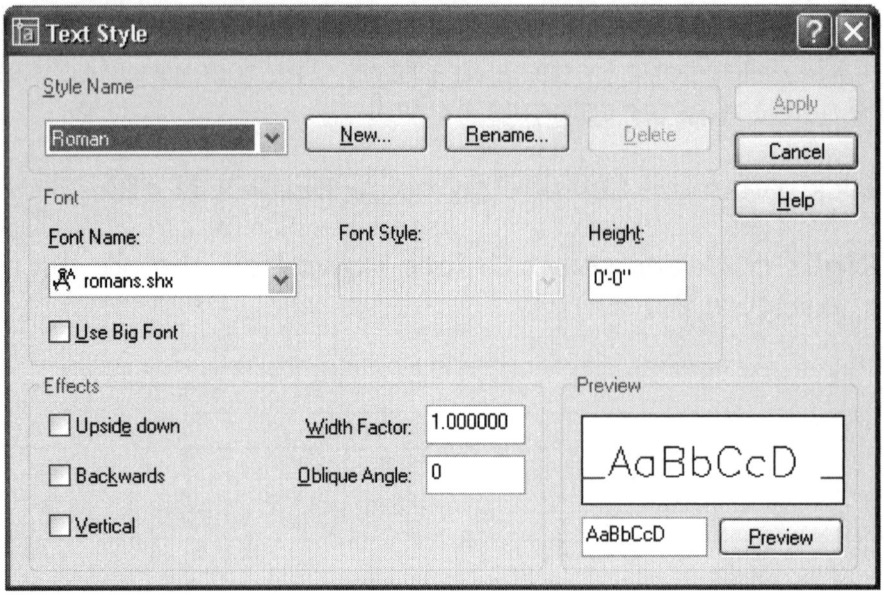

Figure 9-1.18
Text Style dialog; initial view

36. Click the down-arrow, next to the *Style Name*, to see that only two Styles exist in the current drawing (Standard and Roman).

Now you will create a new Style named Bold.

37. Click the **New** button.

You are now prompted for a name (Figure 9-1.19).

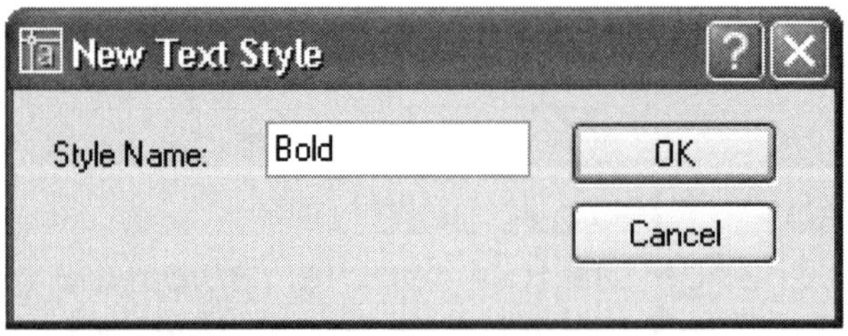

Figure 9-1.19
New Text Style dialog; style name Bold entered

38. Type the new *Style Name* **Bold** and then click **OK.**

39. Make the following adjustments (Figure 9-1.20)
    1. Font Name: **Arial Black**
    2. Width Factor: **.9**

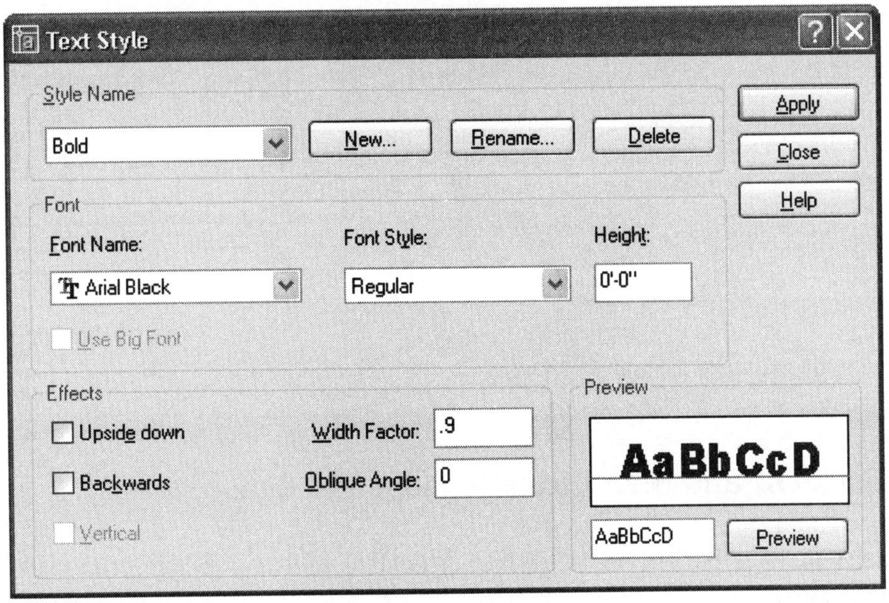

Figure 9-1.20
Text Style dialog; setting for text style named "bold"

40. Click **Apply** to finalize your new *Text Style* settings.

41. Click **Close.**

The new text style is now available for use in the current drawing. If you want regular access to the Bold text style, you would add it to your Drawing Template file.

Now you will modify the *Table Style* title text.

42. From the *Format* menu select **Table Style...**

43. Click the **Modify...** button *(to Modify the Standard table style).*

44. On the *Title* tab, change the following (Figure 9-1.21):
    a. *Text style* to **Bold**
    b. Fill color to **Color 255**

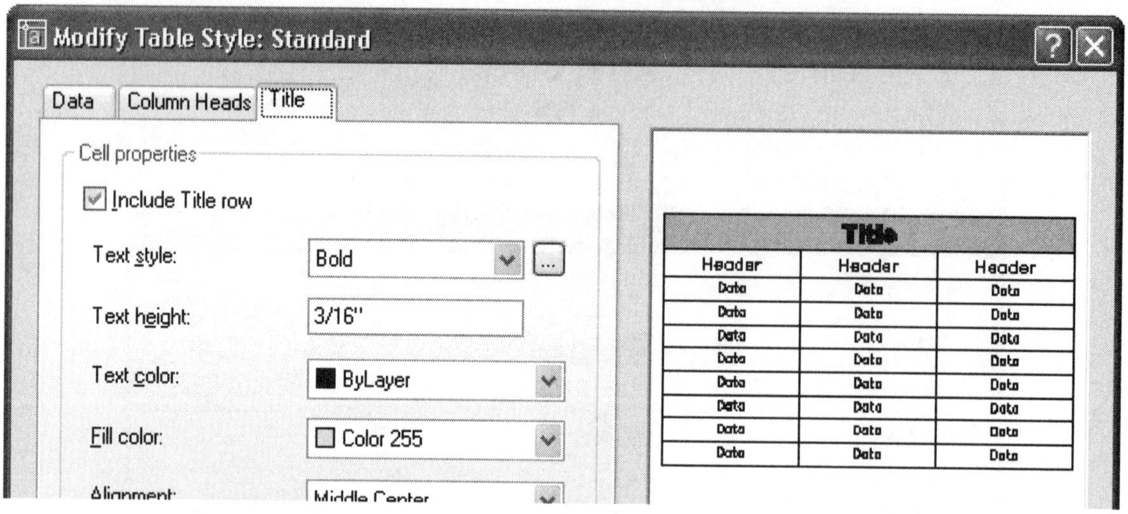

Figure 9-1.21
Modify Table Style; Text style for title set to "bold"

45. Click **OK** and then **Close** to close the dialog boxes.

You should now notice the text for the title is now Bold and the cell is filled with color 255 (a grey shade) in your Room Finish Schedule (Figure 9-1.22). Similarly, if you had additional tables inserted into the current drawing (and using the standard style), they would all be updated to use the Bold font as well.

ROOM FINISH SCHEDULE											
RM NO	ROOM NAME	FLOOR		WALLS				CEILING		REMARKS
		FINISH	BASE	NORTH	EAST	SOUTH	WEST	MAT'L	HEGIHT	
001	BASEMENT	SEALED	N/A	CMU	CMU	CMU	CMU	EXP.	–	
100	FOYER	Q.T.	Q.T.	WOOD PNL	WOOD PNL	WOOD PNL	WOOD PNL	GYP BD	8'–6"	
101	LIVING ROOM	WOOD	WOOD	GYP BD	GYP BD	GYP BD	GYP BD	GYP BD	8'–6"	
102	FORMAL DINING	WOOD	WOOD	GYP BD	GYP BD	GYP BD	GYP BD	GYP BD	8'–6"	
103	KITCHEN	Q.T.	Q.T.	GYP BD	GYP BD	GYP BD	GYP BD	GYP BD	8'–6"	
104	FAMILY DINING	CARPET	WOOD	GYP BD	GYP BD	GYP BD	GYP BD	GYP BD	8'–6"	
105	FAMILY ROOM	VINYL	WOOD	GYP BD	GYP BD	GYP BD	GYP BD	GYP BD	8'–6"	
106	BATH	MARBLE	MARBLE	C.T.	C.T.	C.T.	C.T.	GYP. BD.	8'–6"	
107	MUD ROOM	Q.T.	Q.T.	GYP BD	GYP BD	GYP BD	GYP BD	GYP BD	8'–6"	
108	GARAGE	SEALED	–	GYP. BD.	GYP BD	GYP BD	GYP BD	GYP BD	8'–6"	
200	HALLWAY	WOOD	WOOD	GYP BD	GYP BD	GYP BD	GYP BD	GYP BD	8'–0"	
201	MASTER BEDROOM	WOOD	WOOD	GYP BD	GYP BD	GYP BD	GYP BD	GYP BD	8'–0"	
202	CLOSET	WOOD	WOOD	GYP BD	GYP BD	GYP BD	GYP BD	GYP BD	8'–0"	
203	MASTER BATH	MARBLE	MARBLE	C.T.	C.T.	C.T.	C.T.	GYP. BD.	8'–0"	
204	BATH	C.T.	C.T.	C.T.	C.T.	C.T.	C.T.	GYP. BD.	8'–0"	
205	STORAGE	WOOD	–	GYP BD	GYP BD	GYP BD	GYP BD	GYP BD	8'–0"	
206	BEDROOM #1	CARPET	WOOD	GYP BD	GYP BD	GYP BD	GYP BD	GYP BD	8'–0"	
207	BEDROOM #2	CARPET	WOOD	GYP BD	GYP BD	GYP BD	GYP BD	GYP BD	8'–0"	

Figure 9-1.22
Modify Table Style; Text style for title set to "bold"

46. **Save** your drawing as **ROOM FINISH SCHEDULE.DWG.**

What does this setting do in this dialog box?

Occasionally you will come across a setting in a dialog box that you are not quite sure what it does. One option is to try various values and see if you notice any changes (to the table in this example). AutoCAD provides explanatory "tips" in many of its dialog boxes. To see this "hidden" information you first click on the "?" icon in the upper right corner and then click the setting/control you want more information about. The following shows all the "hidden" information available in the *Table* dialog.

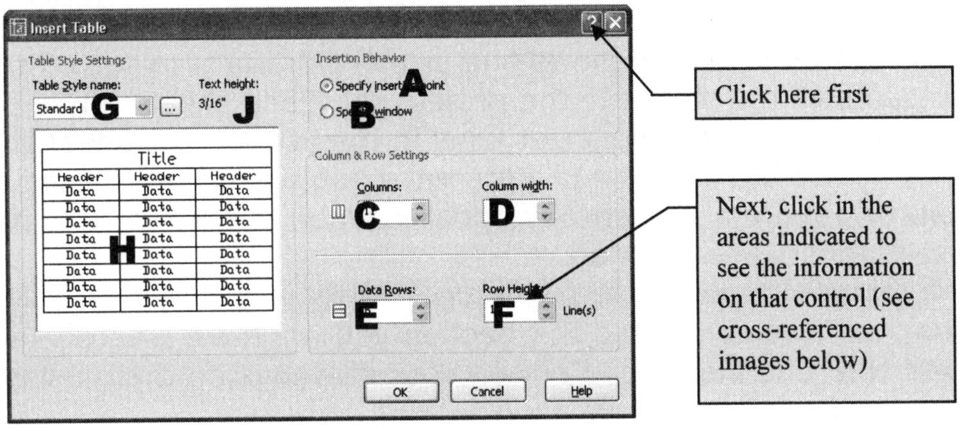

A

Specifies the location of the upper-left corner of the table. You can use the pointing device or enter coordinate values on the command line. If the table style sets the direction of the table to read from the bottom up, the insertion point is the lower-left corner of the table.

B

Specifies a size and a location for the table. You can use the pointing device or enter coordinate values on the command line. When this option is selected, the number of columns and rows and the column width and row height depend on the size of the window and the column and row settings.

C

Specifies the number of columns. When the Specify Window option is selected and you specify a column width, the Auto option is selected, and the number of columns is controlled by the width of the table.

D

Specifies the width of the columns. When the Specify Window option is selected and you specify the number of columns, the Auto option is selected, and the column width is controlled by the width of the table. The minimum column width is one character.

E

Specifies the number of rows. When the Specify Window option is selected and you specify a row height, the Auto option is selected, and the number of rows is controlled by the height of the table. A table style with a title row and a header row has a minimum of three rows. The minimum row height is one line.

F

Specifies the height of the rows in lines. The height of a line is based on the text height and the cell margin, which are both set in the table style. When the Specify Window option is selected and you specify the number of rows, the Auto option is selected, and the row height is controlled by the height of the table.

G

Specifies the table style. The default style is STANDARD.

H

Displays an example of the current table style.

J

Displays the text height specified in the current table style for data rows (read-only).

Exercise 9-2:
Sheet Setup and Management (Sheet Sets)

Introduction:

This exercise covers a new AutoCAD 2005 feature called Sheet Sets, which represents a very powerful feature previously found only in more advanced, architecture specific, programs like Autodesk Revit.

The Sheet Set Manager allows one or more drafters to see a list that represents all the sheets in the project set. Each sheet can be opened by double-clicking on the sheet label in the list. Once a sheet is open, you can place drawings on it. Reference bubbles can be placed on sheets which are automatically updated when the drawing numbers or sheet numbers are changed.

When you have completed this section you will have created several sheets with title blocks and placed your drawings on them using the Sheet Set Manager.

Procedural & Organizational overview:

The following information outlines the basic procedure and organization of a Sheet Set. This will give you a good understanding of this feature before you actually try it.

Sheet Sets pivot around three types of files:

- Resource Drawings
- Sheet Files
- A Sheet Set Data File

In addition to the three types of files listed above, other files are used as well (e.g., callout blocks and template files). Next you will take a closer look the three files types listed above and what role they play in the Sheet Set feature.

<u>Resource Drawings</u>:

- Drawing files (DWG's)
  - Each floor plan, elevation, detail, etc., in a drawing file, has a *Named View* associated with it.
  - These files are the files you have created thus far in this book.
  - You will cover Named Views later in this exercise.

- Any text or dimensions drawn in a *Resource Drawing* needs to be scaled appropriately based on the scale that drawing will ultimately be plotted at.

Sheet Files:

- Drawing files (DWG's)
  - Each of these files represents a sheet in a set of drawings (e.g., 24"x36" sheet)
- *Named Views*, from various *Resource Drawings*, are placed on these sheets.
- *Named Views* can be placed at various scales at the time of insertion. A drawing title tag is automatically inserted below the drawing view; the tag is even automatically filled out with the view's number (if/when one is provided in the *Sheet Set Manager*), and scale (i.e., the scale you selected when the view was placed on the sheet). The image below describes the default drawing tag:

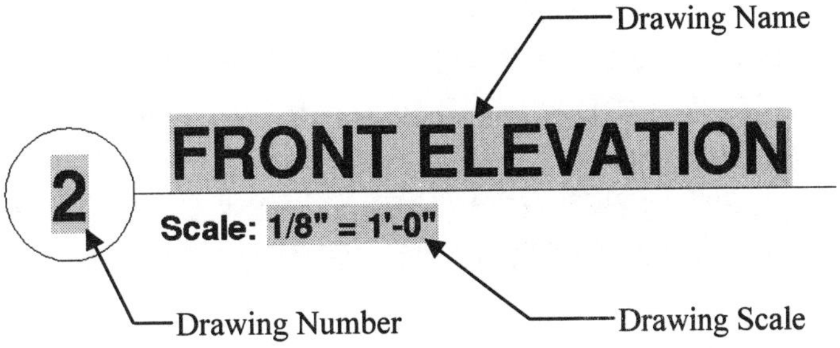

- Once a *View* has been placed on a sheet, you can specify a Drawing Number; you can also change the Drawing (view) Name. This must be done in the *Sheet Set Manager* to insure all sheets and views are correctly cross-referenced.
- *Callout Bubbles* (elevation and detail) can be placed on sheets. The bubbles reference a Named View from a Resource Drawing. The reference bubble is automatically filled out with the View's number and the sheet number the view is placed on (all of which is stored in the Sheet Set Data file). The image below describes the basic components of a callout bubble:

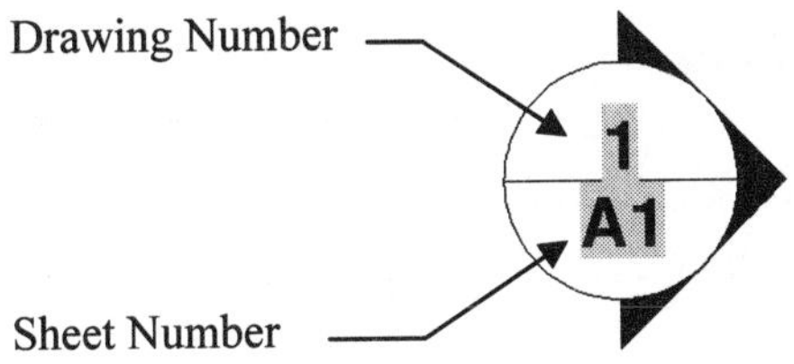

- The shaded rectangle behind the text lets you know that the text is updated automatically and should not be modified manually. Specifically, they are called *Fields*, and are updated at key points while working on a drawing (e.g., Open, Save, Plot, Regen). These are similar to the *Fields* in *MS Word*, the *Date Field* is shaded and automatically updated.

A Sheet Set Data File:
- File name and extension: *filename*.dst.
- This file is a database that maintains information about the Sheet Set and detail/sheet numbering and cross-references.
- The file can be located anywhere on your system (including a network drive). This file should be stored in your project folder for easy backup.

Creating Named Views in your Resource Drawings:

As mentioned above, the various plans, elevations, sections and details you wish to place on a sheet, each need to be identified by a Named View; which is simply defined by an imaginary rectangular area within a drawing file. If you move a door detail, for example, to another part of *Model Space*, the *Named View* does NOT move and would be "looking" at an empty potion of the drawing at that point.

You will start with the exterior elevations.

1. Open your **Exterior Elevations** drawing created in Lesson 5.

If created per the tutorial outlined in Lesson5, you have all four elevations in one drawing. You will create one Named View for each elevation in the *Exterior Elevation* Drawing.

2. **Zoom** into the South Elevation.

3. Select **Named Views...** from the *View* menu.
TIP: You can also type V and Enter to load Named Views.

South Elevation

You are now in the Named Views dialog. (Figure 9-2.1)

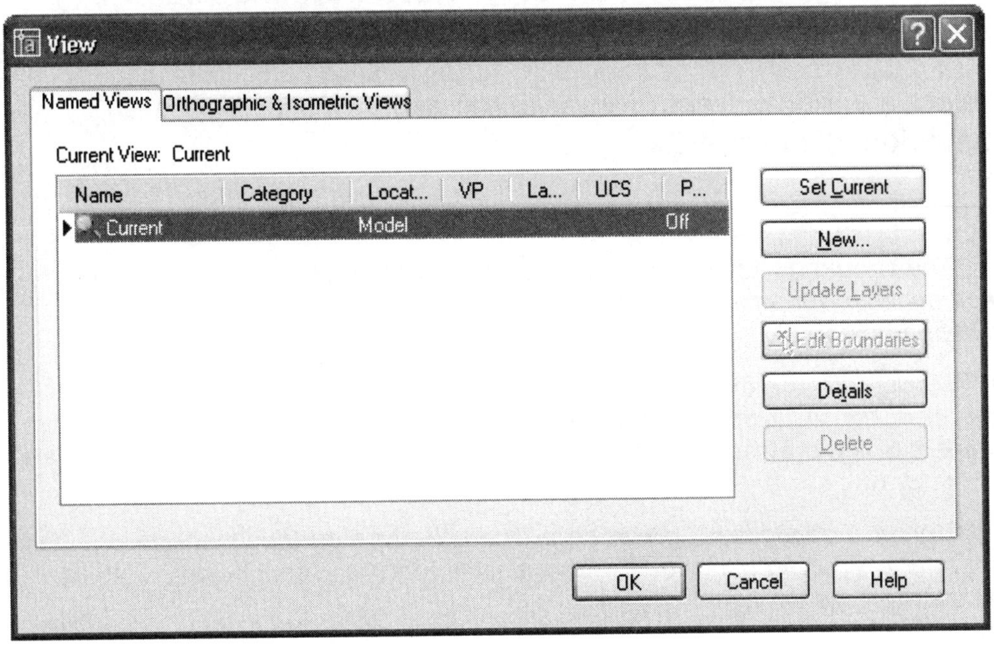

Figure 9-2.1
View dialog box; click "New..." to create a named view

4. Click **New** to create a Named View.

You are now in the *New View* dialog (Figure 9-2.2), where you can create a Named View.

5. Enter **South Elevation** for the *View* name. (Figure 9-2.2)

   TIP: *The name entered here is the default name used in the drawing title tag, when the view is placed on a sheet.*

6. Click **Define window** in the *Boundary* area. (Figure 9-2.2)

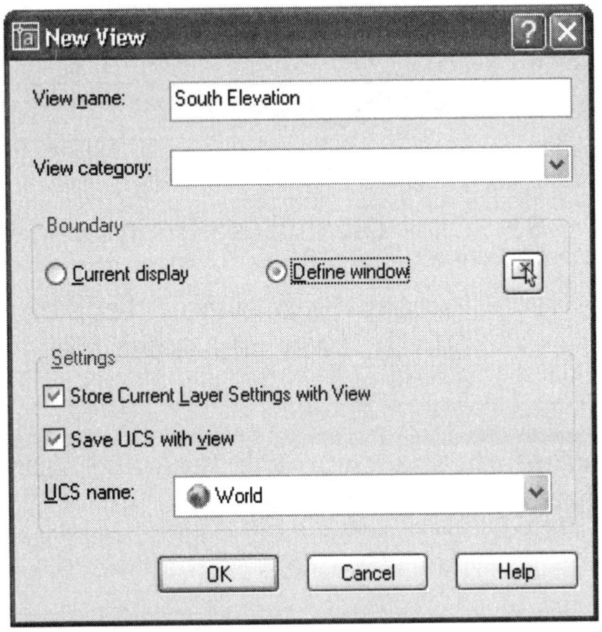

Figure 9-2.2
New View dialog; create a view named "South Elevation"

Immediately after clicking *Define window* you are temporarily brought back to the drawing to select a boundary window around your south elevation.

7. Select a window (rectangular area) around your south elevation. (Figure 9-2.3)

   TIP: *Note the following regarding your boundary window selection:*

   ****You should try to pick a window as tight to the drawing as possible; leaving room for any anticipated additions to the drawing (e.g., more building or notes).*

   ****By default, the drawing title tag is placed just below the lower left corner of the view when it is placed on a sheet; so too much extra space to the left of the drawing would position the title tag so that it is not under any of the drawing.*

   ****If your drawing does grow larger than the Named Views specified boundary, you can use the Edit Boundaries feature (see Figure 9-2.1) to resize the boundary.*

Figure 9-2.3
South Elevation; select window as shown to define view

8. Click **OK** to close the *New View* dialog and create the view.

9. Repeat the previous steps to create a *Named View* for the **North, East** and **West** elevations in your *Exterior Elevations* drawing.

When finished, you will see each *Named View* listed in the View dialog box. (Figure 9-2.4)

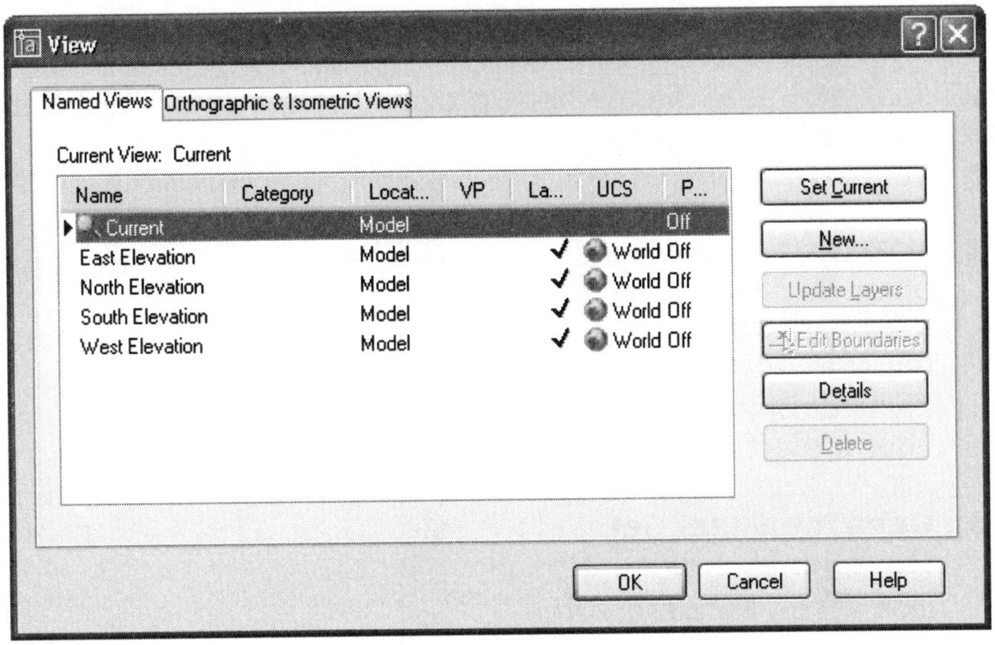

Figure 9-2.4
View dialog; a named view created for each elevation in the Exterior Elevations drawing

10. **Open** your other drawings and create *Named Views* per the chart below.

Drawing name	Named View to create
Flr-B.dwg	Basement Floor Plan
Flr-1.dwg	First Floor Plan
Flr-2.dwg	Second Floor Drawing
Building Section.dwg	Building Section
Wall Section.dwg	Wall Section
Bathroom Elevation.dwg	Bathroom Elevation
Room Schedule.dwg	Room Finish Schedule
Additional Task dwg's	*Name Views appropriately*

FYI: *Remember, these drawings will be referred to as the Resource Drawings in the Sheet Set Manager.*

11. **Save** your drawings.

Next you will create the Sheet Set Data file via the Sheet Set Manger.

Setting up a Sheet Set:

You will look at one of the methods provided to set up a Sheet Set. This involves using the Create Sheet Set Wizard.

12. Make sure a drawing is open. You must have at least one drawing open to get started; it can be a blank drawing or one of your project files.

13. **Open** the **Sheet Set Manager** by clicking its icon on the *Standard Toolbar.*

14. At the top of the *Sheet Set Manager* palette, click the down-arrow and then select **New Sheet Set...** from the menu.

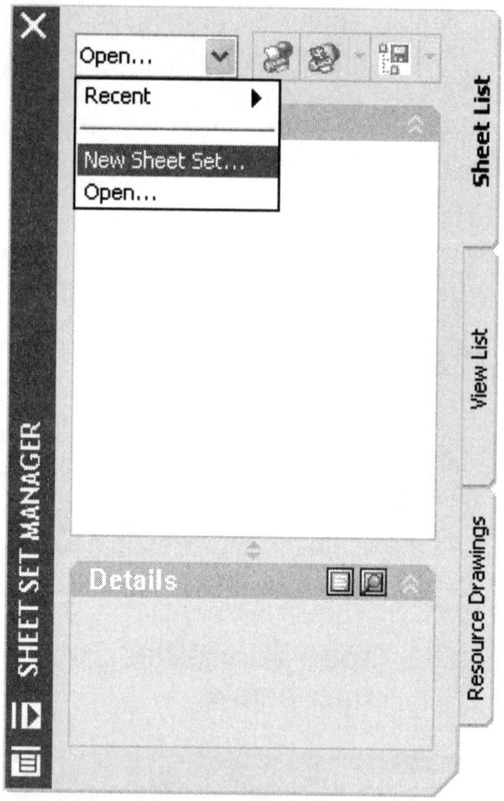

Figure 9-2.5
Sheet Set Manager; click the Down-Arrow and select "New Sheet Set..." to start a new Sheet Set

This starts the *Sheet Set Manager Wizard*. (Figure 9-2.6)

15. Click **Next.**

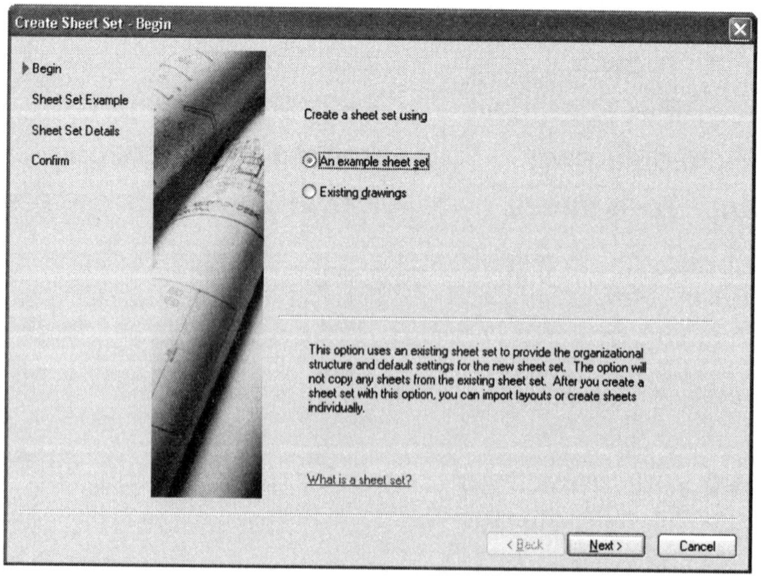

Figure 9-2.6
Create Sheet Set Wizard; Begin screen

16. Next, make sure **Architectural Imperial Sheet Set** is selected and then click **Next.** (Figure 9-2.7)

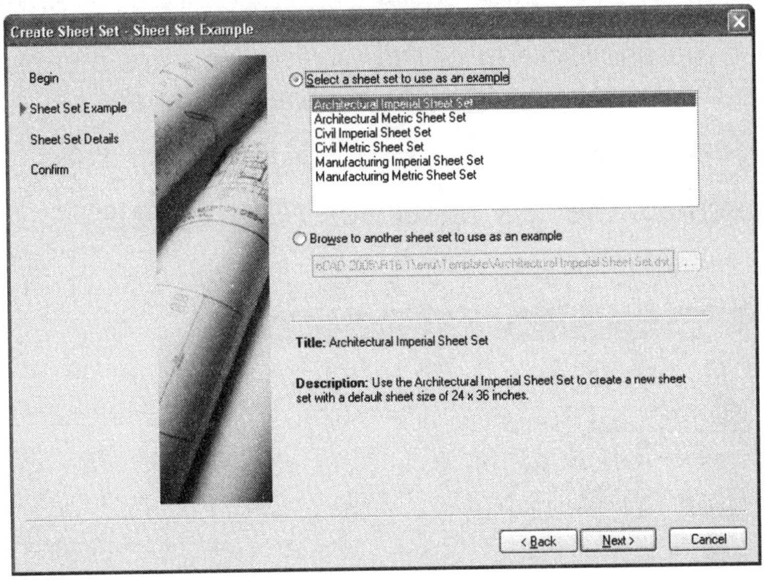

Figure 9-2.7
Create Sheet Set Wizard; Sheet Set Example screen

17. Enter the name of new sheet set; use your last name (e.g., *lastname* Residence). See Figure 9-2.8.

18. Click the " ... " button to change the location where the *sheet set data file* will be stored; **a.**) Create a subfolder named Sheet Set Files in the folder that contains the files created in this book. **b.**) Select the new folder.

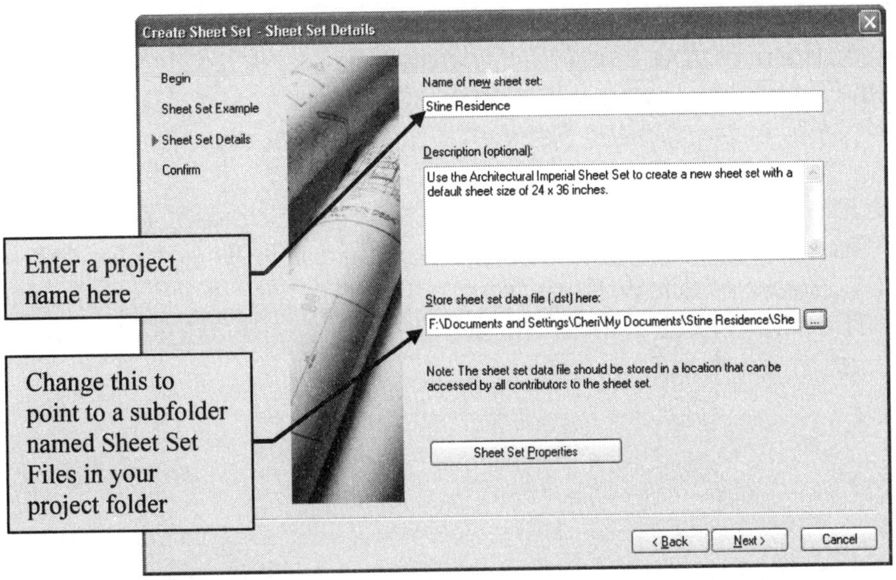

Figure 9-2.8
Create Sheet Set Wizard; Sheet Set Details screen

TIP: *To insure the remainder of this lesson proceeds smoothly, you should make sure all your project files are located in one folder. Just the current files, with no backup DWG files or old copies.*

You are now at the final screen of the wizard. You are given detailed information on the "what and where" for the new sheet set about to be created.

Click **Finish** to create the new *Sheet Set.* (Figure 9-2.9)

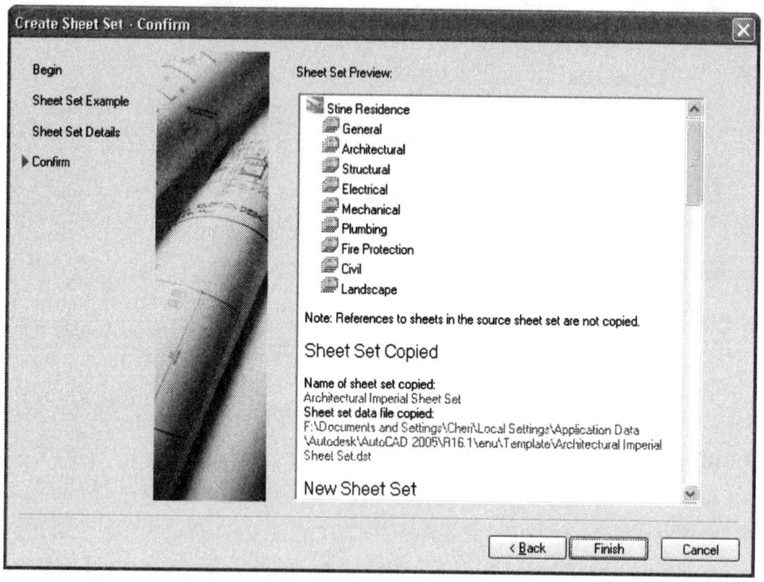

Figure 9-2.9
Create Sheet Set Wizard; Confirm screen

The wizard closes and the *Sheet Set Manager* is populated with the specified information. If you use *MS Windows Explorer* to browse to your *Sheet Set Files* folder, you will see a new file named "*Lastname* Residence.dst", this is the *Sheet Set Data* file previously discussed.

The *Sheet Set Example* file used contained several *Subsets* (e.g., Architectural, Structural, etc.), which are seen on the *Sheet List tab* (Figure 9-2.10). *Subsets* allow *Sheets* to be organized; by discipline in this example. The right-click menu allows you to easily add, rename or remove a *Subset* at anytime.

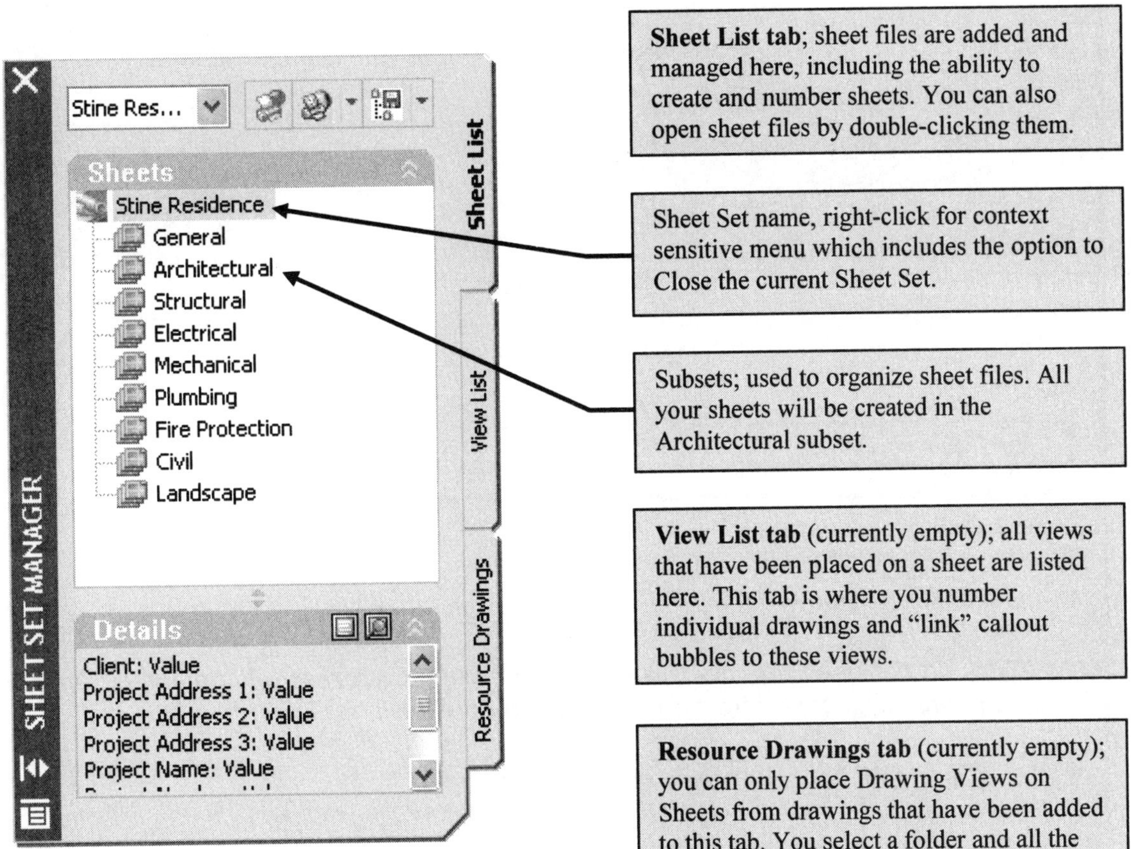

Figure 9-2.10
Sheet Set Manager; Sheet List tab

Adding project info to the Sheet Set Properties:

The Sheet Set Properties dialog contains key information that AutoCAD needs to properly manage and control the Sheet Set. Next you will enter the project name and address, which is automatically placed in the title block of each sheet in the set!

Note: For the remainder of this lesson, substitute your last name for Stine when referring to the sheet set/project name.

19. In the *Sheet Set Manager*, on the *Sheet List* tab, right click on the sheet set name (Stine Residence) at the top of the list and select **Properties** from the pop-up menu.

20. In the *Sheet Set Custom Properties* section, add information similar to that shown in **Figure 9-2.11.**

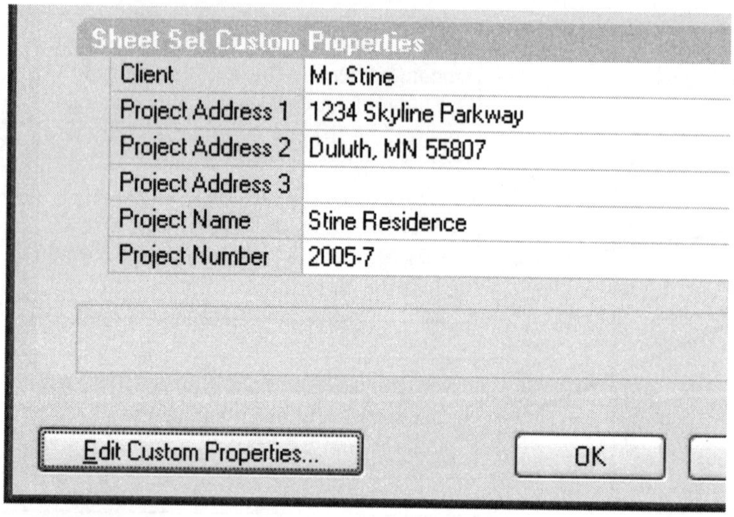

Figure 9-2.11
Create Sheet Set Properties; partial view of dialog

TIP: *If you do not need one field, such as the "Project Address 3" line above, leave it blank, otherwise any text entered will show up on drawings.*

21. Click **OK** to complete the changes.

Creating sheets to place Named Views on:

Creating a sheet with a title block, a number and client information has NEVER been easier! In just minutes you will have all the empty sheets setup and ready for *Named Views* to be placed on them.

As you create sheets in the *Sheet Set Manager*, AutoCAD creates a drawing file in the specified folder (<u>Sheet Set Files</u> sub-folder in this example). This file IS the sheet. If the file is erased or corrupt, that sheet will no longer be available. Therefore, you should backup the files in the <u>Sheet Set Files</u> sub-folder, just as you would your Resource Drawings.

Next you will setup the entire set of sheets, starting with the project Title Sheet.

22. On the *Sheet List* tab, in the *Sheet Set Manager*, right-click on the *Architectural* Subset, and then click **New Sheet...** from the pop-up menu (Figure 9-2.12)

You are now in the New Sheet dialog box where you enter the sheet title and number, as well as specify the name of the drawing file that will be created.

23. Enter the following:
    a. Number: **A0**
    b. Sheet title: **Title Sheet**
    c. File Name: *see tip below*
    d. See **Figure 9-2.13**

TIP*: As you can see, the File name was automatically filled in using the sheet number and title. Unfortunately, you do not want the number as part of the file name. The reason for this is if you want to change the sheet number at a later time, the File Name will still have the original number associated with it, which would be confusing.*

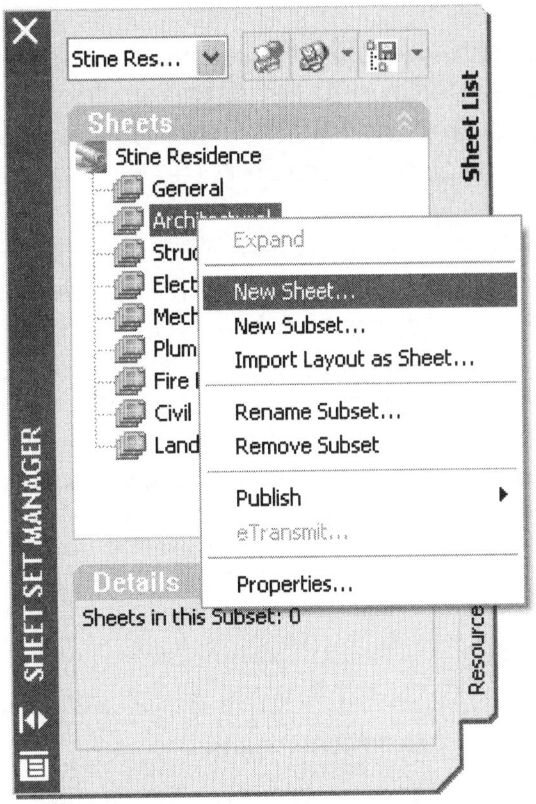

Figure 9-2.12
Sheet Set Manager; create new sheet

24. Delete the *Sheet Number* from the **File Name.**

25. Click **OK** to create the sheet.

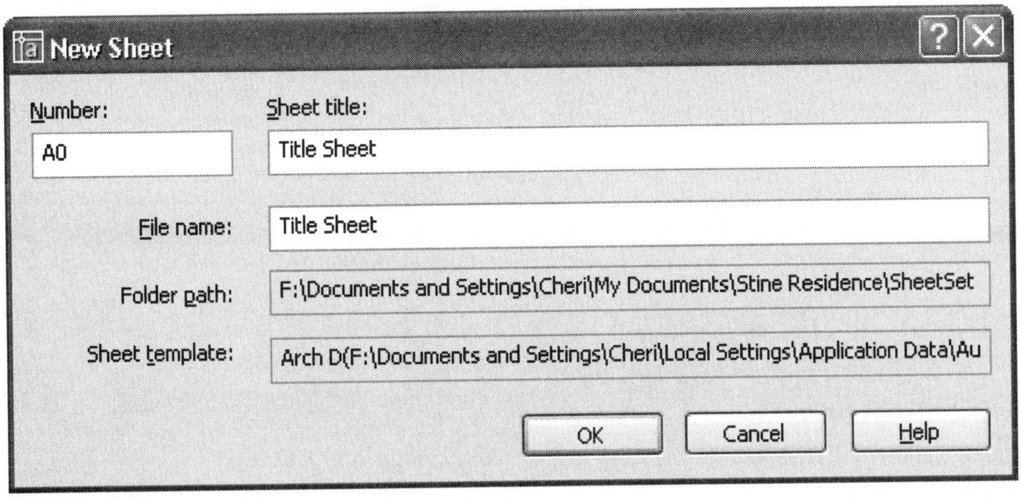

Figure 9-2.13
New Sheet dialog; enter sheet number, title and file name

You have just created your first sheet! You now see the sheet listed under the *Architectural Subset* in the *Sheet Set Manager* (Figure 9-2.14).

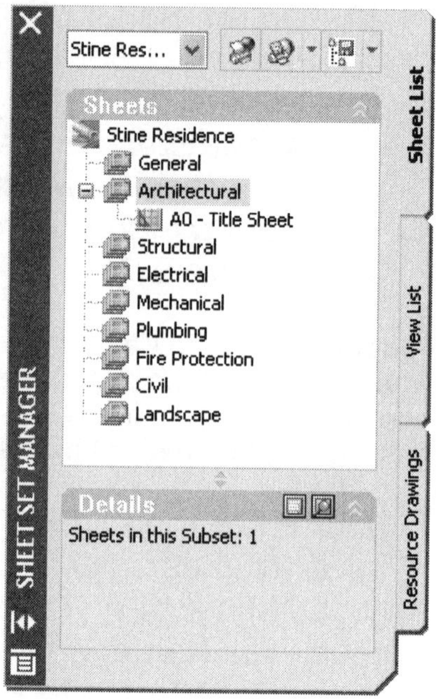

Figure 9-2.14
New Sheet Manager; first new sheet created in Architectural subset

26. Per the steps above, create new sheets so that you have all the sheets listed in the table below. (also see Note below):

***NOTE**: The two Exterior Elevations sheets that you need to create need to have different file names. Also, a Sheet File name cannot be the same as a Resource File name; name (i.e., file name) the elevation sheets Exterior Elevations 1 and Exterior Elevations 2.*

***REMINDER**: Don't forget to remove the sheet number from the file name.*

Sheet name	Sheet number
Title Sheet	A0
Basement Floor Plan	A1
First Floor Plan	A2
Second Floor Plan	A3
Exterior Elevations	A4
Exterior Elevations	A5
Building Sections	A6
Wall Sections	A7
Interior Elevations	A8
Schedules	A9

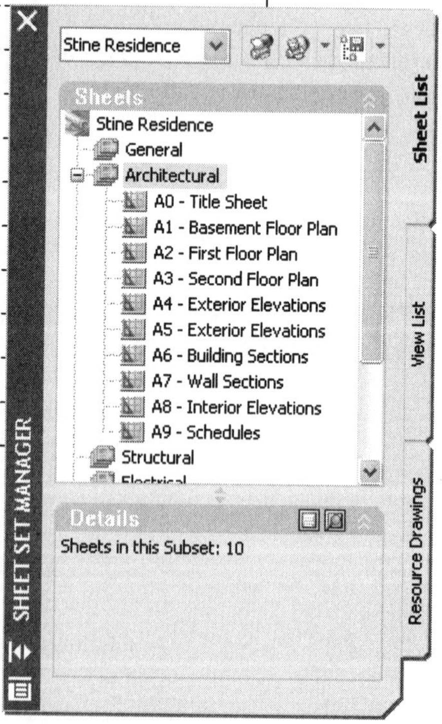

Once finished, all the sheets will be listed in the Sheet Set Manager as shown in Figure 9-2.15.

Figure 9-2.15
New Sheet Manager; all sheets created in Architectural subset

Figure 9-2.16
Window Explorer view of your *Sheet Set Files* sub-folder you created in your project folder; files automatically created with the Sheet Set Manger

Take a minute to browse to the Sheet Set Files folder you previously created and notice an AutoCAD file has been created for each sheet. (Figure 9-2.16)

These files can be opened here, by double-clicking, or from File → Open within AutoCAD.

Next you will see how the Sheet Set Manager allows you to do this.

Opening Sheets from the Sheet Set Manager:

In the *Sheet Set Manager* you can double-click on a sheet title (on the *Sheet List* tab) to open the drawing file that represents that sheet. Once the drawing is open you can save and close it just like any other drawing file.

Next you will open the exterior elevation sheet A4 to place one of your drawings on it.

27. On the *Sheet List* tab, in *Sheet Set Manager*, double-click on the sheet title **A4 – Exterior Elevations.**

The drawing **Exterior Elevations** (located in your *SheetSet Files* sub-folder) is now open.

28. **Zoom** in to the lower right corner of the sheet to see the information that was automatically entered in the title block. (Figure 9-2.17)

29. Notice that the sheet number, project name and date have been automatically added to the title block.

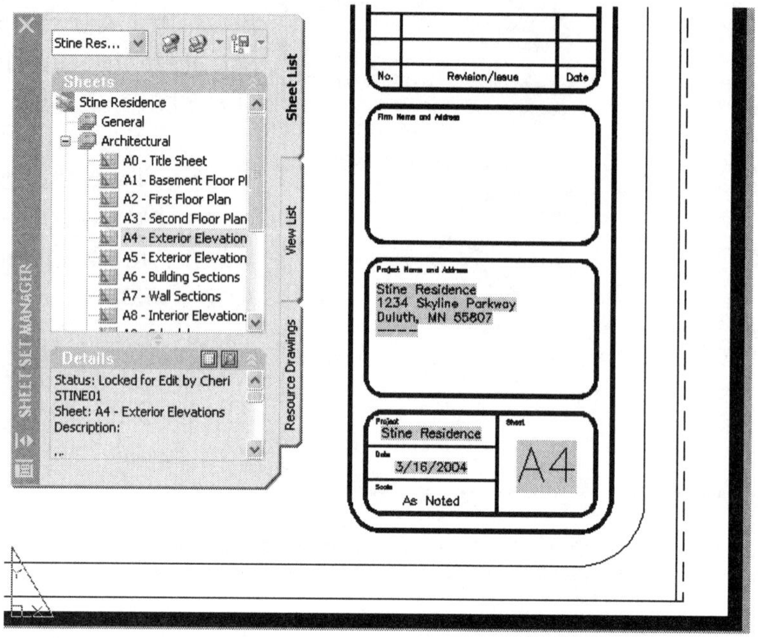

Figure 9-2.17
Sheet A4 – Exterior Elevations; Shaded text are fields which are modified/updated using the Sheet Set Manager

30. **Zoom Previous** so you see the entire sheet.

Contos Residence

Image courtesy of Anderson Architects
Alan H. Anderson, Architect, Duluth, MN

Specifying resource drawing locations:

You are just about ready to start placing drawings on sheets. But first you need to tell the Sheet Set Manager where to look for your drawing files that contain the Named Views. You will do this next.

31. Click on the *Resource Drawings* tab in the *Sheet Set Manager.*

32. Double-click the **Add New Location...** icon. (Figure 9-2.18)

33. Browse to the location where all your drawings, created in the book, are stored and then click **OK.**

Figure 9-2.18
Resource Drawings tab; no folder listed yet

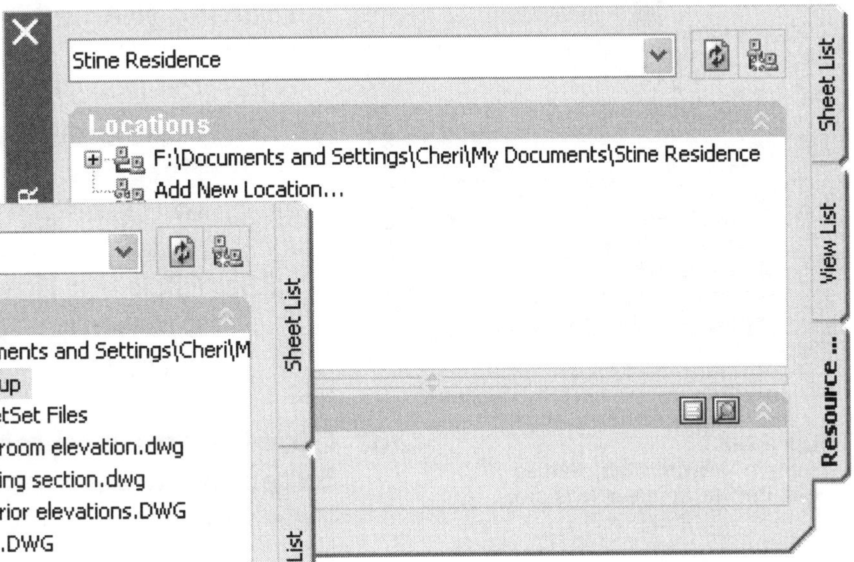

Figure 9-2.19
Resource Drawings tab; stine residence folder now selected

Notice in Figure 9-2.19 that the folder you selected is now listed in the Location pane (on the Resource Drawings tab).

The "plus" symbol next to the new Locations Folder allows you to expand the view to show the drawings listed in that folder. After clicking the plus symbol, the drawings and folders are displayed and the "plus" changes to a "minus" symbol. (Figure 9-2.20)

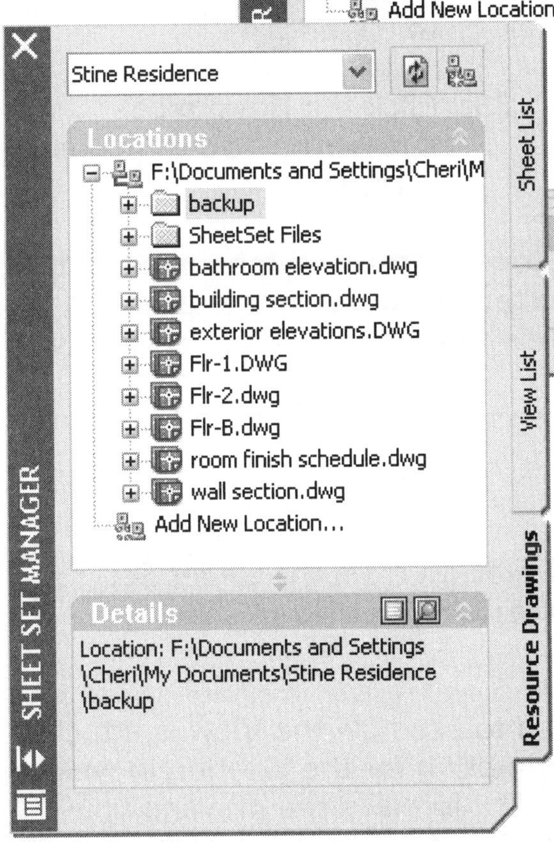

Figure 9-2.20
Resource Drawings tab;
Stine Residence folder expanded

Adding Named Views to Sheets:

You are now to the point where you can start placing drawings (*Named Views*) on your *Sheets*. Basically, you drag on a *Named View* from a *Resource Drawing* onto your *Sheet*.

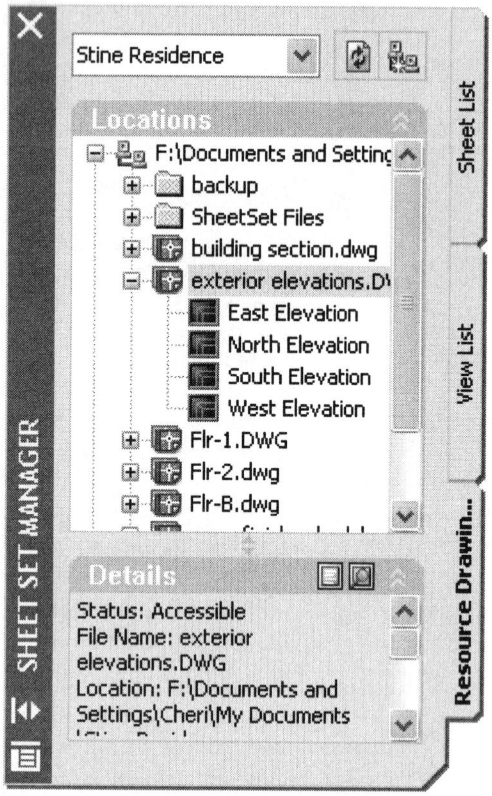

Figure 9-2.21
Resource Drawings tab; Named Views in *exterior elevations.dwg*

Similar to the previous discussion on how the "plus" symbol expands the Locations folder, the "plus" symbol next to the drawings (listed in the Locations folder) expands that drawings view to display its Named Views.

First you will open a sheet to place a drawing (Named View) on…

34. On the *Sheet List* tab, double-click the **A4 – Exterior Elevations** sheet to open it.

35. Click the **Resource Drawings Tab** to make it current.

36. Click the "**plus**" symbol next to the **Exterior Elevations** drawing to view that drawings *Named Views.*

You can now see the four *Named Views* you created in the Exterior Elevations drawing (Figure 9-2.21).

37. Click and drag the **South Elevation** from the *Sheet Set Manager* onto **your A4 – Exterior Elevations** sheet. (Figure 9-2.22)

Move your cursor about the screen to see how the View is attached to your cursor and AutoCAD is prompting for the location in which to place the drawing. Before you click to place the drawing you need to specify the scale you want the drawing printed at.

38. **Right-click** to display the *Insertion Scale* pop-up menu. (Figure 9-2.20)

39. Select **1/4" = 1'-0"** from the list.

Notice how the size of the drawing changes to correspond to the selected scale. Displaying the drawing at the correct scale helps you to correctly position the drawing on the sheet. You should also notice that a drawing title tag is position below and to the left of your view; which you will look at closer after the view is placed.

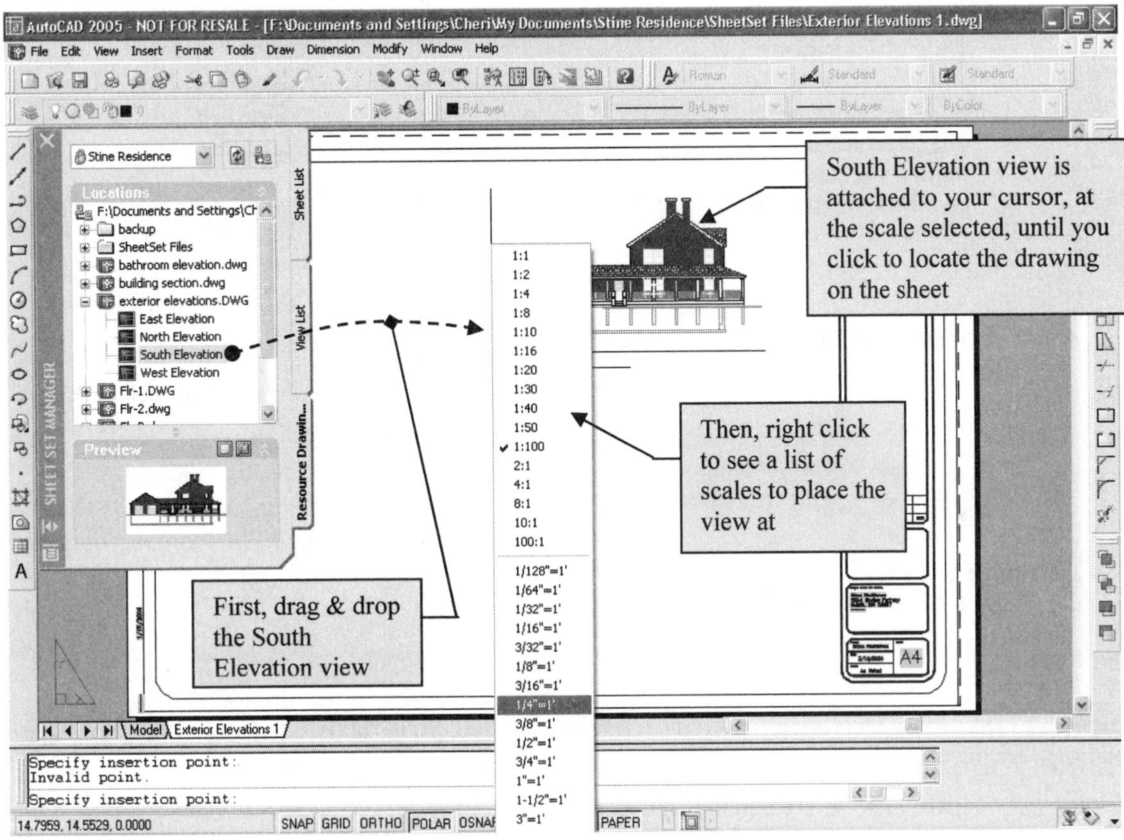

Figure 9-2.22
A4 - Exterior Elevations; placing the South Elevation view and right-clicking to see scale options

40. Position your mouse so the elevation is centered on the sheet and then click to place the view on the sheet.

You have placed your first drawing on a sheet (Figure 9-2.23)! In just minutes you could have all the Named Views placed, but first you will explore a few other options and see how they are affected when you change a few sheet numbers.

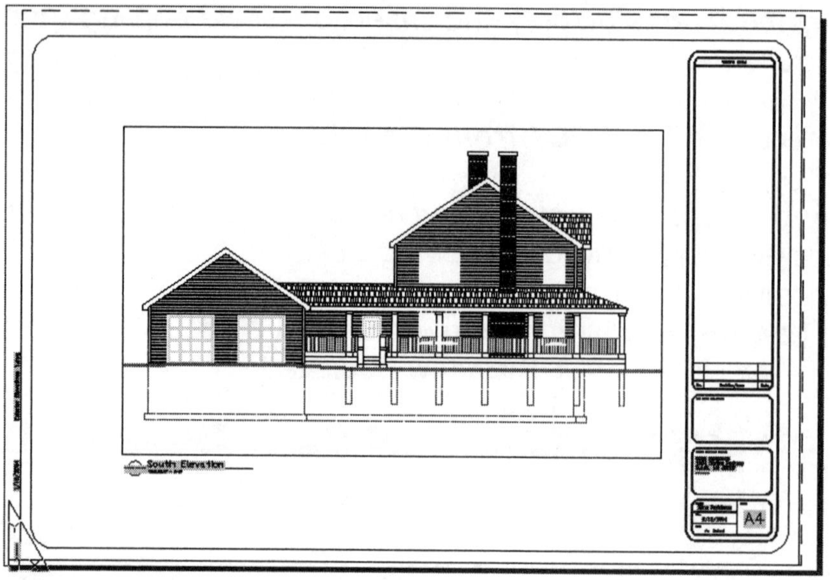

Figure 9-2.23
A4 - Exterior Elevations; South Elevation placed at ¼"=1'-0"

41. **Zoom In** on the *Drawing Title* tag. (Figure 9-2.24)

Figure 9-2.24
A4 - Exterior Elevations; zoomed in on drawing title tag

Notice that the drawing name has been automatically filled in using the name you provided when you created the *Named View* in the *Resource Drawing* (exterior elevations.dwg).

Also notice that the drawing scale has been added and, of course, corresponds to the scale you selected when you placed the view.

The only field not filled out yet is the drawing number. You enter the drawing number for a view, once it is placed on a sheet, in the *Sheet Set Manager*. Next you will provide the sheet number via the Sheet Set Manager.

***WARNING**: Do not change the number in the drawing as it will be overwritten by the Sheet Set Manager.*

42. Select the **View List** tab.

Notice that the South Elevation view is listed. Eventually all your Named Views will be listed here; once they are all placed on sheets. (Figure 9-2.25)

43. Right-click on the *South Elevation* view and select **Rename & Renumber...** from the pop-up menu.

44. Enter number **1** in the Number text box. (Figure 9-2.26)

45. Click **OK** to apply the change.

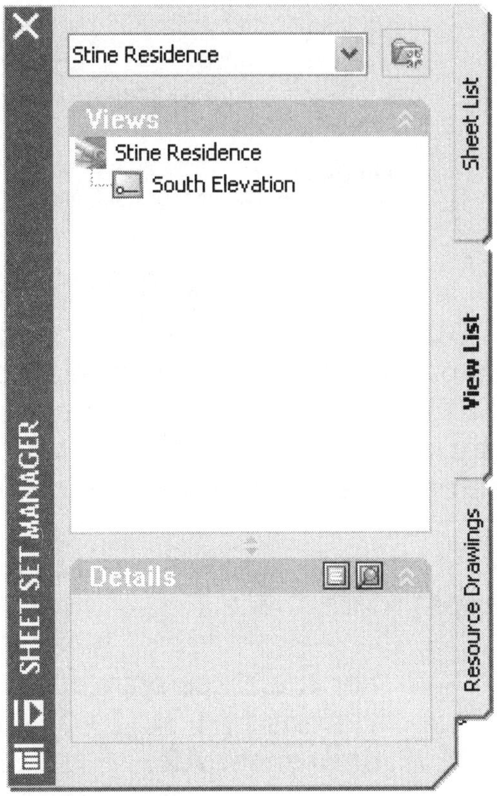

Figure 9-2.25
Sheet Set Manager; view list tab

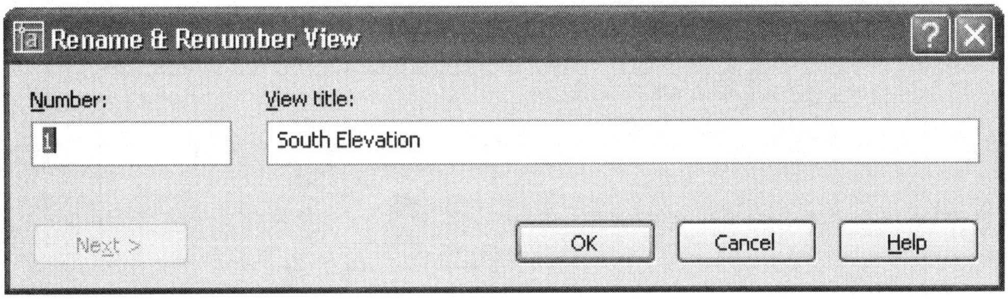

Figure 9-2.26
Rename and Renumber View; enter number 1

You will notice that your drawing has not updated yet. The following step will cause the drawing title tag to update.

46. From the *View* pull-down menu, select **Regen.**

The drawing title tag now has the number 1 in the circle (Figure 9-2.27). A few other key events cause AutoCAD to update the tags. A few examples are opening and plotting a drawing.

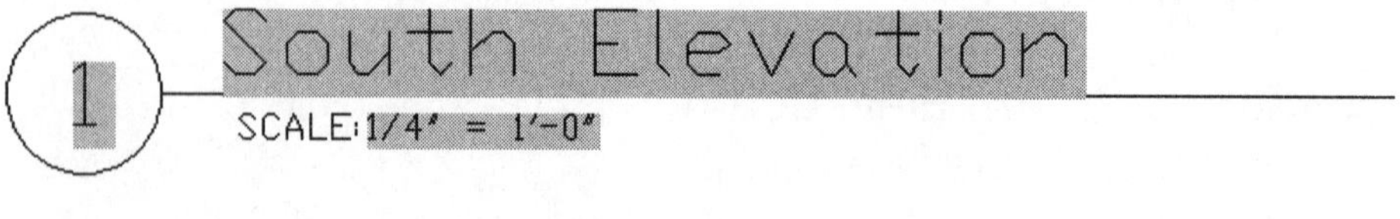

Figure 9-2.27
A4- Exterior Elevations; field updated automatically

Placing Callout tags:

Another powerful feature related to *Sheet Sets* is the ability to place *Callout* tags that are automatically cross-referenced with a sheet and drawing number. Next you will place an elevation Callout tag (that references the south elevation) on the floor plan.

First, though, you will need to place the first floor plan on the appropriate sheet.

47. Per the steps previously outlined, place the **First Floor Plan** view at **1/4" = 1'-0"** (from the Flr-1.dwg resource drawing) onto sheet **A2 – First Floor Plan**. (Figure 9-2.28)

    TIP*: Open the sheet from the Sheet List tab and then drag the view from the Resource Drawing tab.*

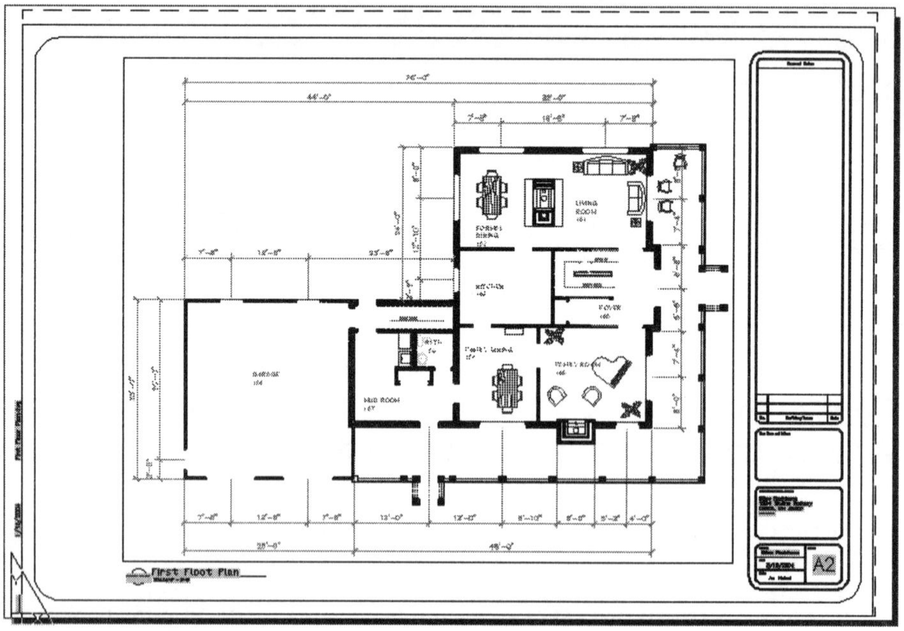

Figure 9-2.28
A2- First Floor Plan; First floor plan view placed on sheet at 1/4"

48. **Zoom** into the bottom center of the floor plan sheet.

49. On the *Sheet List* tab, right-click on the South Elevation view, and then select **Place Callout Block → Elev. Indicator Ext. – Up.** (Figure 9-2.29)

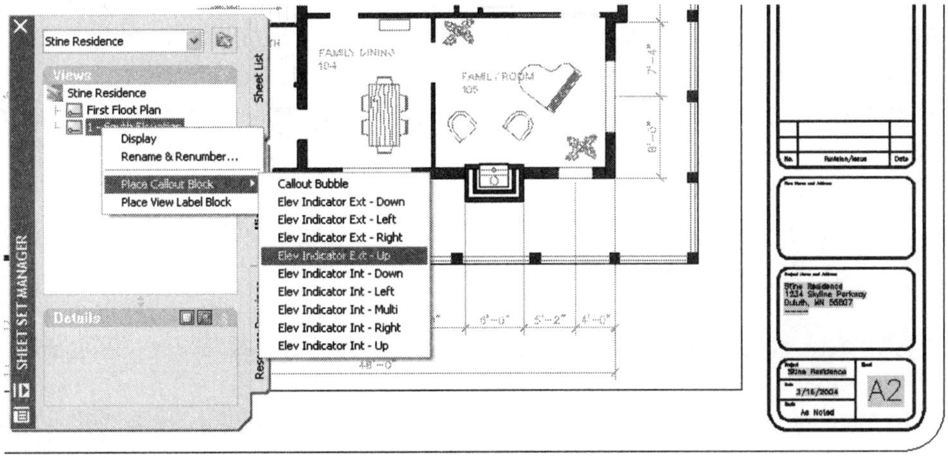

Figure 9-2.29
View List tab; right click on '1 – South Elevation'

50. Click to place the elevation tag approximately as shown in Figure 9-2.30.

Notice that the Elev. Indicator has been automatically fill out. It referenced both the sheet and drawing number where the elevation (i.e., the elevation the tag is pointing at) can be found.

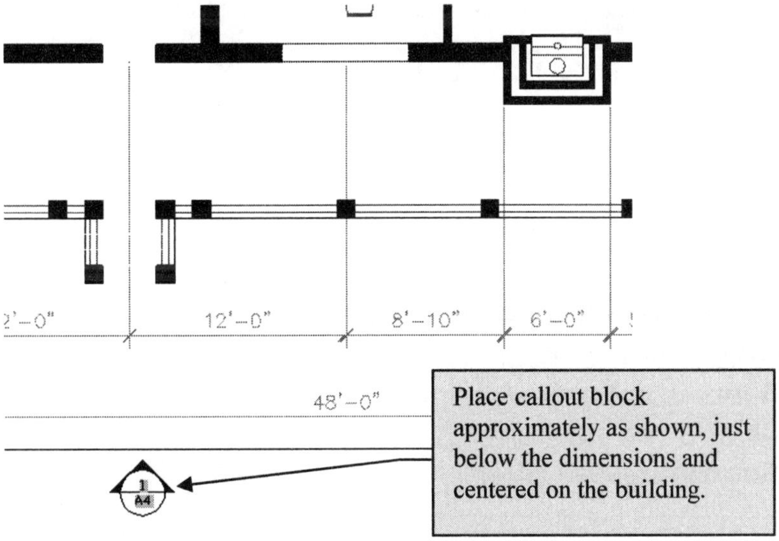

Figure 9-2.30
First Floor Plan sheet; elevation callout placed

51. **Save** both your elevation and plan sheet (*select File → Save*); don't forget to save often so you don't lose any work.

Changing sheet numbers:

Looking at Figure 9-2.23, you realize that you will need two more exterior elevation sheets because one elevation takes up most of the sheet at 1/4" = 1'-0". Next you will increment all the sheets that come after the exterior elevation sheets by 2 and then add two more exterior elevations sheets; all this is done in the *Sheet Set Manager*.

52. On the *Sheet List* tab, right click on sheet **A9 – Schedules** and select **Rename & renumber.**

53. Change the Number to **A11** and click **OK.** (Figure 9-2.31)

This is similar to renumbering and renaming a view on the *View List* tab (look back at Figure 9-2.25). Once the sheet is created you can't change the file name in the Sheet Set Manager; and, of course, you should not change the file in Windows Explorer because the Sheet Set Manager will not be able to find it.

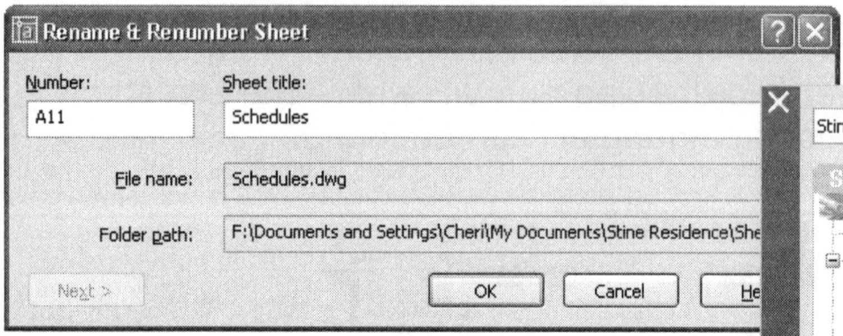

Figure 9-2.31
Rename & Renumber Sheet; change sheet A9 to A11

54. **Renumber** all the sheets after sheet *S3 – Second Floor* to make room to insert two new sheets numbered A4 and A5 (you will add the new sheets later) (See Figure 9-2.32).

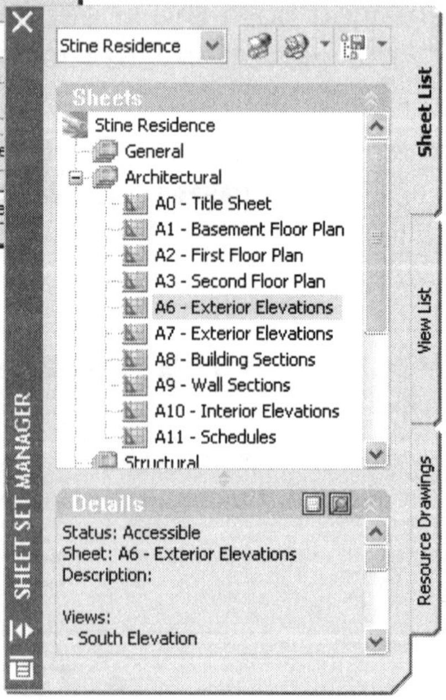

Figure 9-2.32
Sheet View tab; last six sheets renumbered, making room to insert two sheets

Normally, changing sheet numbers is not a good idea because, no mater how hard you look, you will usually miss one reference bubble; leaving the bubble pointing to the wrong sheet. This leads to confusion and possible loss of time and money.

AutoCAD has provided a solution to this problem. The callout bubbles, drawing titles and sheet borders are all linked to the information in the Sheet Set Manager. So once you changed the sheet numbers in the Sheet Set Manager, all the sheets were (or will be) updated automatically. You will verify this next.

55. In the **A6 – Exterior Elevations** sheet, zoom into the lower right corner to see the sheet number. (Figure 9-2.33)

    TIP*: You may need to Regen the drawing to see the change.*

As you can see the sheet number has been updated automatically! What about the elevation tag you placed on the floor plan sheet?

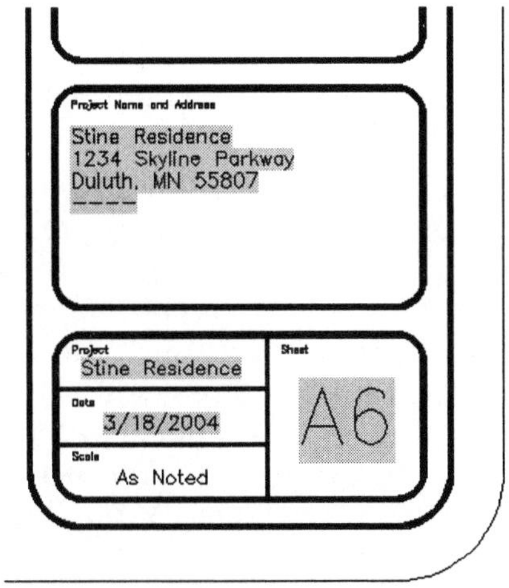

Figure 9-2.33
A6 – Exterior Elevations sheet; sheet number in title block has been updated automatically

56. On the **A2 – First Floor Plan** sheet, zoom in on the callout bubble (elev indicator). See Figure 9-2.34.

As you can see the elevation callout tag has been updated automatically! Thus, eliminating the possibility of cross-reference errors when this system is used.

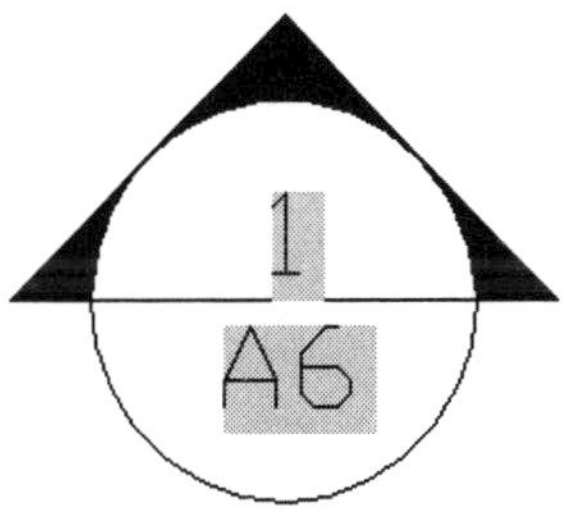

Figure 9-2.34
A2 – First Floor Plan sheet; sheet number in callout block has been updated automatically.

57. Add the following sheets to complete the set:

Sheet name	Sheet number
Exterior Elevations *Filename: Exterior Elevations 3*	A5
Exterior Elevations *Filename: Exterior Elevations 4*	A6

58. Place the remaining views (see step 10) on the appropriate sheets
__FYI__: The room schedule view should be placed at a scale of 1:1.

59. On the *View List* tab, give each view a number (see tip below).

Tip:

Drawings are typically numbered in the direction indicated below. The first drawings are placed in the upper right, and fill in the sheet toward the left. The main reason for starting on the right is this: if a sheet is only half full (for example), you would not have to open the set all the way to see the drawings on that sheet.

Also, it is usually a good idea to wait until the sheet is mostly full before numbering drawings. That way you can organize the drawings neatly on the sheet and avoid a situation where the drawing numbers are not in sequence.

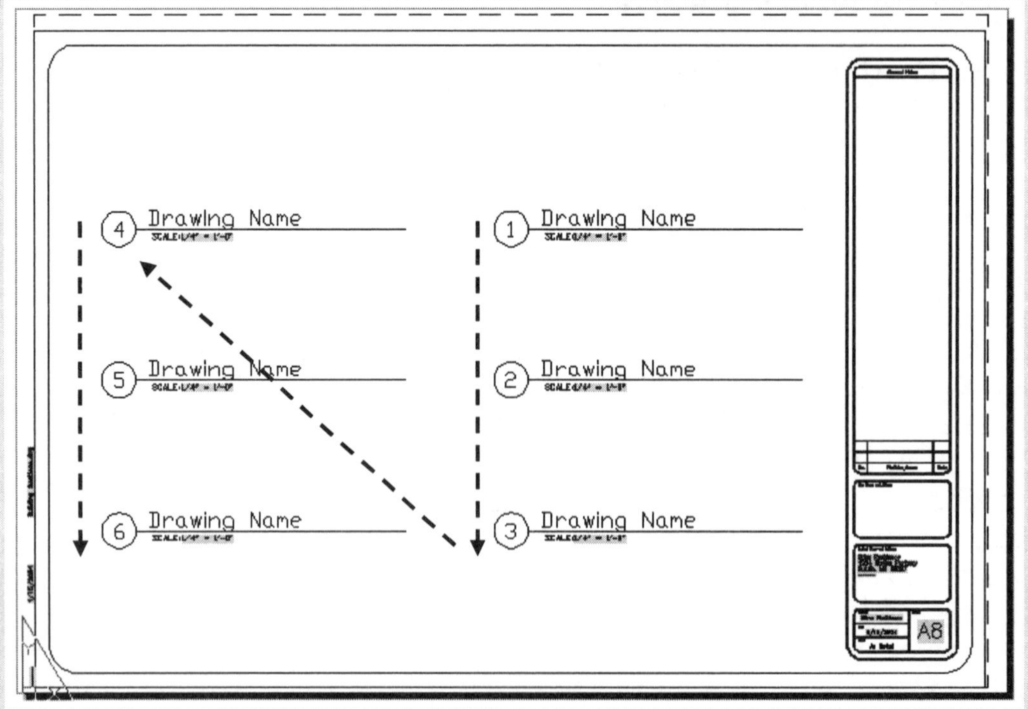

60. Place **Callout** blocks on your floor plan sheets to reference all your elevations (interior and exterior). See Figure 9-2.35.

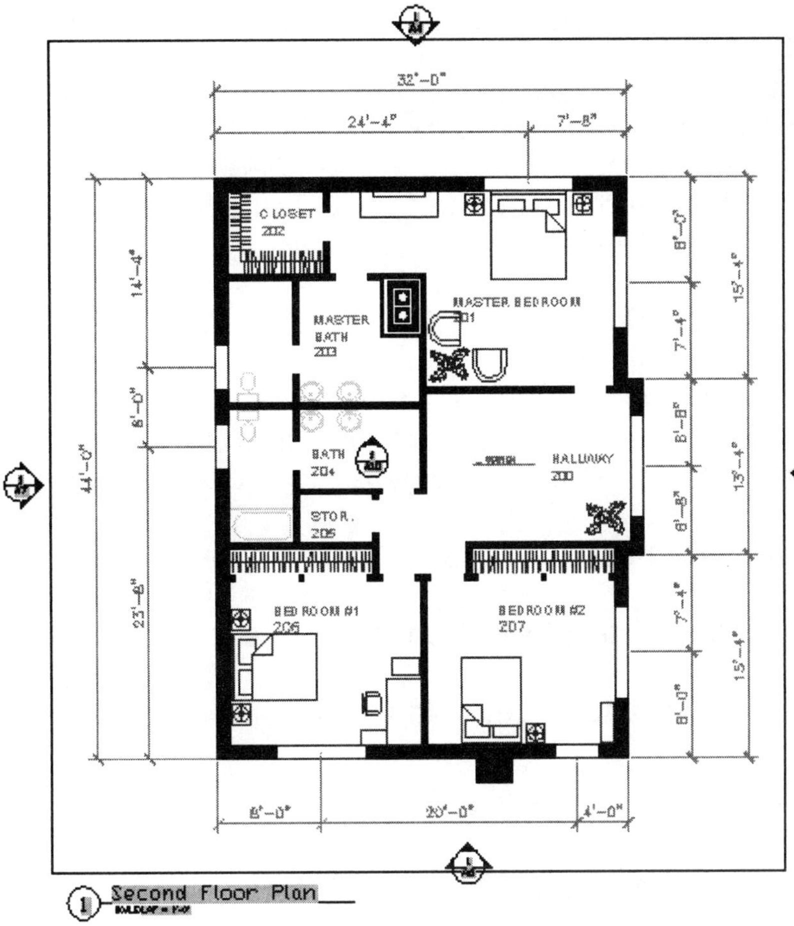

Figure 9-2.35
A3 - Second Floor Plan sheet; callout bubble added

TIP: *The rectangle surrounding your drawings when placed on a sheet (cf. Figure 9-2.35) is called a viewport. This line cannot be erased, but it can be moved to its own layer (e.g., viewport) and then that layer can be Frozen; the drawing will still be visible but the rectangle (viewport) will not.*

61. **Save** and close all your open drawing files.

62. **Close** the Sheet Set data file via the *Sheet Set Manager.*

This concludes the study on Sheet Sets.

Exercise 9-3:
Sheet Index

Introduction:

In this exercise you will take a look at the *Sheet Index* feature that takes advantage of both *Sheet Sets* and *Tables*. The *Sheet Index* feature extracts information stored in the *Sheet Set Data* file (sheet name and number) and then generates a *Table* to be place on one of your sheets in the *Sheet Set*.

Similar to placing *Callout Bubble*, the *Sheet Index* also has hyperlinks embedded in each listing; thus, you can 'Ctrl + click' on a room name or number to open that sheet. As you will see in the next Lesson, these hyperlinks transfer to the electronic set (DWF file) which allows a client or consultant to easily navigate the set of drawings.

1. **Open** you Sheet Set Data file (*yourname* Residence.dst).

2. Open **A0 – Title Sheet** from the *Sheet List* tab.

3. Using *Mtext*, add large, bold text as shown in **Figure 9-3.1.**

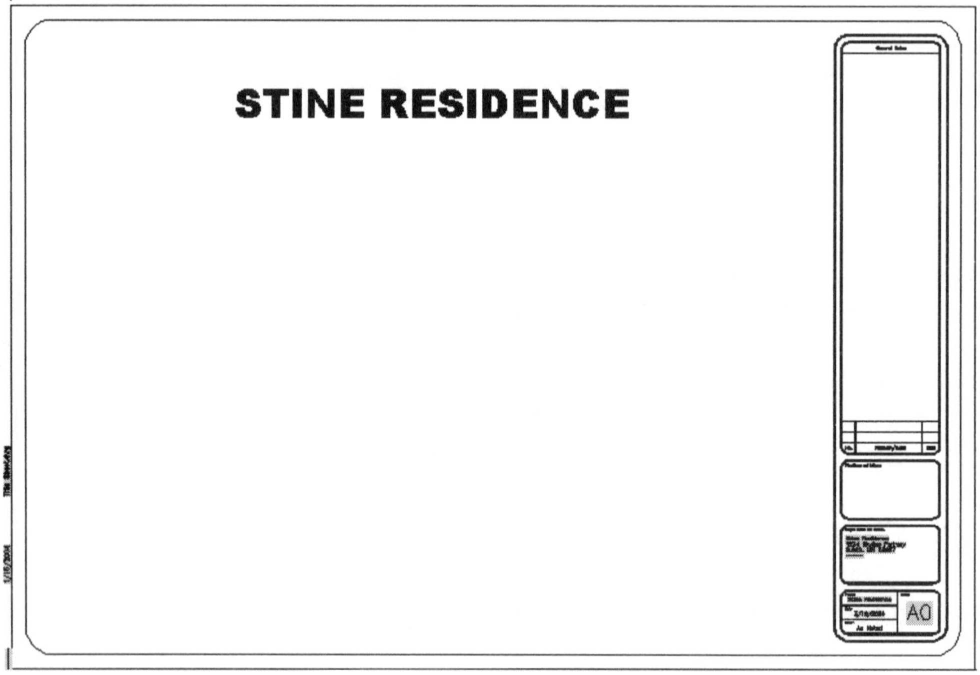

Figure 9-3.1
A0 – Title Sheet; text added to sheet

FYI: A title sheet usually has the project title as its focal point. Additionally, you will typically find the following information:

- Rendering or picture of a model of the project
- Sheet Index
- Abbreviation Legend (e.g., TYP. means TYPICAL)
- Symbol Legend (e.g., show a swatch of AR-CONC hatch pattern and identify it as the symbol for concrete)
- Building Code / Zoning Summary
- Site Plan (typically on smaller projects)

The Legends, which are used over and over, with out modification, can be created in a separate drawing and inserted as a block on the Title Sheet.

Next you will insert a sheet index.

4. Right click on the Sheet Set project title (at the top of the list on the Sheet List tab).

5. Select **Insert Sheet List Table...** from the pop-up menu. (Figure 9-3.2)

6. Click on your **A0 – Title Sheet** sheet to indicate which sheet you want to insert the table on.

You are now in the Insert Sheet List Table dialog. (Figure 9-3.3)

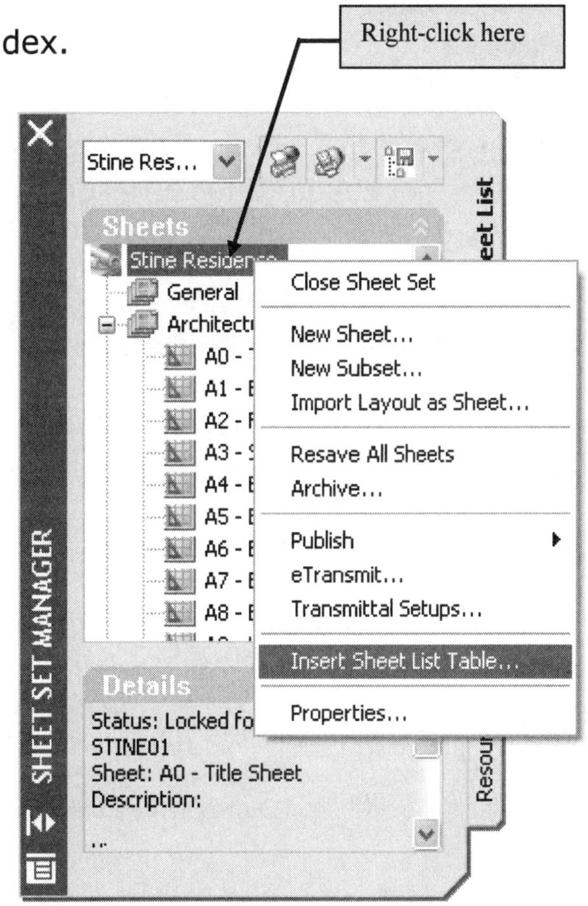

Figure 9-3.2
Sheet Set Manager; right click on project title (Stine Residence in this example)

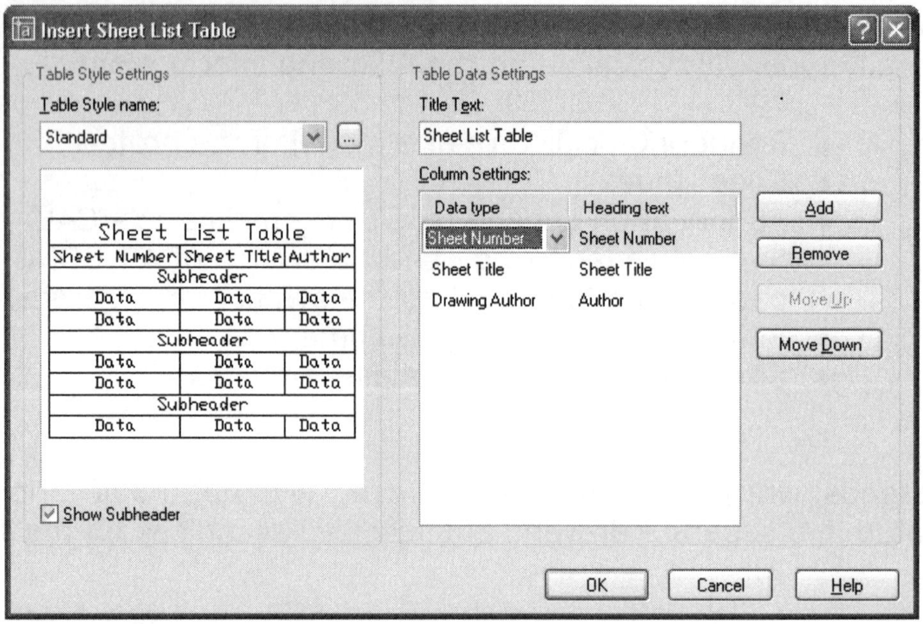

Figure 9-3.3
Insert Sheet List Table dialog

The default Sheet List table style has a column for the author of each sheet. This is not required for a residential project. Next you will delete the Drawing Author column before closing the dialog.

7. In the *Column Setting* area, select **Drawing Author** from the list and then click the **Remove** button to the right.

You will notice the preview has updated to reflect your requested change.

8. Click **OK** to close the dialog.

9. Click **OK** to the prompt warning you not to change the sheet list manually. (Figure 9-3.4)

***FYI:** If you do not get this prompt, you or someone else using your workstation, selected the "don't show this again" check box.*

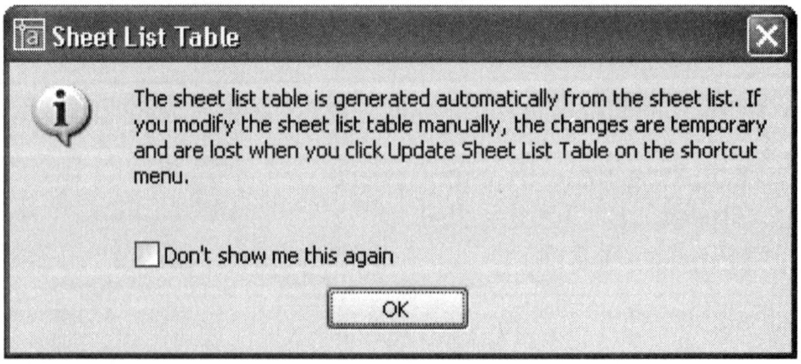

Figure 9-3.4
Sheet List Table prompt prior to placing the table

10. Click anywhere on your *A0 - Title Sheet* to place the Sheet List table.

The table is now placed on your Title Sheet. (Figure 9-3.5)

Sheet List Table	
Sheet Number	Sheet Title
Architectural	
A0	Title Sheet
A1	Basement Floor Plan
A2	First Floor Plan
A3	Second Floor Plan
A4	Exterior Elevations
A5	Exterior Elevations
A6	Exterior Elevations
A7	Exterior Elevations
A8	Building Sections
A9	Wall Sections
A10	Interior Elevations
A11	Schedules

Figure 9-3.5
A0 – Title Sheet; inserted sheet list table

After inserting the Sheet List, you decide to change the justification of the data cell so that everything is left justified. You will make this change now…

11. Click on the table to select it.

12. Right-click and select **Edit Sheet List Table Settings…** from the pop-up menu.

    FYI: *Also notice above the Edit… command is the Update Table tool, which will update the list to include any sheets recently added.*

13. Click the "..." " to modify the Standard Table style.

14. Select the **Standard** style and click the **Modify** button in the *Table Style Manager.*

15. On the *Data* tab, set the *Alignment* to **Top Left.**

16. Click **OK** to close all the open dialog boxes.

As you can see, this is the same process previously described in the Room Finish Schedule exercise, because the Sheet List is a table!

Sheet List Table	
Sheet Number	Sheet Title
Architectural	
A0	Title Sheet
A1	Basement Floor Plan
A2	First Floor Plan
A3	Second Floor Plan
A4	Exterior Elevations
A5	Exterior Elevations
A6	Exterior Elevations
A7	Exterior Elevations
A8	Building Sections
A9	Wall Sections
A10	Interior Elevations
A11	Schedules

Figure 9-3.6
A0 – Title Sheet; modified sheet list table

If you change a sheet number via the *Sheet Set Manager*, the Sheet List will be automatically updated (you need to Regen to see the changes on any open sheets).

17. **Save** your **A0 – Title Sheet** drawing.

That completes the introduction to sheet list tables.

Self-Exam:

The following questions can be used as a way to check your knowledge of this lesson. The answers can be found at the bottom of this page.

1. The Table Manager is where you change a table's text height. (T/F)

2. You need to create Named Views for each drawing/detail that you want to place on a sheet. (T/F)

3. Once a Sheet List table is placed you have to manually update it if you add or remove any sheets. (T/F)

4. When dragging a view, from the Sheet Set Manager onto a sheet, you

   ______________ to get a listing of scales to insert the view at.

5. In the Named Views dialog, you can change the views boundary. (T/F)

Review Questions:

The following questions may be assigned by your instructor as a way to assess your knowledge of this section. Your instructor has the answers to the review questions.

1. Once a Table is created, you cannot add rows or columns. (T/F)

2. It is not possible to combine two or more table cells into one. (T/F)

3. AutoCAD creates a drawing file each time you create a new sheet in the Sheet Set Manager. (T/F)

4. Views are placed on sheets by dragging the view name from the

   ______________ tab; views are numbered (and renamed) on the

   ________________ tab in the Sheet Set Manager.

5. You cannot specify where the Sheet Set Data file is stored. (T/F)

6. The bottom number, in an elevation callout bubble, indicates the

   ________________ number the elevation is located on.

7. This icon () allows you to insert a ________________________.

8. In a Sheet Set, sheets can be organized using ________________.

9. You should not move or rename the files created by the Sheet Set Manager (except what you are able to do in the Manager itself). (T/F)

10. You right-click on the ____________ to see the insert Sheet List option. (T/F)

Self-Exam Answers:
1 - T, **2** - T, **3** - F, **4** – right-click, **5** – T

Additional Tasks:

Task 9-1 Create a Door Schedule:
Using the techniques learned in lesson 9-1, create a door schedule and place it on the Schedules sheet. You will need to number the doors in your plans. Typically, a door has the same number as the room it swings into. If a door has more than one door (like the master bedroom), you add letters to the number (i.e., 201A and 201B). Include the following columns in your schedule: Door number, Door Size, Door Material, Door Type, Frame Material, Frame Type, Jamb Detail, Head Detail, Sill Detail, Fire Rating, Remarks.

Task 9-2 Place additional views you may have created:
If you have been creating the drawings suggested in the previous "additional tasks", you can place them on the appropriate sheets; adding sheets if necessary.

Task 9-3 Place callout blocks to reference your drawings:
You can add additional callout blocks:

- Any other interior elevations you may have drawn.
- Building Section; you can draw a line through your floor plan, where your building section is cut, and place an elevation callout block at one end of the line to reference the building section.
- You can add a note to your floor plan that says "For room finish schedule see" and place the "basic" callout block next to the note.
- Wall Section; draw a rectangle (fillet its corners and change the linetype to dashed) around a portion of you building section that represent the extents of your wall section and then place a "basic" callout bubble with a line drawn from the bubble to the rectangle.

Lesson 10
Residential Project: Lineweights & Plotting::

In this final lesson you will look at how lineweights work in AutoCAD. Finally, you will take another look at plotting; this time plotting to scale from the Sheet Set Manager.

When finished with this chapter you will have a formidable part of a set of residential working drawings.

Exercise 10-1:
Lineweights

Introduction:

As previously discussed, lineweights are an important part of a set of architectural drawings. They help to differentiate between the many lines contained in a drawing; more specifically, lineweights show what part of the drawing is in section versus elevation.

Hand drafters would create different line thicknesses as they drew, whereas CAD drawings typically don't show the actually lineweight until the drawing is printed.

AutoCAD has three primary ways to handle lineweights. This book will describe all three and then give an overview of two methods. Then, you will use one method on your floor plan drawings.

Three methods described:

<u>Color Dependent Plot Style</u>:

With this method the thickness of the plotted line is based on the color of the line; whether the color is set By Layer or By Entity. This used to be the only method available in AutoCAD and is probably still the most used.

<u>Named Plot Style</u>:

With this method you assign a Named Plot Style to each Layer (and even By Entity – not recommended). A Named Plot Style has a name, like Heavy, and has several settings assigned to it (i.e., line thickness, screened, etc.). A group of Named Plot Styles are stored in a file call a "Named Plot Style Table".

Lineweight by Layer:

With this method a Plot Style Table is not used (neither color nor named). Rather, the lineweight is set by the Lineweight column in the Layer Manager (or ByEntity in the Properties Dialog – not recommended). Note that the Lineweight column only applies when a Plot Style Table is not selected in Page Setup (Page Setup will be covered shortly).

Example of the "Lineweight ByLayer" method:

Here you will take a look at a sample drawing, installed with AutoCAD, which uses this method. Because of the nature of this sample drawing, it has the lineweights set *ByEntity* rather than the preferred *ByLayer* method. However, we will use this drawing to understand this method of applying lineweights and why the *ByLayer* method is more preferable.

1. **Open** the drawing file:
   C:\Program Files\AutoCAD 2005\Sample\Lineweights.dwg

By default, you should be on the Layout Tab titled "**ISO A4 Size**" and see the image shown in Figure 10-1.1. However, you may not see the actual line thickness of each line yet; if not, you will set this next.

2. To toggle the Lineweight on-screen visibility, on or off, click the **LWT** button on the *Status Bar* (Figure 10-1.2).

Figure 10-1.2
Status Bar; LWT stands for Lineweights

The LWT button works for any of the methods of defining lineweights discussed.

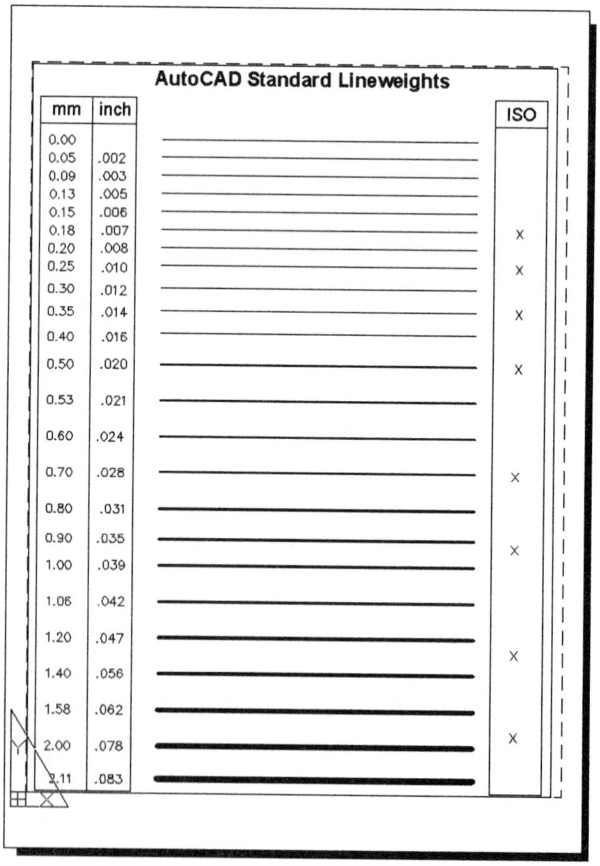

Figure 10-1.1
Sample Drawing; Lineweights.dwg

3. Switch to **Model** Space.

The line thicknesses in Model Space are exaggerated. Most users do not typically have the lineweight visibility turned on when doing day-to-day drafting.

4. Click the **LWT** button on the *Status Bar* to turn **off** the onscreen lineweight visibility.

The Lineweight column in the Layer Properties Manger controls the lineweight for each Layer. So anything drawn on a Layer, which has its lineweight property set to 0.13mm, will always print at 0.13mm (unless the lineweight has been changed for one of more lines in the Properties dialog – this overrides the Layer setting.

5. **Open** the **Layer Properties Manager** (Figure 10-1.3).

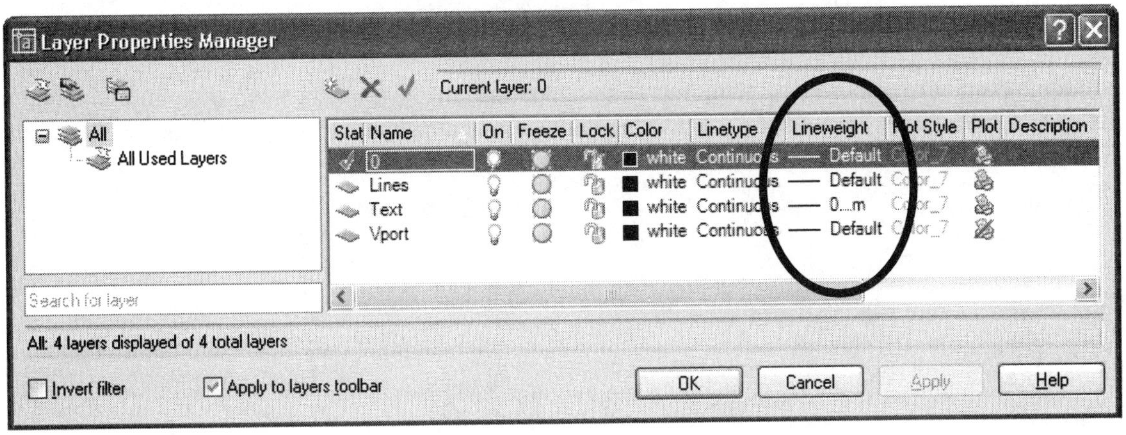

Figure 10-1.3
Lineweights Sample Drawing; Lineweight column used when a Plot Style Table is not used.

The circled area in Figure 10-1.3 is the Lineweight column that you would adjust to various lineweights. So if you want everything drawn on *Layer* Lines to be 0.70mm, you would adjust the Lineweight setting for the Lines Layer to 0.70mm.

As mentioned earlier, for AutoCAD to use these settings you need to make sure that a Plot Style Table is not selected in Page Setup. You will verify this next.

6. Close the *Layer Manager* and then select **Page Setup Manager...** from the **File** pull-down menu.

7. Click **Modify...** to adjust the default settings for the Model tab. (Figure 10-1.4)

Notice, in the image below (Figure 10-1.5) that a Plot Style Table is not specified; that is, it is set to None.

8. Close the open dialogs.

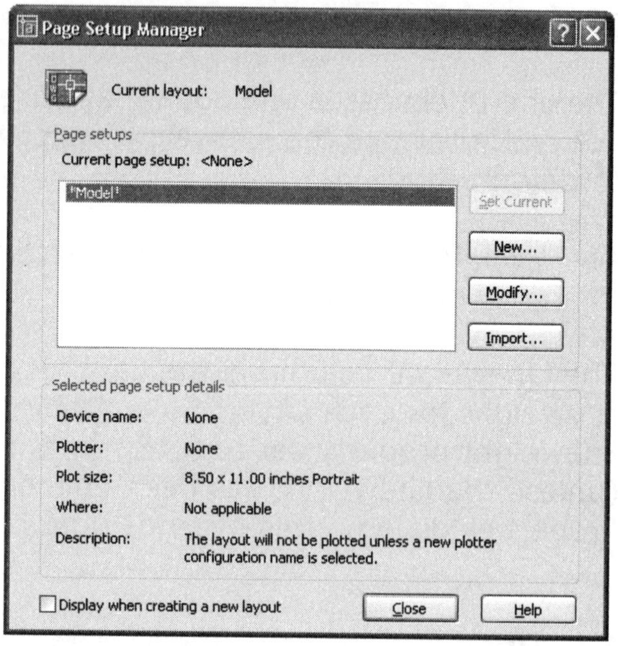

Figure 10-1.4
Page Setup Manager

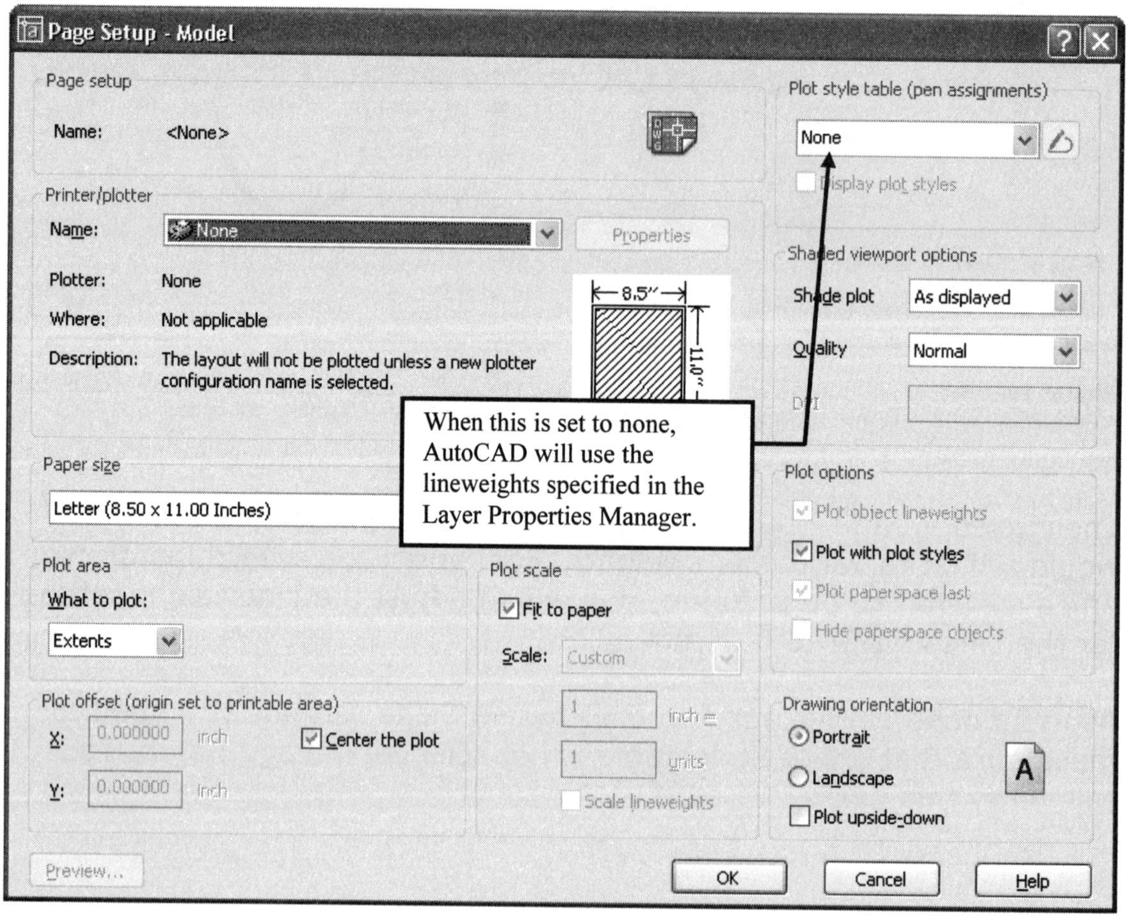

Figure 10-1.5
Lineweights Sample Drawing; Page Setup

The last variation on this method is setting the lineweight *ByEntity*, which overrides the setting in the *Layer Manager*. It is generally recommended that you do not change settings (such as color, lineweight, etc.) *ByEntity*. The reason for this is that it is difficult to change the settings of several lines that have been changed *ByEntity*. Whereas, when you want to change the color of all the lines on Layer A-Wall, all you have to do is change the color one time in the Layer Manager. Finally, having all the settings for an entity set to *ByLayer* allows for more control over *Externally Referenced* drawings.

Even though changing settings *ByEntity* is not recommended, the sample drawing is setup this way. Next you will look at this "*ByEntity*" type of modification to better understand what has been described.

9. Select the **0.35mm** line (i.e., the horizontal line to the right of the 0.35mm label). (Figure 10-1.1)

10. Right-click and select **Properties.** (Figure 10-1.6)

Notice that the Lineweight setting for the selected line is set to 0.35mm; so, no matter which Layer this line is on, it will always print 0.35mm thick

The lineweight for the selected entity could be changed via the *Properties* dialog shown in Figure 10-1.6. In addition to several other lineweights, you can select *ByLayer*; this setting uses the lineweight assigned to the *Layer* – this is generally the preferred method of assigning lineweights (i.e., *ByLayer*).

11. Select a few other lines and look at their Properties; notice that each line has its Lineweight setting changed (to match its corresponding label in the case of this drawing).

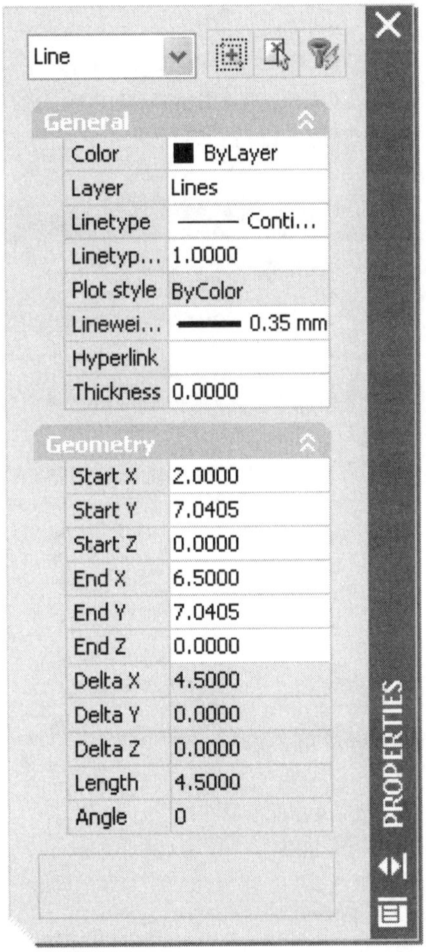

Figure 10-1.6
Properties; 0.35mm line selected

TIP: *You may want to print the Lineweight.dwg sample drawing so you have a reference sheet showing what each line thickness really looks like printed on paper. Switching to the Letter Size tab should be all set to print to an 8 ½" x 11" paper; you should only have to select the printer.*

12. Exit the Lineweight.dwg drawing file without saving.

Example of the "Named Plot Style" method:

Here you will also take a look at a sample drawing, installed with AutoCAD, which uses this method.

The file you will look at is a large Stadium Floor plan which is 4.69 MB. This file will take a minute or two to open depending on the speed of your computer.

13. **Open** the drawing file:
    C:\Program Files\AutoCAD 2005\Sample\Stadium Plan.dwg
    (Figure 10-1.7)

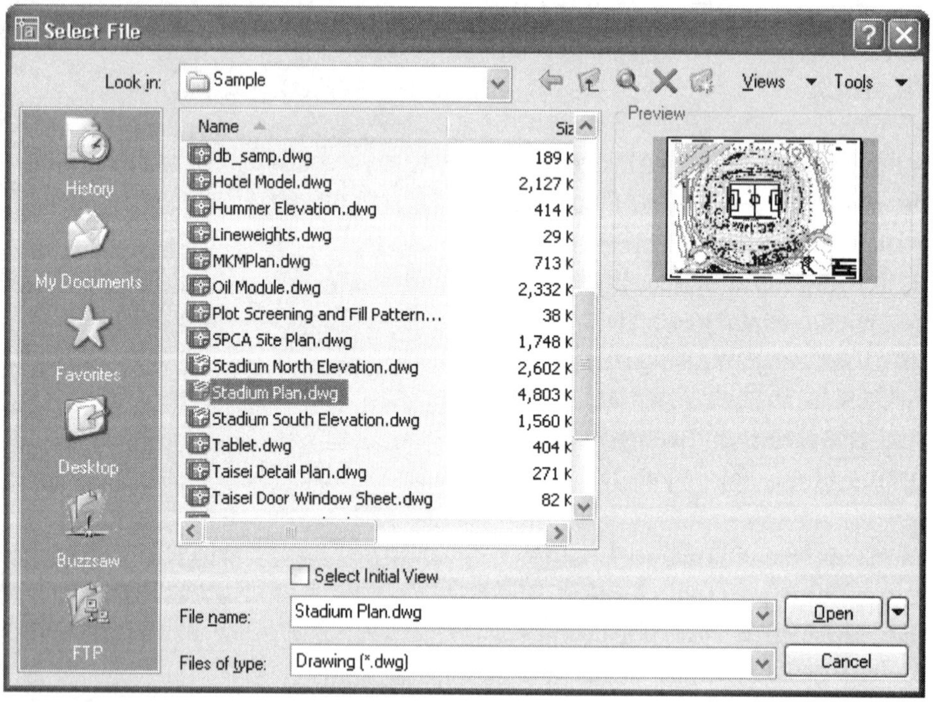

Figure 10-1.7
Select File to Open; stadium plan drawing selected

Why do the "Stadium" drawings have a different icon?

The extra mark in the upper right corner of the AutoCAD icon represents a feature introduced in AutoCAD 2004 which allows you to Digitally Sign a drawing file. This has nothing to do with the Architect/Engineer signature required on some drawings by building officials; rather, it is a way of marking a file at a certain phase. If the drawing is saved with any changes, the mark goes away. Thus, you can give a Digitally Signed drawing to a product supplier and require them to produce the Signed drawing in the future if they make a claim against the project, claiming the drawings provided were incorrect and the reason for a mistake.

14. Click **Close** to acknowledge that the drawing is *Digitally Signed*. (Figure 10-1.8)

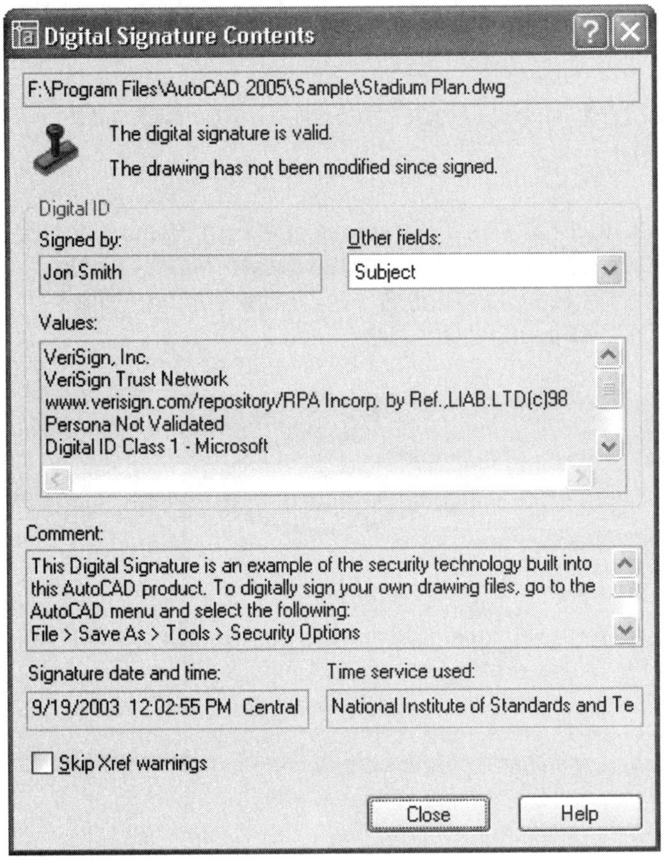

Figure 10-1.8
Digital Signature Contents prompt selected

***TIP:** See AutoCAD's Help system for more information on Digital Signatures. You should know that a fee is required by a third party (such as VeriSign), which is the company that verifies you are a real person/company and maintains your record (certificate). AutoCAD merely provides the ability to use this technology, but does not actually provide ID certificates.*

15. Click on the **Plan-Mono** *Layout Tab* to set it current.

16. Right-Click on the **Plan-Mono** *Layout Tab.*

17. Select **Page Setup Manager...** from the pop-up menu. (Figure 10-1.9)

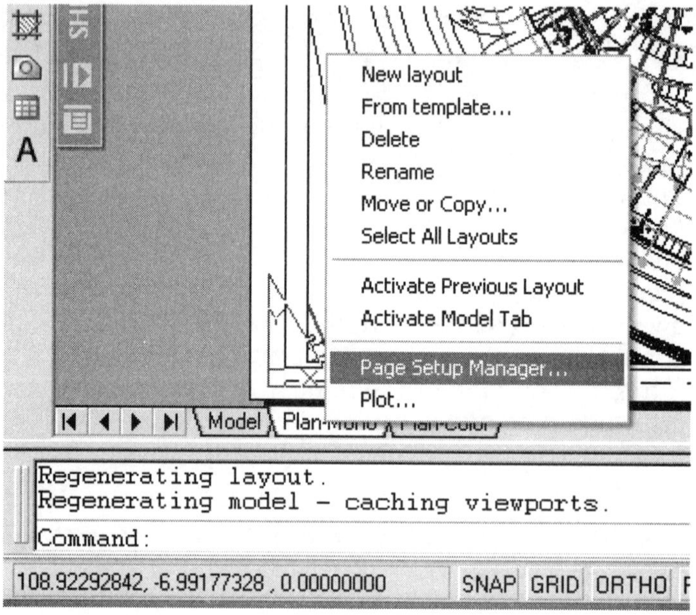

Figure 10-1.9
Right-click on Plan-Mono tab

18. With ***Plan-Mono*** selected in the *Page Setups* list, click the **Modify** button on the right.

You are now in the *Page Setup* dialog for the *Plan-Mono* Layout View (notice title bar). Notice that the *Plot Style Table* is set to **Autodesk-MONO.stb**. The *STB* extension indicates this is a Named Plot Style Table (vs. a Color Dependent Plot Style Table – *CTB*). (Figure 10-1.10)

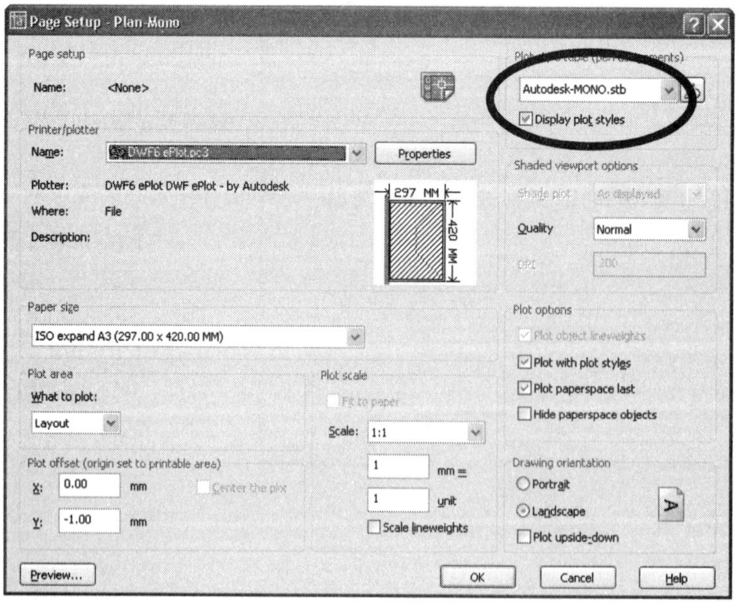

Figure 10-1.10
Page setup; Plan-Mono layout view

Next you will explore the settings for this Plot Style Table.

19. Click on the **Edit icon**  next to the selected *Plot Style Table.* (Figure 10-1.10)

20. Click the **Form View** tab. (Figure 10-1.11)

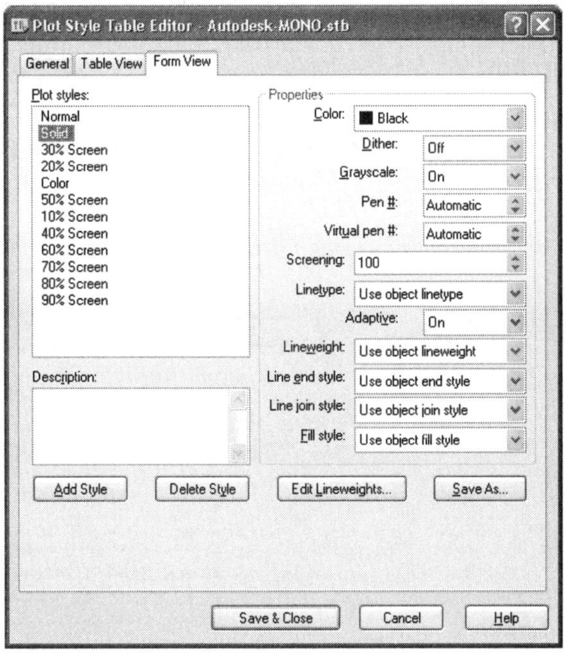

Figure 10-1.11
Plot Style Table Editor; Form View tab

21. Select the *Plot Style* name "**Solid**" to view its *Properties* on the right side of the *Plot Style Table Editor.* (Figure 10-1.11)

Note the following about the selected Plot Style named Solid:

- Because this is a "MONO" *Plot Style table*, the ***Color*** property is set to Black.

  TIP*: The other common Color Property value is "Use Object Color"; so, if the wall lines are Magenta, they will print Magenta on a color plotter.*

- The **Lineweight** is set to "Use Object Lineweight", which means it will use the Lineweight setting in the Layer Manager (or the Lineweight ByEntity).

22. Select **Cancel** to close all open dialog boxes.

Now, to see how this all ties together, you will open the Layer Manager and make a few observations:

23. Open the *Layer Properties Manager* dialog. (Figure 10-1.12)

Note the following about the *Layer* Properties Manager:

- **Plot Style** column has a *Named Plot Style* selected for each *Layer.* (Figure 10-1.12) ***FYI:*** *This column is grayed-out when no Plot Style Table is selected in the Page Setup.*

- The Lineweight is set in the **Lineweight** column of the *Layer Properties Manager.* (Figure 10-1.12)

TIP: *Print the Lineweights drawing for a lineweight reference chart.*

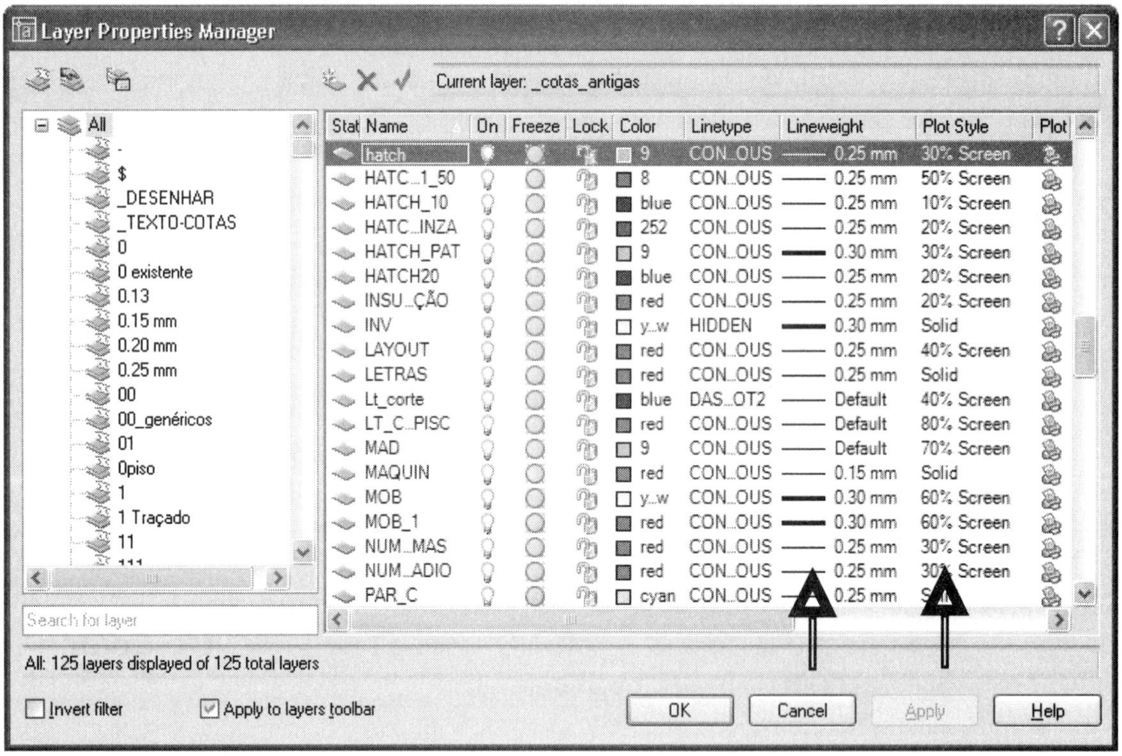

Figure 10-1.12
Stadium Plan sample drawing; Layer Properties Manager

So, the main difference between this method and the previous one is the ability to control the color and screening (in addition to the line weight).

24. **Close** the *Stadium Plan* drawing without saving.

Applying the "Color Dependent Plot Style" method to your drawings:

Now you will apply lineweights to your floor plans. Below, you will take a minute to study lineweight theory; that is, what should be drawn with a heavy line and what should be drawn with a light line.

For floor plans:

- **Heaviest Lines**: Wall lines and openings in floor; any major building component in section (e.g., column) **0.60mm.**
- **Medium Lines**: Objects like cabinets, doors and windows should be the next heaviest **0.30mm.**
- **Lightest Lines**: Any lines on the floor (e.g., furniture) and window sill lines should be the lightest lines **0.05mm.**
- **Light Gray Lines**: Hatch patterns, such as ceramic tile or a recessed slab area, should be a light and gray line so it is not too intense (use one of the screened plot styles) **0.10mm.**

For interior elevations lineweight descriptions see page 7-20.

25. **Open** your **Flr-2** drawing.

26. Right-click on the **Model** tab and select **Page Setup Manager...** from the pop-up menu.

27. Click the **Modify...** button.

28. From the Plot Style Table drop-down list, select **New...** (Figure 10-1.13).

__TIP:__ If you only see tables that end with .STB you started your drawing with the wrong template. You need to copy/paste your drawing into the correct template file per Lesson 3 – page 3-1.

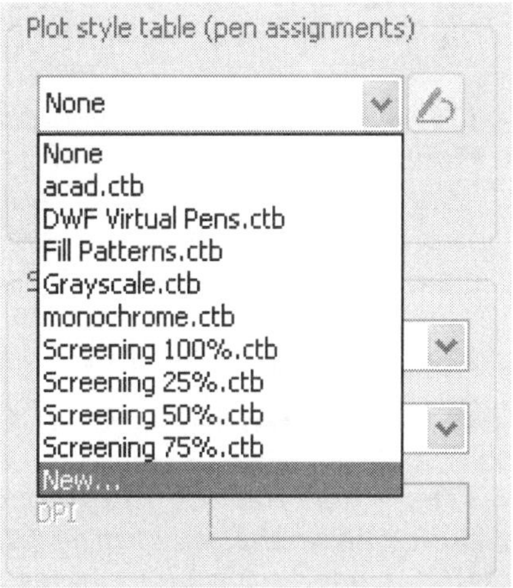

Figure 10-1.13
Page Setup; creating a new Plot Style Table

You are now in the Add Plot Style Table Wizard, which will walk you through the steps and information necessary to create a Plot Style Table.

29. Select **Start from scratch** and then click **Next >.**

30. Type **your last name** for the *Plot Style Table* file name and then click **Next >.**

31. Accept the default settings and click **Finish.**

Your new *Plot Style Table* is now selected as current in *Page Setup.* Next you will modify your new table so that each of the first seven AutoCAD colors equals a particular lineweight.

32. Click the *Edit Plot Style Table* icon. 

33. Click on the **Form View** tab.

34. Modify each of the first seven *Plot Styles* (i.e., Color 1 thru Color 7) so the *Color Property* is set to **Black**

35. Assign each of the first seven colors a lineweight (ranging from 0.1000mm to 1.0000mm) – See figure 10-1.14 for an example; also see the tips below:

    TIP #1: *Divide 1mm by seven and pick the closest lineweight available in the list for each of the 7 colors.*

    TIP #2: *On a separate piece of paper, write down the color number and then the lineweight you assigned to that color; this list will be useful shortly.*

    TIP #3: *If you prefer, you can use the color/lineweight settings shown in Figure 10-1.15, rather than coming up with your own. This is not the "standard" by any means; but, is arranged so the "brighter" lines are heavier lineweights and the "dimmer" lines are lighter lineweights (based on a black drawing area background).*

36. Assign each of the last six colors (250-255) the lineweight **0.1500mm**, least the *Color* property set to **Use Object Color**.

    TIP: *When you set a Layer's color to 250-255, the objects on those Layers will print in five shades of gray (depending on which of the five colors are used). This is used for building lines that are vary far back in the elevation/or existing. Another use would be for a patch pattern that represents brick coursing (which are lines that are close together and can be overpowering if not printed with grayscale lines). One more use might be for a solid hatch that might indicate circulation (i.e., hallways) or sidewalks and driveways.*

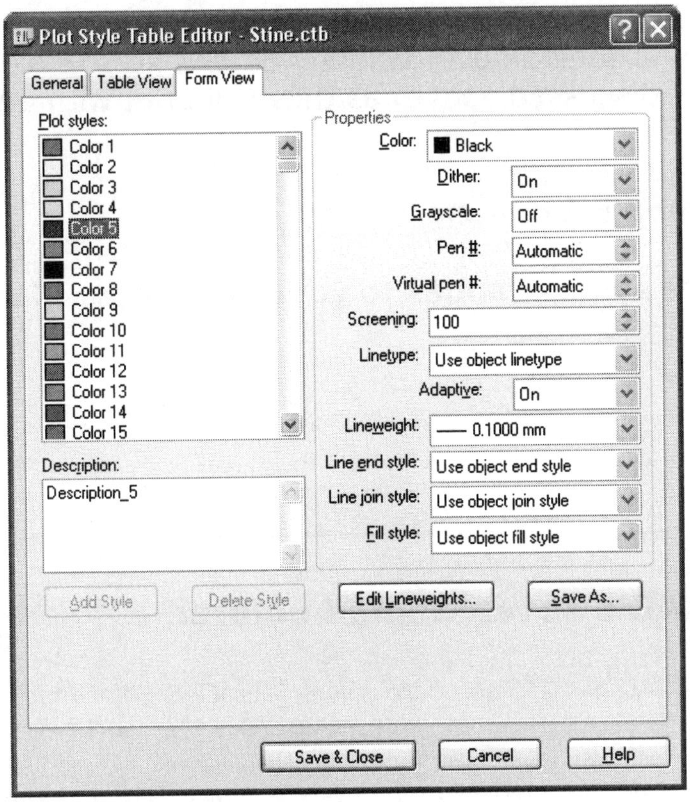

Figure 10-1.14
Plot Style Table Editor; plot style "Color 5" selected

37. Click **Save and Close** to apply these changes to your *Plot Style Table.* (Figure 10-1.14)

38. Click **OK** to close *Page Setup* and then **Close** to exit the *Page Setup Manager.*

Now, in any drawing file, when your *Plot Style Table* is selected in *Page Setup*, any entity that is Color 5 (Blue) will print as a fairly light line (0.1000mm) using the example in Figure 10-1.14.

Once you create a standard, and use it for a while, you will instinctively now what color equals what lineweight.

39. **Open** the **Layer Properties Manager.**

40. Adjust the **Color** for each *Layer.* (Figure 10-1.15)

TIP: *Based on your plot style table, each color now corresponds to a particular lineweight.*

When you are finished, every layer should be assigned a color ranging from 1 to 7; you should never use any other colors (except the "shade" colors discussed above) as they will print with unexpected results.

41. **Save** your **Flr-2** drawing.

42. **Make the same changes to your other floor plans.**

AutoCAD's seven named colors:

FYI: *AutoCAD has 255 standard colors (AutoCAD Color Index – ACI), of which the first seven also have names (see the chart below).*

AutoCAD also has a True Color system which allows for millions of colors. True Colors are great for presentation drawings. They are not controlled by a Plot Style Table; they will always print in the color specified (only on a color printer, of course).

Color number	*Color name*
1	Red
2	Yellow
3	Green
4	Cyan
5	Blue
6	Magenta
7	White (black when background is white)

Backup your plot style table:

You should backup your Plot Style Table to a CD or DVD because you will need it on each computer you print from to get accurate lineweights. You also need to send this file with the drawings, if providing consultants or owners with the drawing files.

43. Backup your *Plot Style Table* file, this file is located at: C:\Documents and Settings*your_login_name*\Application Data\Autodesk\AutoCAD 2005\R16.1\enu\Plot Styles

    FYI: *Substitute your login name for the "your_login_name" placeholder above. Also, the Application Data folder may be hidden – see you system administrator for help.*

Create a lineweight reference chart:

Until you learn which color equals which lineweight, you will benefit from using a reference chart. If you want a line to be thin, you look at the chart, find a thin line you like and then look at what color is associated with that lineweight, and then you modify the line to that color (by changing or creating layers).

44. In a new drawing, named **Reference Chart.dwg**, create the drawing shown in **Figure 10-1.15**;
    a. Adjust drawing to match your color/lineweight settings.
    b. Make all the text set to one of your medium lineweights.
    c. Print the chart, making sure your Plot Style Table is selected in Page Setup.
    d. The lines should be arranged from heaviest to lightest.
    e. Draw everything within a 6"x6" square.

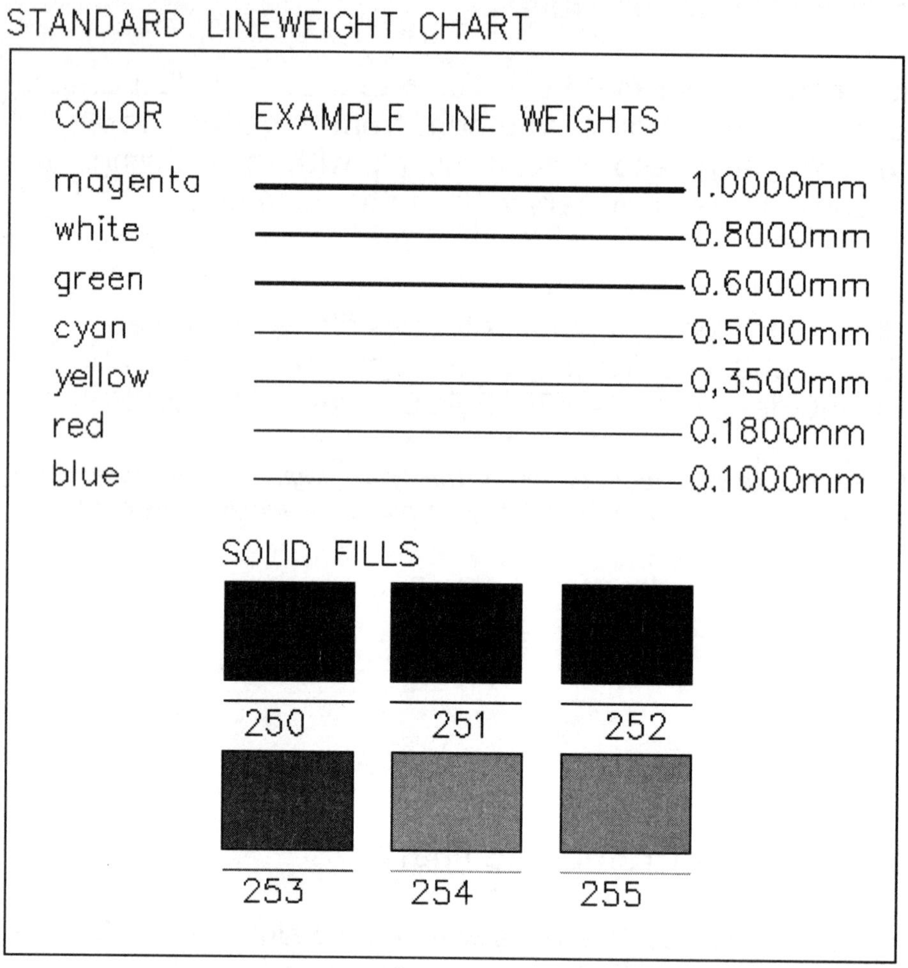

Figure 10-1.15
Lineweight reference chart

45. **Save** and **Close** any open drawings.

Summary:

Most people still use the *Color Dependent Plot Style Tables* because, no matter what drawing/Layer a line is in/on, if it is green (for example), it will always print the same lineweight. Whereas the *Named Plot Style Table* require extra settings in the *Layer Properties Manager* and entities that are green (again, for example) could be different lineweights, even in the same drawing. The visual color / lineweight relationship is very useful, especially when multiple people (or multiple firms) are working on the same set of drawings.

Exercise 10-2:
Plotting: digital set

Introduction:

In this exercise you will learn how to quickly and easily publish your entire set of drawings to a single file that can be viewed by downloading a free viewer from Autodesk.

The file is referred to as a Design Web Format (DWF). A DWF is smaller than the drawing file because it is only for viewing and printing, not editing. They can even be password protected. In fact, one of the best things about DWF's is that they cannot be edited. Thus, you can share the DWF set with a client or contractor and not have to worry about them accidentally (or on purpose) changing the drawings.

The first thing you need to do is adjust the Page Setup in each "sheet" drawing, so the "sheets" are ready to plot.

1. **Open** your sheet **A1 – Basement Floor Plan** from the *Sheet Set Manager* (See Exercise 8-2 for instruction on this).

2. Right-click on the **Basement Floor Plan** *Layout View* tab. (Figure 10-2.1)

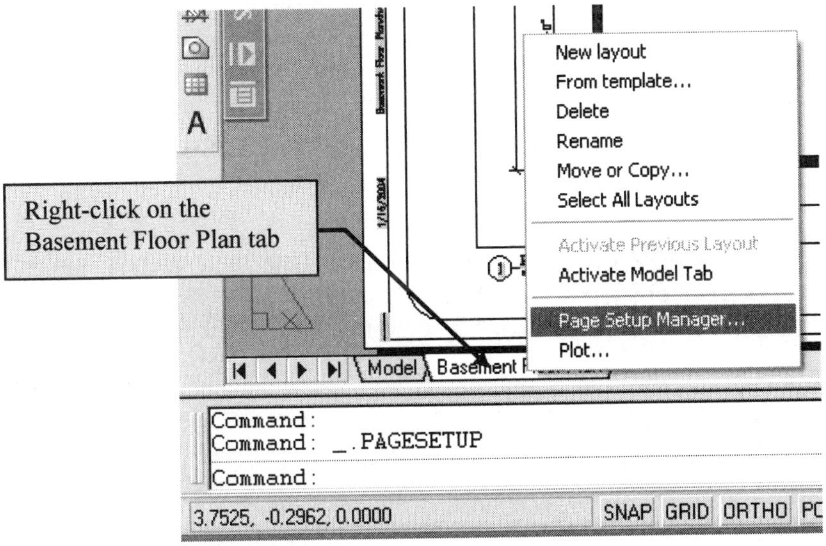

Figure 10-2.1
A1 – Basement Floor Plan; right-click on layout tab

3. Select **Page Setup Manager...** from the pop-up menu.

4. With ***Basement Floor Plan*** selected, click the **Modify...** button. (Figure 10-2.2)

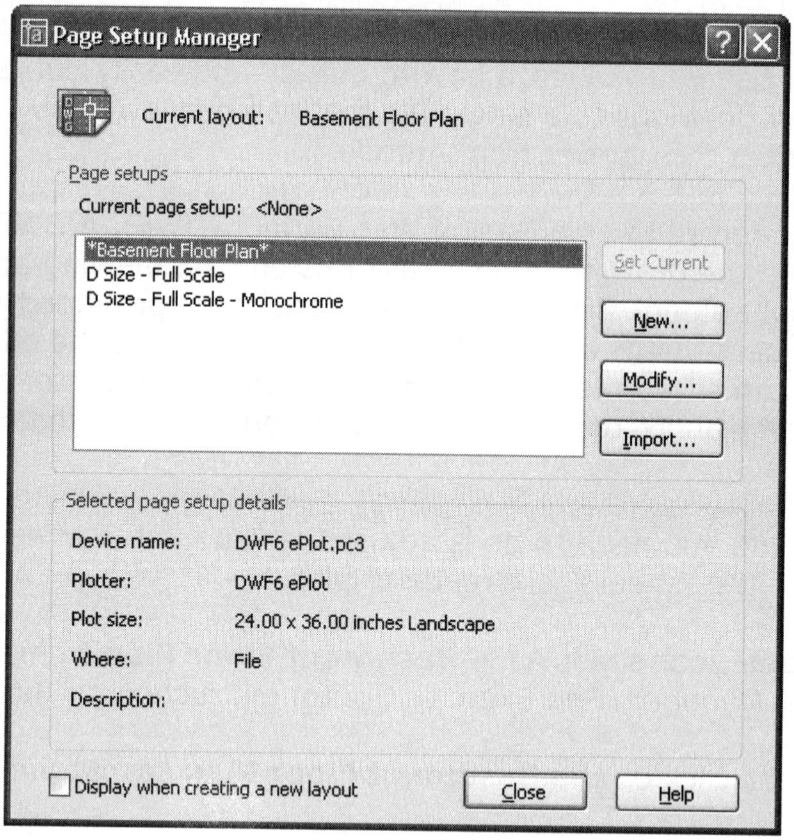

Figure 10-2.2
Page Setup Manager; modify the default layout settings

5. Select your *Plot Style Table* (created in Exercise 10-1); *yourname*.ctb. (Figure 10-2.3)

6. **Check** the "*Display Plot Styles*" option just below the selected *Plot Style Table.* (Figure 10-2.3)

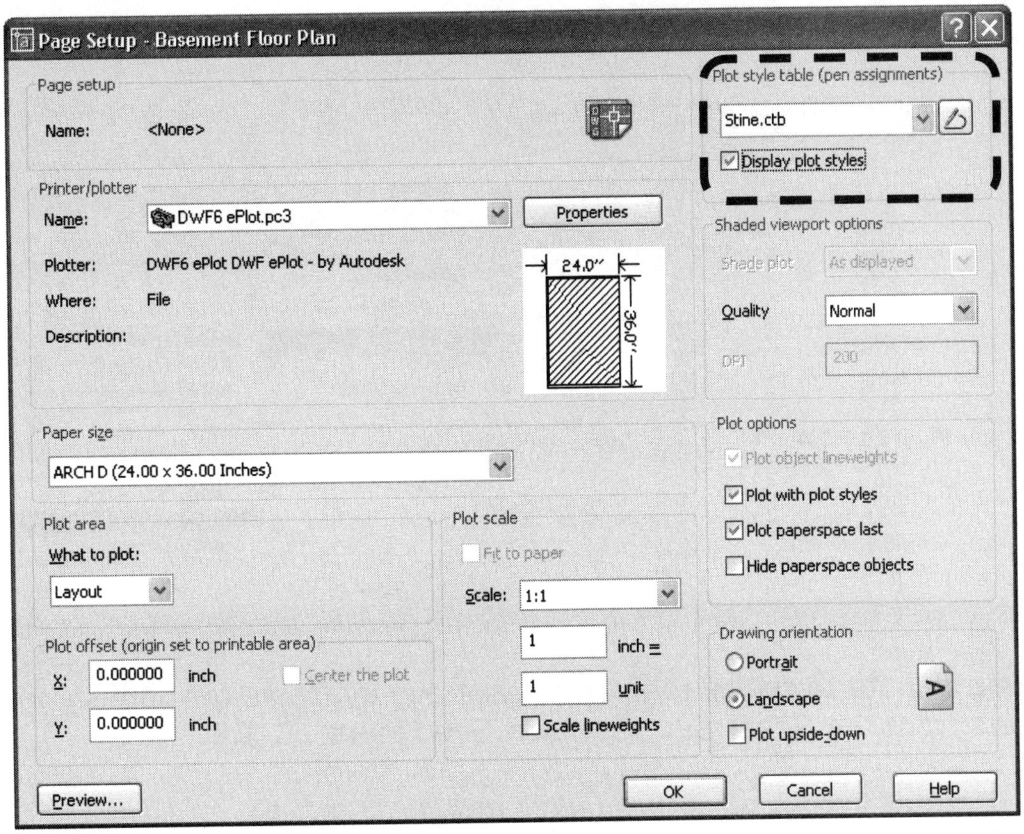

Figure 10-2.3
Page Setup – Basement Floor Plan; select your plot style table

7. Click **OK** and then **Close** to exit the open dialog boxes.

8. **Save** and **Close** the *Basement Floor Plan* drawing.

9. Now open each sheet in your *Sheet Set* and make the same modification; **Save** and **Close** each drawing when done.

Now you will look at the *Options* related to *Publishing* "sheets" from the *Sheet Set Managers*.

10. **Open** your *Sheet Set Data* file (see Exercise 8-2).

11. Right-click on the *Sheet Set* project title (*Stine Residence* in this example) – See **Figure 10-2.4.**

12. Select **Publish → Sheet Set Publish Options...** (Figure 10-2.4)

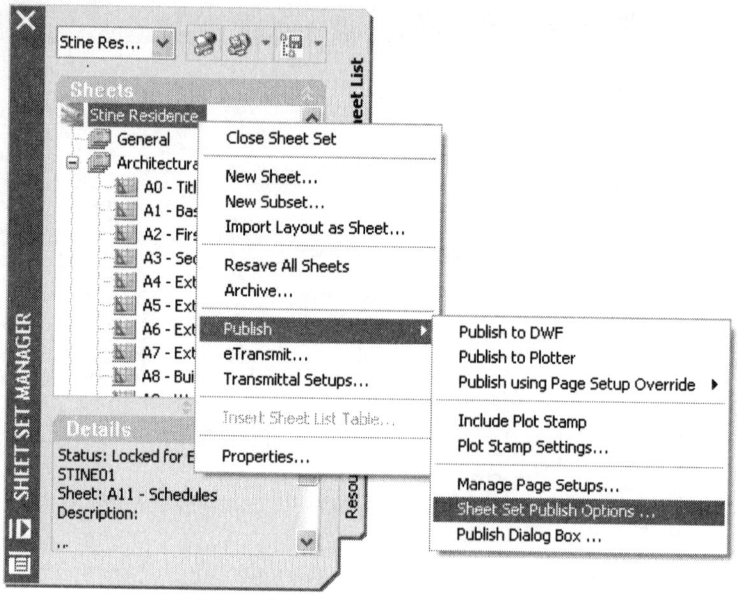

Figure 10-2.4
Sheet Set Manager – right-click menu for sheet set label (Stine Residence in this example)

Take a minute to notice the various options available for publishing sheets from the *Sheet Set Manager*; See Figure 10-2.5.

- **Default output directory (DWF and plot-to-file)**
  Here you can specify a default location to save the DWF file to. The other option is to Publish to Autodesk's online collaboration web site, called Buzzsaw, which requires a contract where the cost is based on space and # of users.

- **DWF type**
  When "single-sheet" is selected, each sheet is created as a separate DWF file. When "multi-sheet" is selected, all sheets are Published into one DWF file.

- **Multi-sheet DWF**
  Here you can specify the file name or have AutoCAD prompt you for the name each time you Publish; this option is only available if Multi-sheet is selected above.

- **DWF security**
  Allows you to assign a password to the DWF file. When a password is assigned, you, and anyone you send the file to, will need to know the password to view the DWF file.

- **DWF data**
  Allows you to include the AutoCAD layer in the DWF file. With this option selected, you can control layer visibility in the DWF file viewer; example – turn of dimensions and notes then print.

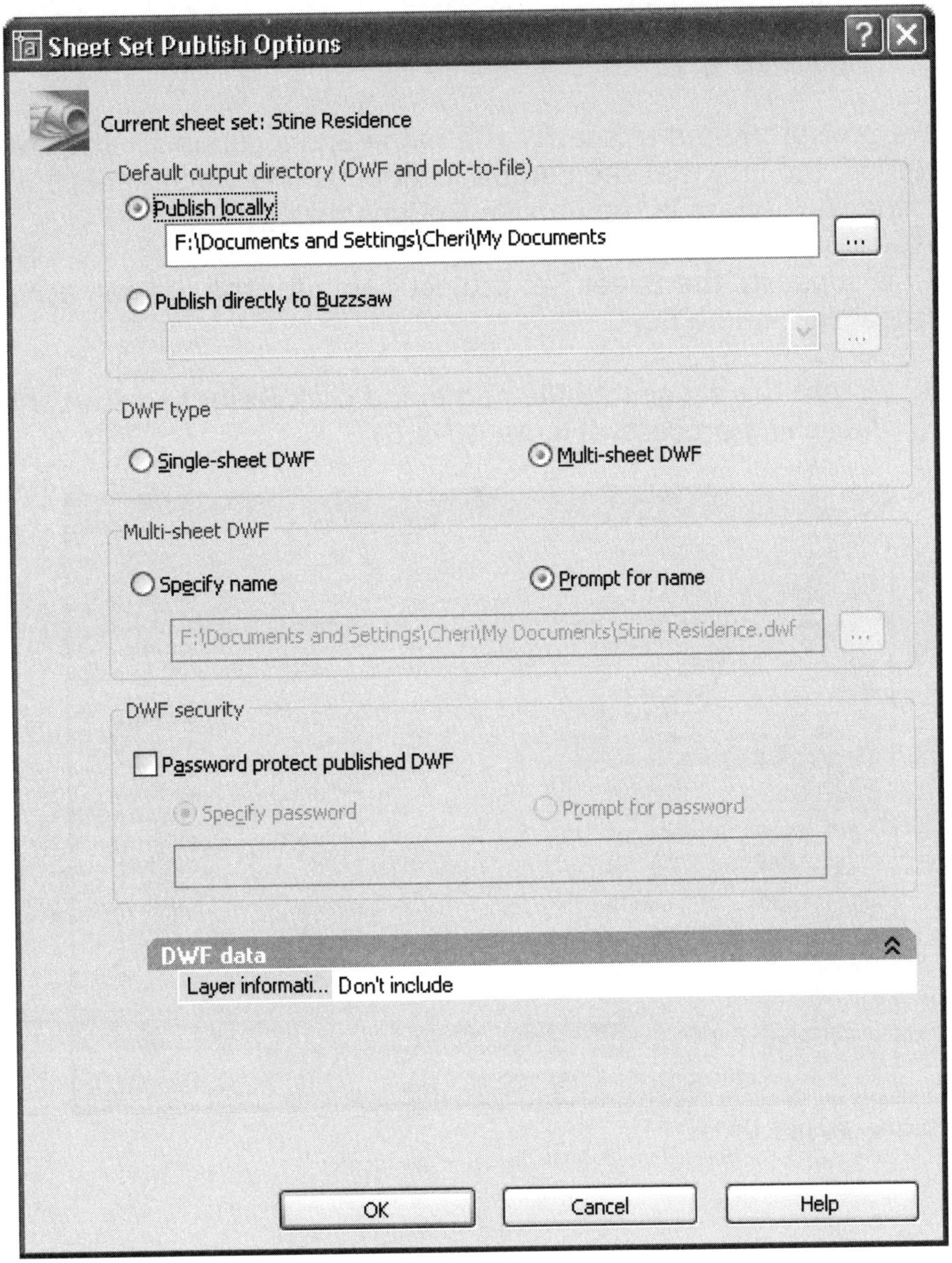

Figure 10-2.5
Sheet Set Publish Options – default settings shown

13. Accept the default options and click **OK.**

14. Right-click on the *Sheet Set* project title (*Stine Residence* in this example). See **Figure 10-2.4.**

15. **Publish → Publish to DWF.**
(Figure 10-2.4)

You are now prompted to specify the name and location for the DWF file. Notice, though, that the default location is "My Documents", which is the specified folder in the Publish Options dialog.

AutoCAD suggests the Sheet Set project name for the file name; you will accept that name next.

16. Accept the suggested file name and click **Select** to start the Publishing process. (Figure 10-2.6)

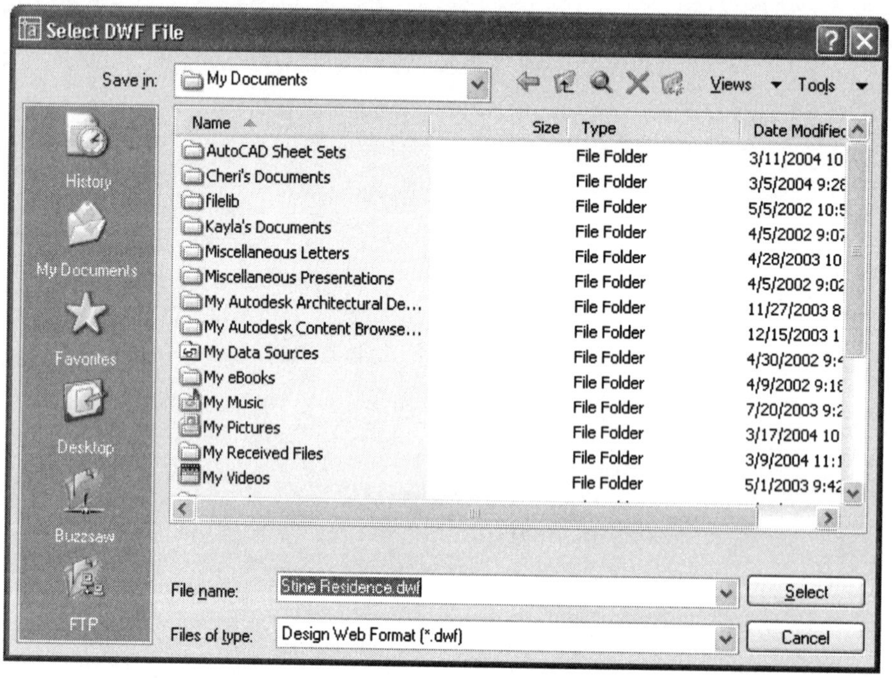

Figure 10-2.6
Select DWF File dialog– specify DWF file name and location

AutoCAD now begins to Publish each drawing to the DWF file you specified. The Publish routine runs in the background so you can continue to work. Depending on your computer speed, a set this size might take 5 – 15 minutes. AutoCAD has to open each file and plot it.

AutoCAD provides a small "plotter" icon on the right-hand side of the status bar. You can hover your cursor over this icon to see a tool-tip that displays the status of the background Publish project. (Figure 10-2.7)

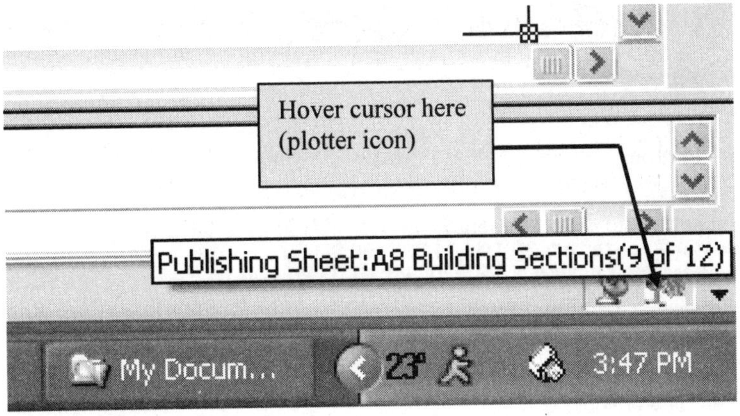

Figure 10-2.7
Plot and Publish Status Icon– hover cursor over icon to display status tool-tip

When the Publishing process is complete, a balloon message will be displayed (Figure 10-2.8) indicating such, and also provides a link to a report. You will take a quick peak at the report before viewing the DWF file.

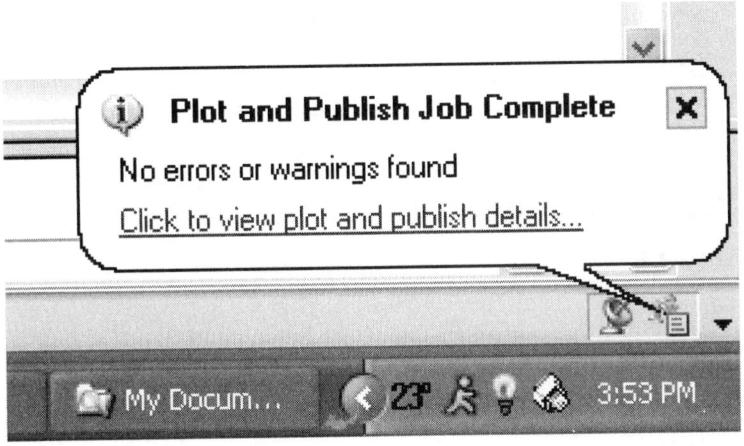

Figure 10-2.8
Plot and Publish Status Icon– balloon notification that job is complete

17. Click on the link *"Click to view plot and publish details..."* in the *Plot and Publish* balloon notification message. (Figure 10-2.8)

Notice the report lists the date, number of sheets, the location of each plotted file and the location of the DWF file. (figure 10-2.9).

18. Click **Close** to close the *Plot and Publish* window.

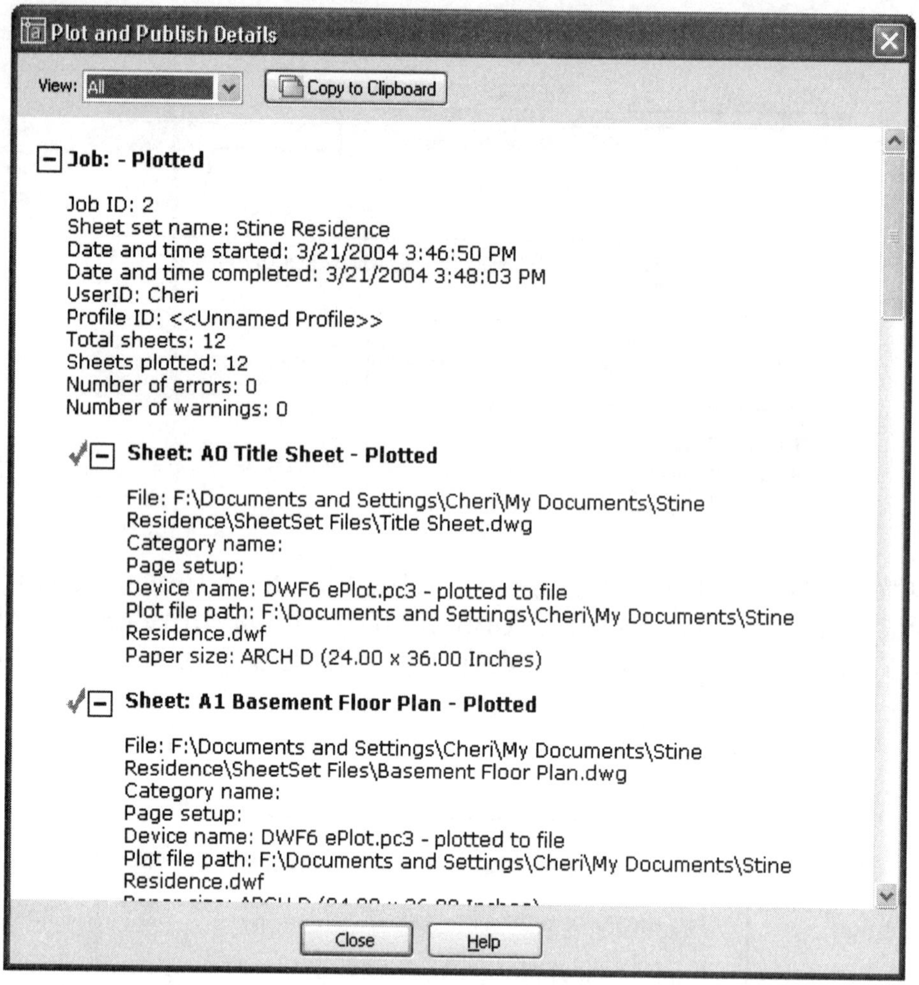

Figure 10-2.9
Plot and Publish Details – report on job just completed

Viewing the DWF file:

Next you will view the DWF file using the *Autodesk DWF Viewer*. You can view this file by double-clicking the file in *Windows Explorer*, or you can access the file from the *Plot and Publish Icon*.

19. Right-click on the *Plot and Publish Icon* on the right side of the *Status Bar.*

20. Select **View DWF File...** from the pop-up menu. (Figure 10-2.10)

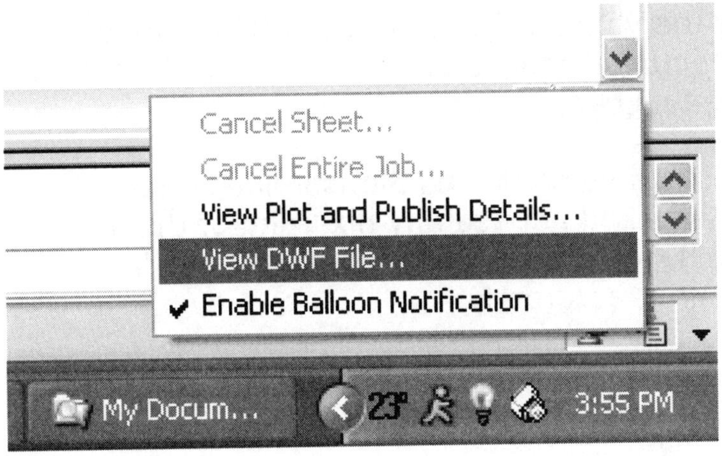

Figure 10-2.10
Plot and Publish Icon Menu; right-click on icon to see menu

A totally separate program (*Autodesk DWF Viewer*) now opens with the DWF project you just created. (Figure 10-2.11)

The Viewer allows you (or a client) to zoom, pan and print the sheets in the multi-sheet DWF file.

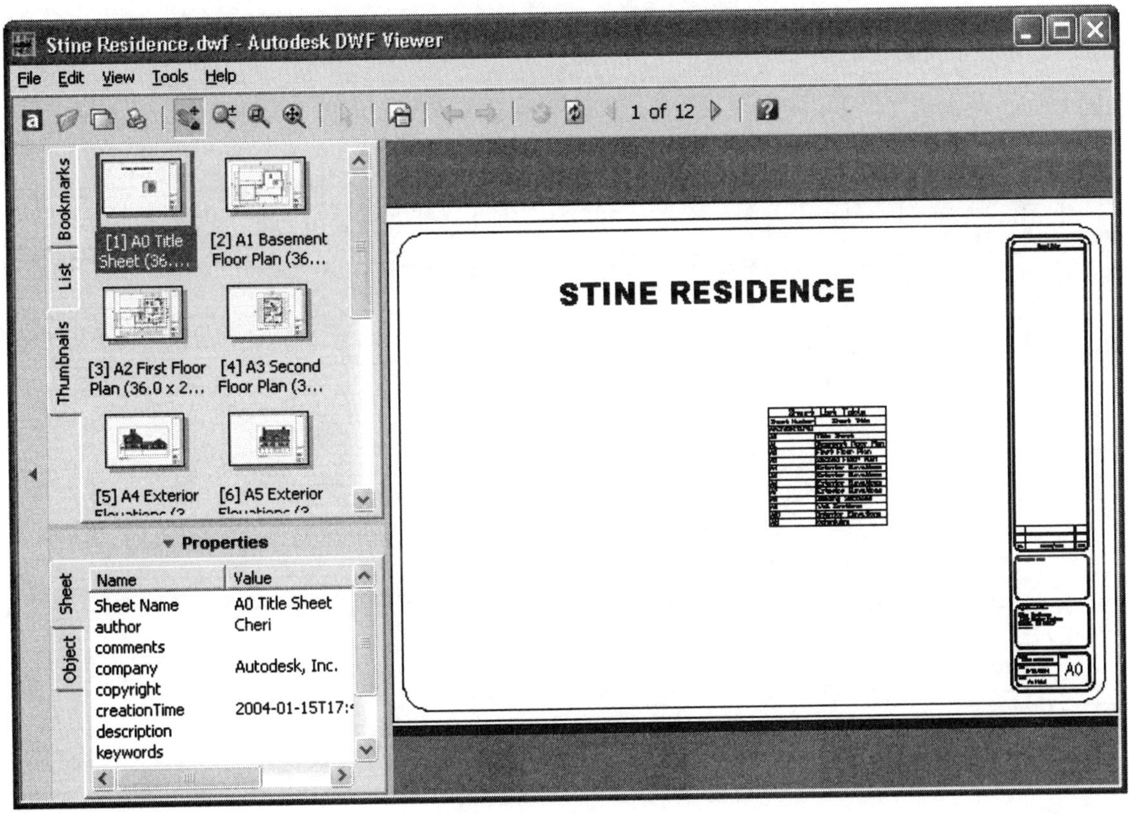

Figure 10-2.11
Autodesk DWF Viewer; your residential project loaded

You can view the various sheets in the DWF file by either clicking on one of the *Thumbnail* images on the left or by clicking the right/left arrows on the tool bar.

A DWF file is still a vector based file, so, like the DWG file, you can zoom in really far and not see any pixilizing of the image. These drawings also have all your lineweights assigned in them so your drawings will print accurately.

Next you will navigate to another sheet and zoom in to see the drawing's lineweights.

21. Scroll down in the *Thumbnails* pane until you see your **A4 Exterior Elevations** sheet.

22. Click on the A4 Thumbnail image to select it.

23. Using your wheel mouse (or the zoom icon), zoom in on the elevation as shown in **Figure 10-2.12.**

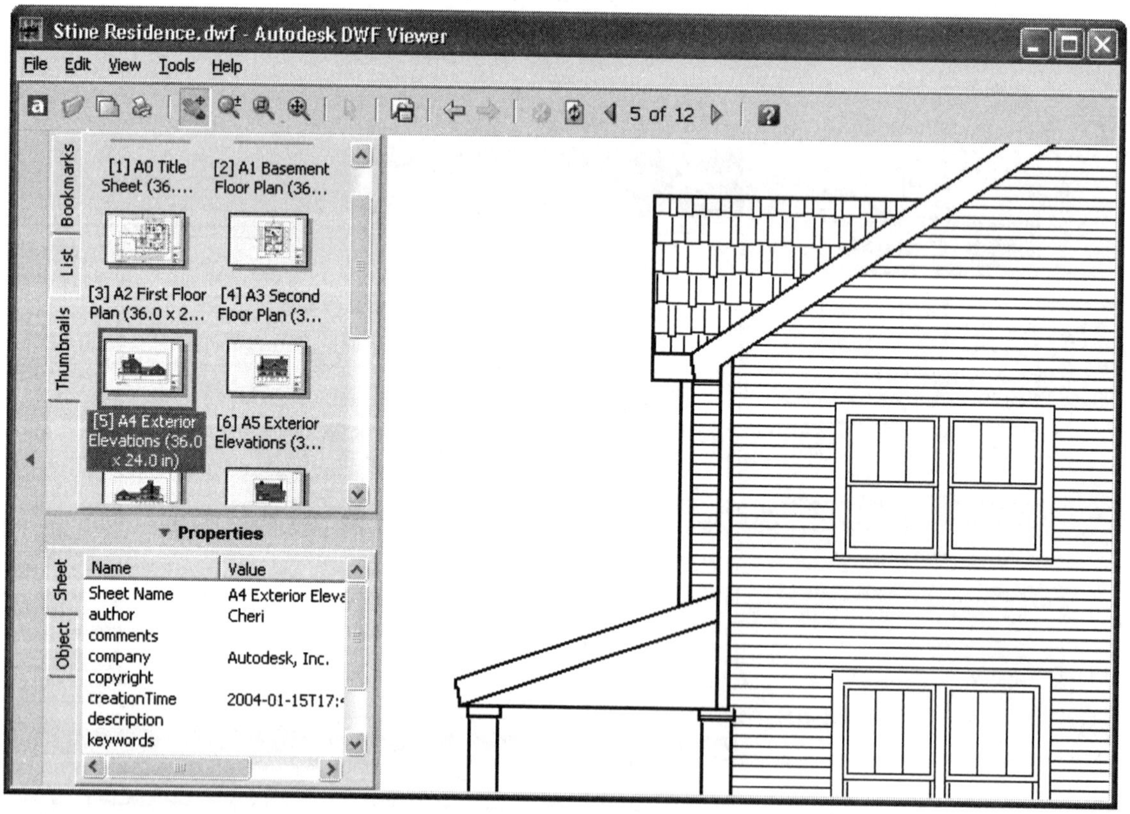

Figure 10-2.12
Autodesk DWF Viewer; sheet A4 – Exterior Elevations displayed

NOTE: *In Figure 10-2.12, that various lineweights can be seen in the elevation drawing.*

Linking feature in the multi-sheet DWF file:

Another amazing feature associated with Sheet Sets and multi-sheet DWF files is the hyper linking embedded in the sheet list and callout bubbles.

24. In your DWF file, switch back to the *Title Sheet* and zoom in on the *Sheet List.*

25. Hover your cursor over the "A2 – First Floor Plan" text to see the pop-up tool tip. (Figure 10-2.13)

The pop-up tool tip displayed in Figure 10-2.13 indicates you can follow a link by holding your Ctrl key and clicking the text. You will try this next.

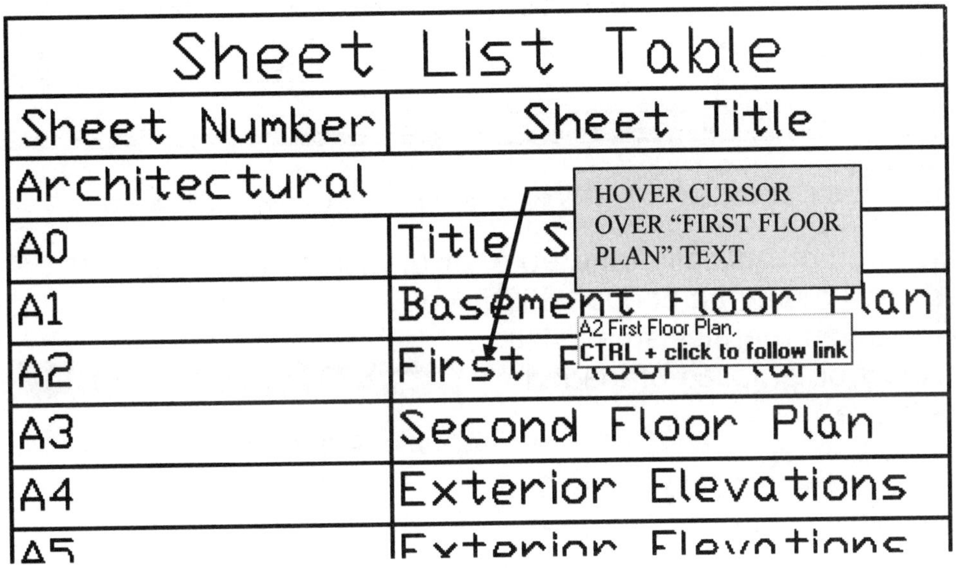

Figure 10-2.13
Multi-sheet DWF file; hyper linked text in Sheet List

26. Holding your **Ctrl** key, on the keyboard, click the "**First Floor Plan**" text in the *Sheet List Table* location on the title sheet.

The DWF Viewer changes the view to the First Floor Plan sheet A2 (Figure 10-2.14). Next you will see how this also applies to your callout bubble.

27. Hold the **Ctrl** key and click on the south elevation bubble (1/A6).

You are now viewing the south elevation drawing on sheet A6!

As you can see this is an easy way for you or a client to navigate a set of drawings.

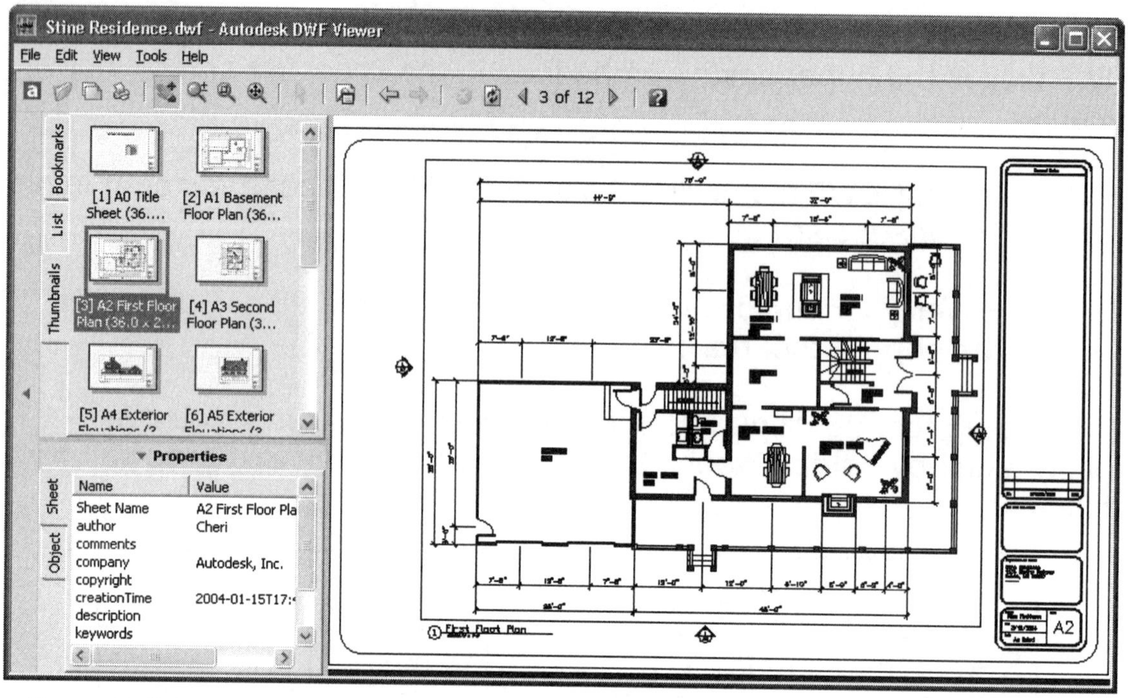

Figure 10-2.14
Multi-sheet DWF file; view displayed by clicking hyper-linked sheet index on title sheet

DWF files do not typically take up a lot of disk space. The DWF file just created should only be about 168kb; you can verify this with Window Explorer. Given the files small size, it can easily be emailed of loaded on a web site.

The Viewer's print dialog (Figure 10-2.15) allows you to print one sheet of the entire set to-scale on 24"x36" paper or "best fit" on 8 1/2" x 11" as you can see in Figure 10-2.15.

FYI: *If you plan to create a DWF file on a project, you can print your hard copy set(s) from this DWF file, eliminating the need to complete the steps outlined in the next section (10-3); which shows how to print directly to the plotter rather than to a DWF file.*

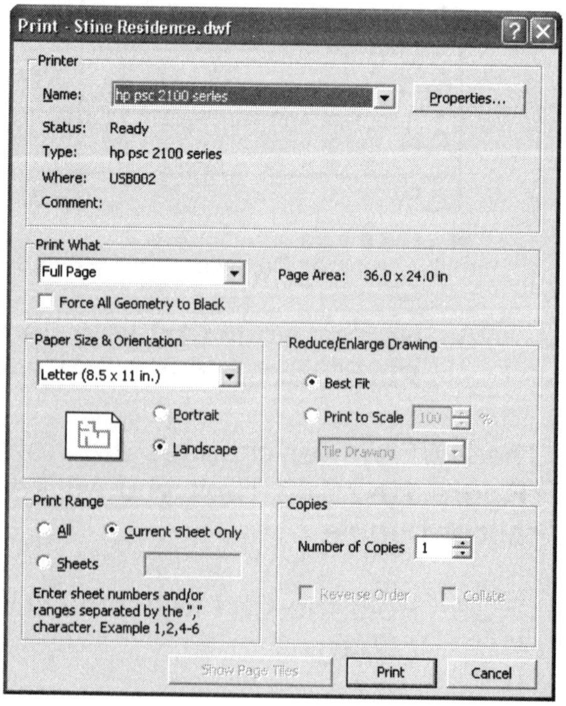

Figure 10-2.15
Autodesk DWF Viewer; print dialog box

Downloading the Autodesk DWF Viewer:

If you will be sharing your DWF files with someone that does not have a DWF Viewer (Note: AutoCAD cannot view DWF files) installed on their computer, you can give them instructions on downloading the free program from Autodesk's web site.

Using an internet browser, such as MS Internet Explorer, go to **www.autodesk.com**. Next, click on **Products** and then click on **Autodesk DWF Viewer** from the list.

From the Product page (Figure 10-2.16), a person can follow the onscreen directions to download and install the program.

28. **Save** and **Close** all files and programs to complete this exercise.

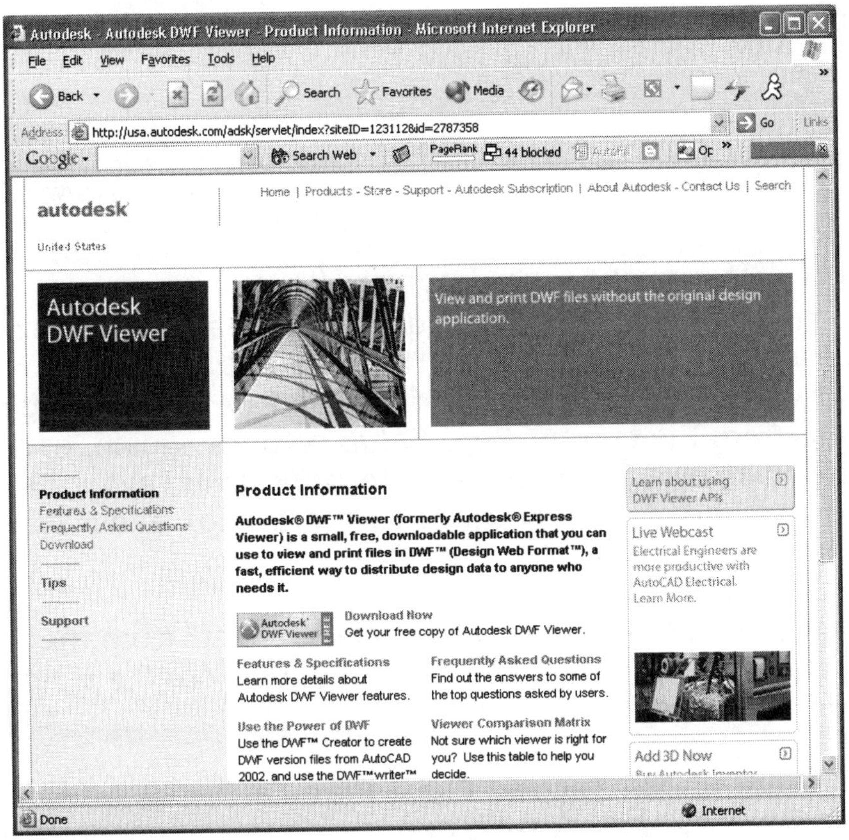

Figure 10-2.16
Autodesk Web Site; DWF Viewer product page

Exercise 10-3:
Plotting: hardcopy set

Introduction:

In this final exercise you will look at a few setting that you should be aware of to create high quality print-outs (i.e., plots). You will look at plotting both from an individual sheet and from the Sheet Set Manager.

Xerox 8850 Digital Solution
High speed B/W plotter + scanner

HP Designjet 1000 series
High quality color and B/W plotter

Page Setup settings for your Layout View:

Page Setup allows you to pre-set things like scale and paper size. Each tab has its own *Page Setup* settings. The *Page Setup* dialog looks almost exactly like the *Plot* dialog. In fact, the *Plot* dialog box gets its initial settings from the current *Page Setup* settings. Again, each drawing file has its own *Page Setup* settings for each *Layout View* tab; this saves time when plotting because each drawing/*Layout View* tab can be pre-set and ready to plot.

1. **Open** your **A3 – Second Floor Plan** "sheet" from the Sheet Set Manager *(this can be opened directly from the Open command as well).*

2. Right-click on the **Second Floor Plan** *Layout View* tab and then select **Page Setup Manager...** from the popup-menu.

You are now in the Page Setup Manager. Here you can create/modify named Page Setups, apply one to the current Layout and Import Page Setups from other drawings. You will modify an existing Page Setup.

3. Select **D Size – Full Scale** from the list and then select **Modify...** (Figure 10-3.1)

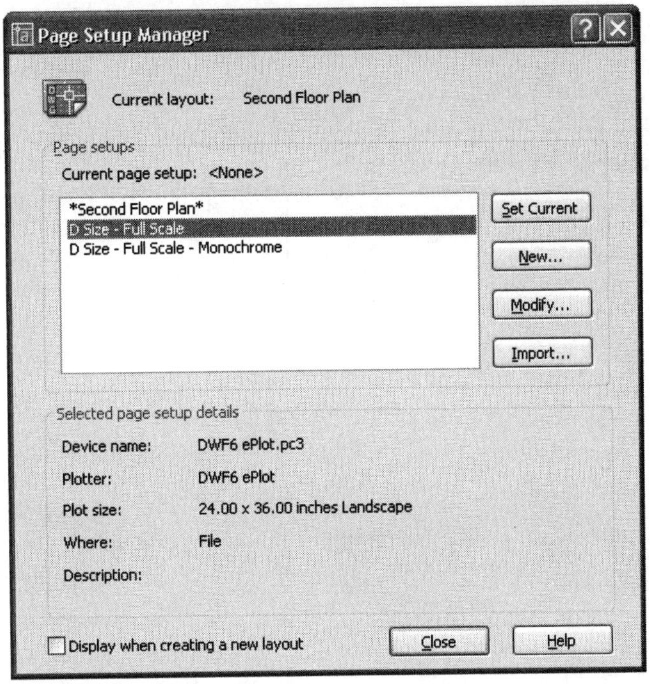

Figure 10-3.1
Page Setup Manager; Page Setup "D Size – Full Scale" selected

You are now in the Page Setup for "D Size – Full Scale".

4. Note and adjust the following settings (**Figure 10-3.2**):

   a. *Select your plotter*; in this case, one that is capable of printing a large sheet like 24"x36".

   b. Make sure your *Plot Style Table* is selected **Stine.ctb** in this example.

   c. Check the box next to "Display plot styles".

      ***FYI**: This setting will make the on-screen display look more like the plotted version of your drawing. (You can also click the LWT toggle on the status bar to see the lineweights on-screen as well.)*

   d. Check the box next to "Scale Lineweights:

      ***FYI:** If the drawing is printed half-scale, for example, the lineweights are adjusted.*

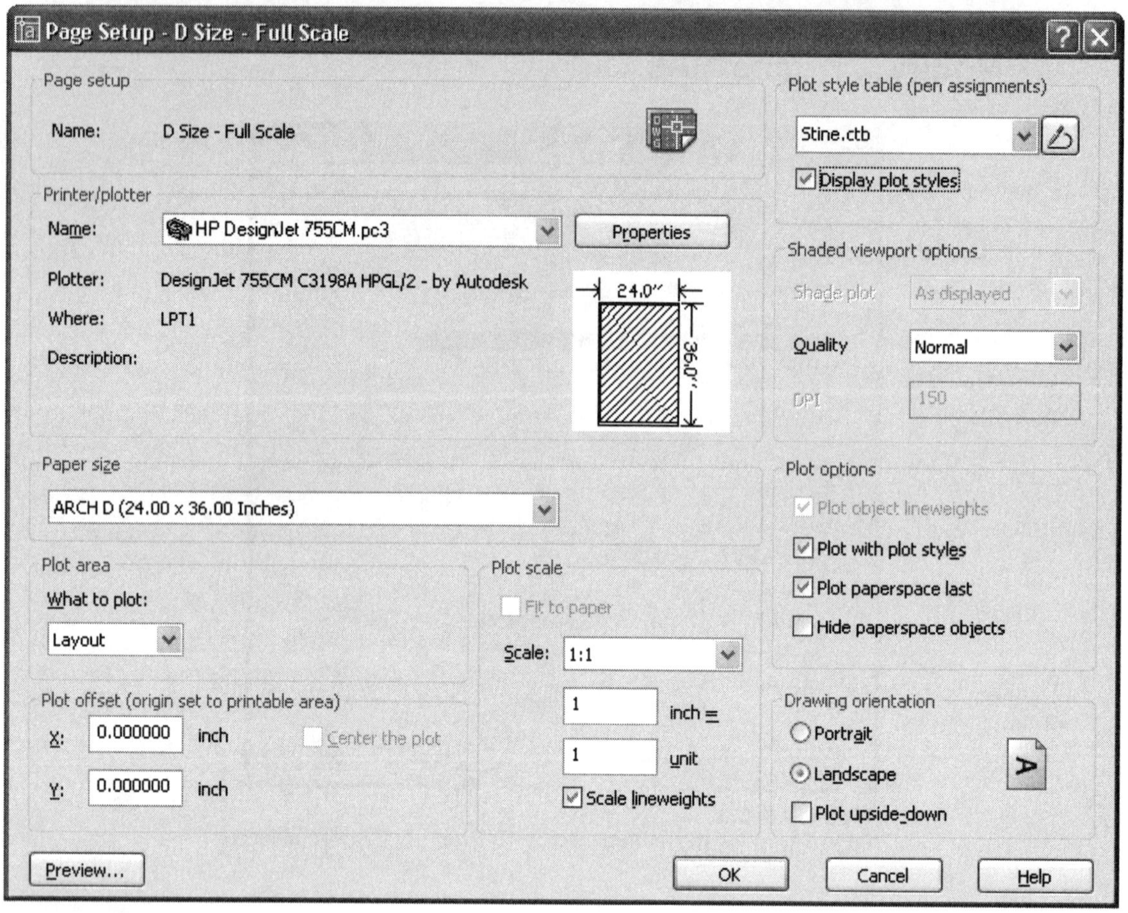

Figure 10-3.2
Page Setup; "D Size – Full Scale" modifications to be made

e. Note these settings as well; they should be set already as they are the default. (Figure 10-3.2)

i. The paper size is set to **24"x36".**
FYI: *This setting controls the size of paper you see on the screen in each Layout View.*

ii. The *Plot Area* is set to **Layout.**

1.	*Layout*	=	*the paper size selected*
2.	*Extents*	=	*all lines selected to print*
3.	*Display*	=	*only lines displayed on screen*
4.	*Window*	=	*user selected area to be plotted*

iii. The *Plot Scale* is set to **1:1**.
FYI: *The 1:1 scale means the 24"x36" sheet will print 24"x36'.*

iv. **Plot with plot styles** is checked.

5. Select **OK** to close the *Page Setup* dialog box.

6. Click **Close** to exit the Page Setup Manager.

Next you will explore the *Plot* dialog box.

7. From the *File* pull-down menu, select **Plot...**

Notice the similarities between the *Plot* dialog and the *Page Setup* dialog (Figure 10-3.3). You should also notice that the settings previously set in *Page Setup* are NOT the defaults in the *Plot* dialog. Your modifications are not the default settings because you did not set the "D Size – Full Scale" page setup to be current (see Figure 10-3.1). However, you can select this on the fly in the plot dialog.

Additional settings on the Plot dialog box (vs. Page Setup):

- **Plot to File**: Creates a "plot file" that can be copied to disk and brought to a print shop (if you don't have a large format printer or color). You need to call the print shop and ask which printer driver to use because the "plot file" is printer specific.
- **Number of copies**: You can specify the number of prints here.

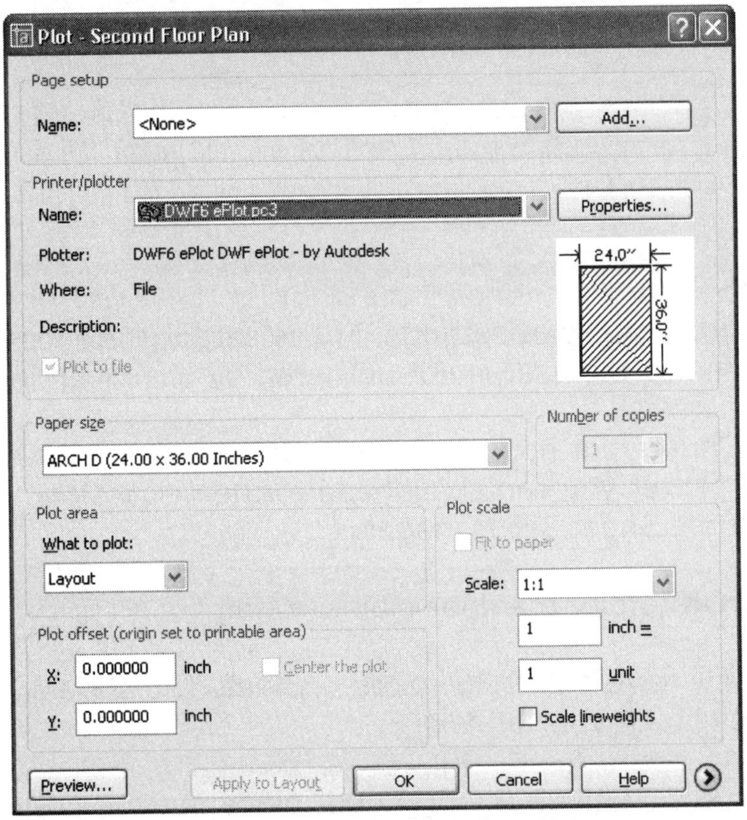

Figure 10-3.3
Plot dialog; initial settings; no page setup selected

8. Select **D Size – Full Scale** from the Page Setup drop-down list near the top of the dialog. (Figure 10-3.3)

Notice how all your settings change to correspond with the selected Page Setup. (Figure 10-3.4)

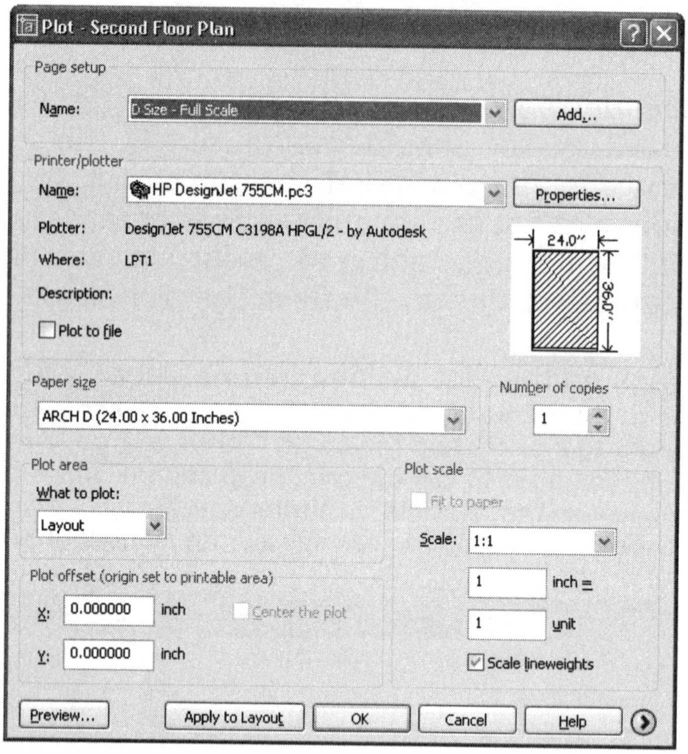

Figure 10-3.4
Plot dialog; page setup applied

If you click the arrow pointing to the right, in the lower right corner, you will see additional plot settings. These settings are less used, so they are hidden so the user is not bothered by too much information.

Next you will print your floor plan sheet. If you do not have access to a large format plotter you can skip ahead to the discussion on how to print sets via the Sheet Set Manager.

9. Click **OK** to plot the floor plan drawing.

You should now have a 24"x36" plotted sheet. You should also be able to see lineweights in your drawing.

10. Plot the basement and first floor plans per the previous steps.

Plotting sets using the Sheet Set Manager:

The previous steps are useful when printing one or two sheets. However, on large projects with 20-30 sheets it would take a lot of your time to open and plot each sheet. Large commercial projects can have hundreds of sheets.

The Sheet Set Manager allows you to print the entire set of drawings at one time. When printing large sets, it can still take quite a while. But, anytime the computer can do the work and save the user time is well worth the effort. Also, the plotting occurs in the "background", which means you can still work in AutoCAD during this process.

11. Open your *Sheet Set* via the *Sheet Set Manager* (see Exercise 8-2 for information on how to do this).

Similar to the first part of this exercise, the Sheet Set has a Page Setup Manager. Here you can prepare a Page Setup that can be used for all "sheets" in your Sheet Set; this is called a Page Setup Override. The Override option ensures consistency and eliminates the need to open every drawing if a Page Setup change is required.

12. Right-click on the Sheet Set title (Stine Residence in the book example).

13. Select **Publish → Manage Page Setups...** from the pop-up menu. (Figure 10-3.5)

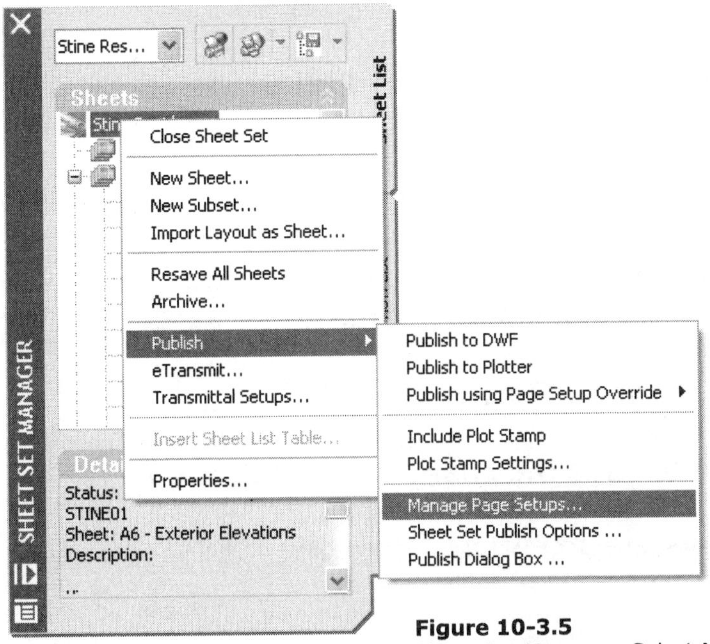

Figure 10-3.5
Sheet Set Manager; Select Manage Page Setups...

You are now in the Page Setup Manager (Figure 10-3.6). This is almost identical to the one previously discussed (see Figure 10-3.1). The difference is this Page Setup Manager applies to the current Sheet Set (Stine Residence) whereas the previous one applied to the Layout View (paper space) in that drawing. Notice one reads "current sheet set" and the other "current layout" at the top of the dialog box.

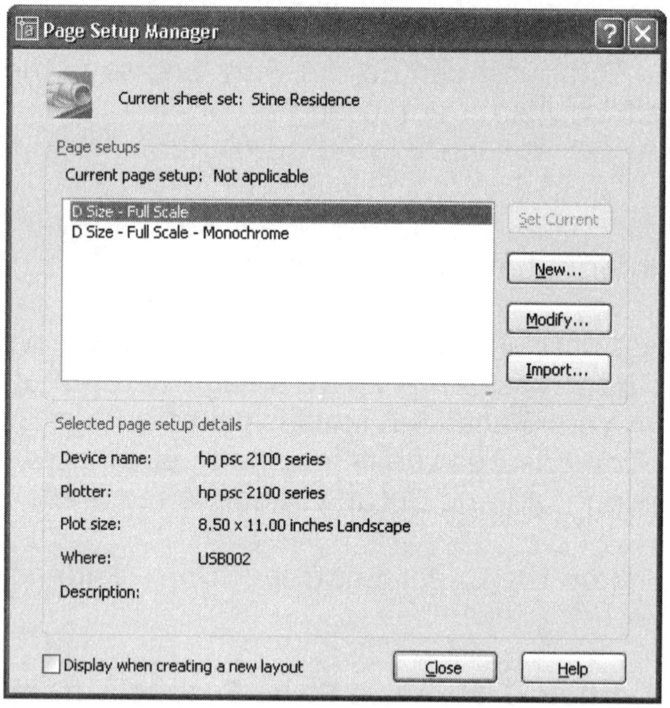

Figure 10-3.6
Page Setup Manager; D Size – Full Scale selected

14. Select the Page Setup named "**D Size – Full Scale**"

15. Click the **Modify...** button

You are now able to adjust the settings for the named page setup. Again, this is identical to what you just did a few pages ago (the difference is the icon next to the page setup name).

16. Make the changes shown in **Figure 10-3.7**

17. Click **OK** and **Close** to save the changes and exit the *Page Setup Manager.*
    TIP*: Select a plotter you have access to.*

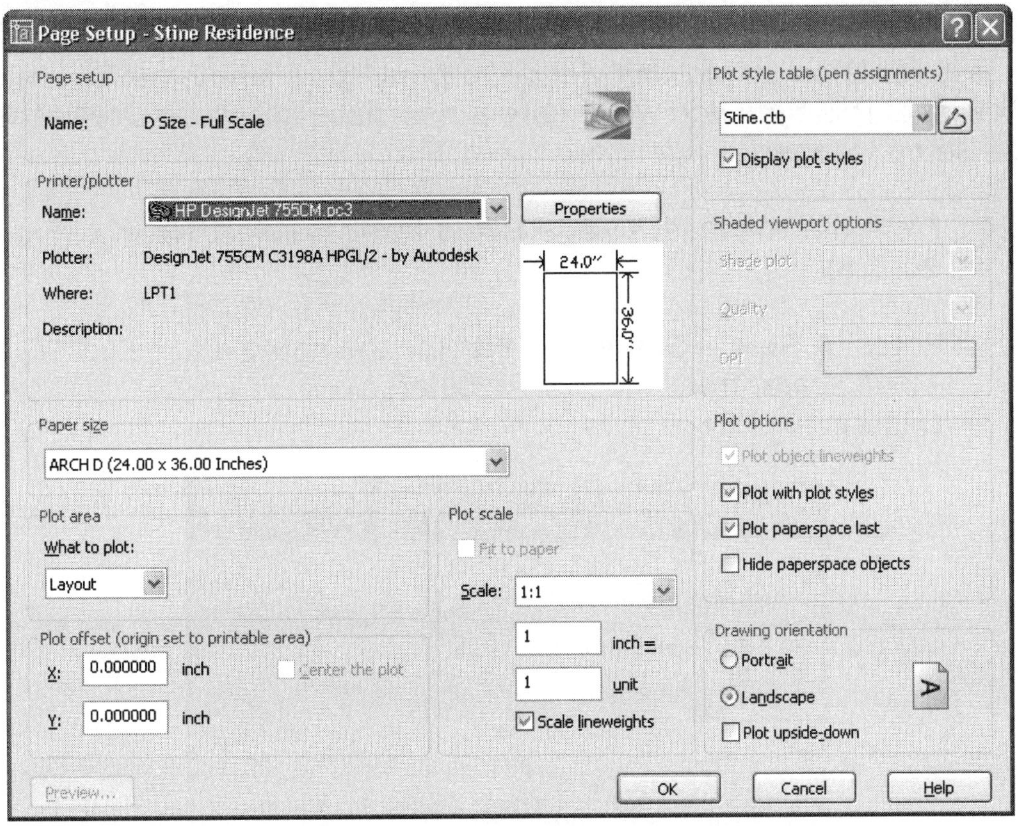

Figure 10-3.7
Page Setup; adjust settings for the selected named page setup

Publishing the sheet set:

Looking back at Figure 10-3.5, notice two things: under the Publish fly-out menu, you have "Publish to Plotter" and "Publish using Page Setup Override". The former uses the current page setup settings in the "sheet" file, whereas the later uses the specified page setup from the sheet set manager. You will try the override option next.

18. Right-click on the sheet set title and select: **Publish → Publish using Page Setup Override** (Figure 10-3.5).

19. From the *Override* fly-out select **D Size – Full Scale**

The plotting process now begins in the background. You will notice the Plot and Publish icon on the right side of the status bar. FYI, you can right-click on it to cancel the current print job at any time.

Drawing should start printing shortly after the process begins!

Publishing a small review set:

The last variation on plotting will be to print out a small, not to scale, review set. This time you will create a new page setup for use in the Page Setup Manger.

20. From the sheet set's *Page Setup Manger* select **New...** (Figure 10-3.6)

21. Enter "**A Size – Scaled to Fit**" for the name and select "*D Size – Full Scale*" from the *Start with* area. (Figure 10-3.8)

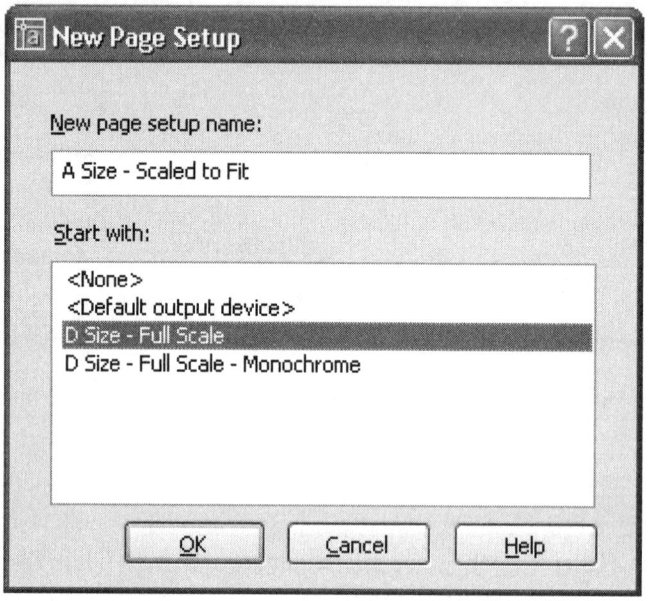

Figure 10-3.8
New Page Setup; creating a new page setup

22. Select **OK** to continue.

23. Make the changes shown in **Figure 10-3.9.**

__FYI__: Notice the "what to plot" is set to Extents; this is a work-around necessary to plot a layout setup for 24x36 onto an 8 ½ x 11 piece of paper.

__TIP__: If you have access to a printer that has 11"x17" paper, you can select that paper size; sets are a little larger and easier to read. Also, on nice thing about using 22" x 34" sheets (rather than 24'x36") is that 11"x17" sets are half-scale which is better than scaled to fit.

24. Select **Save** and then **Close** to complete the open dialog boxes.

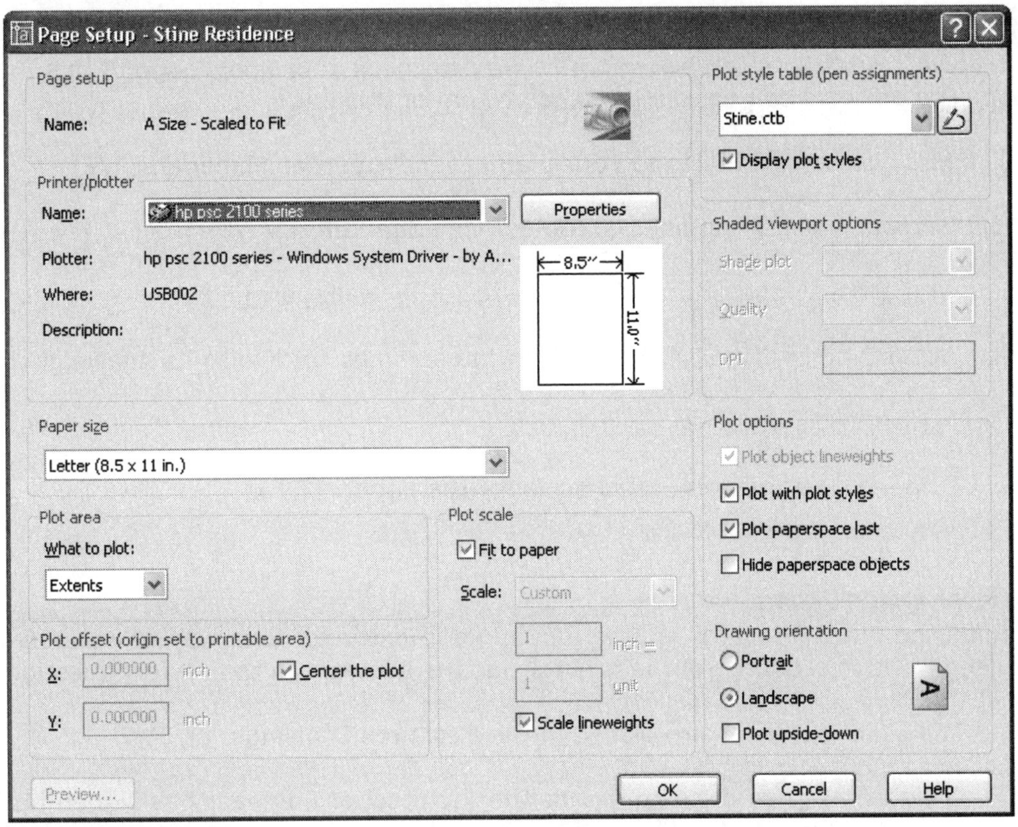

Figure 10-3.9
New Page Setup; make changes shown

25. Now, simply Publish using a page setup override as previously reviewed; selecting the new page setup: "A Size – Scaled to Fit".

Your drawing will begin to print in a moment.

26. **Save** your drawings and close you sheet set.

You have now completed this book (except for the *Additional Tasks and Appendix*)! You should possess the fundamental skills required for most tasks necessary to complete a set of residential drawings.

With the solid foundation you have built using this book you should be able to explore and develop additional commands and techniques on your own. Using the Help system, News Groups and a little "trial and error", you can draw just about anything.

Good luck with your CAD drafting endeavors!

Self-Exam:

The following questions can be used as a way to check your knowledge of this lesson. The answers can be found at the bottom of this page.

1. You access Plot Styles to your plan Layer Properties Manager. (T/F)
2. You can specify "number of copies" via Page Setup. (T/F)
3. You access page setups via the page setup manager. (T/F)
4. What type of Plot Style Table associates a lines color with its lineweight?

   ____

5. The Layout tab is real-word scale for the paper. (T/F)

Review Questions:

The following questions may be assigned by your instructor as a way to assess your knowledge of this section. Your instructor has the answers to the review questions.

1. The callout bubbles are placed in the Resource Drawings. (T/F)
2. A digitally signed drawing means the Architect or Engineer has signed his/her name to that drawing file. (T/F)
3. The LWT button on the Status Bar toggles lineweight visibility. (T/F)
4. The callout bubbles in a multi-sheet DWF file are ______________________

   so you can "jump" to the referenced drawing.

5. You specify which Plot Style Table to use in the Page Setup dialog. (T/F)
6. In a Layout view's Page Setup, the plot scale should be set to __________.
7. This icon () means the drawing is ______________ ____________.
8. Which lines should be light gray in a plan drawing ______________________.
9. You can plot an entire set of drawings from a multi-sheet DWF file. (T/F)
10. You can organize "sheet" in subsets within the sheet set manager. (T/F)

Self-Exam Answers:
1 - F, **2** - F, **3** - T, **4** – Color Dependent, **5** – T

Additional Tasks:

Task 10-1 Apply lineweights to all your drawings:
Using the techniques learned in lesson 10-1, apply lineweights to all your other drawings (or per your instructors direction); including the exterior elevations, sections and interior elevations.

Task 10-2 Plot all your drawings full size:
Using the techniques learned in lesson 8-3, plot each of your drawings that have been setup on a sheet. Plot them full size if your plotter supports large format paper.

Image courtesy of Anderson Architects
Alan H. Anderson, Architect, Duluth, MN

Interior Design, Steven W. Sanborn, A.I.A., Santa Rosa, CA

Notes:

Index